BOLLINGEN SERIES XXVI

HEINRICH ZIMMER

(1890–1943)

Works in English, completed and edited

by Joseph Campbell

1946

MYTHS AND SYMBOLS IN INDIAN ART AND CIVILIZATION

1948

THE KING AND THE CORPSE

Tales of the Soul's Conquest of Evil

1951

PHILOSOPHIES OF INDIA

1955

THE ART OF INDIAN ASIA

Its Mythology and Transformations

IN TWO VOLUMES

HEINRICH ZIMMER

PHILOSOPHIES OF INDIA

EDITED BY JOSEPH CAMPBELL

BOLLINGEN SERIES XXVI

PRINCETON UNIVERSITY PRESS

Published by Princeton University Press, Princeton, New Jersey

Second Printing, 1953
Third Printing, with minor corrections, 1967
First Princeton / Bollingen Paperback printing, 1969
Fourth hardcover printing, 1969

THIS VOLUME IS THE TWENTY-SIXTH IN A SERIES OF BOOKS
SPONSORED BY BOLLINGEN FOUNDATION

Library of Congress Catalogue Card Number: 51-13167
SBN 691-01758-1 (paperback edn.)
SBN 691-09811-5 (hardcover edn.)
Printed in the United States of America
by Princeton University Press, Princeton, New Jersey

EDITOR'S FOREWORD

Dr. Heinrich Zimmer's posthumous chapters for a projected volume on the philosophies of India were found in various stages of completion. Those on the meeting of the Orient and Occident, the Indian philosophy of politics, Jainism, Sāṅkhya and Yoga, Vedānta, and Buddhahood had served as notes for a course of lectures delivered at Columbia University in the spring of 1942, while that on the Indian philosophy of duty had opened the course for the spring of 1943. But since hardly five weeks of the latter term had been completed when Dr. Zimmer was stricken with his final illness, his materials treating of the other phases of Indian thought remained in the uneven condition of mere jottings and preliminary drafts. All were found in a single, orderly file, however, so that the problem of arranging them was not difficult. Lacunae could be filled from other bundles of manuscript, as well as from recollected conversations. The editing of most of the chapters, therefore, went rather smoothly. But toward the end the condition of the notes became so rough and spotty that the merely indicated frame had to be filled in with data drawn from other sources.

I have quoted only from authors suggested either in Dr. Zimmer's outline or in his class assignments, and have named them all clearly in my footnotes. In the chapter on The Great Buddhist Kings, which is the first in which this problem arose, my chief authorities were *The Cambridge History of India,* Vol. I; E. B. Havell, *The History of Aryan Rule in India from the Earliest Times to the Death of Akbar;* Ananda K. Coomaraswamy, *Buddhism and the Gospel of Buddhism;* T. W. Rhys Davids, *Buddhism, Its History and Literature;* S. Radhakrishnan, *Indian Philosophy;* Vincent A. Smith, *Aśoka, The Buddhist Emperor of India;* and L. de la Vallée Poussin's article on the Buddhist Councils and Synods in Hastings' *Encyclopaedia of Religion and Ethics.* The notes for the chapter on Hīnayāna and Mahāyāna Buddhism were quite full, though not yet amplified into a continuously inspired exposition. I simply arranged them and opened the brief sentences into running prose, bridging two short gaps with quotations from S. Radhakrishnan, as indicated in my footnotes. I was particularly distressed, however, to find that the materials for the chapters on The Way of the Bodhisattva, The Great Delight, and Tantra were very sparse and only partially developed; for these were themes to which Dr. Zimmer had been devoting much attention during the latter years of his life, and on which he had been extraordinarily eloquent in conversation. I could find only a few additional bits of paper scattered through the volumes of his library, and these together with what I remembered of our talks had to suffice to eke out the notes. The reader should bear in mind that in these last pages Dr. Zimmer's position may not be quite correctly represented. I have been able to give only a few brief but precious fragments, framed in a setting largely quoted from Swami Nikhilananda's translation of *The Gospel of Srī Rāmakrishna* and Sir John Woodroffe's *Shakti and Shākta.*

Obviously, the history of Indian philosophy here before us is far from what it would have been had Dr. Zimmer lived. The broad sweep of the basic structural ideas carries to completion of itself, however, even where the outlines are no more than indicated, an extraordinary vision not only of the Indian but also of the Western philosophical development. Hence, though the work as it stands is visibly but a fragment (a large and awesome fragment, comparable, one might say, to the unfinished stupa at Borobudur) formally it makes a cogent and prodigious statement. The whole is conceived primarily as an introduction to the subject, each chapter leading to the next, and not as a handbook; but I have supplied cross-references and Mr. William McGuire has prepared a copious index, to serve the reader wishing to study any separate topic. Guidance to further reading will be found in the bibliography and in the titles cited in the footnotes.

My profound thanks go to Swami Nikhilananda for kind permission to quote extensively from his translation of *The Gospel of Srī Rāmakrishna,* to Doña Luisa Coomaraswamy for Plates I, II, III, V, IX, X, and XII, Dr. Stella Kramrisch for Plates VIII and XI, and Dr. Marguerite Block for Plate VIa. The Metropolitan Museum of Art kindly supplied Plates IV and VIb, the Morgan Library Plate VIc, and the Asia Institute Plate VII. I owe much, moreover, to Mrs. Wallace Ferguson for assistance in the final editing of the manuscript, to Miss Elizabeth Sherbon for three years of tireless and painstaking typing, to Mr. William McGuire for his meticulous editing of the proofs and for his above-mentioned index, and to my wife for all her hours of listening and for numberless suggestions.

J. C.

New York City
March 20, 1951

TABLE OF CONTENTS

PART III. THE PHILOSOPHIES OF ETERNITY

LIST OF PLATES

following page 332

(Persian), from a manuscript of Firdausī's *Shāhnāmah,* dated 1602 A.D. (Courtesy of The Metropolitan Museum of Art, New York.)

VIc. Nude bearded hero with a stream flowing over each shoulder, flanked by winged lion-demons and with a star at either side of his head. Hematite cylinder seal. Syria, c. 1450 B.C. (From Edith Porada, *Corpus of Ancient Near Eastern Seals in North American Collections,* The Bollingen Series XIV, New York, 1948, Vol. I, fig. 979E. Reproduced through the courtesy of the Trustees of the Pierpont Morgan Library, New York.)

VII. The Jaina Tīrthaṅkara Ṛṣabhanātha, Relief-stele of alabasterlike marble, from Mount Ābū, Rājputāna, 11th to 13th centuries A.D. Height of central figure, 3 ft. 7⅓ in. Small, kneeling figures at either side, man to right, woman to left, apparently donors; height 5½ to 6¼ inches. Behind these, standing male and female figures, 1 ft. 3¾ in. high; the males with fly-wisps, the female at the right with a cakra-discus and conch, she at the left with nāgas in her hands; probably deities. Above are musicians, worshipers, and two elephants, as well as small, standing images of the Tīrthaṅkaras Neminātha, Pārśvanātha, and Mahāvīra. Nāginīs and yakṣas also are present. The little zebu-bull on the face of the pedestal indicates that the main subject is Ṛṣabhanātha. (Photo, from Karl With, *Bildwerke Ost- und Südasiens aus der Sammlung Yi Yuan,* Basel, 1924.)

VIII. The Jaina saint Gommata (also known as Bāhubalī, "Strong of Arm"), son of the Tīrthaṅkara Ṛṣabhanātha. Monolithic colossus, 56½ ft. high, 13 ft. around the hips, at Śravaṇa Beḷgoḷa, Hāsan District, Mysore; c. 983 A.D. (Photo: Courtesy of Dr. W. Norman Brown.)

IX. The Assault of Māra. Relief from the ruined Buddhist stūpa of Amarāvatī. Āndhra, 2nd century A.D. (Madras Museum. Photo: Archaeological Survey of India.)

TABLE OF PRONUNCIATION

The Consonants

Gutturals:	k	kh	g	gh	ṅ		
Palatals:	c	ch	j	jh	ñ	y	ś
Linguals:	ṭ	ṭh	ḍ	ḍh	ṇ	r	ṣ
Dentals:	t	th	d	dh	n	l	s
Labials:	p	ph	b	bh	m	v	
Aspirate:	h						
Visarga:	ḥ						
Anusvāra:	ṁ						

H combined with another consonant is always aspirated and audible; for example, *th* is pronounced as in boa*th*ook, *ph* as in ha*ph*azard, *dh* as in ma*dh*ouse, and *bh* as in a*bh*or.

The guttural series are the ordinary European *k*- and *g*-sounds and their aspirates (*kh* and *gh*), with a nasal *ṅ,* which is pronounced as *ng* in si*ng*ing.

In the palatal series, *c* is pronounced about like *ch* in *ch*ur*ch* (Sanskrit *ch,* consequently, sounds like chur*ch-h*ouse) and *j* about as in *j*udge. The nasal, *ñ,* is like *ñ* in Spanish *señor.* (An exception is *jñā,* which pronounced by a modern Hindu sounds like *gyah,* with hard *g.*) The palatal semi-vowel, *y,* is about as in English, and *ś,* the sibilant, approximately *sh.*

Linguals are gentler sounds than dentals, pronounced with the tip of the tongue bent back and placed against the roof of the mouth instead of against the teeth. The *r* is untrilled. The *ṣ* is a kind of *sh*-sound.

The dentals and labials are about as in English.

Visarga, *ḥ,* is a final *h*-sound uttered in the articulating position of the preceding vowel. (It is a substitute for a final *s* or *r*.)

Anusvāra, *ṁ,* is a resonant nasal pronounced with open mouth.

The Vowels

Simple vowels	Gutturals:	a	ā
	Palatals:	i	ī
	Labials:	u	ū
	Linguals:	ṛ	ṝ
	Dentals:	ḷ	ḹ
Diphthongs	Palatals:	e	ai
	Labials:	o	au

In general, the vowels are pronounced as in Italian; short *a,* however, is a "neutral vowel," like the vowel-sound of *but, son,* or *blood.* The vowel *ṛ* is an untrilled *r*-sound used as a vowel, as in certain Slavonic languages. The vowel *ḷ* is an *l*-sound similarly uttered.

PART I

THE HIGHEST GOOD

I. THE MEETING OF EAST AND WEST

1.

The Roar of Awakening

WE OF the Occident are about to arrive at a crossroads that was reached by the thinkers of India some seven hundred years before Christ. This is the real reason why we become both vexed and stimulated, uneasy yet interested, when confronted with the concepts and images of Oriental wisdom. This crossing is one to which the people of all civilizations come in the typical course of the development of their capacity and requirement for religious experience, and India's teachings force us to realize what its problems are. But we cannot take over the Indian solutions. We must enter the new period our own way and solve its questions for ourselves, because though truth, the radiance of reality, is universally one and the same, it is mirrored variously according to the mediums in which it is reflected. Truth appears differently in different lands and ages according to the living materials out of which its symbols are hewn.

Concepts and words are symbols, just as visions, rituals, and images are; so too are the manners and customs of daily life. Through all of these a transcendent reality is mirrored. They are so many metaphors reflecting and implying something which, though thus variously expressed, is ineffable, though thus rendered multiform, remains inscrutable. Symbols hold the mind to truth but are not themselves the truth, hence it is delusory to borrow them. Each civilization, every age, must bring forth its own.

We shall therefore have to follow the difficult way of our own experiences, produce our own reactions, and assimilate our sufferings and realizations. Only then will the truth that we bring to manifestation be as much our own flesh and blood as is the child its mother's; and the mother, in love with the Father, will then justly delight in her offspring as His duplication. The ineffable seed must be conceived, gestated, and brought forth from our own substance, fed by our blood, if it is to be the true child through which its mother is reborn: and the Father, the divine Transcendent Principle, will then also be reborn—delivered, that is to say, from the state of non-manifestation, non-action, apparent non-existence. We cannot borrow God. We must effect His new incarnation from within ourselves. Divinity must descend, somehow, into the matter of our own existence and participate in this peculiar life-process.

According to the mythologies of India, this is a miracle that will undoubtedly come to pass. For in the ancient Hindu tales one reads that whenever the creator and sustainer of the world, Viṣṇu, is implored to appear in a new incarnation, the beseeching forces leave him no peace until he condescends. Nevertheless, the moment he comes down, taking flesh in a blessed womb, to be again made manifest in the world which itself is a reflex of his own ineffable being, self-willed demonic forces set themselves against him; for there are those who hate and despise the god and have no room for him in their systems of expansive egoism and domineering rule. These do everything within their power to hamper his career. Their violence, however, is not as destructive as it seems; it is no more than a necessary force in the historic process. Resistance is a standard part in the recurrent cosmic comedy that is enacted whenever a spark of supernal truth, drawn down by the misery of creatures and the imminence of chaos, is made manifest on the phenomenal plane.

"It is the same with our spirit," states Paul Valéry, "as with our flesh: both hide in mystery what they feel to be most important. They conceal it from themselves. They single it out and protect it by this profundity in which they ensconce it. Everything that really counts is well veiled; testimony and documents only render it the more obscure; deeds and works are designed expressly to misrepresent it." [1]

The chief aim of Indian thought is to unveil and integrate into consciousness what has been thus resisted and hidden by the forces of life—not to explore and describe the visible world. The supreme and characteristic achievement of the Brāhman mind (and this has been decisive, not only for the course of Indian philosophy, but also for the history of Indian civilization) was its discovery of the Self *(ātman)* as an independent, imperishable entity, underlying the conscious personality and bodily frame. Everything that we normally know and express about ourselves belongs to the sphere of change, the sphere of time and space, but this Self (*ātman*) is forever changeless, beyond time, beyond space and the veiling net of causality, beyond measure, beyond the dominion of the eye. The effort of Indian philosophy has been, for millenniums, to know this adamantine Self and make the knowledge effective in human life. And this enduring concern is what has been responsible for the supreme morning calm that pervades the terrible histories of the Oriental

[1] "Il en est de notre esprit comme de notre chair; ce qu'ils se sentent de plus important, ils l'enveloppent de mystère, ils se le cachent à eux-mêmes; ils le désignent et le défendent par cette profondeur où ils le placent. Tout ce qui compte est bien voilé; les témoins et les documents l'obscurcissent; les actes et les oeuvres sont faits expressément pour le travestir" (Paul Valéry, *Variété* I, "Au sujet d'Adonis," p. 68).

world—histories no less tremendous, no less horrifying, than our own. Through the vicissitudes of physical change a spiritual footing is maintained in the peaceful-blissful ground of Ātman; eternal, timeless, and imperishable Being.

Indian, like Occidental, philosophy imparts information concerning the measurable structure and powers of the psyche, analyzes man's intellectual faculties and the operations of his mind, evaluates various theories of human understanding, establishes the methods and laws of logic, classifies the senses, and studies the processes by which experiences are apprehended and assimilated, interpreted and comprehended. Hindu philosophers, like those of the West, pronounce on ethical values and moral standards. They study also the visible traits of phenomenal existence, criticizing the data of external experience and drawing deductions with respect to the supporting principles. India, that is to say, has had, and still has, its own disciplines of psychology, ethics, physics, and metaphysical theory. But the primary concern—in striking contrast to the interests of the modern philosophers of the West—has always been, not information, but transformation: a radical changing of man's nature and, therewith, a renovation of his understanding both of the outer world and of his own existence; a transformation as complete as possible, such as will amount when successful to a total conversion or rebirth.

In this respect Indian philosophy sides with religion to a far greater extent than does the critical, secularized thinking of the modern West. It is on the side of such ancient philosophers as Pythagoras, Empedocles, Plato, the Stoics, Epicurus and his followers, Plotinus, and the Neoplatonic thinkers. We recognize the point of view again in St. Augustine, the medieval mystics such as Meister Eckhart, and such later mystics as Jakob Böhme of Silesia. Among the Romantic philosophers it reappears in Schopenhauer.

The attitudes toward each other of the Hindu teacher and

the pupil bowing at his feet are determined by the exigencies of this supreme task of transformation. Their problem is to effect a kind of alchemical transmutation of the soul. Through the means, not of a merely intellectual understanding, but of a change of heart (a transformation that shall touch the core of his existence), the pupil is to pass out of bondage, beyond the limits of human imperfection and ignorance, and transcend the earthly plane of being.

There is an amusing popular fable which illustrates this pedagogical idea. It is recorded among the teachings of the celebrated Hindu saint of the nineteenth century, Śrī Rāmakrishna.[2] Anecdotes of this childlike kind occur continually in the discourses of the Oriental sages; they circulate in the common lore of the folk and are known to everyone from infancy. They carry the lessons of India's timeless wisdom to the homes and hearts of the people, coming down through the millenniums as everybody's property. Indeed India is one of the great homelands of the popular fable; during the Middle Ages many of her tales were carried into Europe. The vividness and simple aptness of the images drive home the points of the teaching; they are like pegs to which can be attached no end of abstract reasoning. The beast fable is but one of the many Oriental devices to make lessons catch hold and remain in the mind.

The present example is of a tiger cub that had been brought up among goats, but through the enlightening guidance of a spiritual teacher was made to realize its own unsuspected na-

[2] Cf. *The Gospel of Śrī Rāmakrishna,* translated with an introduction by Swāmī Nikhilānanda, New York, 1942, pp. 232-233, 259-360. Śrī Rāmakrishna (1836–86) was the perfect embodiment of the orthodox religious philosophy of India. His message first reached America through his pupil, Swāmī Vivekānanda (1863–1902), who spoke for India at the World's Parliament of Religions, held in Chicago, 1893. Today the monks of the Rāmakrishna-Vivekānanda mission maintain spiritual centers and conduct courses of teaching in most of the principal cities of the United States.

ture. Its mother had died in giving it birth. Big with young, she had been prowling for many days without discovering prey, when she came upon this herd of ranging wild goats. The tigress was ravenous at the time, and this fact may account for the violence of her spring; but in any case, the strain of the leap brought on the birth throes, and from sheer exhaustion she expired. Then the goats, who had scattered, returned to the grazing ground and found the little tiger whimpering at its mother's side. They adopted the feeble creature out of maternal compassion, suckled it together with their own offspring, and watched over it fondly. The cub grew and their care was rewarded; for the little fellow learned the language of the goats, adapted his voice to their gentle way of bleating, and displayed as much devotion as any kid of the flock. At first he experienced some difficulty when he tried to nibble thin blades of grass with his pointed teeth, but somehow he managed. The vegetarian diet kept him very slim and imparted to his temperament a remarkable meekness.

One night, when this young tiger among the goats had reached the age of reason, the herd was attacked again, this time by a fierce old male tiger, and again they scattered; but the cub remained where he stood, devoid of fear. He was of course surprised. Discovering himself face to face with the terrible jungle being, he gazed at the apparition in amazement. The first moment passed; then he began to feel self-conscious. Uttering a forlorn bleat, he plucked a thin leaf of grass and chewed it, while the other stared.

Suddenly the mighty intruder demanded: "What are you doing here among these goats? What are you chewing there?" The funny little creature bleated. The old one became really terrifying. He roared, "Why do you make this silly sound?" and before the other could respond, seized him roughly by the scruff and shook him, as though to knock him back to his senses. The jungle tiger then carried the frightened cub to a nearby pond, where he set him down, compelling him to look into the mirror surface, which was illuminated by the moon. "Now look at those two faces. Are they not alike? You have the pot-face of a tiger; it is like mine. Why do you fancy yourself to be a goat? Why do you bleat? Why do you nibble grass?"

The little one was unable to reply, but continued to stare, comparing the two reflections. Then it became uneasy, shifted its weight from paw to paw, and emitted another troubled, quavering cry. The fierce old beast seized it again and carried it off to his den, where he presented it with a bleeding piece of raw meat remaining from an earlier meal. The cub shuddered with disgust. The jungle tiger, ignoring the weak bleat of protest, gruffly ordered: "Take it! Eat it! Swallow it!" The cub resisted, but the frightening meat was forced between his teeth, and the tiger sternly supervised while he tried to chew and prepared to swallow. The toughness of the morsel was unfamiliar and was causing some difficulty, and he was just about to make his little noise again, when he began to get the taste of the blood. He was amazed; he reached with eagerness for the rest. He began to feel an unfamiliar gratification as the new food went down his gullet, and the meaty substance came into his stomach. A strange, glowing strength, starting from there, went out through his whole organism, and he commenced to feel elated, intoxicated. His lips smacked; he licked his jowls. He arose and opened his mouth with a mighty yawn, just as though he were waking from a night of sleep—a night that had held him long under its spell, for years and years. Stretching his form, he arched his back, extending and spreading his paws. The tail lashed the ground, and suddenly from his throat there burst the terrifying, triumphant roar of a tiger.

The grim teacher, meanwhile, had been watching closely and with increasing satisfaction. The transformation had actually taken place. When the roar was finished he demanded gruffly: "Now do you know what you really are?" and to complete the initiation of his young disciple into the secret lore of his own true nature, added: "Come, we shall go now for a hunt together in the jungle."

The history of Indian thought during the period just preceding the birth and mission of the Buddha (c. 563–483 B.C.) reveals a gradual intensification of emphasis on this problem of the rediscovery and assimilation of the Self. The philosophical dialogues of the Upaniṣads indicate that during the eighth century B.C. a critical shift of weight from the outer universe and tangible spheres of the body to the inner and the intangible was carrying the dangerous implications of this direction of the mind to their logical conclusion. A process of withdrawal from the normally known world was taking place. The powers of the macrocosm and corresponding faculties of the microcosm were being generally devaluated and left behind; and with such fearlessness that the whole religious system of the previous period was being placed in peril of collapse. The kings of the gods, Indra and Varuṇa, and the divine priests of the gods, Agni, Mitra, Bṛhaspati, were no longer receiving their due of prayer and sacrifice. Instead of directing the mind to these symbolic guardians and models of the natural and the social orders, supporting them and keeping them effective through a continuous sequence of rites and meditations, men were turning all of their attention inward, striving to attain and hold themselves in a state of unmitigated Self-awareness through sheer thinking, systematic self-analysis, breath control, and the stern psychological disciplines of yoga.

The antecedents of this radical introjection are already discernible in many of the hymns of the Vedas;[3] for example, the

[3] *Editor's note:* For the reader unfamiliar with the chronology of Indian documents, it can be stated, briefly, that the four Vedas (Ṛg, Yajur, Sama, and Atharva) contain the hymns and magical charms of those nomadic Āryan cattle-herding families who entered India through the northwestern mountains during the second millennium B.C., about the time that the

following prayer for power, wherein the divine forces variously manifest in the outer world are conjured to enter the subject, take up their abode in his body, and vivify his faculties.

"The brilliancy that is in the lion, the tiger, and the serpent; in Agni (the god of the sacrificial fire), in the Brāhmans, and in Sūrya (the Sun) shall be ours! May the lovely goddess who bore Indra come to us, endowed with luster!

"The brilliancy that is in the elephant, the panther, and in

Achaeans (to whom they were somehow related and whose language resembled Vedic Sanskrit) were descending into Greece. The Vedic hymns are the oldest extant literary and religious monument of the so-called Indo-European family of languages, which comprises all of the literatures of the following traditions: Celtic (Irish, Welsh, Scottish, etc.), Germanic (German, Dutch, English, Norse, Gothic, etc.), Italic (Latin, Italian, Spanish, French, Romanian, etc.), Greek, Balto-Slavic (Old Prussian, Lettish, Russian, Czech, Polish, etc.), Anatolic (Armenian, Ancient Phrygian, etc.), Iranian (Persian, Afghan, etc.), and Indo-Āryan (Sanskrit, Pāli, and the modern languages of northern India, such as Hindi, Bengali, Sindhi, Panjabi, and Gujarati—as well as Romany or Gypsy). Many of the gods, beliefs, and observances of the Vedic age closely parallel those of the Homeric. The hymns seem to have been fixed in their present form c. 1500–1000 B.C.

The term *Veda* includes, however, not only the four hymn collections, but also a class of prose composition appended to them and known as *Brāhmaṇa,* composed in the centuries immediately following and representing an age of meticulous theological and liturgical analysis. The Brāhmaṇas contain long, detailed discussions of the elements and connotations of the Vedic sacrifice, as well as a number of priceless fragments of very ancient Āryan myths and legends.

Following the period of the Brāhmaṇas came that of the Upaniṣads (mentioned above), which opened in the eighth century B.C. and culminated in the century of the Buddha (c. 563–483 B.C.). Compare the dates of the Greek age of philosophy, which began with Thales of Miletus (640?–546 B.C.) and culminated in the dialogues of Plato (427?–347 B.C.) and the works of Aristotle (384–322 B.C.).

For the convenience of the reader a brief historical appendix has been prepared, which contains notices of the dates of most of the topics treated in the present volume; see Appendix B.

gold; in the waters, in cattle, and in men shall be ours! May the lovely goddess who bore Indra come to us, endowed with luster!

"The brilliancy that is in the chariot, the dice, and the strength of the bull; in the wind, in Parjanya (Indra as the lord of rain), and the fire of Varuṇa (lord regent of ocean and of the western quarter) shall be ours! May the lovely goddess who bore Indra come to us, endowed with luster!

"The brilliancy that is in the man of royal caste, in the stretched drum, in the strength of the horse, and in the shout of men shall be ours! May the lovely goddess who bore Indra come to us, endowed with luster!" [4]

The fully developed Adhyātmam-adhidaivam system of the period of the Upaniṣads utilized as a means for arriving at absolute detachment a thorough-going scheme of correspondences between subjective and objective phenomena.[5] As an instance: "The divinities of the world having been created, they said to Ātman (the Self as the Creator): 'Find out for us an abode wherein we may be established and may eat food.' He led up a bull to them. They said: 'Verily, this is not sufficient for us.' He led up a horse to them. They said: 'Verily, this not sufficient for us.' He led up a person to them. They said: 'Oh! Well

[4] *Atharva Veda* VI. 38. (Translated by Maurice Bloomfield, Sacred Books of the East, Vol. XLII, pp. 116-117; cf. also, Harvard Oriental Series, Cambridge, Mass., 1905, Vol. VII, p. 309.)

"The lovely goddess who bore Indra" is Aditi, mother of the gods of the Vedic pantheon, corresponding to Rhea, mother of the Greek Olympians. Indra, the chief and best beloved of her sons, corresponds to the Greco-Roman lord of the gods, Zeus-Jove, while Varuṇa is comparable to the Greek Ouranos (heaven), and Sūrya to Phoebus-Apollo.

[5] Adhyātmam (*adhi* = "over"; *ātman* = "self or spirit"): the Supreme Spirit manifest as the Self of the individual; adhidaivam (*daivam*, from *deva* = "divinity"): the Supreme Spirit operating in material objects. These two are equated in this system as the dual aspects of one sole Imperishable, known respectively from the subjective and the objective points of view.

done!'—Verily, a person is a thing well done.—He said to them: 'Enter into your respective abodes.' Fire became speech, and entered the mouth. Wind became breath, and entered the nostrils. The sun became sight, and entered the eyes. The quarters of heaven became hearing, and entered the ears. Plants and trees became hairs, and entered the skin. The moon became mind, and entered the heart. Death became the out-breath, and entered the navel. Waters became semen, and entered the virile member." [6]

The pupil is taught to apply his knowledge of correspondences of this kind to such meditations as the following: "Just as a jug dissolves into earth, a wave into water, or a bracelet into gold, even so the universe will dissolve into me. Wonderful am I! Adoration to myself! For when the world, from its highest god to its least stem of grass, dissolves, that destruction is not mine." [7]

There is evident here a total disjunction of the phenomenal self (the naïvely conscious personality which together with its world of names and forms will in time be dissolved) from that other, profoundly hidden, essential yet forgotten, transcendental Self (*ātman*), which when recollected roars out with its thrilling, world-annihilating, "Wonderful am I!" That other is no created thing, but the substratum of all created things, all objects, all processes. "Weapons cut it not; fire burns it not; water wets it not; the wind does not wither it." [8] The, sense-faculties, normally turned outward, seeking, apprehending, and reacting to their objects, do not come into touch with the sphere of that permanent reality but only with the transient evolutions of the perishable transformations of its energy. Will power, leading

[6] *Aitareya Upaniṣad* 2. 1-4. (Translated by Robert Ernest Hume, *The Thirteen Principal Upanishads,* Oxford, 1921, p. 295.)

[7] *Aṣṭāvakra Saṁhitā* 2. 10-11. (Translated by Swāmī Nityaswarūpānanda, Mayavati, 1940, pp. 22-23.)

[8] *Bhagavad Gītā* 2. 23.

to the achievement of worldly ends, can therefore be of no great help to man. Neither can the pleasures and experiences of the senses initiate the consciousness into the secret of the fullness of life.

According to the thinking and experience of India, the knowledge of changing things does not conduce to a realistic attitude; for such things lack substantiality, they perish. Neither does it conduce to an idealistic outlook; for the inconsistencies of things in flux continually contradict and refute each other. Phenomenal forms are by nature delusory and fallacious. The one who rests on them will be disturbed. They are merely the particles of a vast universal illusion which is wrought by the magic of Self-forgetfulness, supported by ignorance, and carried forward by the deceived passions. Naïve unawareness of the hidden truth of the Self is the primary cause of all the misplaced emphases, inappropriate attitudes, and consequent self-torments of this auto-intoxicated world.

There is obviously implicit in such an insight the basis for a transfer of all interest not only from the normal ends and means of people of the world, but also from the rites and dogmas of the religion of such deluded beings. The mythological creator, the Lord of the Universe, is no longer of interest. Only introverted awareness bent and driven to the depth of the subject's own nature reaches that borderline where the transitory superimpositions meet their unchanging source. And such awareness can finally succeed even in bringing consciousness across the border, to merge—perish and become therewith imperishable—in the omnipresent substratum of all substance. That is the Self (*ātman*), the ultimate, enduring, supporting source of being. That is the giver of all these specialized manifestations, changes of form, and deviations from the true state, these so-called *vikāras:* transformations and evolutions of the cosmic display. Nor is it through praise of and submission to the gods, but through knowledge, knowledge of the Self, that the sage passes from involvement in what is here displayed to a discovery of its cause.

And such knowledge is achieved through either of two techniques: 1. a systematic disparagement of the whole world as illusion, or 2. an equally thoroughgoing realization of the sheer materiality of it all.[8a]

This we recognize as precisely the non-theistic, anthropocentric position that we ourselves are on the point of reaching today in the West, if indeed we are not already there. For where dwell the gods to whom we can uplift our hands, send forth our prayers, and make oblation? Beyond the Milky Way are only island universes, galaxy beyond galaxy in the infinitudes of space—no realm of angels, no heavenly mansions, no choirs of the blessed surrounding a divine throne of the Father, revolving in beatific consciousness about the axial mystery of the Trinity. Is there any region left in all these great reaches where the soul on its quest might expect to arrive at the feet of God, having become divested of its own material coil? Or must we not now turn rather inward, seek the divine internally, in the deepest vault, beneath the floor; hearken within for the secret voice that is both commanding and consoling; draw from inside the grace which passeth all understanding?

We of the modern Occident are at last prepared to seek and hear the voice that India has heard. But like the tiger cub we must hear it not from the teacher but from within ourselves. Just as in the period of the deflation of the revealed gods of the Vedic pantheon, so today revealed Christianity has been devaluated. The Christian, as Nietzsche says, is a man who behaves like everybody else. Our professions of faith have no longer any discernible bearing either on our public conduct or on our private state of hope. The sacraments do not work on many of us their spiritual transformation; we are bereft and

[8a] Respectively, as in the Vedānta (*infra,* pp. 409-463) and the Sāṅkhya (*infra,* pp. 280-332).

at a loss where to turn. Meanwhile, our academic secular philosophies are concerned rather with information than with that redemptive transformation which our souls require. And this is the reason why a glance at the face of India may assist us to discover and recover something of ourselves.

The basic aim of any serious study of Oriental thought should be, not merely the gathering and ordering of as much detailed inside information as possible, but the reception of some significant influence. And in order that this may come to pass—in line with the parable of the goat-fosterling who discovered he was a tiger—we should swallow the meat of the teaching as red and rare as we can stand it, not too much cooked in the heat of our ingrained Occidental intellect (and, by no means, from any philological pickle jar), but not raw either, because then it would prove unpalatable and perhaps indigestible. We must take it rare, with lots of the red juices gushing, so that we may really taste it, with a certain sense of surprise. Then we will join, from our transoceanic distance, in the world-reverberating jungle roar of India's wisdom.

2.

The Steely Barb

Before entering upon a study of philosophy one should clear the mind with the question: What, really, do I expect from philosophy? There are many, secretly afraid, who spontaneously resist its revelations. They find philosophy difficult to enjoy—occasionally exciting, but in the main complex, long-winded, abstract, and apparently of no great practical value. For such persons, metaphysics is vague and lofty nonsense, only fit to give one vertigo; its uncontrolled speculations are contrary to the findings of modern science and have been discredited (for all but the inadequately informed) by the publications of the latest thinkers. Working hypotheses have at last begun to dispel the mysteries of the universe and man's existence. By means of calculations based on sober, controlled experiment, and verified not only in the facts of the laboratory but also through the applied techniques of everyday life, the traditional mysteries of the mystics are being systematically dissipated. The Eucharist has been transmuted back into bread. And so, although philosophy may be allowed its due in so far as it is subservient to civilization and follows the usual habits of the modern mind, it cannot be taken seriously if it conflicts with the current formulations of physical science or recommends a different mode of conduct from that today made general by the universal progress of technology. Metaphysics and such airy meditations as those of the philosophy of history and religion may be sensitively tolerated as a genteel embellishment of education, but they are not of any vital use.

Minds of the type represented by this sort of up-to-date apotropaic cerebration teach philosophy as a synthesis of scientific information. They reject everything that cannot be linked into this context. They are concerned to control and harmonize the findings from the various fields of research, outline a comprehensive pattern, and formulate methodical principles, without encroaching on the authority of the specialist—the research fellow in direct touch with the microbe, asterism, or conditioned reflex; but as for the methods, goals, and so-called truths of every other system of thought: these are either rejected or patronized, as the quaint, outmoded prepossessions of a superseded world.

There is, however, another type of modern thinker, diametrically opposed and sometimes overtly antagonistic to the first, who cherishes a hope that contemporary philosophy may some day utter a word to him somewhat different from the communications continually coming from all departments of the sprawling scientific workshop. Touring as a searching student through the laboratories, peering through the various instruments, tabulating, classifying, and becoming very tired of the infinitude of minutely specialized responses to questions of detail, he is seeking an answer to some query that the research fellows seem not to be concerned with and that the comprehensive philosophers are systematically avoiding. Something beyond critical reasoning is what he requires; something that someone of adequate mind should have realized intuitively as a Truth (with a capital T) about man's existence and the nature of the cosmos; something to enter the breast and pierce the heart with what Baudelaire called "the steely barb of the infinite," *la pointe acérée de l'infinie.* What he requires is a philosophy that will confront and resolve the task once performed by religion; and this is a need from which no number of college courses on the validity of inference can emancipate him.

Philosophy as the handmaid of empirical research, thought wearing the blinders of the standards of contemporary science, and metaphysics open to rational criticism from every quarter —in short, reason infallible: this is the ideal and requirement of the practical-minded thinker. Whereas the other is simply not convinced by all the plausible searching and discovering. Neither is he unwilling to accept the reproach of being somewhat mysterious in his personal demands. He does not ask that a philosophy should be comprehensible to every level-headed contemporary; what he wants is a response (if only so much as the hint of one) to the primary questions in his mind.

The sages of India side with the second of these two points of view. They have never intended their teachings to be popular. Indeed, it is only in recent years that their words have become generally accessible through printed texts and translations into popular tongues. They insist on first determining whether a candidate applying for admission to the sanctum of their philosophy is endowed with the necessary spiritual qualifications. Has he fulfilled the preliminary disciplines? Is he ripe to benefit from a contact with the guru? Does he deserve to take a place at the guru's feet? For the solutions of the Indian sages to the enigmas of life and their approaches to the mystery of the universe are worked out along lines completely different from those being followed by the leaders of modern research and education. They neither deny nor apologize for the fact that their teachings are hard to grasp and therefore—necessarily—esoteric.

What the specific requirements are for the Indian pupil (*adhikārin*) qualified to specialize in one or another of the traditional departments of learning, we shall presently see;[9] but first, let us introduce ourselves to this subject by way of two entertaining anecdotes about the preliminary trials and tests of Indian pupils. These will demonstrate that even when a candidate has proved himself and been accepted as an adept well entitled to be instructed, he must not suppose that he is already ripe to understand even the first principles of the wisdom of reality. His superior character and accomplishments (though of an order not known to the multitude, or even to the privileged normal minority) are by no means an adequate safeguard against the pitfalls and curious dangers of the deceptive way to the concealed goal of truth.

The first tale, which is told of a king who had been accepted as a pupil by the famous Vedāntic philosopher Śaṅkara (c. 788–820 or 850 A.D.), is one that will give some idea of the supernal loftiness of the basic conceptions of India's classic philosophy and illustrate their incompatibility with common sense.

[9] *Infra*, pp. 51-56.

They are revelations from "the other shore," from "over Jordan"; or as the Mahāyāna Buddhist tradition phrases it: they are clues to the "Transcendental Wisdom of the Far Bank" (*prajñā-pāramitā*), reflections from beyond these broad and wildly turbulent waters of the stream of life which are to be crossed in the boat (*yāna*) of the enlightening practice of the Buddhist virtues. Not the detailed description of our hither shore, but transport to the shore beyond—through transformation—is to be the supreme goal of human research, teaching, and meditation. This is the ideal on which all the great philosophies of India come to accord.[10]

[10] *Editor's note:* The Buddha (c. 563–483 B.C.) did not accept the authority of the Vedas; hence the doctrine that he taught was heterodox and developed apart from the orthodox Vedic line, producing schools and systems of its own. Two great divisions of Buddhist thinking are distinguished. The first was dedicated to the ideal of individual salvation and represented the way to this end as monastic self-discipline. The second, which seems to have matured in northern India during and following the first and second centuries A.D. (long after the other had been disseminated as far southward as the island of Ceylon), proposed the ideal of salvation for all and developed disciplines of popular devotion and universal secular service. The earlier is known as the *Hīnayāna,* "the lesser or little (*hīna*) boat or vehicle (*yāna*)," while the second is the *Mahāyāna,* "the great (*mahat*) boat or vehicle," i.e., the boat in which all can ride. Hīnayāna Buddhism is supported by an extensive body of scripture that was set down in Pāli (an Indo-Āryan dialect of the Buddha's time), c. 80 B.C., by the monks of Ceylon (the so-called Pāli canon). While the Mahāyāna recognized this canon, it produced, in addition, a body of scriptures of its own, in Sanskrit (the traditional sacred and scholarly language of Vedic India, which has been preserved with little change to the present day). Among the chief of these Buddhist writings in Sanskrit are the so-called *Prajñā-pāramitā* texts, mentioned above and discussed *infra,* pp. 483-552. Mahāyāna Buddhism spread northward into China, Tibet, and Japan, carrying the "Transcendental Wisdom of the Far Bank" to those lands; the Hīnayāna survives chiefly in Ceylon, Burma, and Siam.

Meanwhile, the Vedic-Upanisadic tradition did not cease to develop, but produced its own series of creative and systematizing philosophers. The most celebrated of these was the brilliant genius Śaṅkara c. 788–820

The Vedāntic doctrine, as systematized and expounded by Śaṅkara, stresses a concept which is rather puzzling, namely that of māyā.[11] Māyā denotes the unsubstantial, phenomenal character of the observed and manipulated world, as well as of the mind itself—the conscious and even subconscious stratifications and powers of the personality. It is a concept that holds a key position in Vedāntic thought and teaching, and, if misunderstood, may lead the pupil to the conclusion that the external world and his ego are devoid of all reality whatsoever, mere nonentities, "like the horns of a hare." This is a common error in the early stages of instruction, to correct which, by vivid example, is the purpose of numberless comical anecdotes told of the Indian adhikārins and their gurus.

The king of the present story, who became the pupil of the philosopher Śaṅkara, was a man of sound and realistic mind

or 850 A.D.) whose commentaries on the basic orthodox Vedic scriptures stand as the supreme monument of the late period of Indian philosophy. The term *Vedānta* (=*Veda*+*anta* end: "end of the Veda," i.e., the goal or terminal development of Vedic thought) is applied to the works and concepts of this late period of orthodox Hindu scholasticism (cf. *infra*, pp. 409-463).

[11] *Editor's note: Māyā,* from the root *mā,* "to measure, to form, to build," denotes, in the first place, the power of a god or demon to produce illusory effects, to change form, and to appear under deceiving masks. Derived from this is the meaning, "magic," the production of an illusion by supernatural means; and then, simply, "the production of an illusion," for example in warfare, camouflage, etc. (cf. *infra,* p. 122). *Māyā* in the Vedāntic philosophy is, specifically, "the illusion superimposed upon reality as an effect of ignorance"; for example: ignorant of the nature of a rope seen lying on the road, one may perceive a snake. Śaṅkara describes the entire visible cosmos as *māyā,* an illusion superimposed upon true being by man's deceitful senses and unilluminated mind (compare Kant, *The Critique of Pure Reason;* note also that to the modern physicist a minute unit of matter may appear either as a particle or as a wave of energy, according to the instrument with which it is observed). Cf. Heinrich Zimmer, *Myths and Symbols in Indian Art and Civilization,* The Bollingen Series VI, New York, 1946, index, under "Māyā."

who could not get over the fact of his own royal splendor and august personality. When his teacher directed him to regard all things, including the exercise of power and enjoyment of kingly pleasure, as no more than equally indifferent reflexes (purely phenomenal) of the transcendental essence that was the Self not only of himself but of all things, he felt some resistance. And when he was told that that one and only Self was made to seem multiple by the deluding-force of his own inborn ignorance, he determined to put his guru to the test and prove whether he would behave as a person absolutely unconcerned.

The following day, therefore, when the philosopher was coming along one of the stately approaches to the palace, to deliver his next lecture to the king, a large and dangerous elephant, maddened by heat, was let loose at him. Śaṅkara turned and fled the moment he perceived his danger, and when the animal nearly reached his heels, disappeared from view. When he was found, he was at the top of a lofty palm tree, which he had ascended with a dexterity more usual among sailors than intellectuals. The elephant was caught, fettered, and conducted back to the stables, and the great Śaṅkara, perspiration breaking from every pore, came before his pupil.

Politely, the king apologized to the master of cryptic wisdom for the unfortunate, nearly disastrous incident; then, with a smile scarcely concealed and half pretending great seriousness, he inquired why the venerable teacher had resorted to physical flight, since he must have been aware that the elephant was of a purely illusory, phenomenal character.

The sage replied, "Indeed, in highest truth, the elephant is non-real. Nevertheless, you and I are as non-real as that elephant. Only your ignorance, clouding the truth with this spectacle of non-real phenomenality, made you see phenomenal me go up a non-real tree."

The second anecdote also turns on the undeniable physical impression made by an elephant; this time, however, the adhikārin is a very earnest seeker who takes precisely the opposite attitude to that of the materialistic king. Śrī Rāmakrishna used often to recite this tale to illustrate the mystery of māyā. It is an apt, surprising, and memorable example, touched with the gentle humor characteristic of so many Indian popular narratives.

An old guru—so we hear—was about to conclude the secret lessons that he had been giving to an advanced pupil on the omnipresence of the divine Spiritual Person. "Everything," said the wise old teacher, while his pupil listened, indrawn and full of the bliss of learning, "is God, the Infinite, pure and real, boundless and beyond the pairs of opposites, devoid of differentiating qualities and limiting distinctions. That is the final meaning of all the teachings of our holy wisdom."

The pupil understood. "God," he responded, "is the sole reality. That Divine One may be found in everything, unaffected by suffering or any fault. Every You and I is Its abode, every form an obscuring figuration within which that unique, unacting Activator dwells." He was elate: a wave of feeling swept through him tremendously, and he felt luminous and immense, like a cloud which, increasing, has come to fill the firmament. When he walked, now, it was nimbly and without weight.

Sublime, like the only cloud, in all-pervading solitude, he was walking, keeping to the middle of the road, when a huge elephant came from the opposite direction. The mahout, or driver, riding on the neck, shouted, "Clear the way," and the numerous tinkling bells of the net-covering of the great animal rang with a silvery peal to the rhythm of its soft inaudible tread. The self-exalted student of the science of Vedānta, though full of divine feeling, yet heard and saw the coming of the elephant. And he said to himself, "Why should I make way for that elephant? I am God. The elephant is God. Should God be afraid of God?" And so, fearlessly and with faith, he continued in the middle of the road. But when God came to God, the elephant swung its trunk around the waist of the thinker and tossed him out of the way. He landed hard and was a little hurt, but more greatly shocked. Covered with dust, limping, bruised, and unsettled in his mind, he returned to the teacher and recounted his confusing experience. The guru listened serenely, and when the tale was told, simply replied, "Indeed, you *are* God. So is the elephant. But why did you not listen to God's voice calling to you from the mahout, who is also God, to clear the way?"

To some extent, real philosophical thinking must always be difficult to grasp in the whole range of its implications. Even though expressed with utter clarity and the most precise logical consistency, it yet remains elusive. If the words of Plato and Aristotle, for example, had been finally mastered by their interpreters during the centuries that have elapsed since their first inspired expression, they would certainly not be the vital topics of ever-renewed, passionate debate and research that they remain to this very moment. A profound truth, even though comprehended by the most penetrating intellect and expressed in accurate terms, will be read in conflicting fashions during subsequent periods. Apparently assimilated and integrated, it will yet continue to be a source of new and startling discoveries for generations to come. Antiquity possessed the whole text of Heraclitus, not merely the few scanty fragments and stray references that have survived to us, and yet he was known even then as the "obscure one." He is nevertheless the first master in Western literature of the trenchant sentence and the succinct, crystal-clear aphorism.

It is said that Hegel, that most lofty and powerful of the Romantic philosophers—at once clear and cryptic, abstract and realistic—was being comforted by one of his pupils when he was lying on his deathbed in 1831, prematurely stricken by cholera. The comforter was one of his most intimate friends and distinguished followers; and he was seeking to reassure the master by telling him that, should he be taken away before completing his encyclopedic, gigantic work, there would remain his faithful pupils to carry on. Hegel, serene as the antarctic silence, on the very point of death, only raised his head a little. "I had one pupil who understood me," he was heard to mutter; and while everyone present became alert to hear the venerated teacher pronounce the name, his head relaxed again to the pillow. "One pupil," he went on, "who understood—and he misunderstood."

Such cutting anecdotes need not be literally true. In a kind of mocking pictorial script, nevertheless, they usually mirror something of the truth. The biographies in Plutarch's *Lives* are largely fables of this sort, told of the famous men of the ancient world. Like the Hindu tales, they sharpen the point of what is true.

Occidental philosophy, as developed through the long and stately series of its distinguished masters, from Pythagoras to Empedocles and Plato, from Plotinus and the Neoplatonic thinkers to the mystics of the Middle Ages, and again in Spinoza and Hegel, deals with problems beyond the sphere of common sense, such as can be expressed only in cryptic difficult formulae, and by paradox. Indian philosophy does the same. The Oriental thinkers are as fully aware as the Western of the fact that the means offered by the mind and the powers of reason are not adequate to the problem of grasping and expressing truth. Thinking is limited by language. Thinking is a kind of soundless interior talk. What cannot be formulated in the current words or symbols of the given tradition does not exist in current thinking. And it requires, therefore, a specific creative effort on the part of a bold, fervent mind to break through to what is not being said—to view it at all; and then another effort to bring it back into the field of language by coining a term. Unknown, unnamed, non-existing as it were, and yet existing verily, the truth must be won to, found, and carried back through the brain into speech —where, inevitably, it will again be immediately mislaid.

The possibilities for thought, practical or otherwise, at any period, are thus rigidly limited by the range and wealth of the available linguistic coinage: the number and scope of the nouns, verbs, adjectives, and connectives. The totality of this currency is called, in Indian philosophy, *nāman* (Latin *nomen,* our word "name"). The very substance on and by which the mind operates when thinking consists of this name-treasury of notions. *Nāman* is the internal realm of concepts, which corresponds to the external realm of perceived "forms," the Sanskrit term for the latter being *rūpa,* "form," "shape," "color" (for there are no shapes or forms without color). *Rūpa* is the outer counterpart of *nāman; nāman* the interior of *rūpa. Nāma-rūpa* therefore denotes, on the one hand, man, the experiencing, thinking individual, man as endowed with mind and senses, and on the other, all the means and objects of thought and perception. *Nāma-rūpa* is the whole world, subjective and objective, as observed and known.

Now, all of the schools of Indian philosophy, though greatly diverging in their formulations of the essence of ultimate truth or basic reality, are unanimous in asserting that the ultimate object of thought and final goal of knowledge lies beyond the range of nāma-rūpa. Both Vedāntic Hinduism and Mahāyāna Buddhism constantly insist on the inadequacy of language and logical thought for the expression and comprehension of their systems. According to the classical Vedāntic formula, the fundamental factor responsible for the character and problems of our normal day-world consciousness, the force that builds the ego and leads it to mistake itself and its experiences for reality, is "ignorance, nescience" (*avidyā*). This ignorance is to be described neither as "being or existent" (*sat*), nor as "non-being, non-existent" (*a-sat*), but as "ineffable, inexplicable, indescribable" (*a-nirvacanīya*). For if it were "unreal, non-existent"—so the argument runs—it would not be of force sufficient to bind consciousness to the limitations of the individual and shroud from man's inner eye the realization of the immediate reality of the Self, which is the only Being. But on the other hand, if it were "real," of absolute indestructibility, then it could not be so readily dispelled by knowledge (*vidyā*); the Self (*ātman*) would never have been discovered as the ultimate substratum of all existences, and there would be no doctrine of Vedānta capable of guiding the intellect to enlightenment. "Ignorance" cannot be said to *be,* because it changes. Transiency is its very character—and this the seeker recognizes the moment he transcends its deluding spell. Its form is "the form of becoming" (*bhāva-rūpa*)—ephemeral, perishable, conquerable. And yet this "ignorance" itself differs from the specific transient phenomena within its pale, because it has existed—though ever changing—from time immemorial. Indeed, it is the root, the very cause and substance, of time. And the paradox is that though without beginning it can have an end. For the individual, bound by it to the everlasting round-of-rebirth, and subject to what is popularly called the law of the transmigration of the life-monad or soul, can become aware of the whole sphere of "ignorance" as an existence of no final reality—simply by an act of interior awareness (*anubhava*), or a moment of the uncomplicated realization, "I am nescient" (*aham ajña*).

Indian philosophy insists that the sphere of logical thought is far exceeded by that of the mind's possible experiences of reality. To express and communicate knowledge gained in moments of grammar-transcending insight metaphors must be used, similes and allegories. These are then not mere embellishments, dispensable accessories, but the very vehicles of the meaning, which could not be rendered, and could never have been attained, through the logical formulae of normal verbal thought. Significant images can comprehend and make manifest with clarity and pictorial consistency the paradoxical character of the reality known to the sage: a translogical reality, which, expressed in the abstract language of normal thought, would seem inconsistent, self-contradictory, or even absolutely meaningless. Indian philosophy, therefore, frankly avails itself of the symbols and images of myth, and is not finally at variance with the patterns and sense of mythological belief.

The Greek critical philosophers before Socrates, the pre-

Socratic thinkers and the Sophists, practically destroyed their native mythological tradition. Their new approach to the solution of the enigmas of the universe and of man's nature and destiny conformed to the logic of the rising natural sciences—mathematics, physics, and astronomy. Under their powerful influence the older mythological symbols degenerated into mere elegant and amusing themes for novels, little better than society gossip about the complicated love-affairs and quarrels of the celestial upper class. Contrariwise in India, however: there mythology never ceased to support and facilitate the expression of philosophic thought. The rich pictorial script of the epic tradition, the features of the divinities whose incarnations and exploits constituted the myth, the symbols of religion, popular as well as esoteric, loaned themselves, again and again, to the purpose of the teachers, becoming the receptacles of their truth-renewing experience and the vehicles of their communication. In this way a co-operation of the latest and the oldest, the highest and the lowest, a wonderful friendship of mythology and philosophy, was effected; and this has been sustained with such result that the whole edifice of Indian civilization is imbued with spiritual meaning. The close interdependence and perfect harmonization of the two serve to counteract the natural tendency of Indian philosophy to become recondite and esoteric, removed from life and the task of the education of society. In the Hindu world, the folklore and popular mythology carry the truths and teachings of the philosophers to the masses. In this symbolic form, the ideas do not have to be watered down to be popularized. The vivid, perfectly appropriate pictorial script preserves the doctrines without the slightest damage to their sense.

Indian philosophy is basically skeptical of words, skeptical of their adequacy to render the main topic of philosophical thought, and therefore very cautious about trying to bring into a purely intellectual formula the answer to the riddle of the universe and man's existence. "What is all this around me, this world in which

I find myself? What is this process carrying me on, together with the earth? Whence has it all proceeded? Whither is it tending? And what is to be my role, my duty, my goal, amidst this bewildering breath-taking drama in which I find myself involved?" That is the basic problem in the mind of men when they start philosophizing and before they reduce their aspirations to questions of methodology and the criticism of their own mental and sensual faculties. "All this around me, and my own being": that is the net of entanglement called māyā, the world creative power. Māyā manifests its force through the rolling universe and evolving forms of individuals. To understand that secret, to know how it works, and to transcend, if possible, its cosmic spell—breaking outward through the layers of tangible and visible appearance, and simultaneously inward through all the intellectual and emotional stratifications of the psyche—this is the pursuit conceived by Indian philosophy to be the primary, and finally undeniable, human task.

3.

The Claims of Science

WHEN I was a student, the term "Indian philosophy" was usually regarded as self-contradictory, a *contradictio in adjecto,* comparable to such an absurdity as "wooden steel." "Indian philosophy" was something that simply did not exist, like a "mare's nest," or, as Hindu logicians say, like the "horns of a hare" or the "son of a barren woman." Among all the professors holding permanent chairs in philosophy at that time there was but one lone enthusiast, a follower of Schopenhauer, old Paul Deussen, who regularly delivered lectures in Indian philosophy. Of course, to some extent, the orientalists were providing information by redacting texts—assisted perhaps by some solitary pupil; but they never troubled to investigate the problem of whether there was such a thing as "Indian philosophy." Whatever they encountered in their documents they interpreted on a philological basis, and then they moved along to the following line. Meanwhile the philosophy professors were agreeing unanimously—some politely, some impolitely—that such a thing as philosophy, in the proper sense of the term, simply did not exist outside of Europe. And as we shall presently see, this was an attitude not without a certain technical justification.

But on the other hand, another group of historians was developing at that time a broader and more inspiring view of the history of ideas and the evolution of the human mind. Foremost among these was Wilhelm Dilthey. Such men felt the necessity, though they lacked the ability, to incorporate the philosophies of India and China, at least in any work pretending to be a universal history of human thought. They argued—as has been generally admitted since—that if a thinker of the order of Hobbes is to be admitted to your list of significant minds, then you cannot disregard Confucius on education, state policy, government, and ethics. Or if Machiavelli is to be treated as the first modern political thinker, something must be said about the Hindu system represented in the *Arthaśāstra*.[12] Similarly, if St. Augustine, St. Thomas Aquinas, and Pascal are to be called religious philosophers, then the great Hindu divines like Śaṅkara and Rāmānuja[13]—who, with a fully fledged scholastic technique, expounded the philosophic foundations of orthodox Vedāntic theology—cannot be left aside. And the moment you recognize Plotinus or Meister Eckhart as a philosopher, Lao-tse cannot be ignored, nor

[12] *Infra,* pp. 35-38 and 87-139.

[13] *Infra,* pp. 414ff.; 458-459.

the masters of Hindu and Buddhist yoga. References to China and India, therefore, were added to our Western histories of thought, as footnotes, side-glances, or preliminary chapters, embellishing the story of "real" philosophy, which began with the Ionian Greeks, Thales, Anaximander, and Heraclitus, in the sixth and fifth centuries B.C.[14]

In spite of the influence of this point of view, many remained reluctant, even in the first years of the present century, to confer on Hindu thought the dignifying title "philosophy." "Philosophy," they claimed, was a Greek term, denoting something unique and particularly noble, which had sprung into existence among the Greeks and been carried on only by Western civilization. To support this contention, they could refer to the authority of the giant Hegel, who, a full century before them, with a masterly intuition and thorough command of the information then available, had discussed India and China in his *Philosophy of Religion* and *Philosophy of History*. Hegel coined certain formulae that are still unsurpassed for the study of history, and have been corroborated by our most recent knowledge of facts and sources (which is vastly more than what was available to him). Second to none in his intuitive grasp, he yet banished India and China, together with their philosophies, from the principal chapters of his thought, regarding the achievements of those almost unknown civilizations as a kind of prelude to the rise of the curtain on "real" history, which began in the Near East, and "real" philosophy, which was an invention of the Greeks. Hegel's argument—and it is still the argument of those who entertain

[14] Georg Misch, a pupil of Dilthey and the editor of his mounds of posthumous manuscripts, who is now [1942] in Cambridge, England, has compared the steps and stages of Greek philosophy during the period before Plato with parallel developments in Chinese and Indian history. He has brought together from each of the three traditions texts dealing with similar problems, and has presented these in a series of choice [German] translations, together with commentaries. (Georg Misch, *Der Weg in der Philosophie,* Leipzig, 1926.)

the old reluctance to confer the title "philosopher" upon the immortal thinkers of India and China—is that something is missing from the Oriental systems. When they are compared with Western philosophy, as developed in antiquity and in modern times, what is obviously lacking is the ever renewed, fructifying, close contact with the progressive natural sciences—their improving critical methods and their increasingly secular, non-theological, practically antireligious, outlook on man and the world. This is enough, we are asked to agree, to justify the Western restriction of its classic term.

Here, it must be admitted, the Old Guard are quite correct. A close and continuous interrelationship with rational science has been a distinguishing trait of Western philosophy; consider, for instance, the role of applied mathematics in Greek astronomy, mechanics, and physics, or the approach to zoology and botany of such thinkers as Aristotle and Theophrastus—methodical, and unclouded by any theological or mythical conceptions. It has been argued that Indian thought, at its best, may be compared not with the great line of Western philosophy, but only with the Christian thinking of the Middle Ages, from the Fathers to St. Thomas Aquinas, when philosophical speculation was kept subservient to the claims of the "revealed" faith and compelled to enact the part of helpmate or handmaid of theology (*ancilla theologiae*), and was never permitted to challenge or analyze the dogmatic foundations laid down and interpreted by the decrees of the popes and maintained by the persecution of all heretics and freethinkers. Greek philosophy, and then likewise modern philosophy—as represented by Giordano Bruno (who perished at the stake) and Descartes—has invariably brought intellectual revolution in its wake, effecting a radical and ever increasing disentanglement of thought from the meshes of religious traditionalism. Already in the middle of the fifth century B.C. Anaxagoras was banished from Athens for declaring that the sun was not the sun-god Helios but an incandescent celestial sphere. Among the crimes of which Socrates was accused, and for which he had to drain the deadly cup, was a lack of faith in the established religion, that of the local tutelary deities of Athens. While from the days of Bruno and Galileo on, our modern sciences and philosophy have arrived at their present maturity only by battling at every step the doctrines of man and nature that were the tradition and established treasure of the Church. Nothing comparable, or at least nothing of such a revolutionizing and explosive magnitude, has ever shown itself in the traditional East.

Western philosophy has become the guardian angel of right (i.e., unprejudiced, critical) thinking. It has earned this position through its repeated contacts with, and unwavering loyalty to, the progressive methods of thought in the sciences. And it will support its champion even though the end may be the destruction of all traditional values whatsoever, in society, religion, and philosophy. The nineteenth-century thinkers who declined to accept Indian philosophy on the par level did so because they felt responsible to the truth of the modern sciences. This had been established by experiment and criticism. And philosophy, as they conceived it, was to expound the methods of such rational progress, while safeguarding them against dilettantism, wishful thinking, and the ingrained prepossessions of any undisciplined speculation conducted along the discredited lines of archaic man.

There is, on the other hand, an attitude of hallowed traditionalism conspicuous in most of the great documents of Eastern thought, a readiness to submit to the authoritative utterances of inspired teachers claiming direct contact with transcendental truth. This would seem to indicate an incorrigible preference for vision, intuition, and metaphysical experience rather than experiment, laboratory work, and the reduction of the exact data of the senses to mathematical formulae. There was never in India any such close affinity between natural science and philosophy as to bring about a significant cross-fertilization. Nothing in

Hindu physics, botany, or zoology can compare with the mature achievements of Aristotle, Theophrastus, Eratosthenes, and the scientists in Hellenistic Alexandria. Indian reasoning has remained uninfluenced by such criticism, new raw material, and inspiration as the Occidental thinkers have continually received from sources of this kind. And if the Indian natural sciences cannot be said ever to have equaled those known to Europe even in the time of the Greeks, how much greater is the inequality today!

Under the impact of the sweeping achievements of our laboratories, modern philosophy has completely refashioned its conception of its problems. Without the development of a modern mathematics, physics, and astronomy, through the work of Galileo, Torricelli, and their contemporaries, the new way of thought represented by Descartes and Spinoza would never have been found. Spinoza earned his livelihood as an optician, making lenses—a modern, advanced tool of the newest sciences. The versatile lifework of Leibnitz exhibited most conspicuously the close interrelationship, nay fusion, of mathematics and physics with seventeenth-century philosophy. And one cannot study Kant without becoming aware of Newton. During the nineteenth century, science found its counterpart in the positivistic, empiristic philosophies of Comte, Mill, and Spencer. Indeed, the whole course of modern Western thought has been established by the pacemaking, relentless progress of our secularized, rational sciences, from the day of Francis Bacon and the rise of the New Learning, even to the present moment, when the staggering theories of Einstein, Heisenberg, Planck, Eddington, and Dirac, on the structure of the atom and the universe, have projected the new task for the philosophers not only of today but of generations to come.

Absolutely nothing of this kind will be found in the history of India, though in classical antiquity a corresponding situation is marked by the grand sequence from Thales to Democritus, and through Plato and Aristotle to Lucretius. Not a few of the pre-Socratics were distinguished in mathematics, physics, and astronomy, as well as in philosophical speculation. Thales won more fame when he predicted an eclipse of the sun by means of mathematics applied to problems of cosmology than he ever gained among his contemporaries by declaring water to be the primary element of the universe—an idea that had been common to various earlier mythologies. Pythagoras, similarly, is celebrated as the discoverer of certain basic principles of acoustics. Aristotle writes of the followers of Pythagoras that they "applied themselves to the study of mathematics and were the first to advance that science."[15] Regarding the principles of number as the first principles of all existing things, Pythagoras, by experiment, discovered the dependence of the musical intervals on certain arithmetical ratios of lengths of string at the same tension; and the laws of harmony thus discovered he applied to the interpretation of the whole structure of the cosmos. Thus in ancient Greece, as in Europe today, philosophical speculation concerning the structure and forces of the universe, the nature of all things, and the essential character of man was already largely actuated by a spirit of scientific inquiry; and the result was a dissolution of the archaic, established, mythological and theological ideas about man and the world. Traditionalism based on revelation and time-honored visions became discredited. A series of intellectual revolutions followed, which were in part the cause and spiritual prototype of the collapse, centuries later, of our established social systems—from the French Revolution in 1789 to the Russian and Central European revolutions of the present century, and, last but not least, the recent upheavals in Mexico, South America, and China.

Indian philosophy, on the contrary, has remained traditional. Supported and refreshed not by outward-directed experiment, but by the inward-turned experiences of yoga-practice, it has in-

[15] Aristotle, *The Metaphysics* I. v. (Loeb Classical Library, Vol. I, p. 33).

terpreted rather than destroyed inherited belief, and in turn been both interpreted and corrected by the forces of religion. Philosophy and religion differ in India on certain points; but there has never been a dissolving, over-all attack from the representatives of pure criticism against the immemorial stronghold of popular belief. In the end, the two establishments have reinforced each other, so that in each may be found characteristics which in Europe we should attribute only to its opposite. This is why the professors in our universities who for so long were reluctant to dignify Indian thinking about our everlasting human problems with the Greek and Western title "philosophy" were far from being unjustified. Nevertheless—and this is what I hope to be able to show—there exists and has existed in India what is indeed a real philosophy, as bold and breath-taking an adventure as anything ever hazarded in the Western world. Only, it emerges from an Eastern situation and pattern of culture, aims at ends that are comparatively unfamiliar to the modern academic schools, and avails itself of alien methods—the ends or goals being precisely those that inspired Plotinus, Scotus Erigena, and Meister Eckhart, as well as the philosophic flights of such thinkers of the period before Socrates as Parmenides, Empedocles, Pythagoras, and Heraclitus.

4.

The Four Aims of Life

THE FACT remains: there is no one word in Sanskrit to cover and include everything in the Indian literary tradition that we should be disposed to term philosophical. The Hindus have several ways of classifying the thoughts which they regard as worth learning and handing down, but no single heading under which to comprehend all of their basic generalizations about reality, human nature, and conduct. The first and most important of their systems of classification is that of the four aims, or ends, or areas, of human life.

1. Artha, the first aim, is material possessions. The arts that serve this aim are those of economics and politics, the techniques of surviving in the struggle for existence against jealousy and competition, calumny and blackmail, the bullying tyranny of despots, and the violence of reckless neighbors. Literally, the word *artha* means "thing, object, substance," and comprises the whole range of the tangible objects that can be possessed, enjoyed, and lost, and which we require in daily life for the upkeep of a household, raising of a family, and discharge of religious duties, i.e., for the virtuous fulfillment of life's obligations.[16] Objects contribute also to sensuous enjoyment,[17] gratification of the feelings, and satisfaction of the legitimate requirement of human nature: love, beautiful works of art, flowers, jewels, fine clothing, comfortable housing, and the pleasures of the table. The word *artha* thus connotes "the attainment of riches and wordly prosperity, advantage, profit, wealth," also, "result"; in commercial life: "business-matter, business-affair, work, price"; and in law: "plaint, action, petition." With reference to the external world, *artha,* in its widest connotation, signifies "that which can be perceived, an object of the senses"; with reference to the interior

[16] Religious and social duties are regarded in India as a debt contracted through coming into existence in the community and remaining in it as a member. The debt is to be paid to the gods who protect and favor us, the ancestors to whom we owe our existence, and our fellow creatures, with whom we share life's joys and sorrows. The virtuous fulfillment of one's life-role (*dharma*) will be discussed below (pp. 40-41 and 151-177), as the third of the Four Aims.

[17] Pleasure (*kāma*) is another of the Four Aims; cf. *infra,* pp. 38-41 and 140-150.

world of the psyche: "end and aim, purpose, object, wish, desire, motive, cause, reason, interest, use, want, and concern"; and as the last member of a compound, *-artha*: "for the sake of, on behalf of, for, intended for." The term thus bundles together all the meanings of 1. the object of human pursuit, 2. the means of this pursuit, and 3. the needs and the desire suggesting this pursuit.

There exists in India a special literature on the subject wherein the field of the inquiry is narrowed to the specific area of politics: the politics of the individual in everyday life, and the politics of the gaining, exercise, and maintenance of power and wealth as a king. This art is illustrated by the beast fable—a most remarkable vehicle for the presentation of a realistic philosophy of life. Case histories from the animal realm develop and illuminate a ruthless science of survival, a completely unsentimental craft of prospering in the face of the constant danger that must ever lurk in the clandestine and open struggle of beings for life and supremacy. Like all Indian doctrines, this one is highly specialized and designed to impart a skill. It is not confused or basically modified by moral inhibitions; the techniques are presented chemically pure. The textbooks are dry, witty, merciless, and cynical, reflecting on the human plane the pitiless laws of the animal conflict. Beings devouring each other, thriving on each other, maintaining themselves against each other, inspire the patterns of the thought. The basic principles are those of the deep sea; hence the doctrine is named *Matsya-nyāya,* "The Principle or Law (*nyāya*) of the Fishes (*matsya*)"—which is to say, "the big ones eat the little ones." The teaching is also called *Arthaśāstra,* "The Authoritative Handbook (*śāstra*) of the Science of Wealth (*artha*)," wherein are to be found all the timeless laws of politics, economy, diplomacy, and war.

The literature of the subject thus comprises, on the one hand, beast fables, and on the other, systematic and aphoristic treatises. Of the former, the two best known are the *Pañcatantra,* "The

Five (*pañca*) Looms or Warps (*tantra*)," i.e., "The Five Treatises," and the *Hitopadeśa,* "Instruction (*upadeśa*) in What Is Advantageous and Beneficial (*hita*)." Of the systematic treatises, by far the most important is an encyclopedic work known as the *Kauṭilīya Arthaśāstra,* named after and traditionally attributed to Cāṇakya Kauṭilya, the legendary chancellor of Candragupta Maurya, who flourished at the end of the fourth century B.C. At the time of Alexander the Great's raid into northwestern India, 326 B.C., the northeastern provinces were governed by the Nanda dynasty: some five years following the raid, Candragupta, whose father may have been a Nanda, but whose mother was a woman of inferior birth, overthrew this house and founded the empire of the Mauryas, one of the most powerful of Indian history. The political handbook attributed to the wise and crafty Brāhman who is supposed to have advised and supported him in his enterprise gives an extensive, detailed, and vivid picture of the style and techniques of Hindu government, statecraft, warfare, and public life, in the period in question.[18] A much briefer treatise, the so-called *Bārhaspatya Arthaśāstra,* is a compact collection of aphorisms supposed to have been revealed by the divinity Bṛhaspati, the mythical chancellor, house-priest, and chief adviser in world politics of Indra, king of the gods.[19] Still another summary is Kāmandaki's *Nītisāra,* "The Extract, Juice, or Essence (*sāra*) of Government, or Proper Conduct (*nīti*)."[20] This is a

[18] *Kauṭilīya Arthaśāstra,* edited by R. Shamasastry, Mysore, 1909; 2nd edition, revised, 1919. A translation by the same hand was published in Bangalore, 1915; 2nd edition, 1923.

[19] *Bārhaspatya Arthaśāstra,* edited and translated by F. W. Thomas, Punjab Sanskrit Series, Lahore, 1921. For Brhaspati, cf. *infra,* pp. 76-77.

[20] *Kāmandakiya Nītisāra,* translated by M. N. Dutt, Wealth of India Series, Calcutta, 1896. The verb *nī* means "to lead, convey, conduct, guide, govern, direct," and the noun *nīti:* "direction, guidance, management; behavior, propriety, decorum; course of action, policy; prudence, political wisdom, statesmanship." *Nītisāra* therefore is a synonym for *arthaśāstra.*

much later work than Kauṭilya's, composed, sometimes delightfully, in didactic verse, and claiming to contain the extract or essence of the earlier compilation. Valuable materials appear also in many of the didactic dialogues, tales and fables of the great national epic, the *Mahābhārata*—stray bits and fragments from treatises now lost, coming down from the Indian feudal age of the eighth and seventh centuries B.C. And we have some other minor works in which the science is modified, occasionally, to accord somewhat with the claims of ethics and religion.[21]

From such sources a vigorous, resourceful, and absolutely realistic philosophy of practical life is to be extracted, as well as a theory of diplomacy and government that is certainly comparable to the statecraft of Machiavelli and Hobbes. The Indian *Arthaśāstra* bears comparison and shares many features, also, with Plato's *Republic* and *Laws,* and Aristotle's *Politics.*

2. *Kāma,* the second of the four ends of life, is pleasure and love. In Indian mythology, Kāma is the counterpart of Cupid. He is the Hindu god of love, who, with flower-bow and five flower-arrows, sends desire quivering to the heart. Kāma is desire incarnate, and, as such, lord and master of the earth, as well as of the lower celestial spheres.

The principal surviving classic of India's Kāma teaching is Vātsyāyana's celebrated *Kāmasūtra.*[22] This work has earned India an ambiguous reputation for sensuality that is rather misleading; for the subject is presented on an entirely secularized and technical level, more or less as a textbook for lovers and courtesans. The dominant attitude of the Hindu, in actuality, is aus-

[21] A review of the literature and discussion of the whole topic will be found in M. Winternitz, *Geschichte der indischen Litteratur,* Leipzig, 1920, Bd. III, pp. 504-536.

[22] *Sūtra,* a thread, string of rules, aphorisms (compare Latin *sutura,* English "suture" and "sew"). A sūtra is a handbook, or book of rules. There are sūtras for every department of Indian life. The great period of composition of these aphoristic summaries was c. 500–200 B.C.

tere, chaste, and extremely restrained, marked by an emphasis on purely spiritual pursuits and an absorption in religious and mystical experiences. Kāma teaching came into existence to correct and ward off the frustration in married life that must have been all too frequent where marriages of convenience prevailed and marriages of love were the rare exception. Through the centuries, marriage became increasingly a family affair. Bargains struck by the heads of families, based on the horoscopes cast by astrologers and on economic and social considerations, determined the fate of the young bride and groom. No doubt there were many dull and painful households where a little study of the courtesan's science could have been of immense service. It was for a society of frozen emotions, not libertine, that this compendium of the techniques of adjustment and stimulation was compiled.

Though the Kāma literature that has come down to us is thus excessively technical, nevertheless some basic insights concerning the attitude of the sexes toward each other can still be extracted from it—some notion of the Hindu psychology of love, analysis of the feelings, and manners of emotional expression, as well as a view of the recognized task and sphere of love. Better, however, than the *Kāmasūtra* for this purpose is another class of textbooks devoted to the various arts of pleasure, namely the handbooks of poetics and acting, the so-called *Nāṭyaśāstras,* which are summaries, for professionals, of the techniques of dancing, pantomime, singing, and the drama. The standard Hindu types of hero and heroine are here presented and discussed. The traits of their psychology are delineated, and the sequences of feeling described which they normally experience in different standard situations. We find reflected in these texts an exquisitely developed psychology of the heart, comparable to the typology and tapestry of human emotions and reactions that developed in the West with the Italian opera and the French tragedy of the seventeenth and eighteenth centuries. The works continually remind one of the essays and aphorisms of such French littérateur-psychologists as La Bruyère, La Rochefoucauld, Chamfort, and Vauvenargues—revivers of the Greek tradition of Theophrastus, who in his turn had been inspired by the Greek art of the stage.

3. Dharma, the third of the four aims, comprises the whole context of religious and moral duties. This too is personified as a deity, but he is one of comparatively abstract character.

The texts are the *Dharmaśāstras* and *Dharmasūtras,* or Books of the Law. Some are attributed to mythical personages such as Manu, forefather of man, others to certain eminent Brāhman saints and teachers of antiquity. The style of the most ancient—for example, that of Gautama, of Āpastamba, and of Baudhāyana, who belong to the fifth and following centuries B.C.[23] —resembles that of the later Vedic prose tradition. These earlier works are filled with social, ritual, and religious prescriptions intended for one or another of the Vedic schools. But the later law books—and most notably the great compendium assigned to Manu[24]—reach out to cover the whole context of orthodox Hindu life. The rituals and numerous social regulations of the three upper castes, Brāhman (priest), Kṣatriya (noble), Vaiśya (merchant and agriculturalist), are meticulously formulated on the basis of immemorial practices ascribed to the teaching of the Creator himself. Not the king or the millionaire, but the sage, the saint, the Mahātma (literally "magnanimous": "great (*mahat*) Self or Spirit (*ātman*)"), receives the highest place and honor in this system. As the seer, the tongue or mouthpiece of the timeless truth, he is the one from whom all society derives its order. The king is, properly, but the administrator of that order; agriculturalists and merchants supply the materials that give embodiment to the form; and the workers (*śūdras*) are those who contribute the necessary physical labor. Thus all are co-ordinated

[23] Translated by G. Bühler in the Sacred Books of the East, Vol. II (Āpastamba and Gautama) and Vol. XIV (Baudhāyana).

[24] *Mānava Dharmaśāstra,* translated by Bühler in *ib.,* Vol. XXV.

to the revelation, preservation, and experience of the one great divinely-intended image. Dharma is the doctrine of the duties and rights of each in the ideal society, and as such the law or mirror of all moral action.

4. Mokṣa, apavarga, nirvṛtti, or *nivṛtti,* the fourth of the Four Aims, is redemption, or spiritual release. This is regarded as the ultimate aim, the final human good, and as such is set over and against the former three.

Artha, Kāma, and Dharma, known as the *trivarga,* the "group of three," are the pursuits of the world; each implies its own orientation or "life philosophy," and to each a special literature is dedicated. But by far the greatest measure of Indian thought, research, teaching, and writing has been concerned with the supreme spiritual theme of liberation from ignorance and from the passions of the world's general illusion. *Mokṣa,* from the root *muc,* "to loose, set free, let go, release, liberate, deliver; to leave, abandon, quit," means "liberation, escape, freedom, release; rescue, deliverance; final emancipation of the soul." *Apavarga,* from the verb *apavṛj,* "to avert, destroy, dissipate; tear off, pull out, take out," means "throwing, discharging (a missile), abandonment; completion, end; and the fulfillment, or accomplishment of an action." *Nirvṛtti* is "disappearance, destruction, rest, tranquility, completion, accomplishment, liberation from worldly existence, satisfaction, happiness, bliss"; and *nivṛtti*: "cessation, termination, disappearance; abstinence from activity or work; leaving off, desisting from, resignation; discontinuance of worldly acts or emotions; quietism, separation from the world; rest, repose, felicity." All of which dictionary terms taken together suggest something of the highest end of man as conceived by the Indian sage.

India's *paramārtha*—"paramount (*parama*) object (*artha*)"—is nothing less than the basic reality which underlies the phenomenal realm. This is apprehended when the mere impressions conveyed by the physical senses to a nervous brain in the service of the passions and emotions of an ego no longer delude. One is then "dis-illusioned." *Paramārtha-vid,* "he who knows (*vid*) the paramount object (*paramārtha*)," is consequently the Sanskrit word that the dictionary roughly translates "philosopher."

5.

Release and Progress

THE GIST of any system of philosophy can best be grasped in the condensed form of its principal terms. An elementary exposition must be concerned, therefore, with presenting and interpreting the words through which the main ideas have to be conceived. Indian thought is excellently adapted to such an approach; for all of its terms belong to Sanskrit and have long served in the everyday language of poetry and romance as well as in such technical literatures as that of medicine. They are not terms confined to the strange and unfamiliar atmosphere of the specialized schools and doctrines. The nouns, for example, which constitute the bulk of the philosophic terminology, stand side by side with verbs that have been derived from the same roots and denote activities or processes expressive of the same content. One can always come to the basic meaning through a study of the common uses of the word in daily life and by this means ascertain not only its implied shades and values, but also its suggested metaphors and connotations. All of which is in striking contrast with the situation in the contemporary West, where by far the greater number of our philosophical terms have been borrowed from Greek and Latin, stand detached from actual life, and thus suffer from an inevitable lack of vividness and clarity. The word "idea" means very different things, for example, according to whether it is Plato, Locke, the modern history of ideas, psychology, or everyday talk that one is trying to understand. Each case, each authority for the term, every author, period, and school, must be taken by itself. But the Indian vocabulary is so closely connected with the general usage of the civilization that it can always be interpreted through the way of the general understanding.

By reviewing the whole range of values covered by any Sanskrit term one can watch Indian thought at work, as it were from within. This technique corrects the unavoidable misinterpretations that arise, even in the best intended translations, as a result of the vastly differing range of associations of our European terms. Actually, we have no precise verbal equivalents for translations from Sanskrit, but only misleading approximations resounding with Occidental associations that are necessarily very different from those of the Indian world. This fact has led the West to all sorts of false deductions as to the nature, ends, and means of Oriental thought. Even the most faithful interpreter finds himself spreading misinformation simply because his words slip into a European context the moment they leave his lips. It is only by referring continually to the Sanskrit dictionary that one can begin to perceive something of the broader backgrounds of the phrases that for centuries have served to carry the living burden of Indian thought.

For example, the emphasis placed by the ascetic philosophies on the paramount ideal and end of mokṣa, and the consequent mass of literature on the subject, leads the Western student to an extremely one-sided view of Indian civilization. The true force of the ideal cannot be understood out of context—and that context is the traditional Indian, not the modern industrial, world. Mokṣa is a force that has impressed itself on every feature, every trait and discipline, of Indian life and has shaped the entire scale of values. It is to be understood, not as a refutation, but as the final flowering, of the success of the successful man. Briefly: the greater part of Indian philosophy proper is concerned with guiding the individual during the second, not the first, portion of his life. Not before but after one has accomplished the normal worldly aims of the individual career, after one's duties have been served as a moral member and supporter of the family and community, one turns to the tasks of the final human adventure. According to the Hindu dharma, a man's lifetime is to be divided into four strictly differentiated stages (*āśrama*). The first is that of the student, "he who is to be taught" (*śiṣya*), "he who attends, waits upon, and serves his guru" (*antevāsin*). The second is that of the householder (*gṛhastha*), which is the great period of a man's maturity and enactment of his due role in the world. The third is that of retirement to the forest for meditation (*vanaprastha*). And the fourth is that of the mendicant wandering sage (*bhikṣu*). Mokṣa is for the latter two; not for the first or second.

Grāma, "the village," and *vana,* "the forest": these stand as opposites. For grāma, men have been given the "group of three" (*trivarga*), and the handbooks of the normal aims and ends of worldly life; but for vana—the forest, the hermitage, the work of getting rid of this earthly burden of objects, desires, duties, and all the rest—a man will require the other disciplines, the other way, the other, quite opposite, ideals, techniques, and experiences of "release." Business, family, secular life, like the beauties and hopes of youth and the successes of maturity, have now been left behind; eternity alone remains. And so it is to that—not to the tasks and worries of this life, already gone, which came and passed like a dream—that the mind is turned. Mokṣa looks beyond the stars, not to the village street. Mokṣa is the practical discipline of metaphysics. Its aim is not to establish the foundations of the sciences, evolve a valid theory of knowledge, or control and refine methods of scientific approach to either the spectacle of nature or the documents of human history, but to rend the tangible veil. Mokṣa is a technique of transcending the senses in order to discover, know, and dwell at one with the timeless reality which underlies the dream of life in the world. Nature and man, in so far as they are visible, tangible, open to experience, the sage cognizes and interprets, but only to step through them to his ultimate metaphysical good.

On the other hand, in the Occident, we have had no metaphysics—practical or otherwise—since the middle of the eighteenth century. In diametric contrast to the dominant Oriental view of the insubstantiality of the world of change and decay, our materialistic minds have developed and favored an optimistic view of evolution and, together with this, a fervent faith in the perfectibility of human affairs through better planning, technology, a wider spread of education, and the opening of opportunities for all. Whereas the Hindu feels himself to be utterly at the mercy of the destructive forces of death (diseases, plagues, warfare, human tyranny and injustice), and the inevitable victim of the relentless flow of time (which swallows individuals, wipes out the bloom of realms and towns, and crumbles even the ruins to dust), we feel the power of human genius to invent and organize, the sovereign strength of man to achieve collective discipline, and both the urge and the capacity to control the moving forces of nature. *We* are the ones who work changes; nature remains ever the same. And this nature, conquered by scientific analysis, can be compelled to submit to the harness of the triumphant chariot of our human advance. Europe's eighteenth-century thinkers believed in progressive collective enlightenment: wisdom as a dispeller of darkness, making society perfect, noble, and pure. The nineteenth century believed in collective material and social progress: the conquest of nature's forces, the abolition of violence, slavery, and injustice, and the victory over not only suffering but even premature death. And now the twentieth century feels that only by intense and extensive planning and organization can our human civilization hope to be saved.

The frailty of human life does not really obsess us, as it did our ancestors in the fifteenth and sixteenth centuries. We feel more sheltered than did they against vicissitudes, better insured against setbacks; decay and decline do not fill us with such despair and resignation. We believe that it is we ourselves who constitute our providence—as we all press onward in the historic human battle to dominate the earth and its elements, to control its mineral, vegetable, animal, and even sub-atomic kingdoms. The secret forces of existence, the complex chemistry and organic alchemy of the life process, whether in our own psyches and physiques or in the world around, we are now gradually unveiling. No longer do we feel caught in the meshes of an unconquerable cosmic web. And so, accordingly, we have our logic of science, experimental methods, and psychology, but no metaphysics.

The airy flights do not really interest us any more. We do not found our lives on fascinating or consoling total interpretations of life and the universe, along lines such as those of traditional theology or meditative speculation; rather, we have all these questions of detail in our numerous systematic sciences. Instead of an attitude of acceptance, resignation, and contemplation, we cultivate a life of relentless movement, causing changes at every turn, bettering things, planning things, subduing to schedule the spontaneous wild growths of the world. In place of the archaic aim of understanding life and the cosmos as a whole, by means of general speculation, we have for our thought the ideal of a multifarious, ever more refined activity of highly specialized understandings, and the mastery of concrete details. Religion and philosophy have become transformed into science, technology, and political economics. Since this is so, and since the main object of Indian philosophy, on the other hand, is mokṣa, we may well ask whether we have any qualifications at all for the understanding of that remote doctrine—fixed as we are to our pursuit of artha, kāma, and dharma, and feeling fully satisfied to be this way.

And so here we hit upon another of the fundamental differences between the philosophies of the modern West and the traditional East. Viewed from the standpoints of the Hindu and Buddhist disciplines, our purely intellectual approach to all theoretical matters that are not directly concerned with the trivarga would seem dilettante and superficial. Through the course of its evolution during comparatively modern times, Western thought has become completely exoteric. It is supposed to be open to the approach and accredited investigation of every intellectual who can meet the general requirements of a) a basic education, and b) some specialized intellectual training to enable him to keep up with the argument. But this was not the way in Plato's ancient time. Μηδεὶς ἀγεωμέτρητος εἰσίτω ἐμὴν στέγην: "Nobody untrained in mathematics may cross this my threshold."[25] Plato is said to have inscribed this warning above his door in homage to Pythagoras and the contemporary revolutionary mathematicians of Sicily—such men as Archytas of Tarentum; whereas in modern times, a high-school education and four years of college are supposed to open an access to the sanctum sanctorum of ultimate Truth. India, in this respect, is where Plato was; and that is another of the reasons why the professors of the European and American universities were justified in refusing to admit Indian thought to *their* temple of "philosophy."

[25] Tzetzes, *Chiliades* 8. 973.

II. THE FOUNDATIONS OF INDIAN PHILOSOPHY

1.

Philosophy as a Way of Life

IN ANCIENT India each department of learning was associated with a highly specialized skill and corresponding way of life. The knowledge was not to be culled from books primarily, or from lectures, discussions, and conversation, but to be mastered through apprenticeship to a competent teacher. It required the wholehearted surrender of a malleable pupil to the authority of the guru, its elementary prerequisites being obedience (*śuśrūṣā*) and implicit faith (*śraddhā*). *Śuśrūṣā* is the fervent desire to hear, to obey, and to retain what is being heard; it implies dutifulness, reverence, and service. *Śraddhā* is trust and composure of mind; it demands the total absence of every kind of independent thought and criticism on the part of the pupil; and here again there is reverence, as well as strong and vehement desire. The Sanskrit word means also "the longing of a pregnant woman."

The pupil in whom the sought truth dwells as the jungle-tiger dwelt within the cub [1] submits without reserve to his guru,

[1] *Supra,* pp. 5-8.

paying him reverence as an embodiment of the divine learning to be imparted. For the teacher is a mouthpiece of the higher knowledge and a master of the special skill. The pupil in his religious worship must become devoted to the presiding divinity of the department of skill and wisdom that is to be the informing principle, henceforward, of his career. He must share the household of the teacher for years, serve him in the home and assist him in his work—whether the craft be that of priest, magician, ascetic, physician, or potter. The techniques must be learned by constant practice, while the theory is being taught through oral instruction supplemented by a thoroughgoing study of the basic textbooks. And most important of all, a psychological "transference" between the master and pupil has to be effected; for a kind of transformation is to be brought to pass. The malleable metal of the pupil is to be worked into the pattern of the model teacher, and this with respect not only to matters of knowledge and skill but also, much more deeply, to the whole personal attitude. As for the life and morals of the guru himself: it is required that there should be an identity—an absolute, point-for-point correspondence—between his teachings and his way of life; the sort of identity that we should expect to find in the West only in a monk or priest.

No criticism, but a gradual growing into the mold of the discipline, is what is demanded. The training is accepted and followed, as it were, blindfold; but in the course of time, when the pupil's grasp of his subject increases, understanding comes of its own accord. Such blind acceptance and subsequent intuitive comprehension of a truth through the enactment of its corresponding attitude is known to Europe primarily in the practice of the Roman Catholic church. In one of the novels, for example, of Flaubert, *Bouvard et Pécuchet,* the case is described of two freethinkers, disappointed with their way of life, who, following an attempt at suicide, become reconverted to the faith of their childhood and early peasant environment.

They turn to the priest and assail him with unsettled doubts and skepticism, but he replies merely, *"Pratiquez d'abord."* That is to say: "Take up and practice first the orthodox, established way of the ritualistic duties—attending mass regularly, praying, going to confession and communion. Then gradually you will understand, and your doubts will vanish like mist in sunshine. You need not fathom the great depths of the dogma of the Trinity, nor the other mysteries, but you must indeed profess and feel an implicit faith that ultimately, somehow, these must be true. Then abide with the hope that their meaning may dawn upon you with the increasing operation within you of supernatural grace."

Precisely in this way, Oriental philosophy is accompanied and supported by the practice of a way of life—monastic seclusion, asceticism, meditation, prayer, yoga-exercises, and daily devotional hours of worship. The function of the worship is to imbue the devotee with the divine essence of the truth; this being made manifest under the symbolic thought-directing forms of divinities or other superhuman holy figures, as well as through the teacher himself, who, standing for truth incarnate, reveals truth continually, both through his teaching and in his way of daily life. In this respect Indian philosophy is as closely linked with religion, sacraments, initiations, and the forms of devotional practice as is our modern Western philosophy with the natural sciences and their methods of research.

This Indian view of the identity of personality and conduct with teaching is well rendered in the apt comment of a Hindu friend of mine in criticism of a certain popular book on Oriental philosophy. "After all," said he, "real attainment is only what finds confirmation in one's own life. The worth of a man's writing depends on the degree to which his life is itself an example of his teaching."

2.

The Qualified Pupil

THE ATTITUDE of the Indian pupil toward his subject, no matter what it may be, is conveniently illustrated in the special field of orthodox Brāhman philosophy by the first few pages of a little treatise for beginners, dating from the middle of the fifteenth century A.D., known as the *Vedāntasāra,* "The Essence (*sāra*) of the Doctrines of Vedānta." [2] Of course one may read this translated text precisely as one reads any essay of Locke, Hume, or Kant; but it should be borne in mind that the stanzas were not intended to be assimilated this way. In fact we are warned at the very outset by being confronted with a discussion of the preliminary question: "Who is competent, and consequently entitled, to study the Vedānta in order to realize the truth?" The question may be readily answered, so far as we ourselves are concerned: "Not we Westerners. Not intellectuals." This much will soon be very clear.

The "competent student" (*adhikārin*), when approaching the study of Vedānta, should feel an attitude not of criticism or curiosity, but of utter faith (*śraddhā*) that in the formulae of Vedānta, as they are about to be communicated to him, he shall discover the truth.[3] He must furthermore be filled with a yearning for freedom from the encumbrances of worldly life, an earnest longing for release from the bondage of his existence as an individual caught in the vortex of ignorance. This is known as

[2] *Vedāntasāra of Sadānanda,* translated with introduction, text, and comments by Swāmī Nikhilānanda, Mayavati, 1931. For "Vedānta," see *supra,* p. 18, Editor's note.

[3] *Vedāntasāra* 24.

mumukṣutva, or *mokṣa-icchā:* "the desire for release."[4] Just as a man carrying on his head a load of wood that has caught fire would go rushing to a pond to quench the flames, even so should the adhikārin, scorched with the mad pains of the fire of life in the world, its birth, its death, its self-deluding futility, go rushing to a guru learned in the Vedas, who, himself having reached the goal of Vedānta, now abides serene in uninterrupted consciousness of the essence of imperishable being. The adhikārin is to come to this guru bearing presents in his hand, ready to serve, and prepared to obey in every way.

"The competent student is an aspirant, who, through having studied in accordance with the prescribed method the Four Vedas and their 'limbs' (*vedāṅga*),[5] has already a general comprehension of Vedic lore. He must also have already been cleansed of all sins clinging to him from either this or previous existences, through having abstained from all rituals for the fulfillment of worldly desires and the causing of injury to others, while performing faithfully the orthodox daily devotions and the special obligatory rites for such occasions as the birth of a child. He must, moreover, have practiced the special austerities that conduce to the expiation of sin,[6] and all of the usual orthodox meditations designed to conduce to the concentration of the mind.[7] Whereas the daily, special, and peni-

[4] *Ib.* 25.

[5] Auxiliary textbooks on phonetics, rituals, grammar, etymology, prosody, and astronomy.

[6] Viz. reducing the diet gradually with the waning of the moon, until, at the night of no moon, no food is eaten; then increasing the quantity by a fourteenth each day, until, at full moon, the normal diet is again attained (*cāndrāyaṇa*). Such austerities are described in the "Laws of Manu"; *Mānava Dharmaśāstra* 11.217.

[7] Exercises of meditation on the worshiper's special tutelary divinity (*iṣṭadevatā*), which is an "aspect-provided-with-qualities" (*sa-guṇa*) of the highest essence (*brahman*). Brahman in itself is absolutely devoid of qualifications (*nir-guṇa*), and consequently beyond the reach of the powers

tential "rites" above described are for the mind's purification, the "meditations" are intended to bring it to a state of "single-pointedness." [8]

According to the traditional belief, the fulfillment of these prescribed rites and devotions will bring the devotee after death to either the "heaven of the ancestors" (*pitṛ-loka*) or the higher "sphere of truth" (*satya-loka*). But such pleasurable results are not regarded by the adept of Vedānta as important or even desirable; they are the mere by-products of the discipline, stopping-stations along the way, in which he is no longer interested. They are still within the worlds of birth, and represent no more than a continuance of the round of being (*saṁsāra*), though indeed an extremely blissful episode of the round, enduring, it is said, for innumerable millenniums. Rather than the beatitudes of heaven, what the Vedāntist desires is to see through and past the illusory character of all existence whatsoever, no less that of the higher spheres than that of the gross terrestrial plane. He has sacrificed completely all thought of the enjoyment of the fruits of his good deeds; any rewards that may be accruing to him as a result of his perfect devotion he surrenders to the personal divinity that he serves. For he knows that it is not himself who acts, but the Spiritual Person dwelling omnipresent within himself and all things, and to whom he, as worshiper, is devoted utterly—the God who is the Self (*ātman*) within his heart.

The necessary means for the transcending of illusion which the student must be competent to bring to bear are, first of all, "discrimination between the permanent and things transient"

---

of the normal human mind. The various *iṣṭadevatās,* images and personifications, consequently, are only preliminary helps, guides, or accommodations, which serve to prepare the spirit of the worshiper for its final, form-transcending realization.

[8] *Vedāntasāra* 6-13.

(*nitya-anitya-vastu-viveka*).[9] "Brahman alone," we read, "is the permanent substance, everything else is transient." [10] All objects in this world that are pleasant to the senses, garlands of flowers, perfumes, beautiful women, gratifications of every kind, are merely transient; they come as the result of our actions (*karma*). But the pleasures of the next world too are non-eternal and the mere result of acts.

An unwavering disregard for all such illusoriness, once it has been recognized as such, is the second requisite of the student of Vedānta. He must renounce, sincerely and efficaciously, every possible fruit of his virtuous acts. This is true renunciation: *ihāmutrārthaphalabhogavirāgaḥ*, "indifference (*virāgaḥ*) to the enjoyment (*bhoga*) of the fruits (*phala*) of action (*artha*) whether here (*iha*) or in the world to come (*amutra*)." [11]

The third of the necessary means is concentration, and this is discussed under the heading of "The Six Treasures," the first of which is *śama*, "mental quietness, pacification of the passions." [12] Śama is the attitude, or mode of behavior, that keeps the mind from being troubled by sense objects—the only sense activity permitted to the student of philosophy being that of listening eagerly to the words of his guru. The second treasure, *dama*, stands for a second stage of self-restraint, "the subjuga-

[9] *Ib.* 15.

[10] *Ib.* 16.

[11] *Ib.* 17.

Renunciation of the fruits of action is the basic formula of Karma Yoga, the way of release through action, which has received its classic statement in *Bhagavad Gītā* 3. All actions are to be performed as pertaining to one's duty (*dharma*), enacted as the role of an actor on the stage of life. They belong to the play (*līlā*), not to the actor's real Self (*ātman*). "Therefore always do without attachment the work you have to do; for a man who does his work without attachment attains the supreme" (*Bhagavad Gītā* 3. 19). Cf. *infra*, pp. 386-389.

[12] *Vedāntasāra* 18-19.

tion of the senses." [13] According to the classical Hindu science of the mind, man has five perceiving faculties (hearing, touch, sight, taste, smell), five acting faculties (speech, grasping, locomotion, evacuation, generation), and a controlling "inner organ" (*antaḥ-karaṇa*) which is made manifest as ego (*ahaṅkāra*), memory (*cittam*), understanding (*buddhi*), and cogitation (*manas*).[14] Dama refers to the decisive turning away of this entire system from the outer world. The next treasure, *uparati*, is "complete cessation" of the activity of the perceiving and acting sense-faculties.[15] The fourth, *titikṣā*, "endurance, patience," represents the power to endure without the slightest discomposure extremes of heat and cold, weal and woe, honor and abuse, loss and gain, and of all the other "pairs of opposites" (*dvandva*).[16] The pupil is now in a position to bring his mind past the distractions of the world. The fifth of the treasures, therefore, becomes now attainable: *samādhāna*, "constant concentration of the mind." The pupil is able to keep his attention fixed on the teachings of the guru, and can dwell without interruption on the holy texts, or on the symbols and ineffable themes of his intense meditations.[17] *Sam-ā-dhā* means "to put together, unite, compose, collect; to concentrate, to fix, to apply intently (as the eye or the mind)." *Samādhāna* is the state attained as well as the activity itself. It is a fixing of the mind on something in absolutely undisturbed—and undisturbable—contemplation: "deep meditation, steadiness, composure, peace of mind, perfect absorption of all thought in the one object." After this the sixth treasure can be achieved, which is perfect faith.[18]

Discrimination, renunciation, the "six treasures," and a

[13] *Ib.* 20.

[14] These are discussed *infra*, pp. 314-332.

[15] *Vedāntasāra* 21.

[16] *Ib.* 22.

[17] *Ib.* 23.

[18] *Ib.* 23; for faith (*śraddhā*), cf. *supra*, pp. 48-50.

yearning for release (*mumukṣutva*),[19] are the very means by which the Indian philosopher comes to his goal of understanding. The neophyte must be competent to command them. His heart and mind must already have been cleansed by the preliminary rituals and austerities of the orthodox religious practices of his community. He must be sufficiently trained in the Holy Scriptures. And he must then be able to bring himself to gain possession of these "necessary means" for the transcending of illusion. "Such an aspirant," we read, "is a qualified student." [20]

3.

Philosophy as Power

IN THE Orient, philosophic wisdom does not come under the head of general information. It is a specialized learning directed to the attainment of a higher state of being. The philosopher is one whose nature has been transformed, re-formed to a pattern of really superhuman stature, as a result of being pervaded by the magic power of truth. That is why the prospective pupil must be carefully tested. The word *adhikārin* means, literally, as adjective, "entitled to, having a right to, possessed of authority, possessed of power, qualified, authorized, fit for"; also, "belonging to, owned by"; and as noun, "an officer, a functionary, head, director, rightful claimant, master, owner, a personage qualified to perform some sacrifice or holy work."

Philosophy is but one of many kinds of wisdom or knowl-

19 *Supra*, pp. 51-52.

20 *Vedāntasāra* 26.

edge (*vidyā*), each leading to some practical end. As the other vidyās lead to such attainments as belong to the special masterships of the craftsman, priest, magician, poet, or dancer, so philosophy ends in the attainment of a divine state both here and hereafter. Every kind of wisdom brings to its possessor its specific power, and this comes inevitably in consequence of the mastery of the respective materials. The doctor is the master of diseases and drugs, the carpenter the master of wood and other building materials, the priest of demons and even of gods by virtue of his charms, incantations, and rituals of offering and propitiation. Correspondingly, the yogī-philosopher is the master of his own mind and body, his passions, his reactions, and his meditations. He is one who has transcended the illusions of wishful thinking and of all other kinds of normal human thought. He feels no challenge or defeat in misfortune. He is absolutely beyond the touch of destiny.

Wisdom, in the Orient, no matter what its kind, is to be guarded jealously and communicated sparingly, and then only to one capable of becoming its perfect receptacle; for besides representing a certain skill, every department of learning carries with it a power that can amount almost to magic, a power to bring to pass what without it would seem a miracle. Teaching not intended to communicate such a power is simply of no consequence, and the communication to one unfit to wield the power properly would be disastrous. Furthermore, the possession of the wisdom and its special potencies was in ancient times regarded as one of the most valuable portions of the family heritage. Like a treasure, it was handed down with all care, according to the patrilineal order of descent. Charms, spells, the techniques of the various crafts and professions, and, finally, philosophy itself originally were communicated only in this way. Son followed father. For the growing generation there was little leniency of choice. This is how the instruments of family prestige were kept from slipping away.

And so it is that the Vedic hymns originally belonged exclusively to certain great family lines. Of the ten books of the *Ṛg-veda* (which is the oldest of the Vedas and indeed the oldest extant document of any of the Indo-European traditions)[21] the second and those following it are the so-called "Family Books." They contain groups of potent verses which formerly were the guarded property of the ancient families of priests, seers, and holy singers. The ancestors of the various clans composed the stanzas in order to conjure gods to the sacrifice, propitiate them, and win their favor—the hymns having been revealed to those ancestral singers during their intercourse (in vision) with the gods themselves. The owners then occasionally marked their property, either by letting their names appear somewhere in the verses or, as was more frequently the case, by a characteristic closing stanza, which would be generally recognized as an earmark. Just as the ranging herds of the cattle-breeding Āryan families in Vedic times were distinguished by some brand or cut on the ear, flank, or elsewhere, so likewise the hymns—and with the same aristocratic sense of the force, and consequent preciousness, of property.

For if the wisdom that produces a special art and mastery is to be guarded jealously, then the higher the powers involved the more careful the guardianship must be—and this particularly when the powers are the gods themselves, the moving forces of nature and the cosmos. Cautious, complex rituals designed to conjure them and link them to human purposes occupied in Vedic (as also in Homeric) antiquity precisely the place held today by such sciences as physics, chemistry, medicine, and bacteriology. A potent hymn was as precious for those people as the secret of a new super-bomber is for us, or the blueprint of the latest device for a submarine. Such things were valuable not only for the art of war but also for the commercial competition of the times of peace.

[21] Cf. *supra,* p. 8, Editor's note.

The early as well as later history of India was characterized by a state of practically continuous battle, invasions from without as well as strife for supremacy among the feudal barons and the later kingly despots. In the midst of all this turmoil the religious formulae of the Vedic Brāhmans were regarded and utilized as a most precious secret weapon—comparable to that of the tribes of Israel, when they entered Canaan under their chieftain Joshua and destroyed the walls of Jericho with a magic blast of their ram's horns. It was because of superior wisdom that the Āryan invaders of India were able to defeat the native pre-Āryan populations, maintain themselves in the land, and ultimately spread their dominion over the sub-continent. The conquered races then were classified as the fourth, non-Āryan, caste of the Śūdra, excluded ruthlessly from the rights and power-giving wisdom of the society of the conquerors, and forbidden to acquire even an inkling of the techniques of the Vedic religion. We read in the early *Dharmaśāstras* that if a Śūdra chances to overhear the recitation of a Vedic hymn, he is to be punished by having his ears filled with molten lead.[22] Those sacred formulae were for the Brāhmans (the priests, wizards, and guardians of sacred power), the Kṣatriyas (kings, feudal chieftains, and warriors), and the Vaiśyas (peasants, craftsmen, and burghers of Āryan lineage)—and for them alone.

This pattern of archaic secrecy and exclusion has maintained itself through all the periods and in all departments of Indian life. It is characteristic of most of the sacred traditions from which the greater part of the elements of Indian philosophy have been derived—particularly those of Āryan origin, but also, in many important details, even those outside the pale of Āryan-Brāhman control. The non-Vedic traditions—Buddhism, Jainism, Sāṅkhya, and Yoga—lack the caste and familial restrictions

[22] Gautama, *Institutes of the Sacred Law* 12-4. (Sacred Books of the East, Vol. II, Part I, p. 236.)

peculiar to the Vedic lines;[23] nevertheless they demand of anyone who would approach their mysteries such an utter surrender to the authority of the spiritual teacher that any return to the former field of life is rendered impossible. Before a student of one of these non-Āryan Indian disciplines can enter the inner temple and really attain the goal of the doctrine, he must put off entirely his inherited family, with all of its ways of life, and become reborn as a member of the order.

[23] *Editor's note:* Like Buddhism (cf. *supra,* p. 18, Editor's note), Jainism, Sāṅkhya, and Yoga do not accept the authority of the Vedas, and are therefore reckoned as heterodox, i.e., doctrines outside of the orthodox Brāhman tradition of the Vedas, Upaniṣads, and Vedānta. It was Dr. Zimmer's contention that these heterodox systems represent the thinking of the non-Āryan peoples of India, who were overcome and despised by the Brāhmans, but nevertheless could boast of extremely subtle traditions of their own.

Dr. Zimmer regarded Jainism as the oldest of the non-Āryan group, in contrast to most Occidental authorities, who consider Mahāvīra, a contemporary of the Buddha, to have been its *founder* instead of, as the Jainas themselves (and Dr. Zimmer) claim, only the last of a long line of Jaina teachers. Dr. Zimmer believed that there is truth in the Jaina idea that their religion goes back to a remote antiquity, the antiquity in question being that of the pre-Āryan, so-called Dravidian period, which has recently been dramatically illuminated by the discovery of a series of great Late Stone Age cities in the Indus Valley, dating from the third and perhaps even fourth millennium B.C. (cf. Ernest Mackay, *The Indus Civilization,* London, 1935; also Zimmer, *Myths and Symbols in Indian Art and Civilization,* pp. 93ff.).

Sāṅkhya and Yoga represented a later, psychological sophistication of the principles preserved in Jainism, and prepared the ground for the forceful, anti-Brāhman statement of the Buddha. Sāṅkhya and Yoga belong together, as the theory and the practice of a single philosophy. Kapila, the reputed founder of Sāṅkhya (cf. *infra,* pp. 281f), may have been a contemporary of the Upaniṣādic thinkers, and seems to have given his name to the city in which the Buddha was born, Kapilavastu.

In general, the non-Āryan, heterodox philosophies are not exclusive in the same sense that the Brāhman philosophies are; for they are not reserved to members of the three upper castes.

The main ideas of the Brāhman secret doctrine, as developed and formulated at the end of the Vedic period (c. eighth century B.C.), are preserved in the Upaniṣads. These represent a sort of highly specialized post-postgraduate training which the teacher was free either to impart or to withhold. The pupil had to be truly an adhikārin to receive such esoteric lore, truly mature and perfectly fit to bear the revealed wisdom. In the period when the books were first conceived the restrictions imposed were even more severe than they came to be in the later ages. One of the main Upaniṣads contains the warning that its teaching is to be handed down, not simply from father to son, but only to the eldest son, which is to say, to the father's youthful double, his reborn alter ego, "but to no one else, whoever he may be." [24] And in the somewhat later stratification of the metrical Upaniṣads we read: "This most mysterious secret shall be imparted to none who is not a son or a pupil, and who has not yet attained tranquility." [25] It must be borne in mind that the equivalent term by which the word *upaniṣad* is everywhere described is *rahasyam,* " a secret, a mystery." For this is a hidden, secret doctrine that discloses *satyasya satyam,* "the truth of truth."

This same ancient character of secrecy, aloofness, and exclusion is preserved in the works even of the most recent great period of Hindu philosophy and teaching, namely that of the Tantras. These represent a development of the medieval period, the Tāntric literature in its present form belonging mainly to the centuries following 300 A.D.[26] The texts, generally, are

[24] *Chāndogya Upaniṣad* 3. 11. 5-6. Compare *Bṛhadāraṇyaka Upaniṣad* 6. 3. 12.

[25] *Maitri Upaniṣad* 6. 29. Compare *Śvetāśvatara Upaniṣad* 6. 22.

[26] *Editor's note:* The orthodox sacred books (*śāstras*) of India are classed in four categories: 1. *Śruti* ("what is heard"), the Vedas and certain Upanisads, which are regarded as direct revelation; 2. *Smṛti* ("what is remembered"), the teachings of the ancient saints and sages, also law books (*dharmasūtras*) and works dealing with household ceremonies and

supposed to represent secret conversations held between Śiva, the supreme God, and his *śakti* or spouse, the supreme Goddess; first one listening as pupil, then the other; each hearkening with all attention as the truth of the world-creating, -preserving, and -guiding secret essence of the other is made known in mighty verses; each teaching the way to break the spell of misknowing that holds individual consciousness bound to phenomenality. The Tāntric texts insist on the secret character of their contents, and are not to be made known to unbelievers or

---

minor sacrifices (*gṛhyasūtras*); 3. *Purāṇa* ("ancient; ancient lore"), compendious anthologies, comparable in character to the Bible, containing cosmogonic myths, ancient legends, theological, astronomical, and nature lore; 4. *Tantra* ("loom, warp, system, ritual, doctrine"), a body of comparatively recent texts, regarded as directly revealed by Śiva to be the specific scripture of the Kali Yuga, the fourth or present age of the world. The Tantras are called "The Fifth Veda," and their rituals and concepts have actually supplanted the now quite archaic Vedic system of sacrifice as the supporting warp of Indian life.

Typical of the Tāntric system is the concept of *śakti:* the female as the projected "energy" (*śakti*) of the male (compare the Biblical metaphor of Eve as Adam's rib). Male and female, God and Goddess, are the polar manifestations (passive and active, respectively) of a single transcendent principle and, as such, in essence one, though in appearance two. The male is identified with eternity, the female with time, and their embrace with the mystery of creation.

The cult of Śakti, the Goddess, plays an immense role in modern Hinduism, in contrast to the patriarchal emphasis of the Vedic, strictly Āryan tradition, and suggests that the Tantra may have its roots in the non-Āryan, pre-Āryan, Dravidian soil (cf. *supra,* p. 60, Editor's note). Noteworthy is the fact that Śiva, the Universal God, and consort of the Goddess (standing to her as Eternity to Time), is also the supreme Lord of Yoga—which is a non-Vedic discipline (cf. *supra, loc. cit.*). Caste, moreover, is not a prerequisite to Tāntric initiation. Dr. Zimmer suggests (*infra,* pp. 601-602) that the Tāntric tradition represents a creative synthesis of the Āryan and native Indian philosophies. It has exercised a prodigious influence on Mahāyāna Buddhism. Furthermore, its profound psychological insight and bold spiritual techniques give it a peculiar interest to the modern analytical psychologist.

even to believers who are uninitiated into the innermost circles of the adept.

In the West, on the other hand, the pride of philosophy is that it is open to the understanding and criticism of all. Our thought is exoteric, and that is regarded as one of the signs and proofs of its universal validity. Western philosophy has no secret doctrine, but challenges all to scrutinize her arguments, demanding no more than intelligence and an open-minded fairness in discussion. By this general appeal she has won her ascendency over the wisdom and teaching of the Church—which required that certain things should be taken for granted as once and for all established by divine revelation, and unquestionably settled by the interpretations of the inspired fathers, popes, and councils. Our popular modern philosophy, sailing in the broad wake of the natural sciences, recognizes no other authority than proof by experiment and pretends to rest upon no other assumptions than those rationally drawn as the logical theoretical result of critically and methodically digested data derived through sense-experience, registered and controlled by the mind and the faultless apparatus of the laboratories.

I wonder to what extent we feel in our civilization that the man who takes up the profession of the philosopher becomes mysteriously powerful. The business people controlling our economics, social life, internal politics, and foreign affairs generally feel suspicious of philosophers. Absorbed with lofty notions not easily applicable to current emergencies, the "professors" tend only to complicate issues with their abstract approach—and besides, they are not conspicuously fortunate themselves as breadwinners or practical managers. Plato, we know, once tried his hand at government. He attempted to assist a tyrant of Sicily who had invited him to come and establish a model government along the highest philosophic lines. But the two soon quarreled, and the tyrant ended by arresting the philosopher, offering him for sale in the slave-market of the very capital that was to have been the birthplace of a golden age and the model city of a righteous order, highly philosophical and representative of a definitely satisfactory state of human affairs. Plato was bought immediately by a friend who set him free, and returned to his homeland—liberal, democratic Athens, whose corrupt, muddling government had always utterly disgusted him. There he availed himself of the one escape and consolation that is always open to the intellectual. He wrote a book, his immortal *Republic*, which was to be followed later by the *Laws*. Through these, the apparently powerless, stranded philosopher made his impression—secret at the time, yet in every sense immeasurable—on the centuries, indeed on the millenniums, yet to come.

Or again: when Hegel suddenly died of the cholera in 1831 his philosophy publicly collapsed; and it was ridiculed for the next eight decades by the philosophy professors of his country. In his own University of Berlin, as late as 1911 when I was a student there sitting at the feet of his fourth successor, Alois Riehl—a noble-minded, charming man, ranking supreme among the interpreters of Hume's and Kant's theories of the criticism of human understanding—we had to listen to a series of mere jokes the moment the professor embarked on a review of Hegel's philosophy. And yet, that same Hegel was on the point of being rediscovered by my own generation—following the inspiring leadership of old Wilhelm Dilthey, who had just resigned his chair to Riehl and retired from teaching. The Neo-Hegelians sprang into existence, and the philosopher won the official, academic recognition that was his due.

But meanwhile, outside the universities, outside the channels of official doctrine, Hegel's ideas had been exerting an influence on the course of world events, beside which the importance of the academic seal of approval dwindles to nothingness. Even the faithful Hegelianism of G. J. P. J. Bolland and his followers, in the Netherlands, which continued and developed after the philosopher's reputation had collapsed in Germany, and the Hegelian tradition in southern Italy, which culminated in the work of Benedetto Croce, seem insignificant in comparison with the weight of Hegel's influence on modern world affairs. For Hegel's system was the inspiration of Karl Marx; his dialectical thinking inspired the political and psychological strategy of Lenin. Also, his thinking was the inspiration of Pareto, the intellectual father of Fascism. Thus the practical impact of Hegel's ideas upon the non-democratic powers of Europe—and that means, of course, on the affairs of the whole modern world—is perhaps second to none. At the present moment it is comparable in magnitude to the power of the lasting authority of the philosophy of Confucius in China—which shaped the history of that land from the third century B.C. to the revolution of Sun Yat-sen; or to the force of Aristotle's thought in the Middle Ages and (by virtue of the influence of the Jesuits) in modern times. Though philosophers, to their neighbors, almost invariably seem to be harmless stay-at-homes, unaggressive, perhaps even shipwrecked academic teachers, despicable to the hard-headed man of action—sometimes they are far from being so. Ghostlike, rather, and invisible, they are leading the battalions and nations of the future on battlefields of revolution, soaked with blood.

India, dreamy India, philosophical, unpractical, and hopelessly unsuccessful in the maintenance of her political freedom, has always stood for the idea that wisdom can be power if (and this is an "if" that must be kept in mind) the wisdom permeates, transforms, controls, and molds the whole of the personality. The sage is not to be a library of philosophy stalking about on two legs, an encyclopedia with a human voice. Thought itself is to be converted in him into life, into flesh, into being, into a skill in act. And then the higher his realization, the greater will be his power. The magic of Mahātma Gandhi is to be understood, for example, in this way. The force of his model presence on the Hindu masses derives from the fact that in him is expressed an identity of ascetic wisdom (as a style of existence) with politics (as an effective attitude toward worldly issues, whether of daily life or of national policy). His spiritual stature is expressed and honored in the title bestowed upon him: Mahātma: "whose essence of being is great," "he in whom the supra-personal, supra-individual, divine essence, which pervades the whole universe and dwells within the microcosm of the human heart as the animating grace of God (*ātman*), has grown to such magnitude as to have become utterly predominant (*mahat*)." The Spiritual Person has swallowed and dissolved in him all traces of ego, all the limitations proper to personal individuation, all those limiting, fettering qualities and propensities that belong to the normal human state, and even every trace remaining from ego-motivated deeds (*karma*), whether good or evil, whether derived from this life or from deeds in former births. Such traces of personality bias and distort a man's outlook on worldly affairs and prevent his approach to divine truth. But the Mahātma is the man who has become transformed in his being through wisdom; and the power of such a presence to work magic we may yet live to see.[27]

4.

"The Dying round the Holy Power"

THE SAGE is both worshiped and feared because of the miraculous soul-force that he radiates into the world. A man of

[27] *Editor's note:* This lecture was delivered in 1942.

learning who has transformed himself through wisdom is more like a primitive medicine man than like the usual Doctor of Philosophy; or like a Vedic priest or sorcerer-magician. Or again, he is like an Indian ascetic who through self-inflicted austerities has overcome his human limits and acquired such powers that even the gods governing the forces and spheres of the universe stand under his control. In most of the Vedic texts precise statements are given of the specific miraculous rewards or magic powers that one can expect to derive from the various sorts of learning communicated. *Yo evam veda,* "who knows thus," is a formula continually encountered. "Who knows thus —assimilates into himself the superhuman powers of which he has come to understand the secret efficacy and essence through his study and practice of this lesson."

We may select from the vast store one illustration which will sufficiently show what worship was paid to every kind of knowledge, and to the possessor of the knowledge. This is a text that is at once a document of metaphysics and a curious power-recipe, a terrible secret weapon of the arthaśāstra, the wisdom of politics.[28] It has survived to us from the feudal battlefields of the deep Indo-Āryan past—the chivalrous age that is reflected in the disastrous war of the *Mahābhārata.*[29] This war, which has

[28] Cf. *supra,* pp. 35-38.

[29] *Editor's note:* The most celebrated examples of India's vast body of *Purāṇa* (cf. *supra,* p. 61, Editor's note) are the two folk epics known as the *Rāmāyaṇa* and *Mahābhārata* (the latter is eight times as long as the *Odyssey* and *Iliad* combined), which appear to have assumed their present form during the years between 400 B.C. and 400 A.D. (cf. M. Winternitz, *Geschichte der indischen Litteratur,* Vol. I, pp. 403 and 439-440). This interval—one of immense transformations in India (cf. *infra,* pp. 494-507) —stretches as a bridge between two Golden Ages; the first, the period of the Indo-Āryan political and spiritual conquest of the Indus, Jumna, and Gangetic plain (c. 1500–500 B.C.), was marked by the Vedas, Brāhmanas, and Upaniṣads, and culminated in the period of the Buddha; the second, the age of the Gupta dynasty (320–647 A.D.), represents India's classic statement of her synthesized Hindu-Buddhist civilization, and is the highest

become so famous in the annals of Indian civilization, took place in a period when the prose writings of the Brāhmaṇa texts

---

of an impressive series of summits of medieval Indian creativity, which are known to history by the names of the various imperial houses in different parts of India under which they arose; for example: the Early Cāḷukya dynasty in the western Deccan (550–753 A.D.), and the dynasty of the Rāṣṭrakūṭas who succeeded them; the Pallava dynasty in South India (third to ninth centuries A.D.), and their colonial branches in Java and Cambodia; the Rājput kingdom of Kanauj in the northwest (ninth to eleventh centuries A.D.); the dynasty of the Later Cāḷukyas, who in their turn unseated the Rāṣṭrakūṭas and remained in power until the end of the twelfth century; the Coḷas, who succeeded the Pallavas in the south (c. 850–1287 A.D.); the Hoyśala dynasty in Mysore (zenith, twelfth and thirteenth centuries A.D.); and the little oasis of the Rāya dynasty at Vijayanagar (c. 1370–1565), which was the last nucleus of Hindu civilization to survive the sandstorm of the Mohammedan invasion.

In contrast to the numerous architectural and literary remains of these imperial ages, tangible monuments from the first Golden Age are almost non-existent; for the early Indo-Āryans, like the early Greeks, neither built in stone nor committed their traditions to writing. The Vedas, Brāhmaṇas, and Upaniṣads, as well as the teachings of the Buddha and his contemporaries, were preserved orally, until rendered into writing sometime following the third century B.C. Everything not regarded as worthy of a special school of rememberers was therefore lost, either totally or in part.

The earliest Purānic compositions—the epics, romances, and heroic lays of the Indo-Āryan feudal age—have all thus disappeared. The *Rāmāyaṇa* and *Mahābhārata,* as well as the twenty-odd other extant Purāṇas of the late period, preserve only fragments of the older heroic compositions, mingled with oceans of miscellaneous folklore, ascetic moralizing and learning, popular religious tales, and the sentiments of a comparatively late period of religiosity in which Viṣṇu—who was a rather unimportant deity in the Vedic period—is the supreme personification of the absolute. The *Bhagavad Gītā,* which is introduced in Book VI of the *Mahābhārata* and announced as the teaching of Viṣṇu incarnate in the hero Kṛṣṇa, is so late that it can bring together in one rounded statement the doctrines of the Sāṅkhya and Upaniṣads, and thus prepare the ground (as Dr. Zimmer shows, *infra,* pp. 378-409) for the final, full-fledged syntheses of the Vedānta and the Tantra.

Nevertheless the consensus of scholarly opinion places the epic battle

and early Upaniṣads were being fixed in the forms in which they are preserved to the present day. Our example of metaphysical magic, therefore, may well have been employed by one or more of the actual contenders. It is preserved in an exegetic prose compilation belonging to the tradition of the *Ṛg-veda,* known as the *Aitareya Brāhmaṇa,* and is called "The Dying round the Holy Power." [30]

---

described in the *Mahābhārata* in the early years of the Āryan conquest of India, c. 1100 B.C. (see, for example, *Cambridge History of India,* Vol. I, p. 276). The field of the battle, Kurukṣetra, lies in a region between the Sutlej and the Jumna, which was the center of Indo-Āryan culture in the period of the Brāhmaṇas, while the character of the fighting is continually suggestive of the *Iliad.* What must once have been a comparatively brief and brilliant chivalrous epic drew to itself, in the course of the centuries, all the lore and wonder-tales of the various worlds of Indian life, growing like an avalanche until it encompassed, and in turn became the supreme inspiration of, the whole civilization of "the land of the Bharatas." For the past fifteen hundred years this prodigious folk-epic, in its present form, has supplied the prayers and meditations, popular plays, princely entertainments, moral admonitions, fables, romances, puppet plays, paintings, songs, poetic images, yogī-aphorisms, nightly dreams, and patterns for daily conduct of the hundreds of millions dwelling between the Vale of Kashmir and the tropical Isle of Bali. As they say in India today: "If you do not find it in the *Mahābhārata* you will not find it in the world."

[30] *Aitareya Brāhmaṇa* 8. 28. (Translated by Arthur Berriedale Keith in *The Rigveda Brāhmaṇas,* Harvard Oriental Series, Vol. XXV, Cambridge, Mass., 1920.) This work is a convenient introduction to, and specimen of, the forms of Brāhmaṇa theology and ritual. See especially the remarkable story of the Brāhman youth Śunaḥśepa, through whom human sacrifices were abolished (*Ait. Brahm.* 7. 13 ff.). The story is rendered in an excellent prose. (Hymns ascribed to Śunaḥśepa in *Ṛg-veda* 1. 24-30, by the way, contain no allusion to the predicament depicted in this legend.) These Brāhmaṇa tales are the oldest specimens of prose in any Indo-Āryan language; they are presented in a mixture of prose and verse such as we find again in ancient Celtic poetry and in the Buddhist legends of the *Jātaka.*

A briefer version of "The Dying round the Holy Power" appears in *Taittirīya Upaniṣad* 3. 10.

"Now comes the dying round the holy power (*brahmanaḥ parimaraḥ*). He who knows the dying round the holy power, round him the rivals that vie with and hate him die.

"He who blows here [i.e., the wind, the all-pervading, ever-moving life-breath of the macrocosm, the vital breath (*prāṇa*) of the universe] is the Holy Power (*brahman*). [That *brahman* is the secret life-essence of everything. "Who knows thus," *yo evam veda,* participates in that vital principle's relentless strength, and in his own restricted sphere can enact its overwhelming role.] Round him [who blows here] die these five deities: the lightning, the rain, the moon, the sun, the fire. The lightning after lightening enters into the rain [vanishes into the rain, disappears, dissolves, dies in the rain]; it is concealed; then men do not perceive it."

That is the basic statement of the charm; now the parallel for the human sphere: "When a man dies, then he is concealed, then men do not perceive him."

And on the basis of this macromicrocosmic correspondence we learn the following technique: "He [who practices the charm or ritual of the dying round the holy power, this magic performance (*karma*) which constitutes part of the "way of ritual deeds" (*karma-mārga*) for the attainment of a superhuman status] should say at the death of lightning [i.e., the moment the flash is seen to disappear into the rain]: 'Let my enemy die, let him be concealed, may they not perceive him!' [That is the curse put on the enemy, a charm of destruction by analogy, working at a distance.] Swiftly they [i.e., the friends of the victim, other people] perceive him not."

And now we proceed to the next stage of the charm:

"The rain having rained enters into the moon [for the moon is regarded as the receptacle and main source of the all-enlivening life-sap of the cosmic waters; these in the form of rain feed the vegetable and animal kingdoms, but when the rain ceases the power re-enters the source from which it became manifest, i.e., disappears and dies into King Moon, the vessel of all the waters of immortal life]; it is concealed; then men do not perceive it."

Now again: "When a man dies, then he is concealed, then men do not perceive him. He [the practicer of the charm] should say at the death of the rain: 'Let my enemy die, let him be concealed, may they not perceive him!' Swiftly they perceive him not.

"The moon at the conjunction enters into the sun; it is concealed; then men do not perceive it. When a man dies, then he is concealed, then men do not perceive him. He should say at the death of the moon: 'Let my enemy die, let him be concealed, may they not perceive him!' Swiftly they perceive him not.

"The sun on setting enters into the fire [the sacrificial and household fire which is kept burning by every family father and worshiped as the main presiding and tutelary divinity of the Vedic household; Agni ("fire") is the messenger of the gods; into his mouth are poured the offerings; on the rising flame and smoke he then flies with the offerings to the invisible celestial abodes, where he feeds his brother divinities from his mouth, as a bird its young]; it is concealed; then men do not perceive him." The murderous charm is again projected against the enemy. He shall die as the sun dies every night when its light and heat are reabsorbed into the fire. The sacrificial fire keeps burning from sunset to dawn, and the light that in the morning becomes manifest with the sun is regarded as derived from it. Fire is thus of greater power than the sun.

"The fire, breathing forth and upward, enters into the wind." The wind is air, the highest holy power of the universe, *brahman,* the life-force of the world; for the wind persists in its blowing when all the other powers of the body of the universe have temporarily ceased to exist, when they are no longer manifest but have melted into each other in their regular sequence.

Anyone worshiping one of these minor powers as though it were the highest shares in its weakness and must succumb to him whose superior knowledge of the more comprehensive force has gained unequaled strength for him. "It [the fire] is concealed [in the wind]; men do not perceive it. . . ."

The curse of death is then pronounced for the last time, and this ends the first phase of the charm. But now begins the task of controlling the reverse process:

"Thence are these deities born again; from the wind is born the fire [fire being churned by means of a stick twirled in a hole nicked in a board; the stick is of hard wood, the board of softer; the little flame of fire alights on the board—as it were, out of the air]; for from breath (*prāṇa*) it is born, being kindled by strength. [The wind in the form of the life-breath-energy (πνεῦμα, *spiritus, prāṇa*) within man, joined to bodily strength (*bala*) through man's exertion during the process of churning, actually produces the fire.]

"Having seen it, he should say: 'Let the fire be born; let not my enemy be born; far hence may he hasten away.' "

Then the effect: "Far hence he hastens away.

"From the fire the sun is born; having seen it, he should say: 'Let the sun be born; let not my enemy be born; far hence may he hasten away.' Far hence he hastens away.

"From the sun the moon is born. . . ." and when the moon becomes visible, the operator is to pronounce the same charm.

"From the moon the rain is born. . . ." The worker of magic watches the lightning as it appears, and again puts the curse upon his rival: " 'Let not my enemy be born; far hence may he hasten away.' Far hence he hastens away.

"This is the dying round the holy power. [Its effectiveness is guaranteed by its origin and success; as follows:] Maitreya Kauṣārava proclaimed this dying round the holy power to Sutvan Kairiśi Bhārgāyaṇa. [The first was a priest, the latter a king.] Round him died five kings; then Sutvan attained greatness (*mahat*)." He became, that is to say, a mahārāja, having reduced all other rājas to vassalage or forced allegiance.

There is a special observance or vow (*vrata*) that accompanies this magic ritual, and this must be kept by the one who performs it. "He should not sit down before the foe; if he think him to be standing, he should stand also. Nor should he lie down before the foe; if he think him to be sitting, he should sit also. Nor should he go to sleep before the foe; if he think him awake, he should keep awake also."

Then at last, the result of all these painstaking observances: "Even if his enemy has a head of stone, swiftly he lays him low—lays him low."

This is a vivid specimen of the magic of him "who knows thus," *yo evam veda.* In so far as it depends on knowledge—the knowledge of *brahman*—it is an archaic example of *jñāna-mārga,* the "way of knowledge," but in so far as it can be successful only when accompanied by a performance of the special observance or vow (*vrata*), it belongs also to *karma-mārga,* the "way of ritual action," the main thing being that it is to be practiced without fail on the five occasions of the birth and death of the five cosmic powers.

Anyone undertaking such an enterprise of magic for the gaining of supremacy over unfriendly neighbors—rival feudal chieftains, perhaps one's own cousins (as in the *Mahābhārata*) or step-brothers (as in the case of the constant battle for cosmic supremacy between the gods and the anti-gods or titans)—will have a complicated task. It will keep him busy all the while, what with the fire, the sun rising and setting, and the moon appearing and again disappearing. Particularly during thunderstorms the man will have to be on the alert—the rain starting and ceasing and the lightning now flashing and immediately vanishing. He will have to be quick to mutter his curses at precisely the correct instant if he is to cast his spells at the distant enemy with any hope of success. And with all this business of remaining on one's feet, not lying down while the enemy is sitting, and not going to sleep before the rival, the one practicing the charm must have had much the look of a neurotic caught by a strange obsession. Yet, obviously, all would be well worth the trouble if the secret weapon got rid of the ring of enemies and opened to him, *yo evam veda,* the dominion of paramount royal rule.

This is a sample of magic arthaśāstra[81] from as terrible an age of internecine warfare as any period in Indian history: for that matter, any period in the history of the world. It was an age that ended with the mutual slaughter, the self-extermination, of the whole of Indian chivalry, terminating the older style of Āryan feudal kingship. The great blood-bath depicted in the *Mahābhārata* marked at once the climax and the close of the Vedic-Āryan feudal age. In the following period, which was that of the Upaniṣads, the Sanskrit term for "hero," *vīra,* was no longer applied primarily to the man of action but instead to the saint—the sage who had become the master, not of others, not of the surrounding kingdoms of the world, but of himself.

5.

Brahman

THE TERM *brahman,* which in the translation above is rendered "holy power" (*brahmanaḥ parimaraḥ,* "the dying round

[81] Note that this term (cf. *supra,* p. 36) refers both to the literature of the science in general and to a particular volume on the subject written by Cānakya Kauṭilya.

the holy power"), has been from Vedic times to the present day the most important single concept of Hindu religion and philosophy. As we proceed in our present study, the meaning of *brahman* will open out and become clear; it is not a word that one can simply translate into English. Nevertheless, we may prepare the ground by a brief preliminary investigation, conducted along lines that have been held in high esteem in Vedic theology, and in the later Hindu sciences, as a technique for discovering not only the meaning of a term (*nāman*) but also the essential nature of the denoted object (*rūpa*); by a review, that is to say, of the etymology of the vocables in question.

Taking the phrase, *brahmanaḥ parimaraḥ:* the root *mar,* "to die," is related to "mortal," and the prefix *pari* corresponds to the Greek περι, "around" (viz. *peri*-meter, "measurement around, i.e., circumference"; *peri*-scope, "an instrument for looking around"). The ending *-aḥ,* which is added to the root, forms a verbal noun. And so we read this term *parimaraḥ* "the dying around."

As a translation of *brahman* in the above context, Professor Keith's rendering, "the holy power," seems to me an apt and happy choice—a circumscription of the term that fits very well the special case of the magic text. In the noun *brah-man, brah-* is the stem, *-man* the ending (the form *-manaḥ,* of the text, is the genitive). This ending *-man* will be recognized in *āt-man, kar-man, nā-man;* its force is the formation of a noun of action (*nomina actionis*). For example, *āt-man,* from the root *an,* "to breathe" (some believe, rather, from *at,* "to go") is the principle of breathing (or of going), which is life. Similarly, *kar-man,* from the root *kṛ,* "to make," is "work, action, rite, performance"; and *nā-man,* from the root *jñā,* "to know," means "name." [32]

Now the stem *brah-* occurs in a shorter, weaker form as *bṛh-;*

[32] *Nāman* is the form of the stem, *nāma* the form of the nominative singular; so also, *karman, karma;* the nominative of *ātman* is *ātmā.* Com-

and both formations appear in the alternate names of the Vedic deity *Bṛhas-pati,* called also *Brahmaṇas-pati,* who is the house-priest and guru of Indra, king of the gods. Just as every human king has as guru a Brāhman house-priest who serves also as court-magician—defending the king from demons, diseases, and the black magic of his enemies, while working counter-magic in turn, to make the king paramount, a mahārāja—so too was Indra served by this divine Bṛhaspati, the enactor of the traditional role of the king-god's spiritual and political adviser. It was, indeed, by virtue of the power-wisdom of Bṛhaspati that Indra conquered the anti-gods or titans (*asuras*) and held them at bay in their subterranean mansions.

Bṛhaspati is the heavenly archetype of the caste of the Brāhmans—a divine personification of ritual skill and inventiveness, unfailing in cunning devices, embodying the very quintessence of the highly developed intellectual faculties of the Hindu genius. He is regarded as the first of the divine priestly ancestors of one of the two most ancient Vedic priestly families, the Aṅgiras, whose descendants, in close friendship with the heavenly powers during the dim ages at the beginnings of time, beheld the gods in visions and gave expression to their visions in the potent stanzas (*ṛc, ṛg*) of the *Ṛg-veda.*[33] That is why the wisdom-power of these stanzas is capable of conjuring gods to sacrificial rites, gaining their good will, and winning their assistance for the ends of man—or rather, for the ends of the particular family in control of the Vedic hymn. The Sanskrit ending *-pati* of the word *Bṛhas-pati* means "lord" (compare the Greek πόσις, "husband, spouse," fem. πότνια, "mistress, queen"). Literally then, *Bṛhas-pati* is "the Pot-ent One," the one with the

---

pare *yogin, yogī.* Scholars have not been consistent in their selection of the form in which to carry over these Sanskrit nouns. For example, *ātman* is more commonly seen than *ātmā, karma* than *karman.*

[33] The Sanskrit word *aṅgiras* is related to the Greek ἄγγελος, whence "angel."

power of wielding *bṛh* or *brah*. And so what is *brah?* As we shall see—it is something far from "intellect."

Bṛh occurs as a verb of which only the present participle survives, this being employed as an adjective: the commonly encountered *bṛh-ant,* meaning "great." Furthermore, there is a derivative form (with an inserted nasal: *bṛṁh*) which appears in the verb *bṛṁh-ayati,* "to make *bṛh,* to render *bṝh,*" i.e., "to make or render great"; for *bṛh* means "to grow, to increase" and, when referring to sounds, "to roar." *Bṛṁhita,* which, as we have just seen, signifies "made great," when referring to sounds denotes "the roaring of an elephant"—that mighty trumpeting which, whether angry or triumphant, is the greatest of all animal noises. *Bṛh*—the word itself—has a highly sonorous ring.

Bṛṁhayati in classic Hindu medicine denotes the art of increasing the life-strength in weak people; the art of making fat. The doctor "fattens" (*bṛṁhayati*) those who are thin. Similarly, divinities become *bṛṁhita,* "fattened, swollen, puffed up," by hymns and praises; and men, in return, by blessings. There is a prayer pronounced over one setting forth on a journey: *Ariṣṭam vraja panthānam mad-anudhyāna-bṛṁhitā:* "Proceed along your path, and may it be free of obstacles and harm. You are increased (*bṛṁhitā*) by my soul-force, which accompanies you in the form of my inward vision." To which is pronounced the reply: *Tejo-ṛdha-bṛṁhitaḥ:* "These (enemies) I shall slay, being swollen or increased, by the half of your fiery life-strength." [34]

Bṛṁhayati means "increase, strengthen, fortify, intensify," and the Vedic noun *barhaṇā,* from the same root, denotes "power, strength." Thus it appears that, in the Vedic vocabulary, *brahman* corresponded exactly to what the Hinduism of subsequent centuries terms *śakti:* "energy, force, power, potency." [35] A

[34] *Editor's note:* I have not been able to locate the source of this quotation.

[35] *Editor's note:* It has become customary in the Occident to designate the orthodoxy of the first great Indo-Āryan period (the religion of the

person who is *śak-ta* is "potent to do something." Indra, king of the gods, is *śak-ra,* "the potent one," the one endowed with strength;[36] and his queen, Indrāṇī, is correspondingly *śacī,* "the potent female." Professor Keith, therefore, was being quite exact when he chose the term "holy power" to render *brahman,* in his translation of the old Vedic charm.

Power, the supreme aim and instrument of magic, was in fact the great and determinative element in all Vedic priestcraft. As we have seen, he who knows and can avail himself of the highest power in the universe is all-powerful himself. The power is to be found everywhere and assumes many forms, many manifestations. It abides with man—not in the outermost stratifications of his nature, but at the very core, in the innermost sanctum of his life. From there it wells up. It increases, floods into man's body and brain. And it can be made to grow, so that it takes form and bursts into the mind as a vision, or to the tongue in the lasting form of the powerful magic spell, the potent stanza. The word *brahman* in the Vedic hymns simply means, in many cases, "this stanza, this verse, this line." For example: "By this stanza (*anena brahmaṇā*) I make you free from disease." [37]

Brahman as the charm, or sacred magic formula, is the crystallized, frozen form (the convenient, handy form, as it were) of the highest divine energy. This energy is perennially latent in man, dormant, yet capable of being stirred to creative wakefulness through concentration. By brooding upon it, hatching it,

---

Vedas, Brāhmaṇas, and Upaniṣads) by the name "Brāhmanism," and that of the post-Buddhistic period and modern India (the religion of the *Bhagavad Gītā,* and of the Vedāntic, Purāṇic, and Tāntric teachers) by the name "Hinduism." For the term *śakti,* cf. *supra,* p. 61, Editor's note.

[36] *Śak-ra,* "endowed with *śak*"; compare *dhī-ra,* "endowed with *dhī,*" i.e., with the virtue of *dhyāna,* profound religious meditation. *Dhīra* means "steady, steadfast, strong-minded, courageous, calm, energetic, wise, deep, agreeable, gentle"; but then also, "lazy, dull, headstrong, bold."

[37] *Atharva Veda, passim.*

the wizard priest makes it available to his mind and purpose, bringing it to crystallization in the charm. Not yet so crystallized, in its unprecipitated, liquid or ethereal state, it is the powerful urge and surge that rises from man's unconscious being. Brahman, in other words, is that through which we live and act, the fundamental spontaneity of our nature. Proteus-like, it is capable of assuming the form of any specific emotion, vision, impulse, or thought. It moves our conscious personality by premonitions, flashes of advice, and bursts of desire, but its source is hidden in the depth, outside the pale of sense-experience and the mind-process. Brahman transcends these, hence is "transcendental" (what in modern psychology we term "unconscious"). Brahman properly is that which lies beyond the sphere and reach of intellectual consciousness, in the dark, great, unmeasured zone of height beyond height, depth beyond depth.

Brahman, then, the highest, deepest, final, transcendental power inhabiting the visible, tangible levels of our nature, transcends both the so-called "gross body" (*sthūla-śarīra*) and the inner world of forms and experiences—the notions, ideas, thoughts, emotions, visions, fantasies, etc.—of the "subtle body" (*sūkṣma-śarīra*). As the power that turns into and animates everything in the microcosm as well as in the outer world, it is the divine inmate of the mortal coil and is identical with the Self (*ātman*)—the higher aspect of that which we in the West style (indiscriminately) the "soul."

For in our Occidental concept of the "soul" we have mixed up, on the one hand, elements that belong to the mutable sphere of the psyche (thoughts, emotions, and similar elements of ego-consciousness), and on the other, what is beyond, behind, or above these: the indestructible ground of our existence, which is the anonymous Self (Self with a capital S; by no means the bounded ego), far aloof from the trials and history of the personality. This invisible source of life is not to be confused with the tangible matter, nerves and organs, receptacles and vehicles, of the manifest life-process, which constitute the gross body; neither with any of the various highly individualized faculties, states of reasoning, emotions, feelings, or perceptions that go to make up the subtle body. The true Self (*ātman; brahman*) is wrapped within, and not to be confused with, all the "spiritual" and "material" stratifications of its perishable covering.

Brahman—cosmic power, in the supreme sense of the term—is the essence of all that we are and know. All things have been precipitated wonderfully out of its omnipresent all-transcending omnipotence. All things bring it into manifestation—but only the holy wisdom of the competent wizard-sage deserves its name; for this sage is the one being in the universe devoted to making *conscious* in himself, and *consciously* manifest in action, that which in all else is deeply hidden. Bṛhas-pati, Brahmaṇas-pati, is the potent knower and bringer into form of every kind of sign and instrument of sacred wisdom: charms, hymns, and rites, as well as exegetical interpretations and elucidations. In him the bubbling waters from the hidden source (which is the divine power in us all) flow freely, abundantly, and with unremitting force. To tap and live by those waters, fed by their inexhaustible force, is the alpha and omega of his priestly role. And he is able to maintain himself in that role because of the yoga technique that has always attended, guided, and constituted one of the great disciplines of Indian philosophy.

Every being dwells on the very brink of the infinite ocean of the force of life. We all carry it within us: supreme strength—the plenitude of wisdom. It is never baffled and cannot be done away, yet is hidden deep. It is down in the darkest, profoundest vault of the castle of our being, in the forgotten well-house, the deep cistern. What if one should discover it again, and then draw from it unceasingly? That is the leading thought of Indian philosophy. And since all the Indian spiritual exercises are devoted seriously to this practical aim—not to a merely fanciful contemplation or discussion of lofty and profound ideas—they may well be regarded as representing one of the most realistic, matter-of-fact, practical-minded systems of thought and training ever set up by the human mind. How to come to Brahman and remain in touch with it; how to become identified with Brahman, living out of it; how to become divine while still on earth—transformed, reborn adamantine while on the earthly plane; that is the quest that has inspired and deified the spirit of man in India through the ages.

Still, we cannot say that this is exclusively an Indian objective; for it is reflected in many myths throughout the world. The ancient Mesopotamian hero Gilgamesh set forth to seek the Watercress of Immortality. The Arthurian knight Owein found the Fountain of Life; Parsifal, the Holy Grail. So likewise, Herakles overcame the guardian monster-dog of the realm of death, and after numerous deeds of valor ascended in the flame of the funeral pyre to a seat of immortality among the gods. Jason and the Greek heroes of his day, in their stout vessel Argo, gained the Golden Fleece. Orpheus sought Eurydice, his cherished soul, hoping to bring her back from among the shadows. And the Chinese emperor Shih Huang sent forth an expedition (which never returned) into the vast Eastern Sea, to secure the Plant of Immortality from the Isles of the Blest. Such tales represent in the universally known picture-language of mythology the one primal and final, everlasting human quest. The adventure was continued in medieval Europe in the secret laboratories of the mysterious alchemists, who were concerned with the transmutation of vile matter into imperishable gold and the production of the philosophers' stone—that materialized Brahman, containing a supreme power over all phenomena, which should be potent to change everything into anything. Throughout the world we find men striving for this *summum bonum:* the gold, the pearl, the watercress of deathlessness. Maui, the trickster-hero of Polynesia, lost his life attempting to win immortality for mankind by diving down the throat of his ancestress Hine-nui-te-po. The search has been pursued in many ways. We of the West are continuing it, even today, through the science of our doctors of medicine. The unique thing about the quest as conducted in India is its formulation and pursuit in terms of thought. Indian philosophy, therefore, does not contradict, but rather elucidates and corroborates the universally known mythological symbols. It is a practical mental and physical discipline for their realization in life through an awakening and adjustment of the mind.

Before embarking, however, on our study of the Indian techniques for this perennial human adventure, we must gain some sense of the general state of Indian human affairs. This can be done by tracing in brief outline India's three philosophies of worldly life—those of the so-called *trivarga:* [38] the political doctrines of the arthaśāstra, psychological of the kāmaśāstra, and ethical of the dharmaśāstra. For what men have to transform into divine essence are precisely the vicissitudes that afflict their tangible personalities—the bondages of their desires and sufferings, possessions (*artha*), delights (*kāma*), and virtues (*dharma*). It is to these, which are the very life of the Old Adam, that the hero-adventurer dies when he passes from the known and familiar to what is beyond and underneath it, omnipresent but normally out of reach. Rebirth, release, means to go beyond what is known.

One cannot but feel that such a sublime flight as India's into the transcendental realm would never have been attempted had the conditions of life been the least bit less hopeless. Release (*mokṣa*) can become the main preoccupation of thought only when what binds human beings to their secular normal existences affords absolutely no hope—represents only duties, burdens, and obligations, proposing no promising tasks or aims that

[38] Cf. *supra,* p. 41; the fourth sphere of philosophy, *mokṣa,* "release," is to be the topic of Part III.

stimulate and justify mature ambitions on the plane of earth. India's propensity for transcendental pursuit and the misery of India's history are, most certainly, intimately related to each other; they must not be regarded separately. The ruthless philosophy of politics and the superhuman achievements in metaphysics represent the two sides of a single experience of life.

PART II

THE PHILOSOPHIES OF TIME

I. THE PHILOSOPHY OF SUCCESS

1.

The World at War

WHEN, in August 1939, I read of the German-Russian non-aggression pact, which just preceded the opening of the present war,[1] I was as much surprised as many who were supposed to understand more than Indologists about political affairs and who might have known better. Yet as soon as I learned of this startling alliance between two powers that had been thought to be natural enemies, professing conflicting interests and ideals of life, I was reminded of a Hindu tale, a beast fable figuring in the epic *Mahābhārata*—that unique and inexhaustible treasury of spiritual and secular wisdom. It was the parable of a cat and a mouse. And its teaching was that two sworn and deadly enemies, such as Hitler's Germany and Stalin's Russia, might very well enter into an alliance and present a united front, if such an arrangement suited the temporary interests of both.

Once upon a time—so runs this timely tale [2]—there lived a wildcat and a mouse; and they inhabited the same tree in the

[1] *Editor's note:* The lectures of this chapter were delivered in the spring of 1942.

[2] *Mahābhārata* 12. 138.

jungle, the mouse dwelling in a hole at its root, and the wild tomcat up in the branches, where it lived on bird's eggs and inexperienced fledglings. The cat enjoyed eating mice also; but the mouse of the tale had managed to keep out of reach of its paw.

Now one day a trapper placed a cunning net beneath the tree, and the cat that night became entangled in the meshes. The mouse, delighted, came out of its hole and took conspicuous pleasure in walking around the trap, nibbling at the bait, and generally making the most of the misfortune. When lo! it became aware that two other enemies had arrived. Overhead, in the dark foliage of the tree, perched an owl with sparkling eyes, who was just about to pounce, while on the ground a stalking mongoose was approaching. The mouse, in a sudden quandary, decided quickly on a surprising stratagem. It drew in close to the cat and declared that if it were permitted to slip into the net and take shelter in the cat's bosom it would repay its host by gnawing through the meshes. The other agreed. And the little animal, having delayed only long enough to receive the promise, gladly darted in.

But if the cat expected a prompt release it was disappointed; for the mouse nestled comfortably in against its body, hiding as deeply as possible in the fur in order to disappear from the sight of the two watchful enemies without, and then, safely sheltered, decided to have a quiet nap. The cat protested. The mouse declared there was no hurry. It knew that it could slip from the trap in an instant, and that its disgruntled host would simply have to be patient, with the hope of getting free. So it frankly told its natural enemy that it thought it would wait until the trapper appeared; the cat, then threatened in its turn, would not be able to take advantage of its freedom by catching and devouring its deliverer. There was nothing the larger animal could do. Its little guest took a nap between its very paws. The mouse peacefully waited for the coming of the hunter, and then, when the man could be seen approaching to inspect his traps, safely fulfilled its pledge by quickly gnawing through the net and darting into its hole, while the cat, with a desperate leap, broke free, got up into the branches, and escaped the death at hand.

This is a typical example from the vast treasure store of India's beast fables of political wisdom. It gives an idea of the cold-blooded cynical realism and sophistication that is the very life-sap and flavor of the ancient Indian style of political theory and casuistry. The quick-witted mouse, completely unprejudiced in his forming of alliances to stave off danger, was, besides being bold, a master of the art of timing. But the episode of the net was not the end of this affair. The further course of the tale presents the particular point intended for the instruction of the Hindu kings and their chancellors.

Following the departure of the disappointed huntsman from the scene with his shattered net, the cat came down from the branches and, approaching the mousehole, called in sweetly to the mouse. He invited it to come up and rejoin its old companion. The common predicament of the night just past (so the cat maintained) and the assistance that the two had so loyally given to each other in their common struggle for survival had forged a lasting bond that expunged their former differences. Henceforward the two should be friends forever, and trust each other implicitly. But the mouse demurred. It remained cold to the tomcat's rhetoric, stoutly refusing to come out of its secure abode. The paradoxical situation that had thrown the two together in a queer temporary co-operation having passed, no words could induce the canny little creature to draw near again to its natural enemy. The mouse brought forth in justification of its rejection of the other's insidious kindly sentiments the formula that is intended to be the moral of the tale, which is, frankly and simply, that on the battleground of politics there is no such thing as lasting friendship.

There can be no traditional bond, no cordial alliance, no sticking together in the future because of common experiences, perils, and victories in the past. In the course of the unremitting struggle of political powers—which is like that of beasts in the wilderness, preying and feeding upon each other, each devouring what it can—friendships and alliances are but temporary expedients and attitudes, enforced by common interests and suggested by need and desire. The moment the actual occasion for mutual assistance has passed, the reason for as well as the safety of the companionship has also passed. For what governs politics is never friendship, but only temporary co-operation and assistance, inspired by common threats or by parallel hopes of gain, and supported by the natural selfishness of each of the allies. There is no such thing as an altruistic alliance. Loyalties do not exist. And where friendship is pleaded, that is only a mask. There must be no "Union Now."

So it was that Japan, at the beginning of the present century, wooed and gained the support of Britain to weaken Russia in Persia, in the Near East, and at the Dardanelles. Then, in the first World War, Japan became the ally of England *and* Russia, together with France, in order to drive Germany out of China (Kiaochow) and take possession of Germany's Pacific islands. Whereas in the present struggle, Japan has become the ally of Germany, has conquered France in Indo-China, and seems to be seriously threatening the colonial empire of England. Apparently the ancient Hindu political wisdom of the first millennium B.C. is still a good key to the political thinking of Asiatic peoples.

It is a remarkably good key, also, to international politics throughout the world; for its utterly unmoral, premoral point of view brings out, and formulates with the cold precision of a kind of political algebra, certain fundamental natural laws that govern political life, no matter where. England, for example, before the first World War, discovered that she had to ally herself with Russia to check the rise of Germany—even though Russian and British imperialism were themselves at odds and had been in collision throughout the better part of the nineteenth century. From 1933 to 1938, on the other hand, following Hitler's coming into power and until the Munich collapse of the appeasement policy, England tolerated and even favored the rise of Nazism as a possible safeguard against the danger of the spread of Communism over Middle Europe. After Munich, England again sought alignment with Russia—against what was now the Nazi peril. And so today [March, 1942] we have liberal, democratic, capitalistic England hand in hand with Communist Russia against a common foe.

Such fluctuations in our modern international situation indicate that the theories of politics evolved in Indian antiquity may be by no means out of date. They have remained unnoticed, largely because overshadowed by the world-wide reputation of India's great metaphysical and religious philosophies of release—Buddhism, Vedānta, and the rest; but this does not mean that they could be of no use or interest to the modern mind. It is only in the past few decades that these hard-headed political doctrines have been brought to our attention, as a result of the recent editions and translations by scholarly specialists. And it appears that they really might figure usefully among the required studies of the modern foreign service offices. Composed by astute Brāhmans trained in the complex formalities and perilous rituals of commerce with the superhuman powers, they were intended for use in a very real, intricate, and ruthless political game. Specifically, they were composed for the guidance of chancellors and ministers. These, mostly of Brāhman extraction, were the advisers of the Hindu despots in secular life as well as in their spiritual affairs. They are textbooks, that is to say, written for and by professionals, and, as such, are as technical and thoroughgoing as the handbooks, or sūtras,[3] of any of

[3] Cf. *supra,* p. 38, note 22.

the other Indian crafts: carpentry, medicine, witchcraft, priestcraft, or the dance.

The popular Hindu tradition of the beast fables, which runs parallel in doctrine to the more technical professional treatises, became known to the Occident centuries ago. The vivid case histories—presenting, under the entertaining guises of the animal kingdom, the perplexing situations and issues of policy that everywhere confront kings, states, and private individuals, both in the great struggle for survival and in the lesser emergencies of everyday life—have been the delight of many generations in the West. But their value for the interpretation of current situations, and for the understanding of international politics in general, has not yet been realized. To the Hindu mind, on the other hand, the pertinence of the beast fable to the high art of intrigue and defense has always been apparent.

The best known collection, the *Pañcatantra,* entered Europe as early as the thirteenth century A.D. through the medium of Semitic translations (Arabic and Hebrew), and finally became known, as La Fontaine phrases it, *"en toutes les langues."* [4] But the systematic *Arthaśāstra* of Cāṇakya Kauṭilya was not made available until 1909. I can still remember vividly what a surprising discovery this was for all concerned—the rather restricted

[4] The *Directorium humanae vitae,* c. 1270, was a Latin translation made by the Jew, John of Capua, from a Hebrew version, which in turn had been translated from an Arabic translation of a Persian translation from the Sanskrit. An Old Spanish rendering had appeared in 1251, taken from the same Arabic version. John of Capua's Latin was translated into German in the fifteenth century (*Das buch der byspel der alten wysen,* c. 1481), and into Italian in the sixteenth (A. F. Doni, *La moral filosophia,* Venice, 1552). Sir Thomas North translated the Italian into English (*The Morall Philosophie of Doni,* London, 1570), and in the seventeenth century numerous printed versions appeared in many tongues. La Fontaine drew most of the subjects of his second volume of *Fables* from the *Pañcatantra*—which he describes in his preface as "les fables de Pilpay, sage indien."

circle, that is to say, of scholarly specialists in Europe, the United States, and India. The caustic and sententious style, literary facility, and intellectual genius displayed do high credit to the master of political devices who composed this amazing treatise. Much of the material was quarried from older sources, the work being founded on a rich tradition of earlier political teachings, which it superseded, but which is still reflected through its quotations and aphorisms; and yet the study as a whole conveys the impression of being the production of a single, greatly superior mind. We know little—or perhaps nothing—of the author. The rise of Candragupta, the founder of the Maurya dynasty, to paramount kingship over northern India in the third century B.C., and the important role of his dynasty during the following centuries, have contributed a practically impenetrable glow of legend to the fame of the fabled chancellor, Kauṭilya, whose art is supposed to have brought the whole historical period into being.[5]

2.

The Tyrant State

WHEN we review the theories and devices of the Hindu master statesman, we behold the ancient style of despotism in all its power and weakness, and begin to understand something of the

[5] Cf. *supra*, p. 37, and Appendix B. For a history of this period, cf. Sir George Dunbar, *A History of India, from the earliest times to the present day,* 2nd edition, London, 1939, pp. 35-57, "The Maurya Empire."

Kauṭilya is one of the very few historical individuals who have been

sinister backgrounds of the Indian political scene: the ever-recurrent tragedy, the constant perils of the individual, the total lack of security, and the absence of all those rights which we cherish today as pertaining to our basic human freedom. The world depicted was that of the lonely monarch-dictator, supported by a vast and costly military machine and a monstrous system of secret espionage and police—which included informants, prostitutes, sycophants, thugs, sham ascetics, and professional poisoners; a terrible organization of despotism similar to that described by the Greek historians in their accounts of the Basileus of ancient Persia, "the King of Kings."

For it was the empire of Persia—as established by Cyrus the Great (550–529 B.C.), and as carried on magnificently until its sudden collapse when Darius III (336–330) was defeated by Alexander the Great—that set the model for the monarchies in neighboring India.[6] Persia was the first state in history to bring kingship to an absolute, unquestionable, and overwhelming position of power through sheer military might. Within three generations—from Cyrus through Cambyses to Darius I (521–486)—the armies of the Persians shattered all of the known ancient kingdoms in every direction (civilizations of highly divergent character), so that the tyrant's control soon extended from the Black Sea and the Caucasus in the north, southward to the mouth of the Tigris and Euphrates and even into Egypt, and from Syria and Asia Minor in the west, eastward through Afghanistan to the Indus Valley and into India proper. No such

immortalized in Indian poetry. He appears in the *Mudrārākṣasa,* a play of seven acts by Viśākhadatta (of the fifth, eighth, or ninth century A.D.), the subject of which is the rooting out of the Nanda dynasty by Kautilya, and his winning over of the Nanda chancellor, Rākṣasa, to the cause of his own royal protégé, Candragupta. There is an English translation by H. H. Wilson, *Works,* London, 1871, Vol. XII, pp. 125ff.

[6] Note that the period about to be described is that following the early Indo-Āryan feudal age of the Vedas, Brāhmaṇas, the Upaniṣads. Cf. *supra,* p. 8, Editor's note, and Appendix B.

forcible unification of peoples had ever been achieved before. An astounding variety of independently flourishing populations was conquered and forcibly knit into that single, mighty, brutal system. The army, which was second to none in the world, laid low whatever stood in its way, until it came against the rugged Scythians north of the Dardanelles and the stout Greeks fighting in the heart of their homeland. All the other domains within reach were reduced to the status of mere provinces under the hard control of the single Basileus.

This frightening super-king, dwelling in his sunlike, glorious capital, Persepolis, was described as having his "eyes and ears everywhere"—which meant simply that his unnumbered spies and secret agents were on the alert throughout the empire, to watch and inform upon the enslaved populations (peoples of numerous faiths, languages, and races, multitudinous, and divided among themselves). A complex, efficient system of informants, denouncers, and plain-clothes men—making use also of the demimonde and the underworld—covered the conquered provinces with a close and inescapable network. The frontiers and roads of entry were controlled by a passport service, while all travelers and political ambassadors within the realm were strictly supervised. Vigilance of this kind was absolutely necessary to uphold the achievements won through sheer violence; the forced unification of the whole of Near Eastern Asia could be maintained only by a crushing, suspicious, ruthless administration. Secret agents were delegated to shadow even the high officials of the government.

All of which sounds ominously familiar; for today we are being reintroduced to such things by the reports that are coming steadily from within the new tyrant states of Europe and Asia. Indeed, anyone who may wish to visualize and understand the actual historical model on which the philosophy of Kauṭilya's *Arthaśāstra* was based would do well to study the world-picture of the modern day—as well as that ancient Persian prototype, of which the dynasties in India (rising, spreading and collapsing, towering and vanishing into dust) were the faithful copies. Furthermore, such a consideration would facilitate one's understanding of the basic tendency of escape from secular life which characterizes the tradition of classic Indian thought—the holy way of mokṣa [7]—the serious search for release from the perils and pains of earthly bondage, through the attainment of some kind of metaphysical equanimity.

The records of the Buddhists and Jainas make it possible to study the state of India in the sixth and fifth centuries B.C. At that time the political structures of the Āryan feudal period were disintegrating, thus leaving the way open for the development of the harsher Persian style. The pattern can be compared to that of the late and declining medievalism of the fifteenth century in Italy and Germany: a flowering chaos of petty principalities and free cities, all vying with each other jealously, desperately fighting for survival and struggling for ascendancy, most of them doomed to become absorbed or subordinated in the end by larger, rising states, governed by uncontrollable monarchs. In the period immediately preceding the day of Kauṭilya, this stage of enforced unification seems to have been practically completed—at least for the northern part of India—under the Nanda dynasty, which it was to be his great achievement to overthrow. The model of the Persian techniques for the reduction of extensive areas of formerly independent peoples and the shaping of them into helpless provinces, the sowing of suspicion and mutual distrust among them, disarmament of the conquered populations and the induction of their manhood into the tyrant's army to serve in distant fields, all had already become fundamental to the new Indian conception of statecraft and social discipline. The much older, native Indian ideal

[7] For a discussion of this term, cf. *supra,* p. 41.

of the "divine world-emperor" (*cakravartin*) [8] was to be girded, so to say, with the up-to-date instruments of aggressive militarism, and coarsely parodied through the crushing administration of conquered lands.

The official art of Kauṭilya's Maurya dynasty, as represented by the monuments of King Aśoka's reign (273–232 B.C.), bears witness to the influence of the Persian style (*Plate I*). Such an art, in spite of its iconology, has no real flavor of the religious; it is an art of pomp, secular display, and success. For in terms of the new Persian type of Indian despotism, kingship lacked the idea of sanctity, the idea of a divine mandate bestowed by the gods on the bearer of the crown; rather, the state was a demonstration and reflex of the personal power of the king himself—a prodigious unification of disparate regions by a steel-hard central tyranny, in perpetual danger of disintegration. What it required—and *all* that it required—to survive was a kind of superman in the seat of control, a superdemon, who, by superior talent, intellect, and cunning, could keep the whole impossibly intricate machine running at the peak of power.

This remained the post-feudal Indian view, even though in Persia a new touch was added by Darius I (521–486 B.C.), when he restored the dynasty after Cambyses' death and the conspiracy of Pseudo-Smerdis and the Magians, in the year 521. Darius made bold to claim a divine mandate for himself and his reign. He is represented in an inscription carved on a cliff at Behistun standing triumphant over his enemies and receiving the divine support of the highest Persian god, Ahura-Mazda. This was bold, and yet not quite a new thing either; for it followed the precedent of an ageless, practically universal world tradition. The Chinese emperor, for example, had for centuries been styled "The Son of Heaven" (*t'ien-tse*), and was supposed to embody not only the

[8] *Infra*, pp. 127-139. Cf. also Ananda K. Coomaraswamy, *Spiritual Authority and Temporal Power in the Indian Theory of Government*, New Haven, 1942.

royal but also the priestly principle. He was the mediator between heaven and earth. And should his dominion suffer from defeat, famine, or corruption and himself be overthrown, his fall was to be interpreted as a sign that heaven (*t'ien*) had withdrawn its mandate, dissatisfied because of some personal deficiency in the higher virtues. The usurper who then managed to establish the new dynasty obviously drew to his own house the heavenly favor and bore the Heavenly Mandate (*t'ien ming*) on his victorious brow.

The heads of the later Hindu kings lacked this light of glory. Not the supreme Lord of the World but only the goddess of fortune, *Fortuna,* Śrī Lakṣmī, a fickle and comparatively weak divinity, was regarded as their guarantor of success and continued rule. And she forsook her favorite the moment fate (*daivam*) left him in the lurch. Temporarily she was incarnate in the king's supreme queen, so long as any reason for the connection lasted, but if he dallied away his prosperity in self-indulgence, or fell victim to some mightier rival, she withdrew—reluctantly and in tears—to bestow her favors on her next crowned fondling. Śrī Lakṣmī had nothing to do with virtue, but only with politics and the turn of the wheel of time. The philosophy of life of the Hindu kings and chancellors was fatalistic, skeptical, and unregenerately realistic.

3.

Valor against Time

THERE is an age-long argument that comes down through the Hindu literature of all eras, from the feudal period, as represented in the *Mahābhārata,* to the works of comparatively modern Hinduism. Which (it is asked) is the more potent, the finally decisive factor in life's ceaseless struggle for survival and success, personal valor or the simple, fatal turn of time?[9] Those who speak for the former—*vīrya,* that dauntless prowess and endurance of the hero who never yields but battles through and outlives all reversals, never is downed but has the fortitude to rise again, and thus ultimately masters stubborn, stony, merciless fate —maintain that valor in the end prevails; and this argument is used against the weakling who becomes disheartened, life's exile who gives in, the craven who resigns and abandons the game. We detect in this view of life and destiny something of the British bulldog attitude, though without the Christian belief that the right cause will prevail, and that a humble acceptance of one's own sufferings as punishment for shortcomings and faults will have redeeming power.

The opposite argument is one of blank fatalism, based on sad and long experience. Many of the most valorous fighters in the course of history, it is declared, have failed, time and time again. Brave men have fought in vain, to the last stroke, against rising tides that have swept all away, while men of comparatively little valor, delighted by all the blandishments of Fortune, have sat proudly and safely in the seat of the hero. For in history there are times and tides. There are mounting periods, when everything supports the hero-conqueror. He rides the wave. His very faults and deficiencies turn to his advantage. No reversal can break his career. And his enemies, though great with valor and backed by superior resources, struggle in vain to halt his triumphant march. "Time" (*kāla*), the supreme power, favors him—that is all. But time proceeds in cycles, now expanding, now contracting. The hero's career only happens to coincide with a period of increase.

The gods—so runs this hopeless argument—in their battle with the anti-gods, gained the victory, not because of valor, not by cunning or by the craft of their all-knowing Brāhman-priest ad-

[9] Cf. *Mahābhārata* 12. 25; 13. 6; and *passim.*

visers, but only because time favored them. The moment arrived for the gods to crush their enemies and gain the dominion of the universe, and this carried them to their lofty seats. But time revolves, and they will in time be swept away. Borne from glory into exile, they will then be the ones filled with impotent rage, while the demons, triumphant now, set up their own ungodly rule.

No one can battle time. Its tides are mysterious. One must learn to accept them and submit to their unalterable rhythm. So it was that when divine Kṛṣṇa became incarnate on earth and gave support to his kingly human friend Arjuna, the latter was filled with superhuman power and seemed a hero whom no one could overcome. But the moment the divine friend mysteriously withdrew, returning from this human plane to his supermundane abode, then everything changed in the history of the king. No valor availed. A mere tribe of wild herdsmen, non-Āryan outcasts and forest-dwellers, armed with nothing more than wooden clubs and clods of clay, carried off the widowed queens of Kṛṣṇa, entrusted to Arjuna's care, and the once invincible warrior was unable to stop the rape and defilement of the noble ladies. Time (*kāla*) had turned—that mysterious stream from the waters of which all things appear, and on whose surface they ride until engulfed again, to be swept away in an unfeeling, reeling, indiscriminate flood.

Thus runs this classic argument. No decision has been reached in India between the champions of the two sides—those who accept the decrees of time or destiny with a fatalistic mysticism, and those who stand for the effectuality of valor. Both agree, however, that the gods are in no better position with respect to these two determinative forces than the kings of men, or than individuals in general.

Daivam, the Sanskrit word for "fate," is an adjective that has become a noun, meaning properly "that which pertains to, that which is related to, the gods (*deva*)." It denotes a sexless, anonymous power or factor that is divine; a neuter; the "godly essence" which is a transcendent force antecedent both to such mythical personifications as the gods themselves and to all god-wrought events. *Daivam*, "fate," cannot be personified, brought down to the scale of the human imagination; neither can it be reached by prayer, oblation, or magic spell. *Daivam* is that stony face of life which must be confronted when the comforting illusion of the magic mythological tradition, the consolation of devotional religion, has been outgrown; when at last it is realized what a little day is that of the victory of human arms. An acceptance, sober and brave, of man's position against this mighty background is then required, there being no longer any screening, comforting ideals: neither gods strong enough to defend us, nor satisfying illusions about the nature of the community—illusions, for example, of the nation surviving through the sacrifice and surrender of the individual, or through the sacrifice of a generation, or such flattering notions as those of supremely valuable institutions and ideals that will outlive the doom of the period and the personal disaster of the individual sacrificed for their survival.

A lonely beast of prey, a wounded lion in its den, forsaken by fortune and his fellows, the Hindu king, no matter what his fortune, is doomed to die an exile in the jungle. Fame will scarcely outlive his brief career. His life-spark, his personal soul (*jīva*) will go on, in the vortex of rebirth, to subsequent embodiments, in the heavens or hells—most likely hells; and after the interlude of that yonder-life he will be born again, as man or beast. He may aspire to kingship again, go through the same struggle, the same cycle, thrilled in turn by the anxieties and the merciless triumphs, shaken by foreboding, submitting finally to doom—rising like a rocket, falling like a star, and all the while oblivious of the fact that he has experienced this thing many times before. He will empty once again this cup of life to the last drop, in gluttony and disgust, in surfeit and misery, without understanding the elementary trick—namely that it was himself who mixed the ingredients through his deeds and desires in former existences, and that now again he is preparing his own future.

The situation of the Hindu despot forsaken by Fortune (*śrī*), crushed by Fate (*daivam*), engulfed by Time (*kāla*), is like that of Napoleon on the rocks at Saint Helena. And there is an apposite remark of the Little Corsican on destiny and fortune, which voices an attitude strikingly similar to that of the Hindu. At the period of the climax of his rocketlike career, in 1810, when he was still on tolerable terms with Russia, there was held a congress of kings and princes in the heart of Germany, at Erfurt in the Duchy of Weimar, over which Napoleon presided. The glamour of the gathering was reflected in a remark that his master of ceremonies, the Count Ségur, one day used as an excuse for arriving late to a meeting of his emperor's privy council: he had had difficulties making his way through the antichamber, he declared, for it was so crowded with kings: *"Il y avait tant de rois!"* At the conclusion of the congress, when Napoleon was departing from this spectacular pageant, his host, the Duke of Saxe-Weimar, brave Charles Augustus, the friend and protector of Goethe, was standing at the door of the imperial carriage to see the emperor away. And when the host wished good luck to his departing overlord, whom he heartily disliked, Napoleon, now inside the carriage, practically rebuked him for his levity by replying that in the career of a man of destiny, like himself, there was a time when nothing could stop his rise, but then, unawares, there might come a turn when all was changed, whereupon a straw tossed by a child would suffice for his fall. This was a haughty rejection of the concept of an accidental, personal "luck" (the power of *Fortuna,* fortune, *śrī*) for such men as he, and a cryptic pronouncement pointing to the vast impersonal destiny of the stars.[10]

[10] This idea of the stars or "the star" that presides over the hero-career is one that has been common in the West since the Renaissance. The humanists of that progressive time revived Greco-Roman astrology for the sake of those freethinkers who had just discarded the authority of the

No doubt Napoleon's hint of the stars was only a metaphor suggesting Fate—not referring, specifically, to the questionable matter of stellar influence; in which case the words of the great adventurer and man of destiny would seem to be fairly consistent with the Hindu view of the tides and cycles that bear the strong to victory and then turn to disaster. One must remark, however, a certain important difference. The political genius or master gambler in the West feels himself to be an instrument of something higher, during those moments when he seems to be figuring as a fatal force in history. He is incarnate Fate, a carrier of the powers that govern the growth of civilization and effect its epochal changes. He is the protagonist of certain social forces, or the chief representative of the spirit and ideals of a new and better age, carrying into history high principles for which earlier martyrs have suffered, fought, and died: such principles, for example, as those of liberty, democracy, and the rationalization of human affairs, which inspired the seizure of power by the Third Estate in the French Revolution. Apparently the Western man of action has to regard himself as the noble instrument of a mysterious plan for the history of mankind, the arm of the universal spirit, working changes and driving forward evolution. In this respect, even such an unbeliever and atheist as Napoleon—who had no belief but in his own "star," his own genius—directly sides with those who remain embedded in some established faith and fight "God's War" in their revolutions—men such as Cromwell, who humbly regarded himself as God's chosen vessel and the instrument elect of Providence, upholding true Christianity against popery, the Inquisition, the Jesuits, and whatever else

---

Church and Revelation and were now being "modern" after the Roman fashion of the period of Horace and Tiberius. Astrology was introduced into Rome at the time of the first emperors, as a fascinating fad of Sumero-Babylonian origin. It has never played any great role in shaping the Indian philosophy of fate—the fate of kings and despots—even though there is much horoscope-casting in India and a daily use of astrology.

he chose to consider to be the devilish distortion (as he was not) of Christ's true message. Napoleon was carrying into effect forcibly the mandate of modern thought, as created by Locke, Montesquieu, Voltaire, and Rousseau, and as sounded forth in the "Eroica" of Beethoven. He was the deputy of the New Age. So we regard him, and so we value him, in our Western view of the progress (through ourselves) of the destiny of man.

No such mandate from Providence, history, or mankind descends to form a wreath around the head of the Hindu despot. He is the actual temporary holder of despotic power, but not borne on by the mission of a new idea, some new dream of human affairs with which his age is pregnant and which he fancies himself as chosen to bring into the world. He stands merely for himself—himself and those whom he can pay or bribe, gain with favor, or threaten and bully into his service. And when he falls, it is simply he who falls—together with those who depended on his rule or misrule. Thus in India kingship lacks the prestige of divine right by which it has been supported elsewhere, both in Asia and in Europe. Sanctity such as pertains to the Chinese Son of Heaven, the Mikado of Japan, the Pharaoh of Egypt, and the royal head of the Anglican church, is attributed in India not to the members of the Kṣatriya caste—warriors, kings, aristocrat-adventurers, and conquerors—but to the Brāhmans: the priests, the sages, the knowers and conjurers of the transcendental Brahman. For millenniums the summit of the Hindu social pyramid has been occupied by those born inheritors of the secret wisdom of the Holy Power. They, the living repositories of tradition, the professional wizards and teachers, are the depersonalized intermediators between the divine zones of power and the human world. But as for kings (*il y avait tant de rois!*): their valor, their fate, their agony, is their own.

4.

The Function of Treachery

Kings, from the beginning of Hindu history, as we learn from the Vedic records and all the records since, have always ranked below the caste of the Brāhmans. During the Vedic period and the ensuing feudal age represented in the *Mahābhārata* they stemmed largely from the warrior clans, the families of Kṣatriya caste, but following the disintegration of feudal society in the seventh and sixth centuries B.C., when the strength of the Āryan Kṣatriyas was greatly diminished as a result of incessant internecine warfare and their power over northern India broken, there came the dark age that we have been describing, during which men of various extractions came into power—both the scions of some of the surviving pre-Āryan regal families, and soldiers of fortune of inferior birth. We know, for example, that Candragupta was an adherent of a non-Vedic creed (that of the Jainas), the roots of which go back to pre-Āryan beliefs in northwestern India which had never been quite eradicated by the Brāhmans.[11] And many of the founders of new dynasties were little better, apparently, than desperadoes. The Brāhman records complain in no uncertain terms that adventurers of the lowest origin were to be found holding thrones in the new age of disorder, and that there were kings who did not support the Brāhmans, the Āryan religion, or even the Āryan style of life. Kingship had forfeited the splendor of the Vedic past when the rulers had been lavish in their subservience to the priest-caste and had received in turn the reflection of orthodox approval. But kingship lacked also the glory of the still more remote days

[11] Cf. *supra*, p. 60, Editor's note, and *infra*, pp. 181ff.

of the half mythical pre-Āryan, Dravidian period, when the royal clans of the land had claimed descent from gods and were said to be of the "solar" dynasty or of the "lunar" dynasty.[12] Kingship in the new, dark, miserable, evil age of the so-called Kali Yuga, the last and worst of the four World Ages of the present cycle of time,[13] had assumed the vulgar traits of common despotism. Whatever once had been its spiritual dignity was gone. The power abided only with the strong, the cunning, the daring, and the reckless—those able to inspire greed and fear.

In post-feudal India the weakness of the ruling house derived from the fact that the king and his dynasty were not firmly rooted in the people, as are the kings of England or the mikados of Japan, or as the emperors of Austria formerly were. The principle of kingship in itself, as an institution, was never questioned. It was an unchallengeable constituent of the divine plan of creation, no less an integral portion of the revealed social order than were the moral and religious laws, the caste system, and the traditional sequence of the four stages of life.[14] The institution itself was in accordance with dharma, its function being to serve as the instrument of dharma. The king was to supervise mankind and see that all fulfilled their ordered duties and life-tasks according to the orthodox prescriptions for caste, age, and sex. But though the principle itself, thus, was unquestionable—

[12] As we know from the tombs of ancient Sumer and of Egypt, kings in the archaic civilizations of the fourth to second millenniums B.C. were regarded as incarnate gods. This was the period, in India, of the Dravidian civilization. The principle of divine kingship survived into later Indian history in the genealogies of the non-Āryan royal houses, where descent was traced from the Sun God and from the Moon God. Compare Japan, where the Mikado is regarded as descended from the Sun Goddess, Amaterasu; and compare *supra,* p. 104.

[13] For the Hindu theory of the ages of the world, see Zimmer, *Myths and Symbols in Indian Art and Civilization,* pp. 11-19.

[14] The four stages in the biography of the individual: 1. *brahmacārin,* 2. *gṛhastha,* 3. *vanaprastha,* 4. *sannyāsin.* Cf. *supra,* p. 44; *infra,* pp. 155-160.

unquestionable as a basic law of nature (the notion of a democratic, self-governing republic simply being outside the available assortment of ideas)—the actual individual or family enacting the royal part might be overthrown by a rival and there would be few to care. Some neighboring king of equal rank might invade the realm, or some adventurous upstart seize the throne, or perhaps the chancellor would grow weary of the crowned puppet he was leading by the strings and decide to take to himself the symbols of the power that he was already to a large extent actually wielding. No one would be profoundly concerned unless himself involved in the dynastic collapse. All that the population clung to was the institution. And so the individual king, like the kingly lion among the other beasts of prey in the jungle, had to look out for himself.

Like the military emperors of Rome in its period of decline, or the despots of Byzantium throughout their dramatic history, the Indian kings had to be constantly on the alert for attacks from both within and without, relying largely on their military strength, personal valor, and cunning. Their principal trust had to be in the efficiency and loyalty of the officers whom they elevated to commanding positions; for any form of government by the mandate of the people was unknown. People were only subjects, busy with their private struggles for life, divided into groups and kept apart from each other by their rules of caste, their numerous religious denominations, and the racial taboos of various origin (taboos against intermarriage and even contact; for to some degree, one way or another, the members of the differing castes were almost all mutually "untouchable"). There was no established, constitutional, representative body, either to check the executive power and guard through legislation against encroachments on the people's privileges by willful kings, or to support by general action those kings of whom the people approved. Theoretically, the Indian ruler was supposed to heed the advice of the Brāhmans and old people of the community; these were regarded as the voice of the traditional order. But there was no power that could stop him if he chose to disregard them. If he so wished, he could be a wasteful, ruthless, selfish bully, overtaxing and overburdening his tormented folk. And by the same token, he could expect no effective support from them, no matter how magnanimous he chose to be. His sole trust was his own mighty arm, his wit, his royal wealth, and his self-interested troops.

The mercenaries had to be lavishly paid to fight the king's wars, and would desert him as soon as his fortune failed. One lost battle in ancient Indian history generally meant a kingdom lost, a dynasty overthrown. Intrigue, conspiracy, distrust, treachery, were therefore the very atmosphere of the royal court. "Lucky those kings who at night enjoy a quiet, happy slumber." The more efficient and powerful the favored officers, the less were they to be trusted; for they were the ones who knew the king's weaknesses and resources; they were the holders of the keys. And so it was that high favor and sudden disgrace, intimacy and suspicion, were inextricably joined.

The able minister lived in an everlasting dilemma. He had on the one hand continually to demonstrate his efficiency, but on the other to secure his position against the very monarch he served. He had to be on the alert against calumny bred of envy and the slightest failure on his own part, but also (and this was always an acute danger) against rendering himself superfluous through doing all too well. For if he was too zealous in his work, eradicating without remainder the internal threats to the dominion of his tyrant—those "thorns" (*kaṇṭakas*), as they are called in the Hindu works on politics, the annoyances that prick the king and discompose his royal ease—then he well might find that, having made himself dispensable, he was disposed of.—This is the theme of the following instructive beast fable of the lion, the mouse, and the cat.[15]

[15] *Hitopadeśa* 2. 4.

A certain miserable tomcat, expelled by the villagers and roaming the fields on the brink of starvation, gaunt and helpless, was encountered and rescued from its predicament by a lion; the kingly beast invited the wretched one to share his cave and feed on the leavings of his majestic meals. But this was not an invitation inspired by altruism or any sense of racial loyalty, it was simply that the lion was being annoyed in his cave by a mouse that lived in a hole somewhere; when he took his naps, the mouse would come out and nibble at his mane. Mighty lions are unable to catch mice; nimble cats however can; here therefore was the basis for a sound and possibly agreeable friendship.

The mere presence of the cat in the cave sufficed to keep the mouse at bay, and so the lion took his naps in peace. Not even the squeaks of the little nuisance were heard, for the cat was continually on the alert. The lion rewarded him with lavish courses, and the efficient minister grew fat. But then one day the mouse made a sound, and the cat committed the elementary error of catching and eating it. The mouse vanished; the favor of the lion vanished too. Already tired of the tomcat's company, the king of beasts ungratefully turned his competent officer back into the fields and the jungle, where he had to face again the peril of starvation.

The lesson is summarized in the concluding maxim: "Do your job, but always let something remain to be done. Through this remainder you will remain indispensable."

Here is one of the many secrets of the secret police of every land—one of those witty "secrets that cannot be told." This ironic tale, addressed to the astute ministers and other loyal servants of the fickle Indian despots, reveals the circumstance of the dictator in the clutches of his own Gestapo. Though terribly efficient at tracking down the lurking enemies, the officers manage nevertheless to keep a goodly number always in reserve, and thus ensure both the security of their dictator and the continued importance of themselves. This is a perfectly natural thing for them to do, the world being what it is; and it has the interesting effect of keeping alive under the protection of the monarch whose "eyes and ears are everywhere" an insidious, self-supporting, cross-fertilizing process, by which a continuous mutual regeneration of antagonists, "asking for each other," is maintained. The secret police become the principal support and protection of the underground revolutionaries whom it is their function to suppress. Indeed, they are not only the protection of the opposition but even its cause; for the tyrannical system that has to rely for continuance on a crushing, omnipresent secret police inevitably breeds, through its brutal pressures, new enemies from within, every day. And these subversive elements, often highly idealistic, are in turn under the illusion that they are less visible than they really are. When the ruling power breaks, it sometimes happens that the revolutionaries find themselves justified in their hope that some day their cause should prevail—this much we know from history; but meanwhile, unconsciously, through their sheer budding into existence, they have been warranting the precious indispensability of the cat to the lion. Without mice, the officers of the Gestapo and Ogpu would be at a loss to keep themselves so terribly important. And so here again we find that the view of political intrigue represented in the Hindu philosophy of statecraft bears a remarkable pertinence to contemporary affairs.

The archaic teachings have a curiously modern ring. In Hindu foreign policy, for example, surprise by treacherous assault and sudden onslaught was regarded as one of the best means of successful foreign action, deep secrecy and perfect concealment forming the proper atmosphere for the ripening of schemes and the achievement of perfect preparations. In the political treatises we find the maxim: "Carry your enemy on your shoulder until you have got from him what you want, then throw him off—throw him off and shatter him, like an earthen jar against a rock."[16] Or again: "Whoever, pursuing his own advantage, intends to

[16] *Mahābhārata* 12. 140. 18.

crush somebody, should follow a cautious and deliberate procedure. When he lifts his hand, ready to strike his enemy, he should accost him in a friendly way. [That would be Mr. Nomura, in the conversational prelude to Pearl Harbor!] He should address him even more gently while delivering the deadly blow. [That would be Mr. Kurusu!] And when he has cut off his enemy's head, he should pity and bewail him." [17]

The documents of Indian history contain many examples of the successful practice of this maxim. There is the account, for instance, of a crown prince who proceeded from the capital in a solemn march with his army to welcome his aged father, who was returning crowned with victory following the defeat of a powerful neighbor whose possessions he had seized. An impromptu town with gorgeous tents was erected out on the plain to comfort the victor after the hardships of his campaign, and an elaborate triumphal edifice was set up, in which he was to celebrate his victory. But while the king was reposing under its massive beams, and while the dutiful son, surrounded by his own strongly armed bodyguard, was parading a large company of war-elephants before him, the stately structure collapsed, and the father, with all his attendants, was buried in the ruin.[18]

The lulling of an intended victim to sleep is recommended not only for inner policy (at the court of the despot, or in the conclaves of the groups or parties where the members wielding power are purging rivals) but also for foreign affairs (where it is a weapon second to none). It is known as *māyā,* "the creation of an illusion." We may study it best in the political history of the present day. Nazi policy, for example, in preparation for the overthrow of Poland, first inspired confidence by the non-aggression pact concluded with Marshal Pilsudski in 1933. With that, Poland was taken away from her natural ally, France, and became

[17] *Ib.* 12. 140. 54; cf. also 12. 102. 34; 12. 103. 9-13.

[18] ibn-Batuta, *Voyages,* translated (into French) by C. Defremery and B. R. Sanguinetti, Paris, 1853, Vol. III, pp. 212-213.

isolated. Next the Poles were flattered by being allowed to share the spoils of crippled Czechoslovakia, in the fall of 1938, following the Munich crisis. This was nothing but the still more friendly approach, preceding and screening the deadly blow—which fell like a thunderbolt within a year.

So too the modern techniques for dealing with enemies that have been overcome; these were already known to the ancient Hindu masters. The modern conquered territories left to famine, plague, and rapine—like Poland, the Ukraine, Greece, Norway, under the Nazi occupation—illustrate the general law. "A surviving remnant of the enemy," we read, "is like a remnant of smoldering fire or of unpaid debt; all three are bound to increase with time." [19] The defeated force is therefore to be liquidated: communists in Italy and Nazi Germany, the bourgeoisie in Russia. Inconvenient party chiefs and generals are purged everywhere; leftists and rightists crowd the prisons of the world. This is a merciless natural principle abundantly exemplified, whether in the history of India, the history of bygone Byzantium and the Russia of Boris Godunov and the false Dimitri, or in the comparatively up-to-date shooting of the last Czar with his wife, son, and four daughters, in a cellar, when they were supposed to be on their way to confinement.

Ancient Indian affairs were pervaded by an atmosphere of danger, suspicion, and threat. There was waged a kind of continuous white war of nerves. Precisely the same situation is described in the biographies of the Roman emperors by Tacitus and Suetonius, or in Gibbon's *Decline and Fall of the Roman Empire,* as well as in the Greek accounts of the Achaemenids of ancient Persia, the Moslem records of the caliphates at Bagdad, Cairo, and elsewhere, and the histories of Ottoman power in Constantinople. It is the atmosphere that is general today, particularly in the sphere controlled by the totalitarian states, as it was in that of their numerous forerunners and collaborators

[19] *Mahābhārata* 12. 140. 58.

from 1918 on: King Alexander's Yugoslavia, Voldemaras' Lithuania, Pilsudski's Poland, Kemal Ataturk's Turkey, and the Greece of the general-dictators. Everyone feels always endangered. Every king—utterly vulnerable though armed to the teeth —is watching constantly to forestall surprise. No one is fully master of any situation for any length of time. Sudden changes bring death or disgrace. Intrigues and murder from within, intrigues and aggression from without, threats of surprise, upset the strong. Direct, crushing blows annihilate the weak. Māyā, fratricide, poison, and the dagger constitute the order of the day.

5.

Political Geometry

BRITAIN's balance of power policy will serve to introduce another of the basic principles of the Indian *Arthaśāstra,* that of the *maṇḍala,* or political circles of neighbors. British statesmen have always and everywhere exhibited tact and skill in their manipulation of this weapon of the game. In order to maintain the balance of Europe, when Louis XIV threatened to disturb the political equilibrium by putting his grandson on the throne of Spain, Marlborough (whose life, by the way, supplies several fine examples of the subject of our last discussion) brought England into an alliance with the Netherlands, a number of the German states, Portugal, Denmark, and the house of Hapsburg, waging the War of the Spanish Succession (1701–14) against the threat of the rising empire of France. Shortly after, in the Seven Years' War (1756–63), when France had combined with Austria, Russia, Sweden, and Saxony against the Prussia of Frederick the Great, the British threw their weight on the side of Prussia, and came off so well in the gamble that they shattered the French world-empire and fixed the foundations of their own by winning control of both Canada and India. Then once again Britain joined forces against France when Napoleon's campaigns were the threat, assisting Portugal and Spain in the Peninsular War (1804–14), as well as Russia, Austria, Prussia, and the Netherlands at Waterloo. But the Crimean War (1854–56) saw England united with France (for the first time in some two hundred years), together with Turkey and Savoy, to counterbalance Russia, which now was pressing dangerously to the Dardanelles. Britain supported Japan to weaken Russia in 1903–04, but in the first World War was at the side of Russia—as well as of France again—against the combination of Germany and Austria.

This remarkable game of weights and counterweights is one that was taken very seriously by the ancient kings and princes of India. There the battlefield of the contending powers was the vast landscape of a subcontinent about the size of Europe but much less broken by difficult mountain ranges. Though interspersed with treacherous jungles and deserts, India's various parts were linked by broad rivers and far-stretching plains; almost every kingdom was surrounded by enemy neighbors and open to attack from every side. There prevailed, consequently, a situation of perpetual distrust, such as we know, for example, on the much smaller stage of the Balkans.

The principal Hindu formula for the arrangement of foreign alliances and coalitions is based on a pattern of concentric rings of natural enemies and allies. Each king is to regard his own realm as located at the center of a kind of target, surrounded by "rings" (*maṇḍalas*) which represent, alternately, his natural enemies and his natural allies. The enemies are represented by the first surrounding ring; these are his immediate neighbors, all alert to pounce. The second ring then is that of his natural friends, i.e., the kings just to the rear of his neighbors, who threaten them in turn through the very fact of being neighbors. Then beyond is a ring of remoter danger, interesting primarily as supplying reinforcement to the enemies directly at hand. Fur-

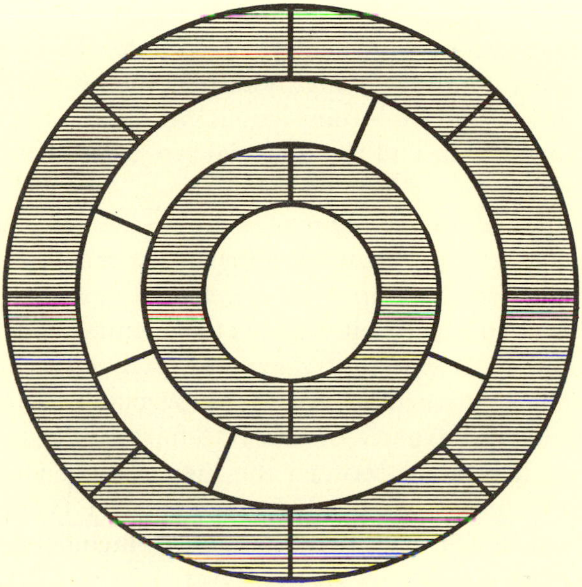

thermore, within each ring are subdivisions signifying mutual natural animosities; for since each kingdom has its own maṇḍala, an exceedingly complicated set of stresses and cross-stresses must be understood to exist. Such a plan of mutual encirclement is to be cast, carefully weighed, and then used as a basis for action. It delineates and brings into manifestation a certain balance and tension of natural powers, as well as touching off periodic, terrific outbursts of widely spreading conflict. Taken for granted as a universal social principle is the propensity of neighbors to be unfriendly, jealous, and aggressive, each biding his hour of surprise and treacherous assault.[20]

This somewhat formal pattern may look to us a bit theoretical and over-sophisticated, yet it well reflects the geographical conditions of the Indian subcontinent. Also it is amply warranted by the modern history of Europe. It is the basic figure of a kind of political geometry that can be applied with few adjustments

[20] The science of the *maṇḍala* ("the circle of states") is discussed in *Kauṭilīya Arthaśāstra* 7.

to the practical reckoning of the stresses in almost any historical scene—a really wonderful achievement of that Hindu genius which so loves to indulge in highly abstract intellectual exercises, yet at the same time has a conspicuous gift for intuitive insight, symbolic expression, and the pictorial language of the parable and the myth.

When applied to the map of Europe the ancient Indian maṇḍala supplies a perfect pattern for the issues and vicissitudes, understandings and seeming misunderstandings, that have underlain our almost incessant wars. At the opening of the modern period, in the sixteenth century, France found herself threatened with encirclement when Spain and the German Empire became united under the dynasty of the Hapsburgs. The subsequent struggle for hegemony between the French kings and the emperors in Vienna—from the time of Francis I (1515–47) and Charles V (1519–56)—continued until the dismemberment of the Austro-Hungarian Empire in the Treaty of Versailles in 1919. Louis XIV (1643–1715)—that "most Christian king," who persecuted the Calvinist Huguenots and expelled them from his realm —secured the support of the Mohammedan Turks in the rear of the Hapsburg dominions in eastern Europe, and these then invaded the enemy territories from what is now Yugoslavia, and through Hungary, while the armies of France fought the German Imperial forces in Flanders and along the Rhine.

The neighbor to the rear, or at the flank, of one's own neighbor and rival is the born ally: that is the supreme principle. Moral and religious considerations, matters of ideology, and common spiritual tradition do not have the force of this simple geometrical fact. The Christian king did not hesitate to betray and endanger the Christian civilization of Europe by inspiring and supporting an invasion by the very power that had been the primary common foe of Christendom for the past thousand years. In precisely the same way, Nazi Germany today betrays the common cause of Europe, i.e., the White Man's colonial empire and civilization, by its co-operation with Japan's attempt to conquer the Far East and the Pacific. And both of these betrayals of the Christian, Western cause for selfish ends have a remarkable precedent and model in an arrangement concluded with the Grand Turk by a pope. Anxious to preserve the political independence of the territory of the Holy See, Alexander VI, supreme shepherd of the Christian flock, vicar of Christ on earth, and the very tongue of the Holy Ghost, joined hands, in 1494, with the sultan Bayazid II, to defeat the imperial ambitions of Charles VIII of France. Half a century later, Suleiman the Magnificent became allied with the French king, Francis I, against the Holy Roman Emperor, Charles V; and the subsequent Moslem advance into eastern Europe (a forerunner of the one in the time of Louis XIV) even enjoyed the tacit approval of Pope Paul III.

In the French maṇḍala of alliances, when the power of Turkey began to decline, that of rising Russia took its place, as the natural ally at the back of the immediate neighbor to the east. Napoleon in 1805 and 1810 accordingly made friends with the emperor of Russia, in order to check Prussia and Austria (the Russian armies having previously fought for years side by side with the Austrians, in Switzerland and along the Riviera, in their common campaign against the French Revolution and Republic). Napoleon also resurrected Poland, as a second ally for himself at the back of Germany, by restoring those portions that had fallen to the share of Austria and Prussia in the partitions of Poland between those powers and Russia at the close of the eighteenth century. And following the same absolutely dependable logic of the maṇḍala, France again won the cooperation of Russia in her policy of encirclement just before the first World War—a classic pincer movement on the chessboard of the powers that would compel her immediate neighbor to fight a war on two fronts. France at the same time supported Serbia against Austria, as the ally at Austria's rear,[21] and then Romania,

[21] Russia, too, supported Serbia against Austria—another pincer movement.

as a dagger in the back at the crucial hour when Germany had failed in the Battle of Verdun and was suffering defeat along the Somme sector of the Western Front. With the Treaty of Versailles a comprehensive maṇḍala policy was inaugurated by France to hold the crushed enemy in check. A ring of Slavic powers, from Poland and Czechoslovakia to Romania and Yugoslavia, was brought into being, threatening the rear of Germany and what was left of Austria. The new allies were provided with loans for armament and development. To which the reply of Germany was the Rapallo Treaty, in 1922, with Russia—a natural ally now, to the rear of Poland and Czechoslovakia.

Following the rise of the Nazis to power, there came a quick series of clever moves on the maṇḍala chessboard, which ended in a total breakdown of the subtle structure that had been designed to guarantee France's hegemony on the continent. The moment Poland agreed to sign the ten-year non-aggression pact, in 1933, the ring was virtually undone. Step by step, then, the Eastern allies of France became estranged, and at last even Belgium withdrew from the plan for immediate and automatic cooperation with France against Germany. And so all was ripe for the new break for power.

The next arrangement of the maṇḍala will make itself apparent in due time.

6.

The Seven Ways to Approach a Neighbor

Nīti, the Sanskrit term for policy, means, literally, "proper conduct." The policy of the king sets the outstanding model in the community for successful conduct amidst the perils of the world. Though he is supreme in the realm, he is nevertheless the most in danger, in his lofty, enviable, and precarious state of splendor. Neighboring kings, his own ambitious ministers and all too successful generals, even the members of his own family —aspiring sons and princes, scheming queens—are on the alert for his throne. And last but not least, the people, often harassed and overtaxed, may at any time be secretly stirred to revolt by some enemy king or some personage of lower lineage ambitious to usurp. In such an atmosphere of threat, dread, and sudden moves, the *matsya-nyāya* prevails, "the law of the fish":[22] the law of life unmitigated by moral decency, as it prevails in the merciless deep.

This is a law no less well known to the West than to India. It is phrased in the popular proverb of old standing, "The big ones eat the little ones," which Pieter Breughel, the sixteenth-century Flemish artist, vividly illustrated in a number of his lively and humorous masterpieces. One sees in these works a multitude of fish of every sort and size, the little swallowed by the big and these caught in turn by fishermen. The bellies of the larger, ripped open by the men, pour out the smaller, and there is an inscription underneath this that gives the proverb. Breughel painted these canvases in a period when the whole of Europe was being made a sea of turmoil by the struggle of Hapsburg, Flanders, world-ruling Spain, and the German Empire to restrain the rising power of France, which was trying to break free from the encirclement of that colossal coalition. It was an age when new weapons (gunpowder and cannon) as well as a new style of warfare (the deploying of large companies of mercenary infantry instead of the combat of knights on horseback) were spreading havoc and terror—just as the new weapons of modern technology are doing today. Breughel's pictorial proverbs display the life of the watery realm of cold-blooded voraciousness as an apt expression of the idea that in the sphere of politics each is out for

[22] *Arthaśāstra* 1. 4. 9; cf. also *Mahābhārata* 12. 67. 16-17, and 12. 89. 21.

himself and feeding greedily on as many of the others as he can. The idea is that politics is, and forever must be, an enterprise of battle, not a decent, orderly courtroom affair, wherein each nation, group, or race is reasonably assigned its due share of the world, according to its size, its contributions to civilization, and its abilities.

In conformity to this same pessimistic way of understanding the problem of life's war for survival, the means and devices proposed in the Indian books of politics are without conscience or regard for mercy. The four chief "means" (*upāya*)[23] of approach to an enemy, for example, are the following:

1. *Sāman,* "conciliation or negotiation." This is the way of appeasement, soothing, or charming.

The snake-charmer appeases the serpent by playing a melody on a pipe; this soothes the dangerous animal. Similarly, the so-called "wrathful" or "terrible" aspect of a divinity (who is always ambivalent and may be dangerous) is charmed, soothed, appeased, or propitiated by the magic melodies on the wings of which the holy incantations of magic stanzas mount to his invisible abode. Our English "charm" is from the Latin *carmen,* "magic song to win the grace of a superhuman being." And in the same spirit, the Sanskrit *sāman* literally means "melody." *Sāman* denotes a special branch of priestly learning in the Vedic tradition of rituals, which treats of the melodies to which the various stanzas (*ṛc*) of the *Ṛg-veda* must be sung. This is a lore loaded with magic, certain parts of it being so dangerous that they may not be imparted inside the village boundary; the master and pupil withdraw to some remote and lonely spot in the wilderness. By singing magic charms of this kind while holding in his hands some of the remainders of the Cosmic Egg after it had opened at the beginning of the world (the upper half of the egg having ascended to become the heavens, while the lower descended and became the earth), Brahmā, the creator, conjured

[23] *Upāya,* from the verb *upa-i,* "to approach."

forth eight celestial elephants, which then were assigned to the four quarters of the world and the four points between, to stand as supports for the upper firmament. Elephants are called, therefore, *sāmodbhava,* "produced by *sāman.*"

We use *sāman* every day in meeting people—when we say, "Hello!" "How do you do!" "So nice to meet you!" and then: "Good-bye!" "Do come see us soon!" *Sāman* in this social context the Sanskrit dictionary renders: "gentle words, mildness, gentleness." *Sāman* applied to politics is translated: "conciliatory or mild means, conciliatory conduct." This would refer in modern practice to such devices as non-aggression pacts, the preliminary talks about them, the definition of respective spheres of influence and exploitation, and the pooling of resources.

2. The opposite pattern of approach is called *daṇḍa,* the rod of punishment—in the hand of the judge, or of a doorman chasing beggars and street-boys. *Daṇḍa* means "chastisement, punishment, attack, assault, violence; a cudgel, stick, staff; an army; control, subjection, restraint." "The king should always keep the rod of punishment (*daṇḍa*) uplifted in his hand," declares the *Mahābhārata.*[24] And we read in the book of Manu: "For the increasing of a kingdom, *sāman* and *daṇḍa* are the two chief means." [25] Briefly: *Daṇḍa* is aggression of whatever kind, whether outright and shameless, or hypocritically justified as punishment for insult or for a threatening attitude. It is an unbearable insult, for example, if an intended victim proceeds to armament, or strikes an alliance with some stronger neighbor.

3. *Dāna* (Latin *donum,* English "donation"), "giving, present, gift," is the third recommended approach. In politics this is simply "bribery." *Dāna* includes arrangements for the division of

[24] *Mahābhārata* 12. 120. 93 and again, 12. 140. 7. "A king should display severity in making all his subjects observe their respective duties. If this is not done, they will prowl like wolves, devouring one another" (*Ib.* 12. 142. 28.). Cf. also the political play *Mudrārākṣasa* 1. 15.

[25] *Mānava Dharmaśāstra* 7. 109.

the spoils of war, as well as presents, decorations, etc., for the neighbor's generals, ministers, and secret agents.

4. *Bheda,* "splitting, dividing, breach, rupture, disturbance, sowing dissension in an enemy's party, treachery, treason." This is the technique of divide and conquer, of boring from within.

These are the four chief means, to which are added:

5. *Māyā,* "deceit, trick, the display of an illusion."

The god Indra displayed his māyā when he assumed the form of an inoffensive Brāhman and appeared among the anti-gods or titans. These enemies of the gods had built a fire-altar in the form of a pyramid by which they were mounting to heaven to seize command of the universe. The harmless Brāhman removed a few bricks from the lowest level of the towering structure, and all the demons were dropped back to the ground.[26] Another Vedic myth tells how the same god, when pursued by a company of the titans who had just defeated his forces in battle, suddenly assumed the shape of a horsehair and thus disappeared from view.

Māyā means "deceit, fraud, any act of trickery or magic, a diplomatic feat." Mr. Kurusu's diplomatic mission to Washington, apparently for appeasement, while the Japanese bombers were on their way to Pearl Harbor, was not an utterly unfair, unprecedented play, according to the completely unmoral code of Indian and Far Eastern policy, but a classic stratagem. The fishes always attack and swallow each other without warning.

Māyā, in diplomacy, would also include the wearing of the mask of moral probity, religious righteousness, and civilized indignation, which has proven itself a powerful weapon in the recent history of the West, where the war leaders have had to draw support from populations bred to philosophies rather of moral duty than of unashamed attack.

6. *Upekṣā,* a second minor device or means, is that of "over-

[26] *Śatapatha Brāhmaṇa* 2. 1. 2. 13-16 (Sacred Books of the East, Vol. XII, pp. 286-287).

looking, taking no notice, taking no account of, neglecting, ignoring." England's attitude when Japan seized Manchuria, Mussolini Ethiopia, and Hitler Austria was that of *upekṣā:* pretending to be unconcerned because one cannot make up one's mind to become involved in the affair.

7. *Indrajāla,* "the net (*jāla*) of Indra," means "conjuring, jugglery, magic trick; stratagem or trick in war." This denotes the creation of an appearance of things that do not exist; for example, the building of a line of fortifications made only of dummies, or the simulation of an attack, say, on the British Isles, while actually an invasion of Russia is being prepared. *Indrajāla* involves the spreading of false information and creation of false belief, and might be said to be a special form of application of the principle of *māyā* to the techniques of war.

These, then, are the seven ways to approach a neighbor in this unsentimental ocean of the fish. I wonder whether we have textbooks of politics in the West that cover the subject with more simplicity and clarity.

We may conclude this introduction to the ancient Indian handbooks of success by glancing at a few typical maxims. The following are taken from the *Mahābhārata,* Book XII.

"Both kinds of wisdom, straight and crooked, should be within call of the king." [27]

[27] *Mahābhārata* 12. 100. 5.

Throughout most of the *Mahābhārata* the teaching is of the "straight" wisdom. Only when hard pressed by the unrelenting questions of the noble Yudhiṣṭhira was the great guru of warriors, Bhīṣma, brought to reveal the dark secrets of the "crooked" way.

"Yudhiṣṭhira said: 'What course of conduct should be adopted by a king shorn of friends, having many enemies, possessed of an exhausted treasury, and destitute of troops, when he is surrounded by wicked ministers, when his counsels are all divulged, and when he does not see his way clearly before him . . .?'

"Bhīṣma said: 'Conversant as thou art with duties, thou hast, O bull of Bharata's race, asked me a question that touches on a mystery. Without

"The last word of social wisdom is, never trust."[28]

"As clouds change form from moment to moment, just so thine enemy of today becomes, even today, thy friend."[29]

"Whoever desires success in this world must be prepared to make deep bows, swear love and friendship, speak humbly, and pretend to shed and wipe away tears."[30]

"Do not fear the results of karma, rely on your strength. No one has ever seen in this world what the fruits are of a good or of an evil deed. Let us then aspire to be strong; because all things belong to the man who is strong."[31]

"Might is above right; right proceeds from might; right has its support in might, as living beings in the soil. As smoke the wind, so right must follow might. Right in itself is devoid of command; it leans on might as the creeper on the tree.

"Right is in the hands of the strong; nothing is impossible to the strong. Everything is pure that comes from the strong."[32]

"Be a heron in calculating thine own advantage, a lion when thou dost attack, a wolf when thou dost prey, a hare when thou takest flight."[33]

"When thou findest thyself in a low state, try to lift thyself up, resorting to pious as well as to cruel actions. Before practicing morality, wait until thou art strong."[34]

---

being questioned, O Yudhiṣṭhira, I could not venture to discourse upon this duty. Morality is very subtle. . . . Listen therefore, O Bhārata, to the means that kings may employ during seasons of distress. From the standpoint of true morality, however, I would not call these means righteous" (*ib.* 12. 130. 1-8).

[28] *Ib.* 12. 80. 12.

[29] *Ib.* 12, 138. 154.

[30] *Ib.* 12. 140. 17.

[31] *Ib.* 12. 134. 2-3.

[32] *Ib.* 12. 134. 5-7.

[33] *Ib.* 12. 140. 25.

[34] *Ib.* 12. 140. 38; cf. also 12. 141. 62.

"If thou art not prepared to be cruel and to kill men as the fisher kills the fish, abandon every hope of great success." [35]

"If men think thee soft, they will despise thee. When it is, therefore, time to be cruel, be cruel; and when it is time to be soft, be soft." [36]

A few selections from Kauṭilya's *Arthaśāstra* will suffice to communicate a sense of the atmosphere within the palace.[37]

"He [the king] should construct his residential palace after the model of his treasure house; or he may have his residential abode in the center of a delusive chamber (*mohanagṛha*), provided with secret passages built into the walls; or in an underground chamber concealed by the figures of goddesses and altars (*caitya*) carved on the wooden door-frame and connected with many underground passages for exit; or in an upper storey, provided with a staircase hidden in a wall, with a passage for exit made in a hollow pillar—the whole building being so constructed with mechanical contrivances that it may be caused to fall down when necessary." [38]

"When in the interior of the harem, the king shall see the queen only when her personal integrity is guaranteed by an old maid-servant. He shall not touch any woman (unless he is assured of her personal integrity); for, hidden in the queen's chamber, his own brother slew king Bhadrasena; hiding beneath the bed of his mother, the son killed king Kārūśa; mixing fried rice with poison, as though with honey, his own queen poisoned Kāśirāja; by means of an anklet painted with poison, his own queen killed Vairantya; with a gem of her zone, bedaubed with poison, his own queen killed Sauvīra; with a look-

[35] *Ib.* 12. 15. 14; again, 12. 140. 50.

[36] *Ib.* 12. 56. 21; again, 12. 102. 33; 12. 103. 33; 12. 140. 65; 12. 142. 32; and *passim.*

[37] *Chānakya Kauṭilya's Arthaśāstra,* translated by R. Shamasastry, with an introduction by D. J. F. Fleet, Bangalore, 1915, 2nd edition, 1923.

[38] *Ib.* 1. 20. 40; transl., p. 45.

ing-glass painted with poison, his own queen killed Jālūtha; and with a weapon hidden under the knot of her hair, his own queen slew Vidūratha. Hence the king should always be watchful for such lurking dangers. He should keep his wives away from ascetics with shaven head or braided hair, as well as from buffoons and prostitutes. Nor shall women of high birth have occasion to see his wives, unless they be appointed midwives." [39]

"Every person in the harem shall live in the place assigned to him, and shall never move to a place assigned to others. No one in the harem shall at any time keep company with an outsider. The passage of commodities of any kind from or into the harem shall be controlled, and only objects marked with a seal (*mudrā*) after careful inspection shall be allowed to reach their destination." [40]

"The king shall partake of fresh dishes only after making an oblation out of them, first to the fire and then to the birds. Fire, birds, the food, and the servants will betray the presence of poison by various reactions, symptoms, and manners of behavior." [41]

"All undertakings depend upon finance. Hence foremost at-

[39] *Ib.* 1. 20. 41; transl., p. 46.

[40] *Ib.* 1. 20. 42; transl., p. 47.

[41] *Ib.* 1. 21. 43; transl., p. 48.

Robert Graves, in *I, Claudius* (a novel of the life of the emperor Claudius, based on Suetonius and Tacitus), tells how Augustus, fearing lest he should be poisoned by Livia, took only figs that he plucked himself. But Livia then had the figs on the trees of the imperial villa-garden coated with poison, and thus the aged Augustus met his death. Claudius was served a plate of mushrooms, his favorite dish, by his wife, Agrippina the younger. The largest mushroom, on the top of the portion, was poisoned. The queen lovingly put the poisoned mushroom on his plate herself, while taking some of the smaller ones from the same dish to keep him confident. We remember, also, that the cupbearers of medieval monarchs had to guarantee the drink they served their sovereign by first pouring a small quantity into the shallow lid of the cup and emptying it before the monarch's eyes with a drink to his health.

tention shall be paid to the treasury. . . . There are about forty ways of embezzlement. [These are described in detail.] Just as it is impossible not to taste honey or poison when it is on the tip of the tongue, so is it impossible for a government servant not to eat up at least a bit of the king's revenue. Just as fish moving under water cannot possibly be detected either as drinking or as not drinking water, so government servants employed in their government work cannot be found out while taking money.

"It is possible to mark the movements of birds flying high in the sky, but it is not equally possible to ascertain the movement of government servants of hidden purpose." [42]

7.

The Universal King

THE BLANK pessimism of the Indian philosophy of politics, untouched as it is by any hope or ideal of progress and improvement, harmonizes with the Indian view of time (*kāla*), as also with the early and medieval Christian notions of the corrupt character of the "world." Indian ethics (*dharma*) recognize that the rule of the fish must be outlawed as far as possible within human society; indeed, within each unit of society it is absolutely outlawed—that is to say, within the province of each king.[43] Ideally, the science of government, as reviewed in the

[42] *Arthaśāstra* 2. 8. 65, 66, 69; transl., pp. 73, 75, 79-80.

[43] "The king should always bear himself toward his subjects as a mother toward the child of her womb. As the mother, disregarding those objects that are most cherished by her, seeks the good of her child alone, even so should kings conduct themselves" (*Mahābhārata* 12. 56. 44-45).

Arthaśāstra, stands for the daṇḍa of dharma. The king is the chief policeman of dharma within the realm that he controls, being the maintainer and staff (*daṇḍa*) of the revealed ritualistic order of civil life. Mutual good will, forbearance, and co-operation among the individuals, groups, trades, and castes are demanded within each state, just as within the fold of a family; but there is no hope, according to the Indian conception, that this peaceful pattern of well-controlled, harmonious human decency should ever become transferred to the larger field of the nations. Between these fiercely antagonistic super-individuals, since they are unamenable to the control of any higher power, the primeval law of nature remains in operation, uncontrolled.

And yet there is an ancient mythical ideal—an idyllic compensatory dream, born of the longing for stability and peace—which represents a universal, world-wide empire of enduring tranquillity under a just and virtuous world-monarch, the *cakravartin,* "owner of the *cakravarta,*" who should put an end to the perpetual struggle of the contending states. *Cakra* is "wheel," a noun related etymologically to the Greek κύκλος, Latin *circus* and *circulus,* and Anglo-Saxon *hwēol. Cakravarta* refers to the circumference of the mighty mountain-range that surrounds the world, out beyond the enveloping world-ocean, like a rim. The Cakravartin conducts his army to the farthest horizon. His war-elephants quench their thirst and bathe in the deep seas at the four quarters. The kings of the rival realms throughout the concentric circles of his maṇḍala bow in acknowledgment of his unchallengeable supremacy, the diamonds of their jeweled tiaras and diadems being reflected in the mirrorlike nails of his toes as they pay obeisance at the platform of the raised throne of his supreme command. For by virtue of his moral supremacy the passage of his army is irresistible. The Cakravartin is the great man, the superman (*mahāpuruṣa*), among kings; and he is preceded on his march by a luminous apparition in the firmament in the form of a wheel (*cakra*)—a duplication of the neolithic symbol of the sun-wheel. The day when this first appeared to him, coming before his pure vision in the concentration of his morning prayer and meditation, it stood as the sign that he was to undertake the campaign of unifying the whole earthly realm. He arose and followed the symbol, which now moves before him as he marches. In this way he makes it "turn and revolve" on his path. Hence he is called the *cakra-vartin*—the root *vṛt* meaning "to turn, to revolve." *Cakram vartayati:* "he sets the sacred wheel (of the world-pacifying monarchy) in motion."

This conception of the *mahāpuruṣa cakravartin,* "the superman turning the wheel," goes back not only to the earliest Vedic, but also to the pre-Vedic, pre-Āryan traditions of India, being reflected in various Buddhist and Jaina writings as well as in the Hindu Purāṇas.[44] According to the Buddhist conception, the Universal Monarch is the secular counterpart of the

[44] *Editor's note:* As stated *supra,* p. 60, note, Dr. Zimmer regarded Jainism, Sāṅkhya, Yoga, and Buddhism (which are heterodox teachings, i.e., teachings rejecting the authority of the Vedas) as representing a non-Vedic, non-Āryan stream of tradition, coming down (with modifications) from pre-Āryan, Dravidian times.

The best description of the Cakravartin appears in the Buddhist Pāli canon of Ceylon, in "The Longer Sermons or Dialogues" (*Dīgha-nikāya*), translated by T. W. and C. A. F. Rhys Davids, *Dialogues of the Buddha,* Vols. II, III (Sacred Books of the Buddhists, Vols. III, IV), London, 1910 and 1921; see especially no. 17, *Mahā-sudassana-sutta* and no. 26, *Cakkavatti-sīhanāda-sutta.* The *Mahā-sudassana-sutta* treats of Sudassana, a legendary Cakravartin to whom the Buddha repeatedly refers in the course of these dialogues (see also, for example, the *Mahā-parinibbāna-suttanta,* "The Great Text of the Final Extinction," *ib.* 16. 5, 15). The *Cakkavatti-sīhanāda-sutta* ("The Lion's Roar of the World Emperor") describes the career of the legendary Cakravartin Dṛdha-nemi (Pāli: *Dalha-nemi*), "He, the felly of whose wheel (*nemi*) is firm (*dṛdha, dalha*), i.e., indestructible." The attributes of a Cakravartin are described in *Dīgha-nikāya* III, *Ambatthasuttanta* 1. 5.

Buddha, the "Enlightened One," who himself is said to have "set in motion the wheel of the sacred doctrine." Like the Cakravartin, the Buddha is the master, not of a national or otherwise limited communion, but of the world. His wheel, the Buddhist dharma, is not reserved for the privileged castes, like the dharma of the Brāhmans, but is for the whole universe; a doctrine of release intended to bring peace to all living beings without exception. The Buddha and the Cakravartin, that is to say, manifest the same universal principle, one on the spiritual, the other on the secular plane; and both bear on their bodies, already at birth, certain characteristic auspicious signs in token of their mission: the thirty-two great marks (*mahāvyañjana*), and the numerous additional secondary marks (*anuvyañjana*). These having been examined by the soothsayers and astrologer-physiognomists shortly following the hour of the nativity, it is announced what destiny awaits the miraculous babe.[45]

The seven great symbols that come to the Cakravartin when the moment arrives for him to fulfill his mission are the following:

1. The Sacred Wheel (*cakra*), denoting universality. The Cakravartin himself is the hub of the universe; toward him all things tend, like the spokes of a wheel. He is the Polar Star about which everything revolves with the order and harmony of the hosts of the celestial lights.

2. The Divine White Elephant (*hastiratna,* "elephant-treasure"). Swift as thought, this divine animal carries the monarch on his world-inspection tours across the firmament. The white elephant was the ancient sacred mount of the pre-Āryan kings.

3. The Milk-white Horse, the valorous sun-steed (*aśvaratna,* "horse-treasure"). The horse was the mount and chariot animal

[45] Those Mahāpuruṣas who at birth are close enough to final enlightenment to become Buddhas have the choice of becoming either Cakravartins or Buddhas, the latter alternative requiring the rejection of secular power and enjoyment for the flinty path of austerity and absolute renunciation.

of the Āryan invaders. This milk-white animal performs the same service for the Cakravartin as the Divine White Elephant.

4. The Magic Jewel (*cintāmaṇi,* "thought-jewel"), i.e., the wishing-stone that turns night into day and fulfills every desire the moment the wish is uttered.

5. The Perfect Queen-Consort (*strīratna,* "treasure of a wife"): the ideal woman, faultless in beauty, as in virtue. Her body has a cooling touch during the hot season and a warming touch during the cold.

6. The Perfect Minister of Finance (*gehapati, gṛhapati,* "householder"). Because of his able and blameless administration, he is never short of funds for the purposes of lavish generosity; charity is dispensed throughout the universe, to alleviate the sufferings of widows, orphans, the aged, and the sick.

7. The Perfect General-in-Chief (*pariṇāyaka,* "the leader").

These seven symbols are shown on Buddhist altars, together with a few additional emblems, to represent the spiritual emperorship of the Enlightened One. A pair of fish also appear frequently—not standing for the *matsya-nyāya,* this time, but for life-abundance. For the fish typifies the breeding force of the sea, the fecundity of the waters out of which come organisms without number, procreative and self-engendering. The fish provides sustenance for all; hence it is used symbolically with the same meaning as the cornucopia, the vessel filled with lotus flowers, and the bowl full of jewels or of gold.

A Buddhist representation of the secular Cakravartin with the seven symbols has been preserved on a stone slab that once formed part of a relic mound (*stūpa*) [46] at Jaggayapeṭa, just east of Hyderabad and not far from the celebrated stūpa of Amarāvatī. The building itself has disappeared; possibly parts of it were incorporated in the later structure of Amarāvatī. The date

[46] The relic mound, or stūpa, is perhaps the most characteristic and striking type of Buddhist edifice. For a discussion, cf. Zimmer, *Myths and Symbols in Indian Art and Civilization,* pp. 199-201.

is certainly not later than the first century A.D., and with reasonable assurance may be assigned even to the second or third century B.C. The style betrays no trace of the Hellenistic influence of Gandhāra, nor any Bactrian or Kuṣāna characteristics. It is definitely Hindu, pre-Mathurā, and more archaic than the lively work of nearby Amarāvatī.[47] This is the earliest rep-

[47] *Editor's note:* Indo-Āryan art (as distinct from the pre-Āryan, Dravidian remains of the Indus Valley civilization; cf. *supra,* p. 60, Editor's note) is almost undocumented before the third century B.C., when it appears suddenly in an abundance of forms, some crude, some refined. Conspicuous among the remains are a number of Greek coins bearing portraits of the Alexandrian emperors of Bactria, as well as the works of a post-Alexandrian school of craftsmen in the Punjab and Afghanistan (Gandhāra) who produced Buddhist statuary in a Hellenistic style. Occidental historians have been zealous to detect the influence of these Greek colonial forms throughout the Orient, and some have gone so far as to assert that all Oriental art whatsoever stems from the influence of the Greek genius. Ananda K. Coomaraswamy, however, has pointed out *(History of Indian and Indonesian Art,* New York, Leipzig, London, 1927, pp. 50ff.) that the art of Gandhāra cannot be dated as early as its first champions supposed, it being impossible to establish any of its sculpture earlier than the first century A.D., and that though its sentimental style is Hellenistic, its iconography and themes are Indian, copying motifs already represented in works of the Maurya period some three to four centuries earlier. Moreover, the vigorous Buddhist and Jaina sculpture that was being produced in the same century in Mathurā (modern Muttra, on the Jumna, between Delhi and Agra) "cannot be derived from any known class of images in Gandhāra" *(ib.,* p. 57, quoting J. Ph. Vogel, "The Mathurā School of Sculpture," *Archaeological Survey of India, Annual Reports,* 1909–10, p. 66).

One of the most curious facts about Gandhāra is that its Hellenistic art did not come to flower while the Greeks were governing that region. As we shall see (*infra,* pp. 505-506), the Greeks were expelled, c. 75 B.C., by a group of invading Scythians, or Śakas, and these in turn, c. 50 A.D., by a tribe of Mongolian nomads known as the Yueh-chi, or Kuṣāṇas. The earliest possible dating of any known Gandhāran work is in the Śaka period, while the culmination of the style took place under the protection of the Kuṣāna emperor Kaniṣka (c. 78–123 A.D.). Under this emperor the vigorous native Indian school of Mathurā flourished also.

Contemporaneous with these developments in the north was the growth

resentation extant of the native Indian ideal and vision of the universal king (*Plate II*).

In "The Great Text on the Final Extinction of the Buddha," [48] the teacher, at the moment of his departure from the world, was questioned by his cousin and favorite pupil, Ānanda. What ceremonies, Ānanda wished to know, were to be performed after his demise? The Enlightened One replied that the disciples should not trouble themselves about it, because there were enough believers in the highest classes of society to honor the remains of the Tathāgata.[49] "They will not fail to honor the remains of the Tathāgata," he said, "in the same way one honors the remains of a Cakravartin"; that is to say, in the noblest manner possible. And then he described to Ānanda the ceremonies traditionally performed after the death of a Cakravartin. The Buddha added that there were four kinds of men worthy of a stūpa: 1. a Tathāgata like himself, who had turned the wheel of the law and taught the universal doctrine, 2. a Pratyeka Buddha, i.e., one who, having found Enlightenment, had not returned to the world to teach, 3. the pupil of a Tathāgata, and 4. a secular Cakravartin. This list does not belong to the earliest

---

of a more gentle and graceful style in the Deccan, in the coastal region governed by the native Āndhra dynasty, between the Godavari and the Kistna. The destroyed stūpa at Jaggayapeṭa (which belongs to this movement) seems to have been built during or before the first century A.D., since the much more sophisticated and exquisite work of nearby Amarāvatī—"the most voluptuous and the most delicate flower of Indian sculpture," it is called by Coomaraswamy (*ib.*, p. 71)—certainly belongs to the second. Dr. Zimmer's example of the Cakravartin comes, therefore, from one of the earliest known monuments of native Indian art.

[48] *Dīgha-nikāya* XVI, *Mahā-parinibbāna-suttanta* 5. 10-12; H. Kern, *Manual of Indian Buddhism* (Grundriss der Indo-Arischen Philologie, Band III, Heft 8), Strassburg, 1896, pp. 43-44; also Davids, *Dialogues of the Buddha,* Vol. III, pp. 154-156.

[49] "Who has come (*āgata*) in truth (*tathā*)." *Tathā,* "such-ness"; the indescribable way or state that can be expressed only by *tathā,* which means simply "thus, such manner," or "yes." The Tathāgata is the Buddha.

stratification of the Buddhist tradition but is a reflection of the fact, apparently, that there were stūpas in existence to the memories of Mahāpuruṣas of these four kinds.

As we have said, the ideal of the Universal Monarch goes back to pre-Āryan times in India (third and fourth millenniums B.C.). But traits have been added from a second, equivalent ideal, associated rather with the horse than with the native Indian elephant, which must have been developed by the Āryan semi-nomads before they moved into India proper from Afghanistan through the Khyber Pass. At that distant period the steppe-domains of the various chieftains were somewhat flexible as to boundaries; power and the possession of lands being understood in terms of claims to certain grazing areas. The ranging herds of cattle and horses were accompanied by armed riders, Āryan cowboys, who went as defenders of their chieftains' claims to both the animals and the grounds on which they grazed. When a king, in those remote times, wished to announce himself as paramount sovereign, he would do so by letting loose to graze a perfect specimen of a horse—one fit to be offered in the most solemn rite of the horse-sacrifice (*aśvamedha*). This beast was to be allowed to go where it liked, followed by an elite-guard of young warriors, ready and fit to overthrow anyone who should attempt to drive the horse from his own grazing grounds, or to make it captive. When this stately animal, in imitation of the horselike sun, had wandered over the earth for the full cycle of a year, extending its adventurous stroll of conquest as far as it pleased and wherever it chose, it was then escorted home again to be slaughtered sacrificially with the most elaborate and solemn rites. This royal sacrifice elevated the king who owned the animal to the supreme position over all his neighbors; for he had demonstrated that he could send his herds to graze as far as they pleased; the world was his grazing ground; no one would dare to interfere. His property, the valor of his knights, and therewith his own supremacy, had been demonstrated and accepted.

The aśvamedha rite is described to the last detail in the texts of Vedic priest-lore (Brāhmaṇas and Śrauta-sūtras),[50] and has been performed solemnly by the Hindu emperors even of comparatively recent periods—for example, by the emperors of the Gupta dynasty, who governed all of northern India from 320 to 480 A.D.[51] Samudragupta, the second of this line, ordered cut in stone a panegyric composed by his court-poet Hariṣeṇa, proclaiming that he had extended his control over an empire at least equal to that of the Mauryas under King Aśoka in the third century B.C. The panegyric was cut on a pillar that already bore the edicts of King Aśoka—the point being that Samudragupta was an orthodox Hindu, whereas King Aśoka had been a Buddhist. The Hindu world-monarch (*cakravartin*), pacifying mankind by incorporating under his sole sovereignty all the kingdoms round about—the "great king" (*mahārāja*), "king above kings" (*rājādhirāja;* compare the Persian: *shāhānām shāh,* "shah of shahs")—was to be proclaimed equal in rank to those world-redeeming Buddhas who, through their doctrines, set in motion the wheel. Samudragupta confirmed and celebrated his position with the supreme ceremonial of the aśvamedha, the primary rite of the Vedic Hindu tradition—and this specifically was the deed that he recorded in his inscription on the stone.

The sun-wheel as the Cakravartin's symbol indicates that this universal shepherd-king is as it were the sun—the life-giver and universal eye, the lord and sustainer of the world. The same sun-disk is borne by the Hindu divinity Viṣṇu: it is the discus in his hand, called *Sudarśana,* "beautiful to see, auspicious to behold"; it gives light and life. The sun-wheel as Viṣṇu's

[50] *Śrauta:* "relating to Śruti," i.e., to the Veda. For Śruti, cf. *supra,* p. 61, Editor's note; for sūtra, cf. *supra,* p. 38, note 22.

[51] Cf. *supra,* p. 67, Editor's note, and Dunbar, *op. cit.,* chapter 3, pp. 68-73.

weapon, as the Cakravartin's symbol, and as the Law set in motion by the Buddha is derived in turn from an immensely old and far-spread solar symbolism. Louis XIV of France parodied the formula when he styled himself the Solar King, *le Roi Soleil.* The sun, the light and life of the world, shines on all alike, without distinction; so too shines the true Cakravartin. His power is that of nature's supreme and culminating manifestation, the enlightenment of Man the King—balanced perfectly in reason, justice, mercy, and understanding.

But what mockeries of this ideal have been the dynasties of the pretenders to the solar virtue! Their roads to victory have all been soaked with blood. For sheer extent, the rich domains of the north Indian Gupta conquerors of the fourth century A.D. might well have qualified those kings for the majestic title that they proudly took unto themselves; but their dynasties were supported by the crafty and violent art of *nīti.* Being themselves nothing if not a manifestation of the primeval *matsya-nyāya* doctrine, they did not transmute the base ocean waters into gold. Nor can anything better be said for that self-styled *Roi Soleil* whose neo-Persian concept of the absolute monarch prepared the social atmosphere of France for the downfall of his vain dynasty. Cromwell in England, at the very moment of Louis' apogee, was laying the foundations of Anglo-Saxon, Protestant democracy across the Channel—also in a sea of blood. The first royal head had already fallen. With the French Revolution the new age released its fury to the downfall of many kings and emperors throughout the world. But where, to this day, is the boon of everlasting peace?

In the recent Occident (during the last two decades of the Western world dominion, 1918–38) a generous attempt was initiated to make come true the millennial dream. Self-control, co-operation, and mutual good will were to prevail against the primeval law. Steps were taken to make effective in the sphere of international competition the laws of human decency that throughout history have prevailed within the individual communities: the moral order of the human family. The League of Nations and the Kellogg-Briand Pact renouncing war made it almost appear, for a moment, as though the day of the Cakravartin were at hand. But the brave attempt broke and the law of the fish prevails again without disguise. What is more, within the totalitarian portion of the world that law is now supreme within the communities themselves, dissolving dharma (civil liberties, religious freedom, the rights of man) to an extent such as never was known in the history of Hindu India.

When the philosophy of the *Arthaśāstra* first became known to the little circle of Western philologians who published and commented upon the documents, our civilization had still some years to go before the outbreak of the first World War. The elder generation of scholars, in those comparatively innocent years, expressed their Christian opinion that we were here confronted with a very interesting document of the Hindu genius, a highly sophisticated, curious, yet characteristic specimen of thought, belonging to a definitely bygone stage of human history—an archaic civilization far away that had never known the blessings of the basic ideals of Europe. The Hindu theories seemed to those good men to be imbued with a pagan wickedness quite their own, to which almost nothing in the Christian Western tradition could be compared. Not even Machiavelli could be compared to them; for he was an Occidental, after all, with a Christian mind.

Machiavelli's *The Prince* (*Il Principe*), with its cynical political advice and point of view, was composed in the cruel period of transition from the Middle Ages to modern times. Machiavelli had distilled his worldly wisdom from his personal experiences and observations as foreign secretary to a town-republic caught in the terrible turmoil of fifteenth-century Italian history; and he had added what he could deduce from studying Livy and the classics. His intention was to prepare the way for the political hero-savior, who, as he earnestly hoped and prayed, should soon appear on the troubled stage of his Italy, to set things right, expel from his native soil the cruel invaders (France and Germany), make an end to their devastating raids and crushing tyrannies, and finally quell even the internecine wars of those upstarts and tyrant-adventurers who were tearing the country to pieces, wrecking all hope for such unification as had been achieved for France in the days of Louis XI. Machiavelli's pages thus are inspired by a fervent patriotism, the like of which cannot be detected in the Hindu doctrines; these lack completely that modern idea and feeling. And so it seemed to the scholars who compared the two works that Machiavelli's seemingly cynical doctrine, ice-cold and immoral though it was, nevertheless glowed with a redeeming sacred fire which was lacking to the heathen—that, namely, of the author's love for a modern Christian folk. But this very love is the power that keeps the law of the fishes operating at its full force in the modern world.

The author of *Il Principe* had been the first strictly scientific Western author on politics and the art of government; his work was an unsurpassed classic, highly specialized, unbiased by popular truisms and prejudices, clear-sighted, accurate, unsentimental, and courageous. The Hindu theories, on the other hand, lacking the sacred fire, and going back to the unbaptized age of Alexander the Great—in part, to centuries even earlier—were judged by their critics to have not the slightest trace of moral worth and decent human sentiment. They seemed to the scholars of those days before the first World War to mirror the primitive, though highly sophisticated, state of human affairs in a pagan civilization—a state superseded, once and for all, by the rise of the Christian society, the humanitarian achievements of modern enlightenment, and the whole tendency of what has been called "progress." Pessimists, like Schopenhauer, Nietzsche, and the Swiss historian Jakob Burckhardt, had already questioned and slightly shaken the complacency of those self-congratulatory times, but not enough to have made any conspicuous impression on the general belief in human melioration and perfectibility. Most of the scholars could look with only pity and disgust on such documents as Kauṭilya's *Arthaśāstra,* which confirmed for them everything they had ever believed about the need for Christian light in the unregenerate lands of the heathen.

Today, however, when we peruse this document handed down to us through more than two thousand years, history forces us to the sad and witty comment of Hamlet when he realized that the time was out of joint: "This was sometime a paradox, but now the time gives it proof." What is going on today in a large portion of the world would seem, in the light of this book, to amount to a total Asiatization of political affairs, both international and domestic. And the laws are seen again to be what they were in ages past. One feels inclined to bestow a new and deep respect on the genius who at that early period recognized and elucidated the basic forces and situations that were to remain perennial in the human political field. The same style of Indian thought that invented the game of chess grasped with profound insight the rules of this larger game of power. And these are rules that cannot be disregarded by anyone seriously preparing to enter the field of political action, whether for motives of rugged individualism or in order to take the world in his hands and see whether it may not be he who is destined to become the Cakravartin—that blessed one who is to lift the sufferings that have always and everywhere marked our sorry history under the government of the sharks.

II. THE PHILOSOPHY OF PLEASURE

KĀMA-DEVA, the Hindu god of love, is no little son of mother Venus, no *putto*—chubby, tender infant—but a brilliant, dexterous youth. His glamorous mate is Ratī, "Lust and Sensual Delight." And like the divine Eros of Hesiod, celebrated by Phaedrus in Plato's dialogue, Kāma was the first-born of the gods.

> First Chaos came, and then broad-bosomed Earth,
> The everlasting seat of all that is,
> And Love.[1]

This dangerous youth's divine military commander-in-chief is Vasanta, "Spring." With a fragrant wind from the south Vasanta brings the landscape into blossom and softens all creatures for the sweet, piercing, irresistible attack of the god of love.

Kāma carries a bow entwined with flowers, and five arrows the points of which are fragrant blossoms. The bow and arrow, it must be borne in mind, were once to be taken very seriously. They were always the classic weapon of Indian warfare, from the remote centuries of the Vedic period, through the age of Epic chivalry, and even through the subsequent period of the contending tyrant-kings, until the Moslem invasions introduced the Chinese-Western invention of gunpowder, cannon, guns, and bullets. Kāma is called *Puṣpa-bāṇa,* "whose arrows are flowers," and *Pañca-sāyaka,* "endowed with five arrows." He

[1] Hesiod, *Theogony* 116ff.; Plato, *Symposium* 178 B.

carries also a noose or lasso (*pāśa*) with which to catch and fetter his victim from afar, as well as a hook with which to drag the victim near. These four instruments of the invincible god—the arrow, the bow, the noose, and the hook—are associated in the magic rituals and diagrams of the medieval Tāntric schools [2] with the four great spellbinding commands that produce love and surrender. These are, respectively, the commands "Open up!" (*jambha*), symbolized by the arrows; "Confuse, drive mad!" (*moha*), the bow; "Paralyze, stupefy, make rigid and immovable!" (*stambha*), the noose; and "Humble, tame, subdue!" (*vaśa*), the hook.

It is told that Kāma once presumed to take his aim at Śiva (the master yogī and archetypal ascetic-solitary of the Hindu pantheon), having been commanded to do so by the king of the gods, Indra, in order to break Śiva's meditation and fill him with love for the goddess Pārvatī, divine daughter of the mountain king Himālaya. Pārvatī was an incarnation of the supreme goddess of the world, Kālī-Durgā-Satī, Śiva's eternal female-counterpart and projected energy, whom the god, for the well-being of the universe, was to be brought to recognize and know.[3] But when the first flower-shaft found its mark and Śiva was aroused from the timeless contemplation of his own innermost supernal luminosity, a lightning flash of anger broke from his third or middle eye, at the point between the brows, and the body of Kāma, the very vision of Charm Irresistible, was reduced to ashes. Ratī, the desolated spouse, prevailed on Śiva to bring her consort back from non-entity, but though the spirit returned, the beautiful body could not be produced again. Therefore Kāma is called *Anaṅga,* "bodiless." He hovers above and between lovers intangibly, invisibly forcing them to each other's embrace.

[2] Cf. *supra,* p. 61, Editor's note, and *infra,* pp. 560ff.

[3] Cf. Heinrich Zimmer, *The King and the Corpse,* The Bollingen Series XI, New York, 1948, Part II.

Kāma-loka, "the realm (*loka*) of desires and their fulfillments (*kāma*)," is the god of love's beautiful paradise of joys, where men and animals dwell spellbound by objects of the senses. Thus allured, the Self-forgetful beings remain fixed to the universal wheel of the round of time, doomed to be born again on earth, in the heavens, or in the purgatories of pain, according to the character of their thoughts and desires. For the fruit of desire is destiny, and so the activated individual, linked to the causal round by the delicate but tough and durable filaments of his own desire, goes on from existence to existence—earthly, celestial, and infernal—now as man, now as beast, now as a god, unable to break away and into the peace beyond.

Kāma-loka comprises in its lower levels the hells or purgatories of pain, as well as the ghostly region of specters (*pretas*), the region of giant-monsters that devour beasts and men (*rākṣasas*), the region of the anti-gods or titans (*asuras*), that of the goblins (*kumbhāṇḍas*), the kingdom of the serpentlike water-gods (*nāgas*), and the domain of the household-deities (*yakṣas:* fertility-gods surviving from the archaic pre-Āryan civilization, who now serve as attendants of the deities Kubera and Śiva). The middle realm of men and beasts is on the earthly plane, while above, still ruled by Kāma (the supreme personification of the allure of the transient world), are the kingdom of the winged birdlike gods of the atmosphere (*garuḍas*) and the paradise of the celestial musicians (*gandharvas*)—the last named being men reborn to the sensual pleasures of the lower heavens, where they enjoy the companionship and love of heavenly damsels (*apsarases*). The progressively rarefied spheres of the gods are represented as superimposed, one upon another, up the terraced slopes of Mount Sumeru, the great central mountain of the world, which, like a gigantic Babylonian ziggurat—a natural, cosmic tower of Babel—lifts its summit into the loftiest spheres of celestial bliss, and then soars beyond. What lies beyond is Brahmā-loka, the realm of formless being and purely spiritual bliss. But the power of Kāma reaches even there. For the universe is the production of the divine will (*icchā*) or desire (*kāma*)—the wish of the One to be many. All spheres of being stand generated and supported by that first creative impulse. On the carnal plane it operates through the mystery of sex; on the highest, it is the will of the Creator. Kāma therefore is "the first of the gods"—but the youngest too, as born again every day in the meeting and mating of creatures throughout the course of time. Kāma is the power and process whereby the One begets Itself as man, beast, or plant, and thus carries forward the continued creation of the universe. Kāma is the conjunction of eternity and time, through which *that* abundance becomes *this* abundance, and the non-manifest is made manifest in all the beings of the cosmos, from Brahmā down to the blade of grass.

In Buddhist (as distinguished from Hindu) iconography three created realms (*lokas*), or ranging-grounds into which beings may descend to be reborn (*avacaras*), are described. The first and lowest is Kāma-loka, "the world of desires"; the next is Rūpa-loka, "the world of pure forms (beyond desire)"; while the highest is A-rūpa-loka, "the world without forms, the formless realm." These conceptions represent and are based on the common experiences of yoga. As the process of introvert absorption deepens and the sphere of extrovert experiences drops away, higher, deeper, more rarefied spheres of experience are attained. And these are themselves then found to be subdivided into many stratifications, each inhabited by a class of subtle celestial beings.

According to the early Buddhist legends, when Gautama Śākyamuni was seated under the Bo Tree, on the point of breaking past all forms and realms whatsoever into the timeless infinite of the Void, Kāma appeared to him in the form of a youth carrying a lute, and sought to tempt him from his world-transcending task. One of the names applied to Kāma in these Buddhist texts is that of an old Vedic demon, Namuci, a word commonly interpreted as "he who does not (*na*) let go (*muc*)." By supplying every creature with something of the joys of life Kāma as Namuci holds all spellbound, so that the produced beings fall prey, again and again, to death. Hence he is also called "The Evil One" (*pāpīyān*), or simply "Death" (*māra*).[4] Kāma and Māra, the joy of life and the grip of death, are respectively the bait and the hook—the delights of the loaded table and the price to be paid—the dinner and the check, which here is mortality, suffering, and tears; *la douloureuse,* "the painful hour of payment," ends the carousel. Thus the supreme seducer, oldest of the gods and supporter of the world, has for all beings a dual aspect—as have all the gods and all the forces of life. They are at once attractive and destructive, merciful and merciless, desirable and appalling. In the picture-languages of the Buddhist and Hindu iconographies, all superhuman beings and presences are ambivalent and ambiguous in this way. Life in the world is described as an excruciating paradox—the more alive, the more difficult to bear: a sea of suffering, delusory delights, deceitful promises, and dismaying realizations: the sea, indeed, of the fecund, self-sustaining, self-consuming madness of the fish.

The Buddha, so the legend tells us, broke the power of the god of death and desire (on whose banner is displayed the emblem of the fish) and passed beyond. The dual delusion dissolved from him, and his released consciousness united with the Reality of the Void. All men are destined for that transcendent end. As we shall see, the whole concern of the major portion of Indian philosophy is the way to such release (*mokṣa*) from the world-bounding, binding power of the divine being "who does not let go," the cosmic magician, Namuci.[5] And throughout

[4] *Māra,* literally "he who kills, or makes 'die' *(mar)*"; compare the Latin *mors, mor-tis,* and *mor*-tal, *mor*-tality.

[5] *Na-muci* and *mokṣa* both are derived from the root *muc:* "let go, release"; the former with the negative prefix *na-*.

the traditional literature on the subject, the first step to this goal of goals is described as the refusal of Kāma's bait, his tempting table, the abundance of the world. This, however, does not prevent the great majority—in India, as everywhere in this vast "grazing ground"—from devoting themselves exclusively to the pursuit of the bitter-sweet delusion.

The Hindu handbooks of the art of love, composed for those who are still dedicated to the work of continuing the creation, strictly disregard the discouraging insights and devastating ascetic prescriptions of those who have broken free—except in so far as sophisticated reflections about the transiency of delight may add to love and life a certain exquisite thrill. The case is similar to that of the Hindu handbooks of the science of politics, where all the principles of virtue are disregarded except in so far as a mask of morality may serve the purpose of the power specialist. Fundamentally, the doctrine and technique of Kāma go back to primitive antiquity. They belong to that science and art of love-magic (the lore of charms, spells, and love-philters) which is a dominant concern of all primitive traditions. In that sense they are definitely pre-Buddhistic, pre-Vedāntic,[6] and are innocent of, rather than antagonistic to, the developed monastic ideal and techniques of renunciation.

Kāma, the Sanskrit noun, denotes the whole range of possible experience within the sphere of love, sex, sensual gratification, and delight. *Kāma* is "wish, desire, carnal gratification, lust, love, and affection." The earliest Indian documents on the subject appear in the most antique stratifications of Vedic popular priestcraft and witchcraft; charms of love being numerous and conspicuous, for example, in the text of the *Atharvaveda.* Love-life here means primarily family life, married life, and the principal and original aim of the doctrine was simply to make this love-life a success, i.e., to produce a happy, harmonious family: a happy husband, happy wife and mother, and

[6] Cf. *supra,* pp. 8 and 18, Editor's notes.

numerous healthy, promising children, preferably sons. For sons are indispensable for continuing the lineage and ensuring the unbroken maintenance of the family cult of ancestor-offerings by which the souls of the deceased "Fathers" are supported in the "Realm of the Fathers" (*pitṛ-loka*). Daughters, on the other hand, are expensive and delicate burdens. One has to arrange and provide for a suitable marriage, with due regard to the requirements of caste and social position; and then one never knows quite what to expect of the son-in-law who has thus been so troublesomely acquired. The house prospers inevitably with sons; whereas with daughters, there is generally anxiety and expense. The hints we have of the earliest Kāma tradition include recipes and rituals for begetting male children, keeping oneself youthful and healthy, becoming and remaining attractive, and making married love-life a success.

A brief review of the list of charms in the *Atharva-veda* devoted to the work of Kāma will suffice to indicate the scope and character of the problems as they were understood and approached in that time. This old Vedic material has never been studied and treated in comparison with the much later formulae preserved to us in such works as Vātsyāyana's *Kāmasūtra,* yet it discloses the originally sacred and authoritative character of the doctrine that appears in the later works in a rather secularized, worldly form—as a kind of *ars amandi* for courtesans and gentlemen-about-town. Roughly, a thirteenth part of the whole of the ancient *Atharva-veda* (41 items out of the 536 hymns, prayers, incantations, and charms—not an overwhelming, but certainly a significant and wholesome, portion of the total compilation) is devoted to the magic of this basic and immensely important human subject. The following list will give a notion of the scope of the early hymns and charms: [7]

[7] The titles are those given by the translators, William Dwight Whitney and Charles Rockwell Lanman, in their *Atharva-Veda,* Harvard Oriental Series, Vols. VII and VIII, Cambridge, Mass., 1905. The numbers in paren-

For successful childbirth (11)
Imprecation of spinsterhood on a woman (14)
A love spell, with a sweet herb (34)
To secure a woman's love (72)
To get a husband for a woman (81)
Against a rival wife, with a plant (117)
For fecundity (127)
To command a woman's love (130)
For recovery of virility, with a plant (149)
(The incantation of the lover entering the girl's home by night:) To put the household to sleep (151)
For successful conception (265)
Two charms, to win a woman's love (287)
For birth of sons (288)
Against premature birth (293)
Against jealousy (293)
For winning a spouse (325)
For matrimonial happiness (339)
For successful pregnancy, with an amulet (341)
To obtain a wife (342)
To win affection (347)
For virile power (354)
To win a woman (355)
Two charms, to win a man's love (379)
To compel a man's love (380)
For progeny (401)
Against a rival woman (411)
Husband and wife to one another (411)
The wife to the husband (412)
To win and fix a man's love, with a plant (412)
To cure jealousy (416)
To destroy one's virile power (454)

---

theses refer to the pages of the Whitney-Lanman volumes; pages 1-470 are in Vol. VII, 471-1052 in VIII.

Against a woman rival, with a plant (467)
To guard a pregnant woman from demons (493)
To Kāma (521)
Magic stanzas for marriage ceremonies (740-753)
Of and to Desire (Kāma) (985)

The worries and difficulties of married life in Vedic times, apparently, were much the same as those that we know in the world today. And the remedies offered by the Kāma-material of the *Atharva-veda* are the classic ones of all ages: medical treatment in the form of herbs, plants, and philters; suggestion and persuasion, enhanced by magic objects (amulets); eugenics; mental and emotional hygiene—attunement, adjustment; all couched in terms of magic, and administered by the priest-magician medicine man—archaic archetype of those modern wizards of the psyche, the consulting psychoanalyst and the family doctor. On the other hand, some of the charms are simply household-medicine, used by man or wife without the assistance of the priest-wizard: love-charms against rivals, etc.

Kāma is of the essence of magic, magic of the essence of love; for among nature's own spells and charms that of love and sex is pre-eminent. This is the witchcraft that compels life to progress from one generation to the next, the spell that binds all creatures to the cycle of existences, through deaths and births. It would be impossible to imagine a compendium of magic lore without its due assortment of love-charms. The Latin *carmen,* "magic priestly song (conjuring up the powers, warding demons away)," our English "charm" (which meant, originally, "magic stanza, the conjuring sing-song that works a spell"), and such kindred terms as "incantation," "enchantment," "enchanting," "enchanter," all point back to the magic song or spell; likewise the French *enchanté, désenchanté,* and *charme.* A singer, a soprano, *une cantatrice,* is an enchantress; so too the tenor who "puts a spell" upon the audience. Love, song, and the divine intoxicating potion that brings the god himself threading through the veins have for millenniums been associated with each other, not only blithely, in the dreams of youth, but also desperately, in the black rites of the witch's art.

The early Indian magic lore of love seems to have been known and preserved in esoteric doctrines by the warrior-clans outside the priestly families themselves. The treatment of the subject was profoundly inspired by a sense of the holy mystery of life, whereas in the highly technical later handbooks on the art of pleasure it is comparatively cut and dried. The famous Brāhman Śvetaketu seems to have been one of the first redactors of handbooks of this kind.He is described in the sixth book of the *Chāndogya Upaniṣad* as receiving from his father, Uddālaka Āruṇi, the key to all knowledge, in the form of the Vedic "great formula" (*mahā-vākya*), "Thou Art That" (*tat tvam asi*). Elsewhere he is celebrated as the model Brāhman of that classic, somewhat one-sided type that we know from many orthodox sources. He was in perfect command of the sacred lore, but, apparently, not equally at home in the sphere of secular philosophy. No doubt it was through such hands as his that the archaic Kāma-wisdom lost its scope and depth. The richness of the topic as it was understood in later Vedic times, when it constituted one of the departments of household wisdom, has been drained away, as the result of much epitomizing and reducing. From this later literature on the art of love there is little to be extracted by way of metaphysics or philosophy.

The major text is the justly celebrated *Kāmasūtra*[8] of the Brāhman Vātsyāyana, composed in the third or fourth century A.D. This is a masterly yet very much condensed and all too abbreviated version of the materials of the earlier tradition. A few later and minor treatises composed in verse, which in part show a more archaic character than the classic *Kāmasūtra*, communicate a greater sense of what the larger doctrine must

[8] "The aphorisms *(sūtra)* of the technique of making love *(kāma)*."

have been. Among these may be named *Pañcasāyaka,* "The God with the Five Arrows," composed some time after the eleventh century A.D.; *Ratirahasya,* "The Secret Doctrine of Love's Delight," which is somewhat earlier than the thirteenth century; and *Anaṅgaraṅga,* "The Stage of the Bodiless God," dating probably from the sixteenth century A.D. Occasional fragments preserved in the Upaniṣads also serve to indicate the rich, profound, and holy awe in which the sacred act was held, through which the God of gods continued his creation, pressing it on through the generations of the great Brāhmanic and the great kingly houses. The knowledge of that erotic practical philosophy is for the present all but lost.[9]

[9] *Editor's note:* Here Dr. Zimmer's notes on this subject break off. His intention was to continue his study with an analysis of the textbooks of acting (cf. *supra,* pp. 39-40), and to amplify his treatment of the earlier tradition by reviewing the pertinent passages in the Upaniṣads. The chapter as given above represents but a preliminary sketch.

III. THE PHILOSOPHY OF DUTY

1.

Caste and the Four Life-Stages

IN INDIA everybody wears the tokens of the department of life to which he belongs. He is recognizable at first glance by his dress and ornaments and the marks of his caste and trade class. Every man has the symbol of his tutelary deity painted on his forehead, by which sign he is placed and kept under the god's protection. Maiden, married woman, widow: each wears a distinctive costume. And to each pertains a clear-cut set of standards and taboos, meticulously defined, scrupulously followed. What to eat and what not to eat, what to approach and what to shun, with whom to converse, share meals, and intermarry: such personal affairs are minutely regulated, with severe and exacting penalties for accidental as well as for intentional infringement. The idea is to preserve without pollution-by-contact the specific spiritual force on which one's efficacy as a member of a particular social species depends.

For in so far as the individual is a functioning component of the complex social organism, his concern must be to become identified with the tasks and interests of his social role, and even to shape to this his public and private character. The whole group takes precedence over any of its components. All self-expression, as we know and care for it, is therefore ruled out, the precondition to participation in the group consisting not in cultivating, but in dissolving, personal tendencies and idiosyncrasies. The supreme virtue is to become assimilated—wholeheartedly and without residue—to the timeless, immemorial, absolutely impersonal mask of the classic role into which one has been brought by birth (*jāti*). The individual is thus compelled to become anonymous. And this is regarded, furthermore, as a process not of self-dissolution but of self-discovery; for the key to the realization of one's present incarnation lies in the virtues of one's present caste.

Caste is regarded as forming an innate part of character. The divine moral order (*dharma*) by which the social structure is knit together and sustained is the same as that which gives continuity to the lives of the individual; and just as the present is to be understood as a natural consequence of the past, so in accordance with the manner in which the present role is played will the caste of the future be determined. Not only one's caste and trade, furthermore, but also all the things that happen to one (even though apparently through the slightest chance), are determined by, and exactly appropriate to, one's nature and profoundest requirement. The vital, malleable episode at hand points back to former lives; it is their result—the natural effect of bygone causal factors operating on the plane of ethical values, human virtues, and personal qualities, in accordance with universal natural laws of elective attraction and spontaneous repulsion. What a person is and what he experiences are regarded as strictly commensurate, like the inside and the outside of a vase.

The correct manner of dealing with every life problem that arises, therefore, is indicated by the laws (*dharma*) of the caste (*varṇa*) to which one belongs, and of the particular stage-of-life (*āśrama*) that is proper to one's age. One is not free to choose; one belongs to a species—a family, guild and craft, a group, a denomination. And since this circumstance not only determines to the last detail the regulations for one's public and private conduct, but also represents (according to this all-inclusive and pervasive, unyielding pattern of integration) the real ideal of one's present natural character, one's concern as a judging and acting entity must be only to meet every life problem in a manner befitting the role one plays. Whereupon the two aspects of the temporal event—the subjective and the objective—will be joined exactly, and the individual eliminated as a third, intrusive factor. He will then bring into manifestation not the temporal accident of his own personality, but the vast, impersonal, cosmic law, and so will be, not a faulty, but a perfect glass: anonymous and self-effacing. For by the rigorous practice of prescribed virtues one actually can efface oneself, dissolving eventually the last quirk of impulse and personal resistance—thus gaining release from the little boundary of the personality and absorption in the boundlessness of universal being. Dharma is therefore fraught with power. It is the burning point of the whole present, past, and future, as well as the way through which to pass into the transcendental consciousness and bliss of the purest spiritual Self-existence.

Everybody is born to his own place (*sva-dharma*) in the phantasmagoric display of creative power that is the world, and his first duty is to show it, to live up to it, to make known by both his appearance and his actions just what part of the spectacle he is. Every feminine being is a manifestation on earth of the universal Mother, a personification of the productive, alluring aspect of the holy mystery that supports and continually creates the world. The married woman is to be all decency; the harlot is to pride herself on her ability to keep her allurements effective and sell her charms. The mother and housewife is to breed sons without cease, and to worship her husband as the human embodiment of all the gods. Husband and wife are to approach each other as two divinities; for he, through her, is reborn in his sons, just as the Creator is made manifest in the forms and creatures of the world through the magical operation of his own power, his śakti, personified in his goddess. And as the male member of the community is co-ordinated to the whole through the particular religious devotions and services proper to his social position, so the wife is co-ordinated to society as the śakti of her spouse. Her service to him is her religion, just as his religion is the service to his "Fathers" and the deities of his vocation. Thus the whole of life is lived as, and understood to be, a service to the Divine, all things being known as images of the one and universal Lord.

Every profession has its special tutelary divinity, who embodies and personifies the very skill of the trade, and wields or exhibits its tools as his distinguishing attributes. The tutelary divinity of writers, poets, intellectuals, and priests, for example, is the goddess Sarasvatī Vāc: the goddess of riverlike, streaming speech. And the patroness of magic priestcraft, Brāhmanhood, is Sāvitrī: not the human princess, daughter of King Aśvapati, who, according to the legend, rescued her husband, Prince Satyavān, from the dominion of King Death, but the female counterpart and divine energy, śakti, of Savitar-Brahmā, the Creator of the world; she is the all-moving, all-inspiring, divine principle of creation. Kāma, the Hindu Cupid, is the tutelary divinity of courtesans, and of those who stand in need of the lessons of the kāmaśāstra, the authorized code of traditional revealed wisdom in the lore of love and sex.[1] While Viśvakarman, the divine "Expert of All Crafts," the carpenter, architect, and master craftsman of the gods, is the patron deity of workmen, artisans, and artists.

Each of these, representing the principle and sum total of a certain highly specialized department of knowledge and skill, is a jealous and exclusive god and master. The human creature called by birth to the deity's service is to dedicate all of his

[1] Cf. *supra,* pp. 140-150.

powers and devotion to worship; the slightest failure can entail disaster. Like a mistress, charming and generous if faithfully and exclusively served, but baleful, wrathful, terrific, if not duly paid her whole requirement, the god blossoms like a flower, yielding sweetness, fragrance, and fruit abundantly for the devotee of perfect concentration, but otherwise is touchy and revengeful. India's static, departmentalized, and mutually cooperative hierarchy of the crafts and professions, that is to say, demands and inculcates the most extreme one-sidedness. There is to be no choice, no floundering around, no sowing of wild oats. From the very first breath of life, the individual's energies are mastered, trained into channels, and co-ordinated to the general work of the superindividual who is the holy society itself.

This depersonalizing principle of specialization is pressed even further by the subdivision of the ideal life-course of the individual into four stages (*āśrama*). The first stage, that of the pupil (*antevāsin*), is ruled exclusively by obedience and submission. The pupil, eager to receive, under the magic spell of the spiritual teacher, the whole charge, the total transference, of the divine knowledge and magic craft of his vocation, seeks to be nothing but the sacred vessel into which that precious essence flows. Symbolically, by the spiritual umbilical cord of the "sacred thread" with which he is solemnly invested, he is linked to his guru as to the one and only, all-sufficient human embodiment and source (for him) of superhuman spiritual nourishment. Strict chastity (*brahmacarya*) is enjoined; and if through any experience with the other sex he violates this interdict, thereby breaking the continuity of the life-generating, life-begetting intimacy and identification with the guru, the most severe and complex punishments descend upon him. This is the period for *śraddhā* (blind faith in the master-technician who knows the path), and *śuśrūṣā* (the will and desire to "hear" (*śru*) and to learn by heart; to hear, to obey, and to conform).

This is the period when the mere natural man, the human animal, is to be absolutely sacrificed, and the life of man in the spirit, the supranormal wisdom-power of the "twice-born," to be made effective in the flesh.

Then, abruptly, when the stage of pupilship is finished, and without any transitional period, the youth, now a man, is transferred—one might say, hurled—into married life, the stage of householdership (*gṛhastha*). Taking over the paternal craft, business, or profession, he receives a wife (chosen for him by his parents), begets sons, supports the family, and does his best to identify himself with all the tasks and ideal roles of the traditional *pater familias,* member of the guild, etc. The young father identifies himself with the delights and worries of married life (*kāma*), as well as with the classic interests and problems of property and wealth (*artha*), so that he may have the means at his disposal, not only to support his growing family according to the standards proper to his birth or human species (*jāti*), but also to meet the more or less costly demands of the orthodox sacramental cycle of rituals. For the house-priest, the Brāhman-guru, whom he now must employ and heed—even as Indra must employ and heed the divine Bṛhaspati [2]—blesses and assists the family on every possible occasion, as a combination spiritual adviser and confessor, family doctor, consulting practical psychologist, exorcist, conjuror, and wizard. And these professional men charge their fees: that is part of the cause of the real effectiveness of their cryptic, holy, psychotherapeutic dealings. The gurus, linking themselves with full surrender (like everyone else in the community) to the privileges and duties of their own immemorial role, serve as conduits of supernatural wisdom and holy power (*brahman*), like nerves of consciousness throughout the social body.

The guru tends to become petrified into an idol—just as everyone tends to become petrified, dehumanized, stabilized, and

[2] Cf. *supra,* pp. 76-77.

purged of spontaneous individuality—in proportion to the degree of perfection he achieves in the intensely stylized enactment of his timeless role. In the second half of the individual's life cycle, therefore, these brittle roles are to be put aside. Having identified himself wholly with the functions of his social personality (his social actor's mask, or *persona*), he must now as radically step away from that—throw off possessions and all the concerns of wealth (*artha*), break from the desires and anxieties of his now flowered and variously fruitful life-in-marriage (*kāma*), turn even from the duties of society (*dharma*) which have linked him to the universal manifestation of Imperishable Being through the stable archetypes of the human tragicomedy. His sons are now bearing the joys and burdens of the world; himself, in late middle life, may step away. And so he enters upon the third āśrama, that of the "departure to the forest" (*vanaprastha*). For we are not only social, professional masks, representing ageless roles in the shadow-world of time, but also something substantial; namely, a Self. We belong, cannot but belong, to the world, yet are not adequately described by our caste marks and costume, not fathomed to our essence by secular and moral functions. Our essence transcends this manifested nature and everything that belongs to it, our property, delights, our rights and duties, and our relationship to the ancestors and the gods. To seek to reach that unnamed essence is to enter upon the path of the quest for the Self; and this is the aim and end of the third of the four life-stages.

The man and wife in the period of the retreat to the forest put off the cares, duties, joys, and interests that linked them to the world and begin the difficult inward quest. And yet, not even this idyl of the life of holiness in the forest can mark the end of their adventure; for, like the first period—that of studenthood—this is only a preparation. In the fourth and last āśrama—that of the wandering holy beggar (*bhikṣu*)—no longer linked to any exercise, no longer linked to any place, but "taking no thought of the future and looking with indifference upon the present," [3] the homeless wanderer "lives identified with the eternal Self and beholds nothing else." [4] "He no more cares whether his body, spun of the threads of karma, falls or remains, than does a cow what becomes of the garland that someone has hung around her neck; for the faculties of his mind are now at rest in the Holy Power (*brahman*), the essence of bliss." [5]

Originally, Jaina saints went about "clothed in space" (*digambara*), i.e., stark naked, as a sign that they did not belong to any recognized group, sect, trade, or community. They had discarded all determining marks; for determination is negation by specialization.[6] In the same spirit, the wandering Buddhist monks were instructed to go clad in rags, or else in an ochre-colored garment—the latter being traditionally the garb of the criminal ejected from society and condemned to death. The monks donned this disgraceful raiment as a sign that they too were dead to the social hierarchy. They had been handed over to death and were beyond the boundaries of life. They had stepped away from the world's limitations, out of all the bondages of belonging to something. They were renegades. Likewise, the Brāhman pilgrim-mendicant has always been likened to the wild goose or swan (*haṁsa*), which has no fixed home but wanders, migrating with the rain-clouds north to the Himalayas and back south again, at home on every lake or sheet of water, as also in the infinite, unbounded reaches of the sky.

Religion is supposed finally to release us from the desires and fears, ambitions and commitments of secular life—the delusions of

[3] Śaṅkara, *Vivekacūḍāmaṇi* 432; compare Luke 12: 22-30.

[4] *Ib.* 457.

[5] *Ib.* 416.

[6] Later on, as a concession, the Jaina holy men donned the white garment and became *śvetāmbara,* "clothed in white." This was the most non-committal dress that they could find. (See, however, *infra,* p. 210, Editor's note.)

our social, professional, and family interests; for religion claims the soul. But then religion is necessarily a community affair, and so itself is an instrument of bondage, tying us more subtly, by less gross and therewith more insinuative delusions. Anyone seeking to transcend the tight complacencies of his community must break away from the religious congregation. One of the classic ways of doing this is by becoming a monk—joining, that is to say, still another institution, this time dedicated to isolation from, and insurance against, the ordinary human bondages. Or people take the step into the forest, becoming hermit-solitaries—tied now to the gentle idyl of the hermitage and the innocent details of its primitive life-ritual. Where in all the world can one be totally free?

What is a man really, behind and beyond all the marks, costumes, implements, and activities that denote his civil and religious status? What being is it that underlies, supports, and animates all the states and changes of his life's shadowlike becoming? The anonymities of the forces of nature that operate within him; the curious performances, successful or unsuccessful, upon which his social character depends; the landscape and life incidental to his time and place of birth; the materials that pass through and constitute for a time his body, charm his fancy, and animate his imagination: none of these can be said to be the Self.

The craving for complete release from limitations, which is identical with the craving for absolute anonymity, one may seek to fulfill by turning homeless beggar-mendicant, with no fixed place to lay one's head, no regular road, no goal, no belongings. But then—one is still carrying oneself around. All those stratifications of the body and psyche that correspond to the demands and offerings of the environment and link one to the world wherever one may be are present, active still. To reach the Absolute Man (*puruṣa*) that is sought, one must somehow discard those garbs and obscuring sheaths. From the skin, down through the intellect and emotions, the memory of things past and the deep-rooted habits of reaction—those acquired spontaneities, the cherished automatisms of one's profoundly rooted likes and dislikes—all must be cast aside; for these are not the Self but "superimpositions," "colorings," "besmearings" (*añjana*), of its intrinsic radiance and purity. That is why before entering upon the fourth āśrama, that of the wandering nonentity, the Hindu practices the psychological exercises of the third, that of the idyl of the forest. He must put off himself to come to the adamantine Self. And that is the work of yoga. Yoga, Self-discovery, and then the absolutely unconditional identification of oneself with the anonymous, ubiquitous, and imperishable ground of all existence, constitute the proper end of the second half of the cycle of the orthodox biography. This is the time for wiping off the actor's paint that one wore on the universal stage, the time for the recollection and release of the unaffected and uninvolved, yet all-sustaining and enacting, living Person who was always there.

2.

Satya

"BETTER is one's own dharma, though imperfectly performed, than the dharma of another well performed. Better is death in the performance of one's own dharma: the dharma of another is fraught with peril." [7] There exists in India an ancient belief that the one who has enacted his own dharma without a single fault throughout the whole of his life can work magic by the simple act of calling that fact to witness. This is known as making an

[7] *Bhagavad Gītā* 3.35.

"Act of Truth." The dharma need not be that of the highest Brāhman caste or even of the decent and respectable classes of the human community. In every dharma, Brahman, the Holy Power, is present.

The story is told, for example, of a time when the righteous king Aśoka, greatest of the great North Indian dynasty of the Mauryas,[8] "stood in the city of Pāṭaliputra, surrounded by city folk and country folk, by his ministers and his army and his councilors, with the Ganges flowing by, filled up by freshets, level with the banks, full to the brim, five hundred leagues in length, a league in breadth. Beholding the river, he said to his ministers, 'Is there any one who can make this mighty Ganges flow back upstream?' To which the ministers replied, 'That is a hard matter, your Majesty.'

"Now there stood on that very river bank an old courtesan named Bindumatī, and when she heard the king's question she said, 'As for me, I am a courtesan in the city of Pāṭaliputra. I live by my beauty; my means of subsistence is the lowest. Let the king but behold my Act of Truth.' And she performed an Act of Truth. The instant she performed her Act of Truth that mighty Ganges flowed back upstream with a roar, in the sight of all that mighty throng.

"When the king heard the roar caused by the movement of the whirlpools and the waves of the mighty Ganges, he was astonished, and filled with wonder and amazement. Said he to his ministers, 'How comes it that this mighty Ganges is flowing back upstream?' 'Your Majesty, the courtesan Bindumatī heard your words, and performed an Act of Truth. It is because of her Act of Truth that the mighty Ganges is flowing backwards.'

"His heart palpitating with excitement, the king himself went posthaste and asked the courtesan, 'Is it true, as they say, that you, by an Act of Truth, have made this river Ganges flow back upstream?' 'Yes, your Majesty.'—Said the king, 'You have power

[8] Cf. *supra*, p. 37.

to do such a thing as this! Who, indeed, unless he were stark mad, would pay any attention to what you say? By what power have you caused this mighty Ganges to flow back upstream?' Said the courtesan, 'By the Power of Truth, your Majesty, have I caused this mighty Ganges to flow back upstream.'

"Said the king, 'You possess the Power of Truth! You, a thief, a cheat, corrupt, cleft in twain, vicious, a wicked old sinner who have broken the bounds of morality and live on the plunder of fools!' 'It is true, your Majesty; I am what you say. But even I, wicked woman that I am, possess an Act of Truth by means of which, should I so desire, I could turn the world of men and the worlds of the gods upside down.' Said the king, 'But what is this Act of Truth? Pray enlighten me.'

" 'Your Majesty, whosoever gives me money, be he a Kṣatriya or a Brāhman or a Vaiśya or a Śūdra or of any other caste soever, I treat them all exactly alike. If he be a Kṣatriya, I make no distinction in his favor. If he be a Śūdra, I despise him not. Free alike from fawning and contempt, I serve the owner of the money. This, your Majesty, is the Act of Truth by which I caused the mighty Ganges to flow back upstream.' "[9]

Just as day and night alternate, each maintaining its own form, and support by their opposition the character of the processes of time, so in the sphere of the social order everyone sustains the totality by adhering to his own dharma. The sun in India withers vegetation, but the moon restores it, sending the revivifying dew; similarly, throughout the universe the numerous mutually antagonistic elements co-operate by working against each other. The rules of the castes and professions are regarded as reflections in the human sphere of the laws of this natural order; hence, when adhering to those rules the various classes are felt to be

[9] *Milindapañha* 119-123. (Cited and translated by Eugene Watson Burlingame, "The Act of Truth (Saccakiriya): A Hindu Spell and Its Employment as a Psychic Motif in Hindu Fiction," *Journal of the Royal Asiatic Society of Great Britain and Ireland,* 1917, pp. 439-441.)

collaborating, even when apparently in conflict. Each race or estate following its proper righteousness, all together do the work of the cosmos. This is the service by which the individual is lifted beyond the limitations of his personal idiosyncrasies and converted into a living conduit of cosmic force.

The Sanskrit noun *dharma,* from the root *dhṛ,* "to hold, to bear, to carry" (Latin *fero;* cf. Anglo-Saxon *faran,* "to travel, to fare"; cf. also, "ferry"), means "that which holds together, supports, upholds." [10] *Dharma,* as we have seen, refers not only to the whole context of law and custom (religion, usage, statute, caste or sect observance, manner, mode of behavior, duty, ethics, good works, virtue, religious or moral merit, justice, piety, impartiality), but also to the essential nature, character, or quality of the individual, as a result of which his duty, social function, vocation, or moral standard is what it is. Dharma is to fail just before the end of the world, but will endure as long as the universe endures; and each participates in its power as long as he plays his role. The word implies not only a universal law by which the cosmos is governed and sustained, but also particular laws, or inflections of "the law," which are natural to each special species or modification of existence. Hierarchy, specialization, one-sidedness, traditional obligations, are thus of the essence of the system. But there is no class struggle; for one cannot strive to be something other than what one is. One either "is" (*sat*) or one "is not" (*a-sat*), and one's dharma is the form of the manifestation in time of what one *is.* Dharma is ideal justice made alive; any man or thing without its dharma is an inconsistency. There are clean and unclean professions, but all participate in the Holy Power. Hence "virtue" is commensurate with perfection in one's given role.

The turbaned queen—so runs another tale—longing to greet the sage, her husband's brother, bade farewell to the king, her husband, and at eventide took the following vow: "At early morn,

[10] The noun *dhar-ā,* "she who bears," denotes the earth; the noun *dhar-aṇam* is "prop, stay, support."

accompanied by my retinue, I will greet the sage Soma and provide him with food and drink; only then will I eat."

But between the city and the forest there was a river; and in the night there was a freshet; and the river rose and swept along, both strong and deep. Disturbed by this, when morning came, the queen asked her beloved husband, "How can I fulfill this my desire today?"

Said the king, "O queen, be not thus distressed, for this is simple to do. Go, easy in mind, with your retinue, to the hither bank; and, standing there, first invoke the goddess of the river, and then, with hands both joined, and with a pure heart, utter these words: 'O river-goddess, if from the day my husband's brother took his vow, my husband has lived chaste, then straightway give me passage.' "

Hearing this, the queen was astonished, and thought, "What manner of thing is this? The king speaks incoherently. That from the day of his brother's vow the king has begotten progeny of sons on me, all this signifies that I have performed to him my vow as a wife. But after all, why doubt? Is physical contact in this case the meaning intended? Besides, women who are loyal to their husbands should not doubt their husbands' words. For it is said: A wife who hesitates to obey her husband's command, a soldier who hesitates at his king's command, a pupil who hesitates at his father's command, such a one breaks his own vow."

Pleased at this thought, the queen, accompanied by her retinue in ceremonial attire, went to the bank of the river, and standing on the shore did worship, and with a pure heart uttered distinctly the proclamation of truth recited by her husband.

And of a sudden the river, tossing its waters to the left and to the right, became shallow and gave passage. The queen went to the farther shore, and there, bowing before the sage according to form, received his blessing, deeming herself a happy woman. The sage then asked the woman how she had been able to cross the river, and she related the whole story. Having so done, she asked the prince of sages, "How can it be possible, how can it be imagined, that my husband lives chaste?"

The sage replied, "Hear me, good woman. From the moment when I took my vow, the king's soul was free from attachment and vehemently did he long to take a vow. For no such man as he could patiently endure to bear the yoke of sovereignty. Therefore he bears sway from a sense of duty, but his heart is not in what he does. Moreover it is said, 'A woman who loves another man follows her husband. So also a yogī attached to the essence of things remains with the round of existences.' Precisely so the chastity of the king is possible, even though he is living the life of a householder, because his heart is free from sin, just as the purity of the lotus is not stained, even though it grow in the mud."

The queen bowed before the sage, and then, experiencing supreme satisfaction, went to a certain place in the forest and set up her abode. Having caused a meal to be prepared for her retinue, she provided food and drink for the sage. Then, her vow fulfilled, she herself ate and drank.

When the queen went to take leave of the sage she asked him once more, "How can I cross the river now?" The sage replied, "Woman of tranquil speech, you must thus address the goddess of the river: 'If this sage, even to the end of his vow, shall always abide fasting, then grant me passage.' "

Amazed once more, the queen went to the bank of the river, proclaimed the words of the sage, crossed the river, and went home. After relating the whole story to the king, she asked him, "How can the sage be fasting, when I myself caused him to break the fast?"

The king said, "O queen, you are confused in mind; you do not understand in what true religion consists. Tranquil in heart, noble in soul is he, whether in eating or in fasting. Therefore: even though a sage eat, for the sake of religion, food which is pure, which he has neither himself prepared, nor caused another to prepare, such eating is called the fruit of a perpetual fast. Thought is the root, words are the trunk, deeds are the spreading branches of religion's tree. Let its roots be strong and firm, and the whole tree will bear fruit." [11]

The visible forms of the bodies that are the vehicles of the manifestation of dharma come and go; they are like the falling drops of rain, which, ever passing, bring into sight and support the presence of the rainbow. What "is" (*sat*) is that radiance of being which shines through the man or woman enacting perfectly the part of dharma. What "is not" (*asat*) is that which once was not and soon will not be; namely, the mere phenomenon that seems to the organs of sense to be an independent body, and therewith disturbs our repose by arousing reactions—of fear, desire, pity, jealousy, pride, submission, or aggression—reactions addressed, not to what is made manifest, but to its vehicle. The Sanskrit *sat* is the present participle of the verbal root *as,* "to be, to exist, to live"; *as* means "to belong to, to be in the possession of, to fall to the share of"; also "to happen to or to befall any one, to arise, spring out, occur"; *as* means "to suffice," also "to tend to, to turn out or prove to be; to stay, reside, dwell; to be in a particular relation, to be affected." Therefore *sat,* the present participle, means, literally, "being, existing, existent"; also "true, essential, real." With reference to human beings, *sat* means "good, virtuous, chaste, noble, worthy; venerable, respectable; learned, wise." *Sat* means also "right, proper, best, and excellent," as well as "handsome, beautiful." Employed as a masculine noun, it denotes "a good or virtuous man, a sage"; as a neuter noun, "that which really exists, entity, existence, essence; reality, the really existent truth; the Good"; and "Brahman, the Holy Power, the Supreme Self." The feminine form of the noun, *satī,* means "a good and virtuous wife" and "a female ascetic." *Satī* was the name assumed by the universal Goddess when she became incar-

[11] *Pārśvanātha-caritra* 3. 255-283; Burlingame, *loc. cit.*, pp. 442-443.

nate as the daughter of the old divinity Dakṣa in order to become the perfect wife of Śiva.[12] And *satī,* furthermore, is the Sanskrit original form of the word that in English now is "suttee," denoting the self-immolation of the Hindu widow on her husband's funeral pyre—an act consummating the perfect identification of the individual with her role, as a living image of the romantic Hindu ideal of the wife. She is the goddess Satī herself, reincarnate; the śakti, or projected life-energy, of her spouse. Her lord, her enlivening principle, having passed away, her remaining body can be only *a-sat,* non-*sat*: "unreal, non-existent, false, untrue, improper; not answering its purpose; bad, wicked, evil, vile." *Asat,* as a noun, means "non-existence, non-entity; untruth, falsehood; an evil," and in its feminine form, *asatī,* "an unchaste wife."

The tale of the queen, the saint, and the king teaches that Truth (*sat-ya*: "is-ness") must be rooted in the heart. The Act of Truth has to build out from there. And consequently, though dharma, the fulfillment of one's inherited role in life, is the traditional basis of this Hindu feat of virtue, nevertheless, a heartfelt truth of any order has its force. Even a shameful truth is better than a decent falsehood—as we shall learn from the following witty Buddhist tale.

The youth Yaññadatta had been bitten by a poisonous snake. His parents carried him to the feet of an ascetic, laid him down, and said, "Reverend sir, monks know simples and charms; heal our son."

"I know no simples; I am not a physician."

"But you are a monk; therefore out of charity for this youth perform an Act of Truth."

The ascetic replied, "Very well, I will perform an Act of Truth." He laid his hand on Yaññadatta's head and recited the following stanza:

[12] Cf. Zimmer, *The King and the Corpse,* pp. 264-285.

For but a week I lived the holy life
With tranquil heart in quest of merit.

The life I've lived for fifty years
Since then, I've lived against my will.

By this truth, health!
Poison is struck down! Let Yaññadatta live!

Immediately the poison came out of Yaññadatta's breast and sank into the ground.

The father then laid his hand on Yaññadatta's breast and recited the following stanza:

Never did I like to see a stranger
Come to stay. I never cared to give.

But my dislike, the monks and Brāhmans
Never knew, all learned as they were.

By this truth, health!
Poison is struck down! Let Yaññadatta live!

Immediately the poison came out of the small of Yaññadatta's back and sank into the ground.

The father bade the mother perform an Act of Truth, but the mother replied, "I have a Truth, but I cannot recite it in your presence."

The father answered, "Make my son whole anyhow!" So the mother recited the following stanza:

No more, my son, do I now hate this snake malignant
That out of a crevice came and bit you, than I do your father!

By this truth, health!
Poison is struck down! Let Yaññadatta live!

Immediately the rest of the poison sank into the ground, and Yaññadatta got up and began to frisk about.[13]

This is a tale that could be taken as a text for psychoanalysis. The opening up of the repressed truth, deeply hidden beneath the years of lies and dead actions that have killed the son (i.e., have killed the future, the life, of this miserable, hypocritical, self-deceiving household), suffices, like magic, to clear the venom from the poor, paralyzed body, and then all of that deadness (*asat*), "non-existence," is truly non-existent. Life breaks forth anew, in strength, and the living is spliced back to what was living. The night of nonentity between is gone.

3.

Satyāgraha

This principle of the power of truth, which we all recognize in our personal histories as well as in what we have been able to fathom of the private histories of our friends, Mahātma Gandhi is applying, in contemporary India, to the field and problems of international politics.[14] Mahātma Gandhi's program of *satyāgraha,* "holding (*āgraha*) to the truth (*satya*)," is an attempt to carry this ancient Indo-Āryan idea into play against what would seem to the eye to be the vastly superior powers of the highly mechanized, industrially supported, military and political equipment of the Anglo-Saxon's victorious machine of universal empire. For when Great Britain, at the opening of the first World

[13] *Jātaka* 44. Burlingame, *loc. cit.,* pp. 447-448.

[14] *Editor's note:* This lecture was delivered in the spring of 1943.

War, promised freedom to India in exchange for co-operation in the European battle to prevent Germany and Austria from breaking the iron ring of their maṇḍala, she committed herself to something which, when the hour of her extremity had passed, she simply brushed aside as inconvenient to her own prosperity. By that failure in truthfulness, the government of India immediately became *a-sat,* "non-existent, evil, not answering its purpose; a nonentity," in other words, tyrannical, monstrous, contrary to nature. English rule in India thereby became cut off from the divine vital sources of true being that sustain all earthly phenomena, and was as much as dead: something large that still might cling, like a dead thing, but could be sloughed off by the operation of a higher principle.

The higher principle is Truth, as manifest in dharma, "law: that which holds together, supports, upholds." Government, "law," based on "untruth" is an anomaly—according to Mahātma Gandhi's archaic, pre-Persian, native Indo-Āryan point of view. Great Britain's perennial punitive aggressions to put down the "lawlessness" of those who challenged the jurisdiction of her "laws" based on lawlessness were to be countered, following Gandhi's program, not in kind, but by the soul force that would automatically come into play as a result of a steadfast communal holding (*āgraha*) to truth (*satya*). The grip of the tyrant nation would disintegrate. The play of its own lawlessness throughout the world would be its own undoing; one had only to wait until it took itself apart. Meanwhile, in piety, decency, and the faultless practice—with faith (*śraddhā*)—of its own ageless dharma, the land of India must remain with its passions of violence rightly curbed, firm in that power which is the mother of power, namely Truth.

"Whatever Sovereign," we read in Kauṭilya's *Arthaśāstra,* "even one whose dominion extends to the ends of the earth, is of perverted disposition and ungoverned senses, must quickly perish. The whole of this science has to do with a victory over the powers of perception and action." [15] That is the other, the secret, side of *matsya-nyāya,* the principle of the fish. To us of the West, such a statement in a work of the kind that we have discussed in our former lectures may seem an insincere simulation of political "idealism." But Kauṭilya's work is absolutely devoid of such pretensions. Hypocrisy is taught as a political device, not employed as an excuse for teaching. To understand how such a realist as the first chancellor of the Maurya dynasty could have intended the above statement to be taken seriously, the Western reader must bear in mind that always, in India, the Holy Power has been taken seriously. The Brāhmans, able to control and deploy it by means of their magic formulae, were indispensable advisers and assistants to the kings; the Holy Power could be a secret weapon in their hands. They did not think of the law of the fish as something contrary to the law of spiritual self-mastery. Might wins, they knew, and might makes right. But, according to their view, there are many kinds of might, and the mightiest might of all is that of the Holy Power. This, furthermore, is also "right"; for it is nothing less than the essence and manifestation of Truth itself.[16]

Ahiṁsā, "non-violence, non-killing," is the first principle in the dharma of the saint and sage—the first step to the self-mastery by which the great yogīs lift themselves out of the range of normal human action. They attain through it to such a state of power that when and if the saint steps again into the world, he is literally a superman. We have heard of this ideal also in the West; [17] but we have yet to see a whole continent attempt to

[15] *Arthaśāstra* 1. 6.

[16] "As regards Unrighteousness, it may be said that, even when of great proportions, it is incapable of so much as touching Righteousness, which is always protected by Time, and shines like a blazing fire" (*Mahābhārata* 13. 164. 7).

[17] "But I say unto you, That ye resist not evil: but whosoever shall smite thee on thy right cheek, turn to him the other also. And if any

bring the principle into action, seriously, in the world—that is to say, in the world that seems to us the really serious one, the world of international affairs. Gandhi's program of satyāgraha, his national "firm grasping of truth," in strict adherence to the first principle of India's yoga mastery, *ahiṁsā,* "non-killing, non-violence," is a serious, very brave, and potentially vastly powerful modern experiment in the ancient Hindu science of transcending the sphere of lower powers by entering that of higher. Gandhi is confronting Great Britain's untruth (*asatya*) with India's truth (*satya*); British compromise with Hindu holy dharma. This is a wizard priest-battle, waged on the colossal, modern scale, and according to principles derived from the textbooks, not of the Royal Military College, but of Brahman.

4.

The Palace of Wisdom

THE SOUL-POWER brought into action by such a technique, and such a thorough system of anonymous identification, as that which characterizes and supports the orthodox Hindu way of life is derived from levels of the deep unconscious that are normally sealed to the self-conscious individual operating in terms of rational values consciously ascertained. The psychological inflation, the feeling of supranormal, suprapersonal significance, that we

man will sue thee at the law, and take away thy coat, let him have thy cloke also. And whosoever shall compel thee to go a mile, go with him twain. Give to him that asketh thee, and from him that would borrow of thee turn not thou away" (Matthew 5: 39-42).

of the modern world can sometimes feel when, in moments of special solemnity, we find ourselves enacting one of those great archetypal roles that it has been the destiny of mankind to keep in play throughout the millenniums (the bride, the madonna, the marching warrior, the judge, the teaching sage), the civilization of India has rendered permanent and normal. The accidents of the individual personality are systematically disregarded: the individual is asked, always, to identify himself with one or another of the timeless, permanent roles that constitute the whole pattern and fabric of society. Traits of personality of course remain and are readily perceptible, but always in strict subordination to the demands of the part. All of life, all the time, has the quality, consequently, of a great play, long known and loved, with its standard moments of joy and tragedy, through which the individuals move both as actors and as audience. All is radiant with the poetry of epic timelessness.

But the other face of the picture—of this wonderful mood and mode of general inflation—is, of course, deflation, hell: the utter wreck and hopelessness of the one who, through no matter what fault, goes off the road. The wife who has failed to keep immaculate her representation of the role of Satī; the field marshal conspicuously incompetent in his duty to the king; the Brāhman who has been unable to resist a lure of love outside the taboo-barriers of his caste: such failures represent threats to the stability of the structure. Should such actions become general, the entire piece would disintegrate. And so these mere individuals, as a group, are simply hurled into outer darkness, where there is weeping and gnashing of teeth. They are nothing (*a-sat*), outcast. Their act was their own; their tragedy is their own. Nobody knows what their state has now come to be, nobody cares. This is the kind of failure that in Japan is the proper cause for hara-kiri. The antithesis of the general dream of life is thus the personal shipwreck (it cannot be called even tragedy) of the individual who has been a failure in his part.

"The road of excess," writes William Blake, "leads to the palace of wisdom."[18] Only when pressed to excess does anything generate its opposite. And so we find that in India, where the pattern of identification with the social roles is carried to such an extreme that the whole content of the collective unconscious is emptied into the sphere of action during the first half of the individual's lifetime, when the period of the first two āśramas has been fulfilled a violent countermovement in the psyche transports the individual to the extreme of the other pole, and he rests, anonymous as ever, but in the antarctic, now, of absolute non-identification. We all, in the West as well as in the Orient, have to identify, if we are to participate at all in the life of our society, the course of history, and the general work of the world. One has always to be something—student, father, mother, engineer. But in the Hindu system respect for this necessity has been carried to such excess that the whole of life has become petrified in a rigid icon based on principle; beyond that, outside the social frame, is the void of the unmanifest, to which one can pass when the lesson of the first half of life has been learned—the lesson of the gods; and to which one then passes automatically, compulsively, as though driven by the whole weight of a counterdrive of commensurate reaction. "I would thou wert cold or hot. So then because thou art lukewarm, and neither cold nor hot, I will spue thee out of my mouth."[19] Only because all has been given is the individual free to enter at last into the sphere beyond possession and belief.

We all have to identify ourselves with something and "belong" —but cannot and should not try to seek fulfillment in this attitude. For the recognition of distinctions between things, the differentiation of this from that, which is implicit in and basic to this natural effort, pertains to the sphere of mere appearance, the realm of birth and death (*saṁsāra*). India's popular deifica-

[18] *The Marriage of Heaven and Hell,* "Proverbs of Hell."

[19] Revelation 3: 15-16.

tion of everything, every style of being, is no less absurd, finally, than the Western scientific irreligiosity, which, with its "nothing but," pretends to reduce all to the sphere of rational and relative understanding—the power of the sun as well as the momentum of love. Relativism and absolutism equally, when total, are perverse—because convenient. They oversimplify for the purposes of fruitful action. They are not concerned with truth, but with results. So long as one does not comprehend that everything includes everything else, or at least that it is also other than it seems, and that such antinomies as the opposites of good and evil, true and false, this and that, profane and holy, may extend as far as to the boundaries of thought but do not belong beyond, one is bound still to the dustbin of saṁsāra, subject to the nescience that retains the consciousness within the worlds of rebirth. So long as one makes distinctions and excludes or excommunicates, one is the servant and agent of error.

"Oho! I am Consciousness itself. The world is like a juggler's show. So how and where can there be any thought in me of acceptance and rejection?

"From Brahmā down to the clump of grass, I verily am all: one who knows this for certain becomes free from conflict, pure, peaceful, and indifferent to what is attained and not attained.

"Completely give up such distinction as 'I am He' and 'I am not this.' Consider all as the Self and be desireless and happy." [20]

Exclusion, the rejection of anything, is sin and self-deception, is the subjection of the whole to a part, is violence enacted against the omnipresent truth and essence, the finite superordinating itself to the infinite. And whoever thus presumes (that is to say, whoever is still behaving like a civilized human being) cripples and abridges the revealed reality, and therewith himself. His punishment fits his crime, the sin itself being its own penalty; for the commission is at once the penalty and expression of the sinner's own inadequacy. "Therefore," as we are wisely warned,

[20] *Aṣṭāvakra Saṁhitā* 7.5; 11.7; 15.15.

"when thou doest thine alms, do not sound a trumpet before thee, as the hypocrites do in the synagogues and in the streets, that they may have glory of men. Verily I say unto you, They have their reward."[21] Herein lies the secret practical joke of reality, working itself out like a chain-effect, world without end—the cruel point of the gods' Olympian laughter.

But, on the other hand, anyone who, in order to be closed to nothing, takes in all without distinction is equally fooled and guilty; for then it is the distinction between things that is being disregarded, and the hierarchy of values. The intoxicating, devastating "All is God" of the *Bhagavad Gītā,* though it recognizes that there exists a difference in the degrees of divine manifestation, yet so insists upon the colossal fact of the divinity of all things that in contrast the distinctions may too easily seem negligible.

There has never been found any definitive, general theoretical solution to this world dilemma, with which one might safely rest. Truth, validity, actuality, subsist only *in actu:* in the unremitting play of enlightened consciousness on the facts of daily life as expressed in the decisions made from moment to moment, the crises of sacrifice and laying hold, the acts of Yea and Nay: only in the work, that is to say, wrought by a being in whom Enlightenment is continuously alive as a present force.[22] And the first step to the attainment of such redemptive alertness is to leave behind, with an irrevocable decision, the way, the gods, and the ideals of the orthodox, institutionalized dharma.

So it was that Jesus while treading the soil of Palestine seemed a temperamental, whimsical savior, in his violent repudiation of the petrified sanctimoniousness, hard-hearted ritualism, and in-

[21] Matthew 6: 2.

[22] This idea is represented in Mahāyāna Buddhism by the ideal of the Bodhisattva, the "One whose quick is Enlightenment," and in Hinduism by the Jīvanmukta, the "One released in life." (Cf. *infra,* pp. 441-455, 534-559.)

tellectual callousness of the Pharisees. Equally shocking today to a congregation in our dignified churches would seem the burning words recorded of him in the gospel according to Matthew: "Verily I say unto you, That the publicans and the harlots go into the kingdom of God before you." [23] The point of this rebuke would be lost, however, in India, where harlotry is strictly institutional, and where the gods and the blessed in heaven, as well as the courtesan, are regarded as linked to the virtue (*dharma*), delights (*kāma*), and attainments (*artha*), of the prodigious round of the created world. There, if one is to escape from the dreadful pall of the self-complacent, sanctified community, the sole recourse is to plunge even below the below, beyond the beyond, to break the mask even of the highest god. This is the work of "release" (*mokṣa*), the task of the naked sage.

[23] Matthew 21: 31.

PART III

THE PHILOSOPHIES OF ETERNITY

I. JAINISM

1.

Pārśva

"At the mere mention of the name of the Lord Pārśva disturbances cease, the sight (*darśana)* of him destroys the fear of rebirths, and his worship removes the guilt of sin." [1]

One should make images of Pārśva and pay them homage for the effect of his darśana, not because of any hope that the great being himself might condescend to assist a worshiper; for the Jaina saviors—the "Makers of the River-Crossing" (*tīrthaṅkaras*) as they are called—dwell in a supernal zone at the ceiling of the universe, beyond the reach of prayer; there is no possibility of their assistance descending from that high and luminous place to the clouded sphere of human effort. In the popular phases of the Jaina household cult the usual Hindu gods are implored for minor boons (prosperity, long life, male offspring, etc.), but the

[1] *Editor's note:* I have not been able to locate the text used by Dr. Zimmer for his version of the Life of Pārśvanātha and so cannot give references for the quotations in the present chapter. The version of the Life in Bhāvadevasūri's *Pārśvanātha Caritra* (edited by Shravak Pandit Hargovinddas and Shravak Pandit Bechardas, Benares, 1912; summarized by Maurice Bloomfield, *The Life and Stories of the Jaina Savior Pārçvanātha,* Baltimore, 1919) agrees in the main, but differs in many minor details.

supreme objects of Jaina contemplation, the Tīrthaṅkaras, have passed beyond the godly governors of the natural order. Jainism, that is to say, is not atheistic; it is transtheistic. Its Tīrthaṅkaras —who represent the proper goal of all human beings, the goal in fact of all living entities in this living universe of reincarnating monads—are "cut off" (*kevala*) from the provinces of creation, preservation, and destruction, which are the concerns and spheres-of-operation of the gods. The Makers of the River-Crossing are beyond cosmic event as well as the problems of biography; they are transcendent, cleaned of temporality, omniscient, actionless, and absolutely at peace. The contemplation of their state as represented in their curiously arresting images, coupled with the graded, progressively rigorous exercises of Jaina ascetic discipline, brings the individual through the course of many lifetimes gradually past the needs and anxieties of human prayer, past even the deities who respond to prayer, and beyond the blissful heavens in which those gods and their worshipers abide, into the remote, transcendent, "cut-off" zone of pure, uninflected existence to which the Crossing-Makers, the Tīrthaṅkaras, have cleaved the way.

The foundation of Jainism has been attributed by Occidental historians to Vardhamāna Mahāvīra, a contemporary of the Buddha, who died c. 526 B.C. The Jainas themselves, however, regard Mahāvīra not as the first but as the last of their long series of Tīrthaṅkaras. The traditional number of these is twenty-four, and their line is supposed to have descended through the centuries from prehistoric times.[2] The earlier of them undoubtedly are mythological, and mythology has been poured abundantly into the biographies of the rest, nevertheless it is becoming increasingly evident that there must be some truth in the Jaina tradition of the great antiquity of their religion. At least with respect to Pārśva, the Tīrthaṅkara just preceding Mahāvīra, we

[2] Cf. *supra,* p. 60, Editor's note, and Appendix B.

have grounds for believing that he actually lived and taught, and was a Jaina.

Pārśvanātha, "the Lord Pārśva," is supposed to have attained liberation about two hundred and forty-six years before Vardhamāna Mahāvīra, the historic "founder" of the Jaina religion. If 526 B.C. be taken as the year of the Lord Mahāvīra's gaining of nirvāṇa,[3] 772 B.C. may then be said to be that of Pārśvanātha's. According to the legend, he dwelt in the world exactly one hundred years, having left home at the age of thirty to become an ascetic; from which it may be concluded that he was born about 872 B.C. and left his palace around 842.[4] Pārśvanātha is reckoned as the twenty-third in the legendary series of the Tīrthaṅkaras, having entered the world eighty-four thousand years after the nirvāna of Bhagavan Ariṣṭanemi, the twenty-second of this long spiritual line. His life, or rather lives, following as they do the pattern typical for the orthodox biographies of Jaina saints, will serve as our introduction to the trials and victories of the last and supreme of the four aims of Indian life, that of spiritual release (*mokṣa*). The saint's biography is offered as a model for all those who would put off the heavy load of earthly birth.

He had been dwelling and ruling as an Indra in the thirteenth

[3] The term *nirvāṇa* belongs by no means exclusively to Buddhist tradition. The metaphor is derived from the image of the flame. *Nir-va* means "to blow out; to cease to draw breath." *Nirvāṇa* is "blown out": the fire of desire, for want of fuel, is quenched and pacified.

[4] One hundred lunar years is regarded as the ideal length of life. The flawless saint and man of virtue is endowed with perfect health by reason of his pure, ascetic conduct; and by reason of his meritorious deeds in former lives he is blessed with a bright karma. The latter results in a well-balanced constitution of unsurpassed strength. Though one hundred years may be an overstatement, Pārśva probably reached, as did the Buddha and many other famous Indian ascetics, a remarkably old age. It may be, therefore, that the Jaina tradition of his hundred years of life is not far from the mark.

heaven [5] when his time to re-enter the world of men arrived and he descended to the womb of Queen Vāmā, the beautiful consort of King Aśvasena. All who beheld the child as he grew to manhood were amazed by his beauty and strength, but particularly by his indifference to the concerns, delights, and temptations of the palace. Neither his father's noble throne nor female loveliness could hold his interest; all that he ever desired was to renounce the world. Unwillingly the family consented to the departure of the prince, and the gods at that moment descended to celebrate the "Great Renunciation." They transported him in a heavenly palanquin to the forest, where he took his vow of *sannyāsa:* complete renunciation of the world—the sign of his irrevocable decision to annihilate his mortal nature. Years passed; and then the gods again descended—for Pārśvanātha now had achieved omniscience, having annihilated his karma. Thereafter, as a Tīrthaṅkara, a living savior, he taught and moved among mankind. And when he had fulfilled his earthly mission, being then one hundred years of age, his life-monad became separated

[5] *Editor's note:* The Vedic Āryans, like the Homeric Greeks, offered sacrifices to deities in human form but of a superhuman order. Indra, like Zeus, was the lord of rain, the hurler of the thunderbolt, and the king of gods; no human being could hope to become either Zeus or Indra. The non-Āryan, Dravidian peoples of India, on the other hand (cf. *supra,* p. 60, Editor's note), for whom reincarnation was a basic law, regarded deities simply as beings (formerly human or animal) who had merited bliss. When the merit expired their high seats were vacated to other candidates and they descended again into human, animal, or even demonic forms.

Following the Vedic period a synthesis of these two beliefs—the Āryan and the non-Āryan—yielded a generally recognized Indian system (recognized by Buddhism and Jainism as well as by orthodox Hinduism) in which the names and roles of the Vedic gods represented the high positions to which virtuous souls attained. Moreover, since in the non-Āryan cosmos there had been a multitude of heavens, Indras (i.e., the kings of the various godly realms) were heaped one above the other, storey above storey. Hence we read that the saint Pārśvanātha "had been dwelling and ruling as an Indra in the thirteenth heaven."

from its earthly coil and rose to the ceiling of the universe, where it now abides forever.

That, briefly, is the tale of the probable life of this ancient teacher—embellished with a few mythological details. But in India, the homeland of reincarnation, one biography is not enough; the lives of saints and saviors are provided with preludes —infinitely expansible—of earlier saintly existences, which follow, in general, a consistent pattern. Showing the spiritual hero first on lower, even animal, planes of existence and experience, enacting his characteristic part of the magnanimous being, they follow his gradual progress (with its blissful interludes between lives, spent in one or another of the traditional heavens, reaping the rewards of earthly virtue), until, having progressed through many levels of experience, he at last arrives at that supreme state of embodied spirituality which distinguished his actual, historical biography. Volumes of such earlier births have been provided for the Buddha, and pious legend has invented a long series also for Pārśvanātha.

One of the most striking features of these tales of the earlier lives of Pārśvanātha is the emphasis throughout on the ruthless opposition of a dark brother whose development is the very antithesis of that of the savior. Pārśvanātha increases in virtue, but his dark brother, simultaneously, in evil, until the principle of light represented in the Tīrthaṅkara finally wins, and the brother himself is saved.[6] The enmity between the two is represented as

[6] *Editor's note:* This clean-cut dualism, if Dr. Zimmer's view of the antiquity of the Jaina tradition is correct, throws a new light on the problem of the backgrounds and nature of the "reforms" of the Persian prophet Zoroaster. It has been customary to regard these, with their rigorous moral emphasis and strictly systematized dualism, as representing the spiritual innovation of a single, great, prophetic personality. If Dr. Zimmer's view is correct, however, the pre-Āryan, Dravidian religion was rigorously moral and systematically dualistic years before the birth of Zoroaster. This would seem to suggest that in Zoroastrianism a resurgence of pre-Āryan factors in Iran, following a period of Āryan supremacy, may be represented

having begun in their ninth incarnation before the last. They had been born, that time, as the sons of Viśvabhūti, the prime minister of a certain prehistoric king named Aravinda. And it so happened that their father, one day thinking: "Transitory surely is this world," went away on the path of emancipation, leaving his wife behind with the two sons and a great store of wealth. The elder son, Kamaṭha, was passionate and crafty, whereas the younger, Marubhūti, was eminently virtuous (the latter, of course, being the one who is to be Pārśvanātha in their final birth),[7] and so when their king one time had to leave his kingdom on a campaign against a distant enemy, he committed the safety of the palace not to the elder brother but to the younger, Marubhūti; and the elder, in sinful anger, then seduced his brother's wife. The adultery being discovered, the king when he returned asked Marubhūti what the punishment should be. The future Tīrthaṅkara advised forgiveness. But the king, commanding that the adulterer's face should be painted black, had him seated, facing backwards, on an ass, conducted through the capital, and expelled from the realm.

Deprived thus of honor, home, property, and family, Kamaṭha

—something comparable to the Dravidian resurgence in India in the forms of Jainism and Buddhism. Of significance in this connection is the fact that the Persian "dark brother"—the tyrant Ḍaḥḥāk (or Azhi Dahāka)—is represented, like Pārśvanātha (*see Plate VI*), with serpents springing from his shoulders.

In the folklore and mythology of the antique, pre-Āryan civilizations of the Old World the motif of the contrary brothers is by no means uncommon. One has only to recall the Old Testament legends of Cain and Abel, Esau and Jacob; and among the most ancient Egyptian tales preserved to us is "The Story of the Two Brothers" (cf. G. Maspero, *Popular Stories of Ancient Egypt,* New York and London, 1915, pp. 1-20), where we find not only a strict opposition of good and evil, but also a startling series of magical rebirths.

[7] Likewise in the Biblical legends of Cain and Abel, and Esau and Jacob, as well as in the Egyptian "Story of the Two Brothers" (cf. Editor's note, *supra*), the evil brother is the elder and the good the younger.

devoted himself in the wilderness to the most extreme austerities, not in a humble spirit of renunciation or contrition, but with the intent to acquire superhuman, demonic powers with which to win revenge. When Marubhūti was apprised of these penances, he thought that his brother had at last become purified, and therefore, in spite of the warnings of the king, paid him a visit, thinking to invite him home. He discovered Kamaṭha standing—as had been his custom day and night—holding on his upstretched hands a great slab of stone, overcoming by that painful exercise the normal states of human weakness. But when the future Tīrthaṅkara bowed in obeisance at his feet, the terrible hermit, beholding this gesture of conciliation, was so filled with rage that he flung down the great stone on Marubhūti's head, killing him as he bowed. The aścetics of the penance-grove, from whom the monster had learned his techniques of self-affliction, expelled him immediately from their company, and he sought refuge among a wild tribe of Bhils. He became a highwayman and murderer, and in due course died, following a life of crime.

This grotesque story sets the stage for a long and complicated series of encounters, full of surprises—a typically Indian affair of deaths and reappearances, illustrating the moral theory of rebirth. The wicked Kamaṭha passes through a number of forms paralleling those of his virtuous, gradually maturing brother, reappearing time and again to repeat his sin of aggression, while Marubhūti, the future Tīrthaṅkara, becoming more and more harmonious within, gains the power to accept his recurrent death with equanimity. Thus the dark brother of this Jaina legend actually serves the light—even as Judas, in the Christian, serves the cause of Jesus.[8] And just as Judas' legendary suicide by hanging parallels the crucifixion of his Lord, so the descents of Kamaṭha into one or another of the many subterranean Indian hells parallel the complementary ascents of his future savior into the

[8] Judas, indeed, is represented in a number of medieval legends as the elder brother of Jesus.

storeys of the heavens. It must be noted, however, that in India the concepts of hell and heaven differ from those of Christianity; for the individual's residence in them is not eternal. They are, rather, purgatorial stations, representing degrees of realization experienced on the way to the ultimate transcendence of all qualitative existence whatsoever. Hence the dark brother is not, like Judas, eternally damned for his service to the Lord, but in the end is redeemed from his bondage in the spheres of ignorance and pain.

According to our serial of tales, then, though both Kamaṭha and Marubhūti have died, this death is not to be the end of their adventure. The good king Aravinda, whom Marubhūti had served as minister, was moved, following the death of his officer, to abandon the world and take up the life of a hermit; the cause of his decision being a comparatively insignificant incident. Always pious, he was planning to build a Jaina sanctuary, when one day he beheld floating in the sky a cloud that looked like a majestic, slowly moving temple. Watching this with rapt attention, he became inspired with the idea of constructing his place of worship in just that form. So he sent in haste for brushes and paints with which to set it down; but when he turned again, the form had already changed. A weird thought then occurred to him. "Is the world," he mused, "but a series of such passing states? Why then should I call anything my own? What is the good of continuing in this career of king?" He summoned his son, installed him on the throne, and departed from the kingdom, became an aimless mendicant, and wandered from one wilderness to the next.

And so he chanced, one day, upon a great assemblage of saints in the depths of a certain forest, engaged in various forms of meditation. He joined their company, and had not been long among them when a mighty elephant, running mad, entered the grove—a dangerous event that sent most of the hermits to the four directions. Aravinda, however, remained standing rigidly, in a profound state of contemplation. The elephant, rushing about, presently came directly before the meditating king, but instead of trampling him, became suddenly calm when it perceived his absolute immobility. Lowering its trunk it went down on its great front knees in obeisance. "Why are you continuing in acts of injury?" the voice of Aravinda then was heard to ask. "There is no greater sin than that of injuring other beings. Your incarnation in this form is the result of demerits acquired at the moment of your violent death. Give up these sinful acts; begin to practice vows; a happy state will then stand in store for you."

The clarified vision of the contemplative had perceived that the elephant was his former minister, Marubhūti. Owing to the violence of the death and the distressing thoughts that had been harbored in the instant of pain, the formerly pious man was now in this inferior and rabid incarnation. His name was Vajraghoṣa, "Thundering Voice of the Lightning," and his mate was the former wife of his adulterous brother. Hearing the voice of the king whom he had served, he recalled his recent human life, took the vows of a hermit, received religious instruction at the feet of Aravinda, and determined to commit no further acts of nuisance. Thenceforward the mighty beast ate but a modicum of grass—only enough to keep its body and soul together; and this saintly diet, together with a program of austerities, brought it down so much in weight that it became very quiet and emaciated. Nevertheless, it never relaxed, even for a moment, from its devout contemplation of the Tīrthaṅkaras, those "Exalted Ones" (*parameṣṭhins*) now serene at the zenith of the universe.

Vajraghoṣa, from time to time, would go to the bank of a nearby river to quench his thirst, and on one of these occasions was killed by an immense serpent. This was his former brother, the perennial antagonist of his career, who, having expired in deep iniquity, had been reincarnated in this malignant form.

The very sight of the saintly pachyderm proceeding piously to the river stirred the old spirit of revenge, and the serpent struck. Its deadly poison ran like fire through the loose and heavy skin. But in spite of terrific pain, Vajraghoṣa did not forget his hermit vows. He died the death called "the peaceful death of absolute renunciation," and was born immediately in the twelfth heaven as the god Śaśi-prabhā, "Splendor of the Moon."

This completes a little cycle of three saintly lives (human, animal, and heavenly), matched by three of the antagonist (human, animal, and infernal), everything about the brothers having been in contrast, even their asceticism. For the rigorous practices of the revengeful Kamaṭha had been undertaken not to transcend, but to guarantee, the projects of ego, whereas those of the pious Vajraghoṣa represented a spirit of absolute self-abnegation. Vajraghoṣa, it should be observed, was here the model of the pious devotee in the earlier stages of religious experience—he was what in Christianity would be termed one of God's sheep. The ideal in India, however, is to begin but not to remain in this simple devotional plane; and so the lives of the future Tīrthaṅkara roll on.

"Splendor of the Moon," the happy deity, dwelt amidst the abundant pleasures of his heaven for sixteen oceans (*sagaras*) of time, yet did not relapse even there from the regular practice of pious acts. He was reborn, therefore, as a fortunate prince named Agnivega ("Strength of Fire"), who, on the death of his father, ascended the throne of his domain.

One day a homeless sage appeared, asking to converse with the young king, and he discoursed on the way of liberation. Immediately Agnivega experienced an awakening of the religious sense, and the world abruptly lost its charm for him. He joined his teacher's monastic following and through the regular practice of graduated penances diminished within himself both his attachment and his aversion to worldly things, until at last all was supplanted by a sublime indifference. Then he retired to a cave in the high Himalayas and there, steeped in the profoundest contemplation, lost all consciousness of the external world—but while in this state was again sharply bitten by a snake. The poison burned; but he did not lose his peaceful equilibrium. He welcomed death, and expired in a spiritual attitude of sublime submission.

The serpent, of course, was again the usual enemy, who, following his murder of the elephant, had descended to the fifth hell where the sufferings for a period of sixteen oceans of time had been indescribable. Then he had returned to the earth, still in the form of a snake, and at the sight of Agnivega committed again his characteristic sin. The hermit-king, at the very moment of his death, was elevated to the status of a god—this time for a period of twenty-two oceans of years; but the serpent descended to the sixth hell, where its torments were even greater than in the fifth.

Once again a cycle has been completed; this time comprising one earthly life and one heavenly-and-infernal interlude. The pattern of three in the early cycle gave stress to the earthly transformation of an individual whose center of spiritual gravity had just been shifted from material to spiritual things. For Marubhūti, the virtuous brother and the trusted minister of the king, was a man of noble disposition in the service of the state, whereas Vajraghoṣa stood at the beginning of a career specifically saintly. Though apparently on a lower plane than the king's minister, the elephant was actually on the first step of a higher series: the sudden death of the man of affairs and the birth, then, of the childlike, wild but tractable lamb-elephant of God symbolizing precisely the crisis of one who has undergone a religious conversion. This crisis begins the series of the soul's mighty strides to the height, the first step being that of spiritual realization—as in the life, just reported, of the kingly hermit, Agnivega; the second that of the Cakravartin, bringer of peace on earth; the third a lifetime of miraculous holiness; and the last the step of the Tīrthaṅkara, breaking the way to the transcendental ceiling of the world.

And so this tale of transformations goes on now to recount, with another sudden shift of circumstance, how Queen Lakṣmīvatī, the pure and lovely consort of a certain king named Vajravīrya ("Having the Hero-Power of the Thunderbolt"), dreamt in one night five auspicious dreams, from which her husband deduced that some god was about to descend to become his son. Within the year she gave birth to a boy, and on his beautiful little body were found the sixty-four auspicious signs of the Cakravartin. He was named Vajranābha ("Diamond Navel"), became proficient in every branch of learning, and in due time began to rule the realm. The world wheel (*cakra*) [9] lay among the weapons in his royal treasury in the form of a discus of irresistible force; and he conquered the four quarters of the earth with this weapon, compelling all other kings to bow their heads before his throne. He also acquired the fourteen supernatural jewels that are the marks of the glory of the Cakravartin. And yet, surrounded though he was by supreme splendor, he did not forget for so much as a day the precepts of morality, but continued in his worship of the Tīrthaṅkaras and of the living Jaina preceptors—fasting, praying, practicing vows, and performing numerous acts of mercy. A hermit whose name was Kṣemaṅkara therefore came to court; and the Cakravartin, hearing the holy man's delectable words, was released from his last attachment to the world. He renounced his throne and wealth, and departed to practice holy penances in the wilderness, absolutely fearless of the howls of the elephants, jackals, and forest goblins.

But his old enemy had returned to the world, this time as a Bhil, a wild tribesman of the jungle. And in due course the savage hunter chanced upon the place of the meditating former

[9] Cf. *supra*, pp. 128-130.

Cakravartin. The sight of the saintly being in meditation aroused again the ancient hatred. The Bhil remembered his last human incarnation, became fired with a passion for revenge, notched his keenest arrow to the bowstring, aimed, and let fly. Vajranābha died peacefully—absolutely unperturbed. And so he ascended to one of the very highest celestial spheres—the so-called *Madhyagraiveyaka* heaven, which is situated in the middle (*madhya*) of the neck (*grīvā*) of the human-shaped world-organism [10]—and there he became an Ahaṁ-Indra ("I am Indra"); [11] whereas the Bhil, when he died, since he was full of vile and sinful thoughts, descended to the seventh hell—again for a period of indescribable pain.

The next appearance of the future Tīrthaṅkara was in the person of a prince of the Ikṣvāku family (the ruling house of Ayodhyā), and his name was Ānandakumāra. Remaining always a perfect Jaina and fervent worshiper of the Tīrthaṅkaras, he became the King of Kings over an extensive empire. Years passed. Then while standing one day before his looking-glass, he perceived that one of his hairs had turned gray. Immediately, he completed arrangements to have his son assume the throne and himself initiated into the order of the Jaina ascetics, and so he quit the world. His preceptor, this time, was a great sage named Sāgaradatta, under whom (and thanks to an unflagging practice of all the prescribed austerities) he became possessed of superhuman powers. Wherever he went, the trees bent with the weight of fruits, there was no grief or sorrow, the tanks were filled with blooming lotuses and clearest water, and the lions frolicked harmlessly with the fawns. Ānandakumāra passed his time in meditation, the atmosphere for miles around him being full of peace. The birds and animals flocked about him without fear. But then one day the royal saint was set upon by an unquelled lion (the old enemy) who tore him to pieces and

10 This will be discussed *infra,* pp. 241-248.

11 Cf. *supra,* p. 184, Editor's note.

ate him up completely. The death was met, however, with perfect calm. He was reborn in the thirteenth heaven as its Indra, the supreme king of gods.

The future savior remained up there for twenty oceans of years, far aloft among the heavenly mansions, yet always restrained himself like a true Jaina, practicing moral acts with uninterrupted concentration. His detachment from the senses and their pleasures had matured to such a degree that he could withstand even the temptation of the most subtle heavenly delights. He worshiped the Tīrthaṅkaras, who were still far above him, and gave example to the gods of the light of the true faith. He was, indeed, more like their spiritual teacher and savior than their king. And so it was evident that he was now prepared to enact the supreme role of a savior of gods and men. Only once again should he ever descend to earth; this time for that final incarnation which was to mark the culmination of his progress through the round of birth and death.

It is recorded that the Indra of the Hall Sudharma (the celestial storey nearest the earth) addressed Kubera, the lord of goblins, who controls all the treasures of jewels and precious stones hidden in the mountains: "The Indra of the thirteenth heaven, high above me, soon will descend to earth and become incarnate as the son of the king of Benares. He will be the twenty-third Tīrthaṅkara of India. Be pleased, therefore, to rain down the Five Wonders on the kingdom of Benares and on the pious monarch and the faithful queen who are to become the parents of the Tīrthaṅkara."

Thus was announced the beginning of that incarnation (in the main perhaps historical) which we considered briefly at the opening of our present chapter. Kubera, the goblin king, prepared to execute the command, and as a result of his activities there came down from the sky every day, during the six months preceding the descent of the savior Pārśvanātha to the womb of the queen, no less than thirty-five millions of diamond-pieces, flowers from the wish-fulfilling trees in the celestial gardens of the gods, showers of clear water of the sweetest fragrance, divine sounds from the great drums of the most auspicious rain-clouds, and the sweet music of the singing of the deities of the sky. The splendor of Benares increased a thousand fold and the joy of the people knew no bounds. For such are the portents that always signal the beginning of the cosmic sacred ceremonies that celebrate the appearance on earth of a Tīrthaṅkara. The entire world rejoices and participates, with the gods, as chorus, glorifying each sublime event in this great culmination of the life-monad's career to perfection, omniscience, and release.

On a supremely auspicious night, the lovely Queen Vāmā dreamt fourteen auspicious dreams, and the moment King Aśvasena was informed of them he understood that his son would be a savior—either a Cakravartin or a Tīrthaṅkara. The pure monad came down to the royal womb of its last earthly mother in the auspicious spring month known as Vaiśākha,[12] descending amidst celestial celebrations, and the moment it imparted life to the embryo, which had already been three months in the womb (this being the moment of its reception of its own life), the thrones of all the Indras trembled in the heavens and the expectant mother experienced the first motion of her child. The deities came down in palatial aerial cars, and, entering the royal city, celebrated the First Kalyāṇa, "the salutary event of the enlivening of the embryo through the descent of the life-monad into its material body" (*garbha-kalyāṇa*). Seating the king and queen on thrones, they joyfully poured sacred water on them from a golden pitcher, offering prayers to the great being within the womb; and Benares resounded with divine music. The foremost goddesses of heaven were delegated to care for the pregnant lady; and to please her they would converse with her on various entertaining themes. For example, they would play-

[12] A lunar month corresponding partly to April, partly to May.

fully propose difficult questions for her to answer: but the queen could always reply immediately; for she had within her no less a personage than the conqueror of omniscience. Moreover, throughout the period of her blessed pregnancy, she was undisturbed by pain.

When the son was born the thrones of all the Indras trembled, and the gods understood that the Lord had seen the light of day. With pomp they descended for the celebration of the Second Kalyāṇa, "the salutary event of the Savior's birth" (*janma-kalyāṇa*). The child was of a beautiful blue-black complexion,[13] grew rapidly in beauty and young strength, and, as a boy, enjoyed traveling from place to place on horseback and on the mighty backs of the great royal elephants. He frequently sported in the water with the water-gods and in the forest with the gods of the trees and hills. But in all this childlike play—though he indulged in it with the greatest spirit—there was manifest the pure moral sweetness of his extraordinary nature. He assumed and began to practice the twelve basic vows of the adult Jaina householder when he reached the age of eight.[14]

Now Pārśva's maternal grandfather was a king named Mahīpāla, who, when his wife died, became so disconsolate that he renounced his throne and retired to the wilderness to practice the severest disciplines known to the penitential groves. There

[13] He was a scion, that is to say, of the non-Āryan, aboriginal stock of India.

[14] The Jaina householder, 1. must not destroy life, 2. must not tell a lie, 3. must not make unpermitted use of another man's property, 4. must be chaste, 5. must limit his possessions, 6. must make a perpetual and a daily vow to go only in certain directions and certain distances, 7. must avoid useless talk and action, 8. must avoid thought of sinful things, 9. must limit the articles of his diet and enjoyment for the day, 10. must worship at fixed times, morning, noon, and evening, 11. must fast on certain days, and 12. must give charity in the way of knowledge, money, etc., every day. (*Tattvārthādhigama Sūtra,* translated with commentary by J. L. Jaini, Sacred Books of the Jainas, Arrah, no date, Vol. II, pp. 142-143.)

was, however, no real spirit of renunciation in this passionate man. He was an example of that archaic type of cruel asceticism—self-centered though directed to lofty ends—which the Jaina ideal of compassion and self-renunciation was intended to supersede. With matted locks and a deerskin loincloth, full of passion and the darkness of ignorance, storing tremendous energies through self-inflicted sufferings, Mahīpāla moved from forest to forest, until one day he was in the neighborhood of Benares, practicing a particularly arduous spiritual exercise known as the penance of the "Five Fires." [15] It was here that he was accidentally encountered by his grandson, the beautiful child of his lovely daughter Vāmā.

The boy came riding on an elephant, surrounded by the playmates with whom he had entered the jungle; and when the lively company broke upon the grim solitude of the passion-ridden old hermit among the fires, Mahīpāla was beside himself. He cried out to the prince, whom he immediately recognized: "Am I not your mother's father? Was I not born of an illustrious family, and have I not given up all to betake myself to the wilderness? Am I not an anchorite, practicing here the severest possible penances? What a proud little fellow you are, not to greet me with a proper salutation!"

Pārśva and the company halted in amazement.

The old man then got up and seized an ax, which he prepared to bring down on a huge piece of timber—no doubt to work off something of his temper, but ostensibly to cut fuel for his great system of fires. But the boy shouted to make him stop; then explained: "There are dwelling in that log a serpent and his mate: do not murder them for nothing."

Mahīpāla's state of mind was not improved by this peremptory advice. He turned and demanded with searing scorn: "And

[15] Four great blazes are kindled close around the penitent, one in each of the four directions, while the heat of the Indian sun (the "fifth fire") throbs down from above.

who are you? Brahmā? Viṣṇu? Śiva?[16] I perceive that you can see everything, no matter where." He raised his ax and deliberately brought it down. The log was split. And there were the two serpents, cut in half.

The boy's heart bled when he beheld the writhing, dying creatures. "Do you not feel compassion?" he demanded of the old man. "Grandfather, you are without knowledge. These austerities of yours are absolutely worthless."

Mahīpāla, at that, lost all control. "I see, I see, I see!" he cried. "You are a sage, a very great sage. But I am your grandfather. Besides, I am a hermit. I practice the penance of the Five Fires. I stand for days on one leg with lifted arms. I suffer hunger; thirst; break my fast only with dry leaves. Surely it is proper that a youngster, such as you, should call the austerities of his grandfather fruitless and unwise!"

The little prince answered firmly, but in a sweet and wonderfully gentle tone. "The spirit of envy," he said, "infects all of your practices; and you are killing animals here every day with your fires. To injure others, even if only a little, is to be guilty of a great sin; but great suffering is the consequence even of a little sin. Such practices as yours, divorced as they are from right knowledge, are as barren as chaff separated from grain. Give up this meaningless self-torture; follow the way of the Tīrthaṅkaras and perform right acts, in right faith and right knowledge: for that is the only road to emancipation."

The Lord Pārśva then chanted a hymn to the dying serpents and they expired in his presence calmly. He returned to his palace and they—following such a meritorious death—were immediately reborn in the underworld: the male was now Dharaṇendra, "Lord of the Earth" (the cosmic snake, Śeṣa, who

[16] The basic Hindu gods are common to all the great religions of India, Buddhism and Jainism as well as the Hindu sects; cf. *supra,* p. 184, Editor's note.

supports the earth on his head), and the female, Padmāvatī (the goddess Lakṣmī). They enjoyed unbounded delight.

Crotchety old Mahīpāla, it must now be told, was none other than the wicked brother. As a lion, he had slain and eaten the savior at the end of his previous incarnation, and in consequence had been hurled to the sufferings of the fifth hell, where he had remained for a period of seventeen oceans of time. After that, for a period of three oceans of time, he had passed through a number of incarnations in the forms of quadrupeds, during the last of which he performed certain meritorious acts, and in reward he was reborn as this old ruffian. But the words of the grandson bore no fruit. The hermit continued in his unproductive practices, and at last expired.

The prince grew to young manhood, and when he arrived at the age of sixteen his father wished to procure for him a bride, but the youth rejected the idea. "My life," he said, "is not to be as long as that of the first Tīrthaṅkara, the Lord Ṛṣabha; for I am to live to be only one hundred. Sixteen of my short years have already been whiled away in boyish play, whereas in my thirtieth I am to enter the Order. Should I marry for a period so brief, in the hope of knowing a few pleasures, which, after all, are but imperfect?"

The king understood. His son was preparing for the Great Renunciation; all efforts to restrain him would be in vain.

The young man thought within his heart, which now was filled with the spirit of renunciation: "For many long years I enjoyed the status of an Indra; yet the lust for pleasure was not abated. Of what use will a few drops of earthly water be to one whose thirst was not quenched by an ambrosial ocean? The desire for pleasure is only heightened by enjoyment, as the virulence of fire by the addition of fuel. Pleasures at the moment are undoubtedly pleasurable, but their consequences are bad; for to satisfy the cravings of the senses, one is forced to range in the realms of pain, paying no heed to moral injunctions and indulging in the worst vices. Hence the soul is compelled to migrate from birth to birth, entering even into the kingdom of the beasts and passing through the spheres of the sufferings of hell. Therefore, I shall waste no more of my years in the vain pursuits of pleasure."

The future Tīrthaṅkara thereupon entered the "Twelve Meditations" and perceived that the chain of existences is without beginning, as well as painful and impure, and that the self is its own only friend. The thrones of all the Indras trembled in the heavens, and the gods descended to celebrate the Third Kalyāṇa: "the salutary event of the Renunciation" (*sannyāsa-kalyāṇa*). They addressed themselves to the young savior, "The world," they said, "sleeps heavily, enveloped in a cloud of illusion. This is the sleep that will not be dispelled except by the clarion-call of your teaching. You, the Enlightened, the waker of the infatuated soul, are the Savior, the great Sun before whom the lamplike words of mere gods, such as ourselves, are insignificant. You are to do now what you have come to do: namely, assume the vows, annihilate the karma-foe, dispel the darkness of unknowing, and open the road to bliss." They scattered heavenly flowers at his feet.

Four Indras descended, together with their retinues; celestial trumpets blew; the nymphs of heaven began to sing and dance; deities cried out, "Victory to the Lord!" and the Indra of the Sudharma-heaven conducted Pārśva to a throne, which had miraculously appeared. Just as a king, at the culminating moment of the ceremonial of the "King's Quickening" (*rājasūya*), is consecrated by an aspersion of water, so was Pārśva by an elixir from the divine Milky Ocean, which was poured from a pitcher of gold. His body being then adorned with celestial ornaments, he returned to his parents to take his leave of them, and he consoled them with gentle words. The gods thereafter conducted him in a heavenly palanquin to the forest.

The company halted beneath a certain tree, and Pārśva, descending from the palanquin, took his stand upon a stone slab. The tumult of the multitude subsided as, with his own hands, he began to remove his ornaments and garments, one by one. When he was completely naked, renunciation filled his heart. He faced the north, and with folded hands bowed in honor of the Emancipated Ones, having divested himself of desire. Plucking from his head five hairs, he bestowed them on Indra. The god accepted these, and, returning to his heaven, reverently tossed them to the Milky Ocean. Thus during the first quarter of the eleventh bright day of the moon of the month of Pauṣa (December-January), the savior assumed his final vows. Standing in a rigid posture, fasting with absolute endurance, and observing with perfect care the twenty-eight primary and the ninety-four secondary rules of the Order, Pārśva became possessed of what is termed the *manaḥparyāya* knowledge: the knowledge of others' thoughts. Lions and fawns played together about him, while in every part of the forest was a reign of peace.

The great goal, however, was not to be attained without further event; for the antagonist had yet to deal his final stroke. One day, while the Savior was standing perfectly still, erect, absorbed in meditation, the car of a god of the luminary order, Saṁvara by name,[17] was stopped abruptly in its airy course—for not even a god can cut through the radiance of a saint of Pārśva's magnitude, absorbed in meditation. Saṁvara, since he had clairvoyant knowledge, realized what had occurred; but then, suddenly, he knew that the saint was Pārśvanātha.

Now the personage in the chariot was the antagonist again—this time in the form of a minor deity, in consequence of powers gained by the penances of old Mahīpāla. The annoyed god determined, therefore, to resume his ancient battle, making use this time of the supernatural forces that he commanded. And so he brought down a dense and terrible darkness and conjured

[17] Called also Meghamālin, viz. in Bhāvadevasūri's *Pārśvanātha Caritra* (cf. Bloomfield, *op. cit.*, pp. 117-118).

up a howling cyclone. Trees splintered and hurtled through the air. The earth was rent, opening with a roar, and the high peaks fell, shattering to dust; a torrential rain descended. Yet the saint remained unmoved, serene, absolutely lost in his meditation. The god, exceedingly wrathful, became as hideous as he could: face black, mouth vomiting fire, and he was like the god of death, garlanded with a necklace of human heads. When he rushed at Pārśva, gleaming in the night, he fiercely shouted, "Kill! Kill!" but the saint never stirred.

The whole subterranean domain of the serpent supporting the earth began to tremble, and the great Dharaṇendra, "King of Earth," said to his consort, the goddess Padmāvatī: "That compassionate Lord to whose sweet teachings at the time of our death we owe our present splendor is in danger." The two came up, made obeisance to the Lord, who remained unaware of the arrival, and stationing themselves at either side of him, lifting their prodigious forms, spread out their hoods, so that not a drop of the torrent touched his body. The apparitions were so large and terrifying that the god Saṁvara turned in his chariot and fled.[18]

Pārśva then broke the fetters of his karma one by one, and became absorbed in the White Contemplation, by which even the last and slightest traces of the human desire for advantage

[18] Or, according to another version: When the Lord Pārśva placed himself beneath an aśoka tree, determined to gain enlightment, an asura named Meghamālin attacked him in the form of a lion, and then sent a storm of rain to drown him. But the serpent king Dharaṇa wrapped his body around him and covered him with his hood. "Then the asura, seeing such great firmness in the Lord, was smitten in his mind with great astonishment and his pride was calmed. He made obeisance to the victorious one and went to his own place. Dharaṇa also, seeing that the danger was gone, returned to his place" (Devendra's commentary to *Uttarādhyayana Sūtra* 23, published and translated by Jarl Charpentier, *Zeitschrift der Deutschen Morgenländischen Gesellschaft,* LXIX, 1915, p. 356).

are dissolved. During the auspicious fourteenth day of the waning moon in the month of Caitra (March-April), the last of the sixty-three ties associated with the four modes of destructive karma broke, and the universal savior gained pure omniscience. He had entered the thirteenth stage of psychical development: he was "emancipated though embodied." From that instant, every particle of the universe was within the purview of his mind.

His chief apostle, Svayambhu, prayed respectfully that the Tīrthaṅkara should teach the world, and the gods prepared an assembly hall of twelve parts, which was named the "Flocking Together" (*samavasaraṇa*), in which there was an allotted place for every species of being. The multitudes that came were tremendous. And to all without distinction—quite in contrast to the way of the Brāhmans—the compassionate Lord Pārśva gave his purifying instruction. His voice was a mysteriously divine sound. The highest Indra desired him to preach the true religion even to the most distant parts of India, and he consented to do so. Wherever he went a "Flocking Together" was erected, and it was immediately filled.

Saṁvara thought: "Is the Lord then truly such an unfailing source of happiness and peace?" He came to one of the vast halls and listened. Pārśva was teaching. And all at once the spirit of hostility that had persisted through the incarnations was appeased. Overwhelmed with remorse, Saṁvara flung himself at the feet of Pārśvanātha with a cry. And the Tīrthaṅkara, inexhaustible in his kindness, gave consolation to the one who from birth to birth had been his foe. Saṁvara's mind, by his brother's grace, opened to right vision; he was placed on the way to liberation. Along with him, seven hundred and fifty ascetics who had been stiff-necked in their devotion to cruel penances—which, according to the Jaina view, are useless—gave up their futile practices and adopted the faith of the Tīrthaṅkara.

Pārśvanātha taught for sixty-nine years and eleven months, and finally, having preached throughout the lands of India, came to the Sammeda hill.[19] He had been in the second stage of contemplation up to this time. He now passed to the third stage. A month elapsed, and he remained absorbed.

The period of the human life of the Tīrthaṅkara was about to end. When no more of it remained than would have sufficed for the utterance of the five vowels, Pārśvanātha passed into the fourth stage of contemplation. Seventy years before, his destructive karmas had been destroyed; now the eighty-five ties associated with the four modes of non-destructive karma were annihilated. This took place in the seventh day of the waxing moon of Śrāvaṇa (July-August), and the Lord Pārśva passed immediately to his final liberation. His life-monad rose to Siddha-śilā, the peaceful region of eternal bliss at the summit of the universe, while his corpse reposed on the summit of the sacred hill.

With their various Indras in the lead, the gods came down to celebrate the Fifth and Last Kalyāṇa: "the salutary event of the Liberation" (*mokṣa-kalyāṇa*). They took up the mortal remains on a diamond palanquin, worshiping them reverently, poured sweet-scented substances on the sacred body, and bowed in obeisance. Then from the head of the god Agni-kumāra ("The Youthful Prince Fire") a blaze shot forth of heavenly flame, and the body was consumed. The gods, following this cremation, rubbed the sacred ashes on their heads and breasts, and marched to their celestial places with triumphant songs and dances.

To this day Mount Sammeda is known as the Hill of Pārśvanātha, reminding the people thus of the twenty-third Jaina Tīrthaṅkara, who there attained his liberation, and thence departed to Siddha-śilā, never to return.

[19] Because of the numerous saints and sages who have attained Enlightenment here, this place is sacred to the Jainas.

2.

Jaina Images

THERE ARE a number of close correspondences between this legend of the last life of Pārśvanātha and the biography of the Lord Buddha. Moreover, certain images of the Buddha, showing him protected by a serpent, can hardly be distinguished from those of the Jaina Tīrthaṅkara (*Plates IV and V*). Unquestionably the two religions share a common tradition. The births of the two saviors are much the same; so too are the anecdotes of the marvelous knowledge they displayed as children. Soothsayers foretold for each the career either of a Cakravartin or of a World Redeemer. Both grew up as princes, but departed from their fathers' palaces to the forest to engage in similar enterprises of ascetic self-realization. And in the culminating episodes of the biographies—the attainment of fulfillment—Saṁvara's attack on Pārśvanātha corresponds to that of Māra, the god of desire and death, on the meditating Gautama Śākyamuni.

For, as we are told, when the Future Buddha had taken his place beneath the Bo Tree, on the Immovable Spot, the god whose name is both Māra ("Death") and Kāma ("Desire") [20] challenged him, seeking to move him from his state of concentration. In the character of Kāma, he deployed the world's supreme distraction before the meditating savior, in the form of three tempting goddesses together with their retinues, and when these failed to produce the usual effect, resorted to his terrible form of Māra. With a mighty host he attempted to terrify and even slay the Buddha—causing mighty storms of wind, showers of rain, flaming rocks, weapons, live coals, hot ashes, sand, boiling

[20] Cf. *supra*, pp. 143-145.

mud, and finally a great darkness to assail him. But the Future Buddha was not moved. The missiles became flowers as they entered the field of his concentration. Māra hurled a keen discus, but it changed into a canopy of blossoms. Then the god challenged the right of the Blessed One to be sitting there, beneath the Bo Tree, on the Immovable Spot; whereupon the Future Buddha only touched the earth with the tips of the fingers of his right hand and the earth thundered, testifying: "I bear you witness!" with a hundred, a thousand, a hundred thousand roars. Māra's army dispersed, and all the gods of the heavens descended with garlands, perfumes, and other offerings in their hands.

That night, while the Bo Tree beneath which he sat rained down red blossoms, the Savior acquired in the first watch the knowledge of his previous existences, in the middle watch the divine eye, and in the last the understanding of dependent origination. He was now the Buddha. The ten thousand worlds quaked twelve times, as far as to the ocean shores. Flags and banners broke from every quarter. Lotuses bloomed on every tree. And the system of the ten thousand worlds was like a bouquet of flowers sent whirling through the air.[21]

Obviously this final victory closely resembles that of Pārśvanātha, except that the serpent, "Lord of the Earth," has not yet appeared. Instead, the Earth herself defends the hero. However, the Buddha legend goes on to relate that the Blessed One sat cross-legged seven days at the foot of the Bo Tree, following this achievement, enjoying the bliss of emancipation, then moved to the Banyan Tree of the Goatherd, where he sat another seven days, and next moved to the so-called Mucalinda Tree. Now Mucalinda was the name of a great serpent, and his abode was among the roots of this very tree. While the Buddha was experiencing there the beatitude of enlightenment, there

[21] *Jātaka* 1. 68. (Reduced from the translation by Henry Clarke Warren, *Buddhism in Translations,* Harvard Oriental Series, Vol. III, Cambridge, Mass., 1922, pp. 76-83.)

appeared a mighty thunderhead out of season, a cold wind blew, and the rain began to pour. "Then issued Mucalinda, the serpent-king, from his abode, and enveloping the body of the Blessed One seven times with his folds, spread his great hood above his head, saying, 'Let neither cold nor heat, nor gnats, flies, wind, sunshine, nor creeping creatures come near the Blessed One!' Then, when seven days had elapsed, and Mucalinda, the serpent-king, knew that the storm had broken up, and that the clouds had gone, he unwound his coils from the body of the Blessed One. And changing his natural appearance into that of a young man, he stood before the Blessed One, and with his joined hands to his forehead did reverence to the Blessed One." [22]

The precise relationship of the Jaina and the Buddhist versions cannot be reconstructed. Both may have originated from the simple circumstance that when the wealthy lay folk of the two denominations began employing craftsmen to fashion images of their saviors, the principal models for the new works of art had to be supplied by older Indian prototypes, chief among which were the yakṣa and the nāga—patterns of the wise superhuman being endowed with miraculous insight and power that had figured prominently in the household cult of India from time immemorial. These were popularly regarded as protecting genii and bringers of prosperity. Their forms appear on every doorpost and on most local shrines. Yakṣas (the earth and fertility spirits) are represented as robust standing figures in human form, whereas nāgas (the semi-human serpent genii), though generally depicted in human shape also, frequently have the head protected by a giant serpent hood as in *Plate III*.[23]

[22] *Mahāvagga,* opening sections, from the translation by Warren, *op. cit.,* pp. 83-86.

[23] Other nāga forms are the serpent, the serpent with numerous heads, and the human torso with serpent tail. Cf. Zimmer, *Myths and Symbols in Indian Art and Civilization,* pp. 59ff.

When the artist-craftsmen who for centuries had been supplying images for the general needs of Indian household worship added to their catalogue the figures of the sectarian saviors, Pārśva and the Buddha, they based their conceptions on the older forms, and sometimes suppressed, but sometimes also retained, the superhuman serpent attributes. These characteristic signs of the supernatural being seem to have supplied the model for the later Buddhist halo (compare *Plate X*); and it is by no means improbable that the special legends of Dharaṇendra and Mucalinda came into existence simply as later explanations of the combination of the figures of the serpent and the savior in Jaina and Buddhist images.

The Jaina version of the legend is more dramatic than the Buddhist and gives the serpent a more important role. More striking still are those Jaina images of Pārśvanātha that represent him with two serpents sprouting from his shoulders (*Plate VIa*): these point to a connection of some kind with ancient Mesopotamian art (*Plate VIc*), and suggest something of the great antiquity of the symbols incorporated in the Jaina cult. In the Near East, following the period of the teaching of Zoroaster (first part of the first millennium B.C.), when the Persian pantheon was systematized in terms of good (heavenly) versus evil (earthly) powers, the serpent became classified among the latter. As such, we find him not only in the Hebrew Bible in the role of Satan, but also in late Persian art and legend as the Ḍaḥḥāk—the great tyrant-villain of Firdausī's medieval Persian epic. *Shāhnāmah* (1010 A.D.). In the latter role, the figure is represented in human form with serpents springing from his shoulders (*Plate VIb*),[24] looking much like an evil or frightful brother of Pārśvanātha.

The first of the twenty-four Jaina Tīrthaṅkaras, Ṛṣabhanātha,

[24] An earlier form of this Persian figure is preserved in the Armenian tradition, where Azhdahak (= Avestan Azhi Dahāka > Pahlavi Dahāk > Modern Persian Ḍaḥḥāk), the dragon lord, is represented in human form with serpents springing from his shoulders. Azhdahak is conquered by

who is supposed to have lived and taught in the remotest prehistoric past, is shown in Plate VII: a typical Jaina vision of the perfected saint, completely detached from worldly bondage because absolutely purified of the elements of karma that color and deform our normal human lives. This piece of sculpture belongs to the eleventh, twelfth, or thirteenth century A.D., and is carved of alabaster—the preferred material for the representation of the clarified state of the Tīrthaṅkara; for it well suggests the sublime translucency of a body purified of the dross of tangible matter. By means of prolonged penances and abstentions the Jaina saint systematically purges himself not only of his egotistical reactions but also of his biological physicality. And so it is said of him that his body is "of a miraculous beauty and of a miraculously pure fragrance. It is not subject to disease, and is devoid of perspiration as well as of all the uncleanliness originating from the processes of digestion." [25] It is a body akin to those of the gods, who do not feed on gross food, do not perspire, and never know fatigue. "The breath of the Tīrthaṅkaras is like the fragrance of water lilies; their blood is white, like milk fresh from the cow." Hence they are of the hue of alabaster—not yellow, rosy, or darkish, like people whose veins are filled with blood that is red. "And their flesh is devoid of the smell of flesh."

This is what is expressed through both the material and the posture of this Jaina statue of the first savior. The stone is milk-white, shining as with a milky glow of divine light, while the rigid symmetry and utter immobility of the stance render a statement of spiritual aloofness. A Tīrthaṅkara is represented, preferably, if not seated in yoga posture, then standing in this

---

Vahagn, just as the Vedic Ahi (or Vṛtra) by Indra, Avestan Azhi Dahāka by Ātar (the Fire God, son of Ahura Mazda), and the Serpent of the Garden of Eden by the Son of Mary.

[25] Helmuth von Glasenapp, *Der Jainismus, Eine indische Erlösungsreligion,* Berlin, 1925, p. 252.

attitude of "dismissing the body" (*kāyotsarga*)—rigid, erect, and immobile, with arms held stiffly down, knees straight, and the toes directly forward. The ideal physique of such a superman is compared to the body of a lion: powerful chest and shoulders, no hips, slim feline buttocks, a tall pillarlike abdomen, and strong toes and fingers, elongated and well formed. The chest, broad and smooth from shoulder to shoulder, fully expanded and without the least hollowness, shows the effect of prolonged breathing exercises, practiced according to the rules of yoga. Such an ascetic is termed a "hero" (*vīra*), for he has achieved the supreme human victory: this is the sense of the title *Mahāvīra,* "the great (*mahat*) hero (*vīra*)," which was bestowed on the Buddha's contemporary, Vardhamāna, the twenty-fourth Tīrthaṅkara. The saint is termed also *Jina,* the "victor," and his disciples, therefore, *Jainas,* the "followers, or sons, of the victor."

In ancient times the Jaina monks went about completely naked, having put away all those caste marks and particularizing tokens that are of the essence of Indian costume and symbolize the wearer's involvement in the web of human bondage. Later on, in Mahāvīra's period, many assumed a white garment as a concession to decency and termed themselves *Śvetāmbara,* "those whose garment (*ambara*) is white (*śveta*)." This raiment denoted their ideal of alabaster-like purity, and so was not too great a departure from the heroic mode of the conservatives, who continued to style themselves *Digambara,* "those whose garment (*ambara*) is the element that fills the four quarters of space (*dig*)." [26] The Tīrthaṅkaras are therefore sometimes de-

[26] At the time of Alexander the Great's raid across the Indus (327-326 B.C.), the Digambara were still numerous enough to attract the notice of the Greeks, who called them gymnosophists, "naked philosophers," a most appropriate name. They continued to flourish side by side with the Śvetāmbara until after 1000 A.D., when, through Moslem rule, they were forced to put on clothes.

Editor's note: Dr. Zimmer's view of the relationship of those "clothed in space" to those "clothed in white" differs from that of the Śvetāmbaras,

picted naked, and sometimes clad in white. Ṛṣabhanātha, in the alabaster monument under discussion, wears a thin silken robe, covering his hips and legs.

But there is a special problem that arises in Jaina iconography as a result of the drastic purity of the ideal of the Tīrthaṅkara. The sculptor cannot be allowed to damage the sense of his representation by modifying in any way the perfect isolation and non-particularity of the released beings. The pristine life-monads are to be represented without fault. How, then, is the worshiper to distinguish one of these "victors" from another, since all—having transcended the sphere of time, change, and specification—are as alike as so many certified eggs? The solution to the difficulty was the simple one of providing every image with an emblem that should refer either to the name or to some distinctive detail of the legend of the Tīrthaṅkara intended. This is why the statue of Ṛṣabhanātha—literally "Lord (*nātha*) Bull (*ṛṣabha*)"—shows a little zebu-bull beneath the savior's feet. The effect of such a juxtaposition is that in dramatic contrast to these accompanying figures, which are reminiscent of the world and life from which the Tīrthaṅkara has withdrawn, the majestic aloofness of the perfected, balanced, absolutely self-contained figure of the saint becomes emphasized in its triumphant isolation. The image of the released one seems to be neither animate nor inanimate, but pervaded by a strange and timeless calm. It is human in shape and feature, yet

---

who regard themselves as representing the original Jaina practice and hold that a schism in the year 83 A.D. gave rise to the Digambaras. The evidence of the Greeks, however, speaks for the existence of gymnosophists at least as early as the fourth century B.C., and tends to support the claim of the Digambaras that it is they who have preserved the earlier practice. According to the Digambara theory of the schism, a sect of lax principles arose under Bhadrabāhu, the eighth successor of Mahāvīra, which in 80 A.D. developed into the present community of the Śvetāmbaras (cf. Hermann Jacobi, "Digambaras," in Hastings, *Encyclopaedia of Religion and Ethics,* Vol. IV, p. 704).

as inhuman as an icicle; and thus expresses perfectly the idea of successful withdrawal from the round of life and death, personal cares, individual destiny, desires, sufferings, and events. Like a pillar of some supraterrestrial, unearthly substance, the Tīrthaṅkara, the "Crossing-Maker," the breaker of the path across the stream of time to the final release and bliss of the other shore, stands supernally motionless, absolutely unconcerned about the worshiping, jubilant crowds that throng around his feet.

At Śravaṇa Beḷgoḷa, Hāsan District, Mysore, is a colossal figure (*Plate VIII*) of this kind that was erected about 983 A.D. by Cāmuṇḍarāya, the minister of King Rājamalla of the Ganga dynasty. It is hewn from a vertical rock needle, a prodigious monolith, on a hilltop four hundred feet above the town. The image measures fifty-six and one-half feet in height and thirteen feet around the hips, and is thus one of the largest free-standing figures in the world; the feet are placed on a low platform. The savior represented is indicated by vines clambering up his body, which refer to an episode in the biography of Gommaṭa (also called Bahūbali, "strong of arm"), the son of the first Tīrthaṅkara, Ṛṣabhanātha. He is supposed to have stood unflinchingly for a year in his yoga posture. The vines crept up to his arms and shoulders; anthills arose about his feet; he was like a tree or rock of the wilderness. To this day the entire surface of this statue is anointed every twenty-five years with melted butter, as a result of which it still looks fresh and clean.

There is a legend to the effect that the image goes back to a date much earlier than 983 A.D., and that for ages it was forgotten, the memory of its location being completely lost. Bharata, the first of India's mythical Cakravartins,[27] is supposed, accord-

[27] For the legend of the birth of Bharata, see Kālidāsa's celebrated play, *Śakuntalā* (Everyman's Library, No. 629). Bharata was the ancestor of the clans of the *Mahābhārata*. The land of India itself is called Bhārata ("descended from Bharata"), as are also its inhabitants.

ing to this account, to have erected it; Rāvana, the fabulous chieftain of the demons of Ceylon, paid it worship; and when it passed, thereafter, from the memory of man, it became covered with earth. The old legend tells us that Cāmuṇḍarāya was informed of its existence by a traveling merchant and so made a pilgrimage to the sacred place with his mother and a few companions. When the party arrived, a female earth-divinity, the yakṣinī Kuṣmāṇḍī, who had been an attendant of the Tīrthaṅkara Ariṣṭanemi, manifested herself and pointed out the hidden site. Then, with a golden arrow, Cāmuṇḍarāya split the hill and the colossal figure could be seen. The earth was cleared away and craftsmen were brought to cleanse the image and restore it.[28]

The emblems of the Tīrthaṅkaras are as follows: 1. Ṛṣabha, bull, 2. Ajita, elephant, 3. Śambhava, horse, 4. Abhinandana, ape, 5. Sumati, heron, 6. Padmaprabha, red lotus, 7. Supārśva, swastika, 8. Candraprabha, moon, 9. Suvidhi, dolphin, 10. Śītala, *śrīvatsa* (a sign on the breast), 11. Śreyāṁsa, rhinoceros, 12. Vāsupūjya, buffalo, 13. Vimala, hog, 14. Ananta, hawk, 15. Dharma, thunderbolt, 16. Śānti, antelope, 17. Kunthu, goat, 18. Ara, *nandyāvarta* (a diagram), 19. Malli, jar, 20. Suvrata, tortoise, 21. Nami, blue lotus, 22. Ariṣṭanemi, conch shell,[29]

[28] Glasenapp, *op. cit.*, pp. 392-393. According to another legend (also noted by Glasenapp), Cāmuṇḍarāya had this image made after the pattern of an invisible model of Bharata, in Potanapura.

There is a statue of Gommaṭa, twenty feet high, on a hill fifteen miles southwest of the city of Mysore. Another was erected in 1432 by Prince Virapāṇḍya of Kārkala, South Kanara, Madras. And in 1604, in the same district, in Vanur (Yenur), still another, thirty-seven feet high, was set up by Timma Rāja, who may have been a descendant of Cāmuṇḍarāya. Some of these figures are supposed to have come into existence without human effort. Others were made by the saints of ancient legends and then, like the colossus of Cāmuṇḍarāya, as described above, rediscovered by miracle.

[29] Ariṣṭanemi, or Neminātha, Pārśva's immediate predecessor, is related, through his half-legendary biography, to Kṛṣṇa, the prophet of the Hindu

23. Pārśva, serpent, 24. Mahāvīra, lion. The standing attitude in which they are commonly shown exhibits a characteristic, puppetlike rigidity that comes of—and denotes—inner absorption. The posture is called "dismissing the body" (*kāyotsarga*). The modeling avoids details and yet is not flat or incorporeal; for the savior is without weight, without throbbing life or any promise of delight, yet is a body—an ethereal reality with milk in its veins instead of blood. The empty spaces left between the arms and the trunk, and between the legs, are consciously intended to emphasize the splendid isolation of the unearthly apparition. There is no striking contour, no interesting trait of individuality, no cutting profile breaking into space, but a mystic calm, an anonymous serenity, which we are not even invited to share. And the nakedness is as far removed as the stars, or as bare rock, from sensuality; for in Indian art nakedness is not intended to suggest either sensuous charm (as it is in the Greek images of the nymphs and Aphrodites) or an ideal of perfect bodily and spiritual manhood, developed through competitive sport (as in the Greek statues of the youthful athletes who triumphed in the sacred contests at Olympia and elsewhere). The nakedness of Indian goddesses is that of the fertile, indifferent mother earth, while that of the stark Tīrthaṅkaras is ethereal. Composed of some substance that does not derive from, or link one to, the circuit of life, the truly "sky-clad" (*digambara*) Jaina statue expresses the perfect isolation of the one who has stripped off every bond. His is an absolute "abiding in itself," a strange but perfect aloofness, a nudity of chilling majesty, in its stony simplicity, rigid contours, and abstraction.

The form of the image of the Tīrthaṅkara is like a bubble: at first sight seemingly a bit primitive in its inexpressive atti-

---

Bhagavad Gītā. Kṛṣṇa belongs to the epical period of the *Mahābhārata*, which marks the conclusion of the Āryan feudal age (cf. *supra*, p. 67, Editor's note).

tude—simply standing on its two legs—but actually highly conscious and rather sophisticated in its avoidance of all the dynamic, glamorous, and triumphant achievements of the contemporary Hindu art [30]—the wonderful, vital sculpture of Elūrā, Bādāmī, and elsewhere. By the Jaina saint—and artist—the restless vitality both of the Hindu gods and of their mythical cosmic display is ignored deliberately, as though in protest. Through a translucent alabaster silence the great Passage-breaking doctrine is revealed of the Jaina way of escape from that universal manifold of enticement and delusion.[31]

For it is important to bear in mind that the Tīrthaṅkaras and their images belong to a totally different sphere from that of the orthodox Hindu devotions. The Hindu gods, dwelling in the heavens that Pārśvanātha transcended, still are accessible to human prayer, whereas the supreme release attained by the Tīrthaṅkaras places them beyond all earthly solicitude. They can never be moved from their eternal isolation. Superficially, their cult may resemble that of the Hindu deities, who not only graciously heed the prayers of man but even condescend to come down into the lifeless temple images—as to a throne or seat (*pīṭha*) [32]—in response to consecrating rituals of conjuration and

[30] For examples of Hindu and Buddhist art, compare Plates I, II, III, IV, IX, X, XI, XII.

[31] The Jainas in their temple building, on the other hand, usually followed the structural tradition of the Hindu sects. The Jaina temples of Rājputāna and Gujarāt belong to the same period to which we owe the magnificent Hindu monuments of Upper India, which were constructed just before the Moslem invasions of the tenth to thirteenth centuries A.D. At that time the Ganga kings erected the Sikhara ("tower") temples of Oṛissā, and the tower temples at Khajurāho were constructed. The Jaina phase of this rich period begins with the structures of Pālitāna (960 A.D.) and closes with the Tejahpāla temple at Mount Ābū (1232 A.D.). Two notable monuments are Vimala Sha's temple at Mount Ābū (c. 1032) and the temple at Dabhoi, in Gujarāt (c. 1254). Cf. Ananda K. Coomaraswamy, *History of Indian and Indonesian Art.*

[32] Cf. *infra,* pp. 351-588.

invitation; for the Jainas pay profound respect to the statues of their Tīrthaṅkaras and recount legends of their miraculous origin. Nevertheless the attitude is not precisely that of worship. The following story, told of the Lord Pārśva in his next to last earthly life, gives the clue to the special character of the Jaina attitude.

The savior's name then, it will be remembered, was King Ānandakumāra.[33] When he had defeated the rulers of the surrounding nations and become a Cakravartin, his minister suggested that he should hold a religious celebration in honor of the Tīrthaṅkara Ariṣṭanemi; but when the king entered the temple to worship he was disturbed by a doubt. "What is the use," he thought, "of bowing before an image, for an image is unconscious?" There was a saint in the temple at the time, however, named Vipulamati, and he removed this doubt. "An image," he told the king, "affects the mind. If one holds a red flower before a glass the glass will be red; if one holds up a dark blue flower the glass will be dark blue. Just so, the mind is changed by the presence of an image. Contemplating the form of the passionless Lord in a Jaina temple, the mind becomes filled automatically with a sentiment of renunciation; whereas at the sight of a courtesan it becomes restless. No one can regard the peaceful, absolute form of the Lord without recalling the noble qualities of the Lord; and this influence is the more forceful if one worships. The mind straightway becomes purified. But given purity of mind, one is already on the way to final bliss."

The sage Vipulamati then illustrated his lesson for the king with a metaphor that has many counterparts in the various traditions of India, non-Jaina as well as Jaina. "In a certain town," he said, "there was a beautiful public woman who died, and her body was brought to the cremation ground. A certain licentious man who chanced to be there looked upon her beauty and thought how fortunate he would have deemed himself could

[33] Cf. *supra*, p. 193. See also, p. 181, note 1.

he, but once in his lifetime, have had the opportunity of enjoying her. Simultaneously a dog that was there, seeing the corpse going into the fire, thought what dainty meals it would have made for him had they not determined to waste it in the flames. But a saint, also present, thought how regrettable that anyone endowed with such a body should have neglected to make use of it in difficult yoga exercises.

"There was but one corpse in that place," said Vipulamati, "and yet it produced three sorts of feeling in three different witnesses. An external thing will thus have its effect according to the nature and purity of the mind. The mind," he concluded, "is purified by the contemplation and worship of the Tīrthaṅkaras. Images of the Tīrthaṅkaras make one fit, therefore, to enjoy the pleasures of heaven after death—and can even prepare one's mind to experience nirvāṇa."

3.

The Makers of the Crossing

JAINISM denies the authority of the Vedas and the orthodox traditions of Hinduism. Therefore it is reckoned as a heterodox Indian religion. It does not derive from Brāhman-Āryan sources, but reflects the cosmology and anthropology of a much older, pre-Āryan upper class of northeastern India—being rooted in the same subsoil of archaic metaphysical speculation as Yoga, Sāṅkhya, and Buddhism, the other non-Vedic Indian systems.[34]

[34] Cf. *supra,* p. 60, Editor's note, and Appendix B. Yoga, Sāṅkhya, and Buddhism will be discussed *infra,* Chapters II and IV.

The Āryan invasion, which overwhelmed the northwestern and north central provinces of the sub-continent in the second millennium B.C., did not extend the full weight of its impact beyond the middle of the Ganges valley; the pre-Āryan nobility of the northeastern states, therefore, were not all swept off their thrones. Many of the families survived, and when the dynasties of the invading race began to show symptoms of exhaustion, the scions of these earlier native lines were able to assert themselves again.

Candragupta Maurya, for example,[35] stemmed from a family of this kind. So did the Buddha. Ikṣvāku, the mythical ancestor of the legendary Solar Dynasty to which Rāma, hero of the *Rāmāyaṇa,* belonged, has a name that points rather to the tropical plant-world of India than to the steppes from which the conquerors descended: *ikṣvāku* means "sugar cane," and suggests a background of aboriginal plant-totemism. Even Kṛṣṇa, the divine incarnation celebrated in the *Mahābhārata,* whose synthesis of Āryan and pre-Āryan teachings is epitomized in the *Bhagavad Gītā,*[36] was born not of a Brāhman but of a Kṣatriya line—the Hari clan—the associations of which are far from orthodox. Kṛṣṇa's religion comprises many elements that were not originally constituents of the Vedic system of thought; and in the celebrated legend of his lifting Mount Govardhan he is actually represented as challenging Indra, the Vedic-Āryan king of the gods, and even putting him to shame.[37] Moreover, Kṛṣṇa's father, Vasudeva, was the brother of the father of the twenty-second of the Jaina Tīrthaṅkaras, the Lord Ariṣṭanemi, and so must have been a recent convert to the orthodox community.

As we shall see in the following chapters, the history of Indian philosophy has been characterized largely by a series of

[35] Cf. *supra,* p. 37.

[36] Discussed *infra,* pp. 378-409.

[37] Cf. Sister Nivedita and Ananda K. Coomaraswamy, *Myths of the Hindus and Buddhists,* New York, 1914, pp. 230-232.

crises of interaction between the invasive Vedic-Āryan and the non-Āryan, earlier, Dravidian styles of thought and spiritual experience. The Brāhmans were the principal representatives of the former, while the latter was preserved, and finally reasserted, by the surviving princely houses of the native Indian, dark-skinned, pre-Āryan population. Since Jainism retains the Dravidian structure more purely than the other major Indian traditions—and is consequently a relatively simple, unsophisticated, clean-cut, and direct manifestation of the pessimistic dualism that underlies not only Sāṅkhya, Yoga, and early Buddhistic thought, but also much of the reasoning of the Upaniṣads, and even the so-called "nondualism" of the Vedānta—we shall treat it first, in the present chapter, and then proceed, in Chapter II, to the closely kindred Sāṅkhya and Yoga. Chapter III will be devoted to the majestic Brāhman development, which constitutes the main line of Indian orthodoxy and is the backbone of Indian life and learning, while Buddhism will be discussed in Chapter IV—first as a vigorous and devastating protest against the supremacy of the Brāhmans, but in the end as a teaching not radically different from that of the orthodox Brāhman schools. Finally, in Chapter V, we shall introduce and briefly review the subject of Tantra: an extraordinarily sophisticated psychological application of the principles of the Āryan-Dravidian synthesis, which shaped both the Buddhist and the Brāhman philosophies and practices of the medieval period, and to this day inspires not only the whole texture of the religious life of India but also much of the popular and esoteric teaching of the great Buddhist nations, Tibet, China, Korea, and Japan.

To return, however, to the Tīrthaṅkaras: as already stated, they represent, in the most vivid manner possible, the life-searing victory of the transcendent principle over the forces of the flesh. Pārśva and those other colossi whose towering forms, carved in alabaster, point like arrows to the heavens, broke free from the spheres of human fear and desire to pass to a realm remote from the conditions, the victories, and the vicissitudes of time. Standing in their posture of "dismissing the body," or seated in the inturned "lotus posture" of the concentrated yogī, they represent an ideal very different indeed from that of the roaring, world-affirmative, Vedic "Dying round the Holy Power." [38]

Twenty-two of these life-negating Jaina Tīrthaṅkaras belong to the ancient, semi-mythical Solar Dynasty, from which the Hindu savior Rāma is supposed to have descended and which is far from Āryan in its backgrounds, while the other two belong to the Hari clan, the family of the blue-black popular hero Kṛṣṇa. All of these figures, Kṛṣṇa and Rāma as well as the Tīrthaṅkaras, represent the resurgence of a world view totally different from that of the triumphant cattle-herders and warlike horsemen who had entered India from the trans-Himalayan plains and whose way of life had swept all before it for nearly a thousand years. The Vedas, like the hymns of the Homeric Greeks, were the productions of a consciousness dedicated to the spheres of action, whereas the figures of the Tīrthaṅkaras stand as the most vivid expressions in all art of the ideal of the world-negating, absolute refusal of life's lure. Here is no bending of the cosmic forces to the will of man, but on the contrary, a relentless shelling off of cosmic forces, whether those of the external universe, or those that pulse in the running of the blood.

Pārśva, the twenty-third Tīrthaṅkara, is the first of the long series whom we can fairly visualize in a historical setting; Ariṣṭanemi, the one just before him, whose brother, Vasudeva, was the father of the popular Hindu savior Kṛṣṇa, is only very dimly perceptible. And yet, even in the biography of Pārśva the element of legend is so strong that one can scarcely sense an actually living, breathing human being. The situation is different, however, in the case of the last Tīrthaṅkara, Vardhamāna Mahāvīra; for he lived and taught in the comparatively

[38] Cf. *supra*, pp. 66-74.

well-documented period of the Buddha. We can readily visualize him moving among the numerous monks and teachers of that age of intellectual ferment. Reflections of his presence and influence can be caught from the Buddhist as well as from the Jaina texts.

Like all the earlier Tīrthaṅkaras, and like his contemporary the Buddha, Mahāvīra was of non-Āryan stock, not related even remotely to those semi-divine seers, sages, singers, and wizards who were the ancestors of the Brāhman families and the source of the wisdom of the orthodox Vedic tradition. He was a Kṣatriya of the Jñāta clan (hence called Jñāta-putra, "a son of Jñāta"), born in Kuṇḍagrāma [39] (*kuṇḍa,* "a hole in the ground for keeping water"; *grāma,* "a village"), which was a suburb of the flourishing city of Vaiśālī (modern Basarh, some twenty-seven miles north of Patna, in the northeastern province of Bihar), and his parents, Siddhārtha and Triśālā, were pious Jainas before him, worshipers of the Lord Pārśva. Mahāvīra was their second son; and they named him Vardhamāna, "Growing, Increasing." He married, in due time, a young woman of their choice, Yaśodā, and had by her a daughter, Aṇojjā. When his parents died in his thirtieth year, and his elder brother, Nandivardhana, succeeded in the direction of the household, Vardhamāna asked and received the permission of his brother to carry out his long-cherished resolve to become a Jaina monk. The monastic authorities also favored his request, and he joined the Order with the usual Jaina rites. Then followed twelve years of severe self-mortification. After the first thirteen months he discarded his clothes, and at the end of a long ordeal achieved the state of "isolation-integration" (*kevala*), which implies omniscience and release from earthly bondage—corresponding to the "enlightenment" (*bodhi*) of the Buddhas. And he lived on earth forty-two years

[39] A town ruled by northeast Indian feudal chieftains, known also from early Buddhist records of the Buddha's itinerary (cf. *Mahā-parinibbāna-suttanta*).

more, preaching the doctrine generally and instructing his eleven principal disciples—the so-called *gaṇadharas,* "keepers of the hosts (of the followers)." When he died at Pāvā, attaining thus the final release (*nirvāṇa*), he was in the seventy-second year of his age. The date is placed by the Śvetāmbara sect (as the beginning of their era) in 527 B.C., by the Digambaras in 509, and by the modern Western scholars (since Mahāvīra passed away only a few years before the Buddha) about 480.[40]

A dialogue recorded in the sacred writings of the Śvetāmbara sect[41] states that in essence the teachings of Pārśva and Mahāvīra are the same. Keṣi, an adherent of Pārśva, is shown asking questions of Sudharma-Gautama, one of the followers of the newer teacher, Mahāvīra; and to all his questions he receives what seem to him to be the wrong answers. He therefore presses his argument. "According to Pārśvanātha the Great Vows are but four in number; why then," he demands, "did Vardhamāna speak of them as five?" To which Gautama replies: "Pārśvanātha understood the spirit of the time and realized that the enumeration of the Great Vows as four would suit the people of his age; Mahāvīra gave the same four vows as five in order to make the Jaina doctrine more acceptable to the people of his time. There is no essential difference in the teachings of the two Tīrthaṅkaras."

The fifth vow, which Keśi, the adherent of the teaching of Pārśva, was calling into question, was the one about the clothes, and is what led to the schism; for it involved a number of revisions of attitude and conduct. The conservatives not only insisted on remaining sky-clad, but also rejected all the other reforms of Mahāvīra. Women, for example, were permitted by

[40] This biography is based upon, and follows closely, the account given by Jacobi, "Jainism," in Hastings, *Encyclopaedia of Religion and Ethics,* Vol. VII, pp. 466-467.

[41] *Uttarādhyayana Sūtra* 23 (Sacred Books of the East, Vol. XLV, pp. 119ff). The authenticity of this text is denied by the Digambaras.

Mahāvīra to take ascetic vows, whereas by the sky-clad sect they were debarred from doing so, having to wait for a later, masculine incarnation. Nevertheless, it is certain that Mahāvīra preached nothing absolutely new; he only modified and developed what had already been taught by Pārśvanātha—and no doubt by numerous even earlier saints and sages.[42]

The writings of the Jainas mention as contemporaries of Mahāvīra the same kings of northeastern India as those who according to Buddhist sources reigned during the Buddha's career. The canonical texts of the Buddhists, dating from the first centuries B.C., mention the Jaina frequently under their old name of *Nirgrantha,*[43] "without knot, tie, or string," i.e., "the unfettered ones"; and refer to them as a rival sect, but nowhere as one newly founded. Their leader is called Jñātaputra Vardhamāna ("Vardhamāna, son of the Jñāta clan"), Mahāvīra (the "Great Hero"), and Jina (the "Victor"), and, in contrast to the Buddha, is never described as having first become a disciple of

[42] *Editor's note:* The reader may experience some difficulty in following Dr. Zimmer's argument, since in the text to which he refers (*Uttarādhyayana Sūtra* 23. 29) the statement about the clothes is precisely the reverse of what he would lead one to expect. "The law taught by Vardhamāna," we read, "forbids clothes, but that of the great sage Pārśva allows an under and upper garment." I confess that I do not know how Dr. Zimmer planned to deal with this inconsistency; for he left no pertinent notes, and I do not recall his having discussed the point. His manuscript for this portion of his history of Jainism is incomplete. However, since he stresses the fact that "the authenticity of this text is denied by the Digambaras" (footnote *supra*), it may be that he intended to suggest that the Śvetāmbaras inverted the historical situation to give to their own customs the prestige of the earlier master. This would make the Digambaras seem to be the followers of a later and merely temporary ruling, whereas it was the contention of the Digambaras that the Śvetāmbaras represented the later form. As noted above (p. 210, Editor's note), Dr. Zimmer adheres to the Digambara version of the historical sequence of the sky-clad and the white-clad modes.

[43] *Nirgrantha* is Sanskrit; the Pāli word, in the Buddhist texts, is *Nigaṇṭha.*

teachers whose doctrines failed to satisfy him. Mahāvīra remained faithful to the tradition into which he had been born and which he embraced fully when he became a Jaina monk. By attaining to the highest goal envisioned in this tradition—a very rare achievement—he did not refute it, but only gained new fame for the ancient way.

Again in contrast to the Buddha, Mahāvīra is never declared to have received through his enlightenment the understanding of any new philosophical principle or any special insight not already familiar to his period. He was not the founder of a new ascetic community but the reformer of an old one. He was not the teacher of a new doctrine, but is represented as having gained at the time of his illumination the *perfect* knowledge of something which both he and his community had known before only imperfectly and in part. He simply entered an existing, time-honored order and some twelve years later attained fulfillment. Thus he realized to the full extent what had been promised—what his tradition had always indicated as the ultimate reference of its sacred, complex, and most detailed system of representing the nature of man and the universe.

The Buddhist historical records, then, would seem to support the traditional Jaina representation of Mahāvīra as the last—not the first, as Western scholars until recently have insisted—of the Jaina "Crossing-Makers through the torrent of rebirth to the yonder shore." And there is good reason, as we have seen, to concede that the Crossing-Maker just preceding him, Pārśvanātha, may also have been an actual historical personage. But before Pārśvanātha stands Ariṣṭanemi (or Neminātha), the twenty-second Tīrthaṅkara of the present so-called "descending" (*avasarpiṇī*) phase of the universal cycle of cosmic time,[44] whose

[44] The cycle of time continually revolves, according to the Jainas. The present "descending" (*avasarpiṇī*) period was preceded and will be followed by an "ascending" (*utsarpiṇī*). *Sarpiṇī* suggests the creeping movement of a "serpent" (*sarpin*); *ava-* means "down" and *ut-* means "up." The

distinguishing emblem is the Hindu battle-trumpet, the conch-shell, and whose iconographic color is black.[45] His existence is not substantiated through historical records, but only reflected through legendary accounts, which link him with the heroes of that feudal period of Indo-Āryan chivalry depicted in the *Mahābhārata* and the Kṛṣṇa legend. He is described as a first cousin of Kṛṣṇa; his father, Samudravijaya ("Conqueror of the Whole Earth, as far as to the Shores of the Oceans"), having been the brother of Kṛṣṇa's father, Vasudeva. Since he is heterodox,[46] he is ignored by the Hindu Kṛṣṇa cycle, which, in spite of its own heterodox traits, has become incorporated in the great body of orthodox legend; but the Jainas claim that Neminātha was far superior to Kṛṣṇa both in physical prowess and in intellectual attainments. His unostentatious, mild disposition, as well as his rejection of luxury and adoption of the ascetic life, are depicted in such a way as to show him to have been exactly the reverse of Kṛṣṇa. His full name, Ariṣṭanemi, is an epithet of the sun-wheel or the sun-chariot, "the felly of whose wheel (*nemi*) is undamaged (*ariṣṭa*), i.e. indestructible," and thus suggests that he belonged to the ancient Solar Dynasty.[47]

With this Tīrthaṅkara, Jaina tradition breaks beyond the bounds of recorded history into the reaches of the mythological past. And yet it does not follow that the historian would be justified in saying that some great renewer and teacher of the Jaina faith—perhaps named Ariṣṭanemi—did not precede Pārśvanātha. We are simply not in a position to know how far back

---

serpent-cycle of time (the world-bounding serpent, biting its own tail) will go on revolving through these alternating "ascending" and "descending" periods forever.

[45] Just as each of the identical Tīrthaṅkaras has a distinguishing emblem (cf. *supra,* p. 213), so also a color. That of Mahāvīra, whose animal is the lion, is golden; that of Pārśvanātha, blue (cf. Jacobi, *loc. cit.,* p. 466).

[46] Cf. *supra,* p. 60, Editor's note.

[47] Cf. *supra,* p. 106.

the imagination should be permitted to go in following the line of the Tīrthaṅkaras. Obviously, however, the dates assigned by Jaina tradition have to be rejected once we pass beyond Pārśvanātha; for Ariṣṭanemi is said to have lived eighty-four thousand years before Pārśvanātha, which would place us back somewhere in the Lower Paleolithic, while the preceding Tīrthaṅkara, Nami (whose emblem is the blue lotus and whose color is golden), is supposed to have died fifty thousand years before Ariṣṭanemi—back, that is to say, in the Eolithic; Suvrata, the twentieth (whose animal is the tortoise and whose color is black), is dated eleven hundred thousand years before that. With Malli, the nineteenth (whose emblem is the jar and whose color is blue) we pass well into the pre-human geologic ages, wnile Ara, Kunthu, Śānti, Dharma, Ananta, Vimala, etc., transport us beyond the reaches even of geological calculation.

The long series of these semi-mythological saviors, stretching back, period beyond period, each illuminating the world according to the requirements of the age yet in strict adherence to the one doctrine, points to the belief that the Jaina religion is eternal. Again and again it has been revealed and refreshed, in each of the endlessly successive ages, not merely by the twenty-four Tīrthaṅkaras of the *present* "descending" series, but by an endless number, world without end. The length of life and the stature of the Tīrthaṅkaras themselves in the most favorable phases of the ever-revolving cycles (the first periods of the descending and the last of the ascending series) are fabulously great; for in the good old days the bodily size and strength as well as the virtue of mankind far exceeded anything that we know today. That is why the images of the Tīrthaṅkaras are colossal. The dwarfish proportions of the men and heroes of the inferior ages are the result and reflex of a diminution of moral stamina. Today we are no longer giants; indeed, we are so small, both physically and spiritually, that the religion of the Jainas has become too difficult, and there will be no more

Tīrthaṅkaras in the present cycle. Moreover, as time moves on to the conclusion of our present descending age, the scale of humanity will decline still further, the religion of the Jainas will disappear, and the earth, finally, will be an unspeakable morass of violence, bestiality, and grief.

This is a philosophy of the profoundest pessimism. The round of rebirths in the world is endless, full of suffering, and of no avail. Of and in itself it can yield no release, no divine redeeming grace; the very gods are subject to its deluding spell. Therefore, ascent to heaven is no less a mere phase or stage of delusion than descent to the purgatorial hells. As a result of meritorious conduct, one is reborn a god among the gods; as a result of evil conduct, a being among the beings of hell or an animal among the beasts; but there is no escape, either way, from this perennial circulation. One will continue to revolve forever through the various spheres of inconsequential pleasures and unbearable pains unless one can manage somehow to release *oneself*. But this can be accomplished only by heroic effort—a long, really dreadful ordeal of austerities and progressive self-abnegation.

4.

The Qualities of Matter

ACCORDING to Jaina cosmology, the universe is a living organism, made animate throughout by life-monads which circulate through its limbs and spheres; and this organism will never die. We ourselves, furthermore—i.e., the life-monads contained within and constituting the very substance of the imperishable great body—are imperishable too. We ascend and descend through various states of being, now human, now divine, now animal; the bodies seem to die and to be born, but the chain is continuous, the transformations endless, and all we do is pass from one state to the next. The manner in which the indestructible life-monads circulate is disclosed to the inward eye of the enlightened Jaina saint and seer.

The life-monads enjoying the highest states of being, i.e., those temporarily human or divine, are possessed of five sense faculties, as well as of a thinking faculty (*manas*) and span of life (*āyus*), physical strength (*kāya-bala*), power of speech (*vacana-bala*), and the power of respiration (*śvāsocchvāsa-bala*) In the classic Indian philosophies of Sāṅkhya, Yoga, and Vedānta, the same five sense faculties appear as in the Jaina formula (namely touch, smell, taste, hearing, and sight); however, there have been added the so-called "five faculties of action." These begin with speech (*vāc,* corresponding to the Jaina *vacana-bala*), but then go on to grasping (*pāṇi,* the hand), locomotion (*pāda,* the feet), evacuation (*pāyu,* the anus), and reproduction (*upastha,* the organ of generation). *Manas* (the thinking faculty) is retained, but is linked to further functions of the psyche, namely *buddhi* (intuitive intelligence) and *ahaṅkāra* (ego-consciousness). Also added are the five *prāṇas,* or "life breaths." [48] Apparently the Jaina categories represent a comparatively primitive, archaic analysis and description of human nature, many of the details of which underlie and remain incorporated in the later, classic Indian view.

[48] These classic categories are discussed *infra,* pp. 317-332. In Jainism the term *prāṇa* is used in the sense not of "life breath" but of "bodily power," and refers to the ten faculties above noted. Dr. Zimmer is suggesting that the analysis of the psyche that prevailed in the classic period of Indian philosophy, in the synthesis of the so-called "Six Systems," was originally not a Brāhman contribution but non-Āryan, having come in through Sāṅkhya and Yoga, and that its categories are prefigured in the Jaina view. For the Six Systems, cf. Appendix A.

Frogs, fish, and other animals not born from the womb are without a thinking faculty (*manas*)—they are called, therefore, *a-sañjñin* ("insensible"); whereas elephants, lions, tigers, goats, cows, and the rest of the mammals, since they have a thinking faculty, are *sañjñin*. The various beings in the hells, and the lower gods, as well as human beings, also are *sañjñin*.

In contrast to those views that represent the soul as being minute, like an atom (*aṇu*), or of the size of a thumb, and dwelling in the heart, Jainism regards the life-monad (*jīva*) as pervading the whole organism; the body constitutes, as it were, its garb; the life-monad is the body's animating principle. And the subtle substance of this life-monad is mingled with particles of karma, like water with milk, or like fire with iron in a red-hot, glowing iron ball. Moreover, the karmic matter communicates colors (*leśyā*) to the life-monad; and these colors are six in number. Hence there are said to be six types of life-monad, in ascending series, each with its color, smell, taste, and quality of tangibility,[49] as follows:

6. white (*śukla*)
5. yellow, or rose (*padma,* like a lotus)

4. flaming red (*tejas*)
3. dove-grey (*kapota*)

2. dark blue (*nīla*)
1. black (*kṛṣṇa*)

These six types fall into three groups of two, each pair corresponding precisely to one of the three *guṇas,* or "natural qualities," of the classic Sāṅkhya and Vedāntic writings.[50] The Jaina

[49] It is not particularly difficult even for us to imagine a smelly or sour life-monad, or a sweet and fragrant one.

[50] *Editor's note:* Here again Dr. Zimmer is pointing to the prefigurement in Jainism of the classic Indian categories. An extensive discussion of the guṇas will be found *infra,* pp. 295-297; the reader unfamiliar with the concept would do well to return to the present paragraph following his

leśyās 1 and 2 are dark; they correspond to the guṇa *tamas,* "darkness." Leśyā 3 is smoky grey while 4 is of the red of flame; both pertain to fire, and thus correspond to the guṇa *rajas* (fire = *rajas,* "red color"; cf. *rañj,* "to tinge red"; *rakta,* "red"). Leśyās 5 and 6, finally, are clear and luminous, being states of comparative purity, and thus are the Jaina counterparts of the classic guṇa *sattva:* "virtue, goodness, excellence, clarity; ideal being; the supreme state of matter." In sum, the six Jaina leśyās seem to represent some system of archaic prototypes from which the basic elements of the vastly influential later theory of the guṇas was evolved.

Black is the characteristic color of merciless, cruel, raw people, who harm and torture other beings. Dark-blue characters are roguish and venal, covetous, greedy, sensual, and fickle. Dove-grey typifies the reckless, thoughtless, uncontrolled, and irascible; whereas the prudent, honest, magnanimous, and devout are fiery red. Yellow shows compassion, consideration, unselfishness, nonviolence, and self-control; while the white souls are dispassionate, absolutely disinterested, and impartial.

As water flows into a pond through channels, so karmic matter of the six colors flows into the monad through the physical organs. Sinful acts cause an "influx of evil karma" (*pāpa-āsrava*), and this increases the dark matter in the monad; virtuous acts, on the other hand, bring an "influx of good or holy karma" (*puṇya-āsrava*), which tends to make the monad white. But even this holy

---

completion of that section. In advance, however, it can be stated that according to the classic Indian view, matter (*prakṛti*) is characterized by the three qualities (*guṇas*) of inertia (*tamas*), activity (*rajas*), and tension or harmony (*sattva*). These are not merely qualities, but the very substance of the matter of the universe, which is said to be constituted of the gunas, as a rope of three twisted strands—*tamas guṇa* being, as it were, black, *rajas* red, and *sattva* white. A predominance of *tamas guṇa* in an individual's disposition makes him dull, sluggish, and resentful, *rajas* makes him aggressive, heroic, and proud, while *sattva* conduces to illuminated repose, benignity, and understanding.

karma keeps the life-monad linked to the world.[51] By increasing the yellow and white karmic matter, virtuous acts produce the gentler, more savory ties—but these are ties, even so; they do not suffice to consummate release. "Influx" (*āsrava*) of every type has to be blocked if nirvāṇa is to be attained, and this arrestment of life can be affected only by abstention from action—all action whatsoever, whether good or bad.[52]

A basic fact generally disregarded by those who "go in" for Indian wisdom is this one of the total rejection of every last value of humanity by the Indian teachers and winners of redemption from the bondages of the world. "Humanity" (the phenomenon

[51] Compare *Bhagavad Gītā* 14. 5-9. "The guṇas—sattva, rajas, and tamas—which are born of matter, bind the immortal dweller-in-the-body fast in the body. Sattva, being stainless, is luminous and of the nature of peace and serenity; it binds by creating attachment to happiness and to knowledge. Rajas, the essence of passion, is the cause of thirst and fascination; it binds the dweller-in-the-body by attachment to action. Tamas, finally, is born of ignorance, and bewilders all embodied beings; it binds by inadvertence, indolence, and sleep. Thus, while tamas darkens judgment and attaches to miscomprehension, rajas attaches to action, and sattva to happiness."

[52] The Jaina Tīrthaṅkara, by virtue of his boundless intuition, or omniscience, which is based on the crystal purity and infinite radiance of the life-monad released from its karmic matter, directly perceives, in the case of each and all, the precise color, taste, fragrance, and quality of the matter infecting the life-monad; he knows exactly the degree of pollution, obscurity, or brightness of every individual that he sees. For the luminosity of the monad pervades the whole organism, and is thought of as emanating even beyond the strict circumference of the bodily frame, in such a way as to form around it a subtle halo, invisible to the average mortal but clearly perceptible to the enlightened saint. Here we have the archaic background of the halo—the "aura' of the Theosophists—which encompasses every living form, and which, through its shadings, darkness, or radiance, betrays the status of the soul, showing whether one is steeped in obscuring animal passions and bedimming ego-propensities, or advanced along the path toward purification and release from the bondages of universal matter.

of the human being, the ideal of its perfection, and the ideal of the perfected human society) was the paramount concern of Greek idealism, as it is today of Western Christianity in its modern form; but for the Indian sages and ascetics, the Mahātmas and enlightened Saviors, "humanity" was no more than the shell to be pierced, shattered, and dismissed. For perfect non-activity, in thought, speech, and deed, is possible only when one has become dead to *every* concern of life: dead to pain and enjoyment as well as to every impulse to power, dead to the interests of intellectual pursuit, dead to all social and political affairs—deeply, absolutely, and immovably uninterested in one's character as a human being. The sublime and gentle final fetter, virtue, is thus itself something to be severed. It cannot be regarded as the goal, but only as the beginning of the great spiritual adventure of the "Crossing-Maker," a stepping place to the superhuman sphere. That sphere, moreover, is not only superhuman but even superdivine—beyond the gods, their heavens, their delights, and their cosmic powers. "Humanity," consequently, whether in the individual or in the collective aspect, can no longer be of concern to anyone seriously striving for perfection along the way of the ultimate Indian wisdom. Humanity and its problems belong to the philosophies of life that we discussed above: the philosophies of success (*artha*), pleasure (*kāma*), and duty (*dharma*); these can be of no interest to one who has literally died to time—for whom life is death. "Let the dead bury their dead":[53] that is the thought. This is something that makes it very difficult for us of the modern Christian West to appreciate and assimilate the traditional message of India.

The sentimental or heroic divinization of man along the lines of the classic and modern humanitarian ideals is something totally foreign to the Indian mind. From the Indian point of view, the special dignity of the human being consists solely in the fact that he is capable of becoming enlightened, free from bondage,

[53] Matthew 8:22.

and therewith competent, ultimately, for the role of the supreme teacher and savior of all beings, including the beasts and the gods. The life-monad mature enough for this super-godly task descends to earth from the high realm of heavenly beatitude, as did the monad of the Jaina Savior, Pārśvanātha,[54] the temporary delights and powers of the gods having become meaningless for his ripened insight. And then, in a final existence among men, the savior himself achieves perfect enlightenment and therewith release, and by his teaching renews the timeless doctrine of the way to reach this goal.

This amazing ideal, expressed in the legendary biographies of the Buddhas and Tīrthaṅkaras, was taken seriously and literally as an ideal for all. It was actually regarded as open to man, and steps were taken to realize it. Apparently, it was a non-Brāhman, pre-Āryan vision of man's role in the cosmos native to the Indian sub-continent. The way of perfectibility taught was that of yogic asceticism and self-abnegation, while the image constantly held before the mind's eye was that of the human savior as the redeemer even of the gods.

In the West such thinking has been suppressed systematically as heresy—a heresy of titanism. Already for the Greeks, it was the classic fault of the suffering hero, the ὕβρις of the anti-gods or titans, while in the Christian Church such presumption has been mocked as simply incredible.[55] Nevertheless, in our modern Western Christian poetry there can be pointed out at least one great instance of the idea of the coming of a human being to the rescue of God. For when Parsifal, in the third act of Wagner's opera, brings back the holy spear, cures Amfortas, the sick guardian of the holy grail, and restores the grail itself to its beneficent func-

[54] *Supra,* pp. 194-195.

[55] See, for example, the accounts of Simon Magus given by Justin Martyr (*Dial. cum Tryph.* cxx. 16), Tertullian (*De Idol.* 9, *de Fuga,* 12, *de Anima,* 34, *Apol.* 13), and Origen (*C. Celsum,* i. 57. vi. 11), or any modern Christian missionary's account of Indian belief.

tion, the voices of the angels sing out from on high: "Redemption to the Redeemer." The sacred blood of Christ, that is to say, has been redeemed from the curse or spell that was nullifying its operation. And again, in Wagner's cycle of the *Ring of the Nibelung,* a pagan parallel to this motif is developed in almost identical terms. Brünnhilde quiets Wotan's sufferings, putting to rest the All-Father of the universe, when she returns the Ring to the primeval waters and sings to Wotan: *"Ruhe nun, ruhe, du Gott!"* —"Rest now, rest, thou God!" The enlightened individual, perfected through suffering, all-knowing through compassion, self-detached through having conquered ego, redeems the divine principle, which is incapable, alone, of disengaging itself from its own fascination with the cosmic play.[56]

5.

The Mask of the Personality

ULYSSES, in the Homeric epic, descended to the netherworld to seek counsel of the departed, and there found, in the murky twilight land of Pluto and Persephone, the shades of his former companions and friends who had been killed at the siege of Troy or had passed away during the years following the conquest of the town. They were but shadows in that dim realm; yet each could be recognized immediately, for all preserved the features that had been theirs on earth. Achilles declared that he would prefer the hard and joyless life of an obscure peasant in the broad daylight of the living to the melancholy monotony of his present

[56] Cf. Zimmer, *The King and the Corpse,* pp. 51-52.

half-existence as the greatest of the heroes among the dead; nevertheless, he was still perfectly himself. The physiognomy, the mask of the personality, had survived the separation from the body and the long exile from the human sphere on the surface of the land.

Nowhere in the Greek epic do we find the idea of the dead hero being divested of his identity with his former, temporal being. The possibility of losing one's personality through death, the slow dissolution, melting away, and final fading out of the historic individuality, was something not considered by the Greeks of Homer's time. Nor did it dawn on the medieval Christian mind. Dante, like Ulysses, was a wayfarer in the world beyond the grave; conducted by Virgil through the circles of hell and purgatory, he ascended to the spheres; and everywhere, throughout the length of his journey, he beheld and conversed with personal friends and enemies, mythical heroes, and the great figures of history. All were recognizable immediately, and all satisfied his insatiable curiosity by recounting their biographies, dwelling at great length, in spun-out tales and arguments, upon the minute details of their trifling, short-lived individual existences. Their personalities of yore seem to have been only too well preserved through the long wandering in the vastness of eternity. Though definitely and forever severed from the brief moments of their lifetimes on earth, they were still preoccupied with the problems and vexations of their biographies and haunted by their guilt, which clung to them in the symbolic forms of their peculiar punishments. Personality held all in its clutches—the glorified saints in heaven as well as the tortured, suffering inmates of hell; for personality, according to the medieval Christians, was not to be lost in death, or purged away by the after-death experiences. Rather, life beyond the grave was to be but a second manifestation and experience of the very essence of the personality, only realized on a broader scale and in a freer style, and with a more striking display of the nature and implications of the virtues and the vices.

For the Western mind, the personality is eternal. It is indestructible, not to be dissolved. This is the basic idea in the Christian doctrine of the resurrection of the body, the resurrection being our regaining of our cherished personality in a purified form, worthy to fare before the majesty of the Almighty. That personality is thought to go on forever—even though, by a curious inconsistency, it is not believed to have existed anywhere, in any state or form, previous to the carnal birth of the mortal individual. The personality did not exist in extra-human spheres, from all eternity, before its temporal earthly manifestation. It is declared to have come into being with the mortal act of procreation, and yet is supposed to go on after the demise of the procreated mortal frame: temporal in its beginning, immortal in its end.

The term "personality" is derived from the Latin *persona*. *Persona,* literally, means the mask that is worn over the face by the actor on the Greek or Roman stage; the mask "through" (*per*) which he "sounds" (*sonat*) his part. The mask is what bears the features or make-up of the role, the traits of hero or heroine, servant or messenger, while the actor himself behind it remains anonymous, an unknown being intrinsically aloof from the play, constitutionally unconcerned with the enacted sufferings and passions. Originally, the term *persona* in the sense of "personality" must have implied that people are only impersonating what they seem to be. The word connotes that the personality is but the mask of one's part in the comedy or tragedy of life and not to be identified with the actor. It is not a manifestation of his true nature, but a veil. And yet the Western outlook—which originated with the Greeks themselves and was then developed in Christian philosophy—has annulled the distinction, implied in the term, between the mask and the actor whose face it hides. The two have become, as it were, identical. When the play is over the *persona* cannot be taken off; it clings through death and into the life beyond. The Occidental actor, having wholly identified himself with the enacted personality during his moment on the stage of the world, is unable to take it off when the time comes for departure, and so keeps it on indefinitely, for millenniums—even eternities—after the play is over. To lose his *persona* would mean for him to lose every hope for a future beyond death. The mask has become for him fused, and confused, with his essence.

Indian philosophy, on the other hand, insists upon the difference, stressing the distinction between the actor and the role. It continually emphasizes the contrast between the displayed existence of the individual and the real being of the anonymous actor, concealed, shrouded, and veiled in the costumes of the play. Indeed, one of the dominant endeavors of Indian thought throughout the ages has been to develop a dependable technique for keeping the line clear between the two. A meticulous defining of their interrelationships and their modes of collaboration, as well as a practical, systematic, and courageously enforced effort to break from the confines of the one into the unfathomed reaches of the other, has been carried on for ages—primarily through the numerous introspective processes of yoga. Piercing and dissolving all the layers of the manifest personality, the relentlessly introverted consciousness cuts through the mask, and, at last discarding it in all of its stratifications, arrives at the anonymous and strangely unconcerned actor of our life.

Although in the Hindu and Buddhist texts vivid descriptions of the traditional hells or purgatories are to be found, where appalling details are dwelt upon minutely, never is the situation quite the same as that of the afterworlds of Dante and Ulysses, filled with celebrities long dead who still retain all of the characteristics of their personal masks. For in the Oriental hells, though multitudes of suffering beings are depicted in their agonies, none retain the traits of their earthly individualities. Some can remember having once been elsewhere and know what the deed was through which the present punishment was incurred, nevertheless, in general, all are steeped and lost in their present misery.

Just as any dog is absorbed in the state of being precisely whatever dog it happens to be, fascinated by the details of its present life—and as we ourselves are in general spellbound by our present personal existences—so are the beings in the Hindu, Jaina, and Buddhist hells. They are unable to remember any former state, any costume worn in a previous existence, but identify themselves exclusively with that which they now are. And this, of course, is why they are in hell.

Once this Indian idea has struck the mind, then the question immediately presents itself: Why am I bound to be what I am? Why have I to wear the mask of this personality, which I think and feel myself to be? Why must I endure its destiny, the limitations, delusions, and ambitions of this peculiar part that I am being driven to enact? Or why, if I have left one mask behind me, am I now back again in the limelight in another, enacting another role and in a different setting? What is compelling me to go on this way, being always something particular—an individual, with all of these particular shortcomings and experiences? Where and how am I ever to attain to another state—that of not being something particular, beset by limitations and qualities that obstruct my pure, unbounded being?

Can one grow into something devoid of any specificity of shade and color, undefined by shape, unlimited by qualities: something unspecific and therefore not liable to any specific life?

These are the questions that lead to the experiment of asceticism and yoga practice. They arise out of a melancholy weariness of the will to live—the will grown tired, as it were, of the prospect of this endless before and after, as though an actor should become suddenly bored with his career. The doom of this timeless course of transmigration: forgotten past and aimless future! Why do I bother being what I am: man, woman, peasant, artist, rich or poor? Since I have impersonated, without remembering, all of the possible attitudes and roles—time and time again, in the lost past, in the worlds that have dissolved—why do I keep going on?

One might very well come to loathe the hackneyed comedy of life if one were no longer blinded, fascinated, and deluded by the details of one's own specific part. If one were no longer spellbound by the plot of the play in which one happened to be caught for the present, one might very well decide to resign—give up the mask, the costume, the lines, and the whole affair. It is not difficult to imagine why, for some, it might become simply a bore to go on with this permanent engagement, enacting character after character in this interminable stock company of life. When the feeling comes of being bored with it or nauseated (as it has come, time and time again, in the long history of India) then life revolts, rebels against its own most elementary task or duty of automatically carrying on. Growing from an individual to a collective urge, this leads to the founding of ascetic orders, such as those of the Jaina and the Buddhist communities of homeless monks: troops of renegade actors, heroic deserters, footloose and self-exiled from the universal farce of the force of life.

The argument—if the renegades would bother to justify themselves—would run like this:

"Why should we care what we are? What real concern have we with all those parts that people are continually forced to play? Not to know that one has already enacted every sort of role, time and time again—beggar, king, animal, god—and that the actor's career is no better in one than in another, is truly a pitiable state of mind; for the most obvious fact about the timeless engagement is that all the objects and situations of the plot have been offered and endured in endless repetition through the millenniums. People must be completely blind to go on submitting to the spell of the same old allurements; enthralled by the deluding enticements that have seduced every being that ever lived; hailing with expectation, as a new and thrilling adventure, the same trite deceptions of desire as have been experienced endlessly;

clinging now to this, now to that illusion—all resulting only in the fact that the actor goes on acting roles, each seemingly new yet already rendered many times, though in slightly differing costumes and with other casts. Obviously, this is a ridiculous impasse. The mind has been bewitched, trapped by the pressures of a blind life-force that whirls creatures along in a cycling, never-ending stream. And why? Who or what is doing this? Who is the fool that keeps this dim-witted entertainment on the boards?"

The answer that would have to be given to you should you be unable to find it for yourself would be simply—Man: Man himself: each individual. And the answer is obvious. For each goes on doing what has always been done, continually imagining himself to be doing something different. His brain, his tongue, his organs of action, are incorrigibly possessed by a drive to be doing something—and he does it. That is how he builds up new tasks for himself, contaminating himself every minute with new particles of karmic matter, which enter into his nature, flow into his life-monad, sully its essence, and bedim its light. These involvements fetter him to an existence murky with desire and ignorance; and here he treasures his transitory personality as though it were something substantial—clings to the short spell of confused life which is the only thing of which he is aware, cherishes the brief passage of individual existence between birth and the funeral pyre—and thus unconsciously prolongs the period of his own bondage indefinitely into the future. By being active in the pursuit of what he conceives to be his own or someone else's welfare and happiness, he only makes his own bonds, as well as everyone else's, the tighter.

6.

The Cosmic Man

THAT GOD has a human form was a prevailing tenet of the pre-Christian Near East. The Hebrews, for example, though forbidden to produce graven images of their deity, nevertheless conceived of him as anthropomorphic. Jehovah made the first man after his own likeness, and we are all in human form, as descendants of Adam, because Jehovah has that form. Jehovah is the FIRST MAN, divine and eternal, whereas Adam is only the *first man*—made in the image of Jehovah, but of earth and consequently perishable. Jesus, finally, is the *second man,* or the MAN'S son, who came down to restore the perfection of the created image.

In contrast to these Near Eastern conceptions, which are of Sumero-Semitic origin, the aboriginal, pre-Āryan Indian tradition—which is what is represented in the religion of the Jainas—regards as the FIRST MAN not God (God distinct from matter, creating the universe out of matter as out of a second principle different from his own essence) but the organism of the universe itself. The entire cosmos, according to this belief, has a human form, never had a beginning, and will never end. Not "spirit" distinct from "matter," but "spiritual matter," "materialized spirit," is the FIRST MAN. The philosophy of Jainism, in this respect, is monistic.

In its analysis of the psychology and destiny of *man,* on the other hand, Jainism is dualistic. The life-monad *(jīva)* is regarded as absolutely different from the "karmic matter" *(a-jīva,* "non-*jīva"*) of the six colorings,[57] by which it is bound down and with-

[57] Cf. *supra,* p. 229.

held from liberation. This is a view that Jainism shares with the Sāṅkhya philosophy, which is likewise non-Āryan, non-Vedic, and rooted in the world view of aboriginal India;[58] for in the Sāṅkhya, the life-monads (there called *puruṣas*) are strictly distinguished from lifeless matter (there called *prakṛti*), and the goal of man's spiritual effort is conceived of as the realization of the separation of the two.

This radical dualism of the early Jaina and Sāṅkhya views is in striking contrast to the well-known "nondualism" of classic Brāhmanism, as developed in the Upaniṣads and *Bhagavad Gītā* and supremely stated in the Vedānta;[59] for according to the Vedāntic teaching, matter (*prakṛti*) is materialized energy (*prāṇa, śakti*), which, in turn, is the temporal manifestation of that incorporeal, supra-spiritual, eternal essence which is the innermost Self (*ātman*) of all things. The Self (*ātman*) both evolves the phenomenal realm of matter (*prakṛti*) and simultaneously enters into it under the form of the life-monads, or individual selves (*jīvas, puruṣas*). In other words, all things, in all their aspects, are but reflexes of that one eternal Self—Ātman-Brahman—which is in essence beyond all definition, name and form.[60]

"The non-existent, verily, was here in the beginning," we read, for example, in one of the basic Brāhmanic texts.[61] That "non-existent" is not to be regarded simply as a nothing; for then one would not have declared that it "was." Hence the text goes on

[58] Cf. *supra,* p. 60, Editor's note.

[59] *Editor's note:* This subject will be discussed at length, *infra,* pp. 355-463. Dr. Zimmer's present point will be simply that though the Jaina-Sāṅkhya view is dualistic and the Vedic-Vedāntic nondualistic with respect to the relationship of the life-monad (*jīva, puruṣa*) to matter (*karma, prakṛti*), both traditions represent the Cosmic Man as identical with the universe—not as an external God-Creator of something absolutely separate from himself.

[60] Cf. *supra,* pp. 74-83.

[61] *Śatapatha Brāhmaṇa* 6. 1. 1. 109.

to ask: "What was this non-existent?" To which it gives the answer: "Life energy (*prāṇa*)."

Now the seven life energies (*prāṇas*) spoke together: [62] "Truly, in the state in which we now find ourselves," they said, "we shall never be able to bring forth. Let us make, therefore, out of these seven men [i.e., themselves], one man. They made those seven men [themselves] into one man. . . . He it was who became the Lord of Progeny.

"And this MAN, the Lord of Progeny, felt the desire within himself: 'I would be more! I would bring forth!' He travailed and created heat within. When he had travailed and created heat, he brought forth from himself, as his first creation, Holy Power, that is, the 'threefold wisdom' [the Vedas]. This threefold wisdom became a solid 'standing place' on which he was able to stand firm. . . .

"On this solid place he then firmly stood and glowed within. He brought forth the waters, out of himself, out of speech (*vāc*), to be the world. Speech indeed was his; it was brought forth from him. It filled everything here, whatever is here it filled."

This is an example of a mythological rendition of the classical Brāhmanic view of the procession of all creation, in all its aspects, from the One. Speech (*vāc,* i.e., the Word, λόγος) and the waters (compare Genesis 1:2) are here the self-duplication of the one unqualified Reality—its self-manifestation as the multifariously qualified. The world of names and forms (*nāmarūpa*),[63] and of the subject-object polarity, has been produced; the state of the pairs-of-opposites (viz. "spirit" and "matter") has been created as an emanation, or self-splitting, of the nondual FIRST MAN. All partakes of, and participates in, his being. What would seem

[62] *Prāṇa,* "life breath": the seven (usually five) prāṇas constitute the vital energies in every creature; their departure marks the death of the individual being; cf. *infra,* pp. 318-319. In the present text they are personified as seven holy sages, or Ṛṣis.

[63] Cf. *supra,* pp. 23-24.

to the eye to be a sphere of dual principles has proceeded from that unique Reality and *is* that one Reality. The Brāhmans in their meditation, therefore, seek to resolve all back again to that "one without a second"—whereas the Jainas, in theirs, separate (within the confines of that one FIRST MAN) the element of spirit (the life-monad, *jīva*) from that of matter (*karma, ajīva*). Nevertheless in both cases—both according to the non-Āryan Jainas and according to the Indo-Āryan Brāhmans—the Universal God (who is at the same time the universe) is himself both "matter" and "spirit." This cosmic monism sets these beliefs far apart from the orthodox Judeo-Christian view.

The Christian notion of God as a giant human form is rendered by the Swedenborgians, however, in a figure that somewhat suggests the cosmic MAN of the Jainas. Emanuel Swedenborg (1688–1772) experienced in his visions the whole of heaven in this anthropomorphic way. His work, *Heaven and Its Wonders, the World of Spirits, and Hell: from Things Heard and Seen,*[64] states: "That heaven as one whole represents one man, is an arcanum not yet known in the world, but very well known in the heavens." [65] "The angels," Swedenborg continues, "do not, indeed, see all heaven, collectively, in such a form, for the whole of heaven is too vast to be grasped by the sight of any angel; but they occasionally see distant societies, consisting of many thousands of angels, as one object in such a form; and from a society, as a part, they form their conclusion respecting the whole, which is heaven." [66] "Such being the form of heaven, it is also governed by the Lord as one man, and thus as one whole." [67]

In the same great visionary's *Angelic Wisdom concerning the Divine Love and the Divine Wisdom* (1763), where the heavens

[64] First published in Latin, London, 1758. Translation by the Rev. Samuel Noble, New York, 1883.

[65] *Ib.*, § 59.

[66] *Ib.*, § 62.

[67] *Ib.*, § 63.

are again described as a human organism, we read: "The heavens are divided into two kingdoms, one called celestial, the other spiritual; in the celestial kingdom love to the Lord reigns, in the spiritual kingdom wisdom from that love. The kingdom where love reigns is called heaven's cardiac kingdom, the one where wisdom reigns is called its pulmonic kingdom. Be it known, that the whole angelic heaven in its aggregate represents a man, and before the Lord appears as a man; consequently its heart makes one kingdom and its lungs another. For there is a general cardiac and pulmonic movement throughout heaven, and a particular movement therefrom in each angel. The general cardiac and pulmonic movement is from the Lord alone, because love and wisdom are from Him alone";[68] i.e., heaven has the form of a giant man, and this form is enlivened through the cardiac movement which is divine love, incessantly proceeding from God, as well as by the pulmonic, or respiratory, which is divine reason. God is not identical with the giant anthropomorphic organism formed of all the stratifications of heaven, yet pervades it with his love and wisdom, and these, in turn, pervade the organism, as the blood from the heart and the air from the lungs pervade the human frame.

The most significant difference between this Western and the Indian Cosmic Man is that whereas in Swedenborg's vision only heaven is shaped according to the divine human image (which is a likeness of the archetypal form of God himself), in Jainism the whole universe, including even its infrahuman stratifications, is comprised in the divine anthropomorphic organism—beasts and plants, which are devoid of man's higher faculties of love, wisdom, and spirituality, and also inorganic matter and the mute elements. This accords with the universal scope of India's doctrines of perfection, transformation, and redemption: not only human beings, but all existences are included. Though steeped in darkness, the beasts and even the atoms are looking for salva-

[68] Published by the American Swedenborg and Publishing Society, New York, 1912, § 381.

tion. They are meant to be taught and guided by the universal saviors, enlightened and redeemed; for they are members of the all-comprehending brotherhood of life-monads. Their destiny is to ascend, at last, beyond the bondages of the karma of the six colorings.

"Because God is a Man," we read again in Swedenborg's *Divine Love and Wisdom* (and here it becomes clear that the human shape of the heavens can be identified with God himself), "the whole angelic heaven in the aggregate resembles a single man, and is divided into regions and provinces according to the members, viscera, and organs of man. Thus there are societies of heaven which constitute the province of all things of the brain, of all things of the facial organs, and of all things of the viscera of the body; and these provinces are separated from each other, just as those organs are separated in man; moreover, the angels know in what province of man they are. The whole heaven has this resemblance to man, because *God is a Man. God is also heaven,* because the angels, who constitute heaven, are recipients of love and wisdom from the Lord, recipients are images." [69] The corollary, of course, is that the human organism is a reflection of heavens: "The multitude of these little glands [which constitute the human brain] may also be compared to the multitude of angelic societies in the heavens, which also are countless, and, I have been told, *are in the same order as the glands.*" [70]

"It has not been granted me to see of what form hell is in the whole: it has only been told me, that as the universal heaven, viewed collectively, is as one man, so the universal hell, viewed collectively, is as one devil, and may also be exhibited to view in the shape of one devil." [71] "It has hitherto been supposed in the world, that there is a certain individual devil who rules over the hells; and that he was created an angel of light, but afterwards

[69] *Ib.*, § 288. The italics are Dr. Zimmer's.

[70] *Ib.*, § 366. The italics again are Dr. Zimmer's.

[71] Swedenborg, *Heaven and Its Wonders and Hell,* § 553.

became a rebel, and was cast, with his crew, into hell. The reason that such a belief has prevailed is, because mention occurs in the Word of the devil and Satan, and also of Lucifer, and the Word has been understood in those passages, according to the literal sense: whereas the truth is, that by the devil and Satan is there signified hell; by the devil being meant that hell which is at the back, and which is inhabited by the worst sort of spirits, who are called evil genii; and by Satan, the hell which is in front, the inhabitants of which are not so malignant, and who are called evil spirits: whilst by Lucifer are signified such as belong to Babel or Babylon, who are those who pretend to extend their authority over heaven itself."[72]

"In the Grand Man, who is heaven, they that are stationed in the head, are in the enjoyment of every good above all others: for they are in the enjoyment of love, peace, innocence, wisdom, and intelligence; and thence of joy and happiness. These have an influx into the head, and into whatever appertains to the head, with man, and corresponds thereto. In the Grand Man, who is heaven, they that are stationed in the breast, are in the enjoyment of the good of charity and faith. . . . In the Grand Man, or heaven, they that are stationed in the loins, and in the organs belonging to generation therewith connected, are they who are eminently grounded in conjugal love. They who are stationed in the feet, are grounded in the lowest good of heaven, which is called spiritual-natural good. They who are in the arms and hands, are in the power of truth derived from good. They who are in the eyes, are those eminent for understanding. They who are in the ears, are in attention and obedience. They in the nostrils, are those distinguished for perception. They in the mouth and tongue, are such as excel in discoursing from understanding and perception. They in the kidneys, are such as are grounded in truth of a searching, distinguishing, and castigatory character. They in the liver, pancreas, and spleen, are grounded in the puri-

[72] *Ib.*, § 544.

fication of good and truth by various methods. So with those in the other members and organs. All have an influx into the similar parts of man, and correspond to them. The influx of heaven takes place into the functions and uses of the members; and their uses, being from the spiritual world, invest themselves with forms by means of such materials as are found in the natural world, and so present themselves in effects. Hence there is a correspondence between them." [73] "In general, the supreme or third heaven composes the head, as far as the neck; the middle or second heaven composes the breast or body, to the loins and knees; the lowest or first heaven composes the legs and feet down to the soles; as also, the arms down to the fingers; for the arms and hands are parts belonging to the lowest organs of man, although at the sides." [74]

The astonishingly close relationship of this anthropormorphic image to the Cosmic Man of Jaina belief will appear in the course of the following exposition of the Jaina way of ascending to the topmost cranial vacancy of that Grand Man which is their universe.

7.

The Jaina Doctrine of Bondage

EVERY thought and act, according to the pessimistic philosophy of the Jainas, entails an accumulation of fresh karmic substance.

[73] *Ib.*, § 96. Compare the Indian idea of the microcosm as a settlement of divine forces enacting the roles of sense and the other faculties; as, for instance, in the hymn from the *Atharva Veda* quoted *supra,* pp. 9-11.

[74] *Ib.*, § 65.

To go on living means to go on being active—in speech, in body, or in mind; it means to go on doing something every day. And this results in the storing up involuntarily of the "seeds" of future action, which grow and ripen into the "fruits" of our coming sufferings, joys, situations, and existences. Such "seeds" are represented as entering and lodging in the life-monad, where, in due time, they become transformed into the circumstances of life, producing success and calamity and weaving the mask—the physiognomy and character—of a developing individual. The process of life itself consumes the karmic substance, burning it up like fuel, but at the same time attracts fresh material to the burning center of vital operations. Thus the life-monad is reinfected by karma. New seeds of future fruits pour in. Two contradictory yet exactly complementary processes are kept, in this way, in operation. The seeds, the karmic materials, are being exhausted rapidly all the time through the unconscious as well as the conscious actions of the psychosomatic system, and yet through those identical actions the karmic storage bins are being continually re-stocked. Hence the conflagration that is one's life goes crackling on.

This self-supporting, continuous, dual process (the karmic seed-substance of the six colorings [75] burning itself out into events that themselves replenish it) is regarded as taking place—in a very literal, physical sense—in the subtle sphere or body of the life-monad (*jīva*).[76] The continuous influx (*āsrava*) [77] of subtle matter into the life-monad is pictured as a kind of pouring in of liquid colorings, which then tinge it; for the life-monad is a subtle crystal, which, in its pristine state, untinged by karmic matter, is stainless, devoid of color, and perfectly transparent; the flow entering the clear body darkens it, infecting it with the color (*leśyā*) corresponding to the moral character of the committed act. Virtuous acts and the lighter, venial offenses impart comparatively

[75] Cf. *supra*, p. 229.

[76] Cf. *supra*, pp. 227-229.

[77] Cf. *supra*, p. 230.

light, less obscuring leśyās (mild whitish shades, through yellow and violent red, down to smoky tones—as we have already seen) whereas major sins bring in much darker stains (dark blue and black). The worst offense possible, according to the Jaina view, is the killing or injuring of a living being: *hiṁsā,* "the intent to kill" (from the verbal root *han,* "to kill"). *Ahiṁsā,* "non-injury," correspondingly (i.e., the infliction of no harm on *any* creature), is the primary Jaina rule of virtue.

This clean-cut principle is based on the belief that all life-monads are fundamentally fellow creatures—and by "all" is meant not only human beings, but also animals and plants, and even the indwelling molecules or atoms of matter. The killing even accidentally of such a fellow being darkens the crystal of the life-monad with a dye of deepest hue. That is why animals of prey, which feed on creatures that they have killed, are always infected with leśyās very dark in shade. So also men who engage in killing professionally—butchers, hunters, warriors, etc.: their life-monads are completely without light.

The color of the monad-crystal indicates the realm of the universe, whether high or low, which the individual is to inhabit. Gods and celestial beings are of the brighter hues; animals and the tortured inmates of hell are dark. And during the course of a lifetime the color of the crystal continually changes according to the moral conduct of the living being. In merciful, unselfish people, inclined toward purity, self-abnegation, enlightenment, and release, the crystal continually brightens, the lighter colorings coming finally to prevail, whereas in the selfish, heedless, and reckless—those doomed to sink in their following birth either to the tortures of hell or to the lower realms of the animal world where they will feed upon each other—the darkness of the crystal thickens into black. And according to its color, the life-monad ascends or falls (quite literally) in the body of the Universal Being.

This literal-minded, gentle doctrine of universal vice and virtue was evolved by an ascetic, self-denying, saintly group of renegades from the struggle for life, and accepted by a peaceful, vegetarian bourgeoisie—merchants, money-dealers, and artisans. Apparently, it goes back to the deepest Indian past. The theory of the karmic colors (leśyās) is not peculiar to the Jainas, but seems to have been part of the general pre-Āryan inheritance that was preserved in Magadha (northeastern India), and there restated in the fifth century B.C. by a number of non-Brāhman teachers. It is an archaic bit of naïvely materialistic psychology diametrically opposed to the main tenets of the Vedic tradition. And yet, the vivid metaphor of the tainted crystal has been carried on in the composite stream of classical Indian teaching, which developed when the ancient Brāhman orthodoxy and the no less ancient non-Āryan traditions at last became synthesized. In the Sāṅkhya system it figures conspicuously, where it is used to illustrate the relationship between the life-monad and the context of bondage in which the monad is held until discriminating knowledge finally dawns and the bonds are dissolved. From the Sāṅkhya it passed then into Buddhist and Brāhman thought.

As represented by the Jainas, the advance of the individual toward perfection and emancipation is the result of an actual physical process of cleansing taking place in the sphere of subtle matter—literally, a cleansing of the crystal-like life-monad. When the latter is freed completely of all coloring karmic contamination it literally shines with a transparent lucidity; for the crystal of the life-monad, in itself, is absolutely diaphanous. Moreover, when made clean it is immediately capable of mirroring the highest truth of man and the universe, reflecting reality as it really is. The instant the karmic darkening substance of the six colorings is removed, therefore, non-knowing too is gone. Omniscience, that is to say, is co-existent with the supreme state of the absolute clarity of the life-monad, and this, precisely, is release. No longer is the monad dimmed with beclouding passions, but open—free—unlimited by the particularizing qualities that constitute individuality. No longer is there felt the otherwise universal compulsion to keep on wearing the mask of some bewildered personality, the mask of man, beast, tortured soul, or god.

8.

The Jaina Doctrine of Release

THE TRANSCENDENTAL wisdom that confers, and is identical with, release from the round of rebirths is regarded as a secret doctrine in the Brāhmanic tradition, into which it was introduced as a new disclosure in the comparatively late period of the Upaniṣads. The Āryan sages of the Vedic Age knew nothing of transmigration; nor was the doctrine alluded to in the complete course of orthodox Vedic studies that was communicated centuries later by the Brāhman sage Āruṇi to his son Śvetaketu.[78] The idea of the sorrowful round really belongs to the non-Āryan, aboriginal inheritance of those noble clans that in Mahāvīra's and the Buddha's time were challenging the somewhat narrow views of Brāhman orthodoxy; and it was imparted freely to spiritually qualified Brāhmans when those haughty conquerors finally condescended to ask for it. For the wisdom of the non-Āryan sages had never been exclusive in quite the same way as that of the Vedic Brāhmans. The Jaina, Buddhist, and other related heterodox Indian teachings [79] are not kept secret like the powerful formulae of the Brāhman families. They are regarded as belonging to all—the

[78] *Chāndogya Upaniṣad* 6; cf. *infra,* pp. 335-337.

[79] For the meaning of the terms "orthodox" and "heterodox" in this context, cf. *supra,* p. 60, Editor's note.

only prerequisite to their communication being that the candidate should have adopted an ascetic way of life after fulfilling the preliminary disciplines of his normal secular duties; that is to say, they are exclusive only in a spiritual, not in a genealogical way.[80]

In Vedic Brāhmanism the domestic cult serves the departed Fathers sent ahead to the Father-world, who require ancestral offerings lest destruction in the form of absolute dissolution (*nivṛtti*) should overtake them. The cult, in other words, serves the end of continued life, defending the dead against the terrible "dying again" (*punar-mṛtyu*) through which their existence would be brought to its final term. This is in diametrical contrast to the chief concern of aboriginal, pre-Āryan India, which was, as we have seen, lest life in its painful round should *not* end. The rituals of the secular cult here were practiced not for the continuance, but for the amelioration, of existence—the averting of ill-fortune and sufferings during the present life, as well as the avoidance of descent to the painful purgatories or rebirth in the kingdom of the beasts. Celestial bliss was desired as infinitely preferable to the agonies of the lower realms, but beyond that, there was the still higher good known to the one who would never again be involved in any form at all.

Omnis determinatio est negatio: all determination of the life-monad through the karmic influx that makes for individualization detracts from its infinite power and negates its highest possibilities. Hence the proper goal is *restitutio in integrum,* restitution of the life-monad to its innate ideal state. This is what is known in Sanskrit as *kaivalya,* "integration," the restoration of the faculties that have been temporarily lost through being obscured. All entities as we see them in the world are in varying degrees imperfect, yet capable of perfection through proper effort and the consequent insight. All beings are intended to be omniscient, omnipotent, unlimited, and unfet-

80 Cf. *supra,* pp. 59-60.

tered; that is what constitutes their secret veiled dignity. Potentially they partake of the plenitude of life, which is divine; essentially they are constituents of the abundance and fullness of blissful energy. And yet they dwell in sorrow. The aim of men must be to make manifest the power that is latent within them by removing whatever hindrances may be standing in the way.

Although this conception was certainly not native to the Āryan religion of the Vedic gods, and was in fact diametrically opposed to its conception of the nature and destiny of man, it became fused with it during the first millennum B.C., and since that time has stood as one of the basic doctrines of classical Indian philosophy. It pervades the whole texture of Brāhmanic thought throughout the period of the Upaniṣads, where the realization of the divine Self within is proclaimed as the sole pursuit worthy of one endowed with human birth. And yet it is important to note that between the Jaina view and that of the Brāhmanic development of the first millennium (as represented, typically, in the Upaniṣads) there is no less difference than resemblance: also the Buddhist doctrine is very different; for whereas the Jaina philosophy is characterized by a strictly mechanical materialism with respect to the subtle substantiality of the life-monad and the karmic influx, as well as with respect to the state of the released, both in the Upaniṣads and in the Buddhistic writings an immaterial, psychological outlook on the same questions is presented. And this fundamental difference touches every detail, not only of the cosmologies and metaphysics in question, but also of the related moral codes.

For example, if a Jaina monk swallows a morsel of meat inadvertently while eating the food that has collected in his almsbowl during his daily begging-tour (at the doors of whatever town or village he may happen to be traversing in the course of his aimless, homeless pilgrimage), the crystal of his life-monad becomes automatically stained by a dark influx, in mechanical consequence of the fact that he has shared in the flesh of some slaughtered being. And wherever the Jaina ascetic walks, he has to sweep the way before his feet with a little broom, so that no minute living thing may be crushed by his heel. The Buddhist monk, on the contrary, goes without a broom. He is taught to be constantly watchful not so much of where he steps as of his feelings and intentions. He is to be "fully conscious and full of self-control" (*smṛtimant samprajānan*), mindful, attentive, and with his sense of responsibility constantly alert. With respect to meat, he is guilty only if he longs for it, or if the animal has been killed expressly for him and he knows it. Should he merely happen to receive some scraps along with the rice that he is offered, he can swallow these with the rest of the dish without becoming polluted.

The Buddhist idea of the progress to purity, self-detachment, and final enlightenment is based on a principle of basically moral watchfulness over one's feelings and propensities. Not the fact but the attitude toward it is the thing that counts. The Buddhist way, in other words, is a discipline of psychological control; and so there will be found no theories about either the subtle karmic influx or the subtle imperishable crystal of the life-monad in the Buddhist doctrine. Both of these ideas are discarded as materialistic errors, caused by primitive ignorance and not verified by inner experience. They are regarded as belonging to that vast morass of abstract metaphysical and biological lore which serves only to involve and trap the human mind—notions that rather fetter one to, than release one from, the spheres of pain and birth. For the outlook on psychic reality of the practicing Buddhist is based on the actual experiences of his own yoga-practice (the techniques of dismissing or doing away with every kind of fixed notion and attitude of mind), and these lead inevitably to a complete spiritualization not only of the idea of release but also of that of bondage. The accomplished Buddhist clings, in the end, to no notion whatsoever, not even that of the Buddha, that of the path of the doctrine, or that of the goal to be attained.

Jainism, on the other hand, is naïvely materialistic in its direct and simple view of the universe, the hosts of monads that fill matter as its elementary living molecules, and the problem of gaining release. The crystal of the life-monad, according to this system of archaic positivism, is actually (i.e., physically) stained and darkened by the various colors of the karmic influx; and this, moreover, has been its condition since immemorial times. To bring the monad to its proper state, every door through which new karmic substance might enter into it must be tightly closed and kept that way, so that the process of the automatic "influx of the six colorings" (*āsrava*) will be blocked. To close the gates means to abstain from action, action of every sort. The beclouding matter already present within will then slowly dwindle, transforming itself automatically into the natural events of the biological life-process.[81] The present karmic seeds will grow and yield their inevitable fruits in the form of sufferings and physical experiences, and so the discoloration will gradually disappear. Then at last, if no fresh particles are permitted to enter, the translucent purity of the life-monad will be automatically attained.

The Jaina monk does not permit himself to respond in any manner whatsoever to the events that afflict his person or take place within his ken. He subjects his physique and psyche to a terrific training in ascetic aloofness, and actually becomes unassailably indifferent to pleasure and pain, and to all objects, whether desirable, repugnant, or even dangerous. An incessant cleansing process is kept in operation, a severe and difficult physical and mental discipline of interior concentration, which burns up with its heat (*tapas*) the karmic seeds already present. Thus the life-monad gradually clears, and attains its intrinsic crystal clarity, while the actor obdurately refuses to participate

[81] Cf. *supra,* pp. 248-249.

any longer in the play on the stage of life. His goal is to achieve a state of intentional psychic paralysis. Rejecting every kind of mask and holding with a sublime stubbornness to his invincible state of non-co-operation, finally he wins. The busy host of players who fill the universe, still enchanted by their roles and eager to go on contending with each other for the limelight, changing masks and lines from life to life, enacting all the sufferings, achievements, and surprises of their biographies, simply turn from him and let him go. He has escaped. So far as the world is concerned, he is a useless fool.

The final state to which the Jaina monk thus wins is termed, as we have said, *kaivalya,* "isolation," "completeness through integration"—which means absolute release; for when every particle of karmic substance has been burnt out, no influx of new seeds having been permitted, there remains no longer any possibility of maturing a new experience. Even the danger of becoming a celestial being has been overcome—a king of gods, an Indra, wielding the thunderbolt and enjoying in domains of heavenly bliss, for periods of numerous oceans of time, the delectable fruits of virtuous conduct in former lives. All the ties that ever fettered the life-monad, whether to higher or to lower realms of being, have been dissolved away. No coloring remains as a hue of kinship to prompt one to assume the garb of some element, plant, animal, human or superhuman being; no hue of ignorance to make one move. And though the body may remain intact for a few more days, until its metabolism has completely ceased, the center of attraction of the life-monad has already lifted far beyond this mortal coil.

For karmic matter, subtle though it is, is a weight that pulls the monad down, retaining it in one or another of the spheres of ignorant action, the precise placement of the monad in these spheres being dependent upon its density or specific gravity—which is indicated by its hue. The darker leśyās—deep blue or black—hold the monad in the lower storeys of the universe, the subterranean chambers of hell or the worlds of mineral and plant existence, whereas when the hue brightens the monad is relieved somewhat of weight and mounts to one or another of the more elevated spheres, ascending perhaps to the human kingdom—which is situated on the surface of the earth, the middle plane of the numerously stratified universe—or even to the higher, supernal abodes of the godly beings. When, however, the supreme state of isolation (*kaivalya*) has been attained and the monad has been purged absolutely, relieved of every ounce of karmic ballast, then it lifts itself with unresisted buoyancy beyond all the strata of the six colors to the zenith, like a bubble of air, destitute of weight. There it abides above the cycling flow of the currents of life that agitate, one way or another, all the realms below. It has left permanently behind the active theater of the continually changing masks.

The metaphor of the bubble is one that is used frequently in the Jaina texts. The life-monad rises, passing through the celestial regions of the gods where radiant beings still burdened by the weight of virtuous karma enjoy the fruits of former lives of benignant thought and action. Self-luminous, transparent, the balloon ascends to the dome of the world—that highest sphere, called "slightly inclined" (*iṣat-prāgbhāra*), which is whiter than milk and pearls, more resplendent than gold and crystal, and has the shape of a divine umbrella. Another metaphor compares the life-monad to a gourd that has been made into a flask or bottle; its marrow has been removed and its surface covered with layers of clay to render it the more solid. Such an empty vessel if placed in the water will sink to the bottom because of the weight of the clay; but as the covering slowly dissolves, the gourd regains its natural lightness, and since it is filled with air it becomes lighter than the water, rising automatically from the bottom to the surface of the pond. With just such an automatic movement, the life-monad, once rid of karmic substance, rises from the depths of its imprisonment—this submarine world of the coating layers and masks of individual existence. Divested of the characteristic features of this or that particular existence-form—the nature of this or that man, woman, animal, or divine being—it becomes anonymous, absolutely buoyant, and absolutely free.

The universe through which the bubble or gourd ascends is pictured in the form of a colossal human being: a prodigious male or female, whose macrocosmic organism comprises the celestial, earthly, and infernal regions, all of which are peopled by innumerable beings.[82] The male colossus appeals to the manly asceticism of the Jaina monks and saints, while the female reflects an old pre-Āryan concept of the Universal Mother. The cult of the Mother Goddess goes back to the Neolithic Age, when it was distributed throughout western Asia and the lands surrounding the Mediterranean. Images of this goddess have been found even from the Paleolithic period. And to this day her worship survives in popular Hinduism. The Jaina conception is of a prodigious human form, male or female, the bounds of which constitute the limits of the universe. The surface of the earth, the playground of the human race, is regarded as situated at the level of the waist. The regions of the hells are beneath this plane, in the pelvic cavity, thighs, legs, and feet, while those of celestial beatitude, stratified one above the other, fill the chest, shoulders, neck, and head.[83] The region of supreme isolation (*kaivalya*) is at the crown of the dome inside the hollow of the skull.[84]

[82] Compare the vision of Swedenborg, *supra*, pp. 244-248.

[83] There is, for example, a class of exalted divine beings called *graiveyaka*, "belonging to or dwelling in the neck (*grīvā*)." Cf. *supra*, p. 193.

[84] These spheres within the body of the macrocosmic being are approximately paralleled (though not exactly) by the "centers" (*cakra*) of the human body as described in Haṭha Yoga and Kuṇḍalinī Yoga (cf. *infra*, pp. 584-585). The techniques of yoga go back, like the doctrines of the Jainas, to pre-Āryan Indian antiquity. They are not included among the original Vedic teachings of Brāhman-Āryan orthodoxy.

After its pilgrimage of innumerable existences in the various inferior stratifications, the life-monad rises to the cranial zone of the macrocosmic being, purged of the weight of the subtle karmic particles that formerly held it down. Nothing can happen to it any more; for it has put aside the traits of ignorance, those heavy veils of individuality that are the precipitating causes of biographical event. Decisively, once and for all, it has broken free from the vortex. It is now deathless, birthless, suspended beyond the cyclic law of karmic causation, like a distilled drop of water clinging to a ceiling or to the underside of the lid of a boiling pot. There, among all the other released life-monads clinging to the interior of the dome of the divine World Being, it remains forever—and the monads in that state, of course, are all as alike as so many drops. For they are pure particles, serene existences, purged of those imperfections that make for individuality. The masks, the former personal features, were distilled away, together with the seed-stuff that would have ripened into future experiences. Sterilized of coloring, flavor, and weight, the sublime crystals now are absolutely pure—like the drops of rain that descend from a clear sky, tasteless and immaculate.

Furthermore, since they have been relieved of the faculties of sensation that are inherent in all organisms (those that render sound, sight, smell, taste, and touch), the released life-monads are beyond the bounds of conditioned understanding which determine the modes of being of the various human, animal, plant, and even inorganic species. They neither perceive nor think, but are aware of everything directly. They know Truth precisely as it is. They are omniscient, as the sheer life-force itself would be if it could be relieved of the modifying darknesses of specific organisms, each with its limited range of sense and thinking faculties. For the moment the limitations that make particular experiences possible are eliminated, the perfect intuition of everything knowable is immediately attained. The need of experience is dissolved in infinite knowledge.—This is the *positive* meaning of the term and state of *kaivalya.*

One is reminded of the protest of the modern French poet and philosopher, Paul Valéry, in his novel, *Monsieur Teste.* "There are people," he writes, "who feel that their organs of sense are cutting them off from reality and essence. This feeling then *poisons* all their sense perceptions. What I see blinds me. What I hear makes me deaf. What I know makes me unknowing. In so far and inasmuch as I know, I am ignorant. This light before me is no more than a kind of blindfold and conceals either a darkness or a light that is more. . . . More what? Here the circle closes with a strange reversal: knowledge, a cloud obscuring the essence of being; the shining moon, like darkness or a cataract on the eye! Take it all away, so that I may see!" [85] This outcry, together with the modern theory of knowledge from which it arises, is remarkably close to the old idea to which Jainism holds: that of the limiting force of our various faculties of human understanding.

But the Tīrthaṅkaras have lost even the faculty of feeling; for this too belongs but to the texture of the flesh, the suffering garment of blood and nerves. Hence they are completely indifferent to what goes on in the stratified worlds that they have left beneath them. They are not touched by any prayer, nor moved by any act of worship. Neither do they ever descend to

[85] "Il y a des personnages qui sentent que leurs sens les séparent du réel, de l'être. Ce sens en eux *infecte* leurs autres sens.

"Ce que je vois m'aveugle. Ce que j'entends m'assourdit. Ce en quoi je sais, cela me rend ignorant. J'ignore en tant et pour autant que je sais. Cette illumination devant moi est un bandeau et recouvre ou une nuit ou une lumière plus. . . . Plus quoi? Ici le cercle se ferme, de cet étrange renversement: la connaissance, comme une nuage sur l'être; le mond brillant, comme une taie et opacité.

"Otez toute chose que j'y voie." (Paul Valéry, *Monsieur Teste,* nouvelle édition, Paris, 1946, pp. 60-61.)

intervene in the course of the Universal Round as does, for example, the supreme divinity of the Hindus, Viṣṇu, when he sends down periodically a particle of his transcendent essence as an Incarnation to restore the divine order of the universe upset by reckless tyrants and selfish demons.[86] The Jaina Tīrthaṅkaras are absolutely cut off. Nevertheless, the Jaina devotee pays them unceasing worship, concentrating his pious attention upon their images, as a means to his own progress in inner purification. And they are sometimes even celebrated side by side with the popular Hindu household and village gods; but never in the same spirit. For what the gods provide is temporal well-being, warding away the demons of disease and disaster, whereas the worship of the Tīrthaṅkaras—the "Victors," the "Heroes," the "Makers of the Crossing"—moves the mind to its highest good, which is eternal peace beyond the joys as well as the sorrows of the universal round.

9.

The Doctrine of Maskarin Gosāla

THE Indian ascetic carries a staff: *maskara, daṇḍa.* Vedāntic monks are sometimes called, therefore, *eka-daṇḍin,* "those bearing one staff"; but also *haṁsa,* "wild goose or swan"—because they are wanderers, like the great birds that migrate from the jungles of the south to the lakes of the Himalayas, at home in the lofty sky as well as on the water-surfaces of the earthly plane.

[86] Zimmer, *Myths and Symbols in Indian Art and Civilization,* index, *s.v.* "Vishnu: avatars of."

Daṇḍin, "bearing a staff," denotes, in general, the pilgrim ascetic (*sannyāsin*), whether of the Brāhman or of the Jaina orders. Buddhist monks also carry a staff, but theirs is named *khakkhara;* for it is provided with a set of rings that produce a monotonous clattering (*khak*), which announces the approach of the otherwise silent mendicant as he walks along the street or comes with his begging bowl for his daily meal. The Buddhist monk never asks for alms but halts in silence on the threshold, waiting to know whether he is to be given something; and when the bowl is filled he departs—again without a word. Only the sound of his khakkhara is heard. And this is the same as the sound of the staff of the Bodhisattva named Kṣiti-garbha, "He whose womb was the earth" or "Born from the earth." Kṣiti-garbha, with his khakkhara, wanders eternally through the spheres of hell, comforting the tortured beings and rescuing them from darkness by his very presence, indeed by the very sound of his staff.[87]

Maskarin Gosāla ("Gosāla of the pilgrim staff") was a contemporary of Mahāvīra and the Buddha. His encyclopedic systematization of the universe was akin to the tradition of the Jainas. Apparently the two doctrines were related, being derived from some main tradition of pre-Āryan natural science and psychology. Judging from the evidence available, this must have been a most elaborate, highly classificatory survey of all the divisions of the natural world. Gosāla's interpretation of the teaching can be reconstructed in its main outlines, and in some of its details, from the reports and criticisms contained in the early Buddhist and Jaina texts.

The followers of this much-abused and freely slandered teacher were the so-called *ājīvika*—those professing the doctrine termed *ā-jīva. Jīva* is the life-monad. The prefix *ā-* here signifies

[87] The concept of the Bodhisattva will be discussed at length, *infra,* pp. 534-552.

"as long as." The reference seems to be to Gosāla's striking doctrine that "as long as the life-monad" (*ā-jīva*) has not completed the normal course of its evolution (running through a fixed number of inevitable births) there can be no realization. The natural biological advance cannot be hurried by means of virtue and asceticism, or delayed because of vice; for the process takes place in its own good time. Apparently Gosāla at first collaborated with Mahāvīra. They were the joint leaders of a single community for many years. But they presently disagreed over certain major points of discipline and doctrine, quarreled, and separated, Gosāla leading a movement of secession. His following seems to have been numerous and to have represented a considerable force in the religious life of India for many years.[88] Their existence and importance as late as the third century B.C. is rendered certain by a royal dedicatory inscription on the walls of three rock-cut caves of a monastery on the Nāgārjuna Hill.[89] They were regarded as very dangerous by both the Buddhists and the Jainas.

Even while he was alive Maskarin Gosāla's enemies spared no words in their attacks upon him. The Buddha himself is quoted as having declared this imposing antagonist's teaching to be the very worst of all the contemporary erroneous doctrines. The Buddha compares it to a hempen garment—which not only is disagreeable to the skin but yields no protection against either

[88] There is an alternate interpretation of the origin and meaning of the name *ājīvika,* which points to this quarrel of the sects. Among the various rules against defilement of the saintly life, as defined by the Jainas, there is one called *ājīva,* which forbids the monk to earn his livelihood in any way. It is said that because the followers of Gosāla took to working for their living, disregarding this *ājīva* rule, they came to be styled by the Jainas *ājīvikas.*

[89] Cf. G. Bühler, "The Barābar and Nāgārjunī Hill Cave Inscriptions of Aśoka and Dasaratha," *The Indian Antiquary,* XX (1891), pp. 361ff.

the cold of winter or the heat of summer.[90] That is to say, the garment (the doctrine) is simply useless. The Buddha's reference, specifically, is to the determinism of Gosāla's principal tenet, which allowed no place for voluntary human effort.

For the Ājīvika doctrine that no amount of moral or ascetic exertion would shorten the series of rebirths offered no hope for a speedy release from the fields of ignorance through saintly exercises. On the contrary, a vast and comprehensive review of all the kingdoms and departments of nature let it appear that each life-monad was to pass, in a series of precisely eighty-four thousand births, through the whole gamut of the varieties of being, starting among the elemental atoms of ether, air, fire, water, and earth, progressing through the graduated spheres of the various geological, botanical, and zoological forms of existence, and coming finally into the kingdom of man, each birth being linked to the others in conformity to a precise and minutely graduated order of evolution. All the life-monads in the universe were passing laboriously along this one inevitable way.

The living body of the atom, according to this system, is the most primitive organism in the cosmos, being provided with but one sense-faculty, that of touch, i.e., the sensation of weight and pressure. This is the state in which each life-monad (*jīva*) takes its start. As it then progresses, bodies come to it endowed with more sense-faculties and with higher powers of intellect and feeling. Rising naturally and of itself, it passes through the long slow course of transmigrations into the various conditions of the vegetables, the lower and then the higher stages of animal life, and the numerous levels of the human sphere. When the time at last arrives, and the final term of the series of eighty-four thousand existences has been attained, release simply happens, just as everything else has happened—of itself.

90 *Aṅguttara Nikāya* i. 286. (Translated by T. W. Rhys Davids, *The Gradual Dialogues of the Buddha,* Pāli Text Society, Translation Series no. 22, London, 1932, p. 265.)

The destiny of man is framed by a rigid law, that of the evolution of the life-monad. Gosāla compares the long automatic ascent to the course of a ball of thread thrown through the air which runs out to its very last bit: the curve ends only when the thread is entirely unwound. No divine grace or human zeal can interrupt or interfere with this unalterable principle of bondage, evolution, and release. It is a law that knits all life, links apparently lifeless elemental matter to the kingdoms of the insects and of man, runs through all things, puts on and lays aside the whole wardrobe of the masks or garbs of incarnation, and will not be forced, hurried, cheated, or denied.

This is a vision of an all-embracing, gloomy grandeur, a cool scientific outlook on the universe and its creatures, impressive through its utter self-consistency. The melancholy of the realm of nature is tempered by no ray of redeeming light. On the contrary, this stupendous cosmic view depresses the spirit through the merciless coherence of its complete disregard for the hopes intrinsic to the human soul. Absolutely no concession is made to man's wishful thinking, absolutely no adjustment to our inborn awareness of a possible freedom.

Jainism and Buddhism, on the other hand, the successful contemporary rivals, agree in stressing the possibility of an accelerated release from the cycle as a consequence of effort. Both protest equally against the mechanistic inflexibility of Gosāla's law of evolution, in so far as it touches the sphere of human will. The Buddha, for example, is most emphatic. "There exists," says he, "a 'heroic effort' (*vīryam*) in man; there exists the possibility of a 'successful exertion' (*utsāha*) aimed at the disengaging of man from the vortex of rebirths—provided he strives wholeheartedly for this end." [91] Gosāla's solemn scientific panorama, excluding as it does all freedom of the will, converts the

[91] *Editor's note:* Many statements in praise of effort and exertion appear in the Buddhist scriptures. I have not located, however, the passage cited here by Dr. Zimmer.

whole universe into a vast purgatory of numerous long-lasting stages. Creation becomes a kind of cosmic laboratory in which innumerable monads, by a long, slow, alchemical process of transformation, become gradually refined, enriched, and cleansed; passing from darker, lower modes of being to higher—passing through sufferings ever renewed—until at last they stand endowed with moral discrimination and spiritual insight, in human form, at the threshold of release.

One can understand why such a philosophy vanished from the historical scene after a few centuries. It proved to be unbearable. Teaching a fatalistic patience in a virtually endless bondage, demanding resignation without compensation, conceding nothing to moral and spiritual will-power, it simply offered no answer to the burning questions of the seeking, empty human soul. It left no place for the practice of virtue with the normal human aim of winning some reward, offered no field for the exercise of will-power, and no reason for making life-plans, gave no hope for compensation, the only source of purification being the natural process of evolution; and that simply took time—eons of time—proceeding slowly and automatically, regardless of man's inward effort, like a biochemical process.

And yet, according to this "hempen shirt" doctrine of Gosāla, man's moral conduct is not without significance; for every living being, through its characteristic pattern of reactions to the environment, betrays its entire multibiographical history, together with all that it has yet to learn. Its acts are not the cause of the influx (*āsrava*) of fresh karmic substance, as in the Jaina view, but only reveal its position or classification in the general hierarchy, showing how deeply entangled or close to release it happens to be. Our words and deeds, that is to say, announce to ourselves—and to the world—every minute, just what milestone we have come to. Thus perfect asceticism, though it has no causative, has yet a symptomatic value: it is the characteristic mode of life of a being who is on the point of reaching the goal of isolation (*kaivalya*); and conversely, those who are not readily drawn to it are comparatively low in the human scale. Any pronounced inability to conform to the most advanced ascetic standards simply proclaims how woefully far one stands from the summit of the cosmic social climb.

Pious acts, then, are not the causes, but the effects; they do not bring, but they foretell release. The perfect ascetic shows through the detached austerity of his conduct that he is the being nearest to the exit. He shows that he has all but completed the long course and is now absolutely unwavering in his exalted unconcern both for himself and for the world—indifferent alike to what the world thinks of him, to what he is, and to what he is about to be.

It is not difficult to imagine what a state of impotent self-annoyance this philosophy would cause in those human beings somewhat below the supreme condition, still ambitious for the world's supreme regard.

10.

Man against Nature

Jainism agrees completely with Gosāla as to the masklike character of the personality. Whether in the shape of element, plant, animal, man, celestial being, or tormented inmate of hell, the visible form is but the temporary garb of an inhabiting life, which is working its way through the stages of existence toward a goal of release from the whole affair. Apparently this depiction of the transient forms of life as so many masks taken on and laid aside by an innumerable host of individual life-monads —the monads themselves constituting the very matter of the universe—was one of the major tenets of the pre-Āryan philosophy of India. It is basic to the Sāṅkhya psychology as well as to Patañjali's Yoga, and was the starting point of the Buddhist teachings.[92] Absorbed into the Brāhman tradition, it became blended with other ideas; so that even today in India it remains as one of the fundamental figures of all philosophical, religious, and metaphysical thought. Jainism and the doctrine of Gosāla thus may be regarded as specimens of the way in which the Indian mind, outside the pale of Brāhman orthodoxy, and according to the patterns of an archaic mode of thought rooted in the Indian soil, has from time immemorial experienced the phenomenon of personality. In contrast to the Occidental idea of the everlasting individual, as conceived by the Greeks and passed on to Christianity and modern man, in the land of the Buddha the personality has always been regarded as a transitory mask.

But Jainism, like Buddhism, disagrees with Gosāla's fatalistic interpretation of the graduated roles of the play, asserting that each human individual is free to make his own escape. By a sustained act of self-renunciation one can elude this melancholy bondage—which is equivalent practically to an eternal punishment and is out of all proportion to whatever guilt can possibly appertain to the mere fact of being alive. Gosāla's strictly evolutionary interpretation is rejected on the grounds of the repeated experience of actual release by perfected holy men throughout the ages. Those masterly teachers began, like Mahāvīra, by joining the saintly order of the Jaina monks, and ended as the models of salvation. They offer us in their own lives our prime guarantee of the possibility of release, as well as an example of how the narrow exit is to be passed. Instead

[92] Cf. *supra,* p. 60, Editor's note, and discussions *infra,* Chapters II and IV.

of Gosāla's mechanistic biological order, slowly but automatically working through the eighty-four thousand incarnations, Jainism thus asserts the power and value of the morale of the individual: the force of thoughts, words, and deeds, which, if virtuous, stainless, and unselfish, lead the life-monad to enlightenment, but if bad, egocentric, and unconsidered, fling it back into the darker, more primitive conditions, dooming it to an existence in the animal kingdom or to lives among the tortured inmates of the hells.

Nevertheless, Jainism, too, represents a scientific, practically atheistic, interpretation of existence. For the gods are nothing but life-monads, wearing temporarily favorable masks in supremely fortunate surroundings, whereas the material universe is uncreated and everlasting. The universe is composed of six constituents, as follows:

1. *Jīva:* the aggregate of the countless life-monads. Each is uncreated and imperishable, by nature omniscient, endowed with infinite energy, and full of bliss. Intrinsically the life-monads are all absolutely alike, but they have been modified, diminished, and tainted in their perfection, through the perpetual influx of the second and opposite constituent of the universe, namely:

2. *Ajīva:* "all that is not (*a-*) the life-monad (*jīva*)." [93] *Ajīva* is, firstly, space (*ākāśa*). This is regarded as an all-comprehending container, enclosing not only the universe (*loka*), but also the non-universe (*aloka*). The latter is what lies beyond the contours of the colossal Macrocosmic Man or Woman.[94] *Ajīva* comprises, moreover, countless space-units (*pradeśa*), and is indestructible. Besides being space, however, *ajīva* is also manifest as all four of the following constituents of the world, which are

[93] This elementary dichotomy of *jīva—ajīva* is carried on in the Sāṅkhya philosophy under the categories *puruṣa—prakṛti. Prakṛti* is the matter of the universe, the psychic-and-physical material that enwraps *puruṣa.*

[94] Cf. *supra,* p. 259.

distinguished as the several aspects of this single antagonist to the *jīva*.

3. *Dharma:* the medium through which movement is possible. *Dharma* is compared to water, through and by which fish are able to move.[95]

4. *Adharma:* the medium that makes rest and immobility possible. *Adharma* is compared to earth, on which creatures lie and stand.

5. *Kāla:* time; that which makes changes possible.

6. *Pudgala:* matter, composed of minute atoms (*paramāṇu*). *Pudgala* is endued with odor, color, taste, and tangibility.

Matter exists, according to the Jainas, in six degrees of density: a) "subtle-subtle" (*sūkṣma-sūkṣma*), which is the invisible substance of the atoms; b) "subtle" (*sūkṣma*), invisible also, and the substance of the ingredients of karma; c) "subtle-gross" (*sūkṣma-sthūla*), invisible and yet experienced, constituting the material of sounds, smells, touch (e.g., of the wind), and flavors; d) "gross-subtle" (*sthūla-sūkṣma*), which is visible yet impossible to grasp—e.g., sunshine, darkness, shadow; e) "gross" (*sthūla*), which is both visible and tangible but liquid, as water, oil, and melted butter; and f) "gross-gross" (*sthūla-sthūla*): the material objects that have distinct and separate existences, such as metal, wood, and stone.

Karmic matter clings to the jīva, as dust to a body anointed with oil. Or it pervades and tinges the jīva, as heat a red-hot iron ball. It is described as of eight kinds, according to its effects. a) The karma that enwraps or screens true knowledge (*jñāna-āvaraṇa-karma*). Like a veil or cloth over the image of a divinity, this karma comes between the mind and the truth, taking away, as it were, inborn omniscience. b) The karma that enwraps or screens true perception (*darśana-āvaraṇa-karma*). Like a door-keeper warding people from the presence of the king in his

[95] This specifically Jaina use of the term *dharma* is, of course, not to be confused with that discussed *supra*, pp. 151-177.

audience-hall, this karma interferes with the perception of the processes of the universe, making it difficult or impossible to see what is going on; thus it veils its own operation on the jīva. c) The karma that creates pleasant and unpleasant feelings (*vedanīya-karma*). This is compared to the edge of a keen sword-blade smeared with honey and put into the mouth. Because of this karma all our experiences of life are compounded of pleasure and pain. d) The karma that causes delusion and confusion (*mohanīya-karma*). Like liquor, this karma dulls and dazzles the faculties of discrimination between good and evil. (The kevalin, the "isolated one," cannot be intoxicated. Perfect enlightenment is a state of supreme and sublime sobriety.) e) The karma that determines the length of the individual life (*āyuṣ-karma*). Like a rope that prevents an animal from going on indefinitely beyond the peg to which it is tied, this karma fixes the number of one's days. It determines the life-capital, the life-strength, to be spent during the present incarnation. f) The karma that establishes individuality (*nāma-karma*). This is the determinant of the "name" (*nāman*), which denotes, in the "subtle-gross" form of sound, the mental-spiritual principle, or essential idea, of the thing. The name is the mental counterpart of the visible, tangible form (*rūpa*)[96]—that is why magic can be worked with names and verbal spells. This is the karma that determines to the last detail both the outward appearance and the inward character of the object, animal, or person. It is the fashioner of the present perishable mask. Its work is so comprehensive that the Jainas have analyzed it into ninety-three subdivisions. Whether one's next incarnation is to be in the heavens, among men or animals, or in the purgatories; whether one is to be endowed with five or with fewer receptive senses; whether one is to belong to some class of beings with charming, dignified gait and carriage (such as bulls, elephants, and geese) or with ugly (such as camels and asses), with movable ears and eyes, or with

[96] Cf. *supra*, pp. 23-24.

immovable; whether one is to be beautiful or ugly of one's kind, commanding sympathy or inspiring disgust, winning honor and fame or suffering ill-repute: all of these details are determined by this "karma of the proper name." Nāma-karma is like the painter filling in with his brush the distinguishing features of a portrait, making the figure recognizable and quite particular. g) The karma that establishes the family into which the individual is to be born (*gotra-karma*). This, properly, should be a subdivision of the above, but owing to the enormous importance of the circumstance of caste in India it has been given the weight of a special category. Destiny and all the prospects of life are limited greatly by the house into which one is born. h) The karma that produces obstacles (*antarāya-karma*). Within this category a number of subdivisions are described. i. *Dāna-antarāya-karma:* this prevents us from being as self-detached and munificent in the bestowal of alms on holy people and the poor as we should like to be. ii. *Lābha-antarāya-karma:* this keeps us from receiving alms—a particularly nasty karma, since holy men depend on gifts, as do all religious institutions. (In the West, for example, a university afflicted with this bad influence would be forced to close for lack of funds.) iii. *Bhoga-antarāya-karma:* this keeps us from enjoying events. We arrive late for the party. Or while we are eating the cake we keep wishing that we could keep it too. iv. *Upabhoga-antarāya-karma:* as a result of this frustration we are unable to enjoy the pleasurable objects that are continually around—our houses, gardens, fine clothes, and women. v. *Vīrya-antarāya-karma:* as a result of which we cannot bring ourselves to act: there is a paralysis of the will.

In all, exactly one hundred and forty-eight varieties and effects of karma are described, and these work, in sum, in two directions. 1. *Ghāti-karma* ("striking, wounding, killing karma") subtracts from the infinite powers of the life-monad, and 2. *aghāti-karma* ("non-striking karma") adds limiting qualities which do not properly belong to it. All of these karmic difficulties have been afflicting jīva from eternity. The Jaina system requires no explanation of the beginning of it all, since there is no notion of a time when time was not: the world has always existed. The concern, furthermore, is not the beginning of the muddle, but the determination of its nature and the application of a technique to clear it up.

Bondage consists in the union of jīva with ajīva, salvation in the dissolution of the combination. This problem of conjunction and disjunction is expressed by the Jainas in a statement of seven *tattvas* or "principles."

1. *Jīva,* and 2. *Ajīva:* these have already been discussed. Ajīva includes categories 2-6 of the Six Constitutents that we have just reviewed.

3. *Āsrava:* "influx," the pouring of karmic matter into the life-monad. This takes place through forty-two channels, among which are the five recipient sense-faculties, the three activities of mind, speech, physical action, the four passions of wrath, pride, guile, and greed, and the six "non-passions" known as mirth, pleasure, distress, grief, fear, and disgust.[97]

4. *Bandha:* "bondage," the fettering and smothering of jīva by karmic matter.

5. *Saṁvara:* "stoppage," the checking of the influx.

6. *Nirjarā:* "shedding," the elimination of karmic matter by means of cleansing austerities, burning it out with the internal heat of ascetic practices (*tapas*), as by a sweating cure.

[97] These six, together with two others—resolution and wonder—are the basic moods or "flavors" (*rasa*) of Hindu poetry, dance, and acting. They are all exhibited by Śiva, the Highest God, in the various situations of his mythical manifestations, and thus are sanctified in devotional Hinduism as aspects of the Lord's "cosmic play," revelations of his divine energy under various modes. According to Jainism, on the other hand, they are to be suppressed, since they attract and increase the store of karmic matter and thereby distract one from the perfect indifference that conduces to the purification of the life-monad.

7. *Mokṣa:* "release."

"Jīva and non-jīva together constitute the universe," we read in a Jaina text. "If they are separate, nothing more is needed. If they are united, as they are found to be in the world, the stoppage and the gradual and then final destruction of the union are the only possible ways of considering them." [98]

The Jaina universe itself is indestructible, not subject to periodical dissolutions like that of the Hindu cosmology.[99] Furthermore, there is no hint of that primal, world-generative sacred marriage of Father Heaven and Mother Earth which constitutes a major theme in the tradition of the Vedas. In the great Horse Sacrifice (*aśvamedha*) of the ancient Indo-Āryans, when the chief queen as representative of Mother Earth, the spouse of the world-monarch (*cakravartin*), lay down in the sacrificial pit beside the slaughtered animal that was symbolic of heaven's solar force (the horse having just ended its triumphant solar year of untrammeled wandering),[100] that act of the queen was the mystical reconstitution of the sacred cosmic marriage. But in Jainism the primal male (or the primal female) *is* the universe. There is no history of a gestatory coming into existence, no "golden germ" (*hiraṇyagarbha*), no cosmic egg which divides into the upper and lower half-shells of heaven and earth, no sacrificed and dismembered primeval being (*puruṣa*), whose limbs, blood, hair, etc., become transformed into the constituents of the world; in short, no myth of creation, for the universe has always been. The Jaina universe is sterile, patterned on an ascetic doctrine. It is an all-containing world-mother without a mate, or a lonely man-giant without female consort; and this primeval person is forever whole and alive. The so-called "up-going" and "down-going" world-

[98] *Tattvārthādhigama-sūtra* 4. (Sacred Books of the Jainas, Vol. II, p. 7.)

[99] Cf. Zimmer, *Myths and Symbols,* pp. 3-22.

[100] Cf. *supra,* pp. 134-135.

cycles [101] are the tides of this being's life-process, continuous and everlasting. We are all the particles of that gigantic body, and for each the task is to keep from being carried down to the infernal regions of the lower body, but, on the contrary, to ascend as speedily as possible to the supreme bliss of the peaceful dome of the prodigious skull.

This is an idea obviously contrary to the cosmic vision of the Brāhman seers, and yet it came to play a great role in later Hinduism [102]—specifically, in the myths of Viṣṇu Anantaśāyin, the giant divine dreamer of the world, who bears the universe in his belly, lets it flower as a lotus from his navel, and takes it back again into his everlasting substance.[103] Equally prominent is the Hindu female counterpart, the all-containing Goddess Mother, who brings all beings forth from her universal womb, nourishes them, and, devouring them again, takes everything back.[104] These figures have been adapted in Hinduism to the Vedic myth of the Cosmic Marriage, but the incompatibility of the two sets of symbols still is evident; for though the world of creatures is described as being born, it is also described as constituting the body of the divine being, whereas in the Jaina vision there is no such incongruity since the jīvas are the atoms of life that circulate through the cosmic organism. An omniscient all-seeing seer and saint (*kevalin*) can actually watch the process of unending metabolism taking place throughout the frame, observing the cells in their continual transmutations; for his individual consciousness has been broadened to such a degree that it corresponds to the infinite consciousness of the giant universal being. With his inward spiritual eye he beholds the life-atoms, infinite in number, circulating continually, each en-

[101] *Supra,* p. 224, note 44.

[102] For the term "Hinduism," as distinct from "Brāhmanism," cf. *supra,* p. 77, note 35.

[103] Zimmer, *Myths and Symbols,* pp. 35-53.

[104] *Ib.,* pp. 189-216.

dowed with its own life-duration, bodily strength, and breathing power, as it goes about perpetually inhaling and exhaling.

The life-monads on the elemental level of existence (in the states of ether, air, fire, water, and earth) are provided with the faculty of touch (*sparśa-indriya*). All feel and respond to pressure, being themselves provided with minute extension, and they are known therefore as *ekendriya,* "provided with one (*eka*) sense-faculty (*indriya*)." The atoms of the vegetables also are endowed with one sense-faculty (the sense of touch), though with four life-breaths (they lack speech-power). Such mute, one-sense existences are no less the masks or garbs of jīvas than the more complex forms of the animal, human, and celestial kingdoms. This the kevalin knows and sees by virtue of his universal consciousness. He also knows and sees that the faculties of the higher beings are ten: 1. life-force or duration (*āyus*), 2. bodily strength, substance, weight, tension, and resilience (*kāya-bala*), 3. speech-power, the power to make a sound (*vacana-bala*), 4. reasoning power (*manobala*), 5. breathing power (*ānāpana-prāṇa, śvāsocchvāsa-prāṇa*), and 6.-10. the five receptive senses of touch (*sparśendriya*), taste (*rasendriya*), smell (*ghrāṇendriya*), sight (*cakṣurindriya*), and hearing (*śravaṇendriya*). Some vegetables, such as trees, are provided with a collectivity of jīvas. They impart separate jīvas to their branches, twigs, and fruits; for you can plant a fruit, or slip a cutting, and it will grow into an individual being. Others, such as onions, have a single jīva common to a number of separate stems. Minute animals, worms, insects, and crustacea, which represent the next level of developed living organization, have, besides life-duration, bodily strength, breathing power and the sense of touch, speech-power or the power to make a sound (*vacana-bala*), and the sense of taste (*rasendriya*). Their life-duration falls within the span of twelve years, whereas that of the preceding classes greatly varies. That of the fire-atom, for example, may be a moment (*samaya*) or seventy-two hours; that of a water-atom, a couple of moments (one to forty-eight) or seven thousand years; that of an air-atom, one moment or three thousand years.

This elaborate systematization of the forms of life, which the Jainas share with Gosāla, is based on the distribution of the ten faculties among the various beings, from the living elemental atoms to the organisms of men and gods. The systematization is anything but primitive. It is quaint and archaic indeed, yet pedantic and extremely subtle, and represents a fundamentally scientific conception of the world. In fact one is awed by the glimpse that it gives of the long history of human thought—a view much longer and more imposing than the one that is cherished by our Western humanists and academic historians with their little story about the Greeks and the Renaissance. The twenty-fourth Jaina Tīrthaṅkara, Mahāvīra, was roughly a contemporary of Thales and Anaxagoras, the earliest of the standard line of Greek philosophers; and yet the subtle, complex, thoroughgoing analysis and classification of the features of nature which Mahāvīra's teaching took for granted and upon which it played was already centuries (perhaps even millenniums) old. It was a systematization that had long done away with the hosts of powerful gods and the wizard-magic of the still earlier priestly tradition—which itself had been as far above the really primitive level of human culture as are the arts of agriculture, herding, and dairying above those of hunting and fishing, root and berry gathering. The world was already old, very wise and very learned, when the speculations of the Greeks produced the texts that are studied in our universities as the first chapters of philosophy.

According to the archaic science the whole cosmos was alive, and the basic laws of its life were constant throughout. One should therefore practice "non-violence" (*ahiṁsā*) even upon the smallest, mutest, least conscious living being. The Jaina monk, for example, avoids as far as possible the squeezing or touching of the atoms of the elements. He cannot cease breathing, but to avoid giving possible harm he should wear a veil before his mouth: this softens the impact of the air against the inside of the throat. And he must not snap his fingers or fan the wind; for that disturbs and causes damage. If wicked people on a ferryboat should for some reason throw a Jaina monk overboard, he must not try to make for shore with violent, flailing strokes, like a valiant swimmer, but should gently drift, like a log, and permit the currents to bring him gradually to land: he must not upset and injure the water-atoms. And he should then permit the moisture to drip or evaporate from his skin, never wipe it off or shake it away with a violent commotion of his limbs.

Non-violence (*ahiṁsā*) is thus carried to an extreme. The Jaina sect survives as a sort of extremely fundamentalist vestige in a civilization that has gone through many changes since the remote age when this universal piety and universal science of the world of nature and of escape from it came into existence. Even Jaina lay folk must be watchful lest they cause unnecessary inconvenience to their fellow beings. They must, for example, not drink water after dark; for some small insect may be swallowed. They must not eat meat of any kind, or kill bugs that fly about and annoy; credit may be gained, indeed, by allowing the bugs to settle and have their fill. All of which has led to the following most bizarre popular custom, which may be observed even today in the metropolitan streets of Bombay.

Two men come along carrying between them a light cot or bed alive with bedbugs. They stop before the door of a Jaina household, and cry: "Who will feed the bugs? Who will feed the bugs?" If some devout lady tosses a coin from a window, one of the criers places himself carefully in the bed and offers himself as a living grazing ground to his fellow beings. Whereby the lady of the house gains the credit, and the hero of the cot the coin.

II. SĀṄKHYA AND YOGA

1.

Kapila and Patañjali

Now let us proceed to Sāṅkhya and Yoga. These two are regarded in India as twins, the two aspects of a single discipline. Sāṅkhya provides a basic theoretical exposition of human nature, enumerating and defining its elements, analyzing their manner of co-operation in the state of bondage (*bandha*), and describing their state of disentanglement or separation in release (*mokṣa*), while Yoga treats specifically of the dynamics of the process of the disentanglement, and outlines practical techniques for the gaining of release, or "isolation-integration" (*kaivalya*). As we read in the *Bhagavad Gītā:* "Puerile and unlearned people speak of 'enumerating knowledge' (*sāṅkhya*) and the 'practice of introvert concentration' (*yoga*) as distinct from each other, yet anyone firmly established in either gains the fruit of both. The state attained by the followers of the path of enumerating knowledge is attained also through the exercises of introvert concentration. He truly sees who regards as one the intellectual attitude of enumerating knowledge and the practice of concentration." [1] The two systems, in other words, supplement each other and conduce to the identical goal.

[1] *Bhagavad Gītā* 5. 4-5.

The main conceptions of this dual system are: 1. that the universe is founded on an irresoluble dichotomy of "life-monads" (*puruṣa*) and lifeless "matter" (*prakṛti*), 2. that "matter" (*prakṛti*), though fundamentally simple and uncompounded, nevertheless exfoliates, or manifests itself, under three distinctly differentiated aspects (the so-called *guṇas*), which are comparable to the three strands of a rope, and 3. that every one of the "life-monads" (*puruṣa*) associated with "matter" (*prakṛti*) is involved in the bondage of an endless "round of transmigration" (*saṁsāra*).

These ideas do not belong to the original stock of the Vedic Brāhmanic tradition. Nor, on the other hand, do we find among the basic teachings of Sāṅkhya and Yoga any hint of such a pantheon of divine Olympians, beyond the vicissitudes of earthly bondage, as that of the Vedic gods. The two ideologies are of different origin, Sāṅkhya and Yoga being related to the mechanical system of the Jainas, which, as we have seen, can be traced back, in a partly historical, partly legendary way, through the long series of the Tīrthaṅkaras, to a remote, aboriginal, non-Vedic, Indian antiquity. The fundamental ideas of Sāṅkhya and Yoga, therefore, must be immensely old. And yet they do not appear in any of the orthodox Indian texts until comparatively late—specifically, in the younger stratifications of the Upaniṣads and in the *Bhagavad Gītā,* where they are already blended and harmonized with the fundamental ideas of the Vedic philosophy. Following a long history of rigid resistance, the exclusive and esoteric Brāhman mind of the Āryan invaders opened up, at last, and received suggestions and influences from the native civilization. The result was a coalescence of the two traditions. And this is what produced, in time, the majestic harmonizing systems of medieval and contemporary Indian thought.

Sāṅkhya is said to have been founded by a semi-mythical holy man, Kapila, who stands outside the traditional assembly of the Vedic saints and sages, as an Enlightened One in his own right. Though he plays no such conspicuous role in Indian myth and legend as do many of the other great philosophers, nevertheless, his miraculous power is recognized in a celebrated episode of the *Mahābhārata*.[2] There we read that the sixty thousand sons of a certain Cakravartin named "Ocean" (*sagara*) were riding as the armed guard of their father's sacrificial horse while it wandered over the kingdoms of the land, during its symbolical solar year of victorious freedom.[3] Suddenly, to their profound distress, the animal vanished from before their very eyes. They set to work digging where it had disappeared and came upon it, finally, deep in the earth, down in the underworld, with a saint sitting beside it in meditation. Over-eager to recapture their sacred charge, the young warriors disregarded the saint—who was none other than Kapila—and omitted to pay him the homage traditionally due to a holy man. Whereupon, with a flash of his eye, he burnt them all to ashes.

The solar power of the sage is evident in this adventure. His name, Kapila, meaning the "Red One," is an epithet of the sun, as well as of Viṣṇu. Judging from his influence in the period of Mahāvīra and the Buddha, he must have lived before the sixth century B.C., and yet the classic texts of the philosophical system that he is said to have founded belong to a much later date. The important *Sāṅkhya-kārikā* of Īśvarakṛṣṇa was composed in the middle of the fifth century A.D., while the *Sāṅkhya-sūtras*, the work ascribed traditionally to the hand of Kapila himself, cannot be dated earlier than 1380–1450 A.D.[4]

As for Yoga, the dating of the classic *Yoga-sūtras* of Patañjali is extremely controversial. Though the first three books of this basic treatise may belong to the second century B.C., the fourth is apparently later; for it contains material that seems to refer

[2] *Mahābhārata* 3. 107.

[3] Cf. *supra*, pp. 134-135.

[4] Cf. Richard Garbe, *Die Sāṁkhya-Philosophie*, 2nd edition, Leipzig, 1917, pp. 83-84, 95-100.

to late Buddhistic thought. This final book has been assigned, therefore, to the fifth century A.D.; but the argument is not yet closed. In any case, the four books of Patañjali's *Yogo-sūtras,* together with their ancient commentary (the *Yoga-bhāṣya,* which is attributed to Vyāsa, the legendary poet-sage of the *Mahābhārata*), must be reckoned among the most astounding works of philosophical prose in the literature of the world. They are remarkable not only for the subject matter, but also, and particularly, for their wonderful sobriety, clarity, succinctness, and elasticity of expression.

We possess little information concerning Patañjali himself, and this little is legendary and replete with contradictions. For example, he is both identified with and distinguished from the grammarian—also named Patañjali—who composed the so-called "Great Commentary" (*Mahābhāṣya*) to Kātyāyana's "Critical Gloss" (*Vārttika*) on Pāṇini's Sanskrit Grammar. He is regarded, moreover as an incarnation of the serpent-king Śeṣa, who surrounds and supports the universe in the form of the Cosmic Ocean. Occidental scholars have assigned him to the second century B.C., and yet the system that he is reputed to have founded certainly existed centuries before that time.

2.

Introvert-Concentration

WHEN AMBITION, success, and the game of life (*artha*), as well as sex and the enjoyments of the senses (*kāma*), no longer produce any novel and surprising turns, holding nothing more in store, and when, furthermore, the virtuous fulfillment of the tasks of a decent, normal, human career (*dharma*) begins to pall, having become a stale routine, there remains, still, the lure of the spiritual adventure—the quest for whatever may lie within (beneath the mask of the conscious personality) and without (behind the visible panorama of the exterior world). What is the secret of this ego, this "I," with whom we have been on such intimate terms all these worn-out years, and who is yet a stranger, full of curious quirks, odd whims, and puzzling impulses of aggression and relapse? And what has been lurking, meanwhile, behind these external phenomena that no longer intrigue us, producing all these surprises that are not surprises any more? The possibility of discovering the secret of the workings of the cosmic theater itself, after its effects have become only an intolerable bore, remains as the final fascination, challenge, and adventure of the human mind.

We read at the opening of the *Yoga-sūtras:*

Yogaś cittavṛtti-nirodhyaḥ.

"Yoga consists in the (intentional) stopping of the spontaneous activities of the mind-stuff." [5]

The mind, by nature, is in constant agitation. According to the Hindu theory, it is continually transforming itself into the shapes of the objects of which it becomes aware. Its subtle substance assumes the forms and colors of everything offered to it by the senses, imagination, memory, and emotions. It is endowed, in other words, with a power of transformation, or metamorphosis, which is boundless and never put at rest.[6]

[5] Pantañjali, *Yoga-sūtras* 1. 1-2.

[6] The protean, ever-moving character of the mind, as described both in Sāṅkhya and in Yoga, is comparable to Swedenborg's idea that "recipients are images," i.e., that the receptive organs assume on the spiritual plane the form and nature of whatever objects they receive and contain. (Cf. Swedenborg, *Divine Love and Wisdom,* § 288.)

The mind is thus in a continuous ripple, like the surface of a pond beneath a breeze, shimmering with broken, ever-changing, self-scattering reflections. Left to itself it would never stand like a perfect mirror, crystal clear, in its "own state," unruffled and reflecting the inner man; for, in order that this should take place, all the sense impressions coming from without (which are like the waters of entering rivulets, turbulent and disturbing to the translucent substance) would have to be stopped, as well as the impulses from within: memories, emotional pressures, and the incitements of the imagination (which are like internal springs). Yoga, however, stills the mind. And the moment this quieting is accomplished, the inner man, the life-monad, stands revealed—like a jewel at the bottom of a quieted pond.

According to the Sāṅkhya (and the view of Yoga is the same) the life-monad (called *puruṣa,* "man," *ātman,* "self," or *puṁs,* "man") is the living entity concealed behind and within all the metamorphoses of our life in bondage. Just as in Jainism, so also here, the number of the life-monads in the universe is supposed to be infinite, and their "proper nature" (*svarūpa*) is regarded as totally different from that of the lifeless "matter" (*prakṛti*) in which they are engulfed. They are termed "spiritual" (*cit, citi, cetana, caitanya*), and are said to be "of the nature of sheer, self-effulgent light" (*prabhāsa*). Within each individual, the self-luminous puruṣa, ātman, or puṁs illuminates all the processes of gross and subtle matter—the processes, that is to say, of both life and consciousness—as these develop within the organism; yet this life-monad itself is without form or content. It is devoid of qualities and peculiarities, such specifications being but properties of the masking realm of matter. It is without beginning, without end, eternal and everlasting, and without parts or divisions; for what is compounded is subject to destruction. It was regarded originally as of atomic size, but later as all-pervading and infinite, without activity, changeless, and beyond the sphere of movements, "at the top, the summit" (*kūṭastha*). The monad is unattached and without contact, absolutely indifferent, unconcerned, and uninvolved, and therefore never actually in bondage, never really released, but eternally free; for release would imply a previous state of bondage, whereas no such bondage can be said to touch the inner man. Man's problem is, simply, that his permanent, ever-present actual freedom is not *realized* because of the turbulent, ignorant, distracted condition of his mind.

Here, obviously, we have begun to step away from the Jaina doctrine, with its theory of an actual contamination of the life-monad (*jīva*) by the karmic matter (*a-jīva*) of the six colors.[7] According to the Sāṅkhya and Yoga view, the monad is an immaterial entity, which—in contradistinction to the ātman of Vedānta—is neither possessed of bliss nor endowed with the power of acting as the material or efficient cause of anything. It is a knowledge of nothing. It is uncreative and does not expand, transform itself, or bring anything to pass. It does not participate in any way in human pains, possessions, or feelings, but is by nature "absolutely isolated" (*kevala*), even though it appears to be involved in life because of its *apparent* association with the "conditioning, limiting attributes" (*upādhis*)—which are the constituents, not of the life-monad itself, but of the subtle and gross material bodies through which it is reflected in the sphere of space and time. Puruṣa, because of these upādhis, *appears* as jīva, the "living one," and *seems* to be endowed with receptivity and spontaneity, breathing, and all the other processes of the organism; whereas, in and by itself, "it is not able to bend a leaf of grass."

By its mere inactive, yet luminous, presence the monad thus seems to be the activator, and in this hallucinatory role is known as the "Lord" or "Supervisor" (*svāmin, adhiṣṭhātar*). It does not actually command or control. The conditioning attributes

[7] Cf. *supra*, pp. 227-231; 248-252.

(*upādhis*) work of themselves, automatically and blindly; the real center and governor, control and head, of their life-process being the so-called "inner organ" (*antaḥ-karaṇa*). But the puruṣa, by virtue of its effulgence, illuminates and seems to be reflected in the process. Moreover, this is an association that never had any beginning and has existed from all eternity. It is comparable to the relationship of the uninvolved yet omnipotent Hindu housepriest to the king of whom he is the spiritual guide. The priest is served by the king, as well as by all the officers of the realm, and yet remains inactive and unconcerned. Or the association can be compared to that in the Hindu game of chess, where the role of puruṣa is represented by the "king," while the "king's" omnipresent "general" (*senāpati*)—who is equivalent to the "queen" in our Western game—is in the powerful, serving yet commanding, position of the "inner organ." Again, the relationship resembles the effect of the sun on the earth and its vegetation. The sun suffers no alteration as a consequence of the heat's pervasion of the earth and of the earth's living forms. The self-effulgence of the uninvolved life-monad (*puruṣa*), by suffusing the unconscious material of the realm and processes of lifeless matter (*prakṛti*), creates, as it were, both the life and the consciousness of the individual: what appears to be the sun's activity belongs really to the sphere of matter. Or it is precisely as though an unmoving personage, reflected in a moving mirror, should be thought to move.

Briefly then, according to the Sāṅkhya philosophy, the life-monad is associated in a special sort of "apparent engagement" (*saṁyoga-viśeṣa*) with the living individual, as a natural consequence of the reflection of its own self-effulgence in the protean, ever-moving, subtle matter of the mind. True insight, "discriminating knowledge" (*viveka*), can be achieved only by bringing this mind to a state of rest. Then the life-monad (*puruṣa*) is perceived unobscured by the qualities of agitated matter (*prakṛti*), and in this state its secret nature is suddenly and simply revealed.

It is beheld at rest, which is the way it actually and always is: aloof from the natural processes that are taking place continually round about, in the mind-stuff, in the senses, in the organs of action, and in the animated outer world.

Truth is to be attained only through the recognition of the fact that, whatever happens, nothing affects or stains the life-monad. It remains detached, completely so, even though it may seem to be carrying on individual life-processes, through the round of rebirths and in the present life. Our normal view attributes all the states and transformations of life to the life-monad; they seem to be taking place within it, coloring it, and changing it for better or worse. Nevertheless, this illusion is merely an effect of nescience. The life-monad is not the least affected. In our fiery true Self we remain, forever, serene.

According to the Sāṅkhya-Yoga analysis, the spontaneous activities of the mind-stuff, which have to be suppressed before the true nature of the life-monad can be realized, are five: 1. right notions, derived from accurate perception (*pramāṇa*); 2. erroneous notions, derived from misapprehension (*viparyaya*); 3. fantasy or fancy (*vikalpa*); 4. sleep (*nidrā*); and 5. memory (*smṛti*).[8] When these five have been suppressed, the disappearance of desire, and of all other mental activities of an emotional character, automatically follows.

1. Right notions are based on, a) right perception, b) right inference, and c) right testimony.[9]

a) Right perception. The thinking principle, i.e., the mind, assumes the shapes of its perceptions through the functioning of the senses. It can be compared to an ever-burning fire, concentrated into tips in its flames and reaching its objects through these foremost points. The foremost point of the thinking principle, when meeting objects through the senses, assumes their form. Because of this the process of perception is one of per-

[8] Patañjali, *Yoga-sūtras* 1. 6.

[9] *Ib.* 1. 7

petual self-transformation. The mind-stuff is compared, therefore, to melted copper, which when poured into a crucible assumes its form precisely. The substance of the mind spontaneously takes on both the shape and the texture of its immediate experience.

One effect of this process is a broken, continually changing reflection of the light of the life-monad in the ever-active thinking function, which brings about the illusion that the life-monad is what is undergoing all the transformations. It appears to be taking on, not only the shapes of our various perceptions, but also the emotions and other reactions that we experience in relation to them. Hence we imagine that it is we ourselves who are unremittingly following and responding to whatever affects the flexible tip of the mind—pleasure and displeasure, sufferings without end, changes of every kind. The mind, according to its natural propensity, runs on, transforming itself through all the experiences and accompanying emotional responses of an avid, troubled, or enjoyable life in the world, and this disturbance then is believed to be the biography of the life-monad. Our innate serenity is always overshadowed, tinged, and colored in this way, by the varying shapes and hues of the susceptible thinking principle. Perceptions, however, belong to the sphere of matter. When two material perceptions do not contradict each other, they are regarded as true or right. Nevertheless, even "true" or "right" perceptions are in essence false, and to be suppressed, since they, no less than the "wrong," produce the conception of an "identity of form" (*sārūpya*) between consciousness-as-mind-stuff and the life-monad.

b) Right inference. Inference is that function of the thinking principle, or activity of the mind, which is concerned with the attribution of characteristics to the objects that seem to bear them. Right inference is inference that can be supported by right perception.

c) Right testimony is derived from the traditional sacred

writings and authorities. It is based on the right understanding of a word or text. It corroborates right perception and inference.

2. Erroneous notions through misconception arise as a consequence of some defect in either the object or the perceiving organ.

3. Fancy dwells on purely imaginary ideas, unwarranted by perception; mythical monsters, for example, or the notion that the life-monad itself is endowed with the traits of the thinking-principle, and hence experiences what happens to be taking place in the mind-stuff. The difference between a fancy and a misconception is that the former is not removable by careful observation of the object.

4. In sleep the spontaneous activity of the mind-stuff continues. This is proven by an experience of pleasure that is normally derived from sleep, and which gives rise to such ideas as "I slept soundly and delightfully." Yoga is concerned with the suppression of sleep, as well as of the activities of the mind awake.

5. Memory is an activity of the mind-stuff that is occasioned by a residuum, or "latent impression" (*saṁskāra*), of some former experience undergone either in the present or in a bygone life. Such impressions tend to become activated. They manifest themselves as propensities to action, i.e., tendencies to behave according to patterns established by reactions in the past.[10]

* * *

"In case there are invitations from those in high places," we read in Patañjali's *Yoga-sūtras*, "these should not arouse attach-

[10] This review of the spontaneous activities of the mind is based on Vijñānabhikṣu, *Yogasāra-saṅgraha*. Vijñānabhikṣu lived in the second half of the sixteenth century A.D. Besides writing the *Yogasāra-saṅgraha* ("Summary of the Essence of Yoga") and a commentary on the *Yoga-sūtras*, called the *Yoga-vārttika*, he condensed the Sāṅkhya doctrine in his *Sāṅkhyasāra* and composed an interpretation of the *Sāṅkhya-sūtras*, along the lines of Vedānta and popular Brāhmanism, in his *Sāṅkhyapravacana-*

ment or pride; for then the undesired consequences will recur." [11]

"Those in high places" are the gods. They are not omnipotent, according to the view of Yoga, but are in fact inferior to the accomplished yogī. They are merely highly favored beings, themselves involved in delights—the delights of their supremely favorable, celestial circumstances. The meaning of this curious aphorism is that the temptation of the prospect of heaven is not to be allowed to distract the serious practitioner of Yoga from his effort to transcend the allurements of *all* the worlds of form.

In the commentary on this passage it is stated that there are four degrees of yogic accomplishment and, correspondingly, four types of yogī:

1. There is the so-called "observant of practice," for whom light is just beginning to dawn.

2. There is the practitioner with "truth-bearing insight."

3. There is the one who has subjugated the organs and the elements and is consequently provided with the means to retain his gains (e.g., the insights of the various super-reflective states). He has means commensurate, that is to say, both with what has been cultivated and with what is yet to be cultivated. He has the means to go on to perfection.

4. There is the one who has passed beyond what can be cultivated, whose sole aim now is to resolve the mind into its primary cause.

"The purity of the harmonious consciousness of the Brāhman who has directly experienced the second or so-called 'Honeyed Stage' is observed by those in high places, and they seek to tempt him by means of their high places: 'Sir,' they say, 'will you sit

---

bhāṣya. According to the view of Vijñānabhiksu, all of the orthodox systems of Indian philosophy (of which Sāṅkhya and Yoga are two) contain the highest truth, though leading to it from diverse and apparently antagonistic starting points.

[11] *Yoga-sūtras* 3. 51.

here? Will you rest here? This pleasure might prove attractive. This heavenly maiden might prove attractive. This elixir keeps off old age and death. This chariot passes through the air. Yonder stand the Wishing Trees, which grant the fruits of all desire, and the Stream of Heaven, which confers blessedness. These personages are perfect sages. These nymphs are incomparable, and not prudish. Eyes and ears here become supernal; the body becomes like a diamond. Because of your distinctive virtues, Venerable Sir, all of these things have been won by you. Enter into this high place, therefore, which is unfading, ageless, deathless, and dear to the gods!'

"Thus addressed," continues the commentator, "let the yogī ponder upon the defects of pleasure: 'Broiled on the horrible coals of the round of rebirths and writhing in the darkness of birth and death, I have only this minute found the lamp of yoga, which makes an end of the obscurations of the hindrances, the "impairments" (*kleśa*). The lust-born gusts of sensual things are the enemies of this lamp. How then may it be that I, who have seen its light, should be led astray by these phenomena of sense—this mere mirage—and make fuel of myself for that same old fire again of the round of rebirths, as it flares anew? Fare ye well, O ye sensual things, deceitful as dreams, and to be desired only by the vile!'

"Determined thus in purpose," the commentary continues, "let the yogī cultivate concentration. Giving up all attachments for things of sense, let him not take pride even in thinking that it is he who is being thus urgently desired even by the gods. If such a one in his pride deems himself secure, he will cease to feel that he is one whom Death has gripped by the hair. [He will become a victim, that is to say, of a heavenly inflation.] And therewith Heedlessness—which is always on the lookout for weak points and mistakes, and must be carefully watched—will have found its opening and will arouse the hindrances (*kleśa*). As a result, the undesired consequences will recur.

"But, on the other hand, he who does not become interested, or feel the urge of pride, will attain the secure fulfillment of the purpose that he has cultivated within, and he will immediately find himself face to face with the still higher purpose that he has yet to cultivate." [12]

This absolute goal is described in the concluding sūtra of Book Three: "When the purity of contemplation (*sattva*) equals the purity of the life-monad (*puruṣa*), there is isolation (*kaivalya*)." [13]

Commentary: "When the 'contemplative power' (*sattva*) of the thinking substance is freed from the defilement of the 'active power' (*rajas*) and the 'force of inertia' (*tamas*), and has no further task than that involved in transcending the presented idea of the difference between itself (*sattva*) and the life-monad (*puruṣa*),[14] and when the interior seeds of hindrances (*kleśa*) have all been burned, then the 'contemplative power' (*sattva*) enters into a state of purity equal to that of the life-monad.

"This purity is neither more nor less than the cessation of the false attribution of experience to the life-monad.[15] That is

[12] *Yoga-sūtras* 3. 51, Commentary. (Based on the translation by James Houghton Woods, *The Yoga-System of Patañjali,* Harvard Oriental Series, Vol. XVII, Cambridge, Mass., 1927, pp. 285-286.)

[13] *Yoga-sūtras* 3. 55.

[14] *Sattva, rajas,* and *tamas:* these are the *guṇas,* or "three qualities of matter" (cf. *supra,* p. 229 and *infra,* pp. 295-297). Since the thinking substance is material, it is compounded of the *guṇas.* The goal of Yoga is to purge it of *rajas* and *tamas,* so that only *sattva* remains. This is clear and unagitated, and so reflects the puruṣa without distortion. When the puruṣa is so reflected, only one act remains for the attainment of release, namely that of recognizing that the reflection is not the puruṣa.

[15] That is to say, it is realized that the reflection of the puruṣa in the sphere of matter is not the puruṣa itself. This realization is comparable to the recognition that one has been identifying oneself with one's own reflection in a mirror. One is thereupon released from absorption in the context of the mirror.

the life-monad's 'isolation.' Then the puruṣa, having its light within itself, becomes undefiled and isolated." [16]

3.

The Hindrances

Kleśa, a common word in everyday Indian speech, is derived from the root *kliś,* "to be tormented or afflicted, to suffer, to feel pain or distress." The participle *kliśta* is used as an adjective meaning "distressed; suffering pain or misery; faded, wearied, injured, hurt; worn out, in bad condition, marred, impaired, disordered, dimmed, or made faint." A garland, when the flowers are withering, is kliśta; the splendor of the moon is kliśta, when obscured by a veil of clouds; a garment worn out, or spoiled by stains, is kliśta; and a human being, when the inborn splendor of his nature has been subdued by fatiguing business affairs and cumbersome obligations, is kliśta. In the usage of the *Yoga-sūtras, kleśa* denotes anything which, adhering to man's nature, restricts or impairs its manifestation of its true essence. Patañjali's Yoga is a technique to get rid of such impairments and thereby reconstitute the inherent perfection of the essential person.

What are the impairments?

The answer to this question is one that is confusing to the Occidental mind, for it reveals the breach that separates our usual view of the inherent values of the human personality from the Indian. Five impairments are enumerated:

[16] *Yoga-sūtras* 3. 55; Commentary. Woods, *op. cit.,* p. 295.

1. *Avidyā:* nescience, ignorance, not-knowing-better; unawareness of the truth that transcends the perceptions of the mind and senses in their normal functioning. As a consequence of this impairment we are bound by the prejudices and habits of naïve consciousness. Avidyā is the root of all our so-called conscious thought.

2. *Asmitā* (*asmi* = "I am"): the sensation, and crude notion, "I am I; *cogito ergo sum;* this obvious ego, supporting my experience, is the real essence and foundation of my being."

3. *Rāja:* attachment, sympathy, interest; affection of every kind.

4. *Dveṣa:* the feeling contrary to rāja: disinclination, distaste, dislike, repugnance, and hatred.

Rāja and dveṣa, sympathy and antipathy, are at the root of all the pairs of opposites (*dvandva*) in the sphere of human emotions, reactions, and opinion. They tear the soul unremittingly this way and that, upsetting its balance and agitating the lake-like, mirrorlike surface, thus rendering it incapable of reflecting without distortion the perfect image of puruṣa.

5. *Abhiniveśa:* clinging to life as to a process that should go on without end; i.e., the will to live.

These five hindrances, or impairments, are to be regarded as so many perversions, troubling consciousness and concealing the essential state of serenity of our true nature. They are generated involuntarily and continuously, welling in an uninterrupted effluence from the hidden source of our phenomenal existence. They give strength to the substance of ego, and ceaselessly build up its illusory frame.

The source of all this confusion is the natural interplay of the guṇas, those three "constituents, powers, or qualities" of prakṛti at which we glanced in our study of the leśyas of the Jainas; [17] namely, sattva, rajas, and tamas.

1. *Sattva* is a noun built on the participle *sat* (or *sant*), from

[17] *Supra,* pp. 229-231.

as, the verb "to be." [18] *Sat* means "being; as it should be; good, well, perfect," and *sattva,* accordingly, "the ideal state of being; goodness, perfection, crystal purity, immaculate clarity, and utter quiet." The quality of sattva predominates in gods and heavenly beings, unselfish people, and men bent on purely spiritual pursuits. This is the guṇa that facilitates enlightenment. Therefore, the first aim of the Yoga taught in Patañjali's *Yoga-sūtras* is to increase sattva, and thus gradually purge man's nature of rajas and tamas.

2. The noun *rajas* means, literally, "impurity"; in reference to the physiology of the female body, "menstruation"; and more generally, "dust." The word is related to *rañj, rakta,* "redness, color," as well as to *raga,* "passion." The dust referred to is that continually stirred up by wind in a land where no rain falls for at least ten months a year; for in India, except in the rainy season, there is nothing but the nightly dew to quench the thirst of the ground. The dry soil is continually whirling into the air, dimming the serenity of the sky and coming down over everything. In the rainy period, on the other hand, all this dust is settled. And during the beautiful autumnal season that follows the rains, when the sun has dispelled the heavy clouds, the sky is spotlessly clear.[19] The Sanskrit word for "autumnal," *śarada,* (from the noun *śarad*="autumn"), consequently, connotes "fresh, young, new, recent," and *vi-śārada* ("characterized by a greatness or abundance of *śarada*") means "clever, skillful, proficient, versed in, conversant with, learned, wise." The intellect of the wise, that is to say, is characterized by the far visibility of the autumnal firmament, which is translucent, untainted, and utterly clear, whereas the intellect of the fool is filled with rajas, the ruddy dust of passion.

Rajas dims the outlook on all things, obscuring the view not

[18] Compare English pre*sent,* ab*sent* (*sant*); also, *ess*ence, *ess*ential (*as*).

[19] The Hindu autumn, in this respect, is comparable to the Indian Summer of New England and New York.

only of the universe but of oneself. Thus it produces both intellectual and moral darkness. Among mythological beings rajas predominates in the titans, those anti-gods or demons who represent the Will for Power in its full force, reckless in its pursuit of supremacy and splendor, puffed with ambition, vanity, and boastful egotism. Rajas is evident everywhere among men, as the motivating force of our struggle for existence. It is what inspires our desires, likes and dislikes, competition, and will for the enjoyments of the world. It compels both men and beasts to strive for the goods of life, regardless of the needs and sufferings of others.

3. *Tamas* (cf. Latin *tene-brae,* French *ténè-bres*)—literally, "darkness, black, dark-blue"; spiritually, "blindness"—connotes the unconsciousness that predominates in the animal, vegetable, and mineral kingdoms. Tamas is the basis of all lack of feeling, dullness, ruthlessness, insensibility, and inertia. It causes mental gloom, ignorance, error, and illusion. The stolidity of seemingly lifeless matter, the mute and merciless strife among the plants for soil, moisture, and air, the insensible greed of animals in their search for food and their ruthless devouring of their prey, are among the primary manifestations of this universal principle. On the human level, tamas is made manifest in the dull stupidity of the more self-centered and self-satisfied—those who acquiesce in whatever happens as long as their personal slumber, safety, or interests are not disturbed. Tamas is the power that holds the frame of the universe together, the frame of every society, and the character of the individual, counterbalancing the danger of self-explosion that perpetually attends the restless dynamism of the principle of rajas.

The first of the five impairments, avidyā, lack of true insight, is the main support of the unending play and interplay of these three guṇas. Avidyā permits the blind onrush of life to go on, both lured and tortured by its own principles. The other four impairments (asmitā, the crude notion "I am I"; rāja, attachment; dveṣa, repugnance; and abhiniveśa, the will to live) are but so many transformations or inflections of this primary cause, this persistent delusion that, somehow, the perishable, transitory values of earthly and celestial existence may yet become a source of unmixed and everlasting happiness. Avidyā is the common doom of all living beings. Among men, it casts its spell over the reasoning faculty, impelling it to false predictions and wrong deductions. In spite of the fact that the goods of life are intrinsically impure, and necessarily the causes of suffering because finally devoid of substance, we insist on regarding and discussing them as though they were absolutely real. People believe that the earth is everlasting, that the firmament with the stars and moon is imperishable, that the gods dwelling in celestial mansions are immortal—whereas nothing of the kind is true. In fact, the truth is precisely the contrary of these popular beliefs.

It is to be noted that, whereas, according to the essentially materialistic view of the Jainas, the primary and all-inclusive opposite to jīva was a-jīva,[20] here, where the problem of release is regarded from a psychological point of view, the crucial principle to be combatted is a-vidyā. A constant trend of wishful wrong-thinking is what supplies the motivating force of existence, producing a vigorous, life-supporting manifold of wrong beliefs. Each phenomenal entity, wanting to go on forever, avoids the thought of its own transitory character, and resists observing the many symptoms round about of the liability of all things to death. The *Yoga-sūtras,* therefore, direct attention to the instability of the backgrounds of life: the universe; the celestial bodies, which, by their circling, measure and mark the passages of time; and the divine beings themselves, "those in high places," who are the governors of the round. The undeniable fact that it is in the nature of even these great and apparently long-enduring presences to pass, guarantees the transitory, fleeting, and mirage-like character of all the rest.

[20] Cf. *supra,* p. 270.

The five impairments together distort every object of perception, thus provoking fresh misunderstandings every moment. But the yogī, in the course of his training, systematically attacks them at the root. And they actually fade away, vanishing step by step, with his gradual conquest of that ignorance (*avidyā*) whence they all derive. They become less and less effective, and at last disappear. For whenever he enters into his yogic state of introverted absorption, they are lulled into temporary slumber, and during these moments, while they are inoperative, his mind becomes aware of new insights—whereas in the so-called "normal" states of consciousness, which are the only source of *our* experience, the five impairments constitute the very bounds of knowledge, holding the whole of the universe under a tyrannical spell of helpless fascination.

From the Occidental point of view, the entire category of the "impairments" (*kleśa*) might be summed up in the term, "personality." They are the bundle of life-forces that constitute the individual and implicate him in the surrounding world. Our clinging to our ego, and our usual concrete conception of what our ego is; our spontaneous self-surrender to the likes and dislikes that guide us daily on our way and which, more or less unconsciously, are the most cherished ingredients of our nature—these are the impairments. And through all runs that primitive craving of the living creature, which is common to both men and worms: abhiniveśa, the compulsion to keep the present existence going. From the depths of the nature of every phenomenal being comes the universal cry: "May I not cease to exist! May I go on increasing!"[21] Face to face with death, this is the ultimate desire "even in the wise." And such a will to live is strong enough, according to the Indian theory of rebirth, to carry an individual across the gulf of death into a new incarnation, compelling him to reach out again for a new body, another mask, another costume, in which to carry on. Moreover, the craving

[21] *Yoga-sūtras* 2. 9; Commentary, Woods, *op. cit.*, p. 117.

wells up spontaneously, of itself; it is not an effect of thought. For why should a creature just born, and without any experience of death, shrink back from death? [22]

This elemental cry and craving to expand, even to multiply in new forms in order to circumvent the inevitable doom of individual death, is rendered vividly in the pictorial script of one of the great Hindu myths of the Brāhmaṇa period (c. 900–600 B.C.), in which we are told of the first, world-creative impulse of Prajāpati, the "Lord of Creatures." This ancient god-creator was not an abstract divine spirit, like the one in the first chapters of the Old Testament, who, floating in the pure void, beyond and aloof from the confused welter of the dark world of matter, created the universe by the sheer magic of the commands of his holy voice, summoning all things into being by the mere utterance of their names. Prajāpati, rather, was a personification of the all-containing life-matter and life-force itself, yearning to develop into teeming worlds. And he was impelled to create, we are told, by a twofold impulse. On the one hand, he felt lonely, destitute, and fearful, and so brought forth the universe to surround himself with company; but on the other hand, he also felt a longing to let his substance overflow, wherefore he said to himself: "May I give increase; may I bring forth creatures!" [23]

This double attitude of destitution and longing, at once forlorn amid the utter Nought and surging to put forth the creative life-strength within, represents in mythical form the whole meaning of the primal, universal cry. The Hindu god-creator is a personification of the dual tendency that inhabits all living things, everywhere. A timorous shrinking from possible dissolution, with, at the same time, the valiant impulse to increase, to multiply indefinitely and thus become a complete universe through prog-

[22] Cf. *ib.*, p. 118.

[23] *Śatapatha Brāhmaṇa* 2. 2. 4; 6. 1. 1-9; 11. 5. 8. 1. Compare *Bṛhadāraṇyaka Upaniṣad* 1. 2, 1-7 and 1. 4. 1-5.

eny, are the two complementary aspects of the one fundamental impulse to keep going on and on.

The five kleśas, then, comprise that heritage of tendencies on which creatures thrive, and on which they have always thrived. These "impairments" are involuntary, unconscious propensities, effective within every living creature, which sweep it along through life. According to the Indian view, moreover, they are inherited from former existences. They are the very forces that have brought about our present birth. Hence the first work of Yoga is to annihilate them, root and branch.

This requires a resolute dissolving, not only of the conscious human personality, but also of the unconscious animal drive that supports that personality—the blind life-force, present "both in the worm and in the wise," that avidly clings to existence. For only when these two spheres of natural resistance (the moral and the biological) have been broken can the yogī experience, as the core of his being, that puruṣa which is aloof from the cries of life and the constant flow of change. The serene substratum is reached, released, and made known to consciousness, only as a result of the most severe and thoroughgoing yogic process of disentanglement and introversion. To which end, three lines or ways of yogic discipline have been developed: 1. asceticism, 2. "learning in the holy teaching," and 3. complete surrender to the will and grace of God.

1. Asceticism is a preliminary exercise to purge away the impurities that stain our intrinsic nature. These dim all experience and expression by impregnating everything with the traces of former acts of the body and mind. The obscuring traces are like scars; they have been cut by passion (*rajas*) and spiritual inertia (*tamas*), the two forces of the animal portion of our nature. Ascetic exercises heal us of such wounds. Ascetic practices dispel the impairments, just as a wind dispels the clouds that hide the sky. Then the crystalline limpidity of the inner firmament of the soul—that mirror-calm of the deep inner sea, unstirred by emo-

tional gales, unfurrowed by feeling—illuminates the consciousness. This is the releasing, trans-human illumination which is the goal of all the cruel, and otherwise inexplicable, practices of Yoga.

2. "Learning in the holy teaching" means, first, getting the sacred texts by heart, and then, keeping them alive in the memory through a methodical recitation of holy prayers, sentences, formulae, and the various symbolical syllables of the religious tradition. This practice imbues the mind with the essence of the teaching, and so draws it away from worldly things, steeping it in a pious atmosphere of religious detachment.

3. Complete surrender to the will and grace of God is the adoption by the whole personality of an attitude of devotion toward the tasks and events of daily life. Every act of one's diurnal routine is to be performed with disinterest, in a detached way, and without concern for its effect upon, or relationship to, one's conscious ego. It should be performed as a service to God, prompted as it were by God's will, executed for the sake of God, and carried through by God's own energy, which is the life-energy of the devotee. By regarding duties in this light, one gradually eliminates egoism and selfishness both from one's actions and from their results. Every task becomes part of a sacred ritual, ceremoniously fulfilled for its own sake, with no regard to the profit that might redound to the individual. This type of preliminary "devotion" (*bhakti*) is taught in the *Bhagavad Gītā* and in many of the later, classical texts of Hinduism. It is a practical exercise, or technique, of spiritual development, based on the device of regarding all work as done through God, and then offering it to Him, together with its results, as an oblation.

The *Yoga-sūtras* teach that through a life perfectly conducted according to these principles, one can attain to a state where the five impairments—that is to say, the whole human personality, together with the unconscious and animal layers that are its foundation and ever-welling source—are reduced to practically nothing.

One can "burn the seeds" of future individual ignorant existences "in the fire of asceticism." The seeds have been accumulated and stored as a result of actions, both voluntary and involuntary, during this and former existences; if not demolished they will sprout into new growths of entanglement, yielding the fruits of still another destiny of delusory performances and rewards. By means of Yoga, however, the human being, congenitally impaired though he is in mind and character, can acquire a sublime, refined understanding, which then opens for him the way to release and enlightenment. Cleansed of the whirling dust of passion that normally bedims the inner atmosphere, as well as of the dulling weight of darkness that besets all phenomenal existence, the material of nature and its innate vital force (*prakṛti*) becomes entirely sattva: calm, transparent, a mirror unobscured by film, a lake without a ripple, luminous in its crystalline repose. The impairments (*kleśa*) having been removed, which normally break and blacken out the view, illumination unfolds automatically to the mind, and the living consciousness realizes that it is identical with light.

Thus the yogic "reduction diet" systematically starves the personality to death. It gives no quarter to that naïve egotism which is generally regarded as the healthy selfishness of creatures, the force that enables men and animals, as well as plants, to survive and succeed in the struggle for existence. It is a "reduction diet" that eradicates even the basic, unconscious plant and animal tendencies of our biological character. And the benefit is that when all this rajas and tamas has been destroyed and sattva alone remains—isolated, pure, and rendered fit to reflect the true nature of our undistorted being—a nucleus (*puruṣa*) comes to view that is detached from the realm of the guṇas and distinct from all that once seemed to constitute the personality: a sublime inhabitant and onlooker, transcending the spheres of the former conscious-unconscious system, aloofly unconcerned with the tendencies that formerly supported the individual biography.[24] This anonymous "diamond being" is not at all what we were cherishing as our character and cultivating as our faculties, inclinations, virtues, and ideals; for it transcends every horizon of unclarified and partly clarified consciousness. It was enwrapped within the sheaths of the body and personality; yet the dark, turbid, thick guṇas could not disclose its image. Only the translucent essence of clarified sattva permits it to become visible—as through a glass, or in a quiet pond. And then, the moment it is recognized, its manifestation bestows an immediate knowledge that this is our true identity. The life-monad is remembered and greeted, even though it is distinct from everything in this phenomenal composite of a body and psyche, which, under the delusion caused by our usual ignorance and undiscriminating consciousness (*avidyā*), we had crudely mistaken for the real and lasting essence of our being.

"Discriminative insight" (*viveka*) is the enemy of avidyā and therefore the chief instrument to disentangle us from the force of the guṇas. It cuts through tamas and rajas like a knife, opening the way to the realization that the core of our identity is separated by a wide gulf from the continuous ebb and flow of the tendencies that capture the attention of the usual individual and are everywhere regarded as pertaining, one way or another, to the Self. Through "discriminative insight" (*viveka*) an abiding state of supreme "isolation" (*kaivalya*) from the living-processes is discerned and attained. This state is an earthly counterpart of that of the transcendent monad itself—which is then disclosed to the inner consciousness of the absolutely quieted yogī, by virtue of its clear reflection in the translucent, unself-assertive sāttvic mirror of his mind. That self-luminous, abiding point amidst the whirlpool of the transient feelings, emotions, delusions, and miragelike superimpositions—that inmost, basic nucleus of nature, crystalline, the very spark of being—stands brilliantly revealed and is known immediately as both the fundament and the

[24] Cf. *supra,* pp. 293-294, and footnotes 14 and 15.

pinnacle of existence. Moreover, once a firm position has been taken on that point, never will it be abandoned; for it is above the whirl of both outer and inner changes, and beyond all event. Thence can be witnessed the life-processes going on in the body and soul—just as from the summit of a high mountain, bright in the sunshine above the welter of a storm, clouds can be witnessed shifting down a valley.

4.

Integrity and Integration

THE STATE of supreme isolation that is intrinsic to the life-monad (*puruṣa*)—aloof from all the self-continuing processes of matter (*prakṛti*), which are the very life of the body and soul—is called *kaivalya,* a term that has a double sense. *Kaivalya* is the state of one who is *kevala*—an adjective meaning "peculiar, exclusive, isolated, alone; pure, simple, unmingled, unattended by anything else; bare, uncovered (as ground)"; and at the same time, "whole, entire, absolute, and perfect" (*kevala-jñāna,* for example, means "absolute knowledge"). *Kaivalya,* consequently, is "perfect isolation, final emancipation, exclusiveness, and detachment," and at the same time, "perfection, omniscience, and beatitude." The noun *kevalin,* furthermore, is a term used specifically to denote the Jaina saint or Tīrthaṅkara. Cleansed of karmic matter, and thereby detached from bondage, this perfected one ascends in complete isolation to the summit of the universe. Yet, though isolated, he is all-pervading and endowed with omniscience; for since his essence has been relieved of qualifying, individualizing features, it is absolutely unlimited. Referring to the Tīrthaṅkara and his condition, the word *kevalin* thus expresses the two meanings of "isolated, exclusive, alone," and "whole, entire, absolute," both being ideas pertaining to the sphere of beatitude in perfection.

The Sāṅkhya-Yoga system shares, as we have seen, many features with the ancient pre-Āryan philosophy preserved in the beliefs of the Jainas. In both contexts the gods are reduced to the rank of celestial supermen; they enjoy the prerogatives of their high position only for a time, then they are reborn among the creatures of the lower kingdoms. Moreover, in both systems, matter (*prakṛti:* composed of the guṇas, according to Sāṅkhya-Yoga; composed of karma of the six colorings, according to the Jainas)[25] is an absolutely indissoluble principle; so that the world, together with its visible, tangible creatures, is understood to be utterly real. It is not a mere production of nescience (*avidyā*), as it is according to the orthodox Vedāntic view. Besides, the life-monads (*puruṣas, jīvas*) also are real. They are separate entities distinct from matter, and they are innumerable. This idea, too, is contrary to the Vedāntic teaching.

For the Vedānta is nondualistic. Instead of founding the universe on a legion of eternal spiritual entities (*jīvas, puruṣas*), embedded in, yet intrinsically antithetical to, the substance of an eternal material sphere (*ajīva, prakṛti*), the Āryan teachers held that there is, finally and fundamentally, but one essence, Brahman, and that this unfolds into the world-mirage of the visible multitude of beings. Every creature appears to be, and regards itself as, a distinct individual, and yet, fundamentally, there is nothing but Brahman. Brahman is the one-without-a-second, all-comprehending, the only "thing" that there is, in spite of the fact that each individual experiences Brahman separately, in its microcosmic, psychological aspect, as the Self.

In the *Yoga-sūtras* the term *kaivalya* has the same double mean-

[25] Cf. *supra,* pp. 229-231.

ing as in the philosophy of the Jainas, notwithstanding that the problem of bondage and release is now regarded from a psychological point of view, which approaches, in a certain way, the psychological illusionism of Vedānta. The term *kaivalya* still denotes both "isolation" and "perfection." The yogī who has got rid of the impairments (*kleśa*) that in normal life diminish the perfection of being is expected to experience fulfillment in his own omniscient isolation—just as did the Jaina kevalin or Tīrthaṅkara; he does not lose himself in the universal Brahman, as does the Vedāntic sage. Unlike the Jaina, however, the yogī achieves kaivalya, not by cleansing himself literally of contaminating karma, but by a simple (yet supremely difficult) act of comprehending that he is, in fact and essence, in spite of all appearances, unimplicated in the spheres of change and toil. Untouched, unaltered by the processes of the natural activities of the guṇas, the puruṣa (in contrast to the Jaina jīva) is never impaired or soiled, but eternally free and self-contained—even in the case of beings of the lowest orders, and in spite of the dismal fact that most creatures will never know (never will integrate into consciousness the realization) that they are in essence kevala: "serene, supreme, omniscient, and alone."

The recollection of this truth about oneself, which comes with the disappearance of the impairments, leads simultaneously to the attainment of supernormal powers. That is to say, these powers seem to be supernormal from the point of view of our naïve and worldly, "normal" life; but when one reads the texts in which they are described, it is impossible not to feel that they should perhaps be regarded not as supernormal at all, but as attributes of the pristine reality of our nature that in the course of yoga become restored to us. They are not extras—miraculous additions bestowed on the perfected saint—but man's original property. They are portions of the human heritage, withheld from us as long as we dwell under the pall of the impairments. To read about these powers is to gain a sense of what we are being deprived of by the kleśas; for when the yogī wins access to them, he comes into possession like someone taking title to rights and faculties that always had belonged to him in his character as Man (*puruṣa, ātman, puṁs*).

The traditional simile is that of the "King's Son" (*rājaputra*) who did not know that he was of royal blood and by rights a king. That is to say, there is no bondage fundamentally, no release; we are by nature free. It is only an illusion that we are bound. When the yogī attains to knowledge, no fundamental change takes place in his essence; only his outlook undergoes the change—his understanding of what is "real." He dismisses the superimposed wrong notions about the underlying reality of himself and everything else, and with that comes into possession of all that he in essence is: *rājaputravat,* "like the King's Son."[26] The reference of the simile is to the following symbolic tale.

"There was a king's son, once upon a time, who, having been born under an unlucky star, was removed from the capital while still a babe, and reared by a primitive tribesman, a mountaineer, outside the pale of the Brāhman civilization [i.e., as an outcaste, uneducated, ritually unclean]. He therefore lived for many years under the false notion: 'I am a mountaineer.' In due time, however, the old king died. And since there was nobody eligible to assume the throne, a certain minister of state, ascertaining that the boy that had been cast away into the wilderness some years before was still alive, went out, searched the wilderness, traced the youth, and, having found him, instructed him: 'Thou art not a mountaineer; thou art the King's Son.' Immediately, the youth abandoned the notion that he was an outcaste and took to himself his royal nature. He said to himself: 'I am a king.'

"So likewise," the text continues, "following the instruction of a merciful being [the guru], who declares: 'Thou didst originate from the Primal Man (*ādipuruṣa*), that universal divine life-monad which manifests itself through pure consciousness and is

[26] *Sāṅkhya-sūtras* 4. 1.

spiritually all-embracing and self-contained; thou art a portion of that,' an intelligent person abandons the mistake of supposing himself to be a manifestation or product of prakṛti, and cleaves to his own intrinsic being (*svasvarūpam*). He then says to himself: 'Since I am the son of Brahman, I am myself Brahman. I am not something different from Brahman, even though caught in this bondage of the round of birth and death.' "[27]

In this version of the ancient tale the figure is expressed according to the nondual formula of Vedānta: Thou art That (*tat tvam asi*). "Thou art the universal, only Self, though unaware of it." This is the Buddhist message too: "All things are Buddha-things."[28] Saṁsāra, the realm of birth and death, is but a vast, spread-out illusion, a cosmic dream from which one must awake. Cast away, therefore, this state of ignorance, be rid of the notion that thou art an outcaste in the wilderness. Mount thy proper throne. This is also the lesson of Sāṅkhya and Yoga—but here, as we have already seen, the puruṣa is not identified with the "First Puruṣa" (*ādipuruṣa*), the Primal Man, the World Ground (*Brahman*), but is detached, isolated, and omnipotent, because alone.

The King's Son becomes aware of what he has always been unconsciously. Nothing changes in the sphere of facts; only consciousness, his notion of what he is, becomes transformed. The instant he acquires "discriminating knowledge" (*viveka*) a distinction is revealed between his true nature and the accidental mask that he took on as a member of his wild and outcaste hunting tribe—like the realization experienced by the tiger-fosterling among the goats.[29] Accepting the reality of his character as now perceived, the King's Son recovers himself and becomes isolated (*kaivalya*) from the earlier biography and all that it contained,

[27] Compare Calderón's seventeenth-century Spanish version of the story of the King's Son in his celebrated play, *La Vida es Sueño,* "Life Is a Dream."

[28] *Vajracchedikā* 19. Cf. *infra,* pp. 545-546.

[29] Cf. *supra,* pp. 5-8.

discarding the mask of that apparent personality. And the past simply falls away. The King's Son rises from his former life as from a dream, and in the broad daylight of his new realization really feels that he is a king's son, possessing royal powers and prerogatives. He is united, at last, with the hidden fullness of his own true nature (*kaivalya*), and is never again to be touched by the crude disfigurements that shrouded his supreme perfection throughout his earlier career.

The relationship of this Indian illustration of a spiritual principle to the modern Western science of psychoanalysis is obvious. Following the dissipation of the repressing factor ("impairment," "fixation"), self-recollection is automatic. A single deep-rooted mistake having been destroyed, a whole context of beclouding ignorance dissolves, and the life is changed. Such an awakening completely and immediately transforms both one's own face and the appearance of the world.

In this Indian tale it is not expressly stated that the prince killed his father, and yet the parallel to the tragedy of Oedipus is apparent. The Oriental prince, we are told, was delivered into exile because he was a threat to his father's reign and realm; which is as much as to say, a threat to his father's life. In Indian history, as everywhere else, the regency of despotic father-kings was always endangered by the birth of a son. Kauṭilya, in his treatise on the science of politics, the *Arthaśāstra,* discussed this danger as a classic problem. In Book I, Chapters XVII–XVIII, he summarized exhaustively the classic techniques for dealing with it. We have already noted the case of the son who killed his father from a hiding place beneath his mother's bed.[30] Oriental history abounds in family romances of this kind.

The great King Bimbisara, in his old age, was blinded by his son Ajātaśatru, who then kept him captive in a dungeon to avoid the capital crime of parricide. And in the Moslem period (according to an account by ibn-Batuta), the sturdy old Shah Ghiyas-

[30] *Supra,* p. 125.

ud-din Tughlak, on his return to Tughlakabad, the capital that he had built for himself south of Delhi, and to his big treasure-house there, was killed by the fall of a roof treacherously planned by his son, Ulugh Khan, who had already (during the Warangal expedition) shown flagrant disloyalty to his sire. Thus, in 1325, Ulugh Khan ascended the throne of Delhi, with the title Mohammed Tughlak, over the corpse of his murdered father.[31] The celebrated Mughul emperor Shah Jahan, the builder of the Taj Mahal, was dethroned by Aurangzeb, his son, in 1658, and kept a prisoner until his death in 1666.[32] And we know that King Aśoka, following the quick advice of his incomparable minister Kauṭilya, forestalled a like danger by having his son Kunāla placed under guard in a frontier fortress, where the young prince was deprived of his eyesight. In this particular instance, apparently, as no doubt in many others of the kind, the catastrophe was the result of an intrigue by the queen—much like the one described in the classic legend of Phaedra and Hippolytos. The youth had rejected his stepmother's love, which presumably would have entailed the murder of his father and his own assumption of the throne with the queen as consort; then, when he had been cast into a cell, the queen sent the guard an ambiguous order, which was read as a command to deprive the young prisoner of his sight.[33]

What the science of psychoanalysis treats as the basic pattern of an ambivalent father-son relationship, relegated more or less to the unconscious but discoverable in dreams and other spontaneous manifestations, has through the ages been a practically

[31] Cf. *supra,* p. 111 (ibn-Batuta, Vol. III, pp. 212-213).

[32] *Encyclopaedia of Islam,* 1934, Vol. IV, p. 257.

[33] *Aśokāvadāna* 2. 3. 1. (Translated by J. Przyluski, *La légende de l'empereur Açoka, dans les textes indiens et chinois,* Annales du Musée Guimet, bibliothèque d'études, tome 32, Paris, 1923, pp. 281ff.) Cf. also Vincent A. Smith, *Aśoka, The Buddhist Emperor of India,* Oxford, 1901, pp. 188-189.

perpetual pattern of kingly life. It is found amply illustrated in Greek mythology, where it is a reflection of the early, pre-Āryan history of the Pelasgian dynasties, and in Roman history too, as rendered in the volumes of Tacitus, Suetonius, and Gibbon. The God Zeus renounced the goddess Thetis when he understood that a son of hers was to do away with him, as he had done away with his own father, Kronos; and the aged king of Argos, Acrisius, confined his daughter Danaë to a tower, when an oracle declared that her son (as yet not even conceived) would kill him.

The motif is a basic one, known to all humanity. And the philosophers have utilized it, practically everywhere, as a telling figure for the individual's coming into his own. The physical father and the sphere of his heritage (i.e., the whole domain of the physical senses and organs of reason, as well as the inherited customs and prejudices of one's race) must be put aside before one can enter into the full possession of one's intrinsic self. In the parable of the King's Son, as in that of the tiger among the herd of goats, this metaphor is softened, but at the same time rendered even more vivid, by a representation of the life to be transcended as that of a foster parent, while the royal and tiger natures remain as symbols of the reality to be reassumed. This is a common transfer and amelioration of the traditional metaphor.[34] The symbolized meaning is that in order to become integrated, isolated, realized, and fully mature (*kevala*), a candidate for wisdom must break the spell of simply everything that his mind and feelings have ever imagined to be his own.

For the ultimate and real task of philosophy, according to Indian thought, and to such classical Occidental philosophers as Plato, transcends the power and task of reason. Access to truth demands a passage beyond the compass of ordered thought. And by the same token: the teaching of transcendent truth cannot be

[34] For a multitude of eloquent examples, cf. Otto Rank, *The Myth of the Birth of the Hero,* Nervous and Mental Disease Monograph Series, No. 18, New York, 1914.

by logic, but only by pregnant paradox and by symbol and image. Where a carefully reasoning thinker, progressing step by step, would be forced to halt (out of breath, as it were, at the confines of the stratosphere, panting for lack of oxygen, swooning with pulmonary and cardiac distress) the mind can still go on. The mind can soar and enter the supernal sphere on the wings of symbols, which represent the Truth-beyond-the-pairs-of-opposites, eluding by those wings the bird-net of the basic principle of earthbound human logic, the pedestrian principle of the incompatibility of opposites. For what "transcendent" means is the transcending (among other things) of the bounding and basic logical laws of the human mind.

"Transcendent" means that a principle is in effect that comprehends the identity of apparently incompatible elements, representing a union of things which on the logical level exclude each other. Transcendent truth comprehends an ever-recurrent "coincidence of opposites" (*coincidentia oppositorum*) and is characterized, therefore, by an everlasting dialectical process. The secret identity of incompatibles is mockingly disclosed through a constant transformation of things into their antitheses—antagonism being but the screen of a cryptic identity. Behind the screen the contending forces are in harmony, the world-dynamism quiescent, and the paradox of a union of contrary traits and forces stands realized *in toto;* for where the One and the Many are identical, eternal Being is known, which is at once the source and the force of the abundant diversity of the world's perpetual Becoming.

Though called the true and only Being (*sat*), this Transcendent is known also as non-Being (*asat*); for it is that ineffable point "wherefrom words turn back, together with the mind, not having attained" [35]—as birds flying to reach the sun are compelled to return. And yet, on the other hand: "He who knows that bliss of Brahman has no fear of anything at all. Such a one, verily, the

[35] *Taittirīya Upaniṣad* 2. 9; cf. Hume, p. 289.

thought does not torment: 'Why did I not do the right? Why did I do evil?' He who knows thus, extricates himself from both of these questions, and secures the Self for himself by setting it free." [36]

5.

Sāṅkhya Psychology

In the form of Sāṅkhya and Yoga the pre-Āryan, dualistic-realistic philosophy and cosmology of the life-monads versus the life-matter of the universe became acceptable, eventually, to Brāhman orthodoxy. It even came to constitute one of the most important portions of the comprehensive classic Hindu philosophical tradition. Nevertheless, Kapila, the mythical founder of the Sāṅkhya doctrine, was at first regarded as heterodox, and the names of no Brāhman teachers of the Vedic line appear among the earlier expounders of Sāṅkhya and Yoga. In fact, the basic incompatibility of the nondual idealism of Vedānta with the dualistic-pluralistic realism of Sāṅkhya and Yoga can still be felt —even in the *Bhagavad Gītā;* though indeed one of the main features of that great synthesizing scripture is its employment, side by side, of the languages of the two contrary traditions, to make the point that they are not intrinsically at variance. In the fifteenth century, in the *Vedāntasāra,*[37] and again in the sixteenth, in the writings of Vijñānabhikṣu,[38] the two philosophies are presented simultaneously, on the theory that they represent the one

[36] *Ib.,* continuation.

[37] Cf. *supra,* pp. 51-56; *infra,* pp. 415ff.

[38] Cf. *supra,* p. 290, note 10.

truth from two points of view. In fact, the protagonists of the two schools have collaborated in India for centuries, borrowing major conceptions from each other for the purpose of expounding the mysteries of the way to their common goal of mokṣa.[39]

It would hardly have been possible for the masters of the orthodox Brāhman tradition to accept and assimilate the teachings of the non-Vedic aboriginal lore without this Sāṅkhya-Yoga spiritualization of the conception of the relationship between life-matter and the life-monads. Jainism, as we have seen, viewed the interaction of the two principles in terms of a kind of subtle chemistry, as a material process of pervasion and suffusion, a tingeing of the crystal of the life-monad by contamination with a subtle karmic substance; but in the *Yoga-sūtras* no such concrete process is described. Here, rather, is a kind of optical effect—a psychological illusion—which makes it appear that the life-monad is in bondage, trapped in karmic meshes, caught in the unceasing activities of the various aspects of matter (the *guṇas*),[40] whereas, actually, it is ever free. Bondage is but an illusion, which our limited and limiting minds entertain concerning the condition of our transcendent, changeless, and untainted Self.

Sāṅkhya and Yoga, however, in contrast to the orthodox Brāhman view, regard the activity of the guṇas as no less real, no less self-sustaining, than the transcendent repose of the life-monad. Matter (*prakṛti,* which is composed of the *guṇas*) *really* shrouds the life-monad; it is no mere illusory, miragelike superimposition. The activities of the guṇas are transitory in so far as their changing details are concerned, but enduring in their continuous passage itself. Nevertheless, within the sphere of each individual, the effects of the guṇas can be brought to a state of "cessation"

[39] The principal link between the two traditions, at least from the period of the Upaniṣads and *Bhagavad Gītā,* has been the doctrine that self-surrender (*bhakti*), should be practiced as a preliminary step to self-detachment.

[40] Cf. *supra,* pp. 295-297.

(*nirodha*): in consequence of a kind of optical readjustment, a realization can be attained of the remoteness of the life-monad from all that appears to be entering into it and giving it color; for though matter and its activities (*prakṛti* and the *guṇas*) are real, the involvement of the life-monad (*puruṣa*) in them is illusory, like the presence of a man within the frame and matter of a mirror. The purusa is separated from the shifting play of the guṇas by a gulf of heterogeneity not to be bridged, even though the puruṣa and the guṇas are equally real. This is a theory substantially at variance with the nondualism of the Vedāntic view.[41]

Yoga can be defined as a discipline designed to yield an experience of the sovereign aloofness and isolation of the suprapersonal nucleus of our being, by stilling the spontaneous activities of matter, which, in the form of the bodily and psychic shell, normally overlie the life-monad. Yoga is founded on, and demonstrates, a doctrine of psychological functionalism. It creates and then transcends and dissolves various planes, or worlds, of experience, and thus makes known the relativity of all states of reality; for when the inner world is seen to be but a function of the inner psychic organs, then the outer, visible and tangible universe can be understood, by analogy, to be but the consequence of an operation outward of the energies of the outer organs. By permitting energies to flow through those organs, and by then withdrawing the same energies to inner spheres, no less immediate and "real," the external world is experienced as something that can be contacted at will, and therewith built up, or cut off by yogic effort, and therewith dissolved. All depends on whether one's sense-faculties are addressed to, or withdrawn from, their usual "planes of projection" (*āyatana*).

A sovereign independence from all the pairs of opposites (*dvandva*) that assail and seduce man from without is prerequisite to the control and experience of this functionalism. Only by an accomplished yogī, in perfect control of the microcosm of him-

[41] Cf. *infra,* pp. 409ff.

self, can the entities belonging to the macrocosmic realm of name and form be dissolved and summoned back again at will. For the human mind, with its contents and wisdom, is conditioned, in every specific case, by the peculiar balance of the guṇas within the character and disposition of the given individual. His ideas, beliefs, and insights, and even the things that he sees around him, are, finally, but the functions or reflexes of his particular manner of not-knowing-better. This avidyā is the bird-net in which he is at once caught and supported as a personality. And even his after-death experiences will be determined by this limitation, which intangibly bounds and binds his being.[42]

According to the analysis of the psyche rendered by the Sāṅkhya, and taken for granted in the disciplines of Yoga, man is "active" (*kartar*) through the five "organs of action" and "receptive" (*bhoktar*) through the five "organs of perception." These two sets of five are the vehicles, respectively, of his spontaneity and receptivity. They are known as the "faculties working outward" (*bāhyendriya*) and function as so many gates and doors, while "intellect" (*manas*), "egoity" (*ahaṅkāra*), and "judgment" (*buddhi*) stand as the doorkeepers. The latter three, taken together, constitute the so-called "inner organ" (*antaḥkaraṇa*); they are the powers that open and close the gates—inspecting, controlling, and registering whatever is carried through.

The body is described as a town or kingly palace in which the king dwells inactive (according to the Oriental style) amidst the activities of his staff. The outer sense-faculties are compared to village chieftains, levying taxes on the householders, collecting and handing the taxes over to the local governor. He, in his turn, hands them to the finance minister; whereupon the latter presents them to the chancellor of the king. The experiences of the senses, that is to say, are collected and registered through

[42] Swedenborg's idea of life and death is an exact counterpart of this karma theory of Sāṅkhya and Yoga.

manas, appropriated by *ahaṅkāra,* and then delivered to *buddhi,* the "chancellor" of the king *puruṣa.*

The various sense-faculties are mutually antagonistic, yet they co-operate automatically—like the flame, the wick, and the oil of a lamp in dispelling darkness and giving light to the shapes and colors round about. The ten "faculties working outward" (*bāhyendriya*) are classed, as we have seen, in two groups: 1. that of the five "faculties of receptivity or apprehending" (*jñānendriya*), which are, namely, seeing, hearing, smelling, tasting, and touch, and 2. that of the five "faculties of spontaneity or action" (*karmendriya*)—speech, grasping, walking, evacuating, and procreating.[43] The faculties themselves are of subtle matter but the organs in which they have their seats are of gross; the faculties (as distinguished from the organs) being not perceptible, yet inferable from their activities. Rajas guṇa prevails in those of action, while in those of perception, sattva guṇa prevails.

Since the "intellect" (*manas*) co-operates directly with the ten faculties, it is reckoned as number eleven and is termed "the inner sense" (*antar-indriya*). As we have said, it is comparable to the local governor who collects the experiences of the outer senses and presents them to the finance minister (*ahaṅkāra,* the ego function), whence they go to the chancellor (*buddhi,* the faculty of judgment). *Manas, ahaṅkāra,* and *buddhi* together constitute the "inner organ" (*antaḥ-karaṇa*), which is declared to be of "medium size" (*madhyama-parimāṇa*), neither small nor immense. And from this threefold organ proceed the activities of the "vital airs," which are known through the following five manifestations: [44] 1. *prāṇa,* the "forward breathing," or exhaling air, which pervades the whole organism, from the tip of the big toe through the navel and heart to the tip of the nose; 2. *apāna,* the "opposite or downward breathing," the inhaling air, which

[43] Cf. *supra,* p. 228.

[44] N.B. These five vital airs are not "gross" but "subtle," and not to be confused with the breathing of the pulmonary system.

prevails in the throat, back ribs, intestinal canal, sex organs, and legs; 3. *samāna,* the "equalizing breath," which digests and assimilates, and is centered in the digestive organs, the heart, the navel, and all the joints; 4. *udāna,* the "ascending breath," which is in the heart, throat, palate, and skull, and between the eyebrows; and 5. *vyāna,* the "pervading breath," which is effective in the circulation, perspiration, and distribution of the life saps, and is diffused throughout the whole physique. These five prāṇas build up and maintain the system of the body, but are competent to do so only by virtue of the kingly presence of puruṣa.

Ahaṅkāra, the ego-function, causes us to believe that we feel like acting, that we are suffering, etc.; whereas actually our real being, the puruṣa, is devoid of such modifications. Ahaṅkāra is the center and prime motivating force of "delusion" (*abhimāna*). Ahaṅkāra is the misconception, conceit, supposition, or belief that refers all objects and acts of consciousness to an "I" (*aham*). *Ahaṅkāra*—"the making (*kāra*) of the utterance 'I' (*aham*)"—accompanies all psychic processes, producing the misleading notion "I am hearing; I am seeing; I am rich and mighty; I am enjoying; I am about to suffer," etc., etc. It is thus the prime cause of the critical "wrong conception" that dogs all phenomenal experience; the idea, namely, that the life-monad (*puruṣa*) is implicated in, nay is identical with, the processes of living matter (*prakṛti*). One is continually appropriating to oneself, as a result of ahaṅkāra, everything that comes to pass in the realms of the physique and psyche, superimposing perpetually the false notion (and apparent experience) of a subject (an "I") of all the deeds and sorrows. Ahaṅkāra is characterized by a predominance of rajas guṇa, since it is concerned, primarily, with doing.

Buddhi, on the other hand, is predominantly sāttvic (characterized by a predominance of sattva guṇa); for it is the faculty of awareness. Buddhi is termed *mahat,* "the great principle or primary substance"; also *mahan,* "The Great One." The verbal root *budh* means "to wake, to rise from sleep, to come to one's senses or regain consciousness; to perceive, to notice, to recognize, to mark; to know, understand, or comprehend; to deem, consider; to regard, esteem; to think, to reflect." *Buddhi* then (the gerund) means "returning to consciousness, recovering from a swoon"; also, "presence of mind, readiness of wit, intention, purpose, design; perception, comprehension; impression, belief, idea, feeling, opinion; intellect, understanding, intelligence, talent; information, knowledge; discrimination, judgment, and discernment."

According to the Sāṅkhya, buddhi is the faculty of what is known as *adhyavasāya,* i.e., "determination, resolution, mental effort; awareness, feeling, opinion, belief, knowledge, discrimination, and decision." All of these spiritual processes take place within man, yet are not at his disposal according to his conscious will. One is not free to feel, to know, and to think precisely as one chooses. This means that buddhi precedes ahaṅkāra both in rank and in power. The modes of judgment and experience, according to which we react to impressions, control us more than we them; we are not in a position to take or leave them. They appear from within, as manifestations of the subtle substance of our own character; they are the very constitution of that character. Hence it is that, though when making a decision we may suppose ourselves to be free and following reason, actually what we are following is the lead of buddhi, our own "unconscious" nature.

Buddhi comprises the totality of our emotional and intellectual possibilities. These stand in store—beyond, and as the background of, our ego-function. They constitute that total nature which is continually becoming conscious (i.e., manifest to our ego) through all the acts denoted by the term buddhi. As a great reservoir of the permanent raw-materials of our nature, which are continually presented to consciousness and the ego-function from within, buddhi is manifold in its products and utterances, wonderful in its all-inclusiveness; that is why it is termed "The Great One," *mahan*. Furthermore, through the synonyms for buddhi in popular literature, the amplitude of its suprapersonal abundance is again declared; for these give expression to the various aspects under which it becomes manifest. Buddhi is popularly known as *manas:* [45] "mind, understanding, intelligence, perception, and cognition"; also as *mat:* "knowledge, judgment, resolution, determination; intention, purpose, design; esteem, regard; counsel, advice; remembrance, recollection." Within this great storehouse of our psychic potentialities, our intellectual, volitional, emotional, and intuitive faculties are assembled side by side. Hence "The Great One" (*mahan*) is known also as *prajñā,* "wisdom, discernment"; *dhī,* "intuition, visualization, imagination, fancy"; *khyāti,* "knowledge, the power of distinguishing objects by appropriate names"; *smṛti,* "remembrance, memory"; and *prajñāna-santati,* "the continuity of knowing." Buddhi renders the unconscious manifest—through every possible kind of creative and analytical psychic process; and these processes are activated from within. That is why we become aware of the sum total of our own nature only a posteriori, through its manifestations and reactions in the forms of feelings, recollections, intuitions, ideas, and the choices that we make through the intellect or will.

Still another common synonym for buddhi is *citta. Citta,* the participle of the verb *cint/cit,* "to think," denotes whatever is experienced or enacted through the mind. Citta comprises 1. observing, 2. thinking, and 3. desiring or intending; that is to say, the functions of both the reasoning faculty and the heart. For, normally, the two behave as one, closely knit in the soul-substance of our nature. Thought, when it surges to the mind, is both directed and colored by our emotional biases and trends; and this to such a degree that a considerable discipline of criti-

[45] The term which properly refers to "intellect"; cf. *supra,* p. 318.

cism and concentration is required before one can learn to separate reasoning (for example, in science) from the movements of the heart.

Buddhi is compounded of the three guṇas, but by means of Yoga sattva guṇa is made to prevail.[46] Yogic training purges buddhi of its original inheritance of tamas and rajas. With the removal of the first, darkness is removed, and the subtle matter of buddhi becomes translucent, like the waters of a mountain lake. With the removal of the second, agitation is removed, and the rippling of the restless surface then is stilled, so that the waters, already cleared, become a steady mirror. Buddhi then reveals the puruṣa in its serene unconcern, aloof from the busy, rippling sphere of prakṛti.

Buddhi both contains and *is* the spontaneity of our nature; the other faculties (ahaṅkāra, manas, and the ten indriyas) are "like bees, which follow the advice of their kings." [47] Yet to all appearances the influence runs in the opposite direction: the outer senses come in contact with their environment; their experiences are digested by manas; the product of manas is brought through ahaṅkāra into relation to one's individuality; and then buddhi decides what is to be done. The primacy of buddhi thus is heavily obscured. Only with the removal of rajas and tamas does the veil become transparent; for the powers that then pour into the human organism are the "supranormal" ones of the King's Son, and buddhi is revealed in its innate strength. Before such an effect can be attained, however, the apparent connection of the life-monad with suffering must be broken. The illusion of a connection is caused, as we have seen, by an absence of discrimination, a failure to recognize the distinction between puruṣa and prakṛti—particularly between purusa and that most subtle of the products of prakṛti, the inner organ and the ten faculties of sense. Since this lack of "discriminative knowledge"

[46] Cf. *supra,* pp. 301-305.

[47] There is no queen bee according to the nature lore of the Hindus.

(*viveka*) is the cause, obviously a sufficiency will be the end of the experience of suffering. Viveka makes it possible for the individual to distinguish between his own life-principle and the indifferent matter that flows around it.

The matter stops being active, furthermore, the moment one becomes identified with puruṣa; therefore prakṛti in action through the guṇas is compared to a dancing girl of the seraglio, who ceases dancing the moment the onlooker loses interest. She withdraws from the presence of the king when he becomes bored with her exhibition of the world's delights and pains. Working through the guṇas, prakṛti exhibits the wonders that we know and love, or feel as suffering, but the eye that gives energy to the spectacle is the all-illuminating eye of puruṣa, and the moment this returns to itself, the world-scene disappears.

Because the subtle matter of the inner organ assumes all the forms presented to it by the senses, objects tend to give to the mind a shape or character and to leave on it an impression, or "memory," more or less permanent. Not only the shape of the object itself, but also the associated feelings and thoughts, as well as the will and determination to act that it aroused, remain as vestiges, and these may be reanimated at a later date by the impingement of something new. In this way memories are excited, images of recollection aroused, and continuities of life-desire, fear, and manners of conduct founded. The psychological process is understood in Sāṅkhya and Yoga, that is to say, in strictly mechanical terms. The unceasing agitation of transformation brought to pass in the inner organ through perception, emotion, thought, and will is not different in kind from the changes observable in the outer world. The transformations are material in both spheres, purely mechanical processes taking place in matter, the sole difference being that in the outer world (which includes, of course, the body of the subject) the matter is gross whereas in the inner it is subtle.

This mechanistic formula is of the essence of the Sāṅkhya,

and not only underlies its system of psychology but also gives the key to its interpretation of the mystery of metempsychosis. Within the gross body, which suffers dissolution after death, every living being possesses an inner subtle body, which is formed of the sense-faculties, vital breaths, and inner organ. This is the body that goes on and on, from birth to birth, as the basis and vehicle of the reincarnated personality.[48] It departs from the sheath of the gross body at the time of death, and then determines the nature of the new existence; for within it are left the traces—like scars or furrows—of all the perceptions, acts, desires, and movements of will of the past, all the propensities and trends, the heritage of habits and inclinations, and the peculiar readinesses to react this way or that, or not to react at all.

The technical terms used to denote these reminders of the past are *vāsanā* and *saṁskāra.* The former word (from the root *vas,* "to dwell in, to abide") can be used to refer to the smell that clings to a cloth that has been perfumed with fragrant smoke. A vessel of unbaked clay retains the smell of whatever it first contained, and in the same way the subtle body is pervaded by the vāsanās ("fragrances, perfumes, the subtle residues") of all its earlier karma. These vāsanās tend to cause saṁskāras, permanent scars that go from life to life.

The noun *saṁskāra,* signifying "impression, influence, operation, form, and mold," is one of the basic terms of Indian philosophy. It is derived from the verbal root *kṛ,* "to make." *Saṁskṛ* means "to make ready, to fashion to some use, to change or transform"; the opposite idea being *pra-kṛ*—cf. *prakṛti:* matter as it is at hand, presented in its raw or virgin state.

[48] This reincarnating subtle body deserves the name of "soul" much more than the life-monad, though the latter is what has been constantly translated "soul" (by Garbe and others). And yet "soul" is not quite correct here either; for the material of the subtle body is essentially lifeless, senseless (*jaḍa*); it is rather a body than a soul.—Better, when translating from the Sanskrit, not to use our animistic Occidental term.

Prakṛti is primal virgin matter, on which no change, transformation, or evolution has yet been brought to pass. Conversely, *saṁs-kṛ* means "to transform something, to adorn, to grace, to decorate." The vernacular speech of the uneducated is known as *prakṛta* (Engl. "Prakrit") while *saṁskṛta* (Engl. "Sanskrit") is the classic language of the rules of established, correct grammar, based on the holy tradition of the priestly language of the Vedas—which in turn was a reflection of the language of the gods, and so a natural vehicle of divine truth. The verb *saṁskṛ* means "to purify a person by means of scriptural ceremonies," i. e., to change him from an ordinary person, a mere human being, into a member of the sacramental, magic community, divested of his former crude impurities, and made eligible to participate in traditional ceremonials. *Saṁskāra* therefore is "purification, purity; investiture with the sacred thread of the twice-born," [49] or, in general, any purificatory rite or sacred ceremony; but also "cooking, the dressing of food (to make it more palatable and attractive, depriving it of its natural, unappetizing, indigestible 'raw nature,' *prakṛti*), the polishing of a stone or jewel; education, cultivation, training, embellishment, decoration, ornament, and make-up" (the lack of make-up is permissible for housework, labor, and rustic toil, but not for meeting people; for it would indicate a lack of respect and self-esteem). *Saṁskāra,* thus, is a rich and highly suggestive term. Its connotations cluster about the concept of "that which has been wrought, cultivated, brought to form." But this, in the case of the individual, is the personality—with all its characteristic adornments, scars, and quirks—which for years, indeed for lifetimes, has been in the process of concoction.

Prakrti, undeveloped, primitive matter, if left to itself, would

[49] The members of the three upper castes are the "twice-born." The ritual of investiture with the sacred thread, performed at puberty, symbolizes the transformation which in the Christian tradition is associated with the baptismal font.

be characterized by a perfect equilibrium of the guṇas. In this state there would be no play of transformation; there would be no world. Tamas (heaviness, sloth, obstruction), rajas (movement, excitation, pain), and sattva (lightness, illumination, joy) would then not work upon each other but lie in perfect balance and remain at rest. According to the Sāṅkhya, the world is not the result of any act of a Creator. It had no beginning in time. It is the result, rather, of an unceasing influence on prakṛti, deriving from infinitely numerous individual puruṣas. These puruṣas are not themselves active; they only contemplate, as spectators, the movement of which they are the perpetual stimulation. Nor do they exert their influence by consciously willing. Their mere presence is what excites prakṛti to move—as a magnet excites iron. "By virtue of its nearness" the life-monad illuminates the field and processes of the guṇas. By its mere radiance, it creates a kind of consciousness in the subtle body. "As fire in a red-hot iron ball, so is consciousness in the material of life."

This dualism is fundamental to Sāṅkhya. The two principles—prakṛti (composed of the guṇas) and puruṣa (the collectivity of irradiant but inactive life-monads)—are accepted as eternal and real on the basis of the fact that in all acts and theories of knowledge a distinction exists between subject and object, no explanation of experience being possible without the recognition of a knowing self as well as of an object known. Accepting this duality as basic and axiomatic, Sāṅkhya then proceeds to develop an "exhaustive analytical enumeration" (*parisaṅkhyāna*) of the "principles or categories" (*tattva:* "thatnesses") of nature, as these have been evolved in the unceasing developments and combinations of inert matter under the uninterrupted influence of the brilliance radiating from the life-monads and producing consciousness. Briefly, this evolution of the tattvas may be summarized in the following way:

SAṄKHYA PSYCHOLOGY

PRAKṚTI
(undifferentiated primal matter)

↓

Buddhi / Mahat
(the suprapersonal potentiality of experiences)

↓

Ahaṅkāra
(egoity: a function appropriating the data of consciousness and wrongly assigning them to puruṣa)

↓

the five karmendriya (the faculties of action)

manas (the faculty of thought)

the five jñānendriya (the faculties of sense)

the five tan-mātra[50] (the subtle, primary elements: realized as the inner, subtle counterparts of the five sense experiences, viz., sound, touch, color-shape, flavor, smell: *śabda, sparśa, rūpa, rāsa, gandha)*

↓

parama-aṇu
(subtle atoms: realized in the experiences of the subtle body)

↓

sthūla-bhūtāni
(the five gross elements, ether, air, fire, water, earth, constituting the gross body and the visible tangible world: realized in sense experiences)[51]

[50] *Tan-mātra:* "merely (*mātra*) that (*tan*)," "mere trifle."

[51] The formation of the gross elements from the subtle is described as follows: "By dividing each subtle element into two equal parts, and sub-

The tattvas emerge from each other gradually. This emergence is the natural process of the unfolding, or evolution, of the "normal" waking state of consciousness from the primal, undifferentiated, quiescent state of prakṛti. By yoga the transformations, or tattvas, are dissolved back again, this reverse movement representing a process of involution. The former process, namely that of the evolution of the tattvas from the subtle (*sūkṣma*) to the gross (*sthūla*), is marked by a continuous increase of tamas guṇa, whereas with the return sattva guṇa comes to prevail. However, puruṣa, the life-monad, remains uninvolved, no matter which way the process runs, and no matter how refined the state of sattva guṇa that is attained. Puruṣa is beyond the system of the guṇas absolutely, whether the latter be in evolution or in involution. Self-radiant, self-subsistent, aloof, it never changes, whereas prakṛti will go on changing forever.

Puruṣa is defined as "pure spirit" (*caitanya*), in token of the fact that it is non-matter, and yet it is far from every Western concept of spirituality—for all of the conditions of what we term the "soul" are effects of the realm of subtle matter, according

---

dividing the first half of each into four equal parts, and then adding to the unsubdivided half of each element one subdivision of each of the remaining four, each element becomes five in one" (*Pañcadaśi* 1. 27). These compounds are what are known as the gross elements. They are named according to whether the preponderant portion is ether, air, fire, water, or earth.

air	ether	ether	ether	ether
fire	fire	air	air	air
water	water	water	fire	fire
earth	earth	earth	earth	water
ether	air	fire	water	earth

Since ether is experienced as sound, air as touch, fire as color and shape, water as flavor, and earth as smell, each gross element (being a compound of all five) affects all the senses.

to the Sāṅkhya, coming to pass in the subtle body. Such a body is not to be identified, in any sense, with the life-monad. About the life-monad nothing can be said (beyond the statement that *it is*) except in negative terms: it is without attributes, without qualities, without parts, without motion—imperishable, inactive and impassive; it is unaffected by pains and by pleasures, devoid of feelings and emotions, completely indifferent to sensations. It abides outside the categories of the world. Puruṣa is comparable to a seer when he is seeing nothing, or to a mirror in which nothing is reflected. Nothing comes to it in that sphere except itself—even though all things this side of it are illuminated, activated, and given consciousness by its pure, untroubled, undeluded radiance.

When perfect knowledge of the puruṣa has been attained, one does not give up one's gross and subtle body immediately; life lingers on for a considerable time. Just as the potter's wheel continues to revolve after the completion of the pot, in consequence of the initial impulses, so the body of the kevalin goes on with all its subtle and gross natural processes, even though the Knower himself, aloof from them, is simply watching with sublime indifference; for the present life is a result of works, the fruit of seeds that were planted before the attainment of emancipation, and these must mature to the fullness of their days. On the other hand, the germinal force of all the seeds that have not yet sprouted is broken and consumed. The Knower knows that there can be no future life or lives for him, because he has withdrawn his impulses from the process. The process is running down. Henceforward, therefore, he simply endures the events of his existence without committing himself to anything new, until finally, when the forces of the works already bearing fruit are exhausted, death overtakes him and there can be no return. The gross body dissolves. The subtle body also dissolves. The inner organ, with its saṁskāras, which have gone on from birth to birth, dissolves. The guṇas are released from their agitation in this vortex, and the disturbance of this individual dissolves.

But the life-monad continues to exist—just as an individual continues to exist when his reflection has disappeared from a shattered glass. Self-consciousness is gone—because the material basis necessary for the processes of knowledge, feeling, and experience now is missing—but the life-monad endures, as an individual entity in and for and by itself. Without the apparatus of the gross and the subtle body, puruṣa is completely out of contact with the sphere of the guṇas; it is not to be reached by anything, it is unattainable, absolutely removed.

This is real "isolation."

Here is apparent the parallel of Sāṅkhya with the Jaina and Ājīvika teachings, as well as its contrast with Vedānta. The idea of a pluralism of life-monads belongs, apparently, to the ancient, native Indian, pre-Āryan philosophy; so too, the theory that the sphere of matter (*prakṛti*) is in itself substantial, not a mere reflex, or mirage, or trick of māyā.[52] Nevertheless there is one aspect of the Sāṅkhya teaching that seems to differ as much from the Jaina notion of release as from the Vedāntic; for in its final state of separation from the instruments of consciousness, the puruṣa abides in eternal *unconsciousness.* During life the same condition was attained temporarily in deep, dreamless sleep, in swoons, and in the state of perfect abstraction that is achieved through disciplined yoga practice. But this is not the state described for the omniscient Jaina Tīrthaṅkara. Whereas Vedānta, precisely to stress the idea that the perfect state is one of pure *consciousness,* speaks of a stage or sphere beyond those of the Gross Body (Waking Consciousness), the Subtle Body (Dream Consciousness), and the Causal Body (Deep Sleep), which it calls the "Fourth" (*turīya*).[53] With this Vedāntic Brāh-

[52] Cf. *supra,* p. 19.

[53] Cf. *infra,* pp. 361-362 and 372ff.

man insight, the *psychological* Sāṅkhyic-Yogic isolation in unconsciousness becomes as archaic as the *physical* isolation of the Jaina Tīrthaṅkaras.

The supreme contribution of Sāṅkhya and Yoga to Hindu philosophy lies in their strictly psychological interpretation of existence. Their analyses of the micromacrocosm, as well as of the whole range of human problems, are presented in terms of a sort of proto-scientific psychological functionalism, which is comparable, in its meticulousness and sober positivism, to the comprehensive system and theory of biological evolution that we discussed in connection with the Jainas and Gosāla. Here the primitive mythical image of the rise of a universe out of the cosmic waters and cosmic egg is reinterpreted and revivified in terms of stages of human consciousness, as these can be observed in the subjective experiences of yoga. From the primal state of self-absorption, or involution, which amounts practically to quiescence and resembles non-being, a state of intuitive inner awareness (*buddhi*) is evolved; this is antecedent to the notion of "I" (*ahaṅkāra*), which is the following transformation; and through intellect (*manas*), consciousness then proceeds to an experience of (and to action upon) the outer world through exterior senses. The cosmogonic process thus is read, in terms of psychological experience, as the unfoldment of a perceived environment from an innermost, all-perceiving center. The naïve myth becomes immediately significantly structuralized: the world is understood as unfolding from a quiescent state of inward absorption; and introspection therewith becomes the key to the riddle of the sphinx.

Finally, it should be observed that the following four features of Sāṅkhya appear in Buddhism as well: an insistence that all life is, necessarily, suffering; an indifference to theism and to Vedic sacrificial ritualism; a denunciation of ascetic extravagances (as represented, for example, in Jainism); and a belief in *pariṇāma-nityatva,* "the constant becoming of the world." [54]

[54] Sāṅkhya is referred to in the Buddhist Pāli canon, and Buddhist legends mention Kapila as one of the predecessors of the Buddha. "There are some recluses and Brāhmans who are eternalists," we read in the *Brahmajālasuttanta* (*Dīgha-nikāya* 1. 30, 34; translated by T. W. Rhys Davids, Sacred Books of the Buddhists, Vol. II, Oxford, 1899, pp. 27-29); "they are addicted to logic and reasoning and give utterance to the following conclusions of their own: eternal is the soul and the world, giving birth to nothing new, it is steadfast as a mountain peak, as a pillar firmly fixed; and the living creatures, though they pass from birth to birth, fall from one state of existence and spring up in another, yet they exist forever and ever."

I. Lion-capital, Sārnāth, 3rd century B.C.

II. Cakravartin, Jagayyapeṭa, 2nd century B.C.

III. Nāga King and Queen, Ajaṇṭā, 6th century A.D.

IV. Gautama Buddha, Cambodia, 11th century A.D.

V. Pārśvanātha, Mathurā, 2nd century A.D.

VIa. Pārśvanātha, West India, 16th or 17th century A.D.

VIb. Ḍaḥḥāk, Persia, 1602 A.D.

VIc. Syrian seal, c. 1450 B.C.

VII. Ṛṣabhanātha, Mount Ābū, 11th to 13th centuries A.D.

VIII. Gommaṭa, Śravaṇa Beḷgoḷa, c. 983 A.D.

IX. The Assault of Māra, Amarāvatī, 2nd century A.D.

X. Gautama Buddha, Mathurā,
5th century A.D.

XI. Vīra and Śakti, Khajurāho, 10th century A.D.

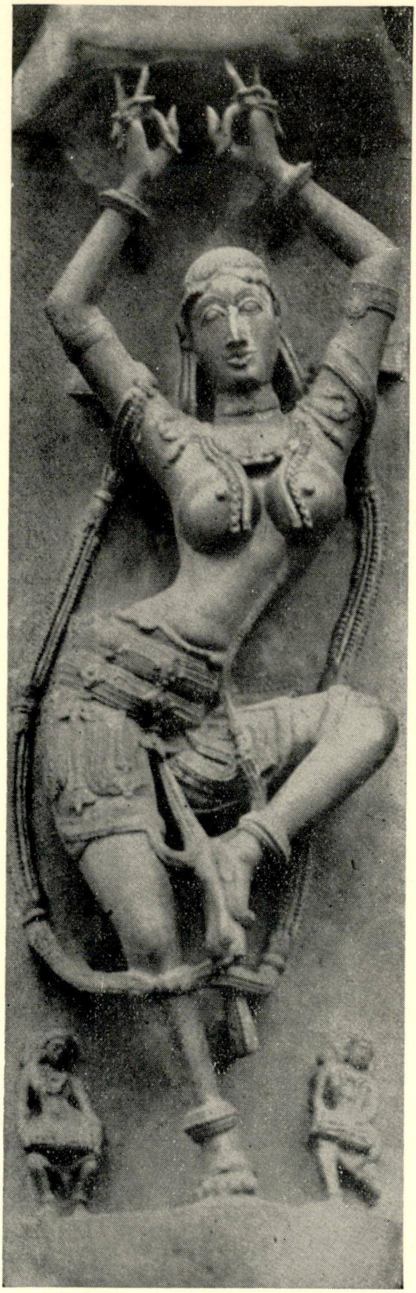

XII. Apsaras, Palampet,
12th or 13th century A.D.

III. BRĀHMANISM

1.

Veda

INDIAN orthodox philosophy arose from the ancient Āryan religion of the Veda. Originally the Vedic pantheon with its host of gods depicted the universe as filled with the projections of man's experiences and ideas about himself. The features of human birth, growth, and death, and of the process of generation, were projected on the course of nature. Cosmic forces and phenomena were personalized. The lights of the heavens, the varieties and aspects of clouds and storm, forests, mountain masses and river courses, the properties of the soil, and the mysteries of the underworld were understood and dealt with in terms of the lives and commerce of divine beings who themselves reflected the human world. These gods were supermen endowed with cosmic powers and could be invited as guests to feast on oblations. They were invoked, flattered, propitiated, and pleased.

In Greece this ancient stage of Āryan belief was represented in the mythology of the Homeric age, which was continued in the tragedy of the Athenian theater. However, with the appearance of Greek philosophical criticism in Ionian Asia Minor and its development by philosophers and sophists from Thales to Socrates (supported then by the advance of the natural sciences, with rational astronomy—i.e., cosmology based on mathematics—in the lead), the primitive, dreamlike, anthropomorphic projections were withdrawn from the natural scene. Myth was no longer accepted as a valid interpretation of the processes of nature. The human features and biographies of the gods were rejected, even satirized; the archaic mythology and religion collapsed; the brilliant community of the Olympians fell. And this debacle was followed, shortly, by the collapse of the Greek city-states themselves, in the period of Alexander the Great.

No such Twilight of the Gods occurred in the sphere of the ancient Hindu thinkers. The guardian deities of the world were not overthrown, but incorporated in an amplified and deepened vision, like local puppet-kings within the empire of a mightier lord. The One Presence, which was experienced as the Self (*ātman*), or Holy Power (*brahman*), within and beyond the many, took to itself the whole charge of the Indian libido, absorbed its entire interest; and this universal spiritual monarchy seriously threatened the reign of the gods, greatly reducing them in significance and prestige. Nevertheless, as viceroys and special emissaries, transcendentally invested, as it were, with their powers and insignia of office, the deities remained in their high seats, only serving a new function. They were recognized as themselves manifestations of that omnipresent, supporting inner Power, to which all serious attention was being turned. This universal ground was understood to be identical within all things—unchanged through the changing forms. It abides supreme within the unfolding shapes of the phenomenal universe, whether in the grosser spheres of normal human experience or in the more rarified of the empyrean. Moreover, it transcends them all, and is infinitely beyond. Gradually, with the development of this type of Brāhmanical speculative thought, the complex polytheistic ritual of the earlier stages of the Vedic tradition fell into disuse, and a way of worship came into favor that was at once less elaborate, more intimate, and more profound.

"*Om!* Now, there was Śvetaketu Āruṇeya. To him his father said: 'Live the life of a student of sacred knowledge. Verily, my dear, from our family there is no one unlearned in the Vedas, a Brāhman by connection as it were.' He then, having become a pupil at the age of twelve, having studied all the Vedas, returned at the age of twenty-four, conceited, thinking himself learned, proud.

"Then his father said to him: 'Śvetaketu, my dear, since now you are conceited, think yourself learned, and are proud, did you also ask for that teaching whereby what has not been heard of becomes heard of, what has not been thought of becomes thought of, what has not been understood becomes understood?'

" 'How, pray, Sir, is that teaching?'

" 'Just as, my dear, by one piece of clay everything made of clay may be known (the modification is merely a verbal distinction, a name; the reality is just "clay")[1]—just as, my dear, by one copper ornament everything made of copper may be known (the modification is merely a verbal distinction, a name; the reality is just "copper")—just as, my dear, by one nail-scissors everything made of iron may be known (the modification is merely a verbal distinction, a name; the reality is just "iron"); so, my dear, is that teaching.'

" 'Verily, those honored men did not know this; for, if they had known it, why would they not have told me? But do you, Sir, tell me it.'

" 'So be it, my dear. . . . Bring hither a fig from there.'

[1] Or: "every modification being but an effort of speech, a name, and the clay the only reality about it" (*vācārambhanam vikāro nāmadheyam—mṛttik-ety eva satyam*).

" 'Here it is, Sir.'

" 'Divide it.'

" 'It is divided, Sir.'

" 'What do you see there?'

" 'These rather fine seeds, Sir.'

" 'Of these, please, divide one.'

" 'It is divided, Sir.'

" 'What do you see there?'

" 'Nothing at all, Sir.'

"Then he said to him: 'Verily, my dear, that finest essence which you do not perceive—verily, my dear, from that finest essence this great sacred fig tree thus arises. Believe me, my dear,' said he, 'that which is the finest essence—this whole world has that as its self. That is Reality. That is Ātman. That art thou (*tat tvam asi*), Śvetaketu.'

" 'Do you, Sir, cause me to understand even more.'

" 'So be it, my dear,' said he. 'Place this salt in the water. In the morning come unto me.'

"Then he did so.

"Then he said to him: 'That salt you placed in the water last evening—please, bring it hither.'

"Then he grasped for it, but did not find it, as it was completely dissolved.

" 'Please take a sip of it from this end,' said he. 'How is it?'

" 'Salt.'

" 'Take a sip from the middle,' said he. 'How is it?'

" 'Salt.'

" 'Take a sip from that end,' said he. 'How is it?'

" 'Salt.'

" 'Set it aside. Then come unto me.'

"He did so, saying, 'It is always the same.'

"Then he said to him: 'Verily, indeed, my dear, you do not perceive Being here. Verily, indeed, it is here. That which is the finest essence—this whole world has that as its self. That is Reality. That is Ātman. That art thou, Śvetaketu.' "[2]

Whereas from the dualistic point of view of Sāṅkhya and Yoga, and the more materialistic non-Āryan philosophies of the Jainas and Gosāla, the universe is interpreted on the basis of two antagonistic eternal principles, puruṣa and prakṛti (or jīva and non-jīva), according to the transcendental nondualism of the Vedic tradition all such oppositions are to be regarded as merely phenomenal. The Brāhmans were not deterred from further thinking by the obvious incompatibility of contradictory functions. On the contrary, they recognized precisely in this dilemma their clue to the nature and meaning of that which is transcendent and therefore divine.

The sage Āruṇi's instruction of his son demonstrated by analogy that the supreme principle transcends the sphere of "names and forms" (*nāmarūpa*), yet is all-penetrating, like the salt. Brahman is as subtle as the seed of the seed within the fruit; it is inherent in all beings, as the potentiality of their unfolding life. And yet, though this invisible entity transforms itself, or at least appears to do so, through all the shapes and processes of the world—as copper and clay are transformed into all the pots and pans in the kitchen—nevertheless, these visible, tangible forms are "mere transformations" (*vikāra*); one should not confine one's attention to the spectacle of their configurations. The names and forms are accidental and ephemeral; in the final analysis, "the reality is just 'clay.' "

According to this Brāhmanical formula, the dialectic of the universe is a manifestation of a transcendent, nondual, transdual, yet immanent principle, which both gives forth the world of names and forms (*nāmarūpa*) and inhabits it as its animating principle. The dualism of *natura naturans* (*prakṛti*) and the

[2] *Chāndogya Upaniṣad* 6. 1; 6. 12-13. (Translated by Robert Ernest Hume, *The Thirteen Principal Upanishads,* Oxford, 1921, pp. 240-241, 247-248.)

transcendent immaterial monad (*puruṣa*) is thus itself trancended.

The chief motivation of Vedic philosophy, from the period of even the earliest philosophic hymns (which are preserved in the later portions of the Ṛg-Veda), has been, without change, the search for a basic unity underlying the manifold of the universe. Brāhmanical thinking was centered, from the beginning, around the paradox of the simultaneous antagonism-yet-identity of the manifest forces and forms of the phenomenal world, the goal being to know and actually to control the hidden power behind, within, and precedent to all things, as their hidden source. This search, or inquiry, was conducted, furthermore, along two main lines, which amounted, fundamentally, to the same. The first—answering the question, "What is the one and only essence that has become diversified?"—sought the highest power behind the formations of the outer world, while the second, directing the gaze inward, asked, "What is the source from which the forces and organs of my own life have proceeded?" The self-analysis of man was thus developed as a parallel discipline, correlative and contributive to the speculative evaluation of external powers and effects.

In contrast to its transitory products or manifestations, the micromacrocosmic essence itself was early regarded as inexhaustible, changeless, and undecaying; for it was experienced inwardly as a well of holy power. To know it, therefore, to gain access to it through knowledge (*jñāna*), meant actually to participate in its fearlessness, bliss, immortality, and boundless strength. Moreover, to attain to these meant to transcend, in some measure, the threat of death and the miseries of life—which was a pressing, very serious, general concern in those ancient times of incessant war, during and just subsequent to the great migration of the Āryan tribesmen into the subcontinent of India, when the struggle of the feudal chieftains for supremacy was in full career, and the world was beset with enemies and demons. From those remote days of nomadic and feudal strife, Vedic inquiry into the secret background of the diversities of the cosmos evolved gradually and without a break, until, in the later centuries of the Upaniṣads, the pictographic reasonings of mythology and theology had been left far behind for the abstract devices of metaphysics. But throughout, through all the transformations of Indian civilization, the Brāhmanical obsession, whether in the comparatively primitive form of early Āryan magic or in the supreme refinements of the later thought, remained the same; namely, fixed on the problem of the nature of the force that continually and everywhere presents itself to man under new disguises.

The task of fathoming this mystery was approached first in the spirit of an archaic natural science. Through comparison and identification diverse phenomena were discovered to stem from the same root, and thus to be basically one. Speculative insight, penetrating the constant metamorphoses, thus recognized a ubiquitous power of self-transmutation, which was termed *māyā* (from the verbal root *mā*, "to prepare, to form, to build") [8] and understood to be one of the characteristic faculties of the supra- and infrahuman world-directing gods and demons. The function of theology then became that of identifying and comprehending the whole series of masks that each divine power could assume, and labeling these correctly, with correct "names." The names were grouped into invocations and litanies, the function of the sacrificial code being to conjure the named forces litanywise, by means of their proper formulae, and thus harness them to the projects of the human will.

A vivid instance of this variety of inquiry is to be found in the Vedic theology of Agni, the god of fire. All Vedic sacrifice centered around this divinity, into whose mouth (the fire of the altar) the oblations were poured. As messenger of the gods, he carried sacrifices along his trail of flame and smoke up to heaven,

[8] Cf. *supra*, p. 19, note 11.

where he fed the celestial beings like a bird its young. Fire in its earthly form, as the presiding power of every Āryan hearth and home, was "Agni Vaiśvānara," the divine being "existing with all (*viśve*) men (*nara*)." The same deity in heaven, as the heat of the sun, was the solar Agni, while in the world-sphere between (*antarikṣa*), where fire abides with the clouds and appears as lightning, he was viewed as the child of the atmospheric waters. Two more important forms of Agni were known here on earth—that associated with wood, and that with the heat of the living cell. Fire was made by the twirling of a stick of hard wood in a hole notched into a softer plank. The rotation produced heat and presently a spark. That was comparable to the process of generation: the twirling spindle and the plank were the fire's parents, respectively male and female; therefore Agni was the son of wood. However, the wood grew and was nourished on water, and so Agni was the "grandchild of the water" (*apāṁ-napāt*), even though also the water's child, born as lightning from the watery womb of the clouds. Fire abides, furthermore, within all living beings—men, quadrupeds, and birds—as one can tell from the temperature of the body. This temperature is perceptible to touch, it is in the skin. Later on, heat was declared to be the cause of digestion—the heat of the bodily juices "cooked" the food in the intestines—and the digestive bile was therefore identified as the principal manifestation in the microcosm of the macrocosmic fire.

A knowledge of such affinities and interrelationships constituted an important department of the earliest Āryan priestly wisdom. It might be described as a kind of intuitive and speculative natural science. Furthermore, just as the speculative sciences of our day give a theoretical background and basis for applied technologies, so did the ancient wisdom of the Vedic priests support an applied technology of practical magic. Magic was the primitive counterpart of modern practical science, and the cogitations of the priests the antecedent of the pure science of our theoretical astronomy, biology, and physics. The archaic Brāhmanical inquiry and application resulted in a far-reaching identification with each other of diverse phenomena in widely differing spheres of the universe. (A) The elements of the macrocosm were identified with (B) the faculties, organs, and limbs of the microcosm (man's organism), and both with (C) the details of the inherited and traditional sacrificial ritual. The ritual was the principal instrument through which the forces of the universe were contacted and brought under control, harnessed to man's need and desire. It gradually vanished into the background, however, as the "path of knowledge" (*jñāna-mārga*) superseded the "path of ritualistic activity" (*karma-mārga*)—that is to say, as the abstract philosophy of the Upanisads became disengaged from the web of ritualistic magic. This development took place among the Vedic divines, in circles devoted to esoteric discussions, meditations, and initiations. Therewith the problem of the equivalences, or parallel structures, of (A) the universe and (B) man's nature became the sole significant key to understanding; the problem of the details of the sacrifice (C) simply dropping away. And so an extraordinary period of speculative research opened, in which the secret identity of the faculties and forces of the human body with specific powers of the outer world was exhaustively studied, from every possible angle, as a basis for a total interpretation of human nature, an understanding of its position in the universe, and a reading therewith of the riddle of our common human fate.

This curious, long-continued comparative study resulted in numerous attempts to sum up the main constituents of the micromacrocosm in co-ordinating lists, or sets of equations.[4]

[4] These can be readily compared in Hume's translation of the Upanisads (*op. cit.*, p. 520) by turning to his index, under "correlation, or correspondence—of things cosmic and personal;—of the sacrifice and the liturgy with life and the world;—of the existential and the intelligential elements."

For example, in the *Taittirīya Upaniṣad* we find that the three elements, earth, fire, and water, correspond to the human breath, sight, and skin, and again, that atmosphere, heaven, the four quarters, and the four intermediate quarters correspond on the one hand to wind, sun, moon, and stars, and on the other to hearing, mind, speech, and touch; while plants, trees, space, and one's body are matched by flesh, muscle, bone, and marrow.[5] Not a few of the identifications were tentative and arbitrary, excessively schematic, and did not prove convincing to posterity. But the practical effect of the movement as a whole was to depersonalize the universe, progressively, and undermine the prestige of the earlier Vedic gods.

As we have said, however, the gods were never dethroned in India. They were not disintegrated and dissolved by criticism and natural science, as were the deities of the Greeks in the age of the Sophists, Anaxagoras, Democritus, Aristotle, and the rest. The gods of Homer became laughable, and were mocked because of their all-too-human love affairs and excesses of wrath, which were regarded as incompatible with the more spiritual and ethical, later concept of divinity. A late and literal-minded style of moral criticism was offended by such symbolic images of the earlier mythical imagination as those of the philanderings of Zeus and the family quarrels of Olympus. India, on the other hand, retained its anthropomorphic personifications of the cosmic forces as vivid masks, magnificent celestial *personae,* which could serve, in an optional way, to assist the mind in its attempt to comprehend what was regarded as manifested *through* them. They remained as useful symbols, full of meaning and interest, through which the ever present powers could be conceived of and dealt with. They served as guides; and they could still be reached, moreover, by means of the ancient sacrificial rites with their unalterable texts, as well as through the private practices

[5] *Taittirīya Upaniṣad* 1. 7. (Cf. Hume, *op. cit.,* p. 279); cf. *supra,* pp. 9-11.

of emotional devotion (*bhakti*) where the "I" addresses itself reflectively to a divine "Thou." What is expressed through the personal masks was understood to transcend them, and yet the garb of the divine *personae* was never actually removed. By this tolerant, cherishing attitude a solution of the theological problem was attained that preserved the personal character of the divine powers for all the purposes of worship and daily life while permitting an abstract, supreme and transcendent concept to dominate for the more lofty, supraritualistic stages of insight and speculation.

Whatever is expressed in divine *personae*—or, for that matter, in any tangible, visible, or imaginable form—must be regarded as but a sign, a pointer, directing the intellect to what is hidden, something mightier, more comprehensive and less transitory than anything with which the eyes or emotions can become familiar. Likewise, concepts and ideas defined and circumscribed by the intellect must also be regarded as merely helpful signs, pointing to what cannot be defined or bounded by name. For both the realm of forms (*rūpa*) and that of names (*nāman*)—both the tangible and the conceptual spheres—are merely reflexes. If they are to be understood they must be recognized as manifestations of something higher than themselves, something infinite, which defies *all* definition—whether through the formulae of an early, wonder-filled theology or in the hypotheses of a later, practical-minded science.

In India the quest for the primal force reached, in soaring flight, the plane of a reality whence everything proceeds as a merely temporal, phenomenal manifestation. This ultimate power in the universe, and in man, transcends both the sensual and the conceptual spheres; it is, therefore, *neti neti,* "neither thus (*neti*) nor thus (*neti*)." [6] It is that "wherefrom words turn

[6] This is the great formula of Yājñavalkya, the paramount thinker of the Upaniṣadic tradition. For its numerous occurrences in the texts, cf. Hume's index under *"neti, neti"* (*op. cit.,* p. 511).

back, together with the mind, not having attained." [7] Yet there is no dichotomy; there is no antagonism between "real" and "unreal" in this strictly nondualistic realization; for the transcendent supreme Reality and its mundane manifestations (whether these be visible or verbal-conceptual) are in essence one.

There is, nevertheless, a hierarchy, or gradation, of the manifestations, states, or transformations of the all-comprehensive, all-evolving essence, according to the differing degrees of their intensities and powers. And this philosophical principle tallies, furthermore, with the principle of order intrinsic to the earlier mythological hierarchy, where the various gods were graded according to the extent of their power-spheres. Some of the gods, such as Indra, Soma, and Varuṇa, ruled as kings; others, like Agni, were endowed with the insignia and faculties of priestly power; many more, such as the wind-gods (the Maruts), of a much lower order, filled the ranks of the divine warrior hosts. Pantheons reflect, always, the local social hierarchies of the family and tribe, and likewise the local social conflicts; groups and generations of divine beings displace and supersede each other, reflecting the crises in civilization and in the ideals of their devotees. Younger gods gain ascendancy over older, as Indra did over Varuṇa, and as Varuṇa, in an earlier age, had superseded the great father Dyaus, Father Heaven. The crucial problem for a theologian is to make contact with the right divinities for the purposes of the time, and to ascertain, if possible, which among the gods is the most powerful in general. But this corresponds to the problem of the later, more philosophic quest of the jñāna-mārga, where again the goal is to single out and establish effective contact with the paramount, all-controlling principle—only now by the way (*mārga*) of knowledge (*jñāna*) rather than that of rite. The highest principle is to be discov-

[7] *Taittirīya Upanisad* 2. 4. (Cf. Hume, *op. cit.*, p. 285); cf. *supra*, pp. 74-83.

ered and mastered through wisdom. The individual is to make himself a part of it through abstract means. And he will then share in its potency, just as a priest in the power of his god. He will become both omnipotent and immortal; he will stand beyond change and all fear, beyond the common doom; and he will be a master of the plenitudes both of earthly life and of the life to come.

As we have seen, the Brāhmanical search proceeded along the two ways of the macrocosmic and the microcosmic quests. An early stage of the former is illustrated in the following hymn from the so-called *Black Yajurveda,* where the highest principle manifests itself as food (*annam*).[8] Food is announced as the source and substance of all things. Brahman, the divine essence, makes itself known to the priestly seer in the following impressive, awe-inspiring stanzas:

I am the first-born of the divine essence.
Before the gods sprang into existence, I was.
I am the navel [the center and the source] of immortality.
Whoever bestows me on others—thereby keeps me to himself.
I am FOOD. I feed on food and on its feeder.[9]

The divine material out of which the living universe and its creatures are composed is revealed here as food, which is matter and force combined. This life-sap builds up and constitutes all the forms of life. Changing its forms it remains nevertheless indestructible. The creatures thrive by feeding on each other—feeding on each other, devouring, and begetting—but the divine substance itself lives on, without interruption, through the ceaseless interruptions of the lives of all the living beings. Thus we find verified in this solemn hymn, verified and experienced

[8] This concept persists as a central theme in the later period of the Upaniṣads. For instances, cf. Hume's index, under "food" (*op. cit.,* p. 523).

[9] *Taittirīya Brāhmaṇa* 2. 8. 8.

in the aspect of its holy mystery, the primary law of the terrible *Arthaśāstra:* the ruthless struggle for life that prevails in innocence in the realm of nature.[10]

> This food is stored [the hymn continues] in the highest of
> the upper worlds.
> All the gods and the deceased ancestors are the guardians
> of this food.
> Whatever is eaten, or spilt or scattered as an offering,
> Is altogether but a hundredth part of my whole body.
>
> The two great vessels, Heaven and Earth, have both been
> filled
> By the spotted cow with the milk of but one milking,
> Pious people, drinking of it, cannot diminish it.
> It becomes neither more nor less.

The life-substance filling the body of the universe circulates through its creatures in a swift, perpetual flow, as they fall prey to each other, becoming to each other both the food and the feeder. The portion made visible in this way is but the hundredth part of the total essence, a mere negligible indication of the totality, by far the greater part of it being hidden from the eye. For it is stored in the highest dominion of the universe, where it is guarded both by the gods and by the deceased ancestors who share the celestial abode. The very nature of that divine store is abundance; the portion manifested as the world is but the yield of a single milking of the sublime source, the great spotted cow. Through the continuous tranformation into the energy and substance of the world the infinite store suffers not the least decrease. The cow suffers no diminution, either of life-substance or of productive vigor, in the yield of a single milking.

[10] Cf. *supra,* pp. 36 and 119.

The ancient hymn goes on:

> FOOD is the exhaling breath; FOOD is the inhaling breath of life;
> FOOD, they call death; the same FOOD, they call life.
> FOOD, the Brāhmans call growing old [decaying];
> FOOD, they also call the begetting of offspring.

Food governs all vital processes. It provides energy for the lifelong breathing process. It produces decay and old age, which end in death and destruction; but it also moves to the begetting of offspring, and it builds up the body of the growing child.

> The foolish man obtains useless food.
> I declare the truth: it will be his death,
> Because he does not feed either friend or companion.
> By keeping his food to himself alone, he becomes guilty when eating it.
>
> I—the FOOD—am the cloud, thundering and raining.
> They [the beings] feed on ME.—I feed on everything.
> I am the real essence of the universe, immortal.
> By my force all the suns in heaven are aglow.

The same divine milk that circulates through creatures here on earth sets aglow the suns—all the suns of the galaxy. It condenses also into the forms of the clouds. It pours down as rain and feeds the earth, the vegetation, and the animals that thrive on the vegetation. The individual initiated into this secret cannot be avaricious for any portion of the abundant food that may come to him. He will share it willingly with his companions. He will not wish to break the circuit by hoarding the substance to himself. And by the same token, anyone keeping food withdraws himself from the animating passage of the life-force which supports the remainder of the universe—all the creatures of the earth, all the clouds in their courses, and the sun. Such a niggardly hoarder cuts himself off from the divine metabolism of the living world. His food avails him nothing: when he eats, he eats his own death.

The command of the hymn, the solemn proclamation made through its stanzas by the holy substance, amounts to a kind of cosmic Communist Manifesto—with respect at least to food. Food is to remain common to all beings. Solemnly, the hymn summons the Truth to witness in the phrase "I declare the Truth"; wherewith a cosmic curse is put upon the head of any rugged individualist who should be concerned to look out only for himself. "It will be his death," the hymn declares; the nourishing substance in his mouth will turn to poison.

The gods are older than men, much older, yet they too were born; they are not eternal or self-existent. They are but the first offspring of the cosmic force-substance which is food, the earliest self-manifestation of that transcendent primary power. And since they were born they must also die. There can be no such thing as eternity for created, individualized forms. But if not for the gods, then how for lesser beings? Inhaling and exhaling the breath of life, begetting offspring and withering away, the numberless organisms of all the spheres of existence support the phases of a single, rhythmic, inevitable process of passage. They make manifest and suffer the metamorphoses of what is intrinsically, in itself, an everlasting freshness—a tireless immortality. Feeding on the divine substance in the form of the others and becoming in turn their food, each is but a moment in a magnitudinous universal play of transformations, a lively shifting-about of masks; for such wild abandonment as characterizes this game of feeding belongs to the state of being a mask. What the masks conceal is everywhere the same: "the source," "the center," the anonymous divine life-force which has no face yet wears the masks of all the faces of life.

The individual's consolation lies in knowing that behind and within his doom is the Imperishable—which is his own very seed and essence. Release from the doom consists in feeling identical not with the mask but with its all-pervading, ever-living substance. To be identified with that through wisdom means to conform to its reality by taking the proper attitude with respect to food and feeders. The mystery of the oneness of all in the divine being will then be made manifest in practice. Disregarding differentiating, discriminatory notions—which set conflicting individuals apart, each ego clinging avidly to itself in isolation, giving battle, according to the way of the fishes, in a selfish sheer maintenance of itself—one no longer feels bound in by the hide of one's personal perishability. All and everything is looked upon as the manifestation of one variously inflected yet permanent essence, of which one's own life is but a passing configuration. Such a realization transforms like magic the view of the seemingly merciless course of life, and bestows immediately a boon of peace.

The Hymn of Food thus gives voice to the same "World Yea" that, centuries later, is to distinguish Tāntrism, with its great formula: "Who seeks Nirvāṇa?" [11] The tangible realm of māyā, which is the veil that occludes Truth, is at the same time the self-revelation of Truth. Everything is a mask, a gesture of the self-revelation. The dark aspects of life (death, bereavement, and sorrow) counterbalance the bright (fulfillment and delight); the two sides check each other, like the celestial and infernal forces in the structure of the universe, the benignity of the gods, and the self-centered, disruptive, ruthless ambitions of the demons. If the kaleidoscopically changing, fleeting aspects of the world are ever to be endured, an acceptance of the totality is necessary; which means, it is necessary to break down the all-too-natural egoistic claim that life and the universe should conform to the shortsighted, asthmatic constitution of a self-centered member of the whole, who excludes from his consid-

[11] Cf. *infra*, pp. 560ff.; also *supra*, p. 61, Editor's note, and Appendix B.

eration everything beyond the range of his own limited personal vision.

Nescience might be called the short-leggedness of man—in contrast to the reach of the divine Cosmic Man, Viṣṇu, who with three gigantic strides created Earth, Atmosphere, and Firmament, simply by setting down the sole of his foot, at each stride, in what was empty space. The cosmic dynamism of which we ourselves are minute manifestations cannot be fitted to the dimensions of our brain, any more than to the brains of ants; for the universe is the holy revelation of an absolutely transcendent essence. We can be glad to understand it even a little, in terms appropriate to the range of our egocentric sensual and mental faculties. Though characterized every moment by perishableness, the universal whirling process in itself is everlasting, even as is the hidden power from which it derives. It is everlasting, indeed, through the very transiency of its continually appearing and vanishing phenomena—all these evanescent forms. And precisely because these break, it is everlasting. The cloud-shadows of death and bereavement darken the face of the world every second; these race across the moonlit, sunlit scene—but they do not outbalance the light, the fulfillment of life's joy in the perpetual begetting of new forms. The world, in spite of its pain, is as it were enraptured by itself, and does not count the hurts that go with the procedure: as though lovers in their rapture should mind whether the kisses hurt, or a child eagerly swallowing ice cream whether the chill was a little painful. Everything depends on where one puts the emphasis. That of the Hymn of Food is on the dionysiac aspect of the world. A continuous blending and transformation of opposites through a relentless vital dynamism—even asking for pains, to balance and enhance the intensity of delight—goes spontaneously, powerfully, and joyously with this terrific Oriental acceptance of the whole dimension of the universe. And this wild affirmative is one that is eminently characteristic, as we shall find, of Hinduism.

Śiva, the cosmic dancer, the divine lord of destruction, is described at once as the model of ascetic fervor and as the type of the frantic lover and faithful spouse.[12] The Alexandrian Greeks recognized in him the Hindu form of Dionysos, and in their typical Western way depicted their own god as having triumphantly entered and conquered India. But we know that the Brāhmans had been giving praise to the dynamic, dionysiac aspect of the universe long before the vine-wreathed, Thracian "Twice-born" entered the vales of Greece with his wild band—to the consternation and scandal of the world-directing, sober personalities of the orthodox Greek Olympus.

The devotee of such a god is asked to adore, not the names and forms (*nāmarūpa*), but the dynamism—this torrential cosmic stream of fleeting evolutions, which is continually producing and wiping out individual existences (this Niagara, of which we are the drops), as it seethes in a roaring, tremendous foam. Such is the attitude that comes to the fore decisively in the Tāntric period of Indian thought: the mortal individual identifies his mind with the principle that brought him into existence, that hurls him along and is to wipe him out, feeling himself to be a part of that supreme force as its manifestation, a part of its veil and play. One submits to the totality. One attunes one's ears to the dissonant as well as to the consonant strains of the cosmic symphony, regarding oneself as a brief passage, a momentary melody, now raised, but soon to fade and be heard no more. Thus comprehending his part and function in the everlasting, joyful-woeful song of life, the individual is not melancholy at the prospect of the pains of death and birth, or because of the frustrations of his personal expectations. Life is no longer evaluated by him in terms of sorrow. Both the sorrows and the joys of the round are transcended in ecstasy.

"Who seeks Nirvāṇa?" The comprehension of the life-patterns that unfold with varying degrees of intensity from the

12 Cf. Zimmer, *The King and the Corpse,* pp. 264-316.

primal, one and only, innermost Self and Core of all existences, the "Holy Power"—Brahman-Ātman—cannot be achieved by means of logic; for logic rejects as absurd, and therefore impossible, whatever goes against the rules of reason. For example, 1 plus 1 logically is 2, never 3 or 5, and can never shrink to 1. Yet things are not that way in the field of the vital processes of nature, where the most alogical developments take place every day, on every side, as a matter of course. The rules of life are not those of logic but of dialectics; the reasonings of nature not like those of the mind, but rather like those of our illogical belly, our procreative faculty, the vegetable-animal aspect of our microcosm. In this sphere, the sphere of biological dialectics, the illogical sphere of nature and life's forces, 1 plus 1 is usually far from remaining merely 2 for very long.

Suppose, for example, that the one 1 is a male and the other 1 a female. When they first meet, they are but the 1-plus-1 that is 2; when they fall in love with each other, however, and throw their destinies together, then they become the 1-plus-1 that is 1, "for better or for worse." The holy sacrament—at least in its more solemn, ancient, and magical form, as preserved in the Roman Catholic ritual—insists emphatically on the idea that now the two are "made one flesh" (*una caro facta est*). This very union, in fact, is what takes away the flaw, the suspicion or tinge of sin, which attaches to every kind of carnal interrelationship between the sexes, according to the ascetic Christian belief. The fact that the two have been transformed into one through the performance of the sacrament makes the married couple exempt from *concupiscentia,* sinfulness; hallows their sexual union. Thus through a magical transmutation, 1 plus 1 emphatically coalesces into 1, the sacramental formula only stating what is actually the basic experience of all true lovers when they have found each other and become joined with an attachment that projects happily the single prospect of their two lives' duration.

The alchemy of nature, melting the two hearts in a mutual fire, reduces the 1-plus-1 to the 1-made-out-of-2. But nature's alchemy does not stop there. Instead of the normal multiplication table, which we learn in school and use in business and practical-minded calculations, nature follows a witches' or wizards' multiplication table—a *Hexeneinmaleins,* as Goethe calls it in his *Faust.* After a brief delay, when 1 plus 1 has become 1, the married couple normally evolves into a triad; the first child is born. And if this evolution is not checked by prudent planning, an uncontrollable series evolves. The 1 that had been made of 1 plus 1 grows into 4, 5, 6—in fact goes on in a virtually indefinite series; the odd fact being, furthermore, that each additional unit contains potentially, and hands down into the future, the plenitude of the biological inheritance of the first fertile unit, for it shows forth features that were latent in both terms of that original 1 made of 1 plus 1.

Mythical thought, when evolving a manifold of godly forces and figures out of the one primal source or essence, proceeds according to this dialectical rationale. And Brāhmanical thought, in its brilliant formulae of psychological self-analysis, which were developed in the Upaniṣadic period, traces the same kind of dialectical evolution in man's consciousness; as follows. Deep sleep (*suṣupti*), when regarded from the point of view either of waking consciousness (*vaiśvānara*) or of consciousness in the web of dream (*taijasa*), would seem to be a state of sheer non-being (*a-sat*); nevertheless, it is from this sheer blank that the dreams emerge, like clouds condensing out of the void of the firmament; and from this same unconsciousness, moreover, the waking state suddenly bursts into being. Furthermore, it is back into this emptiness that the little cosmos of man's waking consciousness dissolves and disappears in sleep.[13] Thus it can be said that the emanation of dreams and the passage of consciousness from sleep to waking are two stages, or two varieties, of a con-

[13] Cf. *infra,* pp. 361-362 and 372ff.

stantly recurrent, daily repeated little cosmogony, or process of world-creation, within the microcosm. Just as the colossal universe evolves from some transcendental secret source—the essence beyond name and form, which remains unaffected by the process of torrential flowing forth—so likewise, the mysterious dream-ego, which in dreams evolves its own landscapes and adventures as well as the visible, tangible individual, who becomes conscious of himself when waking—these temporarily emerge from that innermost secret essence which is called the Self, the bedrock of all human life and experience. In other words, the macrocosmic Self (*brahman*) and the microcosmic (*ātman*) work parallel effects. They are one and the same, only viewed under two aspects. So that when the individual makes contact with the Self that he holds within, he comes into possession of divine cosmic power and stands centered beyond all anxiety, strife, and change. The attainment of this goal is the one and only end of Vedic and Vedāntic thought.

What we have here is a philosophy of life-matter and life-force, a philosophy of the life-process and body, rather than of the mind and spirit. Hence the reasonings of the Brāhmanic tradition were readily compatible with the earlier mythology of the Vedas, which in its turn had been a pictorial representation of the same vital principles and situations. And in so far as we are not sheer mind, sheer disembodied spirit, we are all naturally concerned with this kind of philosophizing. Its main task is to determine and define the true essence of our apparent life; to locate that aspect of our dynamic totality with which we must identify ourselves if we are to come to terms with the problem of existence. Are we identical with our bodily frame? Or is our essence to be sought, perhaps, by way of the purest emotional and spiritual virtues of that intangible entity that we call our soul? Or again, can it be that there is something beyond not only the tangible body but also the apprehended features and processes of the intangible soul, which abides with us as the source and silently guiding force that animates both the body and the soul? What are we? What can we realistically hope for?

These pressing questions cannot be solved by ontological analysis. Metaphysical arguments end in no solution. The root that underlies and gives existence to the analyzing, arguing mind as well as to the body that supports it must be touched. The mind itself is inadequate for this task (cf. Kant, *Critique of Pure Reason*) and has to be put at rest.

In the early Vedic age the work of transcending mind was accomplished by the "way of devotion" (*bhakti-mārga*); wholehearted dedication, that is to say, to the symbolic personalities of the gods and the absorbing rituals of their perpetual worship. During the following centuries the concentration of the philosophers became introverted and the goal was sought along an inner path. But either way, the boon of life's bountiful power was won. A rooted, absolutely firm position was attained, where the dynamism of the phenomenal spectacle and the permanence of the animating principle could be experienced simultaneously as one and the same great mystery—the mystery of that absolutely transcendent, serene being which is immanent, and made partially manifest, in the phenomenal becoming of the world.

2.

Upaniṣad

THE CREATIVE philosophers of the period of the Upaniṣads, examining the problem of the ātman, were the pioneer intellectuals and freethinkers of their age. They stepped beyond the traditional priestly view of the cosmos. Yet, as we have seen, they went beyond it without dissolving or even criticizing it; for the sphere in which they delved was not the same as that which the priests had monopolized. They turned their backs on the external universe—the realm interpreted in the myths and controlled by the complicated rituals of the sacrifice—because they were discovering something more interesting. They had found the interior world, the inward universe of man himself, and within that the mystery of the Self. This transported them far from the empire of the numerous anthropomorphic deities who were the vested governors of both the macrocosm and the sense functions of the microcosmic organism. The introverted Brāhmanic philosophers were therefore spared that head-on collision with the priests and with the past which Democritus, Anaxagoras, and the other scientist-philosophers of Greece experienced when their scientific interpretations of the celestial bodies and other phenomena of the universe began to controvert the ideas held by the priests and supported by the gods. The sun could not be both a divine, anthropomorphic being named Helios and a glowing sphere of incandescent matter; one had to settle for one view or the other. When a philosopher's focus, on the other hand (as was the case in India), is on a mystery the counterpart of which in the established theology is but a metaphysical, anonymous conception, well above and beyond the anthropomorphized powers, and revered simply as the indescribable fountainhead of the cosmos (an *ens entis* with which the polytheistic, more concrete, popular ritual cannot be directly concerned), then there can be neither an occasion nor a possibility for any outright theological-philosophical collision.

The new direction of thought nevertheless brought about a really dangerous devaluation both of the ritualistic theology and of the visible universe with which that theology was concerned; for instead of devoting attention to the gods and the outer world, the new generation was turning its whole consideration to that all-transcending, truly supernatural principle from which the forces, phenomena, and divine directors of the natural world proceeded: furthermore, these creative freethinkers were actually finding and making contact with that principle within themselves. Consequently, such intellectual energy as had formerly been devoted to the study and development of a machinery for the mastery of the demonic and divine forces of the cosmos—through an elaborate system of sacrificial propitiation and appeasing incantation—was being diverted inward, where it had just made contact with the supreme life-force itself. The cosmic energy was being taken at its fountainhead, where it came at its maximum of strength and abundance. As a result, all those secondary, merely derivative streams of energy, which had been dammed, canalized, and put to human use through the magic machinery of priestly ritual, were being left behind. In Indian thought, not only the gods but the whole outer world was dwindling in importance.

"Yājñavalkya," we read, "the great sage, one day came to Janaka, the magnificent emperor of Videha. And the sage thought that he would not reveal anything [he only wished to procure a donation]. However, this same Janaka and Yājñavalkya had talked together on a former occasion, and the sage at that time had granted the emperor a boon. Janaka had begged the liberty of asking, in the future, any question he liked, and Yājñavalkya had acceded to the request. Therefore when the sage now entered upon his audience, Janaka immediately challenged him with a question.

" 'Yājñavalkya,' said the emperor, 'what is the light by which man is served?'

" 'The light of the sun, O Emperor,' said the sage [still intent on revealing as little as possible]; 'for it is by the light of the sun that man sits down, goes out, works, and comes back home.'

" 'Quite so. But when the sun has set, O Yājñavalkya, what then is the light by which man is served?'

"The sage [as though to tantalize his royal pupil] answered: 'The moon then becomes his light; for it is then by the light of the moon that he sits down, goes out, works, and comes back home.'

" 'That is so,' said Janaka; 'but when both the sun and the moon are down, what then, O Yājñavalkya, is the light by which man is served?'

" 'The fire becomes his light,' replied Yājñavalkya; 'for it is then by firelight that he sits down, goes out, works, and comes back home.' "

The emperor again agreed. " 'O Yājñavalkya, that is true; but when the sun and moon have set and the fire has gone out, what then is the light by which man is served?' "

The sage continued to retreat. " 'Sound,' he said, 'then serves as light; for it is with the voice as his light that he then sits down, goes out, works, and comes back home. O Emperor, when it is so dark that one cannot see one's own hand before one's face, if a sound is uttered, then one can follow the sound.'

" 'That indeed is true,' said the Emperor patiently; 'but, O Yājñavalkya, when the sun and moon have set, and the fire has gone out, and there is not a sound–what is then the light by which man is served?' "

The sage was driven to the wall. " 'Ātman, the Self,' he declared, 'becomes his light; for it is by the light of the Self that he sits down, goes out, works, and comes back home.' "

The emperor was pleased; yet the discussion had still to come to his point. " 'That is true, O Yājñavalkya, but of the many principles within man, which is the Self?' "

Only when this question had been asked did the sage at last begin to teach the king.[14]

The Self taught by Yājñavalkya to King Janaka was the same

[14] *Bṛhadāraṇyaka Upaniṣad* 4. 3. 1-7.

as that being taught by all the other great masters of the new wisdom—some notion of which can be gained by a brief review of a number of typical Brāhmanic similes and metaphors, culled at random from the Upaniṣads of that prolific period.

Ghaṭasaṁvṛtam ākāśaṁ nīyamāne ghaṭe yathā,
ghaṭo nīyeta nākāśam tathā jīvo nabhopamaḥ.

"Space is enclosed by earthen jars. Just as space is not carried along with the jar when this is removed [from one place to another], so Jīva [i.e., the Self when contained in the vessel of the subtle and gross body], like infinite space [remains unmoved and unaffected]." [15]

It matters not to Space whether it be inside or outside of a jar. The Self, similarly, does not suffer when a body goes to pieces:

Ghaṭavad vividhākāraṁ bhidyamānaṁ punaḥ punaḥ,
tad bhagnaṁ na ca jānāti sa jānāti ca nityaśaḥ.

"The various forms, like earthen jars, going to pieces again and again, He does not know them to be broken; and yet He knows eternally." [16]

The Self does not become aware of bodies. They can be broken, they can be whole. The Self is the knower of Its own undifferentiated plenitude, beyond form, just as the element ether is beyond form. And just as the element ether, being the first-born of the five elements,[17] contains potentially all the qualities of the other four, as well as everything that can emerge from them (all the objects and figures of sensual experience), so

[15] *Amṛtabindu Upaniṣad* 13.

[16] *Ib.* 14.

[17] Air, fire, water, and earth are supposed to have emanated, in that order, from ether.

likewise the Self, which, being the sole reality, is the source of all.

Yathā nadyaḥ syandamānāḥ samudre
astaṁ gacchanti nāmarūpe vihāya,
tathā vidvān nāmarūpād vimuktaḥ
parātparaṁ puruṣam upaiti divyam.

"As flowing rivers go to rest in the ocean and there leave behind them name and form, so likewise the Knower, released from name and form, goes to that divine Man (*puruṣa*), who is beyond the beyond (*parātparaṁ:* higher than the highest, transcending the transcendent)." [18]

Descriptive metaphors were multiplied to form a string of classic images, surrounding like a garland the mystery of the Self. "Divide the fig"; "Place this salt in water"; "Just as, my dear, by one piece of clay everything made of clay may be known." "The various forms going to pieces, he does not know them to be broken." "This whole world has that as its soul; that is Reality; that is Ātman; that art thou, Śvetaketu." [19]

"That art thou" (*tat tvam asi*), this word of the old Brāhman Āruṇi to his son, which became the "great formula" (*mahāvākya*) of Vedāntic truth, reduced the entire spectacle of nature to its single, all-pervading, most subtle, absolutely intangible, hidden essence. Śvetaketu was taught, by his lesson, to look beyond the visible principle celebrated in the Vedic Hymn of Food; for the idea that food in its various manifestations, visible and tangible, was the highest essence of the universe, had long since been outgrown. The life-essence was now to be conceived of as invisible (like the void within the seed of the fig), all suffusing (like the salt in the pan of water), intangible, yet the final substance of all phenomena. It could be ascertained but not grasped, like the dissolved salt—and was extremely subtle, like the presence within the seed. Therefore, one was not to re-

[18] *Muṇḍaka Upaniṣad* 3. 2. 8.

[19] *Chandogya Upaniṣad* 6. Cf. *supra*, pp. 335-337.

gard oneself as the gross and tangible individual; not even as the subtle personality; but as the principle out of which those had emanated. All manifested things whatsoever were to be known to be *Its* "transformations" (*vikāra*). The forms were accidental. Furthermore, the forms were fragile: pottery breaks, but clay remains. *Tat tvam asi* means: "thou art to be aware of the identity of thine inmost essence with the invisible substance of all and everything"—which represents an extreme withdrawal from the differentiated sphere of individualized appearances. The gross and subtle forms of the world therewith were relegated, in the hierarchy of the gradations of reality, to a radically lower rank than that of the formless void.

> *Dve vāva brahmano rūpe mūrtam cāmūrtam ca,*
> *atha yan mūrtan tad asatyam yad amūrtam tat satyam,*
> *tad brahma yad brahma taj jyotiḥ.*

"There are, assuredly, two forms of Brahman: the formed and the formless. Now, that which is formed is unreal (*asatyam*), while that which is formless is real (*satyam*), is Brahman, is light.

"Light," the text goes on, "that is the sun, and even it [the sun] has this syllable OM as its Self." [20]

It required time to evolve and press to its conclusion the conception of the absolutely formless. The quest for the "really real" rested for a time, therefore, with such phenomena as the sun in the macrocosm (as the primary source of light), the life-breath (*prāṇa*) in the microcosm (as the primary source of life), and the ritual syllable OM. These remain in the texts, and still serve as preliminary holds. But in the end the courageous step was taken, and the goal of absolute transcendence attained.

Three stages, or levels, in the sphere of human consciousness were easily recognized:

1. the waking state, where the sense faculties are turned outward, and the field of cognition is that of the gross body;

[20] *Maitrī Upaniṣad* 6. 3. For *satya* and *asatya,* cf. *supra,* pp. 166-167.

2. the dreaming state, where the field is that of subtle bodies, self-luminous and magically fluid; and

3. the blissful state of dreamless deep sleep.

The second of these three was understood to be a glimpse into the subtle, supra- and infraterrestrial spheres of the gods and demons, which are within, as well as without;[21] a world no less unsatisfactory, however, than that of waking consciousness, because equally fraught with terror, suffering, delusory forms, and incessant change. There was little temptation, consequently, to identify this sphere with that of perfect being. The blissful state of dreamless sleep, however, was different; for it was untroubled by the vicissitudes of consciousness and seemed to represent a perfect return of the life-force to its intrinsic state of "aloofness and isolation" (*kaivalya*), existence in and by itself. This appears to have been the conception of the goal held in the Sāṅkhya.[22] And yet, discussions inevitably arose as to whether this state, which involves an abasement, or even complete annihilation, of consciousness, could really represent the ultimate ideal and condition of spiritual life.[23]

The sage Yājñavalkya, in a celebrated dialogue with his beloved wife Maitreyī, states that for the released and perfect knower there is no consciousness following death, because all pairs of opposites, all dual states, including that of the differentiation of subject and object, have then disappeared.

"When there is a duality, as it were, then one sees another; one smells another; one tastes another; one speaks to another; one hears another; one thinks of another; one touches another; one understands another. But when everything has become just one's own self, then whereby and whom would one see? whereby and whom would one smell? whereby and whom would one taste?

[21] The heavens and hells were regarded as the macrocosmic counterpart of the realm that is entered in dream.

[22] Cf. *supra,* p. 330.

[23] Cf. Hume's index, under "sleep" (*op. cit.,* p. 534).

whereby and to whom would one speak? whereby and whom would one hear? whereby and of whom would one think? whereby and whom would one touch? whereby and whom would one understand? whereby would one understand him by means of whom one understands this All? . . . Lo, whereby would one understand the understander?

"That Self (*ātman*) is not this, not that (*neti, neti*). It is unseizable, for it cannot be seized; indestructible, for it cannot be destroyed; unattached, for it does not attach itself; it is unbound, it does not tremble, it is not injured." [24]

The Self is not easily known. It cannot be realized except by the greatest effort. Every vestige of the normal waking attitude, which is appropriate and necessary for the daily struggle for existence (*artha*), pleasure (*kāma*), and the attainment of righteousness (*dharma*), must be abandoned. The really serious seeker of the Self has to become an introvert, disinterested absolutely in the pursuits of the world—disinterested even in the continuance of his individual existence; for the Self is beyond the sphere of the senses and intellect, beyond even the profundity of intuitive awareness (*buddhi*), which is the source of dreams and the fundamental support of the phenomenal personality. "The Creator, the divine Being who is self-existent (*svayam-bhū*), drilled the apertures of the senses, so that they should go outward in various directions; that is why man perceives the external world and not the Inner Self (*antar-ātman*). The wise man, however, desirous of the state of immortality, turning his eyes inward and backward (*pratyag*, 'into the interior'), beholds the Self." [25]

The Metaphor of the Chariot

"The Self (*ātman*) is the owner of the chariot; the body (*śarīra*) is the chariot; intuitive discernment and awareness (*buddhi*) is

[24] *Bṛhadāraṇyaka Upaniṣad* 4. 5. 15. (Hume, *op. cit.*, p. 147).
[25] *Kaṭha Upaniṣad* 4. 1.

the charioteer; the thinking function (*manas*) is the bridle; the sense-forces (*indriya*) are the horses; and the objects or spheres of sense-perception (*viṣaya*) are the ranging-ground (*gocara:* the roads and pasturages of the animal). The individual in whom the Self, the sense-forces, and the mind are joined is called the eater or enjoyer (*bhoktar*)." [26]

The sense-forces of perception are (in sequence from the finest, or most subtle, to the most tangible and gross):

1. hearing, which is effected through the ear,
2. seeing, which is effected through the eye,
3. smelling, which is effected through the nose,
4. tasting, which is effected through the tongue,
5. touching, which is effected through the skin.

These are the five sense-forces of knowing (*jñānendriyāṇi*), which in living organisms make for the attitude of eater or enjoyer (*bhoktar*). The bhoktar is "he who experiences pleasant and unpleasant sensations and feelings, because endowed with receptivity." We eat, as it were, our sense perceptions, and these then are assimilated by the organism as a kind of food. The eyes swallow objects that are beautiful, the ears become drunk with music and the nose with delicate perfumes. But the contrary principle, that of activity or spontaneity (*kartar*), also is constantly in effect. Just as the bhoktar functions through the receptive senses, so the kartar through the forces of action (*karmendriyāṇi*), which provide for:

1. speaking, which is effected through the organs of speech,
2. grasping, which is effected through the hands,
3. locomotion, which is effected through the feet,
4. evacuation, which is effected through the rectum,
5. generation, which is effected through the genitals.

[26] *Ib.* 3. 3-4.

The bhoktar and kartar, functioning together, enable the healthy organism to carry on the processes of life.[27]

"For one who is devoid of real insight and has not properly and constantly yoked-and-tamed his mind [that is to say: for one who has not disciplined and controlled both his conscious mental faculty (*manas*) and the intuitive awareness (*buddhi*) which is a manifestation of the irrational unconscious], the sense-forces become unmanageable, like the wicked horses of a charioteer. But for him who is always full of intuitive awareness (*vijñānavant*) and who has tamed-and-yoked his mind, the senses are subdued like the good horses of a charioteer.

"He who lacks the proper intuitive awareness, and is thoughtless and impure, does not reach That Place (*pada:* the state of transcendental existence); he tips over into the whirlpool of death and rebirth (*saṁsāra*). But he who is full of intuitive awareness, thoughtful and pure at all times, reaches That Place, whence one is not reborn. The man who has for his charioteer intuitive awareness, and for his bridle the mind, attains the end of his journey—which is a great distance away. That goal is the supreme abode of Visnu [the cosmic, all-pervading Self divine]." [28]

Visnu's celestial paradise, which is situated on the upper surface of the dome of the firmament and is known as his "third step" because it came into existence beneath his foot with the third of his three gigantic, cosmic strides,[29] symbolizes the state of that one who, as an accomplished initiate, has become released from bondage and has been made divine through the realization of his own intrinsic spirituality. Once having broken through the shrouding veils to the Self, by virtue of a conquest of the forces of nature in his own organism, the chariot-rider is no longer in-

[27] Cf. *supra,* p. 317.

[28] *Katha Upanisad* 3. 5-9. Compare Plato's description of the Chariot in the *Phaedrus.*

[29] *Supra,* p. 350; cf. also, Zimmer, *Myths and Symbols in Indian Art and Civilization,* pp. 131-132.

volved in worldly sufferings, pleasures, and pursuits, but has become, now and forever, free.

Ātman: the Controller Within

The Self—"that thread by which this world and the other world and all things are tied together" [30]—is the timeless controller within. "He dwells in the breath, he is within the breath; the breath, however, does not know him: the breath is his body, he controls the breath from within. He dwells in the mind, he is within the mind; the mind, however, does not know him: the mind is his body, he controls the mind from within." He is likewise within speech, the eye, the ear, the skin, the understanding, and the semen. Moreover, in like manner, he is within the elements of the macrocosm. "This Self dwells in the element earth and controls it from within: the earth is his body"; yet the earth is unaware of this principle inherent in its atoms. Earth is the most tangible of the five elements; but in water, fire, and air, and in ether (the most subtle of the five), the Self is equally unknown. "The Self dwells in all beings, he is within all beings; the beings, however, do not know him: all beings are his body, he controls all beings from within. He is unseen, yet seeing; unheard, yet hearing; unthought-of, and yet 'the thinker' (*mantar*). He is unknown, and yet the knower (*vijñātar*, the inner principle of awareness). There is no seer but him, no one to hear but him, no one thinking, no one aware but him. He is the Self, the Ruler within, the One Immortal." [31] The Self, that is to say, is the actual agent of every sense and thinking process, the organs merely serving him as instruments.

"That gigantic divine Being is by nature inconceivable. It appears to be more subtle than the subtlest, much farther off than the farthest, yet here, quite near—deposited right here, within

[30] *Bṛhadāraṇyaka Upaniṣad* 3. 7. 1.

[31] *Ib.* 3. 7. (cf. Hume, *op. cit.*, pp. 114-117).

the cave [the inmost recess of the heart] of those who see."[32] The inner experience of the Self, its visualization by virtue of a descent to the inmost cave, is proof enough that it exists everywhere, as the true core indwelling every being. Indestructible and not susceptible to change, it both transcends the universe and inheres in every particle of it; yet in both aspects remains undisclosed.

"Not for the sake of the husband is the husband loved, but for the sake of the Self is the husband loved. Not for the sake of the wife is the wife loved, but for the sake of the Self is the wife loved. Not for the sake of the sons are the sons loved, but for the sake of the Self are the sons loved. . . . Not for the sake of all is all loved, but for the sake of the Self is all loved. The Self is what is to be beheld, heard, reflected on, and meditated upon with inner concentration. Verily, by beholding, hearing, reflecting upon, and by the intimate knowledge (*vijñāna*) of, the Self, all of the visible and tangible universe becomes known."[33]

"The One God is hidden within all beings. He is the all-pervading, all-filling Inner Self (*antar-ātman*) of all beings; the overseer of all activities [both the inward and the outward, both the voluntary and the involuntary]; the inhabitant (*adhivāsa*) of all beings. He is the witness [ever watching, uninvolved in what is going on], the guardian (*cetar*), complete and alone (*kevala*),[34] beyond the guṇas."[35]

"The sole existing ruler is the Self in the interior of all transi-

[32] *Muṇḍaka Upaniṣad* 3. 1. 7.

[33] *Bṛhadāraṇyaka Upanisad* 2. 4. 5. This again is the sage Yājñavalkya speaking, in conversation with his wife, Maitreyī (cf. *supra*, pp. 362-363). The lesson of the final stanza is that when the unique inner essence of everything is realized within, the various masks that it assumes become translucent. All understanding, as well as all sympathy and love, is based on the intrinsic identity of the Knower and the Known. Hatred arises only from an illusion of diversity.

[34] Cf. *supra*, pp. 305-314.

[35] *Śvetāśvatara Upaniṣad* 6. 11. (cf. Hume, *op. cit.*, p. 409). For the gunas, cf. *supra*, pp. 295-297.

tory creatures; he makes manifold his one form. The wise behold him standing in their own being; hence to them belongs everlasting happiness—and to no one else.

"He is the enduring amidst the non-enduring. He is the intelligence of the intelligent. Though One, he yet produces the desires of many. The wise behold him standing in their own being; hence to them belongs everlasting peace—and to no one else.[36]

Through fear of him the wind blows,
Through fear of him the sun rises,
Through fear of him Agni [the god of fire],
  Indra [the causer of rain and storm, king of the gods],
And Death, the fifth, all hurry
  [to perform their respective tasks].[37]

"A plenitude is that yonder [the transcendental essence which is the source and life of all]; a plenitude is this which is here [the visible, tangible world]. Plenitude is scooped from plenitude [the abundance of the world being drawn from the abundance of the divine], and yet, though the plenitude of plenitude is taken, plenitude remains." [38]

Five Metaphors

"Just as the spider pours forth its thread from itself and takes it back again; just as herbs grow on the earth and hairs from a living man, even so the universe grows from the Imperishable."[39]

[36] *Katha Upanisad* 5. 12-13. (cf. Hume, *op. cit.*, pp. 357-358).

[37] *Taittirīya Upaniṣad* 2. 8. (cf. Hume, *op. cit.*, p. 288). The meaning is that by its mere being the Self keeps everything going.

[38] *Bṛhadāraṇyaka Upanisad* 5. 1.

[39] *Ib.* 1. 1. 7. (cf. Hume, *op. cit.*, p. 367).

Here the emphasis is laid on the contrast between the eternal (*nitya*) and the transient (*anitya*). There is an actual transformation of the eternal transcendental essence into its transitory manifestations. The Imperishable One is the only truly abiding essence, however, in contradistinction to its transient transformations, which make up the phenomenal sphere.

"Just as there shoot out from a blazing fire sparks by the thousands, resembling the fire, so do the various beings (or states: *bhāva*) proceed from that Imperishable; and into It, verily, they return."[40]

"Like the butter hidden in milk, Pure Consciousness (*vijñānam:* the state of Ātman as Brahman, sheer bliss) resides in every being. It is to be constantly churned, with the mind serving as the churning-rod." [41]

The Metaphor of the Two Birds on One Tree

Dvā suparṇā sayujā sakhāyā samānaṁ vṛkṣaṁ pariṣa-svajāte
tayor anyaḥ pippalaṁ svādv atty anaśnann anyo abhicākaśīti

"Two birds of beautiful plumage, close friends and companions, reside in intimate fellowship on the selfsame tree. One of them eats the sweet fruit of the tree; the other, without eating, watches."

The tree with the twin birds, the tree of life or of the human personality, is a well-known motif in Oriental tapestries and carpets. The figure is interpreted and developed in the succeeding stanza:

Samāne vṛkṣe puruṣo nimagno 'nīśayā śocati muhyamānaḥ
juṣṭaṁ yadā paśyaty anyam īśam asya mahimānam iti vītaśokaḥ

"The individual life-monad (*puruṣa*), being deluded, laments, depressed by a feeling of helplessness (*anīśāyā:* of not being a sovereign lord); but when he beholds on the same tree that other, the Lord in whom the pious take delight (*juṣṭam īśam*), and comprehends His greatness, then his grief is gone";[42] for he knows that between himself and that other there is a fundamental identity.

[40] *Muṇḍaka Upaniṣad* 2. 1. 1. (cf. Hume, *op. cit.*, p. 370).
[41] *Amṛtabindu Upaniṣad* 20.
[42] *Muṇḍaka Upaniṣad* 3. 1. 1-2. (cf. Hume, *op. cit.*, p. 374).

The Two Kinds of Knowledge

"Two kinds of knowledge (*vidyā*) are to be known: that of the Brahman-of-sounds (*śabda-brahman*) and that of the Highest Brahman (*param-brahman*)." The Brahman-of-sounds is the aggregate of all the hymns, formulae, charms, incantations, prayers, and exegetical commentaries that constitute the Vedic revelation. This Brahman cannot be the Highest, however, because it is endowed with name and form; names to assist the mind, and the sound-forms of speech, song, melody, and prose (*nāman* and *rūpa*). "But anyone laved (*niṣṇāta*) in Śabda-Brahman goes on to the Highest Brahman. Having studied the books (*grantha*) assiduously (*abhyāsa:* this is the term for constant endeavor in yogic practice), the wise, intent on knowledge solely, and on the plenitude-of-knowledge (*vijñāna*), should discard books completely—just as a person trying to get at rice throws the husks away."[43]

The inferior, preliminary wisdom is like a raft—to be forsaken once it has transported its voyager to his destination. Sacrificial lore and the ethical rituals of life have to be left behind at the brink of the higher realization.[44]

"This is to be attained only by truthfulness (*satya*) and asceti-

[43] *Amṛtabindu Upaniṣad* 17-18.

Vijñāna ("the plenitude-of-knowledge"): the *vi-* here refers to Infinity, which is all-comprehensive and leaves no margin wherein any unincluded, second entity might exist. *Vijñāna* is therefore nondual (*advaita*) knowledge (*jñāna*), and as such synonymous with the state known to Vedānta as *Turīya,* the "Fourth." This is beyond the three planes of waking consciousness, dream consciousness, and deep sleep (cf. *infra,* pp. 372-378). Such would seem to be the meaning of the term *vijñāna* in the *Bhagavad Gītā* also.

[44] Throughout the later periods of the Hindu tradition the term "lower wisdom" (*aparavidyā*) has been regarded as referring to wisdom committed to writing: book lore is to be finally discarded. The injunction resembles that of the European alchemists, *"rumpite libros ne corda vestra rumpantur,"* but lacks the touch of polemic criticism.

cism (*tapas*), real insight (*samyag-jñāna*) and unbroken continence (*brahmacarya*). Consisting of divine light, resplendent, It resides within the body. Ascetics behold It, who have annihilated their defects."[45]

"This Self is not attained through teaching, intelligence, or much learning. It is attained by him only whom It chooses. To such a one this Self discloses Its proper nature (*tanūm svām*)."[46]

"Verily, the Self that is in the three states of waking (*jāgrat*), dream (*svapna*), and dreamless sleep (*susupti*), is to be understood as one and the same. For him who has transcended this triad of states, there is no rebirth.

"Being verily one, the Self-of-all-beings-and-elements is present in every being. It is beheld onefold and manifold simultaneously, like the moon reflected in water."[47]

The Union of the Life-Monad with the Spiritual-Self

"Just as a man fully embraced by his beloved wife does not know anything at all, either external or internal, so does this man (*puruṣa:* the individual life-monad), embraced fully by the supremely knowing Spiritual-Self (*prajñātman*), not know anything at all, either external or internal. That is his form devoid of sorrows, in which all desires are fulfilled; in which his only desire is the Self [which he has now attained]; in which he is without desire. In that state a father is no father, a mother no mother, the worlds no worlds, the gods no gods, . . . a thief no thief, an ascetic no ascetic. Unattended by virtuous works, unattended by

[45] *Muṇḍaka Upaniṣad* 3. 1. 5. (cf. Hume, *op. cit.*, p. 374).

[46] *Ib.* 3. 2. 3. (cf. Hume, *op. cit.*, p. 376). Compare the Christian doctrine of Grace.

[47] *Amṛtabindu Upaniṣad* 11-12.

There is but one moon in the nightly firmament, yet it is reflected in numerous water jars standing in the moonlight. The jars, perishable clay, are compared to individuals.

evil works, he has crossed to the other shore, beyond the sorrows of the heart."[48]

Turīya: "The Fourth"—and the Meaning of the Syllable OM

The very short *Māṇḍūkya Upaniṣad,* which consists of but twelve verses, has come to be regarded as the concentrated extract and epitome of the teaching of the entire corpus of the one hundred and eight Upaniṣads. Its theme is the syllable OM, which is written ओं or ॐ, and through which the mystery of Brahman is gathered to a point. The text first treats of OM in terms of the Upaniṣādic doctrine of the three states of waking, dream, and sleep, but then passes on to the "Fourth" (*turīya*), thus transporting us beyond the typical Upaniṣādic sphere into that of the later, classic, Advaita Vedānta.

We may well conclude the present chapter, and at the same time prepare ourselves for the next development of the orthodox tradition, by reviewing this extraordinary text in its entirety.

1. OM!—This imperishable sound is the whole of this visible universe. Its explanation is as follows. What has become, what is becoming, what will become—verily, all of this is the sound OM. And what is beyond these three states of the world of time—that too, verily, is the sound OM.

There are two spheres, that is to say, which are identical: 1. the phenomenal, visible sphere (that of change [*jagat*], the Heraclitean flux), wherein the manifestations of time appear and perish, and 2. the transcendent, timeless sphere, which is beyond yet one with it (that of imperishable Being). Both of these are symbolized and present in the holy syllable OM.

2. *All of this* (with a sweeping gesture, pointing to the universe round about) *is Brahman. This Self* (placing the hand on the heart) *also is Brahman.*

Here again is the nondual doctrine. The essence of the numer-

[48] *Bṛhadāraṇyaka Upaniṣad* 4. 3. 21-22. (cf. Hume, *op. cit.*, pp. 136-137).

ous phenomena of the macrocosm is one, and is identical, moreover, with the essence of the microcosm. The mystery of the universe, with all its stratifications of the gross and subtle, life in all its forms, matter in all its modifications, may be approached, therefore, either from within or from without.

This Self (the verse continues) *has four portions* (pāda: *foot, part, quarter*—"like the four feet of a cow," states the commentary of Śaṅkara to this verse). We are about to embark on a review of the relationship of the four states of the microcosm to those of the macrocosm.

3. The first portion is Vaiśvānara, "The Common-to-all-men." Its field is the waking state. Its consciousness is outward-turned (through the gates of the senses). *It is seven limbed and nineteen mouthed. It enjoys* (bhuj, *"eats, or lives on"*) *gross matter* (sthūla).

This is the Self in the waking state, the phenomenal individual moving and living in the phenomenal world. The reference of the number seven, however, is obscure. Śaṅkara, in his commentary, seeks to interpret it on the basis of *Chāndogya Upaniṣad* 5. 12. 2., where the limbs of the universal Ātman are described as 1. the head (heaven), 2. the eye (the sun), 3. breath (the wind), 4. the torso (space), 5. the kidneys (water) and 6. the feet (the earth). In the same verse the sacrificial area is likened to the breast of the universal Ātman, the sacrificial grass to his hair, and the three fires of the Agnihotra sacrifice to his heart, mind, and mouth. Śaṅkara, therefore, to complete his catalogue of seven, selects the last of these enumerated fires, and writes: 7. the mouth (the Āhavanīya fire). One feels that the explanation is a bit contrived, yet it vividly renders the basic idea—which is that Vaiśvānara is manifest equally in the physical universe and in the human physique.

The nineteen mouths mentioned in the text are identified by Śaṅkara as the five faculties of sense (*jñānendriya*), the five faculties of action (*karmendriya*), the five vital airs (*prāṇa*), and the four constituents of the inner organ; i.e., *manas* (the mind), *buddhi* (the determinative faculty), *ahaṅkāra* (egoity), and *citta* (the "mind-stuff," of which all the other eighteen mouths are but the various agents). *Citta* is that "mind-stuff" which it is the function of Yoga to bring to rest.[49]

4. The second portion (of the Self) is Taijasa, "The Shining One." Its field is the dream state. Its consciousness is inward turned. It is seven limbed and nineteen mouthed. It enjoys subtle objects (pravivikta: *"the choice; the exquisite; that which is set apart"*).

This is the Self when it is dreaming, beholding the luminous, subtle, magically fluid, and strangely enthralling objects of the world behind the lids of the eyes. Taijasa feeds on the stored-up dream memories, just as Vaiśvānara on the gross objects of the world. His "limbs" and "mouths" are the subtle counterparts of those of the enjoyer of the field of waking consciousness.

5. But where a sleeper neither desires anything desirable nor beholds any dream, that is deep sleep (suṣupta). *Prājña, "The Knower," who has become undivided in this field of dreamless sleep, is the third portion of the Self. He is an undifferentiated mass* (ghana: *"a homogeneous lump"*) *of consciousness, consisting of bliss and feeding on bliss (as the former two fed on the gross and the subtle). His (only) mouth being spirit* (cetomukha).

This verse is a climax. In the following the glory of Prājña, "The Knower," the Lord of the field of dreamless sleep, is described.

6. This is the Lord of All (sarveśvara); *the Omniscient* (sarvajñā); *the Indwelling Controller* (antaryāmī); *the Source* (yoni: *the Generative Womb) of All. This is the beginning and End of beings.*[50]

But now comes the supreme culmination of the series. The

[49] Cf. *supra*, pp. 284-285.

[50] Compare this with the vision of Īśvara, the Lord, in the eleventh chapter of the *Bhagavad Gītā*, where, having been addressed by Arjuna, his devotee, the divine incarnation, Kṛṣṇa, discloses himself in his "uni-

Real Self, which is to be finally known, is announced as that indescribable "fourth" portion of the Self, which is beyond the sphere of the Lord of the field of dreamless sleep, i.e., beyond the Beginning and End of beings.

7. What is known as the fourth portion—neither inward- nor outward-turned consciousness, nor the two together; not an undifferentiated mass of dormant omniscience; neither knowing nor unknowing—because invisible, ineffable, intangible, devoid of characteristics, inconceivable, undefinable, its sole essence being the assurance of its own Self (eka-ātma-pratyaya-sāram); *the coming to peaceful rest of all differentiated, relative existence* (prapañca-upaśamam); *utterly quiet* (śāntam); *peaceful-blissful* (śivam); *without-a-second* (advaitam): *—this is Ātman, the Self, which is to be realized.*

The four portions dissolved into each other as the process of discernment moved from one to the next; nevertheless, all four together constitute the whole of the "four-footed," "four-square," gradated, sole existence, which is the Self. Each quarter is on an equal footing, somehow, with the others (just as the Kali Yuga, the worst of the four ages of the world, is no less a part of the cycle of time than the best, the holy Kṛta Yuga—shorter in length and of less perfect form, indeed, yet an equally indispensable portion of the cycle). During the course of the spiritual adventure inward, the emphasis shifts from the outer world to the inner, and finally from the manifest to the unmanifest, and there is a prodigious increase in the powers gained; nevertheless, the inferior, as well as the superior, states remain as constituents of the totality. They are, as Śaṅkara pictures it, "like the four feet of a cow."

The self-transforming change of emphasis becomes a well-known and controllable experience for the skilled practitioner of yoga. He can make the states come and go, their spheres appear

versal form" as Viṣṇu, the omniscient regent of the macrocosm, the source, support, and end of all beings.

and disappear, according to his will. Which leads him, as we have said, to a philosophy of phenomenalism. Through his sovereign yogic power the gross aspect of reality is, for him, devaluated; for he can produce the subtle, fluid forms of the inward state of vision whenever he likes, fix them and retain them as long as he requires, and after that, again according to his wish, come temporarily back into touch with the exterior world. Such a virtuoso is not subject and exposed helplessly to the waking state, but enters into it only when and as he wishes—his real abode or homestead, meanwhile, being the "fourth," at the opposite end of the series. Yoga makes this deep zone the basis and bedrock of existence for him, from the standpoint of which the other experiences and attitudes are completely reinterpreted and reevaluated. What normally is the sole possible waking attitude of man becomes merely optional, an everyday mirage (*lokayātrā*) into which the master of consciousness enters by a gesture of compliance with the world's course (just as the Supreme Being is represented in mythology as complying with the course of the universe by descending, periodically, in an incarnation, "whenever there is a decline of dharma").[51]

The five final verses of the *Māṇḍūkya Upaniṣad* bring the analysis of the four portions, feet, or states of the Self into connection with the syllable OM, which, as made known at the beginning, is identical with the Self. In Sankrit the vowel *o* is constitutionally a diphthong, compounded of *a* + *u;* hence OM can also be written AUM. We read, consequently, in the text:

8. This identical Ātman, or Self, in the realm of sounds is the syllable OM, the above-described four portions of the Self being identical with the components of the syllable, and the components of the syllable being identical with the four portions of the Self. The components of the syllable are A, U, M.[52]

[51] *Bhagavad Gītā* 4. 7.

[52] As will immediately appear, the silence that follows and surrounds the syllable is the fourth component. The identification of these three

9. Vaiśvānara, "The Common-to-all-men," whose field is the waking state, is the sound A, because this encompasses all, and because it is the first.[53] *He who knows thus* (ya evaṁ veda) *encompasses all desirable objects; he becomes the first.*

10. Taijasa, "The Shining One," whose field is the dream state, is the second sound, U, because this is an extract, and contains the qualities, of the other two.[54] *He who knows thus, extracts from the flow of knowledge and becomes equalized; in his family there will be born no one ignorant of Brahman.*

11. Prājña, "The Knower," whose field is deep sleep, is the third sound, M, because this is the measure, and that into which all enters.[55] *He who knows thus, can measure all and partakes of all.*

12. The Fourth is soundless: unutterable, a quieting down of all the differentiated manifestations, blissful-peaceful, nondual. Thus OM is Ātman, verily. He who knows thus merges his self in the Self—yea, he who knows thus.

A the waking state, U the dream, M deep sleep, and the SILENCE, Turīya, "The Fourth"; all four together comprise the totality of this manifestation of Ātman-Brahman as a syllable. Just as the sound OM manifests itself, grows, becomes trans-

letters and the silence with the four states or portions of the Self is to be taken with the utmost literal seriousness; for all things—sound and silence as well as states of human consciousness—are Brahman-Ātman.

[53] A is regarded as the primal sound, which is common to all the others. It is produced at the back of the open mouth, and is therefore said to include, and to be included in, every other sound produced by the human vocal organs. A is the first letter of the Sanskrit alphabet.

[54] The open mouth of A moves toward the closure of M. Between is U, formed of the openness of A but shaped by the closing lips. So dream is compounded of the consciousness of waking life shaped by the unconsciousness of sleep.

[55] It is from the position of the closed mouth that all begins; the mouth is opened to produce A, and in another way to produce U. The closed mouth is thus the fundament from which all sound of speech takes its measure, as well as the end back to which it devolves.

formed in its vocal quality, and finally subsides into the silence that follows (and which must be regarded as forming part of its sound in a latent, meaningful state of repose), so likewise the four "states," or components, of being. They are transformations of the one existence which, taken together, constitute the totality of its modes, whether regarded from the microcosmic or from the macrocosmic point of view. The A and U are as essential to the sound as M, or as the SILENCE against which the sound appears. Moreover, it would be a mistake to say that A U M did not exist while the SILENCE reigned; for it would be still potential. The actual manifestation of the syllable, on the other hand, is fleeting and evanescent, whereas the SILENCE abides. The SILENCE, indeed, is present elsewhere duṛing a local pronunciation of AUM—that is to say (by analogy), transcendentally during the creation, manifestation, and dissolution of a universe.

3.

Bhagavad Gītā

It was in the great paradoxes of the epoch-making *Bhagavad Gītā* [56] that the non-Brāhmanical, pre-Āryan thought of aboriginal India became fruitfully combined and harmonized with the Vedic ideas of the Āryan invaders. In the eighteen brief chapters was displayed a kaleidoscopic interworking of the two traditions that for some ten centuries had been contending for the control and mastery of the Indian mind.

[56] The full title is *Śrīmad-bhagavad-gītā-upaniṣadas,* "The teachings given in the song of the Sublime Exalted One."

As we have seen, the non-Āryan systems (Jainism, Gosāla's teaching, Sāṅkhya, and Yoga) were characterized by a resolutely logical, theoretical dichotomy, which insisted on a strict distinction between two spheres, that of the life-monad (*jīva, puruṣa*) and that of matter (*a-jīva, prakṛti*), the pure and crystal-like, immaterial essence of the pristine individual and the polluting, darkening principle of the material world. The process of life was read as an effect of the interpenetration of these polar principles —an everlasting blending of two antagonistic forces, bringing to pass a perpetual procreating and disintegrating of compound, unsubstantial forms. The conjunction was compared to the mingling of fire with iron in a red-hot iron ball; it was a result of proximity and association, not proper to either principle *per se*. And the two could be understood in their distinct, mutually contrary, intrinsic natures only when separated and allowed to return to their simple, primary states—the corollary of all this in practice being a doctrine of asceticism (or rather, a number of varying doctrines of asceticism) aiming at the separation of the two incompatible principles. The process of life was to be halted. Purification, sterilization, was to be the great ideal of human virtue; and the goal, the attainment of absolute motionlessness in crystal purity—not the dynamism of the incessant processional of life. For the processes of nature (generation, digestion, assimilation, elimination, the dissolution of the dead body as it begets swarming tribes of worms and insects, metabolism, gestation) are all unclean. The will is to purge the whole thing away. Whether in the microcosmic alchemical retort of the individual, or in the macrocosm of the universal laboratory, the unclean process of elements forever uniting, forever sundering, is equally deplorable, a sort of general orgy of indecencies from which the self-recollecting spirit can only resign.

Contrast with this the vigorous, tumultuous, and joyous life-affirmative of the Vedic Hymn of Food.[57] The new thing that the

[57] *Supra*, pp. 345-347.

Brāhmans brought to India was a jubilant, monistic emphasis on the sanctity of life: a powerful and persistent assertion that the One Thing is always present as two. "I am both," asserts the Lord of Food; "I am the two: the life-force and the life-material —the two at once." The jejune disjunction of the world into matter and spirit derives from an abstraction of the intellect and should not be projected back upon reality; for it is of the nature of the mind to establish differences, to make definitions and discriminate. To declare, "There are distinctions," is only to state that there is an apprehending intellect at work. Perceived pairs-of-opposites reflect the nature not of things but of the perceiving mind. Hence thought, the intellect itself, must be transcended if true reality is to be attained. Logic is a help for preliminary clarification, but an imperfect, inadequate instrument for the final insight; its orderly notions, oppositions, and relationships must be overcome if the searching mind is to attain to any direct conception or realization of the transcendent truth. The One Thing that is the first, last, and only reality (this is the basic Brāhman thesis) comprises all the pairs-of-opposites (*dvandva*) that proceed from it, whether physically, in the course of life's evolution, or conceptually, as logical distinctions occurring to the intellect coincident with thought.

Founded in this realization of an all-unifying, transcendent principle, Brāhmanical thought of the period of the Upaniṣads was well fitted to absorb not only the divine personalities of the earlier Vedic pantheon but also the much more sophisticated philosophic and devotional formulae of the non-Āryan, aboriginal tradition. The *Bhagavad Gītā* is the classic document of the first stages of this adjustment. Its teaching is styled an esoteric doctrine, yet it has become the most popular, widely memorized authoritative statement of the basic guiding principles of Indian religious life. The text, an episode of eighteen brief chapters inserted in the *Mahābhārata* at the point of epic action where the two great armies are about to join in battle,[58] is by no means all of a piece. Numerous contradictions have been pointed out by the Western critics, yet to the Indian mind these contradictions are precisely the value. For they represent the beginning of the great *rapprochement* and, besides, are readily resolved by a realization of the One in all.

The ranks of the warriors of the two rival armies of the *Mahābhārata* had been drawn up against each other, and all was prepared for the opening trumpet blast, when the leader of the Pāṇḍavas, Arjuna, desired to be driven by his charioteer into the field between, so that he might review, at a glance, both his own forces and those of his enemy cousins, the Kauravas. However, the moment he beheld, in both ranks, his friends and teachers, sons and grandfathers, nephews, uncles, and brothers, an emotion of the greatest pity and regret assailed him. His spirit was unmanned, and he doubted whether he should permit the battle to begin.

At this critical juncture his charioteer spoke and gave him heart. And the words uttered under these heroic circumstances, on the verge of the most tremendous battle of Indian epic history, are what have been termed the *Bhagavad Gītā,* "The Song of the Blessed Lord"; for the charioteer was none other than the god Kṛṣṇa, an Incarnation of the Creator, Preserver, and Destroyer of the world. The revelation was given by a friend to a friend, the young god to his companion, the prince Arjuna. It was an exclusive, an aristocratic, doctrine; for the god Kṛṣṇa, this divine particle of the holy supramundane essence who had descended to earth for the salvation of mankind, was himself a slayer of demons, himself an epic hero, while the noble youth to whom the words were addressed when he was in despair as to what to do (impotent, at the critical moment of his career, to determine what would be for him *dharma,* correct behavior) was the fairest flower of the epic period of Hindu chivalry. It had

[58] *Mahābhārata,* book 6, Bhīṣmaparvan, section 6.

been because of his sympathy for this dispossessed young king that the beautiful, dark Kṛṣṇa had become his adviser in the somewhat allegorical role of charioteer, when he was about to enter battle for the recovery of his usurped throne and the winning of the sovereignty of the land of India. Kṛṣṇa wished not only to play the part of spiritual adviser to his friend, but also to utilize this vivid moment to proclaim to all mankind his doctrine of salvation *in* the world—which is known as the "Yoga of Selfless Action" (*karma-yoga*)—and all that it entails in the way of self-surrender and devotion (*bhakti*) to the Lord who is identical with the Self within all. The doctrine is "very difficult to grasp"; this is a fact emphasized again and again. For example: "The innermost principle of man's nature [the so-called 'Owner of the Organism': *dehin śarīrin*] is unmanifest, unthinkable, unchangeable. . . . One person beholds this Self as a marvel. Another speaks of It as a marvel. Still another hears-and-learns of It as a marvel [being instructed in the sacred esoteric tradition by a guru]. Yet, though having heard and learned, no one has any real understanding of what It is." [59]

The circumstances of the dialogue are described in vigorous, simple terms.

"Arjuna said: 'Place my chariot, O Changeless One, between the two armies, so that in this moment of impending battle I may behold those standing eager for war, with whom I have to fight. . . .'

"Thus addressed, Krsna drove the incomparable chariot between the two armies drawn up for battle, facing Bhīsma, Drona, and all the rulers of the earth. And he said: 'Behold, O son of Pṛthā, the Kauravas here assembled!'

"Then Arjuna gazed upon the two peoples: fathers, grandfathers, teachers, maternal uncles, brothers, sons, grandsons, companions, fathers-in-law, and friends. . . ." And he was overcome

[59] *Bhagavad Gītā* 2. 25 and 29.

with horror at the thought of the dreadful fratricidal fury that was about to seize them all. On the one hand he was unwilling to precipitate the battle that should annihilate "those," as he said, "who are my own people," while on the other he was bound by the code of chivalry to avenge the injuries that he and his brothers had sustained from their cousins, and to assist his brethren in their just effort to recover their dominion. Not knowing what he should do, mind whirling, unable to distinguish the right from the wrong, Arjuna, in despair, turned to his friend and charioteer, Krsna; and as the divine words of God poured into his ears and heart, he was set at ease as to the mysteries of right and wrong.[60]

Krsna's message culminates in the "supreme utterance," which commences in Chapter X.

"Now give ear to my supreme utterance. Because thou art dear to Me, I will proclaim it to thee for thy good. Neither the hosts of the gods nor the great seers know My source. Altogether more ancient than they am I. He who knows Me as the Unborn, the Beginningless, the Great Lord of the World, he among mortals, free from delusion, is released from all his sins. From Me alone arise the manifold states of mind of created beings: power of judgment, knowledge, purity of spirit, forbearance, true insight, discipline, serenity, pleasure and pain, well-being and distress, fear and reliance, compassion, equanimity, contentment, self-control, benevolence, glory and infamy. Likewise, the seven great Ṛṣis of old and the four Manus [61] arose from Me alone, generated by My spirit; and from them descend these creatures in the world. He who knows in truth this manifestation of My might and My creative power is armed with unshakable constancy. I am the Source of all, from Me everything arises. Whosoever has insight,

[60] *Ib.* 1. 21-47.

[61] *Ṛṣi:* holy sage, inspired poet of Vedic hymns. *Manu:* the first man at the beginning of each new race of beings.

knows this. And with this insight the wise worship Me, overwhelmed by awe. . . .[62]

"Time (*kāla*) am I, the Destroyer great and mighty, appearing here to sweep all men away. Even without thee [and thine act of leadership] none of these warriors here, in their ranks arrayed, shall remain alive. Therefore, do thou arise, win glory, smite the foe, enjoy in prosperity thy lordship. By Me, and Me alone, have they long since been routed. BE THOU NOUGHT BUT MY TOOL."[63]

This is applied bhakti. The *bhakta,* the devotee, brings into realization in space and time, as the merely apparent cause, what for the time-and-space-transcending God is beyond the categories of the uneventuated and eventuated, the "not yet" and the "already done." The imperishable Self, the Owner of the perishable bodies, is the supreme director of the harrowing spectacle of Time. " 'Having-an-end' are called these bodies of Him, the Eternal, who is the 'Owner of Bodies' (*śarīrin*), who is imperishable, boundless, and unfathomable. . . . Whoever thinks Him to be he who kills, and whoever thinks Him to be he who is killed—these two lack true insight; for He neither kills nor is killed. He is not born, nor does He die at any time; He did not become in the past nor will He spring into existence again at a future moment; He is unborn, eternal, everlasting—the 'Old One' (*purāṇa*); He is not killed when the body is killed. The man who knows Him to be indestructible, eternal, without birth, and immutable—how can he slay; or whom? Even as a man casts off old and worn-out clothes and puts on others which are new, so the 'Owner of the Body' (*dehin*) casts off worn-out bodies and enters into others which are new."[64] "As childhood, youth, and old age in this present body are to Him Who Owns the Body

[62] *Bhagavad Gītā* 10. 1-8.

[63] *Ib.* 11. 32-33.

[64] *Ib.* 2. 18-22.

(*dehin*), so also is the attaining of another body. The Wise are not disturbed by this." [65]

The Self is not affected when its mask is changed from that of childhood to that of youth, and then to that of age. The individual ego, the cherished personality, may feel disturbed, and may have difficulty adjusting itself to the changes and all the losses of life-opportunity that the changes imply, but the Self is unaffected. And it is equally unconcerned when the mask is put aside altogether at the time of death, and a new one assumed at the next birth. There is no death, no real change, for Him. Hence, whether the sequence be that of bodies or of the ages of the body, it weighs no more on Him than do the solstices of the seasons or the phases of the moon. There is no cause for grief. "Weapons do not cut Him, fire does not burn Him, water wet Him, or the wind dry Him away. He cannot be cut, He cannot be burnt, He cannot be wet, He cannot be dried away. He is changeless (*nitya*), all-pervading (*sarvagata*), stable (*sthānu*),[66] unshakable (*acala*),[67] and permanent (*sanātana*)." [68]

The Owner of the Body is beyond event; and since it is He who is the true essence of the individual, one must not pity the perishable creatures for being such as they are. "Thou dost feel pity," says Kṛṣṇa to the confused warrior, "where pity has no place. Wise men feel no pity either for what dies or for what lives. There never was a time when I and thou were not in existence, and all these princes too. Nor will the day ever come, hereafter, when all of us shall cease to be." [69] "There is no existence for nothingness; there is no destruction for that which is. Be assured that the very tissue of this universe is the Imperish-

[65] *Ib.* 2. 13.

[66] Standing motionless, like a pillar, like a rock, or like Śiva, the perfect yogī, in his meditation.

[67] Like a firmly rooted mountain.

[68] *Bhagavad Gītā* 2. 23-24.

[69] *Ib.* 2. 11-12.

able; it lies in no man's power to destroy it. Bodies come to an end, but 'He Who Is Clothed in the Body' (*śarīrin*) is eternal, indestructible, and infinite.—Fight then, O Bhārata!" [70]

Karma Yoga, the great ethical principle incorporated in this metaphysically grounded realism of the Incarnate Divine Essence, requires that the individual should continue carrying on his usual duties and activities of life, but with a new attitude of detachment from their fruits, i.e., from the possible gains or losses that they will entail. The world and its way of actualization is not to be abandoned, but the will of the individual is to be united in action with the universal ground, not with the vicissitudes of the suffering body and nervous system. That is the teaching of the Incarnate Creator and Sustainer. That is the world-balancing crux of his supreme advice to man. "The practice of worship through offerings (*yajña*), the giving of alms (*dāna*), and austerity (*tapas*) should not be abandoned. Indeed, these works should be performed; for worship, charity, and austerity are purifying to the wise. And yet even such selfless works as these are to be performed with a resignation of all attachment to them and their fruits; [71] that is My best and unwavering conviction." [72] "Give thought to nothing but the act, never to its fruits, and let not thyself be seduced by inaction. For him who achieves inward detachment, neither good nor evil exists any longer here below." [73] "Consider pleasure and pain, wealth and poverty, victory and defeat, as of equal worth. Prepare then for the combat. Acting in this way thou wilt not become stained by guilt." [74]

The God himself acts—both as a macrocosm, through the

[70] *Ib.* 2. 16-18.

[71] In this case the fruits are the promised heavenly rewards, or advantages to be enjoyed in a time and birth to come.

[72] *Bhagavad Gītā* 18. 5-6.

[73] *Ib.* 2. 47.

[74] *Ib.* 2. 38.

events of the world, and as a microcosm, in the form of his Incarnation. That fact itself should serve as a salutary lesson. "There is naught in the Three Worlds," declares Krsna, "that I have need to do, nor anything that I have not obtained and that I might gain, yet I participate in action. If I did not do so without relaxation, people would follow my example. These worlds would perish if I did not go on performing works. I should cause confusion [for men would relinquish the tasks and activities assigned to them by birth]; I should be the ruin of all these beings [for the gods, the celestial bodies, etc., would terminate their activities, following the example set by the Highest]. Just as ignorant people act, being attached to actions, even so should the wise man (*vidvān,* the comprehender) also act, though unattached—with a view to the maintenance of order in the world." [75]

The unfatigued activity of the Divine Being controlling the universe is a matter of routine, a kind of ritual that does not deeply concern Him. In the same way, the perfect man should fulfill the duties of his life in a spirit of playful routine, so as not to break the whole course of the play in which the role (from which he has become deeply detached) involves him. "For it is impossible," says Kṛṣṇa, "for any being endowed with a body to give up activity-without-rest; but he who relinquishes the fruits (*phala:* rewards, results) of his acts is called a man of true renunciation (*tyāgin*)." [76]

To suppose that, being endowed with a body, one can avoid involvement in the web of karma is a vain illusion. Nevertheless, it is possible to avoid increased involvement, and possible even to disengage the mind, by disregarding the consequences and apparent promises of one's unavoidable tasks and enterprises—that is to say, by an absolute self-sacrifice. One is to look for no reward in the fulfillment of one's duties as a son or

[75] *Ib.* 3. 22-25.

[76] *Ib.* 18. 11.

father, as a Brāhman or as a warrior, in the performance of the orthodox rituals, in dispensing charity, or in whatever else the work of virtue may chance to be. "One should not give up the activity to which one is born (*sahajaṁ karma:* the duty incumbent on one through birth, caste, profession), even though this should be attended by evil; for all undertakings are enveloped by evil, as is fire by smoke." [77]

The earthly plane is the sphere of imperfection, by definition as it were. Perfection, stainless purity, is to be reached only through disentanglement from the manifest sphere of the guṇas [78] —a spiritual progress that dissolves the individual, the mask of the personality and all the forms of action that pertain to it, in the undefiled, undifferentiated, anonymous, absolutely changeless realm of the Self. Meanwhile, however, the duties and obligations of the life into which one was born are those that are to be clung to. "Better one's own life-task and duty (*dharma*), though worthless and destitute of qualities (*vi-guṇa*), than the duty of another well-performed. He who performs the activities (*karma kurvan*) dictated by his inborn nature [which are identical with those of his place in society] incurs no stain." [79]

Even a person born into an unclean caste (a sweeper, an undertaker, for example) should hold to the inherited career. By performing the work as well as possible, in the ordained way, he becomes a perfect, virtuous member of society; breaking loose and intruding upon other people's duties, on the other hand, he would become guilty of disturbing the sacred order. Even the harlot, as we have seen,[80] though indeed within the hierarchy of society she is far below the state of the virtuous housewife, nevertheless, if she fulfills to perfection the moral code of her despicable profession, participates in the trans-in-

[77] *Ib.* 18. 48.

[78] For the gunas, cf. *supra,* pp. 295-297.

[79] *Bhagavad Gītā* 18. 47.

[80] *Supra,* pp. 161-162.

dividual, suprahuman Holy Power which is manifested in the cosmos—and she can work miracles to baffle kings and saints.[81]

Kṛṣṇa, the divine proclaimer of the doctrine of the *Bhagavad Gītā,* offers himself not only as a teacher but also as a good example. He represents the willing participation of the Supreme Deity itself in the mysterious joy and agony of the forms of the manifested world—these being, finally, no less than Its Own reflection. "Though I am unborn, though my Self is changeless, though I am the Divine Lord of all perishable beings, nevertheless, residing in my own material nature (*prakṛti*), I become a transitory being (*sambhavāmi*) through the magic divine power of playful illusive transformation which produces all phenomena and belongs to my own Self (*ātmamāyayā*). Whenever there occurs a relaxation or weakening of the principle of duty and a rise of unrighteousness, then I pour Myself forth. For the protection of the just and the destruction of the workers of evil, for the confirmation of virtue and the divine moral order of the universe, I become a transitory being among the perishable creatures in every age of the world." [82]

According to the Hindu view, the entrance of God into the strife of the universe is not a unique, astounding entrance of the transcendental essence into the welter of mundane affairs

[81] "Let the scriptures be thine authority in ascertaining what ought to be done and what should not be done. Knowing what is said in the ordinance of the scriptures, thou shouldest act here" (*Bhagavad Gītā* 16. 24). But then, on the other hand: "For the Brāhman who has gained the highest knowledge (*vijānan*), all the Vedas are of as much use as a reservoir when there is a flood everywhere" (*ib.* 2. 46). The scriptural traditions contain the highest truth, but the experience of that truth renders them superfluous. He who Knows has entered the sphere of transcendental reality, and no longer stands in need of guidance. *Before* the moment of realization, the scriptures and the sphere of social duty serve as the necessary guides; *after* realization, they are affirmed voluntarily in a spirit of sublime good will.

[82] *Ib.* 4. 6-8.

(as in Christianity, where the Incarnation is regarded as a singular and supreme sacrifice, never to be repeated), but a rhythmical event, conforming to the beat of the world ages. The savior descends as a counterweight to the forces of evil during the course of every cyclic decline of mundane affairs, and his work is accomplished in a spirit of imperturbable indifference. The periodic incarnation of the Holy Power is a sort of solemn leitmotiv in the interminable opera of the cosmic process, resounding from time to time like a majestic flourish of celestial trumpets, to silence the disharmonies and to state again the triumphant themes of the moral order. These should predominate over, but not eradicate entirely, the numerous melodies and dissonant tones of the complex partition. The savior, the divine hero (the super-Lohengrin, Parsifal, or Siegfried), having set things aright by subduing the demon forces—both in their cosmic aspect and in their human garb of wicked tyrants and evil men—withdraws from the phenomenal sphere as calmly, solemnly, and willingly as he descended. He never becomes the seeming temporary victim of the demon powers (as did Christ nailed to the Cross) but is triumphant in his passage, from beginning to end. The Godhead, in its very aloofness, does not in the least mind assuming temporarily an active role on the phenomenal plane of ever-active Nature.

The descent is represented in Indian mythology as the sending forth of a minute particle (*aṁśa*) of the infinite supramundane essence of the Godhead—that essence itself suffering thereby no diminution; for the putting forth of a savior, the putting forth even of the mirage of the universe, no more diminishes the plenitude of the transcendent and finally unmanifested Brahman than the putting forth of a dream diminishes the substance of our own Unconscious. In fact, it may be said (and now that our Western psychology has begun to search these matters, this is becoming increasingly clear to us) that the Hindu view and symbolism of the macrocosmic universal māyā is based on millenniums of introspection, as a result of which experience the creative processes of the human psyche have been accepted as man's best clues to the powers, activities, and attitudes of the world-creative supramundane Being. In the process of evolving a dream world of dream scenery and dream people—supplying also a heroic dream double of our own ego, to endure and enjoy all sorts of strange adventures—we do not suffer the least diminution, but on the contrary realize an expansion of our personal substance. Unseen forces manifest themselves in all these images and by so doing enjoy themselves, realize themselves. It is likewise with God, when he pours forth his creative māyā-force. Nor is our psychic substance diminished by the sending forth of the sense forces through the gates of the sense organs to grasp the sense objects, swallow them, and present them to the mind; nor again is the mind diminished when it shapes itself to the patterns thus offered by the sense organs, copying them exactly in its own subtle substance—which is clay-like, soft and malleable.[83] Such activities, whether in dream or in waking, are expansive, self-delighting exercises of man's vital essence, which is ready for and easily capable of the facile self-transformations. Man's work therein is a microcosmic counterpart of the creative principle of the universe. God's māyā shapes the universe by taking shape itself, playing through all the transitory figures and bewildering events, and therein it is not the least diminished, but on the contrary only magnified and expanded.

The field of the micromacrocosmic manifestation was characterized in the Sāṅkhya in terms of an unceasing interplay of the three constituents or qualities of prakṛti, the so-called gunas.[84] In the *Bhagavad Gītā,* this idea is taken over but completely assimilated into the Vedic Brāhmanical conception of the one and only Self. "Whatever states there may be of the

[83] Cf. *supra,* pp. 284-285 and 288-289.

[84] *Supra,* pp. 295-297.

qualities of clarity (*sāttvika*), passion and violence (*rājasa*), and darkness-inertia (*tāmasa*), know verily that these proceed from Me; yet I am not in them—they are in Me. This whole universe of living beings is deluded by these states compounded of the three qualities; hence they do not know Me, Who am beyond them and immutable. For this divine illusion (*māyā*) of mine, which is constituted of [and operates through] the guṇas, is exceedingly difficult to traverse. Those who devote themselves exclusively to Me, however, traverse it." [85]

The broad river of ignorance and passion is a dangerous torrent, yet the savior, the divine ferryman, can bring his devotees safely to the other shore. This is an image held in common by all Indian traditions. The Jaina saviors are termed Tīrthaṅkaras, "Crossing-Makers." The Buddha traverses a river by walking on its waves, and his Wisdom is known as the "Knowledge that has Gone to the Other Shore" (*prajñā-pāram-itā*). In the same spirit, the popular Mahāyāna savior Avalokiteśvara (Chinese: Kwan-yin; Japanese: Kwannon) is represented as a winged steed, named "Cloud" (*valāhaka*), who carries to the far-off bank of enlightened freedom-in-extinction all who wish to go.

An amusing allegorical tale, in the Buddhist sūtra known as the *Kāraṇḍavyūha*,[86] represents Cloud as manifesting himself to a company of shipwrecked merchants who had set sail for the Jewel Isle. These had fallen in with certain alluring women on another enchanted island, who had seemed to receive them hospitably and freely allowed them to make love, but finally proved to be man-eating monsters only waiting to devour them.

[85] *Bhagavad Gītā* 7. 12-14.

[86] The full title of this important Mahāyāna Buddhist sūtra is *Avalokiteśvaraguṇakāraṇḍavyūha*, "The Complete Description of the Basket of the Characteristics of Avalokiteśvara." It appears in two versions, an older in prose and a later in verse. See M. Winternitz, *Geschichte der indischen Litteratur*, Vol. II, pp. 238-240, and L. de la Vallée Poussin, "Avalokiteśvara," in Hastings, *Encylopaedia of Religion and Ethics*, Vol. II, pp. 259-260.

The seductresses had consumed many merchants before, who, like those of the present party, had been washed onto their beaches. At once alluring and devouring, they represent in the Buddhist allegory the enticing, destructive character of the sensual world. But over the island of these seductresses, the isle of the life of man's involvement in the world, the figure of "Cloud" (*valāhaka*), the savior, is wont to appear, from time to time, soaring through the sky. And he calls out: *Ko pāraga:* "Who is going to the other shore?" which is a familiar cry in India; for it is the cry of the ferryman when his boat puts in. The ferryman shouts it loudly, so that any travelers tarrying in the village may know that they must hurry; and the voice of Cloud rings loudly too. When the merchants hear it, those who can bring themselves to forsake the perilous pleasures of the island immediately mount the winged steed, and they are transported to the "other shore" of peace. But all who remain meet in time a terrible death. Moreover those, once mounted on the gigantic flying savior, who turn to look back for a last, fond view, inadvertently fall to a sorry death in the pitiless sea below.

The inhabitant of the perishable body—the indestructible life-monad (*puruṣa*), which according to the Sāṅkhya doctrine was to be regarded as the core and life-seed of each living individual—according to the composite system of the *Bhagavad Gītā* is but a particle of the one supreme Divine Being, with which it is in essence identical. Thus, with one bold stroke, the transcendental monism of the Vedic Brāhman doctrine of the Self is reconciled with the pluralistic life-monad doctrine of the dualistic, atheistic Sāṅkhya; and so the two teachings now are understood in India as descriptions from two points of view of the same reality. The nondual Ātmavāda presents the higher truth, whereas the Sāṅkhya is an empirical analysis of the logical principles of the lower, rational sphere of the pairs-of-opposites (*dvandva*). In the latter, antagonistic principles are in force, and these constitute the basis, or termini, of all normal human experience and rational thought. Nevertheless, it is a sign of non-knowing to suppose that because the dualistic argument is logical and accords with the facts of life, it is therefore consonant with the final truth. Dualism belongs to the sphere of manifestation, the sphere of bewildering differentiation through the interaction of the gunas, and is but a part of the great cosmic play of māyā.

The sole Well of Truth, speaking as Kṛṣṇa, declares: "A part of My very Self, an eternal one, becomes a life-monad (*jīva-bhūta*) in the realm of the life-monads (*jīva-loka:* i.e., in the manifested sphere of creation, which is teeming with life-monads). This draws to itself mind and the five sense forces, which are rooted, and which abide, in the matter of the universe. When this Divine Lord (*īśvara*) [87] thus obtains a body, and when again he steps out of it and departs, he carries these six forces or functions along with him from their abode or receptacle [the heart], and goes his way; just as the wind carries scents along with it from their abode. Ruling over the ear, the eye, touch, taste, and the sense of smell, as well as the mind, he experiences the objects of sense. People deluded by ignorance fail to behold Him whether He steps out of the body or remains within it united with the guṇas and experiencing the objects of sense; those do behold Him, however, who possess the eye of wisdom." [88]

"The Lord (*īśvara*) [89] dwells in the region of the heart of all perishable creatures and causes all beings to revolve (*bhrāmayan*) by His divine deluding power (*māyā*) as if they were mounted on a machine (*yantrārūdha:* e.g. on a wheel provided

[87] The life-monad is thus called, for it is a spark from the divine pure light beyond. *Īśvara* means "the potent, all-powerful, sovereign one"; fundamentally, the life-monad partakes of the omnipotence of the Divine Essence.

[88] *Bhagavad Gītā* 15. 7-10.

[89] Here the universal aspect receives emphasis.

with buckets for the irrigation of a rice-field)." [90] "This Owner of the Body, inhabiting the bodies of all, is eternally indestructible: therefore thou shouldest not grieve for any creature." [91]

As stated, the special doctrine of the *Bhagavad Gītā* is Karma Yoga, the selfless performance of the earthly task to be done; but this is not the only road to the freedom and sovereignty of the divine Self. Kṛṣṇa, the warrior-incarnation of the Supreme Being, recognizes many ways, corresponding to the various propensities and capacities of the differing human types. "Some," declares the God, "by concentration, bent on inner visualizations, behold, through their self, in their self, the Self Divine; [92] others [behold or realize It] through the yoga-technique related to the Sāṅkhya system of Enumerative Knowledge; [93] and still others through the yoga of selfless action.[94] Others again, however, not knowing [these esoteric ways of introvert self-discipline and transformation], worship Me as they have been taught to in terms of the orthodox oral tradition; yet even these cross beyond death, though devoted exclusively to the revelation as communicated in the Vedas." [95]

The ancient days of the Vedic, sacrificial, external routines had long passed at the time of the proclamation of the *Bhagavad Gītā*. The ceremonious priestly style of worshiping divine beings was no longer dominant. Nevertheless the value of such exercises for the reaching of the goal could still be acknowledged as a minor way. It long remained sanctified by tradition, but was rather cumbersome and old-fashioned. People not up to date in their philosophical ideas—the country cousins, the *pagani*—continued to practice these rather quaint routines, and

[90] *Ib.* 18. 61.
[91] *Ib.* 2. 30.
[92] This is the way of *Dhyāna,* "contemplation."
[93] Patañjali's Yoga; cf. *supra,* pp. 284ff.
[94] The specific way of the *Bhagavad Gītā.*
[95] *Bhagavad Gītā* 13. 24-25.

of course experienced the usual, long-tested good effects; nevertheless the real adventurers and heroes of the supreme enterprise of the human spirit would follow the direct, much more intense, rapid and dependable, interior, psychological way of the new esoteric dispensation.

The Supreme Being, according to the Hindu view, is not avid to draw every human creature into his supramundane sphere immediately, through enlightenment, nor even to broadcast to everyone identical and correct notions concerning the nature and function of his divinity. He is not a jealous God. On the contrary, he permits and takes benign delight in all the differing illusions that beset the beclouded mind of *Homo sapiens.* He welcomes and comprehends every kind of faith and creed. Though he is himself perfect love, and inclined to all of his devotees, no matter what their plane of understanding, he is also, and at the same time, supremely indifferent, absolutely unconcerned; for he is himself possessed of no ego. He is not of the wrathful nature of the Yahweh of the Old Testament. He makes no totalitarian claim, like the Allah of Mohammed's coinage. Nor does he demand that sinful mankind should be reconciled to him through such an extreme payment as the supreme sacrifice of the Redeemer—the God's own son, his alter ego, Second Person of the Blessed Trinity, who, becoming incarnate as the sole adequate victim, the scapegoat branded as a criminal, the Lamb that takes upon itself the sins of the world, relieves unclean mankind of its merited death by shedding his own precious blood, hanging on the cross as history's most conspicuous victim of judicial murder.

"Whatsoever devotee seeks to worship whatsoever divine form (*rūpa*) with fervent faith, I, verily, make that faith of his unwavering. He, united to that form by that faith, keeps it worshipfully in mind and thereby gains his desires—which, in reality, are satisfied by Me alone. Finite, however, is the fruit of those of little understanding: the worshipers of the gods go to the gods, but My devotees come to Me." [96]

Definite ideas, circumscribed notions and forms, the various personalities of the numerous pantheon of divinities, are all regarded as so many aspects, or reflections, of the shades of man's not-knowing-better. They all convey some truth—approximately and with varying shades of imperfection; yet they are themselves parts and effects of the cosmic play of māyā, representing its operation in the sphere of the intellectual and emotional organs. They share in the qualities of the guṇas. For example, mankind's purer, more spiritual conceptions of the divinities originate where there is a predominance of sattva guṇa (clarity, goodness, purity); wrathful, irascible, emotional views of God (where the deity displays an excess of activity) spring from the impulses of rajas guṇa; while semidivine beings of malevolent character—the gods of death, disease, and destruction—are born of the darkness of tamas guṇa. The aspects and personifications of the divine essence will seem to vary according to the prevalence of one or another of the guṇas in the nature of the devotee; and thus it is that the deities of the various races, culture periods, and levels of society conspicuously differ from each other. The Supreme Being itself, in its absolute aloofness from the interplay of the guṇas—though itself their source—is far from stooping to interfere with the particular propensities of the differing human types, but rather encourages and fortifies every pious inclination, of whatsoever kind, since of every human being it is itself the inner force.

"Whatsoever devotee seeks to worship whatsoever divine form (*rūpa*) with fervent faith. . . ." The "form" (*rūpa*) is the phenomenal manifestation of the transcendent divine essence in the garb of a divine personality, a godly individuality, and this is worshipful because accommodated exactly to the worshiping mind and heart. It may be a divinity of the

[96] *Ib.* 7. 21-23.

most ancient orthodoxy (an Agni, Indra, Varuṇa), of the later Hindu piety (Śiva, Viṣṇu, Kālī), or of one of the still later, intrusive, missionizing systems (Allah and Christ). Casting the spell of delusion upon every creature, displaying through the acts of all his universal māyā, the Supreme Being is ever ready to allow each man to go along his own particular way of ignorance, more or less bedimmed, which he and his circle take for knowledge and wisdom. It is all perfectly all right so far as the Divine Being is concerned if the fish in the deep sea cling to their own two or three ideas about the world and life, if the birds in the lofty air cherish different ones, and if the denizens of the forests and of the cities of mankind have patterns of their own. The magnificent Tenth Chapter of the *Bhagavad Gītā* tells that the Divine Being Himself exists in all. "Whatsoever is the seed (*bīja*) of all creatures, that am I. There is no creature, whether moving or unmoving, that can exist without Me. I am the gambling of the fraudulent, I am the power of the powerful. I am victory; I am effort. I am the purity of the pure." [97] Each is permitted and even encouraged to perpetrate his own particular delusion as long as he can go on believing it to be true. Once he realizes, however, that he is only trudging on a treadmill, keeping the world-as-he-sees-it in motion through his own activity, having to go on simply because he insists on going on yet remaining ever in the same place—just as he would remain if he were doing nothing at all—then the spell is broken; the desire, the need, for freedom comes; and the Divine Being is equally willing now to open the hidden way to the sphere beyond the round.

"The Blessed Lord declared:

" 'Threefold is the vehement faith or desire (*śraddhā*) [98] of the dwellers in bodies, according to their various natures: sāttvic, rājasic, or tāmasic. Hear thou the exposition of their

[97] *Ib.* 10. 39, 36.

[98] *Śraddhā* means both "faith" and "desire." Cf. *supra*, p. 48.

kinds. The śraddhā of each is in accordance with his natural disposition, O Bhārata; indeed the man consists of his śraddhā, he is whatever his śraddhā is. Men in whom serene clarity or goodness (*sattva*) prevails, worship gods; men in whom violent activity and desire (*rajas*) prevail, worship yakṣas and rākṣasas; [99] men in whom darkness and inertia (*tamas*) prevail serve evil spirits, ghosts, and specters; [100] while those who store up vital energy or heat (*tapas*) by glowing, fierce austerities, according to procedures not prescribed by the sacred tradition, are possessed with a demonic determination: they are full of hypocrisy and selfishness; [101] they are full of unconquered sensual longings, desires and passions and animalic strength (*kāma-rāga-bala*); they pull and tear by violence not only the living elements and beings that inhabit their bodies [in the guise of the functions and organs of the life-process], but even the divine Self, the

[99] Yaksas are demigods of riches and fertility, associated in mythology with the local hills and the soil; rākṣasas are goblins or imps, devouring monsters roaming at night, the fiends that disturb and deflect the efficacy of the orthodox sacrifices offered to the gods. Needless to say, one may imagine that one is worshiping a god, while actually serving some yakṣa or rākṣasa. Examples in modern life are not far to seek.

[100] *Pretas* and *bhūtas:* these are members of the host of minor demonic beings presided over by Śiva, the god of demonic terror and cosmic destruction. They represent the forces of night, death, violence, and annihilation.

According to the view of the *Bhagavad Gītā,* a petulent, jealous God, making for himself an exclusive totalitarian claim, or a god of utter mercy and compassion with respect to his lost sheep, would not represent the divine essence in its serene purity and aloofness. Such forms are but cloudy and distorted reflections, mirroring the minds of the devotees, who fancy God to be like themselves. The revengeful, aggressive God is symptomatic of a mixture of rajas and tamas, while the divine being who sacrifices himself out of a superabundance of compassion is a reflex of the mixture of sattva and rajas. The quality of the God speaks of the nature not of Reality, but of the devotee.

[101] Posing as self-detached saints, but being actually full of exacting arrogance.

godly principle [Kṛṣṇa says simply "Me"], which dwells in the interior of the body.' "[102]

The gods that men worship, however, are not the only symptoms of their guṇas. "The food also that is liked by each of them is threefold."[103]

The guṇas, being the constituents of the world substance as it evolves out of its primeval state of perfectly balanced undifferentiation, are inherent in foods, as well as in everything else. "Mild food, full of juice and taste, solid and pleasant, is beloved by men in whom sattva prevails. Acrid, bitter, pungent, sour, salty, sharp, harsh, and very hot food, burning (*vidāhin,* like

[102] *Bhagavad Gītā* 17. 2-6.

The practice of tapas belongs to the pre-Āryan, non-Vedic heritage of archaic Indian asceticism. It is among the most ancient non-Brāhmanic elements of the old Indian yoga. It is a technique for the winning of complete mastery over oneself through sustaining self-inflicted sufferings to the utmost limit of intensity and time; also, it is the way to conquer the powers of the universe itself, the macrocosm, by subduing completely their reflection in the microcosm, one's own organism. What it represents is an expression of an extreme will for power, a desire to conjure the unlimited hidden energies that are stored in the unconscious vital part of human nature.

The practice is termed demonic; for it belongs to the way of the anti-gods or titans. In Hindu mythology the titans are shown, time and time again, practicing terrible austerities of this kind, for the purpose of gaining power enough to overthrow the gods and usurp their seats of universal government. Tapas of this kind represents ambition, selfishness, and egotism, on a gigantic scale. It is full of violent activity (*rajas*) and the darkness of ignorance (*tamas*), clinging with the utmost tenacity to the phenomenal sphere of the ego.

This type of austerity is criticized and rejected by Jainism (cf. *supra,* pp. 196-199), as well as by the *Bhagavad Gītā.* The complaint that these men "pull and tear by violence the living elements and beings that inhabit their organisms," is a reflection of the Jaina fear of harming the atoms of the elements (cf. *supra,* pp. 278-279). Overdoing tapas is regarded as a serious fault by both traditions.

[103] *Bhagavad Gītā* 17. 7.

hot curry) dishes, are preferred by people in whom rajas prevails. This diet gives pain, distress, and diseases [whereas the sāttvic food gives long life, strength, force, comfort, delight, and absence of disease]. Food that is stale, tasteless, and foul-smelling, being overdue, left over [from other meals], and ritually unclean, is liked by people of tāmasic disposition." [104]

The attitude full of sattva asks for no reward (*phala*), and carries out rituals according to prescription, the devotee simply thinking "offerings must be made." When, however, the ceremonial is aimed at some reward or result, or carried out in a manner of sanctimonious arrogance (*dambha*) in order to pose as a perfect, saintly person, the attitude is that of rajas. Rajas produces egotism and ambition. Whereas ceremonials that do not conform to orthodox prescriptions (i.e., which are not included within the pale of the Brāhmanical tradition but are addressed either to malignant demons or to beings foreign to the accepted pantheon), or where the offered dishes are not distributed, later on, to worthy recipients (priests or Brāhmans, as a rule; in brief, any ritual that ignores the Brāhmans and their costly help), show an attitude, according to this priestly judgment, in which tamas prevails.[105]

The balances of sattva, rajas, and tamas can be measured in every detail of human life and practice. Even in the rigorous ascetic austerities (*tapas*) of the traditional hermit groves the operations of all three can be readily discerned. For, as we read: "Sattva prevails in tapas that is performed for its own sake, without an eye to any reward. Rajas prevails when tapas is performed out of reverence [for a deity] and regard for the purpose of worship, and out of sanctimonious arrogance (*dambha*). Austerity of this kind is fickle and unstable. But tamas dominates when the practices are undertaken for some foolish, mistaken idea, with great pain and suffering to oneself,

[104] *Ib.* 17. 8-10.
[105] *Ib.* 17. 11-13.

or with a view to annihilating someone else [i.e., in the service of the destructive forces of death and darkness]." [106]

Similarly threefold are the attitudes toward charity (*dāna*), the giving of gifts. The giving is sāttvic when the gifts are bestowed upon worthy people who can make no return (poor people, orphans, widows, beggars, religious mendicants, saints, etc.), at the correct time and place and with the thought, simply, that one has to make gifts. The charity is rājasic when it is dispensed with an expectation of service in return, or for the sake of some reward from the gods or destiny according to the law of karma (*phalam:* fruit), or when the donation is made with reluctance, or when the gift is in bad condition, worn, or in disrepair. Tāmasic giving is that in which the gift is bestowed at an inappropriate place or time, from improper, wicked motives, or with contempt.[107]

"Arjuna said:

" 'But under what coercion, O Kṛṣṇa, does a man, even against his will, commit sin, driven, as it were, by force?'

"The Blessed Lord replied:

" 'Desire (*kāma*), this furious, wrathful passion (*krodha*), which is born of the guṇa of violent action, is the great evil, the great hunger. Know that in this world this is the foul fiend.[108]

" 'As fire is enveloped by smoke, a mirror by dust, and an unborn child in the womb by the integument that surrounds the embryo, so is understanding by desire. The higher intelligence (*jñāna*) of man—who is intrinsically endowed with perfect insight (*jñānin*)—is enveloped by this eternal fiend Desire, which

[106] *Ib.* 17. 17-19.

[107] *Ib.* 17. 20-22.

[108] *Kāma,* Desire, in the role of the foul fiend, the evil one, figures in exactly the same sense in the legend of the Buddha. A beautiful youth, carrying a lute, appears as the tempter, the "Worst One" (*pāpīyān*), to seduce the Buddha-to-be, first through the alluring charm of his three daughters and then through violence (cf. *supra,* pp. 205-206).

assumes all possible forms at will and is an insatiable conflagration. The sense-forces (*indriyāṇi*), the mind (*manas*), and the faculty of intuitive awareness (*buddhi*), are all said to be its abode. Through these it bewilders and confuses the Owner of the Body, veiling his higher understanding. Therefore begin by curbing the sense organs and slay this Evil One, the destroyer of wisdom (*jñāna*) and realization (*vijñāna*).[109] The sense-forces are superior [to the physical body]; the mind is superior to the senses; intuitive understanding again is superior to the mind; superior to intuitive understanding is He [*sa:* the Owner of the Body, the Self]. Therefore, having awakened to the fact that He is beyond and superior to the sphere of intuitive understanding, firmly stabilize the Self by the Self [or thyself through the Self], and slay the fiend who has the form of desire [or who takes whatever shapes he likes] and who is difficult to overcome.' "[110]

"Through contemplating sense-objects inwardly, visualizing and brooding over them, one brings into existence attachment to the objects; out of attachment comes desire; from desire, fury, violent passion; from violent passion, bewilderment, confusion; from bewilderment, loss of memory and of conscious self-control; from this perturbation or ruin of self-control comes the disappearance of intuitive understanding; and from this ruin of intuitive understanding comes the ruin of man himself."[111]

The technique of detachment taught by the Blessed Kṛṣṇa through the *Gītā* is a sort of "middle path." On the one hand his devotee is to avoid the extreme of clinging to the sphere of action and its fruits (the selfish pursuit of life for personal aims, out of acquisitiveness and possessiveness), while on the other

109 *Vijñāna:* the supreme discriminating insight which realizes the Self as utterly distinct from the personality with all of its cravings, sufferings, and attachments.

110 *Bhagavad Gītā* 3. 36-43.

111 *Ib.* 2. 62-63.

hand the negative extreme of barren abstinence from every kind and phase of action is to be shunned with equal care. The first mistake is that of the normal behavior of the naïve worldly being, prone to act and eager for the results. This only leads to a continuation of the hell of the round of rebirths—our usual headlong and unhelpful participation in the unavoidable sufferings that go with being an ego. Whereas the opposite mistake is that of neurotic abstention; the mistake of the absolute ascetics—such men as the monks of the Jainas and Ājīvikas—[112] who indulge in the vain hope that one may rid oneself of karmic influxes simply by mortifying the flesh, stopping all mental and emotional processes, and starving to death the bodily frame. Against these the *Bhagavad Gītā* [113] brings a more modern, more spiritual, more psychological point of view. Act: for actually you act no matter which way you turn—but achieve detachment from the fruits! Dissolve thus the self-concern of your ego, and with that you will discover the Self! The Self is unconcerned with either the individuality within (*jīva, puruṣa*) or the world without (*a-jīva, prakṛti*).

This formula of Karma Yoga, however, is not the only means; it can be supported and supplemented by the traditional devices of Bhakti Yoga—the way of fervent devotion to some incarnation, image, name, or personification of one's cherished god. Indeed, detachment from the fruits of unavoidable activities is rendered easier through such an attitude of self-surrender to the will of the Personal God—who, in turn, is but a reflex of the very Self that dwells within the heart of every being. "Whatever thou dost do, whatever thou dost eat, whatever thou dost offer in sacrificial oblation, whatever thou dost give away [in charity],

[112] Cf. *supra,* pp. 183-204. Though the Jainas rejected such painful austerities as those ascribed, in the above recounted legend, to the titanic adversaries of Pārśvanātha, their own asceticism, as we have seen, was designed to eliminate all the life-processes, and so to culminate in death.

[113] As also Buddhism; cf. *infra,* pp. 469ff.

whatever austerity thou dost practice, perform the work as an offering to Me [the Divine Being]"; [114] i.e., resign it, hand it over, together with its fruits. Everything that is done is to be regarded as a willing offering to the Lord.

Thus it appears that there are two kinds of Karma Yoga, conducing to the same goal: 1. a primarily mental discipline, conducted on the pattern and basis of the Sāṅkhya, whereby the distinction between the guṇas and the Self is realized, and 2. an emotional, devotional discipline of surrender to the Lord (*īśvara*). The latter is an elementary, more popular, preliminary stage, to be continued until one has realized the phenomenal character of the Lord himself, as well as of the worshiping ego. These two (the Lord and ego) are, as two, annihilated in Brahman-Ātman, which is without form, name, personality, or the gentle movements of the heart.

"Resign mentally all of thine activities to Me. Taking Me as the highest goal, resort to the yoga-practice of inner awareness (*buddhi-yoga*),[115] and keep the mind always fixed on Me." [116]

"To all beings I am the same. To Me there is none either hateful or dear. Yet those who devote [and assign] themselves to Me with utter devotion (*bhakti*)—they are in Me, and I also am in them." [117]

The consoling, enlightening wisdom of Kṛṣṇa is well summarized in the phrase *mattaḥ sarvaṁ pravartate,* "from Me

[114] *Bhagavad Gītā* 9. 27.

The device of making an offering to God of all one's activities is familiar to the Roman Catholic Church, where exercises of mental asceticism and spiritual love (Karma Yoga and Bhakti Yoga) play a prominent role.

[115] Instead of the yoga of bodily penance, self-starvation, and mortification, of Jainism, or those demonic concentrations of energy for the winning of universal power discussed *supra,* pp. 399-400.

[116] *Bhagavad Gītā* 18. 57.

[117] *Ib.* 9. 29.

everything arises." [118] All of man's feelings, worries, joys, calamities, and successes come from God. Therefore, surrender them to him again in thy mind, through bhakti, and attain to peace! Compared with the enduring reality of the Divine Being, thy joys and calamities are but passing shadows. "In Him alone then take thy refuge with all thy being, and by His Grace shalt thou attain Supreme Peace and the Everlasting Abode." [119]

Thus in the *Bhagavad Gītā* the old Brāhmanical way of the Vedic "path of sacrifice" (*karma-mārga*) is left far behind. The routines for gaining access to the Holy Power by virtue of the magic of elaborate sacrificial rites and offerings are definitely and explicitly discredited in favor of the purely mental and psychic ritualism of the "path of knowledge" (*jñāna-mārga*). And the redeeming strength of this knowledge is praised in the highest terms. "The ritual of sacrifice that consists in knowledge is superior to the sacrifice made of material offerings; [120] for all activity [as displayed in the elaborate rituals of traditional sacrifice] attains its consummation in knowledge." [121] "Even if thou art the most sinful of all sinners, yet by the raft of knowledge alone, thou shalt go across all wickedness. Just as a fire, come to full blaze, reduces the fuel to ashes, so does the fire of knowledge reduce all kinds of karma to ashes. For there exists here [in this world] nothing so purifying as knowledge. When, in good time, one attains to perfection in yoga, one discovers that knowledge oneself, in one's Self." [122]

This comes very close to the formula of the *Yoga-sūtras of* Patañjali. The master stroke of the *Bhagavad Gītā,* as we have said, consists in its juxtaposition and co-ordination of *all* the

[118] *Ib.* 10. 8.

[119] *Ib.* 18. 62.

[120] The offering of cakes, butter, mixed beverages (*mantha*), intoxicating liquor (*soma*), etc.

[121] *Bhagavad Gītā* 4. 33.

[122] *Ib.* 4. 36-38.

basic disciplines of the complex religious inheritance of India. The Sāṅkhya, a Brāhmanized form of the old pre-Āryan dualism of life and matter, was, in essence, something very different from the all-affirming monism of the Vedic tradition, and yet the latter, as matured and introverted by the contemplative sages of the period of the Upaniṣads, was also a way of jñāna. Hence the two could be brought together; and in the *Bhagavad Gītā* the union is achieved—the Sāṅkhya idea of the pluralism of the life-monads being accepted as a preliminary view, representing the standpoint of the manifested world. But the theism of the Vedas also remains—as a convenient support for the mind during the earlier stages of its difficult progress toward detachment: the way of bhakti is taught, consequently, though no longer linked necessarily to the specific rituals of the earlier cult of exterior, material sacrifice. It is developed rather in its more personal and introverted, Tāntric form—as we shall observe in a later chapter. And finally, since the goal of all these disciplines is knowledge, the direct path of the absolutely introverted yogī is also accepted as an effective way. "Having in a cleanly spot established his seat, firm, neither too high nor too low, made of a cloth, a skin, and kuśa-grass, arranged in the proper way, there seated on that seat, making the mind one-pointed and subduing the action of the imagining faculty and the senses, let him practice yoga for the purification of the heart. Let him hold his body firmly, head and neck erect and still, gazing at the tip of his nose and not looking around. With the heart serene and fearless, firm in the vow of continence, with the mind controlled and ever thinking of Me, let him sit, having Me as his supreme goal.[123] Thus always keeping the mind

[123] Compare Patañjali: "By sacrificing all to Īśvara comes samādhi" (*Yoga-sūtras* 2. 44). A primary aim of yoga, as we have seen, is to steady the mind by withdrawing the senses from the outer sphere and thus putting them to rest. The mind can be concentrated on an inner object—

steadfast, the yogī of subdued mind attains the peace residing in Me—the peace that culminates in Nirvāṇa." [124]

And as for the state on earth of the one who has attained:

"He who is the same to friend and foe, alike in facing honor and dishonor, alike in heat and cold, in pleasure and pain, who is free from all attachment [to the sphere of conflicting experiences and pairs-of-opposites], to whom censure and praise are equal, and who remains silent and content with anything [good or evil, just as it comes], he who is homeless, steady-minded, and full of devout self-surrender—that man is dear to Me." [125]

"He who sits as one unconcerned, and is not agitated by the guṇas; he who simply knows 'these guṇas are acting of themselves, they are whirling around,' and remains unmoved, not swerving—is said to have gone beyond the guṇas." [126]

" 'Just as a lamp sheltered from the wind does not flicker. . . .' Such is the simile employed to describe the yogī who has subdued his mind, yoking himself in the yoga exercise of concentration on the Self." [127] "He who resigns his activities to the Universal Self (*brahman*) by forsaking attachment to them and their results, remains unstained by evil—just as the lotus leaf remains unstained by water." [128]—This also is a classic simile. Just as the leaves of the lotus, which because of their smooth oily surface are not affected by the water in which they grow

---

some formula or vision—and then kept fixed upon it until this object becomes more or less permanent and remains of itself.

[124] *Bhagavad Gītā* 6. 11-15.

"The mind directed in accordance with the roaming and rambling of the senses in pursuit of their objects carries away man's discriminative awareness and insight (*prajñā*), as a wind carries away a boat drifting on the waters" (*ib*. 2. 67.).

[125] *Ib*. 12. 18-19.

[126] *Ib*. 14. 23-25.

[127] *Ib*. 6. 19.

[128] *Ib*. 5. 10.

and remain, so likewise the man established in the Self; the waves of the world in which he dwells do not destroy him.

"He who sees the Lord Supreme abiding equally in all transitory beings, the Imperishable in the things that perish—he truly sees. And when he beholds the manifold existences all centered in that One, expanding from that One, he then becomes that Brahman." [129]

4.

Vedānta

THE SELF of the Vedic Āryan tradition, the Universal Being, dwells in the individual and is what gives him life. It transcends both the gross organism of his body and the subtle organism of his psyche, has no sense organs of its own through which to act and experience, and yet is the very life-force that enables him to act at all. This paradoxical interrelationship between the phenomenal creature and his anonymous, imperishable nucleus, shrouded by the perishable sheaths, is expressed in riddles and enigmatical stanzas reminiscent of our own nursery rhymes.

> The blind one found the jewel;
> The one without fingers picked it up;
> The one with no neck put it on;
> And the one with no voice gave it praise.[130]

The owner of the body has no eyes, no hands, no neck, no voice, yet accomplishes everything through the instrument of

[129] *Ib.* 13. 27, 30.

[130] *Taittirīya Āraṇyaka* 1. 11. 5.

the gross and subtle bodies that serve as its temporary abode and vehicle. The blind one, without fingers, neck, or voice, carries on the life-process of the self-conscious creature that is its garb. It is the real actor of all the deeds, and yet, simultaneously, remains unconcerned with whatever happens to the individual in the way of either suffering or joy. What for the latter constitutes the reality of life—life with its numberless and exceedingly various visible and tangible features—for the anonymous superindividual are simply "names," so many unsubstantial words.

Words (i.e., Names), words only, nothing but words are with me.
I am no-man, yet I am man and woman;
I am rooted in the soil, yet I move freely;
I am now performing sacrifices, I did perform sacrifices, and I shall perform sacrifices.
The living beings, through me, perform sacrifices;
The living beings are my beasts of sacrifice;
And I am the beast of sacrifice, tied with the rope, filling the entire world.[131]

What this means is that the divine life-force that pervades the universe and inhabits every creature, the anonymous faceless essence behind the numberless masks, is our sole interior reality. Stones, hills, trees and other plants, are "rooted in the soil" and devoid of motion; animals, men, and superhuman beings "move freely" through space: the divine life-force in the form of the life-monads dwells within and vivifies them all simultaneously. Nevertheless, whatever the forms that it puts on and fills, it ever remains indifferent to them, unharmed in them, and uninvolved.

The supreme orthodox religious duty of man with respect to the gods and ancestors has always been to offer sacrifice. The inhabitant of the body, presiding over the works of the indi-

[131] *Ib.* 1. 11. 3-4.

vidual, is the one who enacts this sacred office, as well as all the other deeds of the creatures, whether present, past, or future. The three phases of time are one and the same so far as this inner principle is concerned; for it, there is no time; it is a timeless actor. Moreover, it is not only the perpetrator of sacrifice, fundamentally it is inherent in all the utensils of the holy rite, as well as in those used in the other activities of man. Also, it is present in the "beast of sacrifice"—the victim roped to the sacrificial post and about to be slaughtered. That one being is the offerer, the offering, and the implements of the offering—the all-pervading, universally vivifying, omnipresent principle of phenomenal existence.[132]

For the Brāhman priest—whose wisdom was that of the Vedic sacrificial ritual—the process of the cosmos was a gigantic, ceaseless ceremony of sacrifice. The divine life-substance itself, as the giant victim, filled—nay, constituted—the body of the self-immolating, self-consuming world. The one transcendent essence dwelt anonymously within all—within the officiating priest, the victim offered, and the divinities that accepted the sacrifice, as well as within the pure implements through which the sacrifice was rendered. These were but so many phenomenal forms assumed by the divine force. That unique presence evolved into the shapes of living creatures and dwelt in them as the core of their being, the center of energy prompting them to act, suffer, and partake alternately of the roles of sacrificer and victim in the continuous, never-ending oblation which is the process of the world. Regarded thus as the mere garbs of the one anonymity, the sacrificer and his victim, the feeder and his food, the victor and his conquest, were the same: simultaneous roles or masks of the one cosmic actor.

[132] Cf. *Bhagavad Gītā* 4. 24: "The process of the offering is Brahman. The offering is Brahman. The fire is Brahman. It is by Brahman that the offering is made. He, verily, goes to Brahman, who beholds Brahman in every act."

Such was the orthodox Vedic view of the divine life-force and its unending play—obviously a vision that involves a depreciation of the individual. Any civilization so inspired would tend to overlook the unique and personalizing features of the various men and women who composed it; and indeed we find that the holy wisdom of the Brāhmans largely disregarded the development of the individual. Self-discovery and self-expression were never studied as the means by which one should realize oneself and prepare to make one's contribution to the world. In fact, the whole idea of the Brāhman civilization was precisely the contrary. Fulfillment was sought through self-obliteration; each was all. The one essence inhabiting the colorfully differentiated manifestations, outliving the changes, timeless and featureless, was the only thing to be taken seriously. This, and this alone, the perennial nucleus, was the inner refuge, the ever-waiting homestead, to which each must be ever striving to return.

The early Vedic philosophy, as we have seen, represented the Self as the paramount controller of all the centers of phenomenal activity, and yet, simultaneously, as the unconcerned witness of it all. Between the all-pervading state of action and the opposite state of supreme aloofness there was somehow an identity, most enigmatical and difficult to understand. The Self participated in actions, and yet did not become involved in the processes and consequences. It was all-pervading, and yet unentangled. In other words, it was precisely the counterpart of that Highest Being of the popular Indian mythologies, the Lord-Creator, Maintainer, and Destroyer of the World, who, out of his own boundless transcendent essence evolved the perishable universe and its creatures. Out of that changeless blissful divine Being pour all the transfigurations in this sphere of changes. That One, as the Lord of Māyā, is continually transforming a minute particle of his own immeasurableness into the teeming crowds of beings that go flowing into and out of each other in this terrible, wonderful cycle of rebirth—and yet, being Brahman, he is unconcerned.

The pre-Āryan philosophies of India, on the other hand (as reflected in Jainism and the kindred doctrines, and reinterpreted in Sāṅkhya and Yoga),[133] assigned a completely passive role to the Self, and moreover described the Self not as the force and substance of the cosmos but as the individual life-monad. There was no unique, all-inclusive divine Being emanating energy and substance from a transcendental abyss. All action belonged to the world of matter (*ajīva, prakṛti*). Each life-monad (*jīva, puruṣa*) was an individual entity, a solitary stranger, dwelling, as in Jainism, or reflected, as in Sāṅkhya, in the whirlpool of cosmic matter. And these monads floated (or seemed to float), innumerable, like corks, completely passive, in the great flowing river of the round of birth and death. They were not reflections of the power of a divine, omnipotent and ubiquitous, universal magician—sparks from his eternal flame, substantially one both with him and with each other. Nor was it the aim of the non-Āryan, non-Brāhman yogīs to become annihilated in any One—or in anything else—but only to realize their own intrinsic isolation. Each was concerned with disengaging himself from the matter in which he found himself embedded and afloat, and thus attaining release; which is obviously a very different aim from that of the Vedic hymns, the Upaniṣads, and the teachings of the cosmic song of the *Bhagavad Gītā*.

And nevertheless (this is what is most remarkable) in the final period of the Vedic, Brāhmanical development—that of the post-Buddhistic teachings of the Vedānta—one finds that, though the language of Indian orthodox philosophy is still that of the nondual, paradoxical, Āryan-Brāhman tradition, the mood, ideals, and point of view have become those of the world-renouncing sounders of the call to retreat. The earlier, buoyant, exultant, world-affirmative inflation of the Vedic and Upani-

[133] Cf. *supra*, pp. 181-332.

ṣādic ages has disappeared and a monkish, cold asceticism dominates the field; for the life-chilling theory of the ultimate and absolute inactivity of the Self has come to prevail—only now, instead of the individual life-monad (*jīva, puruṣa*), the Universal Self (*ātman-brahman*) is the inactive principle.

The most important name in this surprising development is that of the brilliant Śaṅkara, the founder of the so-called "Nondualist" (*advaita*) school of Vedāntic philosophy. Little is known of his brief career, which is now supposed to have endured for but thirty-two years, somewhere about 800 A.D. Legends credit his conception to a miracle of the god Śiva, and state that the child was at an early age a master of all the sciences; he is declared to have caused a river to come closer to his mother's door so that she should be saved the trouble of going to fetch water. At an extremely early age he retired to the forest, where he met the sage Govinda and became his pupil. And thereafter he wandered throughout India, engaging everywhere in victorious arguments with the philosophers of the day. Śaṅkara's commentaries on the *Brahmāsūtra, Bhagavad Gītā,* and Upaniṣads, and his original philosophical works (such as the *Vivekacūḍāmaṇi,* "The Crown Jewel of Discrimination"), have exercised an incalculable influence on the history of philosophy throughout the Far and Middle East.

Basing his reasoning on the Vedic formula, *tat tvam asi,* "That art thou," [134] he developed with unwavering consistency a systematic doctrine, taking the Self (*ātman*) as the sole reality and regarding all else as the phantasmagoric production of nescience (*avidyā*). The cosmos is an effect of nescience, and so also is that interior ego (*ahaṅkāra*) which is everywhere mistaken for the Self. Māyā, illusion, mocks the perceiving, cogitating, and intuitive faculties at every turn. The Self is hidden deep. But when the Self is known there is no nescience, no māyā, no avidyā; i.e., no macrocosm or microcosm—no world.

[134] *Supra,* pp. 335-337.

According to an introductory summary of this doctrine, conveniently presented in the *Vedāntasāra* of the fifteenth-century monk Sadānanda,[135] the Self is concealed within five sheaths, five superimposed psychosomatic layers. The first and most substantial is that known as *anna-maya-kośa,* "the sheath (*kośa*) made (*maya*) of food (*anna*)," which is, of course, the gross body and its world of gross matter. This corresponds to the plane of waking consciousness, as described in the *Maṇḍukya Upaniṣad.*[136] The second sheath, *prāṇa-maya-kośa,* "the sheath made of the vital forces (*prāṇa*)," [137] and the third, *mano-maya-kośa,* "the sheath made of mind (and the senses) (*manas*)," together with the fourth, *vijñāna-maya-kośa,* "the sheath made of understanding (*vijñāna*)," compose the subtle body, which corresponds to the plane of dream consciousness; while the fifth, *ānanda-maya-kośa,* "the sheath made of bliss (*ānanda*)," which corresponds to the plane of deep sleep as described in the *Maṇḍukya Upaniṣad,* is what is known as the causal body. This is a dark, very deep covering of ignorance (*avidyā*), which is the fundamental undersheath of the whole created world. Only when *this* has been torn away can the Self be known—that serene Silence beyond the syllable AUM, which from the point of view of Śaṅkara's "Nondualist" Vedānta is the sole actuality, the only really real. "Enveloped by the five sheaths," Śaṅkara writes in his *Vivekacūḍāmaṇi,* "which are produced by its own power, the Self does not shine forth—like water in a tank covered by unbroken masses of sedge (which are produced by its own power). But when the sedge is removed completely the clear water becomes visible to man, allays the pangs of thirst, and bestows happiness to the highest degree." [138]

Nescience (*avidyā*), the "maker" (*māyā*) of the sedge, is not

135 Cf. *supra,* pp. 51-56.

136 *Supra,* pp. 372-378.

137 *Supra,* pp. 318-319.

138 Śaṅkara, *Vivekacūḍāmaṇi* 149-150.

simply lack of insight, a merely negative principle, but also a positive power (*śakti*) [139] which projects or brings forth the illusion of the world and the five sheaths. In its negative function nescience hides the Self, "just as a small patch of cloud conceals the sun"; [140] but in its positive capacity it gives rise to the manifold of the cosmos—overwhelming all our faculties of judgment, stirring our senses and mental powers, rousing our passions of desire and loathing, fear, fulfillment, and despair, causing suffering, and fascinating our bewildered, fatuous consciousness with transient nothings of delight.

As in the Sānkhya, so in the Vedānta, only knowledge (*vidyā*) effects release (*mokṣa*) from the sheaths and bondages of nescience, and moreover this knowledge is not something to be obtained but is already present within, as the core and support of our existence. The water is only screened by the sedge; it is always there and always clear and pure; we do not have to change it, but only to remove the obstruction. Or, as in the story of the King's Son,[141] release is but the realization of our actual nature. This realization can be attained through critical thought, as in the Sāṅkhya, through the mind-amplifying practices of Yoga (applied here to illusionistic monism, as in the *Yoga-sūtras* to the dualistic view), or through any of the other "ways" of the orthodox tradition, but in the end, when found, it amounts to a miracle of Self-recollection—whereupon the apparent creation of the world is immediately undone and the sheathing structures of the body and soul are swept away.

The practice, however, of orthodox moral virtues is meanwhile insisted upon as a preparatory discipline to the final exercise of breaking through. Good works, even such as are merely

[139] *Śakti,* from the verbal root *śak;* "to be able or potent to do something"; cf. *supra,* pp. 77-78, and Zimmer, *Myths and Symbols in Indian Art and Civilization,* p. 25.

[140] *Vedāntasāra* 52.

[141] Cf. *supra,* pp. 308-310.

ceremonial, if performed for pure and proper motives, without attachment to the fruits, the aims and gains, and without desire for reward, afford an excellent preparation for the ultimate enterprise of striving for supreme illumination. Yogic exercises of intensive concentration are the main implement for the realization of the truth communicated by the guru; but these cannot be undertaken by anyone who has not already prepared himself, by means of cleansing austerities and impeccable conduct, in a spirit of virtuous self-abnegation. The candidate for instruction in Vedānta is therefore required to have fulfilled all the normal religious (i.e., social) duties of the Indian way of life (*dharma*). He must be qualified by birth, must have studied the four Vedas and their "limbs," must be able to discriminate between things permanent and things transient, must possess the so-called "six jewels," must have perfect faith, and must have gained the assistance of a qualified spiritual teacher.[142] "This is always to be taught to one," Śaṅkara states, "who is of tranquil mind, who has subdued his sense-forces, who is free from faults, obedient, endowed with virtues, always submissive, and avid for liberation.[143]

"The great theme of all Vedāntic teaching," we read in the *Vedāntasāra,* "is the identity of the individual life-monad with Brahman, which is of the nature of pure consciousness or spirituality." [144] A state of homogeneity wherein all qualifying attributes are transcended, a state of intelligence beyond the pairs-of-opposites, wherein all ideas of separation and variety are effaced, is what is represented by this realization. In other words, the goal of the "Way of Devotion" (*bhakti-mārga*) has to be transcended by the student of Vedānta. The loving union of the heart with its highest personal divinity is not enough. The sub-

[142] All of these requirements are discussed and explained, *supra,* pp. 51-56.

[143] Śaṅkara, *Upadeśasahasrī* 324.

[144] *Vedāntasāra* 27.

lime experience of the devotee beholding the inner vision of his God in concentrated absorption is only a prelude to the final ineffable crisis of complete illumination, beyond the spheres even of the divine form. For the attainment of this highest goal the very last trace, the very seed, of "ignorance" (*avidyā*) must be rooted out. Wherewith the bliss of the nondual Brahman will be present automatically—the experience of this bliss itself being the only direct proof in the world for the *fact* of the transcendental identity. Through thought and rational methods one can establish indirectly, or suggest something of, the final nondual state; but the one purpose of Vedānta is not to suggest, but to make known. This goal is expressed through the frequently quoted Vedic-Upaniṣādic aphorism, *brahmavid brahmaiva bhavati:* "He who realizes Brahman through knowing becomes Brahman."[145]

The basic paradox of the entire discipline is that, though the identity of jīva and Brahman, which is the sole permanent reality, is beyond change, nevertheless it must be realized and reestablished by means of a laborious process of temporal human endeavor. The case is compared to that of a man who has forgotten the precious jewel he wears about his neck and so suffers grief and anxiety, believing it to be lost. When he meets someone who points it out to him, nothing is changed except his ignorance—but this (at least to him) means a great deal.

The direct way to realization is through absorption in the transcendental state beyond qualifications. For this the texts and the teachings of the guru prepare the candidate by the indirect, preliminary, negative way of "the maxim or method (*nyāya*) of the refutation (*apavāda*) of the erroneous imputations or superimpositions (*adhyāropa*)."[146] The verb *adhy-ā-ruh,* "to place one thing on another," also "to cause, to produce, to bring

[145] *Muṇḍaka Upaniṣad* 3. 2. 9; cited in *Vedāntasāra* 29.
[146] *Vedāntasāra* 31.

about," yields the noun, *adhyāropa:* "the act of attributing some state or quality to a thing falsely or through mistake; erroneous knowledge." The term *āropa* is often used to describe the figurative, flattering language of eulogy addressed by court poets to their kings and by lovers to their mistresses. For example, the poet praising a king for having conquered his enemies describes how the subjugated neighbors bend their necks at his feet: "The kings," goes the flattering figure, "carry on their head the lotus flower that is thy foot. Its row of petals is composed of thy rosy toes; its filaments are the rays of thy polished nails." [147]

Here the poet employs the device of superimposition (*āropa*) as a technique of metaphor, comparing the kings prostrate at the throne-steps of the King of kings to devotees placing on their heads the sacred lotus—symbol of their god (Brahmā, Viṣṇu, Lakṣmī, or the Buddha)—in token of absolute submission and service to the Lord. What the poet does intentionally to lend charm and life to a description, mankind in general does unintentionally. The mind in its ignorance (*avidyā*) superimposes a world of duality and plurality on the nondual, unique identity of jīva and Brahman—thus bringing into view, like a wonderful mirage, a multitude of beings, interests, and conflicting opposites. As a snake perceived in the twilight may prove to be a rope (merely a harmless rope, yet it was taken for a snake and inspired fear), or as a glimpse of desirable silver may dissolve into a comparatively worthless piece of mother-of-pearl, even so the world, which inspires both fear and desire, may be caused to vanish into a neutral substratum. "Out of infinite compassion, the guru gives instruction to the pupil by the method of refutation (*apavāda*) of the superimposition (*adhyāropa*)." [148]

[147] This example is given in Daṇḍin's *Kāvyādarśa* ("Mirror of Poetry"), 2. 69-70. Daṇḍin explains: "The poet 'superimposes,' or ascribes to the toes, etc., the nature of petals, etc., and to the foot the nature of a lotus flower."

[148] *Vedāntasāra* 31.

"Superimposition (*adhyāropa*) is the attribution of something unreal to something real." [149]

Having himself "become Brahman by knowing Brahman," the guru understands that there is actually no duality of pupil and guru; in his teaching he is therefore living a double life. But he condescends to this, conforming to the illusory sphere of the manifold which surrounds him as a reflex, out of compassion, accepting again the attitude of duality because of the urgent desire for instruction on the part of the pupil who has come to him. The illumined teacher descends from the transcendental state of being to our lower plane of empirical pseudo-reality for the benefit of the unenlightened. This is comparable to the gracious act of an Incarnation in the mythology of Hinduism, when the highest God descends in the form of an illusory manifestation (Viṣṇu, for example, as Kṛṣṇa) for the sake of the release of devotees, or in the mythology of Mahāyāna Buddhism when a supramundane Buddha likewise descends. By this act the guru conforms to the dictum of the Vedic stanza: "To that pupil who has approached him with due courtesy, whose mind has become perfectly calm, and who has control over his senses, the wise teacher should impart truly the knowledge of Brahman through which one knows the imperishable Man (*puruṣa*), who is truly-and-eternally-existent." [150]

The simple yet paradoxical truth conveyed through the teachings of Vedānta is that Brahman, which is eternal being (*sat*), consciousness (*cit*), and bliss (*ānanda*), is absolutely "without-a-second" (*advayam*); which literally means that all these objects of experience, as well as the creative ignorance that brings them forth, are fundamentally devoid of substantiality—like the snake seen in the rope or the silver in the mother-of-pearl. Reality, in the absolute sense, is denied to them—denied to everything touched and seen, heard, smelled, tasted, thought

[149] *Ib.* 31.

[150] *Mundaka Upanisad* 1. 2. 13; cited in the *Vedāntasāra* 31.

about, recognized, or defined, in the sphere of space and time. This is a verity contrary to man's empirical experience and common sense, and consequently, when represented and interpreted in terms of rational thought and language, it cannot but seem to be full of contradictions. Nevertheless, it can be grasped by the Vedānta-yogī. To grasp it, moreover, means to participate in pure, anonymous, and neuter consciousness devoid of qualifications, and thus to be beyond the individualized personality of any so-called "Supreme Godhead" made manifest with such attributes as omnipotence and omniscience. Brahman, the Self, is consciousness absolutely unqualified. But this is a truth that can be known through experience alone.

Nevertheless the mind can approach the truth; for example, by reasoning that unless the Self were consciousness such a perception as "I am the knower" could not arise in a phenomenal mind. The seeming consciousness of phenomenal beings can be described, approximately, as a reflection, or specification, of the pure and primary consciousness of Brahman—somewhat as reflections of the moon on different surfaces of water all derive from, and seem to limit, the one moon "without-a-second." However, the reality of such phenomenal beings is indefinable. One can describe it by neither of the two contradictory terms "existence" or "non-existence." For man's ignorance cannot be said to be a sheer "nothingness"; if it were, we should perceive no phenomena at all. Ignorance and the material phenomena that it beholds are, in fact, based on Brahman, which is real (just as the illusory snake is based on the real rope); but how (or what this magic *is*) not even the Knowers know.

The truth about ignorance cannot be known, because so long as one remains within the bounds of ignorance, ignorance itself constitutes the limiting horizon of one's thought. And the Knowers cannot know the truth about ignorance, because as soon as their consciousness becomes identical with Brahman, ignorance (for them, at least) no longer exists. Hence ignorance

—together with its world—somehow both is and is not, or perhaps, rather, neither is nor is not. In any case, it is more of an enigma even than Brahman.

Ignorance (*avidyā*), because of which the seeming reality of our empirical experience remains superimposed upon the ultimate reality of Brahman, is thus absolutely inexplicable, through its very nature. It cannot be demonstrated by reasoning, since reasoning itself can never stand apart from ignorance. Analyzing ignorance by reasoning is like searching darkness with the help of darkness. But neither can it be demonstrated by knowledge; for with the awakening of knowledge no trace of ignorance remains. Analyzing ignorance by knowledge is like studying darkness with a blazing light. "The very characteristic of ignorance," declares the Vedāntic philosopher Sureśvara, "is its sheer unintelligibility. It cannot bear any proof; if it could it would be a real thing." [151] It is, on the contrary, a false impression (*bhrānti*). "This false impression is without real support and is contradictory to all reasoning," the same authority states in another text. "It cannot stand against reasoning any more than darkness against the sun." [152]

The existence of ignorance, then, has to be accepted, even though it is inexplicable in itself; otherwise we should deny the undeniable fact that the phenomenal world is experienced. Brahman is experienced, and that experience is the sage's proof of Brahman; but if experience counts in the one context it must be allowed to count also in the other. Hence, ignorance is described as "something" which may be said to have "the form or appearance of a floating or transient reality" (*bhāvarūpa*).[153] In common with the beings and experiences rooted in it, this "something" has the "form of becoming" (also *bhāvarūpa*): it is transient, perishable, conquerable. Having come into exist-

[151] *Bṛhadāraṇyaka-vārtikā* 181. Sureśvara was a direct disciple of Śaṅkara.

[152] *Naiṣkarmyasiddhi* 3. 66.

[153] *Vedāntasāra* 34.

ence at the beginning of time, as the very basis of world experience and ego consciousness, it can go out of existence again. If it were truly existent (*sat,* "real beyond changes") it could never be dispelled, and there would be no experience of Ātman-Brahman as the sole reality; there would be no Vedānta. But on the other hand, if ignorance were non-existent it would not display all these effects. The only thing that can be found out about it, therefore, is that this "something" is "antagonistic to knowledge, incompatible with wisdom," [154] for it vanishes, with all its modifications, at the dawn of knowledge; and furthermore, that the guṇas are inherent in it,[155] for it cannot be separated from them any more than a substance from its attributes. The proof of its existence, finally, is the simple awareness, "I am ignorant."

Like all phenomena, ignorance can be viewed in either of two ways: 1. comprehensively (*sam-aṣṭy-abhiprāyena*), as a whole; or 2. analytically (*vy-aṣṭy-abhiprāyena*), as composed of numerous distinct units.[156] The word *samaṣṭi* means "an aggregate made up of parts that constitute a collective unit," whereas *vyaṣṭi* specifies the units of an aggregate. For example, when a number of trees are considered as an aggregate (*samaṣṭi*) they are denoted as one, that is to say, as "a forest"; or a number of drops of water may be called a "pond," "lake," or "reservoir," depending on the size and nature of their aggregation. When taken as units (*vyaṣṭi*), however, they are so many trees or drops (or gallons).[157] In the same manner, "ignorance" (*avidyā*) can be regarded either as an all-pervading, universal aggregate, or as a multitude of separate occurrences. That is to say, the obvious diversity of ignorance in distinct individuals can be viewed as itself but an aspect of ignorance (which is like saying, "There

154 *Ib.*

155 *Ib.* For a discussion of the guṇas, cf. *supra,* pp. 295-297, 398-402.

156 *Vedāntasāra* 35.

157 *Ib.* 36.

are no trees, there is only a forest"); or, on the contrary, one can insist, just as well, that ignorance exists only in the many (which is like declaring that there is no such thing as a forest, but only so many trees). The end, in either case, however, is ignorance, which, according to the mode of the observation, is experienced as multifarious or as one.

The comprehensive, aggregate (*samaṣṭi*) aspect of ignorance is attributed in myths to a personal divine being, who is revered as the creator, ruler, and maintainer of the cosmos. He is supreme consciousness, Brahman, brought under the spell of a personal role, and as such is a manifestation of the finest, highest, most subtle and sublime aspect or level of ignorance and self-delusion.[158] This god—creator, maintainer, and dissolver—this supreme lord (*īśvara*), is the all-embracing aspect of the life-force (which is ignorance) in its evolution and pervading of the cosmos. He is compared to a forest or an all-containing sea.

Viṣṇu, for example, who through his incarnation in Kṛṣṇa became the revealer of the *Bhagavad Gītā,* is represented in Hindu myth as the Milky Ocean of Immortal Life, out of which the transient universe arises and back into which it again dissolves. This ocean is personified as Ādi-śeṣa, the primordial giant serpent of the abyss, who carries the unfolded universe on his heads and is the life-giving dragon in the depth of space. Meanwhile, in anthropomorphic form, Viṣṇu is pictured as recumbent on this serpent. The serpent is both himself and his living couch, and supports him on the surface of the Milky Ocean, which again is himself in his elemental form. For this divine being is the primary life-sap or substance, which evolves and nourishes all the shapes of all the living creatures in the universe. The god is dreaming. From his navel, as from the universal water, the lotus-calix grows on which Brahmā is seated, the first-born of the universe, who is about to supervise the cosmic process of creation. The shining lotus is the flower of

158 *Ib.* 37-38.

the world, which is the dream of Viṣṇu; and the god upon it, Brahmā, the "Creator," is an emanation from the world womb of Viṣṇu's cosmic sleep.

The meaning of all this is that when the pure, transcendental, metaphysical essence (*brahman*), which is beyond all attributes and personal masks, one-without-a-second, pure bliss, pure sentiency and consciousness, sinks into the state in which, under a personal mask, it fancies itself to be the Universal God, then the clarity of pure spiritual being is clouded, and this cloud is self-delusion on a cosmic scale: universal consciousness, forgetful of the true state and nature of Brahman. It imagines itself to be possessed of a divine personality: this is the crucial mystery of creation. The highest Lord, under this illusion, acquires the consciousness of being the highest Lord; fancies and feels himself to be endowed with omniscience, omnipotence, universal sovereignty, and all the other similar supreme virtues. The possession of these attributes, however (and they are ascribed generally to the Highest Being throughout the world, in Islam and Christianity as well as in the popular cults of India), is itself but a reflex of delusion. Impersonal, anonymous, inactive—Brahman remains untouched, beyond these popular veiling clouds, this supreme eclipse. Only apparently is the universal substance implicated in this highest personal figure, which has been born, as a magnificent superego, out of a sublime state of godly consciousness-in-ignorance.

The Vedāntic adept comes to a point in the course of his yogic progress where he becomes identified with this personal creator of the world illusion. He feels that he is at one with the Supreme Lord, partaking of His virtues of omniscience and omnipotence. This, however, is a dangerous phase; for if he is to go on to Brahman, the goal, he must realize that this inflation is only a subtle form of self-delusion. The candidate must conquer it, press beyond it, so that the anonymity of sheer being (*sat*), consciousness (*cit*), and bliss (*ānanda*) may break upon him as the transpersonal essence of his actual Self. The fascinating personality of the highest godhead will then dissolve and disappear, as the last, most tenuous and tenacious, cosmic illusion. The creator of the world will have been surpassed; and with Him, the entire illusion of the existence of a world.

For the beginner, however, and the religious amateur, the divine superego commonly called "God" is properly and advisedly the center of pious devotional exercises of self-surrender (*bhakti*). By bringing this "God" to focus and making "Him" the center of consciousness, one is enabled to get rid of one's individual ego. This makes it possible to rise above the status of the individual who sees many trees but not the forest and fancies himself to be a tree. One recognizes the all-embracing aspect of the forest, that is to say, the collective identity of all beings in "God." This is a step toward the conquest of the dualism of "I" and "Thou"—the strife with fellow creatures. All are experienced as one, subsumed in the one divine personality. All creatures, everywhere and at all times, are "His" continuously changing manifestations.

But now as for the problem of the Supreme Being himself, as "God," fancying himself to be what the theologians assert him to be: Self-delusion, ignorance, avidyā—the very basis of the erroneous consciousness of God's existence—is of a more subtle character in His vast, omniscient mind than in the grosser, tightly circumscribed little spheres of mortal consciousness. The aggregate of ignorance in God, since it is directly associated with the pure spirituality of Brahman, has a preponderance of sattva guṇa (purest clarity). It is devoid of rajas (uncontrolled passionate activity), as well as tamas (inertia, dullness), which are what preponderate in the spheres of the animals, minerals, vegetables, and normal human beings. God's Ego, the ultimate personal entity, is fundamentally as unreal as the human ego, as much an illusion as the universe, no less unsubstantial than all the other names and forms (*nāmarūpa*) of the manifested world; for "God" is only the most subtle, most magnificent, most flattering false impression of all, in this general spectacle of erroneous self-deceptions. Like the other forms of this floating, transient reality, "God" exists only in association with the power (*śakti, māyā*) of self-misrepresentation. Hence "God" is not real. Furthermore, He is associated with his own self-misrepresentation only apparently—i.e., for us. In short, since he is Brahman—the sole existing essence—he cannot be *really* lost in that ignorance which, in its own turn, is neither "unreal" nor "real."

It is, then, merely to the unenlightened mind that God appears to be real, endowed with such attributes as omniscience, omnipotence, and universal rule, and disposed to the attitudes of benignity and wrath. The pious preoccupations centering around God, the rites of the various religious communities, and the cogitations of their theologians belong to and support an atmosphere of the most subtle and respectable kind of self-deceit. They have, of course, their priceless value as preliminary means. They supply a kind of ladder by which the utterly selfish individual may climb from the dim dungeon of his own ego. But when he attains the final rung, and is now at last capable of transcending the convenient truth of a personal monotheism, the ladder must be left behind.

The Highest Being, as "God," is phenomenal—a majestic, lordly face painted on the sublime blank of Brahman, true being, which is devoid of physiognomy as well as of all other attributes and definitions. Brahman is not actually, but only seemingly, involved in ignorance—and then only in the least dark, least active, most serene state of ignorance, which is brilliant clarity (*sattva*). "God" cannot be said to be taken in by his own illusory attitude of paramount Super-Egoity, great with omniscience, omnipotence, and lordly rule. When the Lord seems to be enacting his cosmic role, he is not implicated in the net of the illusion he creates; the pantomime of the divine part does not fool the actor. Therefore, if "God" is to be conceived of as unfolding, maintaining, and pervading the universe, and directing the mental propensities of finite beings through his universal, all-controlling power, it must be understood that He is performing a sort of play for which there is no spectator—like a child. "God" is the lonely cosmic dancer whose gestures are all beings and all the worlds. These stream forth without end from his tireless, unremitting flow of cosmic energy as he executes the rhythmic, endlessly repetitious gestures. Śiva, the dancing god, is not enthralled; and that is the principal distinction between the Lord (*īśvara*) and the life-monads (*jīva*) that are dancing also in this universal play.

We little beings are trapped in the illusion of all these phantasmagoric forms. We think, actually, that we *are* human beings, that our individual ego *is* a reality, and so cling to ourselves, as well as to the false reality of the other attractive and repulsive phenomena round about. Whereas God knows that his divine personality is a mask, a false impression which he is always capable of removing by a simple return of emphasis to his undifferentiated substance, for us our own personalities are as gross and durable as our ignorance itself, and the personality of God is the great unknown. His nature is, for us in our state of ignorance, unfathomable. And yet he is well called by us the "Inner Guide"; for he can become the illuminator of the whole aggregate of our ignorance. Just as the sun lights the world and dispels darkness, so that Divine Being, once known, lights ignorance and dissipates its product, this phenomenal sphere and all its phenomenal individuals. The sun is never contaminated by darkness; nor is the Divine Being by this world of ignorance in which his grace so miraculously plays.

The pure Self—which is the only really existing entity, sheer consciousness unlimited by any contents or qualifications, and complete bliss—in a cosmic association with ignorance, which is unaware of its own neither real nor unreal true nature, condescends to accept the personality and consciousness of the Lord of the Universe, the all-pervading, omnipotent Supreme One, who is inherent in every particle of creation. And yet, though thus associated with, he is not really subject to, delusion; ignorance with him is wholly sāttvic. He is pervaded ever by the bliss of Brahman, the Self, yet indulges in a curious, childlike game of being aware of the illusory character of his own august personality and the universe, even while playfully bringing them forth, supporting them, and then permitting them to disappear. This is the way of ignorance in its collective, aggregate unawareness—the grandiose ignorance of the forest.

We, the self-centered individual trees, on the other hand, are circumscribed by the individual aspect of ignorance. We fancy ourselves to be a Mr. X, or a Miss Z; we fancy *that* to be a dog, and *this* a cat, distinct and separate from each other and from ourselves. Whereas the Lord experiences ignorance in its grandeur, as one, with us the Self is broken into bits, and associated, moreover, with a nescience that is complex—not made up solely of serenity (*sattva*), but compounded of clarity (*sattva*), violent activity (*rajas*), and dull inertia, mute and dark (*tamas*). The latter two guṇas being predominant, the power of sattva is eclipsed, and so the consciousness of an individual—whether man, tree, bird, or fish—is a poor reflection indeed of the consciousness of the Self. It is not omniscient and omnipotent, but of little knowledge and unlordly; yet it may be called *prājña*, "intelligence,"[159] since it "illuminates" one individual mass of ignorance, one tree in the forest. Such as it is, individual consciousness serves as a light. It cannot dispel the darkness that beclouds the individual completely—as would the sun the darkness of the world—but it serves, nevertheless, as a candle in a house that would otherwise be completely dark.

This darkness within us remains generally unremovable because of its mixed or unclean nature. It is "beset by unpellucid, untransparent, or dull and limiting adjuncts"; it is "not endowed

[159] *Māṇḍūkya Upaniṣad* 5; cited in *Vedāntasāra* 46.

with an utterly brilliant self-effulgence."[160] Nevertheless, the consciousness of the all-comprising, all-pervading supreme Lord of the Universe is an essence identical with the sum total of the consciousness of the manifold of individuals—as the space (*ākāśa*) enclosed by a forest is precisely the same as that enclosed by the circumference of the crowns of all the single trees, or as the one and self-same sky reflected by the collective unity of the lakes and ponds of a region is mirrored in each separate lake or pond.[161] That Highest Lord is sheer, unmitigated self-effulgence, like the pure Self itself, in spite of the fact that a translucent nescience (*sattva-avidyā*) mirrors him. The play of ignorance is hardly as much as a thin veil for him; he sees through it and enacts his role in it, like an adult in a children's game. And so he is identical, not with our ignorance (the limiting adjuncts that keep us apart from each other and constitute the whole difference between that omnipotent, omniscient highest presence and our troubled earthly selves), but with the consciousness, the bliss and the pure being, the brilliant spiritual space (*ākāśa*), that abides within.

Nescience (*avidyā, ajñāna),* we have said, is possessed of a twofold power: 1. that of concealing, and 2. that of projecting or expanding.[162] Through the operation of the former it conceals the true reality of Brahman—timeless existence, pure consciousness, and bliss illimited (*sat-cit-ānanda*)—that is to say, it conceals our own Self from us, the kernel of our nature, while simultaneously through the second power a spectacle of illusory phenomenal entities is produced that is taken for real—the mirage of name-and-form (*nāma-rūpa*), which distracts us from the quest for the really existing entity of the Self.

We tend to resist with every kind of argument the Vedāntic demonstration of the predicament we are in; for at first it seems

[160] *Vedāntasāra* 44.

[161] *Ib.* 47-48.

[162] *Supra,* pp. 415-416; *Vedāntasāra* 51.

unbelievable that unawareness (*avidyā*), if it is in itself neither real nor unreal, should be capable of concealing the utterly real. Until a direct apprehension of spirituality in its own pure form has been achieved, therefore, the practice of exercises is indicated. These conduct the sincere candidate gradually through a series of preparatory, preliminary states of understanding.

1. The first of these states is known as *śravaṇa:* study, listening to the teacher, and thoroughly learning the revealed texts by paying careful attention to what they say. The six characteristics and keys to the understanding of an Indian sacred text are termed: i. *upakrama* ("beginning") and *upasaṁhāra* ("conclusion"): the topic of each text being stated at its beginning and restated at the end; ii. *abhyāsa* ("repetition"): throughout the course of the text the topic is dwelt upon in variations and repetitions; iii. *apurvatā* ("originality"): i.e., the topic cannot be studied elsewhere; iv. *phala* ("result"): the result of the study of the topic is indicated in the text (the result being the knowledge of Brahman): v. *arthavāda* ("eulogy"): the value of the study is pointed out; and vi. *upapatti* ("demonstration"): the truth of the teaching is demonstrated by logical arguments.[163]

2. The second state of spiritual progress is termed *manana:* reflection, meditation, cogitation.[164] This is a continuous, uninterrupted, pondering on Brahman, the one-without-a-second, which has already been heard about from the teacher along with arguments consonant with the purport of Vedānta. Through a sustained and resolute centering of the mind on the teaching and its goal—absolutely undisturbed by extraneous matters of thought, or concepts at variance with Vedānta—the pupil becomes imbued with the spirit of what he has been taught. He thus saturates his being with the attitudes and ideas required for the attainment and realization of the Self.

3. The following state is *nididhyāsanam:* an intense focusing

[163] *Ib.* 182-190.

[164] *Ib.* 191.

on a long-enduring, one-pointed inner vision; a fervent concentration. This step leads beyond the sphere of argument and cogitation. The restlessness of the mind is put at rest because all of its energies have been brought to a single, stable point. *Nididhyāsanam* is defined as "a flow or stream of ideas which are all of the same kind as those of the one-without-a-second; a flow of ideas devoid of all such thoughts as those of a body, a mind, an ego, the duality of subject-object, etc."[165] Having become saturated in the second stage with the ideas and attitudes of Vedānta, to the complete exclusion of all else, the intellect now is urged to dwell incessantly in the truth of Vedānta and concentrate its own spontaneous activities on centers conducing to the goal. The goal, the one-without-a-second, is no longer approached actively, through argument and cogitation, but as though on the waters of a stream or river easily flowing of itself. Consciousness takes the shape of Brahman spontaneously by merging into it.

4. The final state is typified by the classic image of the salt in water. "Just as when salt has been dissolved in water the salt is no longer perceived separately and the water alone remains, so likewise the mental state that has taken the form of Brahman, the one-without-a-second, is no longer perceived, only the Self remains."[166] In this state the distinction between the onlooker and thing looked upon (the subject and object) disappear. The consciousness of the devotee has transformed itself into the substance of the Self. The state would seem to be identical with, or at least closely akin to, deep dreamless sleep, wherein consciousness is totally lost, because in both states there is, to all appearance, no "oscillation of consciousness." Nevertheless, there is in fact a remarkable difference; for whereas there is really no such oscillation in deep sleep, in the state of the merging of consciousness with the being of the Self (*samādhi*) an oscillation is acutely

[165] *Ib.* 192.
[166] *Ib.* 198.

present. Consciousness, though not perceived, yet exists; it has taken the form of the Self (*brahman*); it is vastly alive. It is fixed in a state of transcendent wakefulness—just as awake and fully aware as it is aloof from the semiconsciousness of the body, the mind, the ego, and the power of intuitive discernment. In this experience (which corresponds to "the Fourth" of the *Māṇḍūkya Upaniṣad*)[167] is actualized the meaning of the formula, *tat tvam asi*.[168]

A strictly monastic, ascetic life is required of the Vedāntic candidate seriously aspiring to pass through the first three states to absorption (*samādhi*, "union, completion"). Numerous disciplines are impressed upon him, and these have been classified, conveniently, under heads.[169]

1. *Yama:* the "general discipline" comprises a host of commandments designed to inculcate an unselfish, self-controlled, unworldly habit of behavior. They resemble those of the Buddhist and other ascetic Indian orders dedicated to release from the round of birth and death. The *Vedāntasāra* describes them as follows: a) *ahiṁsā*, non-violence: renunciation of intent to injure other beings by thought, word, or deed (particularly emphatic is the prohibition against taking a creature's life); b) *satya*, truthfulness, honesty, sincerity: the maintenance of identity be-

[167] *Supra*, pp. 372-378.

[168] *Tat* (that) *tvam* (thou) *asi* (art). Cf. *supra*, pp. 335-337.

Tat denotes Brahman, absolute and unlimited; *tvam* the individual, finite and variously limited; *asi* brings the two into apposition. But it is inconsistent with the direct connotations of the two terms to equate them; the identity of "thou" and "that" is not possible unless what is inconsistent in the two terms be rejected and what is consistent in them retained. What is inconsistent is, in the first place, the distinction between them, and in the second place, all such differentiations as "absolute and unlimited" *vs.* "finite and variously limited." What is consistent, on the other hand, is "spirituality, intelligence" (*caitanya*). "Thou" and "that" are identical, therefore, because *caitanya*, the essence of "thou," is the essence, simultaneously, of "that." The rest is not essence but a mere illusion.

[169] *Vedāntasāra* 200-208.

tween thought, word, and deed; c) *asteya,* non-stealing; d) *brahmacarya:* a life of celibacy, like that required of the pupil in the first of his four life-āśramas (*brahmacārin*) when, as a child, he dwelt with his teacher and became imbued with the magic holy substance (*brahman*) of the revealed tradition of the Vedas;[170] and e) *aparigraha,* non-acceptance, rejection, renunciation of all possessions that tie one to the world and its ego and are likely to stand in the way of meditation.

2. *Niyama,* the "particular discipline," which consists in a constant practice of (a) *śauca,* cleanliness of the body and purity of the mind; (b) *santoṣa,* contentment, satisfaction with what comes of itself, equanimity with regard to comfort and discomfort and every kind of happening; (c) *tapas,* austerity, indifference to extremes of heat and cold, pleasure and pain, hunger and thirst; needs, desires, and grievances of the body are to be overruled, so that they may no longer distract the introverted mind from its difficult task of attaining to the Self; (d) *svādhyāya,* study, learning by heart the sacred texts that communicate the principles of Vedānta, keeping them in mind by constant inner recitation, and meditating tirelessly on the meaning of holy formulae and prayers—such, for example, as the mystical syllable OM;[171] (e) *īśvara-praṇidhāna,* surrender to the Lord; the practice, that

[170] Cf. *supra,* pp. 155-156.

If the magic process of turning a youth into a priest, magician, and knower of the essence of the gods requires strict chastity and abstinence, how much more so that of realizing the inner transcendent Self! Sexual life sets free the vital airs (*prāṇa*), and animates the sense-faculties and physical forces of the body. It subsists upon, and strengthens in turn, the outward sheaths of the layered organism, the gross body (*anna-maya-kośa*), the sheath of the vital breath (*prāṇa-maya-kośa*), and the sheath of the senses and mind (*mano-maya-kośa*), i.e., the very zones from which the candidate is striving to withdraw his consciousness. In India this prohibition against sex is not based on the notion that a normal sex life is evil, but on the belief that if energies are to be moved in one direction they should not be sent flowing, at the same time, in another.

[171] Cf. *supra,* pp. 372-378.

is to say, of bhakti, devotion to the personal aspect of the Divine Being as the all-pervading ruler of the world and the "witness" who dwells within every creature, the inner controller (*antaryāmin*) of every action, to whom the fruits (*phala*) of all activities must be resigned.

3. *Āsana,* the particular postures of body, hands, and feet, prescribed for all spiritual exercises and described in detail in the Yoga texts; for example, the "lotus seat" (*padmāsana*), the "swastika seat" (*svastikāsana*). Correct postures are basic to every kind of yogic exercise; they are regarded as elementary physical prerequisites to all meditation, contemplation, and absorption.

4. *Prāṇāyāma,* control and ordered development of the breathing. This is a highly developed technique in India, designed to master and curb the vital air (*prāṇa*) in its three primary states of (a) "filling in" (*pūraka*), (b) "storing, or retention, as if the body were a pot" (*kumbhaka*), and (c) "clearing out" (*recaka*), according to various rhythms and quantities. This too is taught in the Yoga texts.

5. *Pratyāhāra,* withdrawal of the sense functions from their fields of objects to the interior, so that they may be put at rest.[172]

6. *Dhāraṇā,* concentration, firmly fixing the inner sense-faculty (*antar-indriya*) on the One-without-a-second.

7. *Dhyāna,* meditation, an intermittent activity (*vṛtti*) of the inner sense after it has become fixed on the One-without-a-second; an oscillation that proceeds like a stream (*pravāha*) that temporarily ceases and flows on again. The Self is visualized, but then lost again in spite of the concentration of the inner sense. This preliminary realization of the Self is followed by the supreme achievement:

8. *Samādhi,* absorption; which is of two kinds: a) *savikalpa, samprajñāta,* which is absorption with a full consciousness of the

[172] "When, like the tortoise withdrawing its limbs, one can completely withdraw the senses from their objects, then one's insight (*prajñā*) becomes steady" (*Bhagavad Gītā* 2. 58).

duality of the perceiver and thing perceived, the subject and object, the beholding inner sense and the beheld Self; and b) *nirvikalpa, asamprajñāta,* which is nondual absorption, absolutely devoid of any consciousness of a distinction between the perceiver and the thing perceived.

In samādhi of the first type, the mental process, or oscillating vitality of consciousness (*citta-vṛtti*), assumes the form of Brahman, the One-without-a-second, just as in the ordinary waking state it assumes the form of objects apprehended by the sense faculties, [173] and so comes to rest in Brahman; yet it remains conscious of itself, aware of its own activity and attainment of the presence, as well as of the blissful contact and union. Having assumed the form of Brahman by virtue of its protean force of transformation, it yet feels itself to be distinct from its object; the chasm between the two remains, while the subject enjoys the supreme ecstasy of a beatific vision. Numerous elated lyrical utterances of the Vedāntic school express the rapture of this moment. "I am that," we read, for example, "the true nature of which is to be the impassive witness, the paramount being, comparable to the formless, pure, intangible ether that pervades the universe, shining forth and revealing itself: at once the Unborn, the One, the Imperishable, the Untainted and the All-pervading, Without-a-second, the Forever-free-and-released." [174] By the very form of the sentence—the I identifying itself with the That—a line is drawn here between the subject and all the nouns of the extended predicate. What we find expressed is an exquisite consciousness of the union of the two; a fully conscious state of absorption founded on an ecstatic identification of two entities that are still felt to be distinct.

Nirvikalpa samādhi, on the other hand, absorption without self-consciousness, is a mergence of the mental activity (*citta-vṛtti*) in the Self, to such a degree, or in such a way, that the dis-

[173] Cf. *supra,* pp. 284-285.

[174] *Upadeśasāhasrī* 73.

tinction (*vikalpa*) of knower, act of knowing, and object known becomes dissolved—as waves vanish in water, and as foam vanishes in the sea. Properly, savikalpa samādhi should deepen into nirvikalpa. The consciousness of being a subject with certain sublime predicates should dissolve, and the two terms of the vision then deliquesce in each other—now truly One-without-a-second, without predicates, without attributes, and ineffable. The only possible grammar to render the experience and bliss of *this* degree of samādhi is silence.

Four states of mind stand as obstacles to the attainment of nirvikalpa samādhi. The first is *laya,* the obstruction of deep dreamless sleep. Instead of passing on to Turīya, the "Fourth," the mind lapses into unconsciousness, and the candidate mistakes this melting (*laya*) for that of the mergence in the Self. Deep sleep supervenes when the spontaneous activity of the introverted mind (*citta-vṛitti*) fails to grasp and hold to the changeless Total One.[175]

The second, and opposite, obstacle is *vikṣepa,* distraction. The oscillation of the mind cannot be brought to the single-pointedness that leads in the end to samādhi. The mind persists in its normal wakefulness, being distracted by sense-impressions, and so is scattered. Images, ideas, and reminiscences take shape in it through its elementary propensity to become transformed into everything proffered either by the senses or by memory and intuition. Thus remaining a receptacle of transitory floating contents, the candidate is said to be "dispersed" (*vikṣipta*). Vikṣepa is the attitude of the mind in daily life. Though urged to concentration, the faculties cannot be brought to rest. [176] According to the *Yoga-sūtras* this involuntary state must be overcome by a deliberate, relentless effort of concentration before any progress whatsoever can be made along the way of yoga practice.

The third obstacle, blocking the way to the changeless Total

[175] *Vedāntasāra* 210.

[176] *Ib.* 211.

Object after the two elementary hindrances (*laya* and *vikṣepa*) have been overcome, is called *kaṣāya*.[177] The word means "gum, resin, extract or exudation from a tree"; used as an adjective it is both "red, dark-red, or brown" and "fragrant, astringent; improper, dirty." *Kaṣāya,* again as a noun, denotes "astringent taste or flavor"; also, "plastering, smearing, anointing; perfuming the body with unguents (the basic material of unguents being the resinous extracts of certain trees); dirt, uncleanness." With reference to the psyche its meaning is "attachment to worldly objects; passion, emotion, dullness, stupidity." And so it may be said that what *kaṣāya* denotes is something sticky, provided with a strong flavor and aroma, which darkens clarity.

This word is used in Vedānta to denote metaphorically a rigid or hardened state of mind. The candidate is unable to apprehend and come to rest in the Self because the activity of his mind (*citta-vṛtti*) has become stiffened, hardened, paralyzed, or benumbed by the latent predispositions or propensities (literally, "fragrances, perfumes," *kaṣāya*) of his own inclinations, passions, likes and dislikes. These exude like resin from the unconscious hidden store of experiences-in-former-lives that account for all the peculiar personal reactions of the individual to impressions and events. Propensities—one's karmic heritage from earlier days—manifest themselves as lurking desires for renewed gratification. They tinge the inner atmosphere like the fragrant smoke of burnt resin or a perfume reminiscent of things long past, and thus they block the way. They arouse attachments, thoughts of worldly things that should have been left behind. They besmear the field of inner vision like darkish unguents. And so the focus of single-mindedness is dulled, the purpose of approach to the innermost self is deflected, and the intellect stands spellbound in alluring, pungent reminiscences, seductive memories of life, enjoying deep nostalgia. The candidate is unable to steel himself for the effort of release.

[177] *Ib.* 212.

The fourth and last obstacle on the way to nirvikalpa samādhi is that of the bliss of the stage just preceding it—the enjoyment of savikalpa samādhi. The yogī refuses to give up himself and his ecstasy by dissolving in the Self with which now, at last, he is face to face. He remains steeped in the beatific vision, without the will to abandon the duality of seer and seen. This obstruction is called *rasa-āsvāda:* "the tasting or enjoying (*āsvāda*) of the substantial sap or flavor (*rasa*) of the Self." It is as though someone tasting the most palatable food should prolong indefinitely the act of holding it on the tongue. The spirit is caught in the tasting-enjoyment of that celestial state where the Self is divided, as it were, into itself and the consciousness enjoying it, "tasting the juice" (*rasa-āsvāda*), refusing to proceed to the ultimate assimilation of the seer and seen in the state of the changeless Total One.[178] This obstacle arises when the mind has not the strength to give up the bliss of identifying itself with the Self, its supreme vision, and becoming annihilate—swallowing the taste down in a process of unconscious merging, assimilation, and unification.

Nirvikalpa samādhi is known when the mind has pressed beyond the four obstacles. It then stands unmoved—like the flame of a lamp protected from a wind.[179] Changeless and without event, it abides in the "spirituality or consciousness" (*caitanya*) that is "total" (*akhaṇḍa*). Its oscillating ceases—like the flame of the lamp not stirred by any wind. The normal eagerness of the subtle matter of the mind to take the shape of every name, reminiscence, or sensation that comes to it is allayed, has found its rest; it reposes now in its final assumption of the shape of the Changeless Total—a transformation that, owing to its nature, cannot be undone.

The mind has become the Self, having gone beyond the spheres of transiency and changing forms in which it was earlier at home. "As a lamp sheltered from the wind, that does not flicker, so is

[178] *Ib.* 213.
[179] *Ib.* 214.

a yogī's controlled mind."[180] The bliss before the final moment was the last temptation to remain in the sphere of dual forms, the realm of the phenomenal pairs-of-opposites (*dvandva*). That was the final and finest snare, the most subtle nuance of the general delusion that is māyā. For by facing the Changeless Total One without merging (even though the identity was fully realized) the candidate would have missed the meaning of the truth that this Total One is the "One-without-a-second"; that he who beholds It—by beholding It—is maintaining himself as a delusory superimposition upon its unique substance.[181]

There has been given the following advice for the overcoming of the obstacles. "When the activity of the mind melts away, dissolving into the unconsciousness of deep sleep, the yogī should rouse and waken it; when it is dispersed and scattered, he should quiet it down; when it becomes pervaded by the fragrance and impurity of the inherited propensities (*sa-kaṣāya:* the likes and dislikes that arise from the karmic store of predispositions inherited by the individual from former lives), he should be perfectly aware of what is going on within him; when the mind becomes possessed by calmness or steadiness, he should be careful not to shake it up again into dispersion; and he should not linger with the bliss of tasting the juice—going past that, he will be without any attachment whatsoever, enlightened in absolute awareness."[182]

* * *

[180] *Bhagavad Gītā* 6. 19; cited in *Vedāntasāra* 215.

[181] Though in savikalpa samādhi the Self is realized as an anonymous faceless being, identical with oneself, the attitude still has traits akin to those of the preliminary state of the devotee in the stage of bhakti. The latter worships an all-pervading Lord of the Universe (*īśvara*), regarding that Lord as identical with his own Self and yet distinct from him. Savikalpa samādhi is also comparable to the Christian idea of heaven; cf. *supra*, pp. 290-293, where the yogī is being tempted by Those-in-high-places.

[182] *Gauḍapāda-kārikā* 3. 44-45; cited in *Vedāntasāra* 215.

The characteristics of the liberated man, the one "released while living" (*jīvan-mukta*), are stated in many texts of the Vedāntic school. They represent the supreme ideal of the "divine man on earth" as envisioned in the penitential groves—an image of human majesty and serenity that has inspired India for centuries. One may compare and contrast it with the various ideals for man that have served to shape in other lands the raw materials of life: the Hebrew patriarch, the Greek athlete-philosopher, the Roman soldier-stoic, the knight of the chivalrous Middle Ages, the eighteenth-century gentleman, the objective man of science, the monk, the warrior, the king, or the Confucian scholar-sage.

One who has experienced the Universal Self (*brahman*) as the core and substance (*ātman*) of his own nature would be released at once from the spheres of phenomenality, which are woven of ignorance and shroud the Self in layered veils, were it not that a momentum derived from past actions (both from the present and from earlier lifetimes) carries him along, maintaining for a time his phenomenal appearance as a body and its "individual." This karmic momentum fades gradually during the course of his final years; its seeds turn into fruits, becoming the experiences and happenings that affect what remains of the phenomenal individual; yet the released one's consciousness, abiding as it does in the Self, remains unconcerned. Though still associated with a body and its faculties, he is undisturbed by shadows of ignorance. He continues to move among the shapes and events of time but abides forever in peace. When the moment arrives for his ultimate liberation—his supreme isolation (*kaivalya*), his "bodiless liberation" (*videha-mukti*)—and this vestigial shell of his earlier false impression of himself drops away, nothing takes place in the sphere of eternity in which he really dwells—and in which, if we but knew, we all really dwell.

For Vedānta distinguishes three kinds of karma: 1. *Sañcita-karma:* the seeds of destiny already stored as a result of former acts, but which have not yet begun to germinate. Left alone, these would generate in time a set of latent dispositions, which would yield a biography, but they are still in the seed-state; they have not begun to sprout, mature, and transform themselves into the harvest of a life. 2. *Āgāmi-karma:* the seeds that would normally collect and be stored if one were to continue in the path of ignorance basic to the present biography; i.e., the destiny not yet contracted. 3. *Prārabdha-karma:* the seeds collected and stored in the past that have actually begun to grow; i.e., the karma bearing fruit in the shape of actual events. These events are the incidents and elements of our present biography, as well as the traits and dispositions of the personality producing and enduring them; they will continue to shape the present existence until its close.

Now the realization of the Self destroys immediately the latent force of all sañcita-karma, while the detachment that follows makes impossible the accumulation of āgāmi-karma. Though the perfect sage "released in life" may appear to be active in the phenomenal sphere, he is not really putting himself into his actions any longer; at root he is inactive, and so the first two types of karma do not affect him any more. Nevertheless prārabdha-karma, the germs of individual destiny that have been yielding the harvest of his present biography, cannot be done away. These produce the momentum of the continued phenomenal life of the "man liberated-while-yet-alive," but since they are not being refreshed they will die away presently, and the man will disappear.[183]

Meanwhile, the sage liberated-while-yet-alive, who has attained

[183] "The work that fashioned this body prior to the dawn of knowledge is not destroyed by that knowledge until it yields its fruits—like an arrow shot at an object. The arrow that is shot at an object with the idea that it is a tiger does not, when the object is perceived to be a cow, check itself; it goes on and pierces the object with all its force" (Śaṅkara, *Vivekacūḍāmaṇi* 451-452).

the knowledge that the Changeless Total Universal Self is the true form of his proper being, both knows and feels that his ego, and the contents of his mind and senses, are but delusory superimpositions to be disregarded. Only through his earlier ignorance of his own and their true nature did he become entangled and identified with them; they are the realm, merely, of transitory thoughts and pains, possessing no more than a phenomenal substantiality. "By dispelling that ignorance of the true Self he has realized the Changeless Total Universal Self as his own true form, and through this realization ignorance has been destroyed, together with its products or effects, its errors and misapprehensions." [184] He can never be at fault again about the distinction between the real nature of himself and his phenomenality. With his doubts allayed concerning the essence of the universe, and with his seeds of sañcita- and āgāmi-karma sterilized, he is without future, though riding still on the last momentum of the past. Prārabdha-karma goes on producing its effects; and yet his mind, immovably identified with the Self, is not affected. "Free from all the ties of bondage (in which he seems still to move), he is standing firmly in the Universal Self. His state is that expressed by the words of the Upaniṣad: 'The knot of the heart is cut; all doubts are dispelled; the karmas disappear when He Who is both high and low (He who is both the cause and effect, the transcendent and the all-pervading) has been beheld.' " [185]

"Such a liberated man," the *Vedāntasāra* continues, "when his mind is not absorbed in the Self but functioning in the usual state of everyday awareness of the body and outer world, perceives through the body, which is a mere receptacle of flesh and blood containing the impurities of the bowels; by means of the 'village of the sense-faculties,' which is a mere receptacle of blindness, weakness, torpor, incapacity, and other deficiencies; and through the inner organ, which is a mere receptacle of hun-

[184] *Vedāntasāra* 217.

[185] *Muṇḍaka Upaniṣad* 2. 2. 8; cited in *Vedāntasāra* 217-218.

ger and thirst, grief and delusion; the fruits, which are karma of differing sorts brought into effect by predispositions deriving from the remote and still remoter past. And he has to endure these fruits inasmuch as they are the productions of the karma that has begun to transform itself into the fruits of actual happenings, such karma not being checked by enlightening knowledge; nevertheless, though beholding these effects of karma taking place in his own life and in the world about, fundamentally he sees nothing whatsoever taking place, for they mean naught to him, they are inconsequential. He behaves like a man assisting at a magical performance [where the juggler, through various devices, creates the illusion of a conflagration or flood, or of wild animals about to assail the audience], knowing that all is a delusion of the senses wrought by the magic art. Even though he sees something, he does not consider it to be real." [186]

Fundamentally, such a seer does not see what is happening, since he knows that there is nothing to be seen. The man liberated-while-alive perceives his individual frame to be at large in the seemingly real world, yet fundamentally sees neither his body nor his world, being aware that both are illusory, phenomenal tricks of the magic mirror of the mind. He experiences, as an indifferent witness, both his own personality and everything with which it comes in contact, never identifying himself with himself or with anything he seems to see. "Though he has eyes, he is as one without eyes; though he has ears, he is as one without ears." [187]

"As has further been said," states the *Vedāntasāra,* " 'He who sees nothing in the waking state, as though in dreamless sleep; who, though perceiving duality, experiences it as nondual; who, though engaged in work, is inactive: that one, and no one else, knows the Self. This is the truth.' " [188]

[186] *Vedāntasāra* 219.

[187] *Ib.* 220.

[188] *Upadeśasāhasrī* 5; cited in *Vedāntasāra* 221.

"In the case of such a one, the only hidden propensities that remain, in accordance with ingrained habitude, until they are worn out, are those that conduce to virtuous acts—just as the habits of eating, sleeping, and moving around remain as they were before the dawn of knowledge. Or again, one may become entirely indifferent to all action, whether good or evil."[189]

"Following the realization of the Self as the only truly real essence, the qualities that were required as implements for the attainment of this knowledge (humility, non-hatred, non-injury, etc.) are kept, as so many ornaments,"[190] but the very being, the pure Self, of the Enlightened One, stands beyond virtues and qualities. Evil desires were destroyed by ascetic practices, as a preliminary step to the attainment of knowledge, but the good, which carried the Enlightened One to his goal, may remain visible, like jewels on his phenomenal form, before the eyes of the world. They are not actually part of him, any more than jewels are part of the body; and so we read: "Such virtues as non-hatred arise and abide of themselves with one in whom the Awakening of the Self has come to pass. In this case they are not of the nature of requirements or implements necessary to any task."[191]

The man liberated-while-yet-alive experiences, then, only the fruits of the karma that has already begun to yield effects, these final vestiges of the illusion of the world being the only obstacles to his immediate passing away. He experiences them as a terminal chapter of his phenomenal biography—to be lived through, but without identifying himself with the body, mind, and feelings that support them. He observes his own unsubstantial history as a witness unconcerned with what is going on in the phenomenal personality—as one might let one's hair blow in the wind. Or his attitude may be compared to the position of a lamp: the self-effulgent Self illumines the whole psychosomatic system, for it

189 *Vedāntasāra* 222.

190 *Ib.* 224.

191 *Naiṣkarmyasiddhi* 4. 69; cited in *Vedāntasāra* 225.

lights the inner organ, and this in turn sends forth its borrowed light to the outer sheaths of the psychical and physical personality; but just as the lamp that lights a room remains unconcerned with what is going on in it, so the witness of the remaining biography of this house, this individual, this out-lived mask. His Self enacts the role of lighting the phenomenal ex-personality solely for the maintenance of the body, not for the pursuit of any good, any gratification of the senses, or any timely goal. The process is simply permited to go on—until it runs down through the exhaustion of prārabdha-karma. Enlightened-in-life, one moves through the remaining effects of karma, the karma that was generated by one's own will in former times, or by the will of some other, or even against one's own will, knowing that these effects do not concern one's essence.

"And then at last, when the remainder of prārabdha-karma has been exhausted (through the concluding semblances of physical enjoyment and suffering) the life-breath (*prāṇa*) dissolves into the Highest Brahman, which is Inward Bliss."[192] Destroyed is ignorance with all its products, in the forms of the superimpositions of the outward layers of one's being; for since there is no longer ignorance, there can no longer be a phenomenal body or mind to weave delusion. There is no longer the basis of an ego. The sense functions, conveying impressions of outer objects, of a universe all around, no longer build the mirage of any such pseudoentity, endowed with its illusion of inner awareness and producing its pathetic world of visions and dreams; for they no longer bring impressions of outer objects. There is no longer any chance of anything happening in the sphere that used to be called "outside," or in the one that was "the inner realm." Phenomenality is gone. The Self abides wholly in the Self. It has found its "supreme isolation and integration" (*parama-kaivalya*), the taste or sap of which is bliss, and which is devoid of the fallacious

[192] *Vedāntasāra* 226.

appearance of duality, since it is the whole. In this terminal state the Self forever abides.[193]

The condition of him who has reached this goal, the goal of Turīya, the "Fourth,"[194] is expressed, or suggested, in numerous direct statements of accomplished adepts, in the younger Upaniṣads, in certain so-called *Vedānta Gītās* (Vedānta Songs, Hymns, or Rhapsodies), and in many of the stanzas of Śaṅkara.

"From me everything is born; on me everything is supported; into me everything is again dissolved (*layaṁ yāti:* it melts into me, as snow into water). I am this Brahman, One-without-a-second.

"I am smaller than the minutest atom, likewise greater than the greatest. I am the whole, the diversified-multicolored-lovely-strange (*vicitra*) universe. I am the Ancient One. I am Man (*puruṣa:* the first and only, primordial cosmic being), the Lord. I am the Being-of-Gold (*hiraṇmaya:* the golden germ out of which the universe unfolds). I am the very state of divine beatitude.

"Without hands or feet am I; of inconceivable power am I; without eyes I see; without ears I hear; I know all with all-pervading wisdom. By nature detached from all am I, and there is none who knows me. Pure spiritual essence am I, forever."[195]

This has the ring of some sort of holy megalomania, a schizoid inflation of some kind, in which the rational individual consciousness has been swallowed completely by a divine Super-Ego. Actually, however, these formulae are intended for the sober purpose of meditation. They represent the perfect state, which is to be attained, and they teach the candidate how to anticipate its attitude. Through reciting, memorizing, and meditating on such exalted utterances, contemplating what is expressed in them and becoming identified with their purport, the candidate for immortality is to become released from his phenomenal ego.

193 *Ib.*

194 Cf. *supra,* pp. 372-378.

195 *Kaivalya Upaniṣad* 19-20.

These *Vedānta Gītās* celebrate the bliss of the one who has achieved self-divinization through remembering his identity with the Self. They announce in aphoristic stanzas, magnificent outbursts of a kind of transcendental lyric ecstasy, the sovereign experience of the spirit that has found its home.

"I am never born, nor do I die; in me there is no activity, neither holy nor sinful. I am the all-pure divine essence (*brahman*), devoid of all differentiating, limiting, and mutually conflicting qualities (*guṇa*). Then how should there be in me anything like bondage or release?" [196]

The meaning here is that whoever clings to the polarized notions of "bondage and release" has yet to pass beyond the māyā-sphere of the pairs-of-opposites (*dvandva*). His mind still contains differentiating notions, born of the mutually contending guṇas. He does not feel, really, that the One-without-a-second, the Advaita Brahman, is the sole reality. His balanced consciousness has not been transfigured yet in the pure, spiritual, blissful being of the Self.

For as long as a difference can be seen between bondage and freedom, the horizon has not been passed that separates the phenomenal sphere (woven of the display and interplay of the guṇas) from the unqualified (beyond the guṇas). Likewise, in the Buddhist Mahāyāna philosophy there is an unremitting insistence that so long as one can see a distinction between nirvāṇa and the sphere of birth and death, one is still in a state where distinctions are made, and not a Bodhisattva, not yet a being "whose nature is enlightenment." The seemingly nonsensical, paradoxical character of the words of the perfect saint is the proof (and the only possible proof in the range of speech) of his experience of the reality beyond all form and name. Man's thinking function revels in particularities; hence all his rational notions and demands finally are inconsistent with the truth of the divine essence, the

[196] *Avadhūta Gītā* 1. 59. "The Song (*gītā*) of the one who has cast off everything (like dust from his feet or clothes) (*avadhūta*)."

reality of the Inner Self. Whatever can be said about this essence must, by nature, come into collision with the cogitations of the mind (*manas*) and the intuitions of the understanding (*buddhi*). Wild words, therefore, and figures that break beyond the powers of the imagination are the means by which the saint tells of the reality beyond the reach of words.

"In what is night for all transient beings the yogī in perfect control of himself is awake. And that in which the other beings feel awake is night for the saint who really sees." [197]

The truth about what the sage, "the mute one" (*muni*), really sees can be expressed only by a monotony of paradoxical, pompous utterances, defying reason, challenging logic, and shocking normal consciousness out of its complacency. These are intended, on the one hand, to rouse the individual from the false security of his non-awareness in māyā, where he sits gratified by himself and his reasonable mind, and on the other hand, as directed to the initiate well on his way to the goal of the transcendent Self (the true adept of Vedānta), to serve as forecasts of the state that he is striving to attain. These illogical, grandiloquent expressions are intended, in his case, to shape and sharpen consciousness by pressing it toward the pure, translucent spirituality of the Self. They cleanse the ready spirit of the fault of reason (which always flatters itself with its quick perception of contradictions) and thus heal the wound of the knowledge of good and evil, subject and object, true and false—those imperfections of intellectualism, which are the natural effects of the usual compound of sattva and rajas.[198]

"I am free from passion and similar taints. Suffering, a body, and the other limiting peculiarities are not with me. I am the

[197] *Bhagavad Gītā* 2. 69.

[198] Inasmuch as the intellectual attitude, the joy of reasoning, amounts to a passion among intellectuals—philosophers, scientists, writers, etc.—the truth in them is always bent. For a discussion of sattva and rajas, cf. *supra*, pp. 295-297, 398-402.

Self, the Only-lonely-one (*eka*), which is comparable to the infinite sky." [199]

If he were to look to find his own nature, the one released while living would have to ask himself in vain: "Where is anything that has ever been? where anything that will ever come to be in the future? where is what is existing at the present moment? where is space-location (*deśa*), where indeed is the Eternal Essence (*nityam*), when I abide in the glory of my own greatness?" [200]

Past, present, and future belong to transitory beings. Time is a becoming and vanishing, the background and element of the transient, the very frame and content of the floating processes of the psyche and its changing, perishable objects of experience. Under its three aspects of past, present, and future, which exclude and contradict each other, time pertains to the sphere of the pairs-of-opposites (*dvandva*) which is woven of the play of the guṇas; hence it cannot be regarded as of the nature of Eternity. As with Kant in his *Critique of Pure Reason,* time is here seen through and diagnosed as belonging to the phenomenal sphere, the realm of our subjective-human experiences, not that of "things as they are in and of themselves." This point is the one from which Schopenhauer, in *The World as Will and Representation,* took his start when he sought to blend Kant's theoretical criticism with the transcendental wisdom of Indian metaphysics.

The same secondary character must be assigned to the principle of space-location (*deśa*), since this also is a field of contradictory notions. Space for Kant too is one of the fundamental principles of phenomenality.[201] Space is the basic inspiration of our usual logic of mutually exclusive statements, which supports the pas-

[199] *Avadhūta Gītā* 1. 67.

[200] *Aṣṭāvakra Saṁhitā* 19. 3.

[201] Cf. Kant, *Critique of Pure Reason,* Part I, "Transcendental Aesthetic."

sion or frenzy of pure thought, the limiting power of sattva. There is always a "here" and a "not-here"; a "here" and "there."

But in the transcendent state the differentiations known to thought vanish, so that not even the notion of a motionless and unqualified, undynamic Eternal Essence can subsist. This great idea was only meant to inspire the beginner and guide the advanced pupil on the road to the true, concept-shattering experience. In itself, in the end, it proves to be an impediment. Where it stands, the initiate stands and is thus kept within the realm of contradictory pairs-of-opposites; for the notion of Eternity demands its opposite, that of the transient, the phenomenal, the illusory world. And so the initiate who has found "Eternity" still is entangled in the devious net of māyā. His remaining with such ideas gives proof that he has still a certain distance to go. If the one who is finally enlightened uses such a term, it is only by way of accommodation to the partly enlightened, more or less beclouded mind of the pupil who has come to him for help. The guru uses the term out of a mixture of indifference and sublime compassion, his own intrinsic and preferred attitude being silence, the silence of the Self.[202]

The one enlightened-while-living asks: "Where is the Self, or where the non-Self, where what is fair, auspicious, and virtuous, and where what is foul, inauspicious, and sinful, where is thinking-pondering-and-anxiety, and where is not-thinking, non-anxiety—for me who abide in my own glorious greatness?" [203]

The prodigious feeling of relief that comes of getting rid of the obsessing incubus of the phenomenal ego, together with its world of thrilling and painful anxieties, must itself be transcended. It belongs still to the sphere of the qualified conditioned states. It points back to the load of which one has just become disburdened. Its thrill of unraveling is infinitely in-

[202] *Maunam* ("silence"), the quality of the *muni* ("saint").

[203] *Aṣṭāvakra Saṁhitā* 19. 4.

ferior to the motionless, changeless serenity of the Self abiding with Itself—the deep-sea calm that is not to be stirred by any breeze of thought or feeling.

"Where is dream (*svapna*), where dreamless sleep (*suṣupti*), or where the waking state (*jāgaraṇa*), and where is the "Fourth" (*turīya*); where even is fear for me who abide in my own glorious greatness?" [204]

The analysis and experience of the "four states of consciousness"—waking, dream, dreamless sleep, and the "Fourth"—formed the main line, the backbone, of the experimental psychology and self-analysis of the period of the Upaniṣads. Outlining the way of introspective yoga-practice, "the path of knowledge" (*jñāna-mārga*), which had superseded the earlier Vedic way of magic ritualism (*karma-mārga*), the doctrine of the Four States served as a kind of stairway by which the phenomenal ego and its horizon of deluding illusionary experiences was to be transcended, and the personality dissolved. But the moment the goal is attained, the stairway, the instrument, the vehicle, becomes meaningless and is dispensable, nay it is actually nonexistent.[205] There is no fear that these states, or any one of them, should ever again lay a spell over the one who knows.

"Where is far, where near, where outside, where inside, and where is there anything gross (*sthūla*), where is there anything subtle (*sūkṣma*)—for me who abide in my own glorious greatness?" [206]

The horizon of sensual experience (*sthūla*) and the domain of inner spiritual event (*sūkṣma*) have both been surpassed. The perfected saint feels himself possessed of an illimited, far-reaching, all-pervading insight, which amounts actually to a faculty of

[204] *Ib.* 19. 5.

[205] Compare the Buddhist experience of the unreality of the "raft" or "boat" of the doctrine for the Enlightened One who has disembarked on the "Other Shore of Transcendental Wisdom" (*infra*, pp. 477-478).

[206] *Aṣṭāvakra Saṁhitā* 19. 6.

omniscience; for it is indeed a potential omniscience—not a literal, cumbersome, encyclopedic knowledge about every theoretical, so-called scientific, detail of such a classified world system as that, for example, of the Jainas and Ājīvikas, but an infallible intuition about things as they occur in everyday situations, or as they are brought to the attention of the saint, the enlightening teacher, in the questions and problems posed to him by the children of the world. This wonderful surety is the most obvious worldly manifestation in him of the fact that he is in perfect harmony with his own Self, unshaken by the gales of passions, uninhibited by the usual limiting qualifications, not bound to any of the various particular patterns of reaction that characterize the different human types according to the preponderance in them of one or another of the guṇas. He does not wear "besmeared," colored spectacles, like other beings—"besmeared" by their own affections and imperfections. He has become the perfect witness, the Knower of the Field, the Self itself (*ātman*), who observes everything with unwavering gaze because uninvolved, while the world moves around him in a continuous welter of changing phenomena.

"Where is death; where is life; where are the worlds; [207] or where is the realm of earthly entanglements and obligations? Where is the dissolution, the absorption, the melting away; [208]

[207] *Lokās:* both the higher celestial worlds, presided over by phenomenal divinities that are themselves but anthropomorphic superimpositions on the divine, neutral, faceless, impassive essence; and the underworlds, peopled by suffering sinners and the terrifying henchmen of King Death. All originate from the wishful-fearful thinking of deluded consciousness. They are the involuntary projections of its passionate, beclouded dynamism.

[208] *Laya:* the end of the whole many-storeyed universe of upper and nether planes, together with the plane of earth, which is in their midst: the vanishing of it all, as a phenomenal illusion, into the unqualified, uninflected essence of being, when this is experienced in oneself as the Self. Where is the melting of the universe—like snow into the sea?

or where is supreme absorption [209]—for me who abide in my own glorious greatness?

"No more of this talk about the three ends of life; [210] no more of this talk about yoga; no more of this talk about all-pervading wisdom—for me who am reposing in the Self!" [211]

"Where are the five elements; where is the body; [212] where are the sense-faculties; [213] and where is the mind? Where is the supreme, transcendent Void; where is the state beyond expectation—destitute both of hope and of wish; [214]—where indeed, when my true being is unstained, untinged, by any pigment? [215]

"Where is the unfolding and scattering [216] where is the concentrating of my consciousness to one-pointedness; [217] where is the awakening to transcendental reality or where the state of being an unenlightened fool; where is exultation, where dejection—for me who am forever inactive?

[209] *Samādhi:* the final step and experience of yoga; egoity and all that is contained in it being dissolved into the infinite purity of the Self, as the light of a night-candle becomes merged in the bright, triumphant, daylight, after dawn.

[210] *Tri-varga,* "the Triad of Worldly Provinces": 1. *artha:* the pursuit of material possessions, wealth, success in policy, and power; 2. *kāma:* the pursuit of personal happiness through the gratification of the senses; and 3. *dharma:* the fulfillment of the religious and social obligations ordained by the revealed, traditional system of law and order. Cf. *supra,* pp. 87-177.

[211] *Aṣṭāvakra Saṁhitā* 19. 7-8.

[212] Which consists of the five elements.

[213] *Indriyāṇi:* composed of the subtle matter of the five elements and apprehending their manifestations in the outer world.

[214] *Nair-āśya:* the state transcending the pairs of opposites that assail the soul; the state to be devoutly sought.

[215] *Nir-añjane:* untainted by any paint, any touch of impurity to bedim its intrinsic, self-effulgent clarity.

[216] *Vikṣepa:* the diffusion of consciousness over the range of the five fields of the sense experiences, or along with the flow of the internal mental processes.

[217] *Ekāgryam:* the concentrated state of the yogī, firmly focused and abiding in the one inner object of meditation.

"Where is instruction; where is the sacred textbook based on revelation; where is the pupil, where the teacher;[218] where is the highest goal of man—for me who am without distinguishing characteristics[219] and full of bliss?"[220]

* * *

Swāmī Brahmānanda, in his *Spiritual Teachings,*[221] succinctly summarizes the stages of the Advaita Vedānta path to the realization of Brahman. The beginning is *pūjā* (both external and mental worship): the candidate devotes himself to his "chosen and beloved divinity" (*iṣṭa-devatā*) both in thought and with flowers, incense, and *pādya* (water for washing the feet). Then follows meditation and mental *japa* (repetition of the holy name without moving the lips). "In meditation," he writes, "you should think of the form of your *iṣṭam* as effulgent. Imagine that everything is shining through its luster. Think of this effulgence as non-material and possessed with intelligence. This kind of meditation will later on develop into meditation on the formless and infinite aspect of God. In the beginning the aspirant has to take the help of imagination; later on, when he develops his spiritual sense, he will feel the presence of the Divine. Next, when he gets the highest spiritual vision, he will come face to face with Truth. He is then transported into a different realm altogether, of which this world of matter appears to be a mere shadow, and as such something unreal. The mind is then lost in *savikalpa samādhi* (superconscious vision with thought). Next comes *nirvikalpa samādhi* (superconscious vision without thought). There is then the realization of that which

218 *Śiṣya—guru:* the most obvious pair-of-opposites (*dvandva*) in the course of the process of enlightenment.

219 *Nir-upādhi,* beyond *upādhi,* "attribute, condition, limitation, peculiarity," beyond time, space, causality, masking forms, etc.

220 *Aṣṭāvakra Saṁhitā* 20. 1, 9, 13.

221 *Spiritual Teachings of Swāmī Brahmānanda, translated from Conversations and Letters in Bengali,* Mylapore, Madras, 1932, pp. 11-12.

is beyond thought and speech. In this state there is nothing to be seen, nothing to be heard. Everything is lost in the Infinite."

The fundamental thought of Advaita Vedānta is that the life-monad or embodied soul *(jīva)* is in essence the Self *(ātman)*, which, being beyond the changing, transient, phenomenal apparitions of our empirical experience, is none other than Brahman, the sole and universal Eternal Reality, which is beyond change, self-effulgent and ever free, and defined as "one-without-a-second" *(a-dvitīya)*, "really existing" *(sat)*, "purely spiritual" *(cit)* and "sheer bliss" *(ānanda)*. The life-monad is in error about its own true character. It regards itself as bound. But this error vanishes with the dawn of realization. The life-monad *(jīva)* then discovers that it is itself the Self *(ātman)*. Bondage thereupon is non-existent. Indeed, with reference to that which is always free such terms as bondage and liberation are inappropriate. They seem to have meaning only during the preliminary stages of spiritual apprenticeship, when the pupil has still to make the critical discovery. The term "liberation" is used by the guru only in a preliminary sense, as addressed to one in a state of bondage that exists only in his own imagination.

Or, as the ancient Gauḍapāda states the case in his celebrated commentary to the *Māṇḍūkya Upaniṣad:* "There is no dissolution, no beginning, no bondage, and no aspirant; there is neither anyone avid for liberation nor a liberated soul. This is the final truth." [222]

"Only the one who has abandoned the notion that he has re-

[222] *Gauḍapāda-kārikā* 2. 32. Gauḍapāda is supposed to have been the teacher of Govinda, who was the teacher of Śaṅkara. A translation of his commentary (*kārikā*), together with Śaṅkara's commentary on the commentary as well as on the Upaniṣad, will be found in Swāmī Nikhilānanda, *The Māṇḍūkyopanishad with Gauḍapāda's Kārikā and Śaṅkara's Commentary,* Mysore, 1936, where the above quotation, *Kārikā* 2. 32, appears on p. 136.

alized Brahman," we read in Śaṅkara's *Upadeśasahasrī,* "is a knower of the Self; and no one else."[223]

Positing Brahman involves the positing of the experience of liberation; positing liberation involves automatically the positing of bondage; and when this pair-of-opposites is posited all the other pairs-of-opposites are posited too. Illusion, ignorance, and the world of birth and death become thus re-established and nothing has been gained. The speculating mind has again snared itself in its own subtle web of thought. But through the force of paradox the logic of this tenuous web of the mind can be broken, whereupon the great and glamorous tradition of painstaking demonstration disappears—as the splendor of a rainbow into the purity of a translucent firmament. The final, paradoxical, self-annihilating formulae of Advaita Vedānta perfectly harmonize with those of the transcendental "Wisdom of the Other Shore" of the Mahāyāna Buddhist texts and meditations.[224] All agree that the spiritual adventures, conquests, initiations, and experiences met with in pursuit of the goal of liberation are purely phenomenal.

Thus, by the paradox, Indian thought overcame at last its own besetting passion for metaphysics and philosophizing. The impact of the actual experience gained through yogic absorption carried the field against the logical arrangements of the way of speculative knowledge (*jñāna-mārga*). Thought, the mirror of reality, was shattered by the force of reality itself when the truth was realized at the end of the path of introspection. Thought—with all its fine distinctions—was then recognized as only a more subtle horizon of ignorance, in fact the most subtle of all the deluding devices of māyā. For the temptation of thought is another invitation to yield to the fascination of diversity (represented now through individual ideas tending to cluster into pairs-of-opposites) instead of piercing the glitter-

223 Śaṅkara, *Upadeśasahasrī* 115.

224 Cf. *infra,* pp. 478ff.

ing, dynamic sphere of cogency and penetrating to the One-without-a-second.

The force of the conceptions and paradoxes of Advaita Vedānta in the life and history of the Hindu consciousness, and even today in the civilization of modern India, is simply immeasurable. As Richard Garbe states: "Nearly all educated Hindus in modern India, except in so far as they have embraced European ideas, are adherents of the Vedānta; and three fourths of these accept Śaṅkara's interpretation of the Brahma-sūtras, while the rest are divided among the varying explanations of the system offered by one or other of the remaining commentators." [225]

"Among the commentators who dissent from Saṅkara's interpretation of the Vedānta," Garbe proceeds to say, "and who represent one or other of the philosophical and religious standpoints of various sects, the most renowned is Rāmānuja, who lived in the 11th century after Christ. Rāmānuja in his exposition . . . introduces . . . views which are nearly related to the Christian standpoint, but are alien to the true Vedānta doctrine. In his view the individual souls are not identical with the supreme soul, i.e., as he represents it, with God, but are separate and distinct as in the Sāṅkhya-Yoga.[226] The cause of their earthly existence is not 'ignorance,' but unbelief; and deliverance is union with God, to be gained not by 'knowledge,' but by believing love (*bhakti*) towards God." [227] Garbe points out that this point of view approximates to that of the lower knowledge and preliminary understanding described in the Advaita Vedānta of Śaṅkara. It is also that of many of the popular forms of Buddhist worship and belief.

It is interesting to observe that Garbe compares the modified

[225] Richard Garbe, "Vedānta," in Hastings, *Encyclopædia of Religion and Ethics,* Vol. XII. p. 597.

[226] For a discussion of Sāṅkhya and Yoga, cf. *supra,* pp. 280-332.

[227] Garbe, *loc. cit.,* p. 598.

Vedānta of Rāmānuja to the pluralistic-dualistic world-view of Sāṅkhya and Yoga; for, in another sense, the Advaita Vedānta of Śaṅkara is also comparable to Sāṅkhya and Yoga. The unconditioned, illimited state beyond the realm of opposites, as described by Śaṅkara in his "theory of illusory manifestation" (*vivarta-vāda*), reflects, though in a supremely spiritualized form, the state of both the ancient Jaina Kevalin and the absolutely uninvolved Puruṣa of the Sāṅkhya view. As we have heard, from the singer of the *Aṣṭāvakra Gītā:* [228] "Where is exultation, where dejection—for me who am forever inactive (*niṣkriya*)?" Such an epithet as *niṣkriya* ("beyond all activities") revives the whole meaning of the antique, non-Āryan, non-Brāhman, non-Vedic, aboriginal Indian ideal—though now under the guise of a nondual formulation.

And so, we are moved to ask: Has the power of the land triumphed to such a degree that in the very doctrine that pretends, with the most authority, to represent "the gist of the whole meaning of the Vedas" (*vedānta*), the world-feeling not of the Vedic singers but of the conquered folk whom they despised, and whom they sought to shut out from their society of the twice-born, is what has come into its own? Is the passivity of the Self as represented in the Vedānta due to an influence of the Jaina-Sāṅkhya conception of the absolutely passive Jīva-Puruṣa? If so, this points to a most interesting, most ironical, hidden chapter in the history of Indian philosophy and civilization.

Also, it suggests a number of further questions for research. For example, one should look again to see to what extent the Self as "internal controller" (*antaryāmin*) is really active, according to the *Bhagavad Gītā* and the earlier Vedic view. To what extent is Ātman the unconcerned, aloof spectator of the individual's life-process, and to what extent an active all-controlling overseer? To what extent is Ātman comparable to the

[228] *Supra,* p. 454.

Great Self of the universe (*īśvara*) who, though not partaking of any suffering, yet holds all together and interferes with the cosmic dynamism periodically by descending into it—acting thus as a kind of universal unconscious, a cosmic buddhi-mahat,[229] which not only witnesses but also participates in the life-process? That is to say, had the Self more the function of buddhi in ancient times; and was its perfect aloofness, its purification, then effected through a systematic comparison with the Jaina-Sāṅkhya view? The *Bhagavad Gītā* should be the starting point for another investigation of the earlier, more active, ambiverted concept of the Self, wherein participation is combined miraculously with unconcern.[230]

The shining Śaṅkara, to whom we owe Advaita Vedānta—at least in the form in which it has stood for the past thousand years, and in which it prevails today as the typical and best-known philosophy of India—was not only a supreme scholastic thinker but a remarkable religious poet as well. His stanzas praising the Goddess (Śakti-Māyā-Devī) [231] are among the most celebrated examples of Indian devotional verse. They reveal a surprising aspect of his spirituality; for though he dismisses māyā in his philosophical writings and goes relentlessly beyond to the ineffable transcendency of Brahman, the "One-

[229] Cf. *supra*, pp. 319-322.

[230] *Editor's note:* These queries were thrown into Dr. Zimmer's notes together with a brief reference to Rāmānuja (whose theory of the actual "transformation" [*pariṇāma*] of Brahman into the reality of the world, though formulated later than Śaṅkara's theory of "illusory manifestation" [*vivarta*], is nevertheless based, Dr. Zimmer observes, on the works of earlier teachers—Taṅka, Dramiḍa, Guhadeva, Kapardin, and Bhāruci—and may represent a pre-Advaita point of view). Dr. Zimmer intended these notations as suggestions for further projects of research, the present section on Vedānta and those to follow on Buddhism and Tantra having been left by him in a very rough, preliminary state.

[231] For a study of the Goddess, cf. Zimmer, *Myths and Symbols in Indian Art and Civilization*, pp. 189-221.

without-a-second," here he gives devout praise to the "second" —Māyā, Mother of the World—and with all sincerity; expressing the mode of divine dualistic experience on the plane of bhakti, where the devotee regards and understands himself as the creature and servant of the deity-in-human-form.

Thou who bearest the manifold world of the visible and the invisible;
Who holdest the universe in Thy womb!
Who severest the thread of the play we play upon this earth!
Who lightest the lamp of wisdom; who bringest joy to the heart of Thy Lord, Śiva!
O Thou, Queen Empress of holy Benares! Divine Bestower of Food Inexhaustible!
Be gracious unto me and grant me alms.[232]

Other poems of Śaṅkara transport the spirit, however, beyond the sphere of the Holy Name and Blessed Form to the very brink of the experience of Nirguṇa Brahman. These were composed to serve as meditations to press or draw the mind through the final barrier of thought. The collection, "Morning Meditations" (*prātaḥ-smaraṇam-stotram*), opens with the lines:

"At dawn I call to mind the essence of the Self shining forth self-effulgent in my heart, the Fourth (*turīya*), which is existence-eternal, pure spiritual consciousness, and bliss—the goal and salvation of the 'Highest Swans.' [233] The being that regards the states of dream, waking, and deep sleep—that supreme essence

[232] Stanza from the "Hymn to Annapurnā" ("the one overflowing with food"); translated by Swāmī Nikhilānanda, *Self-Knowledge (Ātmabodha)*, New York, 1946, p. 185.

[233] *Paramahaṁsas:* the Vedāntic ascetics, roaming through the world in homeless freedom, are compared to wild swans, or ganders; for these are at home in the trackless lofty sky as well as in the waters of the lakes of the land, just as saints are at home in the formless sphere devoid of attributes as well as in the garb of the human individual, seemingly moving among us in the phenomenal sphere of bondage.

(*brahman*) am I. It is indivisible, without parts; I am not a combination of the five perishable elements. I am neither body, the senses, nor what is in the body (*antar-aṅga:* i.e., the mind). I am not the ego-function; I am not the group of the vital breath-forces; I am not intuitive intelligence (*buddhi*). Far from wife and son am I, far from land and wealth and other notions of that kind. I am the Witness, the Eternal, the Inner Self, the Blissful One (*śivo-'ham:* suggesting also, 'I am Śiva')." [234]

"Owing to ignorance of the rope the rope appears to be a snake; owing to ignorance of the Self the transient state arises of the individualized, limited, phenomenal aspect of the Self. The rope becomes a rope when the false impression disappears because of the statement of some credible person; because of the statement of my teacher I am not an individual life-monad (*jīvo-nāham*), I am the Blissful One (*śivo-'ham*).[235]

"I am not born; how can there be either birth or death for me?

"I am not the vital air; how can there be either hunger or thirst for me?

"I am not the mind, the organ of thought and feeling; how can there be either sorrow or delusion for me?

"I am not the doer; how can there be either bondage or release for me?" [236]

"Neither hatred and aversion nor passionate clinging have I; neither cupidity nor delusion. I am possessed of neither egotism nor self-infatuation. No claim of the ritualistic code of the duties of life (*dharma*), no worldly purpose (*artha*), no desire for any kind of enjoyment (*kāma*), no freedom attained or released to be sought (*mokṣa*), pertains to me.[237] I am Śiva, whose

[234] From the Meditation addressed to Ātman.

[235] Śaṅkara, *Ātmapañcaka* 2.

[236] *Ib.*, conclusion.

[237] I.e., "the three ends of secular life (*trivarga*) mean nothing to me; but the highest goal, release (*mokṣa*), which annihilates their meaning, is

being is spirituality and bliss. I am Śiva, the ever peaceful, perfect being.

"For me there is no death, no fear, no distinction of caste. I have no father, mother, birth, relatives, or friends. For me there is neither teacher nor pupil. I am Śiva ('the peaceful One'), whose form (*rūpa*) is spirituality and bliss." [238]

"I am neither male nor female, nor am I sexless. I am the Peaceful One, whose form is self-effulgent, powerful radiance. I am neither a child, a young man, nor an ancient; nor am I of any caste. I do not belong to one of the four life-stages.[239] I am the Blessed-Peaceful One, who is the only Cause of the origin and dissolution of the world." [240]

The grandiose monotony of these stanzas (to be repeated silently, relentlessly, in the solitary hours of meditation, as aids to the serious intent to break past the barriers of judgment; not to be read, sensitively, from some anthology) functions as a conscious, intentional challenge, directed against skepticism and worldly logic. Such a holy megalomania goes past the bounds of sense. With Śaṅkara, the grandeur of the supreme human experience becomes intellectualized and reveals its inhuman sterility. The stanzas are to be memorized and meditated upon; one is to become imbued with the attitude that they instill. Their mind-destroying paradox, boldly stated, endlessly repeated, is an instrument of guidance to the distant shore of transcendental peace.

---

equally meaningless to me. Were this not so, I should still be entangled in the dynamism of the process toward the goal, still far from the state of perfect, static repose."

[238] Śaṅkara, *Nirvāṇaśatka* 3 and 5.

As we have said, while instructing a pupil the teacher temporarily assumes the state of consciousness that still dwells with the pairs-of-opposites. When all the other opposites have lost their hold, this one of teacher and pupil remains. It is the last to go.

[239] Pupil, householder, hermit, wandering sage; cf. *supra*, pp. 155-160.

[240] Śaṅkara, *Nirvāṇamañjarī.*

IV. BUDDHISM

1.

Buddhahood

Buddhism was the only religious and philosophical message of India to spread far beyond the borders of its homeland. Conquering Asia to the north and east, it became in those vast areas the creed of the masses and shaped the civilization for centuries. This tends to conceal the fact that in essence Buddhism is meant only for the happy few. The philosophical doctrine at the root of the numerous fascinating popular features is not the kind of teaching that one would have expected to see made readily accessible to all. In fact, of the numerous answers that have been offered, during the millenniums, in all quarters of the world, as solutions to life's enigmas, this one must be ranked as the most uncompromising, obscure, and paradoxical.

The Buddhist monks of Ceylon tell us how—according to their tradition—the Order of the Buddha, the "Awakened One," was founded.[1] The great princely yogī, Gautama Śākyamuni, departed in secret from the palace and kingdom of his father

[1] A convenient rendition of the pertinent texts will be found in Henry Clarke Warren, *Buddhism in Translations,* Harvard Oriental Series, Vol. III, Cambridge, Mass., 1922.

and devoted himself to austerities for many years, until he arrived at the threshold of absolute Enlightenment. Sitting then beneath the Bo Tree, he was approached and tempted by the god Kāma-Māra ("Desire and Death"), the master magician of the world illusion.[2] Having overcome the tempter by remaining immovable in introversion, the prince experienced the Great Awakening, since which time he has been known as the "Awakened One," the Buddha. Absorbed in the vast experience, he remained beneath the Bo Tree, unmoved, untouched, for seven days and seven nights, "experiencing the bliss of the Awakening," then arose, as though to depart from that place, but could not depart. He placed himself beneath a second tree, and there again, for seven days and nights, remained merged in the stream of the bliss of the awakening. A third time, under a third tree, a spell of seven days and nights again absorbed him. He moved from tree to tree in this way for seven weeks, and during the fifth was protected by the hood of the serpent-king, Mucalinda.[3] Following the blessed period of forty-nine days, his glorious glance opened again to the world. Then he understood that what he had experienced was beyond speech; all endeavor to talk about it would be vain. He determined, consequently, not to attempt to make it known.

But Brahmā, the Universal Lord of the fleeting processes of life,[4] in his eternal abode at the summit of the egg-shaped cosmos, looking down on the Awakened One, realized that the decision had been made to withhold the teaching. Brahmā, himself a creature, indeed the highest of all creatures, was perturbed to know that the sublime knowledge (knowledge un-

[2] Cf. *supra,* pp. 205-206.

[3] Cf. *supra,* pp. 206-207.

[4] Not Brahman, the anonymous transcendent, but Brahmā, the highest creative being, who supervises the process of the unfolding of the flower of the world; cf. *supra,* pp. 424-425, and Zimmer, *Myths and Symbols in Indian Art and Civilization,* index, under "Brahmā."

known to Brahmā) was not to be revealed. He descended from the zenith and with prayer implored the Buddha to become the teacher of mankind, the teacher of the gods, the teacher of the created world. All were enwrapped in the womb of sleep, dreaming a dream known as the waking life of created beings. Brahmā implored that the truly Awake should open his path to all. For there might be some, the god urged, some happy few among these deluded beings, whose eyes would not be blinded by the dust of passion, and these would understand. As lotus flowers arising from the dark waters of a lake are to be found in various stages of maturity—some with buds still deep under water, some nearing the surface, some already open, prepared to drink the rays of the sun—just so, there might be among mankind and the gods a few prepared to hear.

The Buddha was moved, thus, to teach the path. Disciples came, an Order assumed shape, and the Buddhist tradition was brought into existence. Nevertheless, from the beginning, by the nature of the problem, the doctrine had been meant only for those prepared to hear. It was never intended to interfere with either the life and habits of the multitude or the course of civilization. In time it might even vanish from the world, becoming incomprehensible and meaningless—for the lack of anyone capable of treading the path to understanding; and this, too, would be right. In contrast, in other words, to the other great teachers of mankind (Zarathustra preaching the religious law of Persia; Confucius commenting on the restored system of early Chinese thought; Jesus announcing Salvation to the world) Gautama, the prince of the royal Śākya clan, is known properly as Śākya-muni: the "silent sage (*muni*) of the Śākyas"; [4a] for in spite of all that has been said and taught about him, the Buddha remains the symbol of something beyond what can be said and taught.

In the Buddhist texts there is no word that can be traced with

[4a] Cf. *supra*, p. 451, note 202.

unquestionable authority to Gautama Śākyamuni. We glimpse only the enlightening shadow of his personality; yet this suffices to merge us in a spiritual atmosphere that is unique. For though India in his time, half a millennium before Christ, was a veritable treasure-house of magical-religious lore—to our eyes a jungle of mythological systems—the teaching of the Enlightened One offered no mythological vision, either of the present world or of a world beyond, and no tangible creed. It was presented as a therapy, a treatment or cure, for those strong enough to follow it—a method and a process of healing. Apparently Gautama, at least in his terminology, broke from all the popular modes and accepted methods of Indian religious and philosophical instruction. He offered his advice in the practical manner of a spiritual physician, as though, through him, the art of Indian medicine were entering the sphere of spiritual problems—that grand old arena where, for centuries, magicians of every kind had been tapping powers by which they and their disciples lifted themselves to the heights of divinity.

Following the procedure of the physician of his day inspecting a patient, the Buddha makes four statements concerning the case of man. These are the so-called "Four Noble Truths" which constitute the heart and kernel of his doctrine. The first, *All life is sorrowful,* announces that we members of the human race are spiritually unhealthy, the symptom being that we carry on our shoulders a burden of sorrow; the disease is endemic. No discussion of any question of guilt goes with this matter-of-fact diagnosis; for the Buddha indulged in no metaphysical or mythological dissertations. He inquired into the cause on the practical, psychological level, however, hence we have, as the second of the "Four Noble Truths," *The cause of suffering is ignorant craving* (tṛṣṇā).

As in the teaching of the Sāṅkhya, an involuntary state of mind common to all creatures is indicated as the root of the world-disease. The craving of nescience, not-knowing-better (*avidyā*), is the problem—nothing less and nothing more. Such ignorance is a natural function of the life-process, yet not necessarily ineradicable; no more ineradicable than the innocence of a child. It is simply that we do not know that we are moving in a world of mere conventions and that our feelings, thoughts, and acts are determined by these. We imagine that our ideas about things represent their ultimate reality, and so we are bound in by them as by the meshes of a net. They are rooted in our own consciousness and attitudes; mere creations of the mind; conventional, involuntary patterns of seeing things, judging, and behaving; yet our ignorance accepts them in every detail, without question, regarding them and their contents as the facts of existence. This—this mistake about the true essence of reality—is the cause of all the sufferings that constitute our lives.

The Buddhist analysis goes on to state that our other symptoms (the familiar incidents and situations of our universal condition of non-well being) are derivatives, one and all, of the primary fault. The tragedies and comedies in which we get ourselves involved, which we bring forth from ourselves and in which we act, develop spontaneously from the impetus of our innermost condition of non-knowing. This sends us forth in the world with restricted senses and conceptions. Unconscious wishes and expectations, emanating from us in the shape of subjectively determined decisions and acts, transcend the limits of the present; they precipitate for us the future, being themselves determined from the past. Inherited from former births, they cause future births, the endless stream of life in which we are carried along being greater far than the bounds of individual birth and death. In other words, the ills of the individual cannot be understood in terms of the individual's mistakes; they are rooted in our human way of life, and the whole content of this way of life is a pathological blend of unfulfilled cravings, vexing longings, fears, regrets, and pains. Such a state of suffering is something from which it would be only sensible to be healed.

This radical statement about the problems that most of us take for granted as the natural concomitants of existence, and decide simply to endure, is balanced in the doctrine of the Buddha by the third and fourth of the "Four Noble Truths." Having diagnosed the illness and determined its cause, the physician next inquires whether the disease can be cured. The Buddhist prognostication is that a cure is indeed possible; hence we hear: *The suppression of suffering can be achieved;* and the last of the Four Truths prescribes the way: *The way is the Noble Eightfold Path*—Right View, Right Aspiration, Right Speech, Right Conduct, Right Means of Livelihood, Right Endeavor, Right Mindfulness, and Right Contemplation.

The Buddha's thoroughgoing treatment is guaranteed to eradicate the cause of the sickly spell and dream of ignorance, and thus to make possible the attainment of a state of serene, awakened perfection. No philosophical explanation of man or the universe is required, only this spiritual physician's program of psycho-dietetics. And yet the doctrine can hardly appeal to the multitude; for these are not convinced that their lives are as unwholesome as they obviously are. Only those few who not only would like to try, but actually feel acutely a pressing need to undertake some kind of thoroughgoing treatment, would have the will and stamina to carry to the end such an arduous, self-ordained discipline as that of the Buddhist cure.

The way of Gautama Śākyamuni is called the "middle path"; for it avoids extremes. One pair of extremes is that of the outright pursuit of worldly desires, on the one hand, and the severe, ascetic, bodily discipline of such contemporaries of the Buddha as the Jainas, on the other, whose austerity was designed to culminate in annihilation of the physical frame. Another pair of extremes is that of skepticism, denying the possibility of transcendental knowledge, and the argumentative assertion of undemonstrable metaphysical doctrines. Buddhism eschews the blind alleys to either side and conduces to an attitude that will of itself lead one to the transcendental experience. It rejects explicitly *all* of the contending formulae of the intellect, as inadequate either to lead to or to express the paradoxical truth, which reposes far, far beyond the realm of cerebral conceptions.

A conversation of the Buddha, recorded among the so-called "Long Dialogues," enumerates an extended list of the practical and theoretical disciplines by which people master various skills, crafts, and professions, or seek some understanding of their own nature and the meaning of the universe. All are described and then dismissed without criticism, but with the formula: "Such knowledge and opinions, if thoroughly mastered, will lead inevitably to certain ends and produce certain results in one's life. The Enlightened One is aware of all these possible consequences, and also of what lies behind them. But he does not attach much importance to this knowledge. For within himself he fosters another knowledge—the knowledge of cessation, of the discontinuance of worldly existence, of utter repose by emancipation. He has perfect insight into the manner of the springing into existence of our sensations and feelings, and into the manner of their vanishing again with all their sweetness and bitterness, and into the way of escape from them altogether, and into the manner in which, by non-attachment to them through right knowledge of their character, he has himself won release from their spell." [5]

Buddhism attaches no serious importance to such knowledge as entangles men more tightly in the net of life, knowledge that adds a comfortable material or interesting spiritual background to existence and thereby only contributes additional substance to the maintenance of the personality. Buddhism teaches that the value attributed to a thing is determined by the particular pattern of life from which it is regarded and the personality

[5] *Dīgha-nikāya* 1.

concerned. The weight of a fact or idea varies with the unenlightenment of the observer—his spontaneous commitment to certain spheres of phenomena and ranges of human value. The atmosphere, nay the world, surrounding and overpowering him, is continually being produced from his own unconscious nature, and affects him in terms of his commitment to his own imperfections. Its traits are the phenomenal projections of his inner state of ignorance sent out into the realm of sense-perception and there, as it were, discovered by an act of empirical experience. Hence Buddhism denies, finally, the force and validity of everything that can be known.

A Tibetan author—a Buddhist Dalai-Lama—puts it this way: The one substance, which fundamentally is devoid of qualities, appears to be of various, completely differing flavors, according to the kind of being who tastes it. The same beverage which for the gods in their celestial realm will be the delightful drink of immortality, for men on earth will be mere water, and for the tormented inmates of hell a vile, disgusting liquid which they will be loath to swallow even though tortured with intolerable pangs of thirst.[6] The three qualities of, or ways of experiencing, the one substance are here nothing more than the normal effects of three orders of karma. The senses themselves are conditioned by the subjective forces that brought them into being and hold them under strict control. The world without is no mere illusion—it is not to be regarded as nonexistent; yet it derives its enchanting or appalling features from the involuntary inner attitude of the one who sees it. The alluring hues and frightening shadows that form its very tissue are projected reflexes of the tendencies of the psyche.

One lives, in other words, enveloped by the impulses of the various layers of one's own nature, woven in the spell of their

[6] *Editor's note:* I have not been able to locate the source of this passage. Compare, however, Candrakīrti, *Prasannapadā* 1. 50-54, in Th. Stcherbatsky, *The Conception of Buddhist Nirvana,* Leningrad, 1927, pp. 131-133.

specific atmosphere, to which one submits as to an outside world. The goal of the techniques of the Buddhist therapy is to bring this process of self-envelopment to a stop. The living process is likened to a fire burning. Through the involuntary activity of one's nature as it functions in contact with the outer world, life as we know it goes on incessantly. The treatment is the extinction (*nirvāṇa*) of the fire, and the Budda, the Awake, is the one no longer kindled or enflamed. The Buddha is far from having dissolved into non-being; it is not He who is extinct but the life illusion—the passions, desires, and normal dynamisms of the physique and psyche. No longer blinded, he no longer feels himself to be conditioned by the false ideas and attendant desires that normally go on shaping individuals and their spheres, life after life. The Buddha realizes himself to be void of the characteristics that constitute an individual subject to a destiny. Thus released from karma, the universal law, he reposes beyond fate, no longer subject to the consequences of personal limitations. What other people behold when they look upon his physical presence is a sort of mirage; for he is intrinsically devoid of the attributes that they venerate and are themselves striving to attain.

Buddhist art has attempted to render this paradoxical experience of the Enlightened One in certain curious works of sculpture, which represent the scene of the temptation of the Buddha. The fierce hosts of Kāma-Māra, the tempter, assail the meditation of the one about to be enlightened as he sits beneath the holy tree. They brandish weapons, fling uprooted trees and prodigious rocks against him, and attempt by every means to break the calm of his meditation. By threats they strive to arouse in him some fear of death, the trace of an impulse of self-preservation, a wish to cling to the perishable frame of the body, which they are menacing with destruction. Simultaneously, the charm of life—all its loveliness—in the guise of divine women, is displayed before him; so that the allure of the senses should move him—not literally bring him from his place, but only provoke the least stir of a will to enjoy, which would amount to a step back into the thralldom of life. But both temptations fail. The powers work in vain to discover in his nature some flaw, some last remainder of fear and desire. The menacing and the enticing gestures equally fail to touch him; for he has vanished from the sphere of the currents and cross-currents of delight and despair, which constitute the warp and woof of life. In the works of sculpture in question, this unassailable state of the "one who cannot be reached any more" is expressed by omitting the Buddha-image from the composition. Amid the turmoil of the hosts and the captivating attitudes of the daughters of the tempter, the holy seat beneath the Bo Tree is empty; the Buddha is not to be seen (*Plate IX*).

The De-spirated One [7] is never depicted through visible or tangible features in the early Buddhist monuments; for anything tangible or visible would amount to a description of him —either as a man or as a god. He would be endowed then with such features as befit beings shaped by the influences of former lives, beings brought by the law of karma into human or celestial forms. Any shape would by its nature communicate a wrong notion of his essence, which is on a non-depictable plane. A shape would show him to be tied by the subtle bonds of karma to the sphere of some set of limiting and transitory qualifications, whereas the whole sense of his being is that he is released from such symptoms of ignorance and desire. In viewing these early works of Buddhist sculpture one is to think of the Buddha as truly there, on the throne of Enlightenment, but as though he were a bubble of emptiness. Footprints on the ground and a slight hollowing of the cushion betray his presence, but no visible trait could possibly render the essence of his nature. Visible traits (beauty and grandeur, for example, or the dazzling

[7] This is a term contrived by Dr. Ananda K. Coomaraswamy, a literal rendering of *nir*-(de-)*vāna* (spirated), or "blown out."

charm of a divinity) are the signs of ordinary beings, and reveal their karma. But the Buddha is without karma and therefore must be rendered without determinable form. That is the most consistent, nay the only perfectly adequate way to designate his absolute emancipation from the law that enjoins all to go on assuming the varying transitory garbs of renewed existences.

The Buddha's doctrine is called *yāna.* The word means "a vehicle," or, more to the point, "a ferryboat." The "ferryboat" is the principal image employed in Buddhism to render the sense and function of the doctrine. The idea persists through all the differing and variously conflicting teachings of the numerous Buddhist sects that have evolved in many lands, during the long course of the magnificent history of the widely disseminated doctrine. Each sect describes the vehicle in its own way, but no matter how described, it remains always the ferry.

To appreciate the full force of this image, and to understand the reason for its persistence, one must begin by realizing that in everyday Hindu life the ferryboat plays an extremely prominent role. It is an indispensable means of transportation in a continent traversed by many mighty rivers and where bridges are practically nonexistent. To reach the goal of almost any journey one will require a ferry, time and time again, the only possible crossing of the broad and rapid streams being by boat or by a ford. The Jainas called their way of salvation the ford (*tīrtha*), and the supreme Jaina teachers were, as we have seen, *Tīrthaṅkaras,* "those making, or providing, a ford." In the same sense, Buddhism, by its doctrine, provides a ferryboat across the rushing river of saṁsāra to the distant bank of liberation. .Through enlightenment (*bodhi*) the individual is transported.

The gist of Buddhism can be grasped more readily and adequately by fathoming the main metaphors through which it appeals to our intuition than by a systematic study of the complicated superstructure, and the fine details of the developed teaching. For example, one need only think for a moment about the actual, everyday experience of the process of crossing a river in a ferryboat, to come to the simple idea that inspires and underlies all of the various rationalized systematizations of the doctrine. To enter the Buddhist vehicle—the boat of the discipline—means to begin to cross the river of life, from the shore of the common-sense experience of non-enlightenment, the shore of spiritual ignorance (*avidyā*), desire (*kāma*), and death (*māra*), to the yonder bank of transcendental wisdom (*vidyā*), which is liberation (*mokṣa*) from this general bondage. Let us consider, briefly, the actual stages involved in any crossing of a river by ferry, and see if we can experience the passage as a kind of initiation-by-analogy into the purport of the stages of the Buddhist pilgrim's progress to his goal.

Standing on the nearer bank, this side the stream, waiting for the boat to put in, one is a part of its life, sharing in its dangers and opportunities and in whatever may come to pass on it. One feels the warmth or coolness of its breezes, hears the rustle of its trees, experiences the character of its people, and knows that its earth is underfoot. Meanwhile the other bank, the far bank, is beyond reach—a mere optical image across the broad, flowing waters that divide us from its unknown world of forms. We have really no idea what it will be like to stand in that distant land. How this same scenery of the river and its two shorelines will appear from the other side we cannot imagine. How much of these houses will be visible among the trees? What prospects up and down the river will unfold? Everything over here, so tangible and real to us at present—these real, solid objects, these tangible forms—will be no more than remote, visual patches, inconsequential optical effects, without power to touch us, either to help or to harm. This solid earth itself will be a visual, horizontal line beheld from afar, one detail of an extensive scenic view, beyond our experience, and of no more force for us than a mirage.

The ferryboat arrives; and as it comes to the landing we regard it with a feeling of interest. It brings with it something of the air of that yonder land which will soon be our destination. Yet when we are entering it we still feel like members of the world from which we are departing, and there is still that feeling of unreality about our destination. When we lift our eyes from the boat and boatman, the far bank is still only a remote image, no more substantial than it was before.

Softly the ferryboat pushes off and begins to glide across the moving waters. Presently one realizes that an invisible line has been recently, imperceptibly passed, beyond which the bank left behind is assuming gradually the unsubstantiality of a mere visual impression, a kind of mirage, while the farther bank, drawing slowly nearer, is beginning to turn into something real. The former dim remoteness is becoming the new reality and soon is solid ground, creaking under keel—real earth—the sand and stone on which we tread in disembarking; whereas the world left behind, recently so tangible, has been transmuted into an optical reflex devoid of substance, out of reach and meaningless, and has forfeited the spell that it laid upon us formerly—with all its features, all its people and events—when we walked upon it and ourselves were a portion of its life. Moreover, the new reality, which now possesses us, provides an utterly new view of the river, the valley, and the two shores, a view very different from the other, and completely unanticipated.

Now while we were in the process of crossing the river in the boat, with the shore left behind becoming gradually vaguer and more meaningless—the streets and homes, the dangers and pleasures, drawing steadily away—there was a period when the shoreline ahead was still rather far off too; and during that time the only tangible reality around us was the boat, contending stoutly with the current and precariously floating on the rapid waters. The only details of life that then seemed quite substantial and that greatly concerned us were the various elements and implements of the ferrryboat itself: the contours of the hull and gunwales, the rudder and the sail, the various ropes, and perhaps a smell of tar. The rest of existence, whether out ahead or left behind, signified no more than a hopeful prospect and a fading recollection—two poles of unrealistic sentimental association affiliated with certain clusters of optical effects far out-of-hand.

In the Buddhist texts this situation of the people in a ferryboat is compared to that of the good folk who have taken passage in the vehicle of the doctrine. The boat is the teaching of the Buddha, and the implements of the ferry are the various details of Buddhist discipline: meditation, yoga-exercises, the rules of ascetic life, and the practice of self-abnegation. These are the only things that disciples in the vehicle can regard with deep conviction; such people are engrossed in a fervent belief in the Buddha as the ferryman and the Order as their bounding gunwale (framing, protecting, and defining their perfect ascetic life) and in the guiding power of the doctrine. The shoreline of the world has been left behind but the distant one of release not yet attained. The people in the boat, meanwhile, are involved in a peculiar sort of middle prospect which is all their own.

Among the conversations of the Buddha known as the "Medium-length Dialogues," there appears a discourse on the value of the vehicle of the doctrine. First the Buddha describes a man who, like himself or any of his followers, becomes filled with a loathing of the perils and delights of secular existence. That man decides to quit the world and cross the stream of life to the far land of spiritual safety. Collecting wood and reeds, he builds a raft, and by this means succeeds in attaining the other shore. The Buddha confronts his monks, then, with the question.

"What would be your opinion of this man," asks the Buddha, "would he be a clever man, if, out of gratitude for the raft that has carried him across the stream to safety, he, having reached the other shore, should cling to it, take it on his back, and walk about with the weight of it?"

The monks reply. "No, certainly the man who would do that would not be a clever man."

The Buddha goes on. "Would not the clever man be the one who left the raft (of no use to him any longer) to the current of the stream, and walked ahead without turning back to look at it? Is it not simply a tool to be cast away and forsaken once it has served the purpose for which it was made?"

The disciples agree that this is the proper attitude to take toward the vehicle, once it has served its purpose.

The Buddha then concludes. "In the same way the vehicle of the doctrine is to be cast away and forsaken, once the other shore of Enlightenment (*nirvāṇa*) has been attained." [8]

The rules of the doctrine are intended for beginners and advanced pupils, but become meaningless for the perfect. They can be of no service to the truly enlightened, unless to serve him, in his role of teacher, as a convenient medium by which to communicate some suggestion of the truth to which he has attained. It was by means of the doctrine that the Buddha sought to express what he had realized beneath the tree as inexpressible. He could communicate with the world through his doctrine and thus help his unprepared disciples when they were at the start, or somewhere in the middle, of the way. Talking down to the level of relative or total ignorance, the doctrine can move the still imperfect yet ardent mind; but it can say nothing any more, nothing ultimately real, to the mind that has cast away darkness. Like the raft, it must be left behind, therefore, once the goal has been attained; for it can thenceforth be no more than an inappropriate burden.

Moreover, not the raft only, but the stream too, becomes void of reality for the one who has attained the other shore. When such a one turns around to look again at the land left behind,

[8] *Majjhima-Nikāya* 3. 2. 22. 135.

what does he see? What *can* one see who has crossed the horizon beyond which there is no duality? He looks—and there *is* no "other shore"; there is no torrential separating river; there is no raft; there is no ferryman; there can have been no crossing of the nonexistent stream. The whole scene of the two banks and the river between is simply gone. There can be no such thing for the enlightened eye and mind, because to see or think of anything as something "other" (a distant reality, different from one's own being) would mean that full Enlightenment had not yet been attained. There can be an "other shore" only for people still in the spheres of dualistic perception; those this side the stream or still inside the boat and heading for the "other shore"; those who have not yet disembarked and thrown away the raft. Illumination means that the delusory distinction between the two shores of a worldly and a transcendental existence no longer holds. There *is* no stream of rebirths flowing between two separated shores: no saṁsāra and no nirvāṇa.

Thus the long pilgrimage to perfection through innumerable existences, motivated by the virtues of self-surrender and accomplished at the cost of tremendous sacrifices of ego, disappears like a landscape of dreams when one awakes. The long-continued story of the heroic career, the many lives of increasing self-purification, the picture-book legend of detachment won through the long passion, the saintly epic of the way to become a savior—enlightened and enlightening—vanishes like a rainbow. All becomes void; whereas once, when the dream was coming to pass step by step, with ever-recurrent crises and decisions, the unending series of dramatic sacrifices held the soul completely under its spell. The secret meaning of Enlightenment is that this titan-effort of pure soul-force, this ardent struggle to reach the goal by acts, ever-renewed, of beautiful self-surrender, this supreme, long strife through ages of incarnations to attain release from the universal law of moral causation (*karma*)—is without reality. At the threshold of its own realization it dissolves, together with its background of self-entangled life, like a nightmare at the dawn of day.

For the Buddha, therefore, even the notion of nirvāṇa is without meaning. It is bound to the pairs-of-opposites and can be employed only in opposition to saṁsāra—the vortex where the life-force is spellbound in ignorance by its own polarized passions of fear and desire.

The Buddhist way of ascetic training is designed to conduce to the understanding that there is no substantial ego—nor any object anywhere—that lasts, but only spiritual processes, welling and subsiding: sensations, feelings, visions. These can be suppressed or set in motion and watched at will. The idea of the extinction of the fire of lust, ill will, and ignorance becomes devoid of meaning when this psychological power and point of view has been attained; for the process of life is no longer experienced as a burning fire. To speak seriously, therefore, of nirvāṇa as a goal to be attained is simply to betray the attitude of one still remembering or experiencing the process as the burning of the fire. The Buddha himself adopts such an attitude only for the teaching of those still suffering, who feel that they would like to make the flames extinct. His famous Fire Sermon is an accommodation, not by any means the final word of the sage whose final word is silence. From the perspective of the Awake, the Illumined One, such opposed verbalizations as nirvāṇa and saṁsāra, enlightenment and ignorance, freedom and bondage, are without reference, void of content. That is why the Buddha refused to discuss nirvāṇa. The pointlessness of the connotations that would inevitably seem to be intended by his words would confuse those trying to follow his mysterious way. They being still in the ferryboat framed of these conceptions and requiring them as devices of transport to the shore of understanding, their teacher would not deny before them the practical function of such convenient terms; and yet would not give the terms weight, either, by discussion. Words like "enlightenment," "ignorance," "freedom," and "entanglement" are preliminary helps, referring to no ultimate reality, mere hints or signposts for the traveler, which serve to point him to the goal of an attitude beyond their own suggestions of a contrariety. The raft being finally left behind, and the vision lost of the two banks and the separating river, then there is in truth neither the realm of life and death nor that of release. Moreover, there is no Buddhism—no boat, since there are neither shores nor waters between. There is no boat, and there is no boatman—no Buddha.

The great paradox of Buddhism, therefore, is that no Buddha has ever come into existence to enlighten the world with Buddhist teachings. The life and mission of Gautama Śākyamuni is only a general misunderstanding by the unenlightened world, helpful and necessary to guide the mind toward illumination, but to be discarded when—and if—enlightenment is to be attained. Any monk failing to get rid of such ideas clings (by clinging to them) to the general mundane delusion which he imagines himself to be striving to leave behind. For, briefly, so long as nirvāṇa is looked upon as something different from saṁsāra, the most elementary error about existence still has to be overcome. These two ideas mirror contrary attitudes of the semiconscious individual toward himself and the outer sphere in which he lives; but beyond this subjective range they have no substantiation.

Buddhism—this popular creed which has won the reverence of all Eastern Asia—contains this boldest paradox at its very root; the most startling reading of reality ever whispered into human ear. All good Buddhists tend to avoid, therefore, statements about existence and non-existence. Their "Middle Path" goes between by simply pointing out that the validity of a conception is always relative to one's position along the road of progress from Ignorance to Buddhahood. Attitudes of assertion and negation belong to worldly beings on the hither bank of ignorance, and to pious people making headway in the crowded ferryboat of the doctrine. Such a conception as Voidness (*śūnyatā*) can have meaning only for an ego clinging to the reality of things; one who has lost the feeling that things are real can make no sense of such a word. And yet words of this kind remain in all the texts and teachings. Indeed, the great *practical* miracle of Buddhism is that terms of this kind, used successfully as steppingstones, do not become rocks on which to found and build a creed.

The greater portion of the Buddhist literature that has become available and familiar to us in translation is adjusted in this way, pedagogically, to the general human attitude of partial ignorance. It is intended for the teaching and guidance of disciples. It outlines and points the way along the path of the Buddhas (*buddha-mārga*), depicting the career of the hero "going to enlightenment" (*bodhicarya*). Its position, therefore, is comparable to that of the ferryman inviting people on our hither bank to enter his boat and cross the waters, or guiding his crew in their handling of the craft during the passage. The yonder bank is represented only in a preliminary, very sketchy way; only hinted at and attractively suggested, for the captivation and continued inspiration of those still spellbound by the notions of this dualistic shore—men and women trying to make up their minds to leave, or else in the toilsome stages of crossing to an absolutely contrary point of view, which they will perceive presently to be utterly inconsistent with their expectation.

This pedagogical interest of Buddhism entails, unavoidably, a screening of the ultimate essence of the doctrine. The introductory statements, graded as they are, lead right up to the goal—but then have to be put behind, or the goal itself will never be attained. Anyone wishing to gain some inkling of the transformation of perspective intended will have to turn from the great volumes of initiatory conversations, questions, analyses, and codifications to a somewhat less conspicuous, curious, special branch of Buddhist writings, in which an attempt is made actually to state something of the supreme experience.

One may well marvel at the bold experiment—an effort to represent the ultimate essence of an incommunicable intuition through words and conceptions familiar to the usual philosophical and pious understanding. But, wonderful to relate, a vivid sense of the ineffable reality known in "extinction" (*nirvāṇa)* is actually conveyed in this unexampled body of strange, esoteric texts. They are named *Prajñā-pāramitā:* "The Accomplishment of Transcendental Wisdom," or "The Wisdom (*prajñā*) Gone to the Other Shore (*pāram-itā*)." And they are a series of the most curious dialogues, conducted in a sort of conversation-circle of Buddhas and Bodhisattvas—mostly legendary beings, superhuman saviors, without a single merely human, still half-bewildered aspirant-to-enlightenment among them.

The Illumined Ones behave in a way that should be rather shocking and confusing to any sound thinker, who, from habit and firm determination, is resolved to keep his feet on the ground. In a sort of mocking conversation, these Buddhas and Bodhisattvas entertain themselves with enigmatical statements of the unstatable truth. They delight in declaring, time and again, that there is no such thing as Buddhism, no such thing as Enlightenment, nothing remotely resembling the extinction of nirvāṇa, setting traps for each other and trying to trick each other into assertions that might imply—even remotely—the reality of such conceptions. Then, most artfully, they always elude the cleverly placed hazards and hidden pitfalls—and all engage in a glorious, transolympian laugh; for the merest hint of a notion of nirvāṇa would have betrayed a trace of the vestige of the opposite attitude, saṁsāra, and the clinging to individual existence.

For example, in one of the texts the Buddha makes the following declaration to his pupil Subhūti. "Whosoever stands in the ferryboat of the saviors-who-lead-to-the-far-bank shall bear in mind the rescue of all living beings, conducting them to release-and-extinction in the pure and perfect nirvāṇa. And when, by virtue of this attitude, he has rescued all living beings, no being whatsoever has been made to reach nirvāṇa."

Following this paradoxical remark, the Buddha supplies his explanation. "Why, O Subhūti, is this so? Because, if this savior had the notion of the actual existence of any being, he could not be called a perfect Enlightened One. If there could occur to him the conception of a living being donning the garb of various bodies and migrating through numerous existences, or the idea of an individual personality, then he could not be called a Bodhisattva, 'a being whose essence is Enlightenment.' And why is this so? Because there is no such thing as anything or anybody standing in the vehicle of the Enlightened Ones." [9]

Another text states that on a certain day, when myriads of gods had flocked together to celebrate with a great feast the solemn occasion of the Buddha's preaching of a sermon, they were all saying joyfully: "Forsooth, this is the second time that the wheel of the true law has been set in motion on Indian soil, let us go and watch!" But the Buddha, turning stealthily to Subhūti, whispered something that he would not tell the gods; for it was beyond their power of understanding. "This is not the second time that the wheel of the true law has been set in motion; there is no setting in motion of anything, nor any stopping of the motion of anything. Knowing just that, is the perfection of wisdom (*prajñā-pāramitā*), which is characteristic of the beings whose essence is enlightenment." [10]

These bewildering texts, with their explicit teaching of the Wisdom of the Far Bank (*prajñā-pāramitā*), belong to a later period of the Buddhist tradition, the stage of the so-called "Great Ferryboat," or Mahāyāna, which teaches that the secret meaning and goal of the doctrine is the universal Buddhahood

[9] *Vajracchedikā* 17.

[10] *Aṣṭasāhasrikā Prajñāpāramitā* 9.

of *all* beings. This is in contrast to the earlier doctrine of the so-called "Little Ferryboat," the Hīnayāna, where, though an effective way to *individual release* is disclosed, the accomplishment of *Buddhahood* is regarded as a goal attained only by very few throughout the cycling ages. The *Prajñā-pāramitā* texts of the Mahāyāna were intended to counteract what their authors regarded as a basic misunderstanding, in the Hīnayāna, of the very essence of the wisdom of the Buddha, a misunderstanding caused by thinking that the preliminary teaching was an expression of the Buddha's transcendental realization. The emphasis on the means, the path, the rules of the order, and the ethical disciplines of the ferry-ride was stifling the essence of the tradition within the very fold of Buddhism itself. The Mahāyāna way, on the other hand, was to reassert this essence by means of a bold and stunning paradox.

"The Enlightened One," we read, "sets forth in the Great Ferryboat; but there is nothing from which he sets forth. He starts from the universe; but in truth he starts from nowhere. His boat is manned with all the perfections; and is manned by no one. It will find its support on nothing whatsoever and will find its support on the state of all-knowing, which will serve it as a non-support. Moreover, no one has ever set forth in the Great Ferryboat; no one will ever set forth in it, and no one is setting forth in it now. And why is this? Because neither the one setting forth nor the goal for which he sets forth is to be found: therefore, who should be setting forth, and whither?" [11]

The conceptions that go to make up the communicated doctrine are, from the point of view of the Enlightened One, without corresponding ultimate realities. They are part of a raft, which is good and helpful for the crossing of a stream of ignorance and indispensable for disciples on the way, but they are devoid of meaning for the finished master whose crossing is accomplished. They mirror shapes of the transitory processes of

[11] *Ib.* 1.

life, and so have no lasting substance. They lead to enlightenment, and yet are fallacious, broken reflections of its truth. Indeed, they are different from what is known to the enlightened; just as the boat, or raft, is different from the farther shore. Such helpful concepts emerge, together with all the rest of these visible and thinkable things round about us, from an infinitely pure reality, which is beyond conceptions, void of limiting qualities, undifferentiated, and untouched by the dialectic of the pairs-of-opposites, of which it is the ground—just as the heavens and the atmosphere, which are visible, stand as apparitions on the fundamentally pure void of ether.

"Just as, in the vast ethereal sphere, stars and darkness, light and mirage, dew, foam, lightning and clouds emerge, become visible, and vanish again, like the features of a dream—so everything endowed with an individual shape is to be regarded." Thus we read in one of the most celebrated of these Mahāyāna texts of meditation.[12] From the intangible matter that pervades the universe, tangible shapes emerge as its ephemeral transformations. But their breaking into existence and their vanishing away does not affect the limpid, profound serenity of the basic element, the space of which they fill for their short spell of being. Comparably, the Enlightened Ones, with unruffled self-composure, watch their own sensations, feelings, and other experiences of the outer world and their inner life, remaining untouched by them, beyond the changes continually coming to pass in them, like the reposeful ether beyond the changes of the forms within its infinite space.

So far as the Awakened One is concerned, the notion of Awakening is at bottom as devoid of meaning as the notion that there is a dreamlike state that precedes it (the state of ordinary life—our own attitude and atmosphere). It is unreal. It does not exist. It is the sail of the nonexistent raft. The Buddhist yogī is taught, by means of the disciplines, to realize,

[12] *Vajracchedikā* 32.

within, such a peace as one perceives looking outward into the vast ethereal realm with its sublime display of transient forms. He is taught to experience, gazing inward, through successive stages of self-control and meditation, an ethereal essence of his own—sheer voidness, unsullied by any process of the mind and not changed by any effect of the senses in their contact with the outer world. By imbuing himself completely with an utter aloofness comparable to that of the celestial atmosphere in relation to the various luminous and darkening phenomena that pass through it, he realizes the real meaning of the Buddhist transcendental wisdom, the nature of the view from the yonder shore. He comes to know that fundamentally nothing whatsoever is happening to the true essence of his nature, nothing to give cause for either distress or joy.

The disciple Subhūti said: "Profound, O Venerable One, is the perfect Transcendental Wisdom."

Quoth the Venerable One: "Abysmally profound, like the space of the universe, O Subhūti, is the perfect Transcendental Wisdom."

The disciple Subhūti said again: "Difficult to be attained through Awakening is the perfect Transcendental Wisdom, O Venerable One."

Quoth the Venerable One: "That is the reason, O Subhūti, why no one ever attains it through Awakening." [13]

And the two—we may imagine—roared with laughter. Here is metaphysics as the intellect's greatest game.

[13] *Aṣṭasāhasrikā Prajñāpāramitā* 8.

2.

The Great Buddhist Kings

BY FAR the most original and daring traits of Buddhism are the negative ones—what it has succeeded in omitting. There is no display of encyclopedic omniscience such as we find in the systems of the Jaina and Ājīvika. There is no doctrine of a substantial Self in man or of a cosmic Self as the ultimate world-reality, such as we find, variously, in the Sāṇkhya, in Veda and Vedānta, and in the disciplines of bhakti. There is no description or definition of any blissful state after release and death—in contrast to the rich delineations in the Upaniṣads. And we find no metaphysical inferences proposed, no ontological conclusions; for the Buddha's method was strictly psychological. The traditional schemes of macromicrocosmic comparison (whereby the structures of the universe and the human organism were aligned as parallel manifestations of divine cosmic forces), the Enlightened One ignored as not conducing to illumination, leaving behind him the entire load, or treasure, of precious and intricate insights. In a land where debates and endless hairsplitting discussions, mental tournaments, and metaphysical demonstrations had been for centuries the very entertainment of the educated classes, where the heroes even of the populace were the wise, the doctors in theology and metaphysics (who, indeed, were rewarded to such a degree that they had become a little spoiled and dull with vain self-conceit), and where a contest in the rhetorical stadium before an audience of the learned was a delight to courtiers and townsfolk alike (bringing considerable material wealth, incidentally, to the victor) Gautama Śākyamuni—when at last he had determined to announce what he had found, to the happy few mature enough to grasp it—refused to make any statement about the classic questions every teacher was supposed to solve.

His attitude, however, was so impressive and the teaching so inspiring that he not only escaped contempt and obscurity, but drew an ever increasing multitude of unsought followers. These flocked to him from all classes and professions. Even in the beginning, Brāhmans of the oldest families were conspicuous among the members of the Order, while in later centuries wealthy merchants (the capitalists of the post-feudal, late medieval age), as well as princes and kings, rivaled each other in supporting the Buddhist community with lavish gifts.[14]

After all, to know many things is not so important; the great thing is to know and practice the one thing that matters—which is that one should forsake all to which one is attached. A way is shown in Buddhism, and described with technical details, for the attainment of such release—along the Noble Eightfold Path. And moreover the assurance is given that, in due time, progress along this way will of itself bring the answers to all the questions treated by the popular rhetoricians.

In the course of the twenty-five centuries that have elapsed since the Buddha taught in the parks and villages of northeastern India, many attempts have been made to reconcile his negative attitude with the unquenchable craving for metaphysical philosophizing that characterizes the Hindu mind. The end has

[14] According to one disgruntled orthodox reaction: When the gods were defeated in one of their innumerable cosmic battles with the titans, they sought the protection of Viṣṇu, and he, in answer to their prayers, was born under the delusive form of the Buddha, by whom the titans were then deceived; being induced to abandon the religion of the Vedas, they lost all power as warriors. From that time, the faith of the Buddha has flourished, and many, unfortunately, are the heretics who have forsaken the sacred ordinances of the Vedas.—Lt. Col. Vans Kennedy, *Researches into the Nature and Affinity of Ancient and Hindu Mythology,* London, 1831, p. 251.

been achieved, as a rule, by extracting and developing the metaphysical principles implicit in the psychological teachings and techniques. But though the later thinkers found it imperative to convert Gautama's ungarnished practical advice into a full-blown theoretical system, they did not succeed in eliminating the core-mystery; this remains beyond the reach of their cogent thoughts. And so, whenever in the course of perusing their grave attempts we come to a point where the rational theorizing becomes highly paradoxical, or where a bold enigmatical formula dispenses suddenly with all that a rational mind might have been expected to require, we should allow this to remind us of the fundamental attitude of the Buddha with respect to the possibility of convincing anyone, through talk and teaching, of the truth that he himself gained through Enlightenment alone.

Buddhist metaphysics and the verbal warfare of incipient sects began to trouble the concentration of the disciples even before the death, or *parinirvāṇa* ("the final or perfect nirvāṇa"), of their Master. That the as yet unilluminated followers should have discussed among themselves questions that the Illumined One refused to elucidate was inevitable; the canonical "Dialogues" abound in their finely pointed queries. And there was trouble, also, as to the details of the monastic life. "There is one thing in the world, O monks," the Buddha is said to have proclaimed, "which, in coming into existence, exists to the disadvantage and unhappiness of many people, gods as well as men." "What is this one thing?" they asked. "Dissension in the Order," the Buddha replied. "For in an order that has been divided, there are reciprocal quarrels as well as reciprocal abuses, reciprocal disagreement and desertion, and in such an order they are discontented and enjoy no contentment, and there is diversity of opinion even among those who are content." [15]

[15] *Iti-vuttaka* 18. (Translated by Justin Hartley Moore, *Sayings of the Buddha, the Iti-vuttaka,* New York, 1908, p. 31.)

It is recorded that the following complicated report one day was brought to the Buddha's ears:

"A certain monk, Lord, had committed an offence which he considered as an offence, while the other monks considered that offence as no offence. Afterwards he began to consider that offence as no offence, and the other monks began to consider that offence as an offence. . . . Then those monks pronounced expulsion against that monk for his refusal to see that offence. . . . Then that monk got his companions and friends among the monks on his side, and sent a messenger to his companions and friends among the monks of the whole country. . . . And the partisans of the expelled monk persevered on the side of that expelled monk and followed him."

The Buddha exclaimed piteously: "The Order is divided! The Order is divided!" and delivered words of stern rebuke to those that had taken it upon themselves to excommunicate their fellow. "Do not think, O monks," he declared, "that you are to pronounce expulsion against a monk for this or that, saying, 'It occurs to us to expel this monk.' "[16]

When the founder was no longer alive the party differences grew; and yet, on the whole, we find in Buddhist history an impressive tendency to tolerate minor and even major differences of practice and opinion—perhaps as a result of the warnings of Gautama himself against dissension. The Pāli canon of Ceylon records that immediately following his decease, a certain monk named Subhaddha said to his companions: "Do not grieve, do not lament! We are happily rid of the Great Ascetic. We used to be annoyed by being told, 'This beseems you, this beseems you not'; but now we shall be able to do what we like, and what we do not like we shall not have to do."[17] The great monk Kāśyapa, hearing of this disgraceful utterance, proposed

[16] *Mahāvagga* 10. 1.

[17] *Cullavagga* 11. 1. (As summarized in H. Kern, *Manual of Indian Buddhism,* 1896, pp. 101-102.)

that a council of the Brethren should be called for the purpose of rehearsing and establishing the precepts of their departed Master. Five hundred arhats [18] assembled at Rājagṛha (the ancient capital of Magadha) and in the course of a session that lasted seven months fixed the *Vinaya* ("Discipline") and *Dhamma* (Skr. *Dharma,* "Law"). But when in conclusion they issued a proclamation of their work, there came a celebrated monk named Purāṇa ("The Old One"), with five hundred followers, who refused to adhere to the resolutions of the Council. "The doctrine and the disciplinary rule have been well sung by the Elders," he admitted courteously; "nevertheless, even in such manner as it has been heard by me, and received by me from the very mouth of the Blessed One, in that manner will I bear it in my memory." And neither the Elders nor the recorders of the episode pronounced a single word of rebuke against this manifestation of independence.[19]

A second Buddhist council reported in the Pāli canon is supposed to have been assembled one hundred (or one hundred and ten) years following the parinirvāṇa of the Buddha, at Vaiśālī (modern Basarh, in the Hajipur subdivision of the Muzaffarpur District of Bihar Province),[20] for the purpose of condemning ten heretical practices of the monks of that vicinity. The precise nature of the practices cannot be determined from the brief notices of them given in the record, where they are described simply by such designations as "two fingers," "another village," "dwelling-place," etc.,[21] but they seem to

[18] An arhat is a Buddhist monk who has attained enlightenment.

[19] *Cullavagga* 11. 11; as cited by L. de la Vallée Poussin, "Councils and Synods (Buddhist)," in Hastings, *Encyclopaedia of Religion and Ethics,* Vol. IV, p. 181.

[20] This is the ancient city near which Vardhamāna Mahāvīra, the last of the Jaina Tīrthankaras (cf. *supra,* pp. 221-222), is supposed to have been born.

[21] *Cullavagga* 12.

have been of sufficient importance to split the community in two. The Ceylonese *Dīpavaṁsa* records that following their condemnation for heresy the rebuked monks retired and held a council of their own, and this has been called, significantly enough, even in the orthodox texts of the group against which it was directed, the Mahāsaṅgīti, the "Great Council."

The monks of the Great Council twisted the teaching round.
They broke up the original scriptures and made a new recension,
A chapter put in one place they put in another,
And distorted the sense and doctrine of the Five Nikāyas.
These monks—who knew neither what had been spoken at length
Nor what had been spoken in abstract, neither
What was the obvious nor what the higher meaning—
Put things referring to one matter as if they referred to another,
And destroyed much of the spirit by holding to the shadow of the letter.
They partly rejected the Sutta, and the Vinaya so deep,
And made another rival Sutta and Vinaya of their own.
The Parivāra abstract, and the book of the Abhidhamma,
The Paṭisambhidā, the Niddesa, and a portion of the Jātaka,
So much they put aside, and made others in their place.
They rejected the well-known rules of nouns and genders too,
Of composition and of literary skill, and put others in their place.[22]

Obviously, as T. W. Rhys Davids points out, the animus of this description is that of a group that regards itself as superior; and yet they are compelled to call the council of their opponents the Great Council, "which seems to show that the number of its adherents was not to be despised." [23] Each party possessed its own version of the commonly accepted books, and also,

[22] *Dīpavaṁsa* 5. 32ff.; as translated and cited by T. W. Rhys Davids, *Buddhism, Its History and Literature,* New York and London, 1896, p. 193. The various texts mentioned are portions of the orthodox Pāli canon, as preserved by the Buddhist community of Ceylon.

[23] *Ib.*, pp. 193-194.

apparently, its own notions concerning the essence of the doctrine. "The main point of difference," writes Dr. Radhakrishnan, "between the orthodox and the progressive sections seems to have been on the question of the attainment of Buddhahood. The Sthaviras [the "Elders," i.e., those who had summoned the council of Vaiśālī] held that Buddhahood was a quality to be acquired by a strict observance of the rules of the Vinaya [the recorded Canon Law]. The progressives maintained that it was a quality inborn in every human being, and that by adequate development it was capable of raising its possessor to the rank of a tathāgata." [24] But the whole question of the early councils remains most obscure. It has even been argued that they are inventions of the later chroniclers, intended to give an air of apostolic antiquity to the orthodox texts of the Pāli canon—as though these had been fixed immediately following the Buddha's death and confirmed in solemn council a century later.[25] Had they been invented out of whole cloth, however, would the opposing council have been dignified with the title of the Great Council? And would the detail of the intransigency of Purāṇa and his group of five hundred dissenters, following the recital at Rājagṛha, have been invented and inserted, to make the reader wonder whether the precious heritage of the Master may not have been misremembered after all?

We are on firmer ground in the period of King Aśoka, the grandson of that Candragupta Maurya whose overthrow of the Nanda dynasty (322 B.C.) and organization of the states of the Gangetic plain was facilitated, as we have seen above,[26] by the brilliant genius of Cāṇakya Kauṭilya, author of the *Arthaśāstra*. Candragupta Maurya came to power five years after the raid

[24] S. Radhakrishnan, *Indian Philosophy*, London, 1923, Vol. I, p. 582. For *tathāgata*, cf. *supra*, p. 133, note 49.

[25] R. O. Franke, "The Buddhist Councils of Rājagṛaha and Vesālī," *Journal of the Pali Text Society*, 1908, pp. 1-80.

[26] *Supra*, p. 37.

of Alexander the Great into the northwestern provinces of the Indian subcontinent. Fixing his capital at Pāṭaliputra (modern Patna), he was so successful in his consolidation of the states shattered by the romantic Macedonian, that when Seleucus Nicator (the young Alexandrian general who founded the Seleucid dynasty of Persia, immediately following the death of Alexander in 323) attempted to recover the Greek conquests in India, the native armies made such a convincing showing that the invader, suing for peace and friendship, ceded the Punjab and the Kabul valley in exchange for five hundred elephants, gave his daughter to Candragupta in marriage, and in 302 B.C. dispatched Megasthenes as an ambassador to the Mauryan court.

Bindusāra, Candragupta's son, succeeded him in 297 B.C., and is supposed to have extended the empire southward to Madras. Otherwise his reign was peaceful, and, from the historical point of view, without event. His son, however, King Aśoka (264–227 B.C.), was one of the greatest conquerors and religious teachers of all time.

The conversion of King Aśoka to the Buddhist faith ranks in importance, for the Orient, with the conversion of Constantine the Great to Christianity, for the West. His imperial patronage lifted what had begun as a doctrine of exacting spiritual exercises to the position of a prosperous and popular, widely propagated religion. We are told that when King Aśoka instituted, in place of royal hunting-parties, the pious custom of state pilgrimages to the holy places of the Buddha legend, he let be summoned, to serve as guide, the saint who had converted him to the faith. "The great abbot, Upagupta, came from his forest retreat near Mathurā, traveling by boat down the Jumna and Ganges with eighteen thousand members of the Order as companions. At Pāṭaliputra they joined the Emperor's suite, and with a splendid military escort the imperial procession started for the Lumbīnī Garden. There, as an inscribed standard erected by Aśoka still records, Upagupta pointed to the Buddha's birthplace, saying, 'Here, Great King, the Venerable One was born. Here was the first memorial consecrated to the Enlightened One; and here, immediately after His birth, the Holy One took seven steps upon the ground.' Aśoka then did reverence to the holy place, ordered an imperial standard to be set up there, distributed largesse of gold, and made the village free of state taxes for ever. Kapilavastu, the scene of the great Renunciation, was the next place visited, then the Bo Tree at Gayā under which the Śākya Prince attained Nirvāṇa. There Aśoka built a shrine, probably similar to the one which now exists at the place, and lavished alms upon the crowds of mendicants—a hundred thousand gold pieces, so the story goes. Then the great procession passed on to Sarnāth, the Deer Park or sacred grove in which the Buddha first proclaimed the Dharma, or 'turned the Wheel of the Law'; and next to Śrāvastī, the monastery where the Buddha lived and taught; then to Kuśināgara, where He passed away or reached the goal of Pari-Nirvāṇa. At Śrāvastī Aśoka did reverence to the stūpas [reliquary shrines] of the Buddha's disciples. At the stūpa of Ānanda, the most devoted and beloved, he gave, it is said, largesse of a million pieces of gold, but at that of Vakkula only a single copper coin, for Vakkula had not striven greatly in the Eightfold Path nor had he done much to help his fellow creatures."[27]

King Aśoka is said to have supported sixty-four thousand Buddhist monks; eighty thousand stūpas are credited to him, as well as countless monasteries. He set up memorial columns throughout the empire and engraved on them didactic edicts. Missionaries were sent forth "to the utmost limits of the barbarian countries," to "intermingle among unbelievers" both within the kingdom "and in foreign countries, teaching better things." Taking advantage of the connections with the West, which had

[27] From E. B. Havell, *The History of Aryan Rule in India from the Earliest Times to the Death of Akbar,* New York, no date, p. 97.

been maintained since the coming of Megasthenes to the court of Candragupta, Aśoka sent teachers of the Buddhist Dharma to Antiochus II of Syria, Ptolemy II of Egypt, Magas of Cyrene, Antigonus Gonatas of Macedonia, and Alexander II of Epirus.[28] The force of this Buddhist gesture toward the West is difficult to estimate,[29] but in the Orient the missions of Aśoka mark an epoch of decisive spiritual change.

Nor did the king confine his benefactions to the Buddhist community. "His Sacred and Gracious Majesty," we read in one of his edicts devoted to the subject of tolerance, "does reverence to men of all sects, whether ascetics or householders, by gifts and various forms of reverence. His Sacred Majesty, however, cares not so much for gifts or external reverence as that there should be a growth of the essence of the matter in all sects. The growth of the essence of the matter assumes various forms, but the root of it is restraint of speech, to wit, a man must not do reverence to his own sect by disparaging that of another man without reason. Depreciation should be for specific reasons only, because the sects of other people deserve reverence for one reason or another. . . . Concord, therefore, is meritorious, to wit, hearkening and hearkening willingly to the law of piety as accepted by other people. For it is the desire of His Sacred Majesty that adherents of all sects should hear much teaching and hold sound doctrine." [30]

The king gave practical example of his piety toward living beings by providing for his subjects a reign of peace that ap-

[28] These are recorded in Aśoka's Rock Edict XIII. Cf. Vincent A. Smith, *The Edicts of Aśoka,* London, 1909, p. 20. (This is an exceedingly rare book, only 100 copies having been printed. It revises the translations given by the author in his earlier volume, *Aśoka, The Buddhist Emperor of India,* Oxford, 1901.)

[29] Cf. J. Kennedy, "Buddhist Gnosticism, the System of Basilides," *Journal of the Royal Asiatic Society,* 1902, pp. 377-415.

[30] King Aśoka's Rock Edict XII; Smith, *op. cit.,* p. 17.

The rock-hewn cave sanctuary of the Ājīvikas, which we had occasion to note, *supra,* p. 264, bears a dedicatory inscription of Aśoka.

proached the ideal of the world-ruling Cakravartin.[31] His domain comprised the greater part of India proper, as well as Afghanistan south of the Hindu Kush, Baluchistan, Sind, the valley of Kashmir, Nepal, and the lower Himalaya. Roads were maintained throughout, with inns and protected wells at regular intervals. One reads also of fruit gardens and planted avenues, public granaries, medical aid for animals as well as human beings, special officers to prevent wrongful imprisonment and punishment, to help parents with large families, and to give attention to the aged, courts of justice open to all, and the zeal of the Emperor himself to attend at all times and in all places to the people's business, "whether I am dining or in the ladies' apartments, or in my bedroom or in my closet, or in my carriage or in the palace gardens." [32] Numerous edicts addressed to the populace inculcated devotion, parental and filial love, charity, purity of thought, self-control, generosity to friends, acquaintances, and relatives, and to the Brāhmans as well as to Buddhist monks and nuns. Regulations were instituted for the protection of animals and birds: forests were not to be burnt, not even chaff "containing living things." No animal food was served at the imperial table; and the king himself, even while governing the greatest empire of his time anywhere in the world, assumed and faithfully practiced the vows of a monk.[33]

Aśoka's most important mission was the one that carried the Buddhist teaching to the large southern island-kingdom of Ceylon. The proselytizing party was headed by Mahendra, the King's younger brother (son, according to another version), who was followed presently by the princess-nun Saṅghamittā, the King's daughter, who bore with her a branch of the Sacred Bo Tree, which, being planted, grew, and is growing to this day in Anurādhapura.

[31] Cf. *supra,* pp. 127-135.

[32] Rock Edict VI; Smith, *op. cit.,* p. 12.

[33] Cf. Havell, *op. cit.,* pp. 89-103, and Smith, *op. cit.,* throughout.

In Ceylon, about 80 B.C., the early Buddhist canon was committed to writing. "In former times," the Ceylonese *Mahāvaṁsa* records, "the most learned monks handed down the text and commentary of the Three Piṭakas orally; but since they perceived that the people were falling away from the orthodox teaching, the monks convened; and so that the true doctrines might endure, they wrote them down in books."[34] This corpus of sacred literature—the often cited Pāli canon—is preserved, probably without much alteration, to the present; a comparison with the quotations on King Aśoka's rock-carved monuments reveals that at least a considerable part is now just as it was in that century. But this is not enough to support the orthodox claim that the canon was fixed in its present form at the "First Council" at Rājagṛha, just following the Buddha's death. "Some parts of the texts," wrote Dr. Ananda K. Coomaraswamy, "almost certainly go back to an earlier period, and record the sayings and doctrine of Gautama as remembered by his immediate disciples. . . . However . . . the Buddhist Bible, like the Christian, consists of books composed at different ages, and many or most of the books are compilations of materials by many hands and of various periods."[35]

Nevertheless, in spirit the books of the Pāli canon certainly antedate the great popular movement which we see in full development in Aśoka's time, with its imperial patronage, pilgrimages, veneration of relics, and lavishly sculptured religious monuments. An arresting fact, speaking volumes for the gradual transformation of Buddhist religiosity during the almost unrecorded period between the death of the Enlightened One and the conversion of King Aśoka, is the transfer of emphasis in the inscriptions of the latter's rock-carved edicts from the ideal of *nirvāṇa* to that of *svarga*—heavenly salvation as a reward for good behavior in

[34] *Mahāvaṁsa* 33.

[35] Ananda K. Coomaraswamy, *Buddha and the Gospel of Buddhism*, New York, 1916, p. 262.

the present world: "Let all joy be in effort," states the king, "because that avails for both this world and the next." [36] "The ceremonial of piety is not temporal; for even if it fails to attain the desired end in this world, it surely begets eternal merit in the other world." [37] "And for what do I toil? For no other end than this, that I may discharge my debt to animate beings, and that while I make some happy here, they may in the next world gain heaven." [38] "Even the small man can, if he choose, by exertion win for himself much heavenly bliss." [39] And again: "His Majesty thinks nothing of much importance save what concerns the next world." [40]

This is the attitude of bhakti, and points to a profound change at least in the style of the *teaching* of the doctrine. Buddhist art, which suddenly appears in Aśoka's time, depicts multitudes of earth-divinities, gods and goddesses, serpent kings and queens, tree nymphs, and pious animals, paying obeisance to the various consecrated shrines of the Buddhist community, guarding them, rejoicing in the Enlightenment of the Buddha, and otherwise displaying themselves to the faithful in attitudes of devotion. Stūpas, altars, sacred trees, miraculous events, episodes from the "earlier lives" of the Buddha, clerical processions, and all the classic paraphernalia of popular cult, are depicted in the vividly rendered works of sculpture, together with standing portraits of the wealthy donors and their wives, reverently regarding their own donations. The Enlightened One himself is never depicted in these monuments; as we have observed,[41] the place of his presence is represented by vacuity; or it can be symbolized by the Buddha's footprints, the Wheel of the Doctrine, the Bo Tree it-

[36] Rock Edict XIII; Smith, *op. cit.,* p. 21.
[37] Rock Edict IX; Smith, *op. cit.,* p. 15.
[38] Rock Edict VI; Smith, *op. cit.,* p. 12.
[39] Minor Rock Edict I (Rūpuāth Text); Smith, *op. cit.,* p. 3.
[40] Rock Edict XIII; Smith, *op. cit.,* pp. 20-21.
[41] Cf. *supra,* pp. 472-473.

self, or some other familiar sign. Obviously, the attitude that has come to prevail is one which it would be difficult indeed to draw directly from the teachings of the Master as recorded in the canon. "Instead of the sound of the war-drum," we read in one of the rock-cut inscriptions, "the sound of the drum of the Dharma is heard, while heavenly spectacles of processional cars, elephants, illuminations and the like, are displayed to the people." [42]

And yet we are told that King Aśoka, under whose imperial patronage these patterns of secular devotion prospered, took measures for the suppression of heresy and the settlement of sectarian disputations. As the *Mahāvaṁśa* records: "Heretics assumed the yellow robe in order to share in its advantages; whenever they had opinions of their own they gave them forth as doctrines of the Buddha; they acted according to their own will, and not according to what was right." [43] Aśoka states that he decreed expulsion—"putting in white [i.e., layman's] garments"—against certain monks and nuns; [44] and there is a Buddhist tradition to the effect that he summoned a general council of the Order at Pāṭaliputra in the eighteenth year of his reign, to clear up disputed points of the doctrine, reinforce the rules of discipline among the monks, and defend the faith against the ravages of heresy. We cannot conclude, apparently, that because the way of jñāna (the way of the monks) was now being supplemented by the way of bhakti (the way of the lay community) the fundamental Buddhist principles were being permitted to disappear from the view of those prepared to accept and understand them.

In fact, there is precedent for the growth and development of a Buddhist lay community, devoted to the disciplines of secular religion, in the sermons of the Buddha himself, where it is told how the Enlightened One in former lives dwelt as a layman in

42 Rock Edict IV; Smith, *op. cit.,* p. 9.

43 *Mahāvaṁśa* 38-39.

44 L. de la Vallée Poussin, "Councils and Synods (Buddhist)," in Hastings, *Encyclopedia of Religion and Ethics,* Vol. IV, p. 184.

the world, and how by charitable works one gains the traditional heavenly rewards. "Now I, forsooth, O monks," said the Blessed One, "became Sakkra (Indra), ruler of the gods, thirty-six times; many hundreds of times was I a king, a Universal Monarch (*cakravartin*), a lawful king, victorious in the four quarters, maintaining the security of my dominions, possessed of the seven jewels. Now what was the doctrine of that region and kingdom? This is what I thought of it, O monks: 'Of what deed of mine is this the fruit? Of what deed is it the result, whereby I now have become of such great prosperity and such great might? Truly it is the fruit of three deeds of mine, it is the result of three deeds of mine, whereby I am at this time of such great prosperity and of such great might, namely, the three deeds of Charity (*dāna*), of Self-command (*dama*), and of Self-control (*saññama*).'

"To this effect spake the Blessed One, and hereupon said the following:

" 'One should learn virtue which is of extensive goal,
And which hath the faculty of Happiness;
And one should devote onself to Charity,
To tranquil behavior and to thoughts of Friendship.

Having devoted himself to these three virtues,
Which provide reason for happiness,
A wise man gaineth the world of happiness—
A world all free from distress.'

"Exactly to that effect was it spoken by the Blessed One, so I have heard."[45]

King Aśoka, during the first years of his reign, before his conversion to the faith, had conducted a campaign of military conquest against the powerful neighboring kingdom of Kaliṅga. One hundred thousand of the enemy were slain, fifty thousand

[45] *Iti-vuttaka* 22. (Translated by Justin Henry Moore, *op. cit.*, pp. 35-36.)

carried into captivity, and vast numbers perished from famine and disease. In other words, the king was then just such a one as we are used to reading about in the annals of Christendom and heathenesse—one through whom the Matsya Nyāya, the law of the fishes,[46] operates without suspension. Immediately following his acceptance of the new faith, however, an edict unique in human history was set up in stone; unique, not because of what it says (for many kings have circulated pious proclamations), but because throughout the remainder of this king's career the war drum was no longer heard. "Subsequent to the annexation of the Kaliṅgas," it is declared, "His Sacred Majesty's zealous protection of the Dhamma began, his love of that Dhamma, and his giving instruction therein. Thus arose His Sacred Majesty's remorse for having conquered the Kaliṅgas, because the conquest of a country previously unconquered involves the slaughter, death, and carrying away captive of the people. Thus of all the people who were then slain, done to death, or carried away captive in the Kaliṅgas, if the hundredth or the thousandth part were to suffer the same fate, it would now be matter of regret to His Sacred Majesty. Moreover, should any one do him wrong that too must be borne with by His Sacred Majesty, if it can possibly be borne with. . . . His Sacred Majesty desires that all animate beings should have security, self-control, peace of mind, and joyousness. . . . And for this purpose has this pious edict been written in order that my sons and grandsons, who may be, should not regard it as their duty to conquer a new conquest. If, perchance, they become engaged in a conquest by arms, they should take pleasure in patience and gentleness and regard as the only true conquest the conquest won by piety. That avails for both this world and the next. Let all joy be in effort, because that avails for both this world and the next."[47]

The general laws of history, however, were not as yet undone;

[46] Cf. *supra*, pp. 36 and 119.

[47] Rock Edict XIII; as cited by Coomaraswamy, *op. cit.*, p. 183.

the empire of Aśoka disintegrated shortly following his death. Some fifty years after his passing, the last of his successors, Bṛhadratha, was murdered by his own commander-in-chief on the occasion of a review of the forces,[48] and a new *non*-Buddhist family, stemming from the region of Ujjain (which had just been one of the Maurya dominions) assumed the throne. Puṣyamitra, Bṛhadratha's murderer and the founder of the new Hindu Śuṅga dynasty, released a horse, in preparation for a classic Vedic horse-sacrifice, to wander at will over the domain attended by a hundred young and warlike princes. But somewhere midway to the Punjab the challenge of the ranging symbolic steed was accepted by a company of Greek cavalry.[49] The Europeans were routed, and the imperial Indian sacrifice was completed—but the presence of Greek raiders was enough to signify what was happening toward the west. The regions recovered by Candragupta from the founder of the Hellenistic Seleucid dynasty of Persia had been re-entered by the post-Alexandrian Greek provincial governors of Bactria, and these—Demetrius, Eucratides, and their dynasties—were now battling among themselves. The coins they minted preserve their portraits to the present: vigorous, Mediterranean heads. And, apparently, they were taking generously to their adopted homeland; for we hear of a Greek ambassador to the Śuṅga court at Vidiśā, Heliodorus by name, who was a follower of Viṣṇu,[50] while on the coins of Demetrius (a young king and conqueror whose Indian empire for a moment was more extensive than that of Alexander) one sees the hardy visage crowned by a royal cap in the shape of the head of an elephant. The invaders identified Indra with their own Zeus, Śiva with Dionysos, Kṛṣṇa with Herakles, and the goddess Padmā ("Lotus") with Artemis. Moreover, one of the most celebrated of the non-

[48] *Harṣacarita;* cited in *Cambridge History of India,* Vol. I, p. 518.

[49] Kālidāsa, *Mālavikāgnimitra;* cited in *Cambridge History of India,* Vol. I, p. 520. For a discussion of the horse sacrifice, cf. *supra,* pp. 134-135.

[50] *Cambridge History of India,* Vol. I, p. 558.

canonical Pāli Buddhist scriptures is that called *The Questions of Milinda,*[51] which recounts the religious conversations of a Greek king named "Milinda" (Menander, c. 125 to c. 95 B.C.) with the Buddhist monk Nāgasena. Some of Menander's coins (which are now collected in museums) bear the Buddhist Wheel of the Law, while Plutarch's account of the distribution of his ashes following his death, which echoes the legend of the distribution of the ashes of the Buddha, would seem to indicate that if the Greek king was not himself actually a member of the Buddhist Order, he was at least so great a benefactor that the community looked upon him as one of their own.

But this promising idyl of the marriage of East and West was not destined to endure; for at the very moment of its beginning, when Demetrius was breaking into India, remote events were already preparing the conditions of its close. A group of Huns, ranging the country between the southern reaches of the Great Wall of China and the mountains of Nan Shan, dislodged and launched on a long migration westward the people known to Chinese history as the Yueh-chi. This migration lasted some forty years (c. 165–125 B.C.), causing major shifts of population throughout the neighborhood of Sinkiang; new pressures were brought against the borders of the Greek province of Bactria; the defenses broke, and the wild tribesmen of Scythia, pressed from behind by the Yueh-chi, came pouring through. First the Scythians (Sanskrit, *Śaka*), then the Yueh-chi themselves, took over, one by one, the Greek provinces of Bactria, Afghanistan, Baluchistan, the lower Indus, and the Punjab. During the brief moment of their pause in Bactria the five tribes of the Yueh-chi had come under the leadership of the most powerful of their number, the so-called Kuṣānas; hence it was that they entered India under this appellation. The dominion of the Kuṣānas presently pressed eastward far beyond the bounds of Hellenistic India, traversing

51 *Milindapañha,* Sacred Books of the East, Vols. XXXV-XXXVI.

the whole length of the Gangetic plain and widening southward to the Vindhya hills.

Kaniṣka (c. 78–123 A.D.), the greatest of these Kuṣāna kings, was originally a follower of some non-Buddhist tradition (Brāhmanism, perhaps, or Zoroastrianism), but like Aśoka became a convert to the Gospel. Like Aśoka, he was a generous patron of the Order. And like Aśoka, he concerned himself with the regularization of the texts. Something of the generous character of his reign is made evident by the fact that under his protection one of the earliest known schools of Buddhist art (the Gandhāra school) arose and came to maturity—the craftsmen that produced it being of Greek provenience; while the satraps of his southern provinces were the descendants of those very Scythian (*Śaka*) princes whose dominion the Kuṣānas had overthrown.[52] Kaniṣka's conquests opened again the land routes to the Roman empire; an embassy from India visited Trajan after his entry into Rome, A.D. 99. Also the northern roads to China (the caravan routes through Turkestan) were kept clear for Indian commerce. Pivotal to the whole civilized world in one of the mightiest periods of history—Han China to the east and imperial Rome to the west—the Buddhist empire of the Kuṣāna monarchs flourished for a period paralleling that which we reckon in the West from Caesar's crossing of the Rubicon to the beginning of the decline of Rome under the military tyrants (Maximinus and the rest). The Kuṣānas were overthrown 236 A.D.

But within a century, a brilliant native dynasty arose in Magadha (the Gupta Dynasty, A.D. 320–c. 530),[53] and therewith the

[52] *Cambridge History of India,* Vol. I, p. 585.

[53] The penetration of the Huns into the northwestern provinces, *ca.* 480, broke the peaceful spell of the Gupta reign. The dynasty retained its throne until the beginning of the eighth century, but from the death of Bālāditya, about 530, exercised no general influence. The center of gravity of Indian culture shifted southward for a time, where the great periods followed of the Cāḷuykas of the Deccan (550–753), and the Pallavas of Conjeeveram (c. 400–825).

so-called golden age of Indian religious art, Buddhist as well as Hindu (inspired by the profound psychological realizations of the Tantra), came into being, in a fabulous world of peace, civilized sophistication, universal tolerance, and general prosperity. Once again, the ideal of the Cakravartin seemed to have been all but attained.

3.

Hīnayāna and Mahāyāna

THE VILLAGE LIFE of India was little modified by the rise and fall of the dynasties. The conquerors—even the complacent Greeks—soon recognized the virtues of the native way of being civilized. Alexander took to himself, as guru, the Jaina saint Kalanos, whom he invited to fill the vacancy of his old boyhood tutor Aristotle; while under the Kuṣāna warrior-kings both Buddhist art and Buddhist philosophy moved into a new and richly documented period. The Hellenistic Buddhist sculpture of Gandhāra, as well as the more spiritual and vigorous contemporary native Jaina and Buddhist art of Mathurā, gives ample evidence that under the protection of their foreign overlords the Indian religious systems were continuing to evolve. And we have the testimony of tradition for the statement that at the great Buddhist council assembled by Kaniṣka (the "Fourth Buddhist Council," held according to some reports at Jalandhar in the eastern Punjab, according to others at Kuṇḍalavana in Kashmir), the representatives of no less than eighteen Buddhist sects were in attendance.

The authenticity of the reports of this council has been questioned.[54] Nevertheless it is obvious from many trains of evidence that a critical shift of weight took place in Buddhist teachings about this time. The religious practices of bhakti, which were already evident in the popular art and royal edicts of Aśoka's reign, began to receive the mature support of Buddhist philosophers. A canonical Buddhist literature in Sanskrit (no longer Pāli, the language of the earlier canon treasured in Ceylon) dating from the period of Kaniṣka stands for the view (already represented in Buddhist popular art) that the Buddha is to be reverenced as a divine being, and furthermore that numerous Buddhas (Buddhas of the past, Buddhas of the future) assist the devotee in his attempt to realize the Buddhahood latent within him. For whereas the earlier orthodox view had represented individual enlightenment (arhatship) as the goal to be attained, and this only by means of a literal imitation of the rigorous world-renunciation of the historical princely monk, Gautama Śākyamuni, the newer teaching was that Buddhahood (the status of a World Redeemer) is man's proper end, and furthermore that *since all things in reality are Buddha-things, all things potentially and actually are Saviors of the World.*

"It is as if a certain man went away from his father and betook himself to some other place. He lives there in foreign parts for many years, twenty or thirty or forty or fifty. In the course of time the father becomes a great man, but the son is poor; seeking a livelihood, he roams in all directions." The father is unhappy, having no son, but one day, while sitting at the gate of his palace transacting great affairs, he beholds his son, poor and tattered. The son thinks: "Unexpectedly have I here fallen in with a king or grandee. People like me have nothing to do here; let me go; in the street of the poor I am likely to find food and clothing without much difficulty. Let me no longer tarry in this place, lest I should be taken to do forced labor or should incur

[54] Cf. la Vallée Poussin, *loc. cit.*, p. 184.

some other injury." The father orders his son brought to him, but, before revealing his birth to him, employs him for some years at all kinds of work, first at the meanest kinds, and then at the most important. The father treats his son with paternal kindness, but the son, although he manages all his father's property, lives in a thatched cottage and believes himself to be poor. At last, when his education is completed, he learns the truth.

In the same way we are the sons of the Buddha, and the Buddha says to us today, "You are my sons." But, like the poor man, we had no idea of our dignity, no idea of our mission as future Buddhas. Thus the Buddha has made us reflect on inferior doctrines. We have applied ourselves to them, seeking as payment for our day's work only nirvāṇa, and finding that it is already ours. Meanwhile the Buddha has made us dispensers of the knowledge of the Buddhas, and we have preached it without desiring it for ourselves. At last, however, the Buddha has revealed to us that this knowledge is ours, and that we are Buddhas, like himself.[55]

This is the doctrine that has been termed, somewhat complacently, "The Big Ferryboat" (*mahāyāna*), the ferry in which all may ride, in contrast to "The Little Ferryboat" (*hīnayāna*), the way of those lonely ones, "lights unto themselves," who steer the difficult strait of individual release. The Big Ferryboat, with its pantheons of Buddhas and Bodhisattvas, prayer-wheels, incense, gongs, and graven images, rosaries and muttered syllables, has been disparaged generally by modern Occidental critics as a vulgar popularization of the Buddha's doctrine furthered by the advent into the northwestern provinces of barbaric peoples (not the Greeks, of course, but the Śakas and Yueh-chi), and yet, if anything is clear it is that the entire meaning of the paradox implicit in the very idea of Buddhahood has here come to manifestation. Nāgārjuna (c. 200 A.D.), the founder of the Mādhya-

[55] *Saddharmapuṇḍarīka* ("The Lotus of the True Law") 4. (Sacred Books of the East, Vol. XXI, pp. 98ff.).

mika school of Buddhist philosophy, which is the supreme statement of the Māhayāna view, was by no means a vulgarizer but one of the subtlest metaphysicians the human race has yet produced. While Asaṅga and his brother Vasubandhu (c. 300 A.D.), the developers of the Yogācāra school of the Mahāyāna, likewise merit the respect of whatever thinker sets himself the task of really comprehending their rationalization of Nāgārjuna's doctrine of the Void. And Aśvaghoṣa, the haughty contemporary of Kaniṣka (c. 100 A.D.), can have been no truckler to barbarians, even though his epic of the life of the Buddha, *Buddhacarita,* is graced with many unmonkish charms.

Fa Hsien (c. 400 A.D.), a Chinese Buddhist pilgrim to whom we owe much of our knowledge of the classic Gupta period, states that he found four Buddhist philosophic systems fully developed in India. Two of these, the Mādhyamika and Yogācāra, represented the Mahāyāna, while the others—Vaibhāṣika and Sautrāntika [56]—were of the older Hīnayāna school. Fa Hsien declares that at Pāṭaliputra, the ancient capital of King Aśoka, the Mahāyānists had one monastery and the Hīnayānists another, with some six or seven hundred monks between them. His account of the cities further west reveals that at Mathurā the Bodhisattvas Mañjuśrī and Avalokiteśvara received worship as divinities—which is a Mahāyāna feature. The texts that he brought home with him were of both persuasions. And we learn, furthermore, from a second Chinese pilgrim two centuries later, Hsüan Tsang (629–640), that the two schools were then still in combat with each other. Relations between Buddhism and Hinduism were peaceful, but between the Mahāyāna and the Hīnayāna scholastic debate and mutual abuse, on the verbal level, were at such a pitch that the Buddha himself, had he returned, must certainly

[56] The Sautrāntikas profess to teach the *sūtra-anta,* that is, the "end, gist, secret meaning" (*anta*) of the accounts of the original sermons and dialogues of the Buddha (*sūtras*).

have been compelled to cry out piteously, as eleven centuries before: "The Order is divided! The Order is divided!" [57]

The seeds of the conflict are in the words of the Buddha as recorded in the canon. The unsystematized epistemological, metaphysical, and psychological implications implicit in the program of spiritual therapy prescribed by him whose own one-pointedness had carried him beyond the sphere of simple ratiocination rankled in the minds of those still caught in the nets of thought; or one might say perhaps, in the minds of those who had been originally Brāhmans (rather than Kṣatriyas, like Gautama) and were therefore more disposed than he to adhere to the ways of thought, the ways of jñāna, the processes of *thinking* problems through. Many, it is clear, attained Enlightenment; their formulae are not the vain scrimshaw of unreposeful intellects, but profoundly inspired, original renditions in philosophical terms of the realization promised by the Buddha's cure. Thus we find that just as the Doctrine, when rendered according to the dispositions of the bhakta, yielded a Buddhist art of broad popular appeal, so when apprehended by the Brāhman intellect, its implications opened into the most wonderfully subtle systems of metaphysical philosophy. The Wheel of the Law indeed was turning—churning the whole nature of man to new fulfillment. The Mahāyāna, the big ferryboat, and the Hīnayāna, the little, whether side by side or far apart, have together carried the millions of the Orient through centuries of transformation, secure

[57] *Editor's note:* The above sections, from p. 490 to the present point, have been developed from a single page of Dr. Zimmer's notes, a page containing one line: "The councils of Aśoka and Kaniṣka." The treatment is based on my recollection of conversations with Dr. Zimmer, and on the authorities whom I have been careful to cite in footnotes. Dr. Zimmer's papers from this point forward are extremely sketchy, many carrying simply jottings from texts and critical studies. I have developed them (as briefly as possible) by turning to the texts, and I cite in footnotes all quoted authorities. Where such notices do not occur the passage is based on the notes of Dr. Zimmer.

in the understanding that the Buddha, somehow, in the most intimate, dependable way—no matter what their path of approach to him—was their indestructible, all-embracing Refuge.

"The ocean of tears shed by each being, wandering through life after life, without beginning," we are told, "is vaster than the Four Oceans together.

"The bones of the bodies that a man has worn in countless births, when heaped together would form a hill far larger than the lofty summits of the mountains that strike his eyes with awe." [58]

This is the beginning of the wisdom of release. All life is sorrowful—and there is no beginning or end to it in this vale of tears; yet how substantial, how deep, how real, is this universal sorrow?

A parable is given in the Pāli *Stanzas of the Sister Elders.* There was a mother, we read, who had lost six children; one remained, a daughter. But eventually this child too died, and the mother was disconsolate. The Buddha came to her; and he said: "Many hundreds of children have we buried, you and I, hosts of kindred, in the times that are gone. Do not lament for this dear little daughter; four and eighty thousand with the same name have been burned on the funeral pyre by you before. Which among them is the one for whom you mourn?" [59]

[58] *Saṁyutta-nikāya* 15. 1. 3; 15. 2. 10. (Cf. Mrs. Rhys Davids, *The Book of the Kindred Sayings,* Pāli Text Society, 5 vols., Oxford, 1917?–1930, Part II, pp. 120, 125.)

[59] *Therigāthā* 314.

Compare the idea recorded by Lucian of Samosata (c. 125-180 A.D.) in his biographical essay on the contemporary Cypriotic philosopher, Demonax of Athens. "He went to a man who was mourning the death of a son and had shut himself up in the dark, and told him that he was a sorcerer and could raise the boy's shade for him if only he would name three men who had never mourned for anyone. When the man hesitated long and was perplexed—I suppose he could not name a single one—Demonax said: 'You ridiculous fellow, do you think, then, that you alone

Obviously, there is here implicit an ontological problem; for in what sense can the woman with all the children, the man with all the bones, or the being with all the tears be said to have lived through multitudes of lives, if we are to accept as truth the Buddha's fundamental teaching: "All things are without a self (*an-attā*)"?

The philosophers of the Hīnayāna schools sought to solve the difficulty by contending that the ego-process consists of a series (*santāna, santati*) of moments (*kṣaṇa*) of transient entities (*dharmas*). There is nothing that abides. Not only are all the particles of being perishable (*anitya*), but their duration is infinitesimally short. "All things are as brief as winks" (*yat sat tat kṣaṇikam*). Their springing into existence is almost their ceasing to be. Yet they follow each other in chains of cause and effect that are without beginning and will go on for eternity. These chains, made up of momentary dharmas, are what appear to others, and in some cases to themselves also, as individuals—gods, animals, oceans, men, stones, and trees. Every phenomenal being is to be regarded as such a flux of particles that are themselves ephemeral. Throughout the transformations of birth, growth, old age, death, and the endless chain of rebirths, the so-called individual is no more than the vortex of such a causal sequence—never quite what it was a moment ago or what it is just about to be, and yet not different either. The simile is given of the flame of a lamp. During the first, the middle, and the last watches of the night, the flame is neither the same flame nor a different flame.

Or the simile is given of a bride who was bought from her father by the payment of the bride price when she was a little girl. The buyer thought that when she grew up she would become his wife, but he then went forth on a business voyage, and

---

suffer beyond endurance, when you see that nobody is unacquainted with mourning?' " (From *Lucian,* translated by A. M. Harmon (Loeb Classical Library), Vol. I, "Demonax," p. 159.)

was away for many years. The girl grew up, came to marriageable age and, according to Indian custom, had to be supplied with a husband. The father, coming to a difficult decision, determined to accept a second bride price from a second suitor, and this man then became the actual husband of the girl. Presently, however, the first returned; and he demanded that the wife, now a mature woman, should be returned to him. But the husband replied: "This woman whom I have married is not your bride. The little girl of long ago is not the same as this adult woman who is today my wife." [60] And so it is indeed! Throughout the series of our existences, bounded by death and birth, just as through the differing stages of our present biography, we are both identical with and not identical with ourselves.

The problem, that is to say, was resolved in the schools of the Hīnayāna by the assertion that what are usually taken to be permanent entities do not exist. All that can be said to exist—really—are the dharmas: small and brief realities, which, when grouped in aggregates and chains of cause and effect, create an impression of pseudo-individuals. There is no thinker, there is only thought; no one to feel, but only feelings; no actor, but only visible actions. This is a doctrine of phenomenalism, maintaining the nonexistence of substances and individuals while insisting on the reality of infinitesimal units, of which the world illusion is said to be compounded. The soul, the individual, is no more than a complex of momentary entities; and these are the only reality. Nirvāṇa, the attainment of release, therefore, is simply the cessation of the thought that all these phenomenal effects that we behold and feel constitute the reality that they appear to constitute. The extinction of that wrong idea—which is the leading thought and error of our lives—breaks off the entrainment of falsely grounded hopes and anxieties, life-plans, desires, and resentments. The arhat, the enlightened one, is simply

[60] *Milindapañha* ("The Questions of King Milinda") 2. 2. 6. (Sacred Books of the East, Vol. XXXV, p. 74).

a vortex no longer deluded about itself or about the phenomenality of other names and forms: in him knowledge concerning the conditions of phenomenality has released what once regarded itself as an entity from the consequences of the general delusion. But as to what more might be said about nirvāṇa—this is something the Hīnayāna philosopher does not attempt to face. The term *nirvāṇa* is by him treated strictly as a negative; for as a positive it would fall immediately under the ban of his basic formula, *yat sat tat kṣaṇikam:* whatever is, is momentary—like a wink.

The once extremely widespread Hīnayāna group known as Sarvāstivādins, or "realists" (*sarva,* "all"; *asti,* "exist"; *vāda,* "saying"), distinguish seventy-five dharmas, or "categories," under which, as they declare, every thought and form of being can be comprised. All are "real with regard to their substance" (*dravyato santi*); i.e., all exist as substance even though as ephemeral manifestations they are ever-changing and utterly perishable. They exist in a continuous series of births, durations, and destructions, which terminates when true knowledge puts an end to the restless movement of this contingent process, dissolving it in the quietness of extinction (*nirvāṇa*). This theory marked the climax of the *earlier* Hīnayāna, and supplied the basis for the speculations of the *later* Hīnayāna schools.

The question as to how suffering can be experienced in this world when there are no egos in which the suffering comes to pass, is answered by the thinkers of the later schools in different ways. The Sautrāntikas, for example, attempt to explain the situation in terms of their basic contention that our processes of thought do not represent a direct picture of external reality but follow each other in a thought series of their own—under pressure, as it were, from without, but otherwise autonomously. On the basis of our internal experiences it is to be inferred that external objects exist; yet this does not mean that those objects correspond in character to the internal thoughts generated under their influence. There is no chain of causation from outside to inside by which the suffering is produced that is felt within. The pains of hell, delights of heaven, and mixed blessings of the world, are all equally thoughts, brought about by precedent mental causes, not by outer facts, each chain of thoughts representing the force—more or less enduring—of a particular kind of ignorance or enthrallment. What imagines itself to be a suffering ego is only the continuity of the suffering itself. The continuous sequence of similar mental dharmas goes on simply as a reflex of its own imperfection.

The Vaibhāṣikas, on the other hand, object to this doctrine as "contradictory chatter" (*viruddhā bhāṣā*).[61] They regard it as absurd to speak of inferences about the outer world on the basis of a thought series not in touch with it. For them, the world is open to direct perception. Occasionally, external objects may be known to exist by inference, but as a rule perception is what reveals to us their existence. Hence the objects of experience are of two kinds: 1. sensible or perceived and 2. cogitable or inferred. The laws that govern the causal sequences in these two realms are different, and yet the two interact upon each other. Suffering, for example, represents an actual impingement of the outer world upon the world within, even though the normal inference that an enduring individual is what is undergoing the ordeal is a thought without basis in fact. For whatever the mental stream presents as external does indeed exist without—though not in the mode of substances and enduring entities, as is generally inferred.

According to both of these late Hīnayāna schools of reasoning, the aggregates of experience—whether external or internal—are ephemeral yet real. In the Mahāyāna, on the other hand, they are not even real. A metaphysical substratum of all phenomenality is admitted, but the entire sphere of phenomenality itself

[61] Their name, Vaibhāṣika, is fancifully ascribed to their habit of denouncing the Sautrāntika doctrine of the mere inferability of the outer world as "*viruddhā bhāṣā.*"

(whether mental or physical, inferential or perceived, long-enduring or of briefest moment) is regarded as without substance. The philosophers of the Mahāyāna liken the universe to a magical display, a mirage, a flash of lightning, or the ripple of waves on the sea. The sea itself, the reality beyond and within the rippling forms, cannot be measured in terms of the ripples. Comparably, the objects in the world are of one reality and in reality therefore one; but this reality is beyond description in terms of phenomenality. This one reality, in its ontological aspect, can be termed only *bhūta-tathatā,* "the suchness of beings, the essence of existence." In its relation to knowledge it is known as *bodhi* ("wisdom") and *nirvāṇa.*

That is to say, by treating positively the term and problem to which the Hīnayāna philosophers accorded only a negative description, the Mahāyāna schools transcended the comparatively naïve positivism of their associates and approached the nondualism of the contemporary Vedānta. The Hīnayāna thinkers, in short, never really faced the question of the degree or nature of their so-called "reality." Precisely in what sense were their dharmas and chains of causes and effects being declared to "exist"? How much was being said, after all, when it was insisted that the dharmas were ultimately "real"? The Mahāyāna philosophers, turning their attention to this question, distinguished three aspects in terms of which the reality of any object could be considered: 1. quintessence, 2. attributes, 3. activities. The *quintessence* of a jar is earth or clay; its *attributes,* the coarseness or fineness, fragility or strength, beauty or ugliness, etc. of the form; while its *activities* are the receiving, holding, and discharging of water. Both attributes and activities are subject to laws of change, but quintessence is absolutely indestructible. The waves of the sea may be high or low, but the water itself neither increases nor decreases. And so it is that though all things are born to die—whether as long-lived individuals, or as infinitesimal momentary particles—the quintessence of them all remains unchanged. The universe, the entire world of names and forms, has both its phenomenal and its enduring aspect, but only the latter, this substratum of all things, is what can be known as *bhūta-tathatā,* the "suchness or essence of existence."

According to the basic argument of this metaphysical philosophy (which takes its stand, so to say, in *nirvāṇa*) every dharma is *pratītya-samutpanna,* "dependent on others." It cannot be explained by reference either to itself or to something else, or by bringing the two sets of references into a relationship. Every system of notions terminates in inconsistencies and is therefore simply void. And yet, to assert that all is "non-existent" (*abhāva*) would not be proper either; for that would be only another act of dialectical reasoning, whereas true wisdom is neither an affirmation nor a negation. "Nothing is abandoned, nothing annihilated (*na kasyacit prahānam, nāpi kasyacin nirodhaḥ*)." [62]

The only final truth, then, is the void—an ineffable entity, the state of "being thus" (*tathatā*), which is realized as opposed to the ever-changing mirage of contingent notions. This, and this alone, is the absolute that persists throughout all space and time as the essence of things. Things in their fundamental nature cannot be named or explained; they cannot be discussed; they are beyond the range of perception; they are possessed of absolute sameness; they have no distinctive features; they are subject to neither transformation nor destruction. The realm of their reality is that of "absolute truth" (*paramārtha-tattva*), not of "relative truth" (*saṁvṛti-tattva*)—in other words, precisely what in the Upaniṣads is known as *brahman;* though the negative as opposed to the positive formulation here, in Buddhism, conduces to a different attitude and a different style of thought and teaching.

Nāgārjuna (2nd or 3rd century A.D.) is regarded as the great

[62] Compare Candrakīrti, *Prasannapadā* 1, in Stcherbatsky, *op. cit.,* pp. 83ff. The *Prasannapadā* is a commentary on the *Akutobhayā* of Nāgārjuna, composed, apparently, in the sixth or seventh century A.D.

master of this doctrine. He is described (in a biography that a Hindu sage named Kumārajīva translated into Chinese about 405 A.D.) as a Brāhman of southern India, who, while a mere boy, studied the four Vedas and became adept in all sciences, including those of magic. In his earliest youth he made himself and three friends invisible so that they might slip into the royal seraglio, but the four had hardly begun to take advantage of their situation when they were apprehended. The friends were condemned to die, but Nāgārjuna was allowed to elect the other death, namely, that of the monastic vow.

In ninety days he studied and mastered the whole of the Buddhist Pāli canon. Then he proceeded northward, in quest of further knowledge, until he came to the Himalayas, where a monk of immense age committed to him the Mahāyāna sūtras; after which a serpent king (*nāgarāja*) disclosed an authentic commentary on those pages. All these sacred writings had been preserved in secret—so the story goes—for centuries. They were, in fact, authentic revelations of the doctrine, which the Buddha himself had regarded as too profound for his contemporaries and had therefore put into the keeping of competent guardians. Mankind had required literally hundreds of years of preliminary training (the training of the Hīnayāna) in preparation for this higher law. But now that the world was ready, Nāgārjuna was permitted to spread the final Buddhist teaching of "The Great Ferryboat" throughout the land of India. And he did so (so runs the legend) for three hundred years.

The foundation of the Mahāyāna is thus in legend ascribed to Nāgārjuna. The evidence, however, now seems to show that the basic principles were formulated well before his century. Though practically the whole of the so-called *Prajñā-pāramitā* literature is attributed to him, it now appears that some of these texts preceded, while others followed, his lifetime. And yet it is certain, in spite of the fabulous details of his biography, that

Nāgārjuna was an actual character, and, moreover, a brilliant, crystallizing, and energizing philosophical spirit. Throughout northern India they still speak of him as "the Buddha without his characteristic marks." And the works ascribed to him are revered equally with "the sūtras from the Buddha's own mouth." [63]

We read in the fourteenth chapter of Nāgārjuna's *Mādhyamika Śāstra* ("The Guide-Book of the School of the Middle Way"): "The teaching of the Buddha relates to two kinds of truth, the relative, conditional truth, and the transcendent, absolute truth"; [64]—the meaning of which basic pronouncement is clear enough in the light of what we have already learned concerning the mystery of Enlightenment, as experienced and elucidated in the traditional schools of India. It is not a novel pronouncement, by any means. Nor is there anything surprising in Nāgārjuna's description of the ineffable nature of the supreme experience: "The eye does not see and the mind does not think; this is the highest truth, wherein men do not enter. The land wherein the full vision of all objects is obtained at once has been termed by the Buddha the highest goal (*paramārtha*), the absolute, the truth that cannot be preached in words." [65] Which, as we have said, is nothing new. Nevertheless, in the following verse appears the great key to Nāgārjuna's particular approach:

śūnyam iti na vaktavyam
aśūnyam iti vā bhavet,
ubhayaṁ nobhayaṁ ceti;
prajñāptyarthaṁ tu kathyate.

[63] Bunyiu Nanjio, *A Short History of the Twelve Japanese Buddhist Sects,* Tokyo, 1886, p. 48.

[64] *Mādhyamika Śāstra* 14; cited by Radhakrishnan, *op. cit.,* Vol. I, p. 658.

[65] *Ib.* 3; Radhakrishnan, *op. cit.,* pp. 662-663.

"It cannot be called void or not void, or both or neither, but in order to indicate it, it is called The Void," [66] This negative designation of the transcendent "highest goal," in contrast to the positive which predominates in the Vedic tradition, is what gives to the whole complex of doctrine associated with the name and work of Nāgārjuna its peculiar quality and force. The bold consistency with which this manner of speech has been carried through every phase of thought and feeling, to the very limit, keeps a wonderful, really sublime wind of detachment blowing through all the Mahāyāna discourses.

"A gift should not be given by a Bodhisattva," we read, for example, in the *Prajñāpāramitā sūtra* known as "The Diamond-Cutter" (*Vajracchedikā*), "so long as he believes in objects. A gift should not be given by him, so long as he believes in anything. A gift should not be given by him, so long as he believes in form; a gift should not be given by him, so long as he believes in the special qualities of sound, smell, taste, and touch. Because, O Subhūti, a gift should be given by a Bodhisattva only in order that he should not believe even in the idea of cause. And why? Because that Bodhisattva, O Subhūti, who gives a gift without believing in anything, the measure of his stock of merit is not easy to learn." [67]

"There is a fundamental reality," states Dr. Radhakrishnan, in his elucidation of the Mādhyamika doctrine of the Void, "without which things would not be what they are. Śūnyatā is a positive principle. Kumārajīva, commenting on Nāgārjuna, observes: 'It is on account of śūnyatā (the Void) that everything becomes possible, without it nothing in the world is possible.' It is the basis of all. 'O Subhūti, all dharmas have śūnyatā for their refuge; they do not alter that refuge' (*Prajñāpāramitā*).

[66] *Ib.* 15. 3 (cf. *Mūlamadhyamakakārikās de Nāgārjuna,* Bibliotheca Buddhica IV, St. Petersburg, 1913, p. 264, 11. 9-10); Radhakrishnan, p. 663.

[67] *Vajracchedikā* 4. (Sacred Books of the East, Vol. XLIX, Part II, p. 114).

'Śūnyatā is the synonym of that which has no cause, that which is beyond thought or conception, that which is not produced, that which is not born, that which is without measure' (*Aṣṭasāhasrikā Prajñāpāramitā* 18). . . . 'The absolute is neither existent nor nonexistent, nor both existent and nonexistent, nor different from both nonexistence and existence' (Mādhava, *Sarvadarśanasaṅgraha*). To transfer the finite categories to the infinite would be like attempting to measure the heat of the sun by the ordinary thermometer. From our point of view the absolute is nothing. *Śūnyam tattvam.* We call it śūnyam, since no category used in relation to the conditions of the world is adequate to it. To call it being is wrong, because only concrete things exist. To call it nonbeing is equally wrong. (*Tatra astitā vā nāstitā vā na vidyate nopalabhyate.*) It is best to avoid all descriptions." [68]

"What do you think then, O Subhūti," said the Blessed One, "does the Tathāgata think in this wise: The Law has been taught by me?"

Subhūti said: "No indeed, O Blessed One, the Tathāgata does not think in this wise: The Law has been taught by me."

The Blessed One declared: "If a man should say that the Law has been taught by the Tathāgata, he would say what is not true; he would slander me with some untruth that he has learned. And why? Because, O Subhūti, it is said, The teaching of the Law, the teaching of the Law indeed! O Subhūti, there is nothing that can be perceived by the name of the teaching of the Law."

"What then do you think, O Subhūti, is there anything which has been known by the Tathāgata in the form of the highest perfect knowledge?"

The venerable Subhūti replied: "No indeed, O Blessed One; there is nothing, O Blessed One, that has been known by the Tathāgata in the form of the highest knowledge."

[68] Radhakrishnan, *op. cit.*, pp. 663-664.

"So it is, Subhūti," said the Blessed One, "so it is." [69]

The term *śūnyatā,* as applied to the metaphysical reality, insists on the fact that reason and language apply to only the finite world; nothing can be said of the infinite. But the term is applied also to all things of the phenomenal sphere—and here is the great stroke of the Śūnyavāda. "As applied to the world of experience," writes Dr. Radhakrishnan, "śūnyatā means the ever-changing state of the phenomenal world. In the dread waste of endlessness man loses all hope, but the moment he recognizes its unreality he transcends it and reaches after the abiding principle. He knows that the whole is a passing dream, where he may sit unconcerned with the issues, certain of victory." [70]

In other words, the concept of emptiness, the void, vacuity, has been employed in the Mādhyamika teaching as a convenient and effective pedagogical instrument to bring the mind beyond that sense of duality which infects all systems in which the absolute and the world of relativity are described in contrasting, or antagonistic terms. In the Vedānta Gītas, as we have seen,[71] the nonduality of nirvāṇa and saṁsāra, release and bondage, is made known and celebrated in rhapsodic verses; but in this Buddhist formula, one word, *śūnyatā,* bears the entire message, and simultaneously projects the mind beyond any attempt to conceive of a synthesis. Philosophically, as a metaphysical doctrine, the formula conduces to a thoroughgoing Docetism; the world, the Buddha, and nirvāṇa itself become no more than the figments of an absolutely empty dream. (This is the point that has been attacked, always, in argument, and, of course, it is an easy point to make seem absurd if one takes absolutely the usual categories of reason.) But the circumstance to be borne in mind

[69] *Vajracchedikā* 21-22. (Sacred Books of the East, Vol. XLIX, Part II, pp. 137-138).

[70] Radhakrishnan, *op. cit.,* p. 663.

[71] *Supra,* pp. 447-455.

is that this Buddhist philosophy is not primarily an instrument of reason but an instrument to convert reason into realization; one step beyond the term is the understanding of what it really means.[72] And as a device to effect such a transformation of knowledge—first standing between all the contrarieties of "the world" and "release from the world," then standing between the moment of preliminary comprehension and that of realized illumination—it would be difficult indeed to find a more apt and efficient term. This is why the doctrine is called Mādhyamika, the "Middle Way." And actually, it brings, as far as possible, into systematic philosophical statement the whole implication of the "Middle Doctrine" of the Buddha himself. For as we read in the orthodox Pāli "Basket (*piṭaka*) of the Discourses of the Buddha": "That things have being, O Kaccāna, constitutes one extreme of doctrine; that things have no being is the other extreme. These extremes, O Kaccāna, have been avoided by the Tathāgata, and it is a middle doctrine that he teaches."[73] The Buddha continually diverted the mind from its natural tendency to posit an abiding essence beyond, or underlying, the endless and meaningless dynamism of the concatenation of causes. And this is the effect also of Nāgārjuna's metaphysical doctrine of the void.

Yet the mind will have its say. And so it did in the schools of the Mahāyāna, just as in all other circles, throughout the world, where men have sought to clarify to themselves the riddle of existence. Scholars are undecided as to whether the Yogācāra school of the Mahāyāna preceded or followed the formulation

[72] "The metaphysics of the Mahāyāna in the incoherence of its systems shows clearly enough the secondary interest attaching to it in the eyes of the monks, whose main interest was concentrated on the attainment of release; the Mahāyāna no less than the Hīnayāna is concerned vitally with this practical end, and its philosophy is of value merely in so far as it helps men to attain their aim" (Arthur Berriedale Keith, *Buddhist Philosophy in India and Ceylon,* Oxford, 1923, p. 273).

[73] *Saṁyutta-Nikāya* 22. 90. 17 (Warren, *op. cit.,* p. 166).

of the Mādhyamika theory of the void, but in either case the logical relationship of the two Mahāyāna schools is evident.[74] A foothold for thought is retained in the Yogācāra—a last foothold, but a foothold nevertheless; for the void (*śūnyatā*) here is identified with pure consciousness, pure thought, true wisdom (*prajñā*), as in Vedānta, and a system of reasoning then is developed from this position.

The question is asked, for example, as to how this phenomenal world can have been produced out of the void. If pure thought creates the phantasms called beings and things, which are covered by the categories (*dharmas*), and if pure thought also (as in the experience of the sages) then realizes their voidness and reduces them as it were to nothingness, how does it do this? The Yogācāra thinkers addressed themselves to this question with profound concern.

Their philosophy has been termed the *nir-ālambana-vāda*, the "doctrine (*vāda*) of no (*nir*) support (*ālambana*)," since it denies that any external object exists, apart from our mental processes, to give external support to the constructions of the mind. The doctrine has been termed, also, *vijñānavāda*, "the doctrine (*vāda*) of ideation (*vijñāna*)," since it regards mere mental representations as the sole existence. It insists on the logical primacy not of the created manifold but of the creating principle, pure thought; not the world, but thought, is treated as the positive. Starting from that as the primary substance, the philosophers then reason outward to the ephemeral variety of things. And so they carry to a logical conclusion the idealistic tendency of Buddhist reasoning as initiated by the Hīnayāna Sautrāntikas,[75] and moreover justify their own movement dog-

[74] Cf. *infra*, p. 526, note 77. "The general view places the Śūnyavāda earlier than the Vijñānavāda [= Yogācāra] teaching, though one can never be sure of it. The two perhaps developed side by side" (Radhakrishnan, *op. cit.*, p. 645).

[75] Cf. *supra*, pp. 515-516.

matically by giving emphasis to such formulae from the orthodox Pāli canon as: "Consciousness is luminous, but is defiled by adventitious defilements." [76]

According to the Yogācāra, then, the root of the evermoving *santāna* ("extension": that flowing panorama of successive mental states which constitutes what appears to be, and feels itself to be, an individual) is "ideation" (*vijñāna*). Whatever seems to exist is the result of *parikalpa,* "creation from within," i.e., "imagination." But such magically creative thought is possible only because there exists a kind of eternal repository (*ālaya,* "abode") from which can be drawn the substance of every possible image and idea. This is the so-called *ālaya-vijñāna,* "repository consciousness," which is thought in and by itself; thought without the thing that is thought; thought therefore that is "void" (*śūnya*). This is termed *tathātā,* "the suchness," and is the *positive* aspect of the Void.[77]

The *ālaya-vijñāna* is beyond all conception and imagination, yet at the same time it is the potentiality of all possible thought. Every beheld or discoverable thing, every so-called individual, all the traits of the phenomenal world, are productions of the continuous flow of the imaginings (*parikalpas,* "creations from within") which arise like waves from this ocean, only to vanish again immediately in its infinity. The individual ceases to exist upon contact with this "repository consciousness"; for the rippling mental states that constitute the self-awareness of the ego dissolve in it. The term is practically synonymous, therefore,

[76] *Aṅguttara Nikāya* 1. 10.

[77] "If the Yogācāra be later than the Mādhyamika theory," writes Dr. Radhakrishnan, "we can easily understand the logic of the development. An intellectual account of Nāgārjuna's absolute will lead us to the theory of *ālaya-vijñāna. . . . Ālaya-vijñāna* is spirituality, *vijñāna,* objectifying itself or expressing itself in the object world. The highest way in which thought can envisage the absolute is by looking upon it as consciousness, *cit, vijñāna*" (Radhakrishnan, *op. cit.,* pp. 665-666).

with *nirvāṇa,* as well as with *śūnya*—yet it suggests, always, a positive state. *Ālaya-vijñāna* is a kind of Buddhist *brahman,* which is to be realized by pure mental yoga—absolutely pure consciousness. Indeed, pure consciousness is itself identical with the *ālaya-vijñāna.* And since everything else is but contingent consciousness, this pure consciousness is the ultimate reality, the abstract quintessence of all that is.

"When the Bodhisattvas are possessed of four qualities, then they are practicing the Great Yoga," we read in the *Lankāvatāra-sūtra,* one of the principal texts of the Yogācāra.[78] "These four qualities are as follows: 1. the realization that everything is but a manifestation of our spirit, 2. freedom from the false idea that there is any such thing as the growth, duration, or succession of things, 3. the understanding that the sole characteristic of external objects is nonexistence, and 4. the understanding that the Holy Knowledge is to be realized within ourselves." This fourfold mental yoga rescues the practitioner from the painful whirlpool of saṁsāra, which is otherwise without end. *Prajñā,* "wisdom," dissolves the veil that carries the figures of illusion, shatters the restless display, and thus leads to the "potential universal consciousness in repose, containing all and manifesting nothing" (*ālaya-vijñāna*), which is ineffable. Yoga achieves this end by a gradual process, step by step. Tracing the expansion of thought in action (*santāna*) backward through the continuous flowing of the mental states, it conducts the mind, at last, to the inexhaustible repository whence the expansion is perpetually pouring. And this then, this sheer abundance beyond the contingencies of the world illusion, is nirvāṇa.

But the question remains—a classic problem of metaphysics—as to how the variegated transient processes can arise out of the undisturbed peace of one inactive reservoir of Being. How can

[78] *Laṅkāvatāra-sūtra* 2. 30. According to Mahāyāna usage, adepts are termed Bodhisattvas. (Cf. *infra,* pp. 534ff.)

a "continuous flow of mental states" (*pravṛtti*) proceed from pure thought, which abides in itself absolutely? This question involves, of course, as a corollary, the perennial problem of the origin of evil. How is the pure, absolutely pure, "repository consciousness" perpetually stirred to render out of the quietness that is its nature and essence a phenomenal world both caused and characterized by imperfection (karma, sin), and moreover tainted with every degree and kind of pain?

The enigma is encountered by a practicing yogī every time his state of perfect absorption (*samādhi*) gives way to normal consciousness, with its rational thinking, awareness of ego, and sensations of an exterior world. The entire mirage of phenomenality then closes again around the yogī's consciousness, and even rises from within. Whence does it come?

To suppose that *avidyā* (nescience) and *vāsanās* (imbued and ingrained unconscious tendencies) exist *ab aeterno* as defilement in the *ālaya,* and that these are the ultimate cause of the world's becoming, would be to introduce a dualistic principle—such as is recognized in the Sāṅkhya; which would mean that there must be admitted two independent principles, both of them without beginning or end, *ālaya* and *avidyā,* the former passive, the latter active, the one motionless in its essence while the other is the cause of perpetual movement and unrest. The Sāṅkhya, as we have seen, offers no explanation of the attraction of the life-monads (*puruṣa*) to nature (*prakṛti*). All that is said is that the life-monads are sheer consciousness while prakṛti is mere matter, and the problem is left at that—unresolved. Likewise in the Yogācāra the difficulty remains. No really satisfactory explanation of the relationship between the two principles is proposed. The earlier Yogācāra teaching simply carried within it, in the form of this hidden, implicit dualism, the seeds of its own refutation. But then by the later, classic masters of the doctrine, the celebrated brothers Asaṅga and Vasubandhu

(5th century A.D.), the philosophical impasse was dexterously avoided.[79]

Ālaya they represent as the repository of the bad (*kleśita*), "the distressed and impaired" as well as of the good (*kuśala*), "the happy and auspicious"—thus bringing Buddhist metaphysics directly into line with one of the main conceptions of Hindu mythology and theology. For in Hinduism the Supreme Being (whether under the mask of Śiva, Visnu, or the Goddess) is always represented as the creator of demons as well as of gods. He is the source of everything in the cosmos, whether malevolent or benign, visible or invisible, and himself enacts through them the roles and attitudes that they represent. As the primordial substance from which creatures come, the Universal Being is ambivalent—or rather, polyvalent. As creator and destroyer, comforter and oppressor, teacher and trickster—and yet, at the same time, transcendent, peaceful, and eternally uninvolved—he unites in his one presence all the pairs of opposites; unites and infinitely surpasses them. The same principle appears now again in the interpretation of the *ālaya* by the classic mas-

[79] Asaṅga and Vasubandhu were the first and second of three brothers, of the youngest of whom, Viriñcivatsa, nothing is known. (According to another version, Vasubandhu was the youngest and Viriñcivatsa the second.) They came of a Brāhman family in Gandhāra and took orders in the Sarvāstivāda school of the Hīnayāna (cf. *supra,* p. 515). Asaṅga was the first to transfer his allegiance to the Mahāyāna. He converted his brother, and thereafter the two were distinguished representatives of their communion. They were closely associated with the Gupta court of Ayodhyā (the modern Oudh), where they were contemporaries of King Bālāditya and his father Vikramāditya (= Candragupta II?). Vasubandhu is credited with some twenty-odd works, the two most celebrated and influential of which are the *Abhidharmakośa* ("Compendium of the Supreme Truth"), dating from his Hīnayāna period, and the *Vijñaptimātratā-triṁśikā* ("Treatise in Thirty Stanzas on the World as Mere Representation"), from his later years. The most important of Asaṅga's works are the *Yogācārya-bhūmi* ("Stages of the Yogācāra") and *Mahāyāna-samparigraha* ("Mahāyāna Manual").

ters of the Yogācāra school. Obviously, Buddhist metaphysics does not represent any really fundamental departure from the great principles and problems of orthodox Indian Brāhmanic thought.[80]

The Buddha had begun as a Hindu. Moreover, the Hindu gods had attended him (according to the Buddhist legend) at every stage of his progress. He remained, in other words, within the sphere of India's traditional philosophy, only approaching its classic problem of release (*mokṣa*) from a fresh and revivifying point of view. The range of his interests and effort corresponded precisely to that of the contemporary Brāhmanic

[80] *Editor's note:* The Mahāyāna doctrine of the Trikāya, the Three Bodies of the Buddha, should be mentioned at this point as approaching the Hindu threefold concept (cf. *supra,* pp. 378-409) of 1. the transcendent principle (*brahman-ātman*), 2. the Lord of the created universe (*īśvara*), and 3. the historical incarnation (*avatāra*). The Three Bodies of the Buddha are 1. the Dharmakāya (Essence Body), which is identical with the void (*śūnya*), suchness (*tattva*), divine knowledge (*prajñā*), and wisdom (*bodhi*); 2. Sambhogakāya (Body of Bliss), which is the Essence as made manifest in heaven (or in the various heavens, the "Buddha Fields"), "determined by name and form, but omniscient, omnipresent, and within the law of causality, omnipotent" (Coomaraswamy, *Buddha and the Gospel of Buddhism,* p. 246); and 3. the Nirmānakāya (Body of Transformation), which is the Essence made manifest on earth as a historical Buddha, emanated or projected from the Sambhogakāya.

We may note also, at this point, that in some of the later phases of the Mahāyāna the Dharmakāya is personified as the Ādi-Buddha (the Supreme Buddha), whose consort or śakti is Prajñā-pāramitā (the Wisdom of the Yonder Shore); cf. Coomaraswamy, *op. cit.,* pp. 239-241, 249, and Zimmer, *Myths and Symbols in Indian Art and Civilization,* pp. 98-102, 146. The symbolism of this figure and his consort in embrace (Yab-Yum, cf. *infra,* pp. 552-559) is the Buddhist counterpart of the Tāntric Śiva-Śakti (*infra,* pp. 581-595).

For a discussion of the Trikāya doctrine as inflected in the various Mahāyāna schools of China and Japan, cf. Junjiro Takakusu, *The Essentials of Buddhist Philosophy,* edited by W. T. Chan and Charles A. Moore, 2nd edition, Honolulu, T.H., 1949, pp. 47, 48, 52, 79, 82, 127, 141, 147, 172, 194.

thinkers. And so, in due time, the two systems came practically together. Sharing ideas, problems, and methods, their protagonists argued out the same questions in the same city and village parks and courtly gardens, until, at last, the practical distinctions between their two approaches disappeared. Whether one worshiped Viṣṇu or the Bodhisattva, Śiva or the Buddha, whether one sought release in Brahman or in the all-containing ālaya, the methods to be followed were practically identical, the attitudes toward the divine guru hardly distinguishable, and the grounds for an honest fundamental argument impossible to find.

The universal "repository consciousness"—pure thought, in and of itself—is the wellspring of every possible creative idea, and hence of the unending series of transient thoughts through which are realized both the life-process of each individual and the panorama of the whole phenomenal world. The dynamism of the mental processes is generated by defilement—germs inherent in the ālaya—and yet, fundamentally, the ālaya transcends the defilement. Through wisdom (*prajñā*), obtained in the experience of enlightenment, this truth is realized and understood. The ālaya is tathātā, sheer being—the absolute, forever beyond defilement—and as such is comparable to a jewel. A jewel may be buried in the earth, but when it is recovered, cleaned, and polished, it again shines in its pristine splendor. The moment "the cleansing or doing away" (*vyavadāna*), is effected by the yogī-bodhisattva (as a consequence of his attainment of transcendental wisdom) the blazing splendor is beheld in its motionless, absolutely intact purity. What was thought to be a defilement has disappeared; for the beheld defilement was only an effect of incomplete knowledge, no more than a reflex of the conditions of all earthly cogitation.

Clearly, the problem has not been explained; the argument has been revolving in circles. The defilement (*kleśa*) is an effect of defilement (*avidyā*). The "cleansing away" (*vyavadāna*) that discloses the blaze of the jewel is an effect of the discovery of the blaze of the jewel. The blaze, though absolutely pure, is experienced with defilement, the defilement being, somehow, an effect of purity, a result of the bright essence, a reflex of the blaze itself. The discussion is riddled with paradox. Nevertheless its main function is apparent enough; namely, to lift the mind from the physical and rational sphere and transfer it, in its contemplation, to the metaphysical.

In the light of this metaphysical emphasis all the terms shared with the Hīnayāna become transformed. Karma, for example, can no longer be regarded as solely, or even primarily, a function of the life-ignorance of the individual, representing the continuity of one specific causal chain, a santāna: an individual series, without beginning yet susceptible of termination; for karma now has assumed a cosmic aspect. Instead of an action being a "seed" (*bīja*) which is to bear fruit, it itself is the fruit of a "seed" (*bīja*) in the "repository consciousness." Karma is this universal "seed" of which all action is the fruit; an imaginary seed, fertilizing as it were the unstained immaculate womb of the ālaya-vijñāna, causing it to bring forth imaginary individuals, imaginary universes—phenomenal phantasms, like the figures of a dream. These live and suffer under the illusion that they are living, suffering, and creating karma in the course of time, whereas actually they are themselves the reflexes of imaginary universal ideas sown in eternity. Karma, the real factor in all that we see, feel, experience, and hear, is the apparent creator of the phenomenal world. Its seeds unfold in an endless harvest of individual consciousnesses, which arise, again and again, like grass from seed. The apparently separate chains of consciousness constitute the variety of this world and of the systems of worlds, yet all are rooted in the one repository. Hence life is governed by common laws. There are many lamps yet their light is one; many "streams of consciousness" (*vijñānas*) flowing forth from the ālaya and returning (through release), yet the totality of phenomenal existence, though manifold in its manifestations, in its constitution and process of continuous becoming, is one.

The world in its life is one; nevertheless, since "facts" are never experienced in their reality but only as recorded in variously limited individual systems of consciousness, the character of existence is experienced differently in the different spheres of being. "A river appears to man," writes one of the commentators on Vasubandhu, "as a mass of running water; to the infernal creatures doomed to suffer the torments of hell it appears as a stream of red-hot molten metal; while to the gods among celestial delights, looking down from above, it appears as a necklace of pearls on the breast of the goddess Earth." [81] Each view is conditioned subjectively, as a function of the peculiar nuance of avidyā of each variety of being; for what makes us feel that the world exists at all is simply the magic of "ignorance," and this differs in its effects in each. Hence, all that we see is an appropriate reflex of ourselves, whereas actually the whole context is non-existent. Hell is nothing but a notion of hell, inflicted on us by our peculiar style of imagination. There are no infernal ministers, as Vasubandhu shows in his *Vijñaptimātratā-viṁśatikā;* "yet sinners, owing to their sins, fancy that they see the infernal ministers and the thought arises in them: 'This is hell; this is the place of hell; this is the time of hell. . . . This is an infernal minister. I am a sinner. . . .' As a consequence of their bad karma, they fancy that they see and experience the various infernal tortures." [82] The bad karma is rooted in the pure ālaya, and made manifest as the self-perpetuating impurity of an unreal individual, harassed by correlative unrealities that are no more unreal than himself.

[81] *Editor's note:* Possibly Agotra, commenting on *Vijñaptimātratā-viṁśatikā* 3-5. Compare *supra,* p. 471. I have not been able to locate Dr. Zimmer's sources for these quotations.

[82] Vasubandhu, *Vijñaptimātratā-viṁśatikā* 4.

Such is the paradoxical truth as expressed in the rationalizing terms of the Yogācāra.[82a]

4.

The Way of the Bodhisattva

THE GREAT Mahāyāna Bodhisattva Avalokiteśvara is a personification of the highest ideal of the Mahāyāna Buddhist career. His legend recounts that when, following a series of eminently virtuous incarnations, he was about to enter into the surcease of nirvāṇa, an uproar, like the sound of a general thunder, rose in all the worlds. The great being knew that this was a wail of lament uttered by all created things—the rocks and stones as well as the trees, insects, gods, animals, demons, and human beings of all the spheres of the universe—at the prospect of his imminent departure from the realms of birth. And so, in his compassion, he renounced for himself the boon of nirvāṇa until all beings without exception should be prepared to enter in before him—like the good shepherd who permits his flock to pass first through the gate and then goes through himself, closing it behind him.

Whereas in the Hīnayāna the term *bodhisattva* denotes one

[82a] *Editor's note:* Dr. Zimmer's notes on this subject break off at this point. For further information concerning the doctrines of the Hīnayāna and Mahāyāna schools, see Takakusu, *op. cit.*, pp. 57-73 (Sarvāstivada), 74-79 (Sautrāntika), 80-95 (Yogācāra), and 96-107 (Mādhyamika). See also Daisetz Teitaro Suzuki, *Essays in Zen Buddhism, First Series,* London, no date, pp. 116-160.

who is on the point of consecration into Buddhahood (for example, Gautama was a Bodhisattva prior to his awakening under the Bo Tree), in the Mahāyāna tradition the term designates those sublimely indifferent, compassionate beings who remain at the threshold of nirvāṇa for the comfort and salvation of the world. Out of perfect indifference (egolessness) and perfect compassion (which is also egolessness) the Mahāyāna Bodhisattva does not experience the "real or true enlightenment" (*samyak-sambodhi*) of the Buddha and then pass to final extinction (*parinirvāṇa*), but stops at the brink—the brink of time and eternity—and thus transcends that pair of opposites: for the world will never end; the round of the cosmic eons will go on and on without ceasing; the vow of the Bodhisattva, to remain at the brink till all shall go in before him, amounts to a vow to remain as he is forever. And this is the reason why his vow is world-redemptive. Through it the truth is symbolized that time and eternity, saṁsāra and nirvāṇa, do not exist as pairs of opposites but are equally "emptiness" (*śūnyatā*), the void.

In popular worship the Bodhisattva is invoked because he is possessed of an inexhaustible power to save. His potential perfection is being diffused all the time, in an everlasting act of universal salvage, and he appears in helpful forms—for example as the legendary flying horse-of-rescue, Cloud [83]—to deliver creatures from the darkness of their woeful lives-in-ignorance. He is possessed of a boundless "treasury of virtues" (*guṇa sambhāra*), which was accumulated by means of a prolonged and absolutely faultless practice, through many lifetimes, of the "highest rectitude" (*pāramitā*). During eons, the Bodhisattva-in-the-making progressed along a sublime path of the most especial, most highly refined psychological austerities, cancelling always every notion and emotion of ego. And this is what brought him into possession of that inexhaustible "treasury," which, in the end, as a result of his supreme act of timeless renunciation, became

[83] Cf. *supra*, pp. 392-393.

available forever to every suffering, striving creature in the world.

The peculiar and especial path of the Mahāyāna Bodhisattva represents the final spiritual refinement—the compassionate counterpart, as it were—of the primordial Indian discipline of tapas. This, as we have seen, was a technique for cultivating in oneself a state of glowing psychophysical heat. The internal energies, systematically controlled and retained, and stored within the body, generated a condition of high temperature, comparable to a fever, and bestowed a certain sovereignty over the forces of the macrocosm by virtue of the conquest of the parallel forces in the microcosm; because it is a fact that every form of asceticism results in its own type of freedom from the usual needs and consequent laws of nature, and therefore affords its own boon of independence. The glowing ascetic cannot be crushed or frustrated by the forces of his environment—nature, the weather, animals, or society. Asserting his superior strength, he defies them. He is fearless and cannot be intimidated; he is in control of his own reactions and emotions.

The only peril that can touch such self-sufficiency is that of being surprised or tricked into some involuntary reaction. This could precipitate an unpremeditated outburst of the concentrated store of tyrannically repressed feeling. Indian epics and romances abound in accounts of holy men who explode irritably in this way at some slight annoyance. (They are, in fact, a standard device of the Oriental storyteller for complicating plots.) The old fellows blast with the lightning of a curse any poor innocent who chances to disturb them in their spiritual exercise, letting go the full force of their extraordinary power and thus forfeiting, in a single flash, their hard-won equilibrium. This is a major catastrophe for the holy man as well as for his shattered, unfortunate, and unwitting—often charming—victim. Or (as we also read), whenever Indra, the jealous king of the gods, feels that his cosmic sovereignty is being jeopardized by the increase of some ascetic's spiritual power, he sends a heavenly damsel, incredibly beautiful, to intoxicate the senses of the spiritual athlete. If she succeeds, the saint, in a sublime night (or even eon) of passion, pours away the whole charge of psycho-physical force that he has spent his lifetime striving to accumulate. The consequence for the world, then, is the birth in due time of a child of fabulous endowments, and for the holy man, the wreckage of his power-project.

In the case of a Bodhisattva the requirements of his peculiar spiritual attitude are, humanly speaking, so severe that were he not established perfectly in his knowledge and his mode of being the danger of his subversion would be practically universal. Temptation is concealed in every incident of life, even the slightest detail, yet for the fulfilled Bodhisattva the possibility of relapse is nonexistent. Since he is the one who is truly without ego, he feels no temptation whatsoever to assert the value of his purely phenomenal personality—not even to the extent of a moment's pause for thought when confronted with an arduous decision. The legends of the Bodhisattvas show them sacrificing their limbs, life, and even wives and children, to what would seem to any normal intellect the most unwarranted demands. Possessions that any ordinary man (*pṛthag-jana*) would regard as the most precious and sacred in the world, the Bodhisattva immediately surrenders to some inconsequential or completely indefensible claim—for example, the plea of a troubled bird or tiger-cub, or the command of some wicked, greedy, and lustful old Brāhman.

The tale is told, for example, in the popular story of the Children of King Vessantara,[84] of how this pious monarch, who was an earlier incarnation of the Buddha, took a vow never to refuse anything demanded of him: "My heart and eye, my flesh and blood, my entire body—should anyone ask these of me, I

[84] *Jātaka* 547. (Also, *Jātakamālā* 9; J. S. Speyer, *The Jātakamālā,* Sacred Books of the Buddhists, Vol. I, London, 1895, pp. 71-93; cf. *infra,* p. 543, note 91.)

would give them." Without a second thought he gave away a wonderful elephant on which the well-being of his kingdom depended, and was consequently driven into exile by his indignant people, together with his loyal queen and two little children. And when he was approached in the wilderness by an ugly old Brāhman who demanded the children as slaves, they were given without a qualm; the queen was demanded, and she too was given. But in the end, the Brāhman revealed that he was Indra, the king of the gods, and stated that he had descended to test the saintly human king, and so all ended well. In this case, the temptation of Indra having failed, the god was gracious in defeat.

Even the crudest, most elementary mind cannot but be amazed and outraged by such demonstrations of saintly indifference to the normal values of human welfare—particularly since nothing whatsoever is gained from them. For what does it really matter if a single dove is preserved from the talons of a hawk,[85] a new born litter of tiger-kittens rescued from starvation,[86] or a senile, nasty old Brāhman gratified in his greed and lust by the enslavement of a little prince and princess? The cruel course of nature is not altered. Indeed, the Bodhisattva's absurd sacrifices often support and give voluntary corroboration to the brutal laws that prevail where the struggle for life goes on in its crude, unmitigated, animal-demonic form; while in the case of the Brāhman and the young prince and princess, the first dictate of human morality would seem to have been violated.

In terms, however, of the basic problem and task of the Bodhisattva, it is precisely the apparent senselessness, even indecency, of the sacrifice that makes the difference; for to refuse a paradoxical surrender would be to subscribe (if only by nega-

[85] Aśvaghosa, *Sutrālaṅkāra* 64. (A fine translation will be found in E. W. Burlingame, *Buddhist Parables,* New Haven, 1922, pp. 314-324.)

[86] *Jātakamālā* 1. (Speyer, *op. cit.,* pp. 1-8.)

tion) to the standards and world vision of the passion-bound, ego-ridden, common individual who has presented the demand. The supreme and especial test of the Bodhisattva is that of his readiness and power to expand, time and time again, in boundless giving (*dāna*). This requires of him a continuous abdication—or rather, nonexperience—of ego. Any reaction of shrinking back, even from a nonsensical sacrifice, would confirm and harden a nucleus of ego-consciousness; whereas the whole sense of Bodhisattvahood is that the limited and limiting ego has evaporated. To suppose that a Bodhisattva should give an absurd demand his second thought—or be the least reluctant to abandon body, life, family, and possessions—would be to ask him to show himself as one who subscribed to the intrinsic value and substantiality of things; and this would imply that on the transcendental plane, which he represents, something of the earth is admitted to have a value—one's body or possessions, kingly rank, queen, children, or honor—whereas, on that plane, all things are known to be ephemeral, phenomenal, and so, in reality, nonexistent. Refusal or resistance would throw a candidate for Bodhisatvahood back into the sphere of the unessential and immediately cut him off from true reality. He would no longer be an aspirant to enlightenment, one "whose essence (*sattva*) is (virtually) enlightenment (*bodhi*)," but, like the yogī transfixed by the allure of a seductive heavenly damsel, would have been tempted, tricked, and returned to the realm and multitude of "ordinary beings" (*pṛthagjana*).

The aspirant to Bodhisattvahood must strive to behave as though he were already completely without ego; just as a pupil in any art (the dance, for example) must try to act as though he were already a master of his skill. The nonexistence of all phenomenal values on the transcendental plane must be unremittingly anticipated in both thought and conduct, and the point of view of absolute wisdom relentlessly exercised in numberless acts through numberless lives. In this manner wisdom is incorporated gradually in the candidate. It becomes, first, part and parcel of his personality and then, at last, his whole essence and only state of being. A "superabundant store of forces or virtues" (*guṇa-sambhāra*) is the natural corollary of such a supreme achievement of indifference. By not caring for anything at all, and thus completely transcending himself as man, the absolutely unconditioned being becomes elevated to, and established in, a spiritual sphere of universal omnipotence—and this force thereafter radiates from him eternally, flashing forth for the benefit of all who ask.

The fierce will and the struggle for superhuman power of the old ascetics of the hermit groves thus attain, in the Bodhisattva ideal, to their most benign transfiguration. The infinitely powerful status of saviorship is the purified and perfected, nonegoistic counterpart of that earlier, supremely self-assertive effort—the whole discipline now being devoted to the universal, instead of to the individual, benefit. In every phase, crisis, and realization along the path to perfection of Avalokiteśvara, Kṣitigarbha (Chinese: Ti-tsang; Japanese: Jizo), Amitābha, and the multitude of other Bodhisattvas of Mahāyāna sacred cult and legend, we read the lesson of this absolutely sublimated, omnipotently selfless state of realization.

The brief, extraordinarily compressed Mahāyāna Buddhist text known as the *Prajñā-pāramitā-hṛdaya-sūtra,* "The Manual of the Heart (i.e., the Secret) of the Perfection of the Wisdom of the Other Shore," [87] states that when a Bodhisattva engaging in the deep practice of the Wisdom of the Other Shore considers within himself, "There are the five elements-of-existence," he perceives immediately that they are "void in their very nature." [88] "Here form," it is stated, "is emptiness, and emptiness

[87] Sacred Books of the East, Vol. XLIX, Part II, pp. 147-149.

[88] The five elements of existence are: 1. *rūpa* (form), which comprehends the four elements of earth, water, fire, and air, as well as every form that springs from them, i.e., all physical phenomena, 2. *vedanā* (sensa-

indeed is form. Emptiness is not different from form, form is not different from emptiness. What is form that is emptiness, what is emptiness that is form."

This is what the Bodhisattva perceives with respect to form. His perceptions, then, with respect to each of the other elements of existence—sensations, notions, predispositions, and knowledge—are the same. "All things bear the characteristic marks of emptiness. They do not come into being, they do not cease to be; they are not stainless, they are not stained; they do not become imperfect, they do not become perfect. Therefore, here in this emptiness there is no form, there are no sensations, notions, or mental propensities; there is no consciousness; there is no eye, ear, nose, tongue, body, or mind; no color, sound, odor, taste, or object of touch; no constituent element of vision or of the other sense processes, no constituent element of the mental processes. There is no knowledge, no nescience, no destruction of knowledge, no destruction of nescience. There is no twelvefold concatenation of causes and effects, ending in old age and death.[89] There is no destruction of old age and death; there is neither any coming into existence nor any ceasing of suffering; there is no path to the destruction of suffering. There is no enlightenment, no attainment, no realization—since enlightenment does not exist."

No argument is offered in support of these fantastic observations. They are simply presented as the statements of the Bodhisattva Avalokiteśvara—obviously to show that the paradoxical

tions, sense-perceptions, feelings), 3. *sañjñā* (all the notions that constitute self-conscious intellection), 4. *saṁskāra* (predispositions, inclinations, mental molds), and 5. *vijñāna* (consciousness, discrimination, knowledge). The group 2-5 composes the sphere of *nāman* (name), or mental phenomena.

[89] The twelvefold concatenation of causes and effects (*pratītya-samutpāda)* is represented in Buddhism as follows: 1. ignorance, 2. action, 3. consciousness, 4. name and form, 5. the senses, 6. contact, 7. sensation, 8. craving, 9. attachment, 10. becoming, 11. birth, 12. old age, disease, and death. Cf. Takakusu, *op. cit.,* pp. 29-36.

truth of the Wisdom of the Other Shore lies beyond the range of the vision of this bank. The nature of such a truth may be suggested verbally, but it resists the analysis and arguments of reason. Following, therefore, this suggestion of what is to be known, comes a description of the perfected state itself; and this is the clue to the curious "way of action" of the candidate for Bodhisattvahood:

"There are no obstacles of thought for the Bodhisattva who cleaves to the Wisdom of the Other Shore. Because there are no obstacles of thought, he has no fear; he has transcended all wrong notions; he abides in enduring nirvāṇa. All the Buddhas of the past, present, and future,[90] cleaving to the Wisdom of the Other Shore, have awakened to the highest, perfect, complete awakening.

"Therefore one should know"—and the text now proceeds to its most mysterious and most helpful, culminating statement: "The Wisdom of the Other Shore is the great magic formula (*mantra*), the magic formula of great wisdom, the most excellent magic formula, the peerless magic formula, capable of allaying every suffering. It is truth because it is not falsehood. A magic formula has been given in the Wisdom of the Other Shore. It sounds as follows:

" 'O THOU WHO ART GONE, WHO ART GONE, WHO ART GONE TO THE OTHER SHORE, WHO HAST LANDED ON THE OTHER SHORE, O THOU ENLIGHTENMENT, HAIL!'

"Here endeth the Manual of the Heart of the Wisdom of the Other Shore."

The first requirement of the spiritual pupil in India, as we have seen, is the great virtue of faith (*śraddhā*), trust in the teacher and his words. The faith will be corroborated by the pupil's own experience in the course of his spiritual progress,

[90] According to the Mahāyāna there have been, there are, and there will be numberless Buddhas; cf. *supra*, p. 508.

but meanwhile he cannot presume to argue with his guru in callow criticism of the paradoxical doctrine. He must undergo, first, a transformation; that, not criticism, will be the means of his understanding. He must be brought by a process of evolution to a spiritual level from which to experience the meaning of the enigmatical teaching. And meanwhile, the process of his sublimation will be facilitated by meditation on the magic formula, which is the "Heart of the Wisdom of the Other Shore," and which he is to regard as an expression of his own supreme belief, designed to concentrate and intensify his faith. Though temporarily unintelligible to him, it is nevertheless his credo, to be repeated in constant recitation, as an invocation bidding the Wisdom of the Other Shore to come to him. And the wonder is that this magic formula actually can function as an effective alchemical charm, facilitating the transmutation that duly yields, of itself, the gold of enlightenment.

For meditation on this curious string of words is not the sole means by which the neophyte, filled with faith, is to attempt to bring to pass the all-important transformation in his understanding. The performance of certain characteristic acts is also required, and these, together with the experience of their results, make the formula more meaningful in the course of time, while, in reciprocal effect, the formula, constantly held in mind, serves to extract and bring to a point the lesson of the faithful performance of the necessary acts.

The sense, for example, of the Mahāyānist rerenderings of certain tales from the Jātaka, in the sixth-century collection known as the *Jātakamālā*, "The Garland of Tales from the Earlier Lives of the Buddha," [91] is that one has to assume pecu-

[91] The *Jātakamālā* is a work in Sanskrit attributed to a certain Āryasūra (for translation, see *supra*, p. 537, note 84), which contains 34 Jātakas, or exemplary tales of the earlier lives of the Buddha, adapted, for the most part, from the much earlier, Pāli compendium of more than five hundred Jātakas. The latter is one of the great portions of the orthodox Hīnayāna

liar attitudes, exhibit uncommon reactions in crucial situations, and accomplish very special deeds, if one is ever to come to a new outlook upon life and on oneself. Practice precedes insight; knowledge is the reward of action: therefore, try! That is the thought. For it is by doing things that one becomes transformed. Executing a symbolical gesture, actually living through, to the very limit, a particular role, one comes to realize the truth inherent in the role. Suffering its consequences, one fathoms and exhausts its contents. Knowledge is to be attained, in other words, not through inaction (as in the Jaina and the classic Yoga disciplines) but through a bold and advertent living of life.

This is an idea radically different in its implications from that of the penitential groves, and yet completely consistent with the ancient Indian concept of karma.[92] One attracts the bright karmic substance that cleans away and replaces tamas [93] by sacrificing oneself wholeheartedly, in a spirit of humility and self-effacement, performing virtuous deeds while suppressing relentlessly every impulse to self-aggrandizement and display. The Buddha-in-the-making gradually imbues himself with karmic luminosity by cultivating in action the "highest virtues or perfections" (*pāramitās*), until there is finally no space left within him for any darker, inauspicious karmic force. People who cling to their ego favor instinctively the deceits of the phenomenal illusion, and so bind themselves the more, with every

canon (cf. *The Jātaka, or Stories of the Buddha's Former Births,* translated from the Pāli by various hands under the editorship of E. B. Cowell, 6 vols., Cambridge, England, 1895–1907).

[92] *Editor's note:* The final goal and emphasis—as ever in India—is knowledge, not work; but work, or action, is indicated as the means. Dr. Zimmer's manuscript carries a brief note, indicating his intention to compare this approach with that of the Karma Yoga taught in the *Bhagavad Gītā,* but the paragraph seems not to have been written.

[93] Tamas guna; for a discussion of the guṇas, cf. *supra,* pp. 295-297, 398-402.

act, to the passionate forces of the life-instinct that clings only to itself; but the candidate for the Wisdom of the Other Shore behaves consistently as though he had already left behind the delusion of the world display. In every act of his daily living he makes a decision in favor of the self-transcending alternative, until at last, as a consequence of infinitely numerous deed-experiences of this kind, he does actually transcend the delusions of his phenomenal psychology: thenceforward he behaves instinctively as though his ego, with its false impressions, did not exist. This transmutation is the very sense and essence of the Wisdom of the Other Shore.

Actual acts, meanwhile, are the only things that can set us free. Virtuous, egoless acts release the mind, in the end, from the bondage of its ingrained, normal human attitudes and propensities, which are based on not knowing better. But such egoless, apparently dangerous acts require a faith in the as yet unknown, a humble courage, and a generous willingness to take a blind jump into the dark. Then, as a reward, they open to us a new outlook. A magical change of scenery is produced—a new order of values emerges. Because it is a fact: one is transformed by one's deeds, either for better or for worse: ignorance and knowledge are but the intellectual aspects of the changes wrought upon us by our manner of life.

The manner of life of the Bodhisattva is well summarized in the formula: "A guard I would be to them who have no protection, a guide to the voyager, a ship, a well, a spring, a bridge for the seeker of the Other Shore." [94]

To see the potential Buddhahood in all, the criminal and the animal as well as the virtuous and the human, is the most just approach possible to the beings of the world. All beings, all men, whether virtuous or wicked, as well as inferior creatures even down to the ants, are to be regarded, respected, and treated

[94] Cf. Louis de la Vallée Poussin, *Bouddhisme,* 3rd edition, Paris, 1925, p. 303, and Keith, *op. cit.,* p. 290.

as potential Buddhas. This is a view at once democratic and aristocratic—basically the same view as that of the ancient Jaina system and the doctrine of Gosāla. Indeed, in all of the later Indian philosophic disciplines dedicated to the realization of the hidden truth through an attainment of individual perfection, this view is reflected, one way or another. Its main principle is, that perfection is not something added or acquired from without, but rather, the very thing that is already potential within, as the basic actuality of the individual. The proper metaphor, therefore, for the Indian view of the process of fulfillment is not that of progress, growth, evolution, or expansion into greater external spheres, but Self-recollection. The effort of the pupil is to bring into consciousness what already reposes in a hidden state, dormant and quiescent, as the timeless reality of his being.

This is the basic Indian concept of the way—a fundamentally static view of the "march to enlightenment" (*bodhicaryā*). In the *Yoga-sūtras* the goal is represented as the attainment of "isolation-integration" (*kaivalya*), in the Sāṅkhya as the achievement of "discriminating insight" (*viveka*), in Vedānta as the realization of the "Transcendental Self" (*ātman-brahman*), and in Buddhism as "Enlightenment" (*bodhi*); but in essence these goals are one. Something that was stained, impaired, temporarily inactive and out of contact, polluted, obscured, not shining forth in its supreme light, not manifesting its boundless strength and prodigious faculties, becomes reinstated, restored to its native glory, cleansed, awake, and pristine. The process is compared to that of the polishing of a crystal, or the cleaning of a mirror that has somehow become besmeared and soiled.[94a]

The purification of the gross body is properly the first step, and this is best effected through the physical exercises and processes of Haṭha Yoga: a cleansing of the intestinal canal through

[94a] *Editor's note:* Nāgārjuna's doctrine of the Void rendered this image archaic; nevertheless, it continued to serve as a respected metaphor until

the practices called *basti* and *neti,* and of the bodily channels containing and carrying vital wind (*prāṇa*) through the classic exercises of control of the breath (*prāṇāyāma*). Such disciplines cleanse and rebuild the nervous and glandular systems.[95]

Meanwhile the systematic purification of the subtle body is also undertaken. According to the yogic method of Patañjali, this is effected by a gradual transformation of tāmasic and rājasic qualities and forces into sāttvic,[96] while according to the more ancient, less psychological, more materialistic approach of the Jaina disciplines, it is to be brought about by an inhibiting of the physical influx of darkening karmic color into the crystal of the monad. In either case, the sum and substance of the teaching is the same: not simply that we are meant to be crystal pure and perfect, but that in essence we really are. The psychophysical system is defiled, obscured, and disordered by obstructing matter of some kind, which clogs the channels and vessels of life and consciousness on every level. *Mala,* "dirt, refuse, impurity," fills us; we are "besmeared." Whereas the true and

---

Hui-neng (638–713 A.D.) wrote his celebrated verse on the wall of the Yellow Plum Monastery:

"There is neither Bo Tree
Nor any mirror bright;
Since śūnyatā is all,
Whereon can what dust alight?"

Hui-neng became the Sixth Patriarch of the Ch'an (Japanese: Zen) school of Far Eastern Buddhism. (Cf. Suzuki, *op. cit.,* p. 205; Alan W. Watts, *The Spirit of Zen,* The Wisdom of the East Series, London, 1936, p. 40; and Sokei-an, "The Transmission of the Lamp," in *Cat's Yawn,* published by the First Zen Institute of America, New York, 1947, p. 26.)

[95] *Editor's note:* This paragraph is followed in Dr. Zimmer's papers by a brief note indicating his intention to build it out. Hatha Yoga is a system of physical exercises for the cultivation of perfect health and supernormal bodily powers. Properly, it is a preliminary to other yoga disciplines, but it may be practiced also as an end in itself.

[96] For a discussion of the gunas (tamas guṇa, rajas guṇa, sattva guṇa), cf. *supra,* pp. 295-297, 398-402.

highest state is *nir-añjana:* "without besmearing." Brahman is *nir-añjana.* The Buddha is *nir-añjana.* We ourselves become wholly Brahman, wholly Enlightened, wholly what we are, only by getting rid of the soiling matter (*prakṛti*) which afflicts us from without, purging both the physique and the psyche by means of a continuous and radical cleansing diet.

That is to say: instead of a concept of growth, expansion, evolution, and acquisition, India's thought is that of a draining, scouring, and purification, directed to a *restitutio in integrum:* an integral restitution of the primal state—such as it was before the enigmatic moment or motion that set in action the universe and its microcosmic counterpart, the clouded wit of man. The Self, when cleansed, shines forth of itself, and at this moment our Enlightenment is no longer potential, but a fact. The comparable procedure in Hindu medicine is that of the regimen of preliminary purgatives, enemas, and emetics, to be followed by a light and wholesome, restorative, sāttvic diet.[96a]

[96a] *Editor's note:* "The difference of method between the Indian and the Chinese [Buddhist teachers] often raised the question as to the difference, if there be [any], between the 'Tathāgata Dhyāna' and the 'Patriarchal Dhyāna.' For instance, when Hsiang-yen showed his song of poverty to Yang-shan, the latter said, 'You understand the Tathāgata Dhyāna but not yet the Patriarchal Dhyāna.' When asked about the difference, Mu-chou replied, 'The green mountains are green mountains, and the white clouds are white clouds' " (Suzuki, *op. cit.*, pp. 224-225). The difference of method here noted does not mean that the Far Eastern Buddhist goal is not the same as the Indian, namely, a *restitutio in integrum.* "When the monk Ming came to Hui-neng and asked for instruction, Hui-neng said, 'Show me your original face before you were born' " (*ib.*, p. 224). The "Tathāgata Dhyāna" to which Dr. Suzuki refers was the mode of "contemplation" (Sanskrit, *dhyāna;* Chinese, *ch'an;* Japanese, *zen*) taught by Gautama Śākyamuni (the Tathāgata); the "Patriarchal Dhyāna" was that introduced into China in 520 A.D. by the Indian Buddhist Patriarch Bodhidharma and developed by Hui neng: it is continued to this day in the Zen schools of Japan. For an exposition of this technique of restitution, the reader is referred to Takakusu, *op. cit.*, pp. 153-165, and to the volumes cited *supra,* p. 546, note 94a.

Philosophic theory, religious belief, and intuitive experience support each other in India in the basic insight that, fundamentally, all is well. A supreme optimism prevails everywhere, in spite of the unromantic recognition that the universe of man's affairs is in the most imperfect state imaginable, one amounting practically to chaos. The world-root, the secret veiled reality, is of an indestructible diamond-hardness, even though we—our feelings, minds, and senses—can be in the wrong, and indeed mostly are. Mentally, bodily, and morally, we are far from perfection; hence we are incapable of mirroring truth and becoming aware of our basic serenity. That very truth, however, the highest reality, is ever and universally present, whether our consciousness gets in touch with it or not. Furthermore, even though in the realm of the perishable, in the passage between birth and death, in the sphere of suffering and delight, everything changes, above or beyond all these disturbing changes there remains the possibility of that one, supreme, composing change, which is unique and *sui generis:* the change in our own nature that puts an end to the derangements of change—through knowledge of the Unchangeable, which is the fundament of our own intrinsic, never-changing being.

That abiding presence is compared to the sun obscured from us by the cloud of the mind's unknowing. Suffering, pain, and the disorders of the world do not represent the true state of things, but are the reflexes of our own wrong perspective, and yet they seem to us to be very real, until the obstruction is dissolved and the mind beholds the source of its own light. The cloud between is small, yet it can cover with its little, perishable form the blazing presence. This cloud being blown away, the transcendent light is beheld immediately, of its own power, and yet even while obscured from us—unlooked upon, unrealized, unrevealed—it is ever there in its enduring splendor. And not only is it always there, it is the source and sustenance of everything that is here.

As we have stated many times, and now, for the last time, must state again, the Jainas represented the crystal of the life-monad (*jīva*) as defiled by a physical karmic coloring substance (*leśya*), which, on entering it, darkened its intrinsic light. This subtle physical influx (*āsrava*) had to be literally stopped, and the darkening matter then allowed to evaporate or burn away by becoming converted into experience, biography, suffering, and destiny—which was a comparatively simple, materialistic reading of the problem. The later Indian view, as represented in the classic, semimaterialistic systems of the Sāṅkhya, Yoga, and Upaniṣads, then regarded the life-monad (Sāṅkhya and Yoga: *puruṣa*), or the Self (Upanisads: *ātman*), as forever undefiled, like the sun; only the soul-faculties clustering around it were in darkness—and this was a darkness, furthermore, rather of ignorance than of literal involvement. No longer was karmic matter pouring into the kernel of our being, as in the formula of the Jainas, but a veil of ignorance was cutting off the light. And we had merely to dissolve this cloud by bringing to bear upon it the power of its opposite: *viveka* (discrimination), *vidyā* (knowledge). The unresolved question remained, however, as to the nature of the cloud, and this, as we have seen, furnished a theme for inexhaustible debate. One way or another, no matter how the philosophers turned the problem, a *second* sphere of forces (however defined, however rationalized, however devaluated by unfavorable descriptions) had to be admitted into the system as a counter to the sphere of "That Which Truly Is." And the two had then to be co-ordinated in some kind of not quite satisfying, unrelated relationship.

The mind, for example, is part of the bodily system, though it mirrors, usually imperfectly, the light of the spirit. The mind is not uninvolved. It is not an absolutely unconcerned visitor from a higher realm. On the contrary, most of it is colored, tinged and biased, limited and supported, by the nature and material of the individual body, on and in which it grows, and which it is meant to direct and follow. The mental faculty, in all its operations, is but a function of this bodily whole, prejudiced by the peculiar quality of the gross physical substance that enwraps it, as well as by the subtle substance of which it is itself constituted. The mind is a mirror, but obscured by its own darkness; a pond ruffled by the gales of its own passions, by the winds of the transient emotions, the restlessness of "Him Who Blows." If it were only like a lovely mountain lake, sheltered against the ruffling breath by hill barriers on every side, crystal clear, unaffected by any turbid affluents to stain its clarity and give a ripple to its surface, fed by only an underground source in its own depth—then it might be capable of mirroring, without distortion, the form of truth. And yet, even then, there would remain this dualistic problem (at least so far as metaphysical arguments and explanations are concerned) of the twofold context of the mirror and the light.

The Buddhist approach to the difficulty was based on a formula of negating rather than affirming an abiding essence beyond or beneath the veiling cloud. The Buddha himself initiated this attitude with his fundamental dictum, "All is without a self," and though his followers, in spite of their Master's repeated refusal to engage in metaphysical discourse, soon enough became involved in discussion, both among themselves and with the Brāhmans, and in the end were practically back in the Hindu fold,[97] their basic tendency to negate was nevertheless carried, in the classic, culminating period of the Mahāyāna, to its own, truly wondrous, theoretical consummation in the "Doctrine of the Void." The principle of the paradox here was brought from the meditation grove into the very camp of reason, the academy of philosophical verbalization, where the mind then dismembered itself systematically in a series of thoroughgoing demonstrations, dissolving, one by one, its own supports and leaving the consciousness-beyond-cerebration alone in the

[97] Cf. *supra*, pp. 529-531.

void. And in the same spirit of trust in the transcendent, the way of the Bodhisattva was developed as an ethical application of the principle of unwavering faith in the metaphysically grounded Doctrine of the Buddha. In diametric contrast to the way of the Jaina "Crossing-Maker," whose spiritual passage to the Yonder Shore was achieved by an extreme technique of immobilization, the Bodhisattva, inspired by the immanence on this shore of the transcendency of that, established himself and his world in nondual understanding by the way of truth-revealing acts. The doctrine of the nondual void was applied courageously to the void of life. All things, Buddhas and arhats as well as "momentary particles" (*dharmas*), are void, even unto "nothingness" (*abhāvadhātu*).

5.

The Great Delight

In the mature Mahāyāna the mystery of creation is interpreted in terms of the Bodhisattva idea. When Avalokiteśvara refused nirvāṇa, so that he should remain the savior of all created things, he was filled with the quality known as *karuṇā:* "compassion." This pure compassion is of the essence of the Bodhisattva and is identical with his right perception of the void; or, as one might say, it is the primary reflex of the void. Because of compassion (*karuṇā*) the Bodhisattva assumes the various forms in which he appears for the salvation of beings in the phenomenal realm. He assumes, for example, the divine forms of Viṣṇu for those who worship Viṣṇu and of Śiva for those who worship Śiva. Also, it is by virtue of the compassion of the Bodhisattva that the Buddhas come into the world—which belief represents an important shift and transformation of Buddhist emphasis. "In the excellent Akaniṣṭha heaven, which is beyond the Suddhāvāsa heaven," we read in Śāntarakṣita's *Tattvasaṅgraha,* "the Bodhisattva attains omniscience, and (under his influence) a Buddha is born in this world." [98]

Within the hearts of all creatures compassion is present as the sign of their potential Bodhisattvahood; for all things are śūnyatā, the void—and the pure reflex of this void (which is their essential being) is compassion. Compassion (*karuṇā*), indeed is the force that holds things in manifestation—just as it withholds the Bodhisattva from nirvāṇa. The whole universe, therefore, is karuṇā, compassion, which is also known as śūnyatā, the void.

To a certain extent, this world-supporting condescension of the Bodhisattva is comparable to that of Kṛṣṇa, as represented in the *Bhagavad Gītā,*[98a] and of the Lord of Creation, as revealed in the *Vedāntasāra.*[98b] It is an act of voluntary ignorance; a loving descent or "spiritual sacrifice" (*ātma-yajña*), such as in the Christian tradition is celebrated in the mystery of the Incarnation. However, in spirit and practice it takes us one step further, since it calls for *an unqualified affirmation of "ignorance"* (avidyā) *as in essence identical with "enlightenment"* (bodhi)—which renders archaic the ancient Sāṅkhya-Vedānta-Hīnayāna modes of monkish rejection or acceptance that we have been discussing through hundreds of pages. "Ignorance" (*avidyā*) is still what the Buddha declared it to be, namely the cause of suffering, the cause of the bondage of all beings within the vortex of birth,

[98] Śāntarakṣita, *Tattvasaṅgraha,* as cited by Benoytosh Bhattacharyya, *An Introduction to Buddhist Esoterism,* Oxford, 1932, p. 99.

[98a] *Supra,* pp. 389-392.

[98b] *Supra,* pp. 424-429.

old age, and death. It is still the benighting affliction of those who live in desire and fear, in hope, despair, disgust, and sorrow. But the one whose mind is cleansed, whose "soul," whose selfhood, has become annihilate in the void, is conscious of an enjoyable wonder, like a dream, or like a display set up by magic, with which, as the void, he is identical. The beings who, in their ignorance, experience themselves as engulfed in a sea of pain are themselves non-beings, void and unchanging; only their ignorance makes them feel that *they* are in pain. Mingled with the compassion of the Bodhisattva is a quality, therefore, of "great delight" (*mahā-sukha*); for where others behold pain, disaster, change, poverty, vice, or, on the other hand, honor, pleasure, attainment, luxury, or virtue, the "highest knowledge" (*prajñā*) reveals the void: nameless, absolute, unchanging, stainless, without beginning or end, like the sky. Hence the Bodhisattva wanders everywhere, boundless, fearless, like a lion, roaring the lion-roar of Bodhisattvahood. These three worlds have been created, as it were, for—by—and of—the enjoyment of this immortal: they are his *līlā,* his "play."

Since the candidate for such knowledge must behave like one who has already attained, a programmatic, sacramental breaking of the bounds that normally stand as the limits of virtue was carefully undertaken in certain schools of the Mahāyāna. "By those identical actions by which mortals rot in hell for hundreds of crores of cycles, the yogī" we read in one of the celebrated texts, "is liberated." [99] In spite of all the scandal that has been spread concerning this phase of Buddhist worship, the majority of the sacramental breaches (in a society hedged on every side by the most meticulous taboos) were not such as would give

[99] *Jñānasiddhi* 1. (In *Two Vajrayāna Works,* edited with an introduction by Benoytosh Bhattacharyya, Gaekwad's Oriental Series, No. XLIV, Baroda, 1929, p. xix.)

A crore is ten million.

the slightest pause to the usual modern Christian gentleman or lady. They consisted in partaking of such forbidden foods as fish, meat, spicy dishes, and wine, and engaging in sexual intercourse. The sole novelty was that these acts were to be undertaken not in sensual eagerness or sated boredom, but without egoity and under the direction of a religious teacher, being regarded as concomitants of a difficult and dangerous yet absolutely indispensable spiritual exercise. The Bodhisattva is beyond desire and fear; moreover, all things are Buddha-things and void.

In the sexual act it is possible to recognize a pre-eminent rendition and profound human experience of the metaphysical mystery of the nondual entity which is made manifest as two. The embrace of the male and female principles, and their delight thereby, denote their intrinsic unity, their metaphysical identity. Regarded from the standpoint of logic in the world of space and time, the male and female are two. But in their intuition of their identity (which is the seed of love) the thought of twoness is transcended, while from the mystery of their physical union (their enactment and experience in time of their real and secret nonduality) a new being is produced—as though the corporeal imitation of the transcorporeal, nondual truth had magically touched the inexhaustible spring from which the phenomena of the cosmos arise. Through the sexual act, that is to say, creatures of the visible world actually come into touch, in experience, with the metaphysical sphere of the nondual source. The latter is not absolutely apart and unrelated. It is, rather, their own very essence, which they experience in every impulse of compassion—but supremely in that supreme human realization of compassion which is known in the enactment of the mystery play of the sexes.

śunyatābodhito bījam bījāt bimbam prajāyate
bimbe ca nyāsavinyāsa tasmāt sarvam pratītyajam

"From the right perception of śūnyatā ('the void') comes bīja ('the seed'). From bīja the conception of an icon is developed, and from that conception is derived the external representation of the icon." [100]

"So the entire iconography of the Buddhist," comments Dr. Benoytosh Bhattacharyya to this text, "proceeds from a correct understanding of the doctrine of Śūnyatā." [101] Moreover, one might add, this creation of an icon is an act of the same order as the creation of the world: *ars imitatur naturam in sua operatione.*[102]

Through the contemplation of an icon one's mind is united with the "seed" (*bīja*), and through this seed then returned to the void. The external representation, which is simply the preliminary support of this realization, may be of stone, wood, bronze, or any other lifeless substance, but also, a living being —for example, the guru, or even the devotee himself in some symbolic role; the symbol most appropriately associated with the Mahāyāna doctrine of *mahāsukha,* "the great delight," being the divine male and female (Tibetan: *Yab-Yum*) in embrace.

The primitive idea behind this icon is that of the female as the activating principle. Through her allure she stirs the dormant male element from its quiet; through her embrace she integrates the male energy. In India, as we have seen,[103] the

[100] An alternate rendering: "The void brings forth the seed; this develops into the mental representation; this concretizes externally, and from it springs all that is conditioned-in-existence." *Mahāsukhaprakāśa* ("The Exposition of the Doctrine of the Great Delight"), fol. 32. This is a twelfth-century work by a Bengali expositor, Advayavajra.

[101] Benoytosh Bhattacharyya, *The Indian Buddhist Iconography,* Oxford, 1924, p. xiii.

[102] "For the East, as for St. Thomas [Aquinas], *ars imitatur naturam in sua operatione*" (Ananda K. Coomaraswamy, *The Transformation of Nature in Art,* Cambridge, Mass., 1934, p. 15).

[103] *Supra,* p. 331.

ever-renewed cosmogony of the coming into existence of the universe and its disappearance again is understood, on the basis of yoga experience, as a grandiose psychogeny: the yogī, returning from the transcendental realization of samādhi, enters again into the world of forms presented to consciousness by his inner and outer senses, these phenomenal forms being but functions of the activated sense organs themselves. In the Mahāyāna Buddhist school of the Great Delight (*mahāsukha*) such a process of concentrated meditation on the appearance and disappearance of mental representations is facilitated and given direction by a female form, and the ritual sexual act becomes a kind of *Via crucis* whereby the individual experiences the mystery of the cosmogonic manifestation of compassion. His right perception of śūnyatā enables him to realize a complete self-identification with it, "knower and known, seer and seen, meet in an act transcending distinction," and the initiate thus becomes himself an angel: the angel with two backs—man-woman: the anthropomorphic form of the compassionate void.

This Yab-Yum icon is to be read two ways. On the one hand, the candidate is to meditate on the female portion as the śakti or dynamic aspect of eternity and the male as the quiescent but activated. Then, on the other hand, the male is to be regarded as the principle of the path, the way, the method (*upāya*), and the female, with which it merges, as the transcendent goal; she is then the fountainhead into which the dynamism of enlightenment returns in its state of full and permanent incandescence. And finally, the very fact that the dual symbol of the united couple is to be read in the two ways (with either the male or the female representing transcendent truth) signifies that the two aspects or functions of reality are of perfectly equal rank: there is no difference between saṁsāra and nirvāṇa, either as to dignity or as to substance. Tathatā, the sheer "suchness," is made manifest both ways, and for true enlightenment the apparent difference is nonexistent.

Yab-Yum symbolism thus insists on the dignity of the phenomenal universe. Its genial recognition of the metaphysical implications of the corporeal spirituality of the sexual totality (wherein the tensions and impulses of opposites are at rest, balancing, fulfilling, and nullifying each other) is very different in spirit from the woman-disdaining, world-disdaining arrogance of the mountain sages—whether Jaina, Vedāntic, or Hīnayāna-Buddhist. Apparently, this world-affirmative method of spiritual guidance was a contribution from the aristocratic Kṣatriya caste; perhaps a development of that ancient, profoundly mystical love-lore which became thinned out and practically lost in the late, classic, Brāhmanic *Kāmasūtra*.[104] The origins of the movement are obscure, but there is a tradition that places them in the court circle of a certain Indrabhūti, king of Uḍḍiyāna in the seventh or eighth century A.D. This royal personage is the reputed author of the *Jñānasiddhi*, a basic work in which the Yab-Yum initiation is described.[105] The precise location of his kingdom, however, is a matter of scholarly conjecture, some placing it in the Swat Valley of the North-West Frontier Province, others in Oṛissā, not far from the homeland of the Buddha. We are told that Indrabhūti's gifted daughter, the princess Lakṣmīṅkarā Devī, was the moving spirit of this courtly cult of love.[106]

One thinks immediately of Eleanor of Aquitaine and the Provençal courts of love, four centuries later, when the aristocratic circles of the Occident were being touched by the magic of the Orient, in the period of the Crusades. Simultaneously, in Mahāyāna-Buddhist Japan, the lords and ladies of the Imperial court of Miyako were enacting their poetic romance of the

[104] Cf. *supra*, pp. 140-150.

[105] The Sanskrit text is published in Gaekwad's Oriental Series, No. XLIV (cf. *supra*, p. 554, note 99); a summary of the contents will be found in Bhattacharyya, *Introduction to Buddhist Esoterism*, pp. 38ff.

[106] Cf. Bhattacharyya, *The Indian Buddhist Iconography*, p. xxvi, note.

"Cloud Gallants" and "Flower Maidens," while Persia was singing the songs of Omar, Nizami, and the Sufi poets. A line of Hafiz might be taken as the motto of the movement: "Love's slave am I and from both worlds free." [107] From the castles of Portugal to those of Japan, the civilized world, for some five centuries, resounded to this song; and the echoes are still to be heard in the cloisters of Tibet. The basic Indian doctrine—the doctrine of transcendental monism, which merges opposite principles in timeless union—finds no more striking symbolization anywhere than in the lamasery cult of the icon of the holy bliss (*mahāsukha*) of the united couple.

[107] Hafiz, *Ghazel* ("Odes") 455.

V. TANTRA

1.

Who Seeks Nirvāṇa?

THE LATER Buddhist change of attitude toward the final goal is paralleled exactly by the contemporary Hindu development. As we have seen,[1] in Hīnayāna usage the term *bodhisattva* denoted a great being on the point of becoming a Buddha and so passing from time to nirvāṇa, an archetype of the Buddhist lay-initiate escaping from the world, whereas in the Mahāyāna the concept was translated into a time-reaffirming symbol of universal saviorship. Through renouncing Buddhahood the Bodhisattva made it clear that the task of mokṣa, "release, liberation, redemption from the vicissitudes of time," was not the highest good; in fact, that mokṣa is finally meaningless, saṁsāra and nirvāṇa being equally of the nature of śūnyatā, "emptiness, the void." In the same spirit the Hindu Tāntric initiate exclaims: "Who seeks nirvāṇa?" "What is gained by mokṣa?" "Water mingles with water."

This point of view is rendered in many of the conversations of Śrī Rāmakrishna with his lay disciples.

"Once upon a time," he told them one evening, "a sannyāsin

[1] *Supra,* pp. 534-535.

entered the temple of Jagganāth. As he looked at the holy image he debated within himself whether God had a form or was formless. He passed his staff from left to right to feel whether it touched the image. The staff touched nothing. He understood that there was no image before him; he concluded that God was formless. Next he passed the staff from right to left. It touched the image. The sannyāsin understood that God had form. Thus he realized that God has form and, again, is formless." [2]

"What is vijñāna?" he said on another occasion. "It is knowing God in a special way. The awareness and conviction that fire exists in wood is jñāna, knowledge. But to cook rice on that fire, eat the rice, and get nourishment from it is vijñāna. To know by one's inner experience that God exists is jñāna. But to talk to Him, to enjoy Him as Child, as Friend, as Master, as Beloved, is vijñāna. The realization that God alone has become the universe and all living beings is vijñāna." [3]

And with respect to the ideal of becoming annihilate in Brahman, he would sometimes say, quoting the poet Rāmprasād, "I love to eat sugar, I do not want to become sugar." [3a]

The Mahāyāna Bodhisattva tastes unending saviorship by devoting himself with absolute selflessness to his teaching task in the vortex of the world; in the same spirit, the Hindu Tāntric initiate, by persevering in the dualistic attitude of devotion (*bhakti*), enjoys without cease the beatitude of the knowledge of the omnipresence of the Goddess.

"The Divine Mother revealed to me in the Kālī temple that it was She who had become everything," Śrī Rāmakrishna told his friends. "She showed me that everything was full of Consciousness. The Image was Consciousness, the altar was

[2] *The Gospel of Śrī Rāmakrishna,* translated with an introduction by Swāmī Nikhilānanda, New York, 1942, p. 858.

[3] *Ib.,* p. 288.

[3a] Contrast *supra,* p. 439.

Consciousness, the water-vessels were Consciousness, the door-sill was Consciousness, the marble floor was Consciousness—all was Consciousness. I found everything inside the room soaked, as it were, in Bliss—the Bliss of Satcidānanda.[4] I saw a wicked man in front of the Kālī temple; but in him also I saw the Power of the Divine Mother vibrating. That was why I fed a cat with the food that was to be offered to the Divine Mother."[5]

"The jñānī, sticking to the path of knowledge," he explained again, "always reasons about the Reality, saying, 'Not this, not this.' Brahman is neither 'this' nor 'that'; It is neither the universe nor its living beings. Reasoning in this way, the mind becomes steady. Then it disappears and the aspirant goes into samādhi. This is the Knowledge of Brahman. It is the unwavering conviction of the jñānī that Brahman alone is real and the world illusory, like a dream. What Brahman is cannot be described. One cannot even say that Brahman is a Person. This is the opinion of the jñānīs, the followers of Vedānta philosophy.

"But the bhaktas accept all the states of consciousness. They take the waking state to be real also. They don't think the world to be illusory, like a dream. They say that the universe is a manifestation of God's power and glory. God has created all these—sky, stars, moon, sun, mountains, ocean, men, animals. They constitute His glory. He is within us, in our hearts. Again, He is outside. The most advanced devotees say that He Himself has become all this—the twenty-four cosmic principles, the universe, and all living beings. The devotee of God wants to eat sugar, not to become sugar. (*All laugh.*)

"Do you know how the lover of God feels?" Rāmakrishna continued. "His attitude is 'O God, Thou art the Master, and I am Thy servant. Thou art the Mother, and I am Thy child.'

[4] Brahman as Being (*sat*), Consciousness (*cit*), and Bliss (*ānanda*). Cf. *supra*, p. 425.

[5] *The Gospel of Śrī Rāmakrishna*, pp. 345-346.

Or again: 'Thou art my Father and Mother. Thou art the Whole, and I am a part.' He doesn't like to say, 'I am Brahman.'

"The yogī seeks to realize the Paramātman, the Supreme Soul. His idea is the union of the embodied soul and the Supreme Soul. He withdraws his mind from sense-objects and tries to concentrate it on the Paramātman. Therefore, during the first stage of his spiritual discipline, he retires into solitude and with undivided attention practices meditation in a fixed posture.

"But the Reality is one and the same. The difference is only in name. He who is Brahman is verily Ātman, and again, He is the Bhagavān, the Blessed Lord. He is Brahman to the followers of the path of knowledge, Paramātman to the yogīs, and Bhagavān to the lovers of God.

"The jñānīs, who adhere to the nondualistic philosophy of Vedānta, say that the acts of creation, preservation, and destruction, the universe itself and all its living beings, are the manifestations of Śakti, the Divine Power.[6] If you reason it out, you will realize that all these are as illusory as a dream. Brahman alone is the Reality, and all else is unreal. Even this very Śakti is unsubstantial, like a dream.

"But though you reason all your life, unless you are established in samādhi, you cannot go beyond the jurisdiction of Śakti. Even when you say, 'I am meditating,' or 'I am contemplating,' still you are moving in the realm of Śakti, within Its power.

"Thus Brahman and Śakti are identical. If you accept the one, you must accept the other. It is like fire and its power to burn. If you see the fire, you must recognize its power to burn also. You cannot think of fire without its power to burn, nor can you think of the power to burn without fire. You cannot

[6] Known as māyā in the Vedānta; cf. *supra,* pp. 425-427. Śakti is Yum of the Yab-Yum icon; cf. *supra,* pp. 556-559.

conceive of the sun's rays without the sun, nor can you conceive of the sun without its rays.

"What is milk like? Oh, you say, it is something white. You cannot think of the milk without the whiteness, and again, you cannot think of the whiteness without the milk.

"Thus one cannot think of Brahman without Śakti, or of Śakti without Brahman. One cannot think of the Absolute without the Relative, or of the Relative without the Absolute.

"The Primordial Power is ever at play.[7] She is creating, preserving, and destroying in play, as it were. This Power is called Kālī. Kālī is verily Brahman, and Brahman is verily Kālī. It is one and the same Reality. When we think of It as inactive, that is to say, not engaged in the acts of creation, preservation, and destruction, then we call It Brahman. But when It engages in these activities, then we call It Kālī or Śakti. The Reality is one and the same; the difference is in name and form." [8]

This introductory exposition of the Tāntric point of view was given on the deck of a little excursion-steamer, sailing up and down the Ganges, one beautiful autumn afternoon in 1882. Keshab Chandra Sen (1838–84), the distinguished leader of the semi-Hindu, semi-Christian Brāhmo Samāj,[9] had come, with a number of his following, to visit Śrī Rāmakrishna at Dakshineswar, a suburb of the modern city of Calcutta, where the saintly teacher was serving as priest in a temple dedicated to the Black Goddess, Kālī. Keshab was a modern, occidentalized Hindu gentleman, with a cosmopolitan outlook, and a sāttvic,

[7] This idea of the play (*līlā*) of the Godhead in the forms of the world is fundamental to the Tāntric view and is the Hindu counterpart of the Mahāyāna-Buddhist Mahāsukha (*supra*, p. 554).

[8] *The Gospel of Śrī Rāmakrishna,* pp. 133-135.

[9] For an account of the ideals and history of the Brāhmo Samāj (founded in 1828 by Rājā Rammohan Roy), see Swāmī Nikhilānanda's introduction to *The Gospel of Śrī Rāmakrishna,* pp. 40-42. A distinguished figure in the movement was Devendranath Tagore (1817–1905), father of the Nobel Prize poet, Sir Rabindranath (1861–1941).

humanistic, progressive religious philosophy—not unlike that of his New England contemporary, the Transcendentalist (and student of the *Bhagavad Gītā*), Ralph Waldo Emerson. Rāmakrishna, on the other hand, was a thorough Hindu—intentionally ignorant of English, nurtured in the traditions of his motherland, long-practiced in the techniques of introverted contemplation, and filled with the experience of God. The coming together of these two religious leaders was a meeting of the modern, timely India and the timeless—the modern consciousness of India with the half-forgotten divine symbols of its own unconscious. Noteworthy, moreover, is the fact that on this occasion the teacher was not the Western-educated, tailored gentleman, who had been entertained in London by the Queen, but the yogī in his loincloth, speaking of the traditional Indian Gods out of his own direct experience.

KESHAB (*with a smile*): "Describe to us, sir, in how many ways Kālī, the Divine Mother, sports in this world."

ŚRĪ RĀMAKRISHNA (*also with a smile*): "Oh, She plays in different ways. It is She alone who is known as Mahā-Kālī ["The Great Black One"], Nitya-Kālī ["The Everlasting Black One"], Śmaśāna-Kālī ["Kālī of the Cremation Ground"], Rakṣā-Kālī ["Goblin Kālī"], and Śyāmā-Kālī ["Dark Kālī"]. Mahā-Kālī and Nitya-Kālī are mentioned in the Tantra Philosophy. When there were neither the creation, nor the sun, the moon, the planets, and the earth, and when darkness was enveloped in darkness, then the Mother, the Formless One, Mahā-Kālī, the Great Power, was one with Mahā-Kāla [this is the masculine form of the same name], the Absolute.

"Śyāmā-Kālī has a somewhat tender aspect and is worshiped in the Hindu households. She is the Dispenser of boons and the Dispeller of fear. People worship Rakṣā-Kālī, the Protectress, in times of epidemic, famine, earthquake, drought, and flood. Śmaśāna-Kālī is the embodiment of the power of destruction. She resides in the cremation ground, surrounded by corpses, jackals, and terrible female spirits. From Her mouth flows a stream of blood, from Her neck hangs a garland of human heads, and around Her waist is a girdle made of human hands.

"After the destruction of the universe, at the end of a great cycle, the Divine Mother garners the seeds for the next creation. She is like the elderly mistress of the house, who has a hotch-potch-pot in which she keeps different articles for the household use. (*All laugh.*) Oh, yes! Housewives have pots like that, where they keep sea-foam, blue pills, small bundles of seeds of cucumber, pumpkin, and gourd, and so on. They take them out when they want them. In the same way, after the destruction of the universe, my Divine Mother, the Embodiment of Brahman, gathers together the seeds for the next creation. After the creation the Primal Power dwells in the universe itself. She brings forth this phenomenal world and then pervades it. In the Vedas creation is likened to the spider and its web. The spider brings the web out of itself and then remains in it. God is the container of the universe and also what is contained in it.

"Is Kālī, my Divine Mother, of a black complexion? She appears black because She is viewed from a distance; but when intimately known She is no longer so. The sky appears blue at a distance; but look at air close by and you will find that it has no color. The water of the ocean looks blue at a distance, but when you go near and take it in your hand, you find that it is colorless."

Śrī Rāmakrishna, filled with love for the Goddess, then sang to her two songs of the Bengali devotee and yogī Rāmprasād, after which he resumed his talk.

"The Divine Mother is always sportive and playful. This universe is Her play. She is self-willed and must always have her own way. She is full of bliss. She gives freedom to one out of a hundred thousand."

A Brāhmo Devotee: "But, sir, if She likes She can give freedom to all. Why, then, has She kept us bound to the world?"

Śrī Rāmakrishna: "That is Her will. She wants to continue playing with Her created beings. In a game of hide-and-seek the running about soon stops if in the beginning all the players touch the 'granny.' If all touch her, then how can the game go on? That displeases her. Her pleasure is in continuing the game.

"It is as if the Divine Mother said to the human mind in confidence, with a sign from Her eye, 'Go and enjoy the world.' How can one blame the mind? The mind can disentangle itself from worldliness if, through her grace, She makes it turn toward Herself."

Singing again the songs of Rāmprasād, Śrī Rāmakrishna interrupted his discourse, but then continued. "Bondage is of the mind, and freedom is also of the mind. A man is free if he constantly thinks: 'I am a free soul. How can I be bound, whether I live in the world or in the forest? I am a child of God, the King of Kings. Who can bind me?' If bitten by a snake, a man may get rid of its venom by saying emphatically, 'There is no poison in me.' In the same way, by repeating with grit and determination, 'I am not bound, I am free,' one really becomes so—one really becomes free.

"Once someone gave me a book of the Christians. I asked him to read it to me. It talked about nothing but sin. (*To Keshab Chandra Sen:*) Sin is the only thing one hears of at your Brāhmo Samāj, too. The wretch who constantly says, 'I am bound, I am bound,' only succeeds in being bound. He who says day and night, 'I am a sinner, I am a sinner,' really becomes a sinner.

"One should have such burning faith in God that one can say: 'What? I have repeated the name of God, and can sin still cling to me? How can I be a sinner any more? How can I be in bondage any more?'

"If a man repeats the name of God, his body, mind, and everything become pure. Why should one talk about sin and hell, and such things? Say but once, 'O Lord, I have undoubtedly done wicked things, but I won't repeat them.' And have faith in his name."

Śrī Rāmakrishna sang:

> If only I can pass away repeating Durgā's name;
> How canst Thou then, O Blessed One,
> Withhold from me deliverance,
> Wretched though I may be? . . .

Then he said: "To my Divine Mother I prayed only for pure love, I offered flowers at Her Lotus Feet and prayed to Her: 'Mother, here is Thy virtue, here is Thy vice. Take them both and grant me only pure love for Thee. Here is Thy knowledge, here is Thy ignorance. Take them both and grant me only pure love for Thee. Here is Thy purity, here is Thy impurity. Take them both, Mother, and grant me only pure love for Thee. Here is Thy dharma, here is Thy adharma. Take them both, Mother, and grant me only pure love for Thee." [10]

In Tantra the theistic attitude practically obliterates the abstract ideal of the Formless Brahman (*nirguṇa brahman*) in favor of Brahman-in-the-Guṇas (*saguṇa brahman*)—the Lord (*īśvara*), the personal God; and the latter is represented by the Tāntrics preferably in the female aspect, since in this the nature of Māyā-Śakti is most immediately affirmed.[11] The Tāntric development supported the return to power in popular Hinduism of the figure of the Mother Goddess of the innumerable

[10] *Ib.*, pp. 135-139 (with a few brief omissions).

[11] The Āgamas (Tāntric writings) are divided into five main groups according to the personification celebrated: Sūrya (the sun god), Ganeśa ("Lord of the Hosts," the elephant-headed son of Śiva, who is the Indian counterpart of Hermes, breaker of the way and guide of the soul), Śakti, Śiva, and Viṣṇu, the last three being today by far the most important. Tāntric principles and practices have been applied also to the worship of the Mahāyāna Buddhas and Bodhisattvas; the Yab-Yum symbolism is Tāntric.

names—Devī, Durgā, Kālī, Pārvatī, Umā, Satī, Padmā, Caṇḍī, Tripura-sundarī, etc.—whose cult, rooted in the Neolithic past, had been overshadowed for a period of about a thousand years by the male divinities of the patriarchal Āryan pantheon. The Goddess began to reassert herself in the period of the later Upaniṣads.[12] She is today the chief divinity again. All the consorts of the various gods are her manifestations, and, as the śakti or "power" of their husbands, represent the energy that has brought the latter into manifestation. Moreover, as Mahāmāyā, the Goddess personifies the World Illusion, within the bounds and thralldom of which exist all forms whatsoever, whether gross or subtle, earthly or angelic, even those of the highest gods. She is the primary embodiment of the transcendent principle, and as such the mother of all names and forms. "God Himself," states Rāmakrishna, "is Mahāmāyā, who deludes the world with Her illusion and conjures up the magic of creation, preservation, and destruction. She has spread this veil of ignorance before our eyes. We can go into the inner chamber only when She lets us pass through the door." [13] It is entirely possible that in this reinstatement of the Goddess, both in the popular cults and in the deep philosophy of the Tantra, we have another sign of the resurgence of the religiosity of the non-Āryan, pre-Āryan, matriarchal tradition of Dravidian times.

The Tāntric movement differs from Jainism and Buddhism, however, inasmuch as it adheres to the authority of the Vedas, seeking rather to assimilate and adjust itself to the orthodox tradition than to exclude and refute it. In this it parallels the pattern of popular Hinduism. Indeed, the mixture of Tāntric and Vedāntic traits in modern Hindu life, ritual, and thought

[12] For a discussion both of this development and of the symbolism of the Goddess, cf. Zimmer, *Myths and Symbols in Indian Art and Civilization,* pp. 90-102 and 189ff; also *The King and the Corpse,* Part II, "The Romance of the Goddess."

[13] *The Gospel of Śrī Rāmakrishna,* p. 116.

is so intimate that they present themselves as an organic whole. The Tāntrics speak of their texts as "The Fifth Veda," "The Veda for This Iron Age." "For the first of the four world ages, *śruti* (Veda) was given; for the second, *smṛti* (the teachings of the sages, Dharmaśastra, etc.), for the third, *purāṇa* (the epics, etc.), and for the fourth, *āgama* (the Tāntric texts)." [14]

As has been pointed out by Sir John Woodroffe, whose studies are the most important examinations of the Tantra published in modern times: "The Śākta followers of the Āgama claim that its Tantras [i.e., "books"] contain the very core of the Veda. . . . As men have no longer the capacity, longevity and moral strength required to carry out the Vaidika Karma-kāṇḍa [the ritual section of the Veda], the Tantra Śāstra prescribes a Sādhanā [religious discipline] of its own for the attainment of the common end of all Śāstra, that is, a happy life on earth, Heaven thereafter, and at length Liberation." [15]

Both the Tantra and popular Hinduism accept the truth of Advaita Vedānta but shift the accent to the positive aspect of māyā. The world is the unending manifestation of the dynamic aspect of the divine, and as such should not be devaluated and discarded as suffering and imperfection, but celebrated, penetrated by enlightening insight, and experienced with understanding. The hair of the Goddess is dishevelled in her frantic, self-maddened dance which produces the mirage of saṁsāra, but the perfect devotee is not thereby dismayed. "Though the mother beat him," says Rāmprasād, "the child cries 'Mother! O Mother!' and clings still tighter to her garment." [16] The Vedāntic yogī never tires of stating that *kaivalya*, "isolation-integration," can be attained only by turning away from the distract-

[14] *Kulārnava Tantra*, cited by Sir John Woodroffe, *Shakti and Shākta*, 3rd edition, Madras and London, 1929, p. 7.

[15] *Ib.*, p. 8. For the term *śāstra*, cf. *supra*, p. 36.

[16] Dinesh Chandra Sen, *History of Bengali Language and Literature*, Calcutta, 1911, p. 714.

ing allure of the world and worshiping with single-pointed attention the formless Brahman-Ātman; to the Tāntric, however—as to the normal child of the world—this notion seems pathological, the wrong-headed effect of a certain malady of intellect. By the true lover of the Goddess, not merely the seeking of liberation but even its attainment is not desired. For what is the use of salvation if it means absorption? "I like eating sugar," as Rāmprasād said, "but I have no desire to become sugar." [17] Let those who suffer from the toils of saṁsāra seek release: the perfect devotee does not suffer; for he can both visualize and experience life and the universe as the revelation of that Supreme Divine Force (*śakti*) with which he is in love, the all-comprehensive Divine Being in its cosmic aspect of playful, aimless display (*līlā*)—which precipitates pain as well as joy, but in its bliss transcends them both. He is filled with the holy madness of that "ecstatic love" (*prema*) which transmutes the world.

> This very world is a mansion of mirth;
> Here I can eat, here drink and make merry.[18]

Artha (prosperity), kāma (the fulfillment of sensual desires), dharma (the enactment of the religious and moral rituals of everyday life, with an acceptance of the burden of all the duties), and mokṣa (release from it all) are one. The polarity of mokṣa and the trivarga [19] is transcended and dissolved not in introverted realization alone, but in living feeling as well. By virtue of his talent of love for the merciful Goddess, the true devotee discovers that the fourfold fruit of artha, kāma, dharma, and mokṣa falls into the palm of his hand.

[17] *Supra,* p. 561; cf. E. J. Thompson, "A Poet of the People," *The London Quarterly Review,* CXXX, Fifth Series, XVI (July-October, 1918), p. 71.

[18] *The Gospel of Śrī Rāmakrishna,* p. 139.

[19] Cf. *supra,* p. 41.

"Come, let us go for a walk, O mind, to Kālī, the Wish-fulfilling Tree," wrote Rāmprasād; "And there beneath It gather the four fruits of life." [20] "The mind ever seeks the Dark Beautiful One," he states again. "Do as you wish. Who wants Nirvāṇa?"

Tāntrism, as a matter of course, insists on the holiness and purity of all things; hence, the "five forbidden things" ("the five M's," as they are called) constitute the substance of the sacramental fare in certain Tāntric rites: wine (*madya*), meat (*māṁsa*), fish (*matsya*), parched grain (*mudrā*),[21] and sexual intercourse (*maithuna*). As in the parallel Mahāyāna initiations,[22] the nondualist realization makes all the world one—one, holy, and pure. All beings and things are members of a single mystic "family" (*kula*). There is therefore no thought of caste within the Tāntric holy "circles" (*cakra*). Śūdras, outcastes, and Brahmans alike are elegible for initiation—if spiritually competent. The aspirant must only be intelligent, with his senses controlled, one who abstains from injuring any being, ever doing good to all, pure, a believer in the Veda, and a nondualist, whose faith and refuge are in Brahman: "Such a one is competent for this scripture; otherwise he is no adept." [23]

One's secular social standing is of no consequence whatsoever within the sphere of the truly spiritual hierarchy. Moreover, women as well as men are eligible not only to receive the highest initiation but also to confer it in the role of guru. "Initiation by a woman is efficacious; that by the mother is eightfold

[20] *The Gospel of Śrī Rāmakrishna,* p. 139.

[21] *Mudrā* also denotes the mystic hand postures that play such an important role in Indian ritual and art. This is the only meaning of the word given in the Sanskrit dictionaries. We read, however, in the *Yoginī Tantra* (Ch. VI): "Fried paddy and the like—in fact all such [cereals] as are chewed—are called Mudrā" (cited by Woodroffe, *op. cit.,* p. 571).

[22] Cf. *supra,* pp. 554-559.

[23] *Gandharva Tantra* 2; Woodroffe, *op. cit.,* p. 538.

so," we read in the *Yoginī Tantra*.[24] In striking contrast to the Vedic texts, wherein even the hearing of the Veda is forbidden to a Śūdra, and wherein women are consigned to a secondary (though highly praised and sentimentalized) sphere of spiritual competency and aspiration, the Tantras transcend the limits of social and biological differentiation.

However, it must not be supposed that this indifference to the rules of caste implies any idea of revolution within the social sphere, as distinguished from the sphere of spiritual progress. The initiate returns to his post in society; for there too is the manifestation of Śakti. The world is affirmed, just as it is—neither renounced, as by an ascetic, nor corrected, as by a social reformer. The prerequisite to the initiation being an actual superiority to fear and desire, and the rite itself a confirmation of the understanding that all is divine, the true lover of the Goddess remains content with what She has bestowed, not finding fault with the various traditional proprieties of time and place, but beholding the Divine Power, with whom he is himself identical in essence, within all arrangements.

For the idea of dharma is intrinsic to Indian thought. The sacrament of the "five forbidden things" does not open a way to either libertinism or revolution. On the plane of ego-consciousness, where one operates as an individual member of society, the dharma of one's caste and āśrama [25] still prevails, the height beyond dharma and adharma being ascended only by one in whom the mind has been transcended—in which superior state there can be no question of a desire to enjoy the benefits of illegal practices. The Tāntric ritual of wine, meat, fish, parched grain, and sexual intercourse is accomplished not as a lawbreaking revel, but under the cautious supervision of a guru, in a controlled state of "nondualist" (advaitic) realization, and as the culminating festival of a long sequence of spiritual disci-

[24] *Yoginī Tantra* 1; Woodroffe, *op. cit.*, p. 493.

[25] For the term *āśrama*, cf. *supra*, pp. 155-160.

plines, through many lives. The spiritual emotion of the adept is *prema:* ecstatic, egoless, beatific bliss in the realization of transcendent identity.

Coming down again from this sublime height of form-annihilating realization to the kingdom of phenomenality, differentiation is seen but there is no estrangement; there is no tendency then to deprecate—for there is no guilt, there has been no Fall. The world does not require to be reformed; nor are its laws to be disregarded. All of the various planes of manifestation of the absolute can be beheld in a dispassionate spirit. The solid, the liquid, and the gaseous states of the one substance, under differing conditions, producing differing effects, are accepted without moral or emotional preference. For the whole spectacle of the world, without exception, is generated by the dynamism of Māyā-Śakti, the power of the cosmic dance (*līlā*) of the dark and terrible, sublime, all-nourishing and -consuming Mother of the World. The beings of the world, and all the ranges of experience, are but waves and strata in a single, ever-flowing, universal stream of life.

Obviously, this is the view that we have already encountered many times in our present examination of the philosophies of India. The hymn from the *Taittirīya Brāhmaṇa,* celebrating the substance and energy of the world as food,[26] was based on a nondualism of just this kind. The released-reborn celebrates himself as food-and-eater; for though the gross outer sheath of the organism, the "sheath of food" (*annamayakośa*), is not the whole of the divine manifestation (there being, in the subtle sphere of the several inner sheaths, more subtle formations and incarnations of the Supreme Essence), nevertheless "food is not to be despised." The reality of Brahman was realized in the orthodox Vedic Brāhman tradition progressively, under various manifestations: as the life-matter of the material world, in the Hymn of Food; or as the sun, "he who yonder glows," in a multi-

[26] *Taittirīya Brāhmaṇa* 2. 8. 8; cf. *supra,* pp. 345-347.

tude of other Brāhmanic songs of celebration; or again, as the macrocosmic life-breath (*vāyu*), "he who blows," which is the counterpart of the microcosmic *prāṇa.*

Throughout the history of Brāhman thought there has been a reiterated assertion—either violent and passionate, or vigorously controlled—that the "One is both at once," and in this respect Tāntrism continues the orthodox Vedic line. Everything proceeds from the same supernal source. All beings are members of a single holy family, proceeding from the one and only divine substance. And this view involves, as we have seen, on the one hand a devaluation of the peculiarly personal nuances of individuality, but on the other a bold affirmation of all that may ever come to be. Māyā, the world illusion, is not to be rejected but embraced. The lyricism of the Vedānta-Gītās[27] gave expression to this world-affirmative. The Tantra does so again. And it is reflected today through the whole range of the popular Hindu theologies.

But there is a peculiar and essential trait of the Tāntric Yea which distinguishes it from the earlier philosophies—or at least these as they appear in the orthodox texts and commentaries; for the ideal of Tāntrism is to achieve illumination precisely by means of those very objects which the earlier sages sought to banish from their consciousness. The ancient Vedic cult was world-affirmative, but its rites were primarily those of the vast popular and royal ceremonials in honor of the gods of the macrocosm; they did not invite one to fathom the deep resources of the microcosm. The forest philosophers, on the other hand—devoted to the introvert techniques of Jainism, Yoga, Sāṅkhya, Vedānta, and the Hīnayāna—strove to repress their personal biological impulses by subjecting themselves to a spiritual reducing diet for the conquering of rajas, tamas, and the vāsanās (the vessels of memory and desire); and when this transferred them finally to a plane beyond sin and virtue—they remained

[27] Cf. *supra*, pp. 447-455.

virtuous. Indeed, they had had to cast away the capacity for sinning at the very start, as the first prerequisite of their approach to a guru.[28] But in the Tantra, whereas the goal is that of the meditating yogī (not worldly power, such as was sought by the ancient Brāhman conjurers of the forces of the universe, but enlightenment, absolute consciousness, and the beatitude of transcendental being), the manner of approach is that, not of Nay, but of Yea. That is to say, the world-attitude is affirmative, as in the Veda, but the gods are now addressed as dwelling within the microcosm.

Thus it may be said that if the Vedānta seems to represent the conquest of the monistic Āryan Brāhman heritage by the dualist ideology of the pre-Āryan seekers of integration-isolation (*kaivalya*),[29] in the Tantra we are, perhaps, justified in recognizing just the opposite influence: a rerendering of the pre-Āryan problem of psychophysical transubstantiation in terms of the nondual philosophy of the all-affirmative Brāhmanic point of view. Here the candidate for wisdom does not seek a detour by which to circumvent the sphere of the passions—crushing them within himself and shutting his eyes to their manifestations without, until, made clean as an angel, he may safely open his eyes again to regard the cyclone of saṁsāra with the untroubled gaze of a disembodied apparition. Quite the contrary: the Tāntric hero (*vīra*) goes directly *through* the sphere of greatest danger.

It is an essential principle of the Tāntric idea that man, in general, must rise through and by means of nature, not by the rejection of nature. "As one falls onto the ground," the *Kularnava Tantra* states, "so one must lift oneself by the aid of the ground." [30] The pleasure of love, the pleasure of human feeling, is the bliss of the Goddess in her world-productive dance, the

[28] Cf. *supra,* p. 52.

[29] Cf. *supra,* p. 459.

[30] Cited by Woodroffe, *op. cit.,* p. 593.

bliss of Śiva and his Śakti in their eternal realization of identity; only as known in the inferior mode of ego-consciousness. The creature of passion has only to wash away his sense of ego, and then the same act that formerly was an obstruction becomes the tide that bears him to the realization of the absolute as bliss (*ānanda*). Moreover, this tide of passion itself may become the baptizing water by which the taint of ego-consciousness is washed away. Following the Tāntric method, the hero (*vīra*) floats beyond himself on the roused but canalized current. This is what has discredited the method in the eyes of the community. Its heroic acceptance, without quibble, of the full impact and implication of the nondual celebration of the world as Brahman has seemed far too bold, and too sensational, to those whose view of saintliness embraces the Lord's transcendent repose but omits the detail of His mystery play (*līlā*) of continuous creation.

A right method cannot exclude the body; for the body is *devatā,* the visible form of Brahman as jīva. "The Sādhaka [the Tāntric student]," writes Sir John Woodroffe, "is taught not to think that we are one with the Divine in Liberation only, but here and now, in every act we do. For in truth all such is Śakti. It is Śiva who as Śakti is acting in and through the Sādhaka. . . . When this is realized in every natural function, then, each exercise thereof ceases to be a mere animal act and becomes a religious rite—a Yajña. Every function is a part of the Divine Action (*śakti*) in Nature. Thus, when taking drink in the form of wine the Vīra knows it to be Tārā Dravamayī, that is, 'the Saviour Herself in liquid form.' How (it is said) can he who truly sees in it the Saviour Mother receive from it harm? . . . When the Vīra eats, drinks or has sexual intercourse, he does so not with the thought of himself as a separate individual satisfying his own peculiar limited wants, an animal filching as it were from nature the enjoyment he has, but thinking of himself in such enjoyment as Śiva, saying 'Sivo'ham,' 'Bhairavo'ham' ('I am Śiva')." [31]

Sex, in Tāntrism, has a high symbolic role. The holy fear of the uncontrollable forces in human nature and the consequent strict resistance to the animal instincts and energies, which characterize the common history of man from the earliest taboo to the latest moral tract, can be explained as the result and residue of devastating experiences in the past of the race and the by-product of the successful, historical struggle for independence of a higher, "purer," spiritual principle. The primitive forces, out of the depths of which this principle arose, like the victorious sun, Sol Invictus, climbing the heavens out of the stormy sea (the turbulent abode of the monsters of the deep), had to be checked, held at bay and tied back, like the Greek Titans imprisoned under volcanic Aetna, or like the great Dragon of the Revelation of St. John. The very real peril of an elementary upheaval and rocking outburst led to the construction of protective dichotomic systems, such as those, not only of Jainism and the Sāṅkhya, but also of the Persian Zoroastrian ethical religion, the Gnosis of the Near East, Christianity, Manichaeism, and the usual codes of manners of primitive and civilized mankind. In India, in the ancient world, and among most of the peoples known to anthropologists and historians, there has been, however, an institutionalized system of festivals —festivals of the gods and genii of vegetation—whereby, without danger to the community, the conventional fiction of good and evil could be suspended for a moment and an experience permitted of the mighty titan-powers of the deep. Carnival, the day of masks, revealing all the odd forms that dwell in the profundities of the soul, spills forth its symbols, and for one dreamlike, nightmarish, sacred day, the ordered, timid consciousness freely revels in a sacramentally canalized experience of its own destruction.

[31] Woodroffe, *op. cit.*, pp. 587-588.

The masks are dreamlike. Dreamlike also are the carnival events. Indeed, the world of sleep into which we descend every night, when the tensions of consciousness are relaxed, is precisely that from which the demons, elves, divine and devilish figures of the world mythologies have all been derived. All the gods dwell within us, willing to support us, and capable of supporting us, but they require the submission of consciousness, an abdication of sovereignty on the part of our conscious wills. In so far, however, as the little ego regards its own plans as the best, it resists rigorously the forces of its divine substratum. The gods thereupon become dangerous for it, and the individual becomes his own hell. The ancient peoples made peace with the excluded forces by holding them in worship and allowing them their daemonic carnival—even while cultivating, simultaneously, under the forms of sacrifices to the higher gods, a fruitful relationship with the forces implicated in the social system. And by this means they won the permission, so to speak, of their own unconscious to continue in the conventional conscious attitude of profitable virtue.

But the Tāntric sādhaka is not interested in conventional survival so much as in the fathoming of life and the discovering of its timeless secret. Hence the makeshift of carnival is not enough; for this only supports the general illusion. His goal is to incorporate the excluded forces as well as those accepted generally, and experience by this means the essential nonexistence of the antagonistic polarity—its vanishing away, its nirvāṇa; i.e., the intrinsic purity and innocence of the seemingly dark and dangerous sphere. In this way he breaks within himself the tension of the "forbidden," and resolves everything in light; recognizing in everything the one Śakti which is the general support of the world, macrocosmic as well as microcosmic, the mother of the gods and elves, the weaver of the moon-dream of history. Therewith comes release from the world-illusion—release through its full enjoyment or realization.

Hence the great Tāntric formula (so different from that of the earlier Hindu yogic disciplines): yoga (the yoking of empirical consciousness to transcendental consciousness) and bhoga ("enjoyment," the experience of life's joy and suffering) are the same. Bhoga itself can be made a way of yoga.

But it requires a hero (*vīra*) to confront and assimilate, in perfect equanimity, the whole wonder of the World Creatrix—to make love, without hysterical reactions, to the Life-force, which is the śakti of his own entirety. The "five good things" (*pañcatattva*), which are the "forbidden things" of the ordinary men and women of the herd, serve as sacramental fare for one who not only knows but feels that the World Force (*śakti*) is in essence himself. In Tantra, the worship of the World Creatrix in her own terms is rendered possible; for cohabitation (*maithuna*), her own supreme holy rite, is realized not in the spirit of the *paśu* ("cattle"; the human animal of the herd, desiring, fearing, and enjoying in the usual animal-human way), but of the *vīra* ("hero") who knows himself to be identical with Śiva. "Om," he prays (and knows); "into the Fire which is Spirit (*ātman*) brightened by the pouring on of the ghee of merit and demerit, I, by the path of yoga (*suṣumṇā*), ever sacrifice the functions of the senses, using the mind as the ladle of the offering. Hallelujah!" [32]

The fruit of the rite then is release from illusion, which is the highest gift of Kālī, the dark and beautiful Goddess-Dancer of the Cremation Ground.

[32] *Om*
Dharmādharma-havirdīpte ātmāgnan manasā srucā
Suṣumnāvartmanānityam akṣavṛttīr juhomyaham: Svāhā.
(*Tantrasāra* 698; Woodroffe, *op. cit.,* p. 559.)

2.

The Lamb, the Hero, and the Man-God

"No one who is not himself divine may (successfully) worship the divinity (*nādevo devam arcayet*)." [33] "Having become the deity, one should offer sacrifice to it (*devam bhūtvā devam yajet*)." [34] The identity of the hidden nature of the worshiper with the god worshiped is the first principle of the Tāntric philosophy of devotion. The gods are reflexes in space (which is itself the work of Māyā-Śakti) of that sole reality, Brahman, which is the Śakti of the devotee. Knowing his own Self, then, to be his object of devotion, the Tāntric sādhaka approaches the Goddess in worship (*pūjā*), through the meditative muttering of prayers (*japa:* the recitation of the litany of her names), the unrelenting verbal repetition (again *japa*) of sacred formulae (*mantra:* word-sounds which contain her essence), the making of mental and external offerings (*homa*), and one-pointed meditation on her inner vision (*dhyāna*). He could never hope to experience the final identity if he were not already convinced and aware of it from the first. Meanwhile, to support his preliminary approach, he sets before his eyes and mind an image (*pratīka, pratimā*) of the deity. This may be a statue, painting, symbol of some kind, or yantra; [35] in special cases it may be a living

[33] *Gandharva Tantra.*

[34] *Ib.*

Editor's note: I have not been able to procure copies of some of the Tāntric texts cited in this chapter, hence cannot give for them precise references.

[35] A yantra is a geometrical diagram. For a description of its preparation and use, cf. Zimmer, *Myths and Symbols in Indian Art and Civilization,* pp. 140-148.

being, for example, a virgin (*kumārīpūjā*), or the worshiper's wife.

The first act of devotion consists in contemplating inwardly the mental image of the deity and then projecting the spiritual energy (*tejas*) of that inner subtle form into the gross outer image. This consecration is known as *prāṇapratiṣṭhā,* "the consignment (*pratiṣṭhā*) of the vital breath (*prāṇa*)." It is to be undone again at the conclusion of the period of worship by a "dismissal" (*visarjana*) of the holy presence, following which the image is no longer the seat of a deity (*pīṭha*), and may be thrown away. The worshiper sends forth and takes back again the shining form, just as the Creator sends forth and takes back again into his infinite substance the manifold of the cosmos—and by virtue of the same infinitude (*brahman-ātman*) within, as well as the same miracle of māyā. Later, when the initiate learns to recognize and spontaneously respond to the presence of the divinity everywhere, in all things, he no longer requires the pedagogical assistance of this ritual, but meanwhile his mind and sentiments must be given help. The little miracle of transubstantiation, however, is rather a microcosmic than a macrocosmic crisis. Divinity itself cannot be said to have been actually summoned and dismissed; rather, the *realization* of divinity has been facilitated. For, whereas the adept in the condition of perfect realization beholds and reveres the whole world as an icon or seat (*pīṭha*) of the Universal Presence, the usual member of the human herd (*paśu*) requires all the assistance of religion to bring his mind from the common, animal, economic-political mode of considering things, to the contemplative attitude of a luminous intuition.

The rites performed in the presence of a consecrated image are the counterparts of the secular rituals of daily life. The god is welcomed as a guest, with flowers, obeisance, washing of the feet, food, water for bathing, cloth for garments, jewels, perfume, incense, offerings of various kinds, praise, and conversation.[36] These redound, in turn, to the sanctification of daily life; for a guest is welcomed with the same ceremonial; a parent is honored as a god, and a child attended as a god. The sanctity of the Presence thus perceptibly pervades the social sphere. Ritual gestures (*mudrā*) also are employed in the worship, and these, like words, are the expressions and supports of spiritual resolve. These gestures, or *mudrās,* are identical with those represented in Indian images and utilized in the art of the Indian dance. They constitute a veritable language of the hands, making possible the most subtle amplifications of expression. For example, when presenting, in offering, the vessel of water, the fish gesture (*matsya mudrā*) is made. "This is done as the expression of the wish and intention that the vessel which contains water may be regarded as an ocean with fish and all other aquatic animals. The sādhaka says to the Devatā of his worship, 'this is but a small offering of water in fact, but so far as my desire to honor you is concerned, regard it as if I were offering you an ocean.' "[37] Or again, when the Goddess is invited to take her place, before the moment of worship, the *yoni mudrā* is made, since the yoni, the female organ, is her pīṭha or yantra. The yoni can never be regarded by a Tāntric adept otherwise than as an altar. Therefore, when the sādhaka has attained to perfection in this

[36] According to Woodroffe (*op. cit.,* p. 511), the materials used and things done are called *upacāra* (from *upa-car,* "to approach; to approach with the intention of serving; to assist, wait on, attend; to nurse a patient; to undertake, to begin"). The common number of these is sixteen: 1. *Āsana* (seating the image), 2. *Svāgata* (welcoming the divinity), 3. *Pādya* (water for washing the feet), 4. *Arghya* (offerings), presented in 5. the vessel, 6. *Ācamana* (water for sipping and cleaning the lips—offered twice), 7. *Madhuparka* (honey, ghee, milk and curd), 8. *Snāna* (water for bathing), 9. *Vasana* (cloth for a garment), 10. *Ābharaṇa* (jewels), 11. *Gandha* (perfume), 12. *Puṣpa* (flowers), 13. *Dhūpa* (incense), 14. *Dīpa* (lights), 15. *Naivedya* (food), and 16. *Vadana* or *Namaskriyā* (prayer).

[37] *Ib.,* p. 515.

discipline he can proceed to the most appropriate and congenial form of paying worship to the Goddess, in maithuna.

Bhūtaśuddhi, or "the cleansing (*śuddhi*) of the (five) elements of which the body is composed (*bhūta*)," is an indispensable preliminary to every Tāntric rite. The devotee imagines the divine power *(śakti)* as being asleep within him, withdrawn from operation in his gross physique, coiled away like a sleeping serpent (*kuṇḍalinī*) at the root of his spine, in the deep place known as the *mūlādhāra,* "the root (*mūla*) base (*ādhāra*)." The sādhaka then pronounces mantrā to arouse her, while controlling carefully his inhalations, breathing deeply first through one nostril then the other (*prāṇāyāma*), to clear the way for her through the spiritual channel (*suṣumṇā*) that is supposed to run through the interior of the spine. He is then to think of her as aroused. She lifts her head and begins to move up the suṣumṇā, touching in her passage a number of "centers" or "lotuses" (*cakras, padmas*), which are regarded as the seats of the elements of the body. The mūlādhāra is the seat of "earth"; it is pictured as a crimson lotus of four petals. The next center above, called *svādhiṣṭhāna* (śakti's "own abode"), is at the level of the genitals and is the seat of the element "water"; it is pictured as a vermilion lotus of six petals. The next, at the level of the navel, is known as *maṇipūra,* "the city (*pūra*) of the lustrous gem (*maṇi*)," so called because it is the seat of the element "fire." It is pictured as a blue-black lotus of ten petals. According to the psychology of this system of lotuses: mūlādhāra, svādhiṣṭhāna, and maṇipūra are the centers from which the lives of most people are governed, while the superior centers represent higher modes of experience. The fourth, at the level of the heart, is the lotus in which the first realization of the divinity of the world is experienced. Here, it is said, the god reaches down to touch his devotee. Or again, here the sages hear the sound (*śabda*) of Brahman. Sounds heard by the outer ear are produced by "two things striking together," whereas the sound of

Brahman is *anāhata śabda,* "the sound (*śabda*) which comes without the striking of any two things together (*anāhata*)." [38] This sound is OM; not the OM pronounced by the lips, which is but a mnemonic suggestion produced by the striking of the wind from the lungs upon the organs of the mouth, but the fundamental OM of creation, which is the Goddess herself as sound. Because this is heard in the lotus of the heart, that center is called *anāhata;* it is pictured as a ruddy lotus of twelve petals, and is the seat of the element "air."

"Ether," the fifth and ultimate element, is centered in the cakra of a smoky purple hue and of sixteen petals at the level of the throat. This is the Viśuddha Cakra, "the completely purified." Beyond, at the point between the eyebrows, is the Lotus of Command (*ājñā*), white as the moon, possessing two petals, shining with the glory of perfected meditation, wherein the mind, beyond the zones veiled by the five elements and thus completely free of the limitations of the senses, beholds immediately the seed-form of the Vedas. This is the seat of the Form of forms, where the devotee beholds the Lord—as in the Christian heaven. Beyond is the center beyond duality, Sahasrāra, the varicolored lotus of a thousand petals at the crown of the head. Here Śakti—who is to be thought of as having ascended through all the lotuses of the suṣumṇā, waking each lotus to full blossom in passing—is joined to Śiva in a union that is simultaneously the fulfillment and dissolution of the worlds of sound, form, and contemplation.

The Tāntric worshiper is supposed to *imagine* himself as having purified his body by suffusing all the lotuses with the awakened Śakti in this way (only a perfected yogī being capable of making the kuṇḍalinī actually rise). Meditation (*dhyāna*), the recitation of charms filled with the power of the Goddess in the form of sound (*mantra*), eloquent postures of the hands and

[38] Cf. Arthur Avalon (Sir John Woodroffe), *The Serpent Power,* 3rd revised edition, Madras and London, 1931, p. 120.

body (*mudrā*), and the meditative placing of the tips of the fingers and palm of the right hand on various parts of the body, accompanied by mantra (*nyāsa*),[39] assist him in this process, as well as in that of welcoming the god into the image or yantra. The two processes are reciprocal, and constitute the whole mystery of ritualistic transubstantiation. Hence we read, in the *Gandharva Tantra:* "A man should worship a divinity (*devatā*) by becoming a divinity himself. One should not worship a divinity without oneself becoming a divinity. If a person worships a divinity without becoming himself a divinity, he will not reap the fruits of that worship." [40] And again, in the *Vāśiṣṭha Rāmāyaṇa:* "If a man worships Viṣṇu without himself becoming Viṣṇu, he will not reap the fruits of that worship. If he wor-

[39] An example of *nyāsa* in Christian worship is the making of the sign of the cross, touching first the forehead ("in the name of the Father"), then the breast ("and of the Son"), the left shoulder ("and of the Holy-"), right shoulder ("-Ghost"), and finally bringing the palms together in the position of salutation known to the Hindus as *añjali,* which is the classic Christian mudrā of prayer ("Amen").

The authors of *The Principles of Tantra* (edited by Arthur Avalon, 2 vols., London, 1914–1916), have aptly cited (pp. lxxi-lxxii) the following statement from the Council of Trent: "The Catholic Church, rich with the experience of the ages and clothed with their splendor, has introduced mystic benediction (*mantra*), incense (*dhūpa*), water (*ācamana, padya,* etc.), lights (*dīpa*), bells (*ghaṇṭā*), flowers (*puṣpa*), vestments, and all the magnificence of its ceremonies in order to excite the spirit of religion to the contemplation of the profound mysteries which they reveal. As are its faithful, the Church is composed of both body (*deha*) and soul (*ātman*). It therefore renders to the Lord (*īśvara*) a double worship, exterior (*vāhya-pūjā*) and interior (*mānasa-pūjā*), the latter being the prayer (*vadana*) of the faithful, the breviary of its priest, and the voice of Him ever interceding in our favor, and the former the outward motions of the liturgy." (Interpolations by authors of *The Principles of Tantra.*)

As to the historical relationship of the Christian to the Tāntric service, that is a delicate matter yet to be investigated.

[40] Cited by Arthur Avalon, *The Great Liberation,* Madras, 1927, p. 109, note.

ships Viṣṇu by becoming himself Viṣṇu, an initiate (*sādhaka*) will become Great Viṣṇu (*Mahāviṣṇu,* i.e., the Being that is beyond the personal aspect of the god)." [41] And once again, this time in the *Bhaviṣya Purāṇa:* "A man should not meditate on Rudra without himself becoming Rudra,[42] nor take the name of Rudra (by muttering the "garland" of the god's names) without becoming Rudra; nor will he attain Rudra without becoming Rudra." [43]

The act of worship is meant to facilitate a direct, immediate experience of what the sādhaka already knows theoretically, namely, that jīva and īśvara (the latter preferably in the feminine form of śakti) are in essence one, being the complementary forms through which Brahman becomes manifest in the field of the pairs-of-opposites, the created world. The sādhaka confronts his devatā, which is represented in the form either of an external image or of an interior vision, on the plane and in the state of dualism, yet he knows that what appears as two is actually one. The activity of self-surrender then leads to the perfect realization of this mystery. Surrender of the illusory sovereign nature of the individual transforms him into a servant (*dāsa*) of the divinity, and this state, when brought to perfection, then reveals to him his own fundamental sovereignty as the deity itself. The fervor of daily worship through bhakti yoga thus awakens the hidden divine nature in man, and divine ecstatic beatitude (*prema*) supervenes following the moment of perfect participation. Similarly, the son of the wealthy man, in the above-cited parable of the Mahāyāna-Buddhist *Saddharmapuṇḍarīka,* without knowing it, served his father as a servant, gradually was advanced in his estate, and eventually came to realize that he was himself the son and heir of the master, en-

[41] *Vāśiṣṭha Rāmāyana* (*Yoga-vaśiṣṭha,* cited *ib.*).

[42] Rudra is the violent, world-destructive aspect of Śiva.

[43] *Bhaviṣya Purāṇa.* (Avalon cites, in *The Great Liberation,* somewhat closely, *Agni Purāṇa.*)

titled to all his possessions; indeed, himself the rich man, the alter-ego of his lord.[44]

But the rites and grades of service are governed by the spiritual character of the devotee. This is a basic principle of all Indian psychological training. The personality endowed with rajas (the quality of vigor and action) will require a different sādhana from one steeped in tamas, while the godlike man of brilliant sattva will be fit for still another way. In the Tāntric vocabulary these three types are known, respectively, as *vīra,* the hero, *paśu,* the dark-witted animal of the herd, and *divya,* the godlike, luminous saint.

It is noteworthy, and perhaps a symptom of Kṣatriya provenience, that in the classic Tāntric Āgamas the emphasis is given to the vīra, the man of rājasic disposition. According to the ideal and way of the Vedānta, rajas was to be subdued by sattva, all the disciplines being founded on the principle of the perfect mirror-pond, but in the classic Tāntric realization the victory was achieved by way of the passions themselves: they were challenged, directly faced, and ridden as a mettlesome stallion by a knight. The "five good things," which for the paśu, the pedestrian, the man of the herd, represent only danger, became the pre-eminent vehicles of attainment. "The five essential elements in the worship of Śakti," the *Mahānirvāṇa Tantra* states, "have been prescribed to be wine, meat, fish, parched grain, and the union of man with woman. The worship of Śakti without these five elements is but the practice of evil magic (*abhicāra:* a ritual that injures or destroys); the power that is the object of the discipline is never attained thereby, and obstacles are encountered at every step. As seed sown on barren rocks does not germinate, so worship (*pūjā*) without these five elements is fruitless."[45] These statements are quoted in the text as the words of Śiva to

[44] *Saddharma-puṇḍarīka* 4; cf. *supra,* pp. 508-509.

[45] *Mahānirvāṇa Tantra* 5. 22-24. (Translation by Avalon, *The Great Liberation,* pp. 89-90).

his Śakti, pronounced in the inner chamber of their divinely blissful abode, on the summit of the sacred mountain Kailāsa.

Neither the saintly nor the gentlemanly Hindu of today, however, favors the boldness of this heroic view. Instead, the attitude formerly assigned to the paśu is recommended for all, that namely of worshiping the life force (*śakti*) not as the Bride but as the Mother, and thus submitting, like a child, to a sort of sacramental castration. "The attitude of a 'hero,' " said Rāmakrishna to one of the most worldly of his devotees, Girish Chandra Ghosh, a successful dramatist and the director of the Calcutta "Star Theatre": "The attitude of a 'hero' is not good. Some people cherish it. They regard themselves as Puruṣa and woman as Prakṛti; they want to propitiate woman through their intercourse with her. But this method often causes disaster."

GIRISH: "At one time I too cherished that idea."

Śrī Rāmakrishna gazed at Girish pensively, in silence.

GIRISH: "I still have that twist in my mind. Tell me what I should do."

RĀMAKRISHNA (*following a moment of silent consideration*): "Give God your power of attorney. Let Him do whatever He likes."

Abruptly, the conversation was then turned to a discussion of Rāmakrishna's younger devotees.

RĀMAKRISHNA (*to Girish and the rest*): "In meditation I see the inner traits of these youngsters. They have no thought of acquiring house and property. They do not crave sex pleasure. Those of the youngsters who are married do not sleep with their wives. The truth is that unless a man has got rid of rajas and has acquired sattva, he cannot steadily dwell in God; he cannot love God and realize Him."

GIRISH: "You have blessed me."

RĀMAKRISHNA: "How is that? I said that you would succeed if you were sincere."

Before Girish could respond, Śrī Rāmakrishna cried, with a

shout of joy, "Ānandamayī!" and the company saw him—as they had beheld him many times before—pass abruptly from normal consciousness to the trance state of divine absorption (*samādhi*). He remained abstracted for some time, but presently moved, and soon was back again, vivaciously participating in the conversation.[46]

One of his "youngsters" had inquired, on a former occasion: "Isn't it true that the Tantra prescribes spiritual discipline in the company of women?"

"That," the Master had replied, "is not desirable. It is a very difficult path and often causes the aspirant's downfall. There are three such kinds of discipline. One may regard woman as one's mistress or look on oneself as her handmaid, or as her child. I look on woman as my mother. To look on oneself as her handmaid is also good; but it is extremely difficult to practice spiritual discipline looking on woman as one's mistress. To regard oneself as her child is a very pure attitude." [47]

And on another occasion: "Śakti alone is the root of the universe. That Primal Energy has two aspects: vidyā and avidyā. Avidyā deludes. Avidyā conjures up 'woman and gold,' which casts the spell. Vidyā begets devotion, kindness, wisdom, and love, which lead one to God. This avidyā must be propitiated, and that is the purpose of the rites of Śakti worship.

"The devotee assumes various attitudes toward Śakti in order to propitiate Her: the attitude of a handmaid, a 'hero,' or a child. A hero's attitude is to please Her even as a man pleases a woman through intercourse.

"The worship of Śakti is extremely difficult. It is no joke. I passed two years as the handmaid and companion of the Divine Mother. But my natural attitude has always been that of a child toward its mother. I regard the breasts of any woman as those

[46] *The Gospel of Śrī Rāmakrishna,* p. 682.
[47] *Ib.,* p. 123.

of my own mother. Women are, all of them, the veritable images of Śakti." [48]

In the classic Tāntric Āgamas three varieties of sādhanā are prescribed for the various temperaments. That of the "five good things," as we have described them, is for the vīra. But for the paśu, these are still the "five forbidden things." And so the term "wine" (*madya*) is interpreted in his case to mean coconut water, milk, or some other indicated "substitutional substance" (*anukalpatattva*). Similarly, instead of "meat" (*māṁsa*), he partakes of wheat-beans, ginger, sesamum, salt, or garlic, and instead of "fish" (*matsya*), of red radish, red sesamum, masur (a kind of grain), the white brinjal vegetable, and paniphala (an aquatic plant). "Parched grain" (*mudrā*) in the form of rice, wheat, paddy, etc., is permitted, but instead of maithuna, child-like submission is recommended before the Divine Mother's Lotus Feet.[49]

The divya, the god-man of purest sattva, on the other hand, is far, far beyond both the "substitutional," safe-and-sane sādhanā of the pious lamb, but also beyond the fearless, chivalric experiences of the hero. For him no external image or sacrament whatsoever is required. Hence, in the rereading of the "five good things" as prescribed for the divya, " 'wine' (*madya*) is not any liquid, but that intoxicating knowledge acquired by yoga of the Parabrahman which renders the worshiper senseless as regards the external world. 'Meat' (*māṁsa*) is not any fleshly thing, but the act whereby the sādhaka consigns all his acts to 'Me' (*mām*), that is, the Lord (this, of course, is a pun). 'Fish' (*matsya*) is that sāttvic knowledge by which through the sense of 'mineness' (a play upon the word *matsya*) the worshiper sympathizes with the pleasure and pain of all beings. *Mudrā* is the act of relinquishing all association with evil which results in bondage. While 'coition' (*maithuna*) is the union of the Śakti

[48] *Ib.*, p. 116.

[49] Woodroffe, *Shakti and Shākta,* pp. 569-570.

Kuṇḍalinī, the 'Inner woman' and World-force in the lowest center (*mūlādhāra cakra*) of the sādhaka's own body with the Supreme Śiva in the highest center (*sahasrāra*) in his upper brain." [50]

For, whereas the paśu or vīra devotee practicing bhūtaśuddhi (the ritual purification of the elements of the body in preparation for an act of dualistic worship) [51] has to *imagine* the purifying ascent of the Kuṇḍalinī through the centers or lotuses (*cakras, padmas*) of the suṣumṇa, the divya, adept in the exercises of the Tāntric Kuṇḍalinī Yoga, actually brings this psychosomatic miracle to pass. Āsana and mudrā (proper seat and posture), prāṇāyāma (control of the breath), dhyāna and mantra (interior visualization and the concentrated recitation of certain "seed" sounds and formulae), following a long and severe preliminary training in physical and emotional self-purification, lead actually to a physical effect which is described as the channeling of all the energies of the body into a subtle channel up the interior of the spine (*suṣumṇa*). In this case, the rise of the "Serpent Power" (*kuṇḍalinī*) and awakening of the lotuses (*padmas*) does not have to be imagined, it actually comes to pass. And when the sixth center is attained—the "Lotus of Command" (*ājñā*) between the eyebrows—the Lord (*īśvara*) is actually seen, not simply imagined, and the beholder is completely lost in savikalpa sāmadhi—communion with the Brahman "with limitations" (*savikalpa*), where the distinction between the subject and the personal God is retained.[52] Whereas the moment the rising force then enters the ultimate thousand-petalled lotus at the crown of the head (the sahasrāra), where Śiva and Śakti are one, the knowledge of duality is in sheer experience

[50] Nīlamani Mukhyopadhyāya, *Pañcatattva-vicāra,* p. 85; Woodroffe, *Shakti and Shākta,* p. 567. Other sublimated readings of the pañcatattva appear in other texts; cf. Woodroffe, pp. 495-500, 568-569.

[51] Cf. *supra,* pp. 584-585.

[52] Cf. *supra,* pp. 435-436.

transcended, and the state of the yogī becomes that of nirvikalpa samādhi: realization of the identity of Ātman with the Brahman "beyond all limitations" (*nirvikalpa*), where both the subject and its highest object are annihilate.[53]

"There is one simple test whether the Śakti (= *kuṇḍalinī*) is actually aroused," writes Sir John Woodroffe. "When she is aroused intense heat is felt at that spot, but when she leaves a particular center the part so left becomes as cold and apparently lifeless as a corpse. The progress upwards may thus be externally verified by others. When the Śakti (Power) has reached the upper brain (*sahasrāra*) the whole body is cold and corpselike; except the top of the skull, where some warmth is felt, this being the place where the static and kinetic aspects of Consciousness unite." [54]

"Sometimes the Spiritual Current rises through the spine, crawling like an ant," Rāmakrishna told a circle of his intimate friends. "Sometimes, in samādhi, the soul swims joyfully in the ocean of divine ecstasy, like a fish. Sometimes, when I lie down on my side, I feel the Spiritual Current pushing me like a monkey and playing with me joyfully. I remain still. That Current, like a monkey, suddenly with one jump reaches the Sahasrāra. That is why you see me jump up with a start.

"Sometimes, again, the Spiritual Current rises like a bird hopping from one branch to another. The place where it rests feels like fire. It may hop from Mūlādhāra to Svādhiṣṭhāna, from Svādhiṣṭhāna to the heart, and thus gradually to the head. Sometimes the Spiritual Current moves up like a snake. Going in a zigzag way, at last it reaches the head and I go into samādhi.

"A man's spritual consciousness is not awakened unless his Kuṇḍalinī is aroused. The Kuṇḍalinī dwells in the Mūlādhāra. When it is aroused, it passes along the Suṣumṇa nerve, goes through the centers of Svādiṣṭhāna, Maṇipūra, and so on, and at

[53] Cf. *supra,* pp. 436-437.

[54] Avalon, *The Serpent Power,* pp. 21-22.

last reaches the head. This is called the movement of the Mahāvāyu, the Spiritual Current. It culminates in samādhi.

"One's spiritual consciousness is not awakened by the mere reading of books. One should pray to God. The Kuṇḍalinī is aroused if the aspirant feels restless for God. To talk of knowledge from mere study and hearsay! What will that accomplish?

"Just before my attaining this state of mind, it had been revealed to me how the Kuṇḍalinī is aroused, how the lotuses of the different centers blossom forth, and how all this culminates in samādhi. This is a very secret experience. I saw a boy twenty-two or twenty-three years old, exactly resembling me, enter the Suṣumṇā nerve and commune with the lotuses, touching them with his tongue. He began with the center at the anus and passed through the centers of the sexual organs, navel, and so on. The different lotuses of those centers—four-petalled, six-petalled, and so forth—had been drooping. At his touch they stood erect.

"When he reached the heart—I distinctly remember it—and communed with the lotus there, touching it with his tongue, the twelve-petalled lotus, which was hanging head down, stood erect and opened its petals. Then he came to the sixteen-petalled lotus in the throat and the two-petalled lotus in the forehead. And last of all, the thousand-petalled lotus in the head blossomed. Since then I have been in this state." [55]

"Waken, O Mother!" wrote Rāmprasād, "O Kuṇḍalinī, whose nature is Bliss Eternal! Thou art the serpent coiled in sleep, in the lotus of the Mūlādhāra!" [56]

"In dense darkness, O Mother," runs another wonderful song, "Thy formless beauty sparkles":

> In dense darkness, O Mother, Thy formless beauty sparkles;
> Therefore the yogīs meditate in a dark mountain cave.

[55] *The Gospel of Śrī Rāmakrishna,* pp. 829-830.
[56] *Ib.,* p. 363.

In the lap of boundless dark, on Mahānirvāṇa's waves upborne,
Peace flows serene and inexhaustible.
Taking the form of the Void, in the robe of darkness wrapped,
Who art Thou, Mother, seated alone in the shrine of samādhi?
From the Lotus of Thy fear-scattering Feet flash Thy love's lightnings;
Thy Spirit-Face shines forth with laughter terrible and loud.[57]

3.

All the Gods within Us

In the Jaina and kindred teachings, matter is described as of an inert and lifeless (*ajīva*) character. The ruthless asceticism of the "naked philosophers" (the "gymnosophists" who astounded Alexander's Greeks) followed logically from their resolution to be sterilized of this dead material and thus rendered pristine—pure, luminous, and perfect. Like balloons leaving the earth below—the earth, its atmosphere, and even the ultimate stratospheric envelope—their life-monads were leaving beneath them, trait by trait, the universal bondages of lifeless "life." As we have seen, the force in India of that pre-Āryan, dualistic, yogic point of view was so great that even the exuberant monism of the Brāhmans finally submitted to its life-searing influence. Gradually, the vigorous world-affirmation of the Vedic period underwent a strangely contradictory change, until, in what is generally regarded as the supreme nondualistic designation of Brahman as *sat, cit, ānanda* ("pure being, consciousness, and

[57] *Ib.*, p. 692.

bliss," absolutely uninvolved in the bondage, ignorance, and misery of the world illusion) the yogic principle won its most impressive triumph. For although it is true that instead of the pre-Āryan, Jaina, and Yoga ideal of the "isolation-integration" (*kaivalya*) of separate life-monads (*jīvas, puruṣas*) the new goal was that of reunion with the one Saccidānanda Brahman, "one-without-a-second," nevertheless this nondual reunion, this *re*cognition of an identity which in reality had never been forfeited, was understood as being synonymous with a refutation of the false notion of the existence of a cosmos: a dissolution of the "superimposition" due to "ignorance." "That which is untouched by the sixfold wave [of decay and death, hunger and thirst, grief and delusion], meditated upon by the yogī's heart but not grasped by the sense-organs, which the faculty of intuition (*buddhi*) cannot know, and which is faultless (*anavadyam*): that Brahman art thou—meditate upon this in thy mind." [58] The same, basic ascetic attitude of rejection as that which in the pre-Āryan past has sundered human experience into the spheres of ajīva and jīva, was now discriminating between saṁsāra and nirvāṇa, while striving for identification ("without remainder") with the unimplicated term.

And yet, on the other hand, there flourishes in India, side by side with this attitude of negation, a vigorous affirmation of the world of flux and time, which is just as fearless and absolute, in its own way, as the unflinching self-transcendence of the yogīs. In that land the great human effort, looking either way, seems always to have been to break the all-too-human limitations of the mind by means of "inhuman" techniques. The ideals and disciplines of the castes are "inhuman"—humanistically speaking; and in a sense, every Indian, one way or another, is a yogī; for bhakti, the popular Hindu "path of devotion," is itself yoga: an internal "yoking" of the mind to a divine principle. Wherever bhakti is carried to an ultimate statement, as for instance

[58] Śaṅkara, *Vivekacuḍāmaṇi* 256.

in the *Bhagavad Gītā* and the sacraments of the Tāntric "five good things" (*pañcatattva*), the secular initiate is inspired to a challenge and assimilation of the *immanent* aspect of absolute Being, which is no less audacious than the corresponding effort, in the penitential groves, to assimilate the *transcendent.*

The Brāhman mind, in other words, did not capitulate unconditionally to the principle of world-rejection. The psychophysical problems posed by the Vedic monist philosophy that matured during the period of the Upaniṣads are as open to world-assertive as to negating replies. The more amply documented Indian philosophical tendency, and the one first encountered by the Western scholars, was that represented in the schools of the Vedānta and Hīnayāna, but in recent years the power and profundity of the Tāntric system have begun to be appreciated, and therewith has been facilitated a new understanding of Indian life and art. Indeed, one could only have been amazed had it been found that in the most durable civilization known to history the sole intellectual response to such a dictum as "All Is Brahman" had been that of a monastic renunciation of the manifest for the unmanifest aspect of the metaphysical equation. Had we not learned what we now know of the philosophy of the Tāntric Āgamas, we should have had to posit some such tradition; for as the Indian centuries open their secrets to us we become more and more aware of the power of something very different from the sublimated melancholy of the monks, in the life-loving Hindu contemplation of the delicacies of the world of name and form. In the majestic sculptural rendering of Śiva Trimūrti at Elephanta,[59] in the now well-known South-Indian bronzes of the Dancing Śiva,[60] in the phantasmagoric "foam and mist" style of the great masterpieces of Bhājā,

[59] Cf. Zimmer, *Myths and Symbols in Indian Art and Civilization,* pp. 148-151, and fig. 33.

[60] *Ib.,* pp. 151-175, and fig. 38.

Māmallapuram, and Elūrā,[61] as well as in the Indian aesthetic phenomenon which I have elsewhere described as that of "expanding form," [62] a stupendous dionysian affirmation of the dynamism of the phenomenal spectacle is rendered, which at once affirms and transcends the apprehended traits of the individual and his cosmos. Prakṛti herself (*natura naturans,* not the merely visible surface of things) is here portrayed—with no resistance to her charm—as She gives birth to the oceans of the worlds. Individuals—mere waves, mere moments, in the rapidly flowing, unending torrent of ephemeral forms—are tangibly present; but their tangibility itself is simply a gesture, an affectionate flash of expression on the otherwise invisible countenance of the Goddess Mother whose play (*līlā*) is the universe of her own beauty. In this dionysian vision the individual is at once devaluated and rendered divine, majestic with the majesty of Nature herself and mystically sheltered in the very maelstrom of the world.

Such a view, obviously, is not fit for all. It can appeal to only certain types and tastes: the aristocratic, for example, or the artistic, and the ecstatic. An intellectual temperament, though perhaps appreciative of the torrential magnitude of such a vision, will remain, necessarily, somewhat cool, refusing to respond to it with the whole personality. That is why this view—though certainly perennial in India—is less well documented in literature, theology, and philosophy than in the works of art. The texts are from the hands of intellectuals, by nature endowed for the abstract realizations of the way of disembodied thought (*jñāna-yoga*); but the art works have poured from the hands of craftsmen commissioned by wealthy merchants and aristocrats—all the children, the servants, or the willing heroes of the Goddess; perhaps profoundly respectful of her more thoughtful sons, yet intimately aware, all the time, that there

[61] *Ib.,* pp. 53-54, 117-121, 187-188, and figs. 1, 27, 28, 55, 59, and 60.
[62] *Ib.,* pp. 130-136.

are riches, boons, and wondrous paradoxical insights that She holds in store only for those who truly dote on Her, and which the haughty discriminators, dedicated to the transcendental One-without-a-second, can never share.

Throughout the known history of India these two points of view have operated in a dialectic process of antagonistic cooperation to bring to pass the majestic evolution of art, philosophy, ritual and religion, political, social, economic, and literary forms, which we know today as the miracle of Indian civilization. By and large, it can be said that the nondual world-affirmation of the Vedic Brāhmans, with its wider swing and greater depth, has been the dominant and victorious contributor to the development. To the pluralistic-realistic, idealistic dualism of Jaina-Sāṅkhya stamp we can ascribe only a preliminary and provocative rôle. By virtue of a bold and vigorous technique of philosophizing in paradoxes, continually establishing the essential unity of terms and spheres that would logically appear to be antagonistic, the fertile thought of Brāhmanism unfailingly brought together, fused, and transcended the pairs-of-opposites, which were then allowed to proceed again from each other in a brilliant dialectical play; Brāhmanic thought being the philosophic counterpart and expression of the life-process itself, a reflection in conceptual terms of the paradoxology of life's unceasing dynamism.

Food, flesh, and blood become transformed in a living body into impulses, emotions, feelings, thought, and inspiration. These in turn condition and move the bodily frame. Then the decomposition of the same body after death converts it into the teeming life of worms and vegetation, which again is food. There is a continuous circuit of metabolism, an unending transformation of opposites into each other. And this reality of becoming is what is mirrored in the Brāhmanic monist conception of māyā. The perpetual motion of things turning into each other is the reality denoted by the icon of the Goddess. The female conceives by the male and transforms his seed into their common offspring, a new formation of their substance. Such is the miracle of the enigma, Māyā-Śakti. Hers, therefore, is an erotic life-philosophy, precisely the opposite and exact compliment of the sterilizing, stern, sublime, ascetic thinking of the Jaina-Sāṅkhya schools.

The concern of the latter is to divide, to cleanse of each other, and finally to separate forever, the life-principle, which is incorporeal, and the principle of both gross and subtle matter, which is life-conditioning, life-staining and -obscuring. In the long course of Indian thought, this stern ascetic attitude has been able to celebrate its moments of victory, and these moments have contributed immeasurably to the recoloring and renovation of Indian life. But that life itself, in accordance with its own innate dialectic principle of transformation, has then inevitably brought to pass a new miracle of absorption, assimilation, and restatement: time and time again, great, vigorous, tropical India has adopted the sublime way of sterilization, the way supremely represented in the teachings of the Buddha and in Śaṅkara's Vedānta; but always the power and wisdom of the erotic-paradoxical monism of life—and of the Brāhman understanding—has again successfully reasserted its force.

Brahman, śakti, the force-substance of Indian nondual philosophy, is the principle that enters, pervades, and animates the panorama and evolutions of nature, but as the same time is the animated and pervaded, entered field or matter of nature itself (*prakṛti, natura naturans*); thus it both *inhabits* and *is* the manifested universe and all its forms. As the unceasing dynamism of the transitory sphere of becoming and withering away, it lives in all the changes of birth, growth, and dissolution.

But, simultaneously, it is remote from this sphere of change; for in its quiescent, dormant, transcendent aspect it knows no phases and is detached from both the living and the dead. The names ascribed to it are concessions to the human mind. This mind, however, being itself of the essence of the unutterable, may be touched to Self-recollection by properly hearing one or another of the finally inadequate names. The name Brahman, Saccidānanda Brahman, is misleading; for it suggests that the transcendent *is.* The name Vacuity, Śūnyatā, the Void, is misleading also; for it suggests that the transcendent *is not.* Perhaps, though, the latter is the less misleading and therefore the better term; for it does suggest transcendence, rather than definable existence. Nevertheless, the difference is not seriously worth an argument. As a clue either term will serve, whereas if not properly understood neither means a thing.

Brāhman philosophy produced its last synthesizing statement in the courageous esotericism of the Tantras and in the Tāntric Mahāyāna (the latter surviving today in the snow-clad summits and high dales of Tibet), where the old Āryan frenzy for non-dualism and the paradox, forever asserting the unity of incompatibles, fruitfully combined with its own incompatible—the archaic matrilineal world-feeling of the aboriginal civilization of India. What the Vedic sages had recognized in the heavens of the macrocosm, the Tāntric adept felt dwelling bodily within himself, in the microcosm, and he named it, also, "God." Hence, whereas the members of the Brāhman caste in Vedic times had conjured the holy power (*brahman*) by means of public sacrifices, the Tāntric devotee, of whatever caste, by means of the simple, essentially personal rituals of the circles of Tāntric initiates, sacrificed his own ego and thereby conjured the holy power (*śakti*) of his own phenomenality into manifestation in his life. The gods served by the Brāhmans had been those of the community; the god worshiped by the Tāntrist was his own, his *iṣṭa-devatā,* his chosen beloved—which yet was identical in essence with whatever deity was anywhere adored; for "It is only a fool," states the *Sammohana Tantra,* "who sees any difference between Rāma and Śiva." [63] The eligibility of the Brāh-

[63] *Sammohana Tantra* 9; Woodroffe, *Shakti and Shākta,* p. 53.

man to serve and conjure the gods of the community had rested in the high rank of his caste in that community, whereas the eligibility of the Tāntric devotee reposed in the ripeness of his mind and power of experience. "The Brāhman who is a descendent of a Ṛṣi, or holy sage," we read in the *Śatapatha Brāhmaṇa,* "is all the gods." [64] "I am the Devī and none other," thinks the Tāntric devotee. "I am Brahman who is beyond all grief. I am a form of Saccidānanda whose true nature is eternal Liberation." [65]

The idea of the godhood of the individual is thus democratized in the Tantra, because understood psychologically instead of sociopolitically. As a result, the entire context of the public Indian faith has been reinterpreted. The rites and religiosity of contemporary India exhibit in every trait the profound influence of this Tāntric view; indeed, they have been for centuries more Tāntric than Vedic. In spite of vestigial remains of the archaic snobbism of caste, native Indian life is shot through with the radiance of a realization of universal divinity. In contrast to the attitude of Job who cried out to Yahweh: "What is man, that thou shouldest magnify him?" the Indian, by shattering his ego, equates himself with God, transcends God, and is at peace in the knowledge of himself as Brahman. "The Mother is present in every house," writes Rāmprasād. "Need I break the news as one breaks an earthen pot on the floor?"

[64] *Śatapatha Brāhmaṇa* 12. 4. 4. 6.

[65] Woodroffe, *Shakti and Shākta,* p. 81.

APPENDICES

APPENDIX A: THE SIX SYSTEMS

Sāṅkhya and Yoga, Mīmāṁsā and Vedānta, Vaiśeṣika and Nyāya, the six classic systems, philosophies, or more literally "points of view" (*darśanas;* from the root *dṛś,* "to see"), are regarded as the six aspects of a single orthodox tradition. Though apparently and even overtly contradictory, they are understood to be complementary projections of the one truth on various planes of consciousness, valid intuitions from differing points of view—like the experiences of the seven blind men feeling the elephant, in the popular Buddhist fable. The founders, actual or supposed—Kapila, Patañjali, Jaimini, Vyāsa, Gautama, and Kaṇāda—should probably be regarded rather as schools than as individuals. Nothing is known of them but their names. Their sūtras stand at the beginning of a copious literature of commentators, yet are themselves but the last terms of a long foregoing period of discussion, each of them including arguments against all the others. Moreover, without the commentaries the texts would be unintelligible: they are not the self-sufficient works of independent thinkers, but mnemonic "threads" (*sūtras*) for the guidance of oral teaching in the ancient Indian style of the guru and his adhikārin.[1]

SĀṄKHYA and YOGA have been discussed *supra,* pp. 280-332. They treat of the hierarchy of the principles (*tattvas*) that proceed from the effects of puruṣa in prakṛti and support the experiences of dream and waking consciousness.

[1] Cf. *supra,* pp. 48-49.

The MĪMĀṀSĀ and VEDĀNTA likewise belong together, both representing the point of view of the "Fourth" (*turīya*), that transcendent nondual principle (*brahman*) which is beyond the province of the world-supporting duad (*puruṣa—prakṛti*). The Vedānta has been discussed, *supra,* pp. 409-463, as the final truth or "end" (*anta*) of the Vedas; the Mīmāṁsā is concerned with a clarification of the liturgical aspect of the same sacred books. Indeed, the term *mīmāṁsā*—meaning, literally, "deep thought, consideration, reflection, exposition," and when applied to philosophy, "reflection on, or exposition of, the Vedas"—properly is applied to both of these philosophies: respectively, as 1. *pūrva-mīmāṁsā* ("the first reflection; exposition of the first part [of the Vedas]") or *karma-mīmāṁsā* ("the study of [ritual] action") and 2. *uttara-mīmāṁsā* ("the second reflection; exposition of the second part [of the Vedas]") or *brahma-mīmāṁsā* ("the contemplation of Brahman").

Pūrva-mīmāṁsā, Karma-mīmāṁsā, or more usually simply the Mīmāṁsā, is a kind of scholastic, priestly science, which defines the orthodox patterns of Brāhmanic liturgical life. These inherited patterns are not always clearly designated in the Vedas themselves; hence already in the later Brāhmaṇas [2] the term *mīmāṁsā* occurs, where it already denotes a discussion of some point of ritual practice. During the following centuries, with the proliferation of variant priestly readings, the demand for this science of definitive reasoning must have increased. Somewhere between 200 and 450 A.D.—that is to say, about the time of the crystallization of the Vedānta—its findings were summarized in the *Pūrvamīmāṁsā-sūtra* of Jaimini; but this basic textbook presupposes a long history of argument. "There is evidence," states A. B. Keith, "that the science was in full vogue as early as the middle of the third century B.C." [3]

[2] Cf. *supra,* p. 8, Editor's note.

[3] Arthur Berriedale Keith, *The Karma-Mīmāṁsā,* The Heritage of India Series, London and Calcutta, 1921, pp. 2-3.

The method of the *Pūrvamīmāṁsā-sūtra* resembles somewhat that of Thomas Aquinas' scholastic *Summa Theologica.* Its elementary unit, or subdivision, is the adhikaraṇa ("heading"), which falls into five parts: first, a proposition is formulated; next, the doubt as to its correctness is refuted; third, the erroneous methods of treating it are exhibited; fourth, these are refuted; and finally, the true solution is presented as the inevitable conclusion of the entire discussion.[4] For example, in Sūtra I, two propositions are presented: 1. that Vedic study is obligatory for the upper castes; and 2. that Dharma is a proper subject for study. The first proposition is found to be self-evident in the Vedic precepts, "One should study the Veda" and "One should perform the ritual of the final bath after studying the Veda." A doubt arises, however, with respect to the second proposition, since it may be asked whether one should perform the ritual of the bath immediately after learning the Vedas, and so terminate one's period of studentship. The prima facie view is that the bath should immediately follow the learning of the Veda. The reply is that the real study of the Veda is not satisfied by a mere reading of the text. The true conclusion, consequently, is that the final bath should be postponed until a study of Dharma has brought the student's understanding of the Veda to a state of perfection. Jaimini's volume contains some nine hundred and fifteen of these adhikaraṇas, organized in twelve books.[5]

The Mīmāṁsā darśana supports a theory of the infallibility of the Vedas and a theory of meaning as inherent in sound: Sanskrit, the holy language of the Vedas, that is to say, is not a historical tongue based on convention, but an emanation of Being (*sat*) in sound (*śabda*); hence the power of the sacred mantras and of the Vedic hymns to touch the quick of truth and so to work magic. It is from this potency that the effects of the sacrifice are

[4] R. Garbe, "Mīmāṁsā," in Hastings, *Encyclopaedia of Religion and Ethics,* Vol. VIII, p. 648.

[5] Keith, *op. cit.,* pp. 4-5.

derived, not from divine intervention; for though the offerings are addressed to deities, the deities are themselves supported by the power of the sacrifice. "The Mīmāṁsā," writes Garbe, "does not recognize the existence of God. Nevertheless this fact interferes as little here as in the Sāṅkhya and the other systems with the belief in the supernatural beings of the popular Indian faith." [6] Also rejected is the idea of the periodic creation and dissolution of all things. There is a constant process of becoming and passing away, but no ground for the systematization of this process in terms of cycles of evolution and involution.[7] Moreover, arguing specifically against the Śūnyavāda of the Mahāyāna, the Mīmāṁsā doctrine of knowledge affirms the world as real.[8] This darśana stands in close relationship to Indian law, since its chief object is "to determine injunctions, which are distinct from those of civil law mainly in the fact that they deal with sacrificial rather than civil obligations, and are enforced by spiritual rather than temporal penalties." [9]

VAIŚEṢIKA and NYĀYA, cosmology and logic, the remaining brace of the six philosophies, treat of the data of waking consciousness from the point of view of waking consciousness itself, and are consequently closer in spirit and character than the other Indian darśanas to the academic tradition of the West. The legendary founder of the Vaiśeṣika, Kaṇāda (also known as Kaṇabhakṣa and Kaṇabhuj, all three names meaning "atom eater"), is supposed to have flourished c. 200–400 A.D.[10] His textbook, the *Vaiśeṣika-sūtra* ("the sūtras, or precepts, showing the differences, distinctive characteristics, or manifest nature, of individual things"), distinguishes in nature five categories (*padār-*

[6] Garbe, *loc. cit.*

[7] Keith, *op. cit.*, p. 61. This doctrine is held in opposition to the Vaiśesika and Nyāya view. Cf. *infra*.

[8] *Ib.*, Chapters II, III.

[9] *Ib.*, p. 97.

[10] Garbe, "Vaiśeṣika," in Hastings, *op. cit.*, Vol. XII, p. 569.

thas): 1. substance (*dravya*), comprising earth, water, fire, air, ether, time, space, soul (*ātman*),[11] and mind (*manas*); 2. quality (*guṇa*), comprising color, taste, smell, touch (with temperature), number, extension, individuality, connection, separation, priority, posterity, knowledge, joy, pain, desire, aversion, and will;[12] 3. movement and action (*karma*); 4. association (*sāmānya*); 5. difference (*viśeṣa*); and 6. inherence (*samavāya*).[13] The Vaiśeṣika derives its name from category 5, *viśeṣa,* "difference," because it is an atomistic doctrine (whence the nicknames of its legendary founder). The atoms of the several substances have no extension, yet in combination become extensive and visible. During the periods of world dissolution between the cosmogonic cycles, they are not combined; hence there is then no visible world. The souls, nevertheless, retain their merit and demerit, and in consequence unite, presently, with the various atoms. This renews the movement of the atoms and begins a new cycle of creation. The continuous wanderings and activities of the souls in the manifest world ultimately fatigue them, and so a night, a cosmic night of dissolution, is necessary for their refreshment. The unions of the atoms dissolve, and the universe disappears.

"Both souls and the organ of thought are eternal substances," writes Garbe, describing the psychology peculiar to this system; "but the soul is all-pervading, i.e., not bound down to time and space, while the organ of thought is an atom. The latter is the

[11] I am using the translation "soul" to accord with the quotations (*infra*) from Garbe. See, however, Dr. Zimmer's note, *supra*, p. 324. The term *ātman* here denotes the life-monad (as *jīva* in Jainism, *puruṣa* in the Sāṅkhya) and should not be confused with the *ātman* of the Upaniṣads, *Bhagavad Gītā,* and Vedānta.

[12] Contrast the term *guṇa* as employed in the Sāṅkhya and *Bhagavad Gītā.*

[13] *Samavāya:* "the intimate relationship that unites the substance with its attributes and is itself an attribute of the substance" (René Guénon, *Introduction générale à l'étude des doctrines hindous,* Paris, 1930, p. 237).

intermediary between the soul and the senses, since urged by the soul it betakes itself on each occasion to that sense through which the soul desires to perceive or to act. . . . If it rests motionless in the soul, the union of the latter with the senses ends, and no perception or act or experience is possible. . . . If the organ of thought were omnipresent like the soul, or if the soul could enter into immediate relation with the objects of knowledge, all objects would be simultaneously perceived. As the organ of thought, on the one hand, imparts the quickening power to the soul, so, on the other, it acts as a kind of check by preventing the soul from exercising more than one function at the same time." [14]

Nyāya, logic, the sixth of the classical systems, is attributed to a shadowy figure, Gautama—nicknamed Akṣapāda, "the foot-eyed," that is to say, "with his eyes fixed on his feet"—whose textbook, the *Nyāya-sūtra,* composed perhaps as early as 150 B.C.,[15] but more probably between 200 and 450 A.D.,[16] parallels the Vaiśeṣika in its atomic doctrine, cosmology, and psychology, but is devoted principally to the science of logic. Four sources of true knowledge are recognized: 1. perception (*pratyakṣa*), 2. inference (*anumāna*), 3. analogy (*upamāna*), and 4. credible testimony (*śabda*). Inference, the sole reliable means to philosophical knowledge, is of three kinds: 1. inference from cause to effect (*pūrvavat*), 2. inference from effect to cause (*śeṣavat*), and 3. reasoning from perception to abstract principle (*sāmānyato dṛṣṭa*). Three kinds of cause are recognized: 1. the material or inhering cause (*upādāna-kāraṇa, samavāyi-kāraṇa*), e.g., in the case of a carpet, its threads; 2. the noninhering or formal cause (*asamavāyi-kāraṇa*), in the case of the carpet, the arrangement and knotting of its threads; and 3. the effective or instrumental cause (*nimitta-kāraṇa*): the weaver's tools. The syllogism of the Nyāya

[14] Garbe, "Vaiśeṣika," p. 570.

[15] Garbe, "Nyāya," in Hastings, *op. cit.,* Vol. IX, p. 423.

[16] A. B. Keith, *Indian Logic and Atomism,* Oxford, 1921, p. 24.

darśana comprises five members: 1. the proposition (*pratijñā*), e.g., there is a fire on the mountain; 2. the cause (*hetu*), for the mountain smokes; 3. the exemplification (*dṛṣṭānta*), wherever there is smoke there is fire, as, for example, on the hearth in the kitchen; 4. the recapitulation of the cause (*upanaya*), the mountain smokes; and 5. the conclusion (*nigamana*), therefore there is fire on the mountain. "The conception," writes Garbe, "on which the theory of the syllogism of the Nyāya rests bears the name of 'invariable association' (*vyāpti*). Instead of starting as we do with an affirmative proposition, universally valid—'All smoke presumes the existence of fire'—the Nyāya philosophy asserts the 'invariable association' of smoke with fire. The sign observed (*liṅga*)—in this instance the smoke—is 'invariably associated' (*vyāpya*); the vehicle of the sign which is to be inferred (*liṅgin*)—in this instance the fire—is the 'invariable associate' (*vyāpaka*)." [17] René Guénon points out, however, that abridged forms of this syllogism are used, in which either the first three terms or the last three may appear alone, and that the latter abridgment resembles the syllogism of Aristotle.[18]

Book I of the *Nyāya-sūtra* defines the topics, or categories, to be discussed in the volume; Book II deals with doubt, the four means of proof and their validity, and shows that there are no other valid means of demonstration; Book III discusses the self, the body, the senses and their objects, cognition, and the mind; Book IV disposes of volition, fault, transmigration, the good and evil fruits of human action, pain, and final liberation; then passes to the theory of error and of the whole and its parts; Book V deals with unreal objections (*jāti*) and occasions for the rebuke of an opponent (*nigrahasthāna*).[19]

"When," observes Garbe, "the Vaiśeṣika and Nyāya systems came to be blended together, the combined school adopted the-

[17] Garbe, "Nyāya," p. 423.

[18] Guénon, *op. cit.*, pp. 226-227.

[19] Keith, *Indian Logic and Atomism*, p. 19.

istic views, but never saw in the personal God, whom they assumed, the creator of matter. Their theology is set forth in the *Kusumāñjali* of Udayana [c. 950 A.D.],[20] and in various later works which discuss the two systems in common. According to the view which they hold in harmony with the doctrine of the Yoga, God is a distinct soul like the other individual souls, and these are equally with Him eternal. He is, however, distinguished from them by the fact that He alone possesses the attributes of omniscience and omnipotence, which qualify Him for the government of the universe; and that, on the other hand, He lacks those attributes which result in the entanglement of all other souls in the cycle of existence." [21]

The ideal of liberation presented in Gautama's *Nyāya-sūtra,* Book IV, is that of ascetic detachment, culminating in a condition of absolute unconsciousness, similar to that of the Sāṅkhya, as described *supra,* pp. 329-330. This suggests that in these apparently later doctrines we may have another vestige of the archaic pre-Āryan science represented in Jainism and the doctrine of Gosāla (*supra,* pp. 263-279). Indeed, in a late Jaina text (the *Āvaśyaka*), the Vaiśeṣika is attributed to a Jaina schismatic named Rahagutta.[22]

The "six systems" are considered to be orthodox because they recognize the authority of the Vedas; their co-ordination, however, is not particularly old. Vācaspati-miśra, c. 841 A.D., composed commentaries on the Sāṅkhya, Yoga, Mīmāṁsā, Vedānta, and Nyāya systems, while Udayana, about a century later, combined the views of the Nyāya and Vaiśeṣika in his proof of the existence of God. The culmination of the tendency to syncretize appears in Śivāditya (date uncertain, but probably later than

[20] Garbe gives 1300 A.D., but this is certainly too late, since one of Udayana's works is dated 984 A.D. Cf. Winternitz, *Geschichte der indischen Litteratur,* Vol. III, p. 466.

[21] Garbe, "Nyāya," p. 424.

[22] Keith, *Indian Logic and Atomism,* p. 14.

Udayana), who, though perhaps not the first to amalgamate the darśanas in exposition, must be reckoned the earliest of the authorities of the joint school.[23]

The "six systems," however, never attained the position of an exclusive, dogmatic orthodoxy. The *Sarvadarśanasiddhānta-saṅgraha* ("Epitome of the Doctrines of All the Darśanas"), a tenth- or eleventh-century textbook from the school of Śaṅkara, delineates, with adequate objectivity, the views of the Lokāyatikas (materialists),[24] Jainas, Buddhists (Mādhyamikas, Yogācāras, Sautrāntikas, and Vaibhāṣikas), Vaiśeṣika, Nyāya, Pūrva-

[23] *Ib.*, pp. 29, 31, 37.

[24] *Lokāyata,* literally, "belonging to the world of sense," is the name given to a materialistic system said to have been founded by the sophist Cārvāka (date, of course, unknown). "There are clear indications," states Garbe, "of the presence in India, as early as pre-Buddhistic times, of teachers of a pure materialism; and undoubtedly these theories have had numerous adherents in India from that period onwards to the present day. . . . The Lokāyata allows only perception as a means of knowledge, and rejects inference. It recognizes as the sole reality the four elements, i.e., matter, and teaches that, when a body is formed by the combination of the elements, the spirit also comes into existence, just like the intoxicating quality with the mixture of special materials. With the destruction of the body the spirit returns again into nothingness. . . . The post-operative force of merit and demerit, which, according to the belief of all the other Indian schools, determines the lot of each individual down to the smallest details, has no existence for the Lokāyatika, because this conception is reached only by inference. . . . On the practical side this system exhibits itself as the crudest Eudaemonism; for it represents the gratification of the senses as the sole desirable good. . . . The Vedas are declared to be the idle prating of knaves, characterized by the three faults of untruthfulness, internal contradiction, and useless repetition. . . . The ritual of the Brāhmans is a fraud, and the costly and laborious sacrifices are useful only for providing with a livelihood the cunning fellows who carry them out" (Garbe, "Lokāyata," in Hastings, *op. cit.,* Vol. VIII, p. 138). None of the writings of this school are extant; all that we know of them has been gathered from the writings of their opponents. Cf. F. Max Müller, *Six Systems of Indian Philosophy,* London, 1899, pp. 86, 94ff.

mīmāṁsā (in two schools: that of Prabhākara and that of Kumārila),[25] Sāṅkhya, and Yoga, the philosophy of Vedavyāsa,[26] and the Vedānta of Śaṅkara.[27] Mādhava, an eminent fourteenth-century Vedāntist of the school of Śaṅkara, delineates likewise in his *Sarvadarśanasaṅgraha* ("Epitome of All Systems") [28] sixteen philosophies, adding to the above the Vedānta of Rāmānuja, the doctrines of a number of Śivaite sects, and Pāṇini's treatment of the laws of the metaphysical, eternal, and magical language of the Vedas in his Sanskrit Grammar.[29]

In the final analysis, the orthodoxy of India has never been grounded in a college or academy. Neither can it be defined by any numbering of views. For its life is in the mokṣa of the actual sages: such, for example, as Rāmakrishna (1836–86) in the nineteenth century and Ramaṇa (1879–1950) in our own.[30] These "wild geese" (*haṁsas*), teaching numerously in every part of the land of the Bhāratas, have renewed the ineffable message perennially, in variable terms, which philosophers classify and adhikārins transcend.

J. C.

[25] A sharp divergence in the unity of the Mīmāṁsā-darśana begins with the appearance of these two scholastics, c. 700 A.D. Cf. Keith, *The Karma-Mīmāṁsā,* p. 9.

[26] I.e., the philosophy of the *Mahābhārata.*

[27] Winternitz, *op. cit.,* Vol. III, pp. 419-420.

[28] Translated by E. B. Cowell and A. E. Gough, 2nd edition, Calcutta, 1894.

[29] Winternitz, *op. cit.,* p. 420.

[30] Śrī Ramaṇa Maharṣi ("the Great Ṛṣi") of Tiruvannamalai (an ancient holy city in the south of India) taught no formal doctrine, but with the piercing question "Who are you?" drove his disciples to the Self. Cf. Heinrich Zimmer, *Der Weg zum Selbst; Lehre und Leben des indischen Heiligen Shri Ramana Maharshi aus Tiruvannamalai,* edited by C. G. Jung, Zurich, 1944; cf. also B. V. Narasimha Swami, *Self-Realization, Life and Teachings of Ramana Maharshi,* Tiruvannamalai, 1936, and Śrī Ramaṇa Maharshi, *Who Am I?* (translated by Ramana Dasa S. Seshu Iyer), Tiruvannamalai, 1937.

APPENDIX B: HISTORICAL SUMMARY

B.C.*		B.C.		B.C.	
c. 3500–1450	Minoan Civilization (Crete)			c. 3500–1500	Dravidian Civilization (Indus Valley Ruins)
c. 2000–1000	Hellenic Invasions of Greece	c. 2000–1000	Āryan Invasions of N. India	?	Prehistoric Jaina Saviors
c. 1300?	Moses	c. 1500–800	*Vedas*		
c. 950	Solomon		*Brāhmaṇas*	c. 872–772	Pārśva (23rd Jaina Savior)
800 & after	The Prophets	800 & after	*Upaniṣads*		
	Homer		Early Hero Epics (lost)	?	Kapila (Sāṅkhya)
c. 775	Hesiod				
c. 640–546	Thales			d. c. 526	Mahāvīra (24th Jaina Savior)
611?–547?	Anaximander			?	Gosāla

* In this column: parallel dates in the Western world (for comparison).

B.C.		B.C.		B.C.	
c. 582–c. 500	Pythagoras			c. 563–483	Buddha
fl. 6th cent.	Parmenides				
c. 500–430	Empedocles				
c. 500	Heraclitus	c. 500 B.C.– 500 A.D.	*Sūtras*		
469–369	Socrates				
427?–347	Plato				
384–322	Aristotle		*Laws of Manu*	?	Patañjali (Yoga)
356–323	Alexander the Great	325: Alexander enters N.W. India			
?–287?	Theophrastus				
342?–270	Epicurus			c. 321–297	Candragupta Maurya
336?–264?	Zeno				Cānakya Kauṭilya (*Arthaśāstra*)
276?–195?	Eratosthenes				
c. 600 B.C.?– 200 A.D.	Establishment of *Old Testament canon*	c. 400 B.C.– 200 A.D.	*Rāmāyaṇa* (present form)	c.274–237	Aśoka
264–146	Punic Wars	c. 400 B.C.– 400 A.D.	*Mahābhārata* (present form) (*Bhagavad Gītā*)		
100–44	Julius Caesar			c. 80	*Pāli canon*
70–19	Vergil				Hīnayāna Buddhism

A.D.		A.D.		A.D.	
?–?	Jesus Christ				
53–117	Trajan			c. 78–123	Kaniṣka
121–180	Marcus Aurelius		Medieval Hinduism ⟵	Tantra ⟶	Mahāyāna Buddhism
205?–270?	Plotinus	c. 200/450?	Jaimini (*Mīmāṁsā-sūtra*)	c. 200	Nāgārjuna (Mādhyamika)
272–337	Constantine				
354–430	Augustine	c. 300–500	*Pañcatantra*		*Prajñā-pāramitā*
476	Fall of Rome	?	*Purāṇas*	c. 350	Asaṅga (Yogācāra)
c. 500	Benedictine Monasticism (Monte Cassino)	?	*Tantras*	d. c. 527	Bodhidharma (Dhyāna: Zen)
570?–632	Mohammed	4th–13th centuries	Apogee of Indian Art (Gupta, Cāḷukya, Rāṣṭrakūṭa, Pallava, Pāla, Coḷa, Rājput, Hoyśala styles)	c. 650/750?	Lakṣmīṅkarā Devī (Mahāsukha)

A.D.		A.D.		A.D.	
742–814	Charlemagne	c. 788–820/50?	Śaṅkara (Advaita **Vedānta**)		
		?	"The Six Systems"	c. 983	Cāmuṇḍarāya (Gommaṭa image)
1097	First **Crusade**				
1225?–1274	Aquinas	1175–1250	**Rāmānuja**	?	End of Buddhism in India
1260?–1327?	**Eckhart**				
1469–1527	**Machiavelli**	1400–1500	***Vedāntasāra***		
1596–1650	Descartes				
1712–1778	**Rousseau**	1718–1775	**Rāmprasād**		
1770–1831	**Hegel**				
1809–1882	**Darwin**	1836–1886	Rāmakrishna		
1879–	**Einstein**	**1879–1950**	**Ramaṇa**		

BIBLIOGRAPHY

*BIBLIOGRAPHY**

GENERAL

MACKAY, ERNEST. *The Indus Civilization.* London, 1935.

MARSHALL, SIR JOHN. *Mohenjo-daro and the Indus Civilization.* 3 vols. London, 1931.

PIGGOTT, STUART. *Prehistoric India.* Harmondsworth (Penguin Books), 1950.

DUNBAR, SIR GEORGE. *A History of India, from the earliest times to the present.* London, 2nd edition, 1939.

HAVELL, E. B. *The History of Aryan Rule in India, from the earliest times to the death of Akbar.* New York, no date.

RAFSON, E. J. (ed.). *The Cambridge History of India.* Cambridge and New York, 1922.

SMITH, VINCENT A. *Aśoka, the Buddhist Emperor of India.* Oxford, 1901.

COOMARASWAMY, ANANDA K. *History of Indian and Indonesian Art.* New York, 1927.

FARQUHAR, J. N. *An Outline of the Religious Literature of India.* Oxford, 1920.

HASTINGS, JAMES (ed.). *Encyclopaedia of Religion and Ethics.* 13 vols. New York, 1928.

KRAMRISCH, STELLA. *The Hindu Temple.* Photographs by Raymond Burnier. 2 vols. Calcutta, 1946.

MUIR, J. *Original Sanskrit Texts on the Origin and History of*

* Based on works cited in the text, but with a few additional titles. Further guidance will be found in J. N. Farquhar, *An Outline of the Religious Literature of India,* Oxford, 1920; in C. H. Hamilton, *Buddhism in India, Ceylon, China, and Japan: a Guide to Reading,* Chicago, 1931; and in the bibliographies of the volumes listed.

the People of India, Their Religion and Institutions. 5 vols. London, 1868–74.

WINTERNITZ, MORIZ. *Geschichte der indischen Litteratur.* 3 vols. Leipzig, 1905–22. (English translation by Mrs. S. Ketkar and H. Kohn. 2 vols. Calcutta, 1927–33.)

DASGUPTA, SURENDRA NATH. *A History of Indian Philosophy.* 4 vols. Cambridge, 1922–49.

RADHAKRISHNAN, S. *Indian Philosophy.* 2 vols. London, 1923 and 1927.

TRIVARGA

COOMARASWAMY, ANANDA K. *Spiritual Authority and Temporal Power in the Indian Theory of Government.* New Haven, 1942.

DUTT, MANMATHA NATH (trans.). *Kāmandakiya Nītisāra.* (Wealth of India Series.) Calcutta, 1896.

SHAMASASTRY, R. (trans.). *Kauṭilīya Arthaśāstra.* Bangalore, 1915; 2nd edition, 1923.

THOMAS, FREDERICK WILLIAM (ed. and trans.). *Brihaspati Sūtra.* (Punjab Sanskrit Series.) Lahore, 1921.

COOMARASWAMY, ANANDA K. *The Transformation of Nature in Art.* Cambridge, Mass., 1934.

——. *Why Exhibit Works of Art?* London, 1943.

——. *Figures of Speech or Figures of Thought.* London, 1946.

DANIÉLOU, ALAIN. *Introduction to the Study of Musical Scales.* London, 1943.

HAAS, GEORGE C. O. (trans.). *The Daśarūpa of Dhanamjaya, a treatise on Hindu Dramaturgy.* (Columbia University Indo-Iranian Series.) New York, 1912.

VĀTSYĀYANA. *Kāmasūtra.* Edited (in Sanskrit) by Pandit Durgāprasāda, Bombay, 1891; English translation, Benares, 1883 ("printed for the Hindoo Kama Shastra Society": undependable); French (derived from the English), by E. Lamairesse, Paris, 1891; German, by R. Schmidt, with the commentary of Yaśodhara, Leipzig, 1897; 5th edition, 1915.

BHATTACHARYA, J. N. *Hindu Castes and Sects.* Calcutta, 1896.

BÜHLER, G. (trans.). *The Laws of Manu.* (Sacred Books of the East, Vol. XXV.) Oxford, 1886.

——. *The Sacred Laws of the Āryas.* (Sacred Books of the East, Vols. II and XIV.) Oxford, 1879 and 1882.

COOMARASWAMY, ANANDA K. *The Dance of Siva.* New York, 1918.

——. *Religious Basis of the Forms of Indian Society.* New York, 1946.

GANDHI, M. K. *The Story of My Experiments with Truth.* Ahmedabad, 1927–29.

STEVENSON, MRS. S. *The Rites of the Twice-born.* Oxford, 1920.

——. *Without the Pale. The Life Story of an Outcaste.* Calcutta, 1930.

JAINISM

BLOOMFIELD, MAURICE. *The Life and Stories of the Jaina Savior Pārçvanātha.* Baltimore, 1919.

BROWN, W. NORMAN. *The Story of Kālaka. Texts, History, Legends, and Miniature Paintings of the Śvetāmbara Jain Hagiographical Work: The Kālakācāryakathā.* Washington, 1933.

——. *Miniature Paintings of the Jaina Kalpasūtra, as Executed in the Early Western Indian Style.* Washington, 1934.

——. *Manuscript Illustrations of the Uttarādhyayana Sūtra.* New Haven, 1941.

CHAKRAVARTI, APPĀSVĀMĪ (ed. and trans.). *Kundakundācārya's Pañcāstikāyasāra.* (Sacred Books of the Jainas.) Allahabad, 1920.

FADDEGON, BAREND (trans.). *The Pravacana-sāra of Kundakunda Ācārya.* (Jain Literature Society Series.) Cambridge, 1935.

GLASENAPP, HELMUTH VON. *Der Jainismus, Eine indische Erlösungsreligion.* Berlin, 1925.

GUÉRINOT, ARMAND ALBERT. *La religion djaina.* Paris, 1926.

JACOBI, HERMANN. "Jainism," in Hastings, *Encyclopaedia of Religion and Ethics,* Vol. VII, pp. 465-74.

——. *Jaina Sūtras.* (Sacred Books of the East, Vols. XXII and XLV.) Oxford, 1884 and 1895.

JAINI, JAGMANDAR LAL. *Outlines of Jainism.* Cambridge, 1916.

—— (ed. and trans.). *Tattvārthādhigama Sūtra.* (Sacred Books of the Jainas.) Arrah, no date.

STEVENSON, MRS. S. *The Heart of Jainism.* Cambridge, 1916.

SĀṄKHYA AND YOGA

COLEBROOKE, H. T., and WILSON, H. H. (eds. and trans.) *Sāṅkhya-Kārikā.* Oxford, 1837; Bombay, 1887.

GARBE, RICHARD. "Sāṅkhya," in Hastings, *Encyclopaedia of Religion and Ethics,* Vol. XI, pp. 189-92.

——. *Die Sāṁkhya Philosophie.* Leipzig, 1894.

——. *Sāṁkhya und Yoga.* Strassburg, 1896.

KEITH, ARTHUR BERRIEDALE. *The Sāṁkhya System.* New York, 1918.

SINHA, NANDALAL (Skr. and trans.). *The Sāṁkhya-pravacana-sūtram.* (Sacred Books of the Hindus, Vol. XI.) Allahabad, 1915.

DANIÉLOU, ALAIN. *Yoga: the Method of Re-integration.* London, 1949.

DASGUPTA, SURENDRA NATH. *Yoga as Philosophy and Religion.* London, 1924.

——. *Yoga Philosophy in Relation to Other Systems of Indian Thought.* Calcutta, 1930.

GARBE, RICHARD. "Yoga," in Hastings, *Encyclopaedia of Religion and Ethics,* Vol. XII, pp. 831-33.

WOODS, JAMES HOUGHTON (trans.). *The Yoga-System of Patañjali.* (Harvard Oriental Series.) Cambridge, Mass., 1927.

BRAHMANISM

BLOOMFIELD, MAURICE (trans.). *Hymns of the Atharva Veda.* (Sacred Books of the East, Vol. XLII.) Oxford, 1897.

COOMARASWAMY, ANANDA K. *A New Approach to the Vedas. An Essay in Translation and Exegesis.* London, 1933.

——. *The Ṛg Veda as Land-nāma-bók.* London, 1935.

GRIFFITH, R. T. H. (trans.). *Ṛgveda, Samaveda, White Yajurveda, Atharvaveda.* Benares, 1895–1907.

MACDONELL, A. A. (trans.). *Hymns from the Rigveda.* London, 1922.

——. *Vedic Mythology.* Strassburg, 1897.

——. "Vedic Religion," in Hastings, *Encyclopaedia of Religion and Ethics,* Vol. XII, pp. 601-18.

MÜLLER, F. MAX, and OLDENBERG, H. (trans.). *Ṛg Veda Hymns.* (Sacred Books of the East, Vols. XXXII and XLVI.) Oxford, 1891 and 1897.

OLDENBERG, H. *Religion der Vedas.* Berlin, 1884.

WHITNEY, WILLIAM DWIGHT, and LANMAN, CHARLES ROCKWELL (trans.). *Atharva Veda.* (Harvard Oriental Series, Vols. VII and VIII.) Cambridge, Mass., 1905.

EGGELING, J. (trans.). *Śatapatha Brāhmaṇa.* (Sacred Books of the East, Vols. XII, XXVI, XLI, XLIII, XLIV.) Oxford, 1882–1900.

KEITH, ARTHUR BERRIEDALE (trans.). *The Rigveda Brāhmaṇas.* (Harvard Oriental Series, Vol. XXV.) Cambridge, Mass., 1920.

BESANT, ANNIE (Skr. and trans.). *The Bhagavad Gītā.* 4th and revised edition, London, 1912.

MUKERJI, D. G. (trans.). *The Song of God* [Bhagavad Gītā]. New York, 1931.

NIKHILĀNANDA, SWĀMĪ (trans.). *The Bhagavad Gītā.* New York, 1944.

DEUSSEN, PAUL (trans.). *Sechzig Upanishads des Veda.* Leipzig, 1897.

——. *Philosophy of the Upanishads.* Translated by Rev. A. S. Geden. Edinburgh, 1906.

HUME, ROBERT ERNEST (trans.). *The Thirteen Principal Upanishads.* Oxford, 1921.

KEITH, ARTHUR BERRIEDALE. *The Religion and Philosophy of the Veda and Upaniṣads.* Cambridge, Mass., 1925.

MĀDHAVĀNANDA, SWĀMĪ (Skr. and trans.). *The Bṛhadāraṇyaka Upaniṣad. With the Commentary of Śaṅkarācārya.* Mayavati, Almora, Himalayas, no date.

NIKHILĀNANDA, SWĀMĪ (Skr. and trans.). *The Māṇḍukyopanisad. With Gauḍapada's Kārikā and Śaṅkara's Commentary.* Mysore, 1936.

—— (trans.). *The Upanishads,* Vol. I [Katha, Iśa, Kena, Mundaka]. New York, 1949.

RADHAKRISHNAN, S. *The Philosophy of the Upanishads.* London, 1924.

SHARVĀNANDA, SWĀMĪ (Skr. and trans.). *The Upanishad Series: Isha, Kena, Katha, Prasna, Muṇḍaka, Māṇḍūkya, Aitareya, Taittīrīya.* Mylapore, Madras, no date.

COOMARASWAMY, ANANDA K. *Recollection, Indian and Platonic* and *The One and Only Transmigrant.* New Haven, 1944.

DEUSSEN, PAUL. *The System of the Vedānta.* Translated by C. Johnston. Chicago, 1912.

GARBE, RICHARD. "Vedānta," in Hastings, *Encyclopaedia of Religion and Ethics,* Vol. XII, pp. 597-98.

MĀDHAVĀNANDA, SWĀMĪ (Skr. and trans.). *The Vivekacuḍamaṇi of Śankarācārya.* 3rd edition, Mayavati, Almora, Himalayas, 1932.

NIKHILĀNANDA, SWĀMĪ (trans.). *Self-Knowledge* [The Atmabodha of Śaṅkara]. New York, 1946.

—— (Skr. and trans.). *The Vedāntasāra of Sadānanda.* Mayavati, Almora, Himalayas, 1931.

NITYASWARŪPĀNANDA, SWĀMĪ (Skr. and trans.). *Aṣṭavakra Saṃhitā.* Mayavati, Almora, Himalayas, 1940.

THIBAUT, G. (trans.). *The Vedānta Sūtra. With Śaṅkara's Commentary.* 2 vols. (Sacred Books of the East, Vols. XXXIV and XXXVIII.) Oxford, 1890 and 1896.

——. *The Vedānta Sūtra. With Rāmānuja's Commentary.* (Sacred Books of the East, Vol. XLVIII.) Oxford, 1904.

VIREŚWARĀNANDA, SWĀMĪ (Skr. and trans.). *Brahma-sūtras.* Mayavati, Almora, Himalayas, 1936.

BUDDHISM

BURLINGAME, E. W. *Buddhist Parables.* New Haven, 1922.

COOMARASWAMY, ANANDA K. *Yakṣas.* Washington, 1928–31.

——. *Buddha and the Gospel of Buddhism.* New York, 1916.

——. *Hinduism and Buddhism.* New York, no date.

——. *Elements of Buddhist Iconography.* Cambridge, Mass., 1935.

COWELL, E. B. (ed. and trans.). *The Jātaka, or Stories of the Buddha's Former Births.* 6 vols. Cambridge, 1895–1907.

COWELL, E. B., MÜLLER, F. MAX, and TAKAKUSU, JUNJIRO (trans.). *Buddhist Mahāyāna Sūtras* [Buddha-carita of Aśvaghoṣa; Larger and Smaller Sukhāvatī-vyūhas; Vajracchedikā; Larger and Smaller Prajñā-pāramitā Sūtras; Amitāyur-dhyāna Sūtra]. (Sacred Books of the East, Vol. XLIX.) Oxford, 1894.

DAVIDS, T. W. RHYS. *Buddhism, Its History and Literature.* New York and London, 1896.

—— (trans.). *Buddhist Suttas.* (Sacred Books of the East, Vol. XI.) Oxford, 1881.

—— (trans.). *The Questions of King Milinda.* (Sacred Books of the East, Vols. XXXV and XXXVI.) Oxford, 1890 and 1894.

DAVIDS, T. W. and C. A. F. RHYS (trans.). *Dialogues of the Buddha.* (Sacred Books of the Buddhists, Vols. II, III, IV.) London, 1899, 1910, 1921.

—— (trans.). *Buddhist Birth Stories.* London, 1925.

FAUSBÖLL, V. (trans.). *The Sutta-Nipāta.* (Sacred Books of the East, Vol. X, Part II.) Oxford, 1881.

HAMILTON, C. H. *Buddhism in India, Ceylon, China, and Japan; a Guide to Reading.* Chicago, 1931.

KEITH, ARTHUR BERRIEDALE. *Buddhist Philosophy in India and Ceylon.* Oxford, 1923.

KERN, H. *Manual of Indian Buddhism.* Strassburg, 1896.

—— (trans.). *The Saddharma Puṇḍarīka, or The Lotus of the True Law.* (Sacred Books of the East, Vol. XXI.) Oxford, 1909.

LA VALLÉE POUSSIN, LOUIS DE. *The Way to Nirvāṇa.* Cambridge, 1917.

——. *Bouddhisme.* 3rd edition, Paris, 1925.

MOORE, JUSTIN HARTLEY (trans.). *Sayings of the Buddha, the Iti-vuttaka.* New York, 1908.

MÜLLER, F. MAX (trans.). *The Dhammapada.* (Sacred Books of the East, Vol. X, Part I.) Oxford, 1881.

SPEYER, J. S. (trans.). *The Jātakamālā.* (Sacred Books of the Buddhists, Vol. I.) London, 1895.

STCHERBATSKY, TH. *The Conception of Buddhist Nirvāṇa.* Leningrad, 1927.

THOMAS, E. J. *The Life of Buddha as Legend and History.* New York, 1927.

WARREN, HENRY CLARKE (trans.). *Buddhism in Translations.* (Harvard Oriental Series, Vol. III.) Cambridge, Mass., 1922.

WOODWARD, F. L., and HARE, E. M. *The Book of the Gradual Sayings (Anguttara-Nikāya).* 5 vols. London, 1932–36.

BHATTACHARYYA, BENOYTOSH. *The Indian Buddhist Iconography,* Oxford, 1924.

BHATTACHARYYA, BENOYTOSH. *An Introduction to Buddhist Esoterism.* Oxford, 1932.

BLYTH, R. H. *Zen in English Literature and Oriental Classics.* Tokyo, 1948.

EVANS-WENTZ, W. Y. (trans.). *Tibetan Yoga and Secret Doctrines.* London, 1935.

—— (trans.). *Tibet's Great Yogī, Milarepa. A Biography from the Tibetan.* London, 1928.

NANJIO, BUNYIU. *A Short History of the Twelve Japanese Buddhist Sects.* Tokyo, 1886.

PALLIS, MARCO. *Peaks and Lamas.* New York, 1949.

MCGOVERN, WILLIAM. *Introduction to Mahāyāna Buddhism.* London, 1922.

PRATT, JAMES BISSETT. *The Pilgrimage of Buddhism.* New York, 1928.

SOKEI-AN. *Cat's Yawn.* New York (First Zen Institute of America), 1947.

SUZUKI, DAISETZ TEITARO. *Outlines of Mahāyāna Buddhism.* Chicago, 1908.

——. *Essays in Zen Buddhism.* 3 vols. Kyoto and London, 1927, 1933, 1934.

——. *Studies in the Lankavatara Sutra.* London, 1930.

——. *Introduction to Zen Buddhism.* Kyoto, 1934; New York, 1949.

——. *The Zen Doctrine of No-Mind.* London, 1949.

——. *Living by Zen.* Tokyo, 1949.

—— (trans.). *The Manual of Zen Buddhism.* Kyoto, 1935; London, 1950.

TAKAKUSU, JUNJIRO. *The Essentials of Buddhist Philosophy.* Honolulu, 2nd edition, 1949.

WATTS, ALAN W. *The Spirit of Zen.* (The Wisdom of the East Series.) London, 1936.

——. *Zen.* Stanford, Calif., 1948.

TANTRA AND MODERN HINDUISM

AVALON, ARTHUR (Sir John Woodroffe in collaboration with others). *The Principles of Tantra.* 2 vols. London, 1914–16.

—— (trans.). *The Great Liberation (Mahānirvāṇa Tantra).* 2nd edition, Madras, 1927.

—— (trans.). *The Serpent Power (Ṣaṭ-cakra-nirūpaṇa and Pādukāpañcaka).* 3rd revised edition, Madras and London, 1931.

GLASENAPP, H. VON. *Der Hinduismus, Religion und Gesellschaft im heutigen Indien.* Munich, 1922.

NIKHILĀNANDA, SWĀMĪ (trans.). *The Gospel of Śrī Rāmakrishna.* New York, 1942.

ROLLAND, ROMAIN. *Prophets of the New India.* New York, 1930.

WOODROFFE, SIR JOHN. *Shakti and Shākta.* 3rd edition, Madras and London, 1929.

—— (trans.). *The Garland of Letters (Varnamālā). Studies in the Mantra-Shāstra.* Madras and London, 1922.

ZIMMER, HEINRICH. *Kunstform und Yoga im indischen Kultbild.* Berlin, 1926.

——. *Der Weg zum Selbst; Lehre und Leben des indischen Heiligen Shri Ramana Maharshi aus Tiruvannamalai.* Edited by C. G. Jung. Zurich, 1944. For Jung's introduction, see "The Holy Men of India," *Psychology and Religion: West and East,* Collected Works of C. G. Jung, Vol. 11.

THE SIX SYSTEMS

COWELL, E. B., and GOUGH, A. E. (trans.). *Sarvadarśanasaṅgraha.* 2nd edition, Calcutta, 1894.

FADDEGON, BAREND. *The Vaiçeṣika-System.* Amsterdam, 1918.

GARBE, RICHARD. "Lokāyata," in Hastings, *Encyclopaedia of Religion and Ethics,* Vol. VIII, p. 138.

——. "Mīmāṁsā," *ib.,* Vol. VIII, p. 648.

——. "Nyāya," *ib.,* Vol. IX, pp. 422-24.

——. "Vaiśeṣika," *ib.,* Vol. XII, pp. 568-70.

GUÉNON, RENÉ. *Introduction to the Study of the Hindu Doctrines.* Translated by Marco Pallis. London, 1945.

——. *Man and His Becoming According to the Vedānta.* Translated by Richard C. Nicholson. London, 1945.

——. *La métaphysique orientale.* Paris, 1946.

KEITH, ARTHUR BERRIEDALE. *Indian Logic and Atomism.* Oxford, 1921.

——. *The Karma-Mīmāṁsā.* (The Heritage of India Series.) London and Calcutta, 1921.

MÜLLER, F. MAX. *Six Systems of Indian Philosophy.* London, 1899.

GENERAL INDEX

AND

SANSKRIT INDEX

GENERAL INDEX

Cross-references are given as an aid but do not necessarily indicate exact correspondences. Literary works are printed in italic type. Plate references pertain to the descriptive matter in the List of Plates, pp. xiii-xv, as well as to the pictures. For meanings of Sanskrit terms, see the Sanskrit Index, beginning on the page opposite and running concurrently on the lower part of the pages following.

A

Abel and Cain, legend of, 186n
Abhidharmakośa (Vasubandhu), 529n
Abhinandana, 4th Jaina savior, 213
abhiniviśa, *see* life instinct
absorption (samādhi): dual (savikalpa), 435-36, 440n, 455, 592; nondual (nirvikalpa), 436, 437-40 (obstacles), 455; in Tantra, 562, 590, 592-93; in Yoga, 407n
Ābū, Mount, Jaina temples at, 215n, Pl. VII
Achaeans, 9n
Achaemenids, 112; *see also* Darius I
Achilles, Homeric hero, 234
Acrisius, king of Argos, 312
act of truth (satya), 160-69; parables, 161-62 (courtesan), 163-66 (queen and sage), 167-69 (Yaññadata)
action, faculties of (*usually* karmendriya), 55, 228; Brāhmanism, 364, 373; Buddhism, 541n; Sāṅkhya-Yoga, 228, 317, 318, 327; Vedānta, 228
actions, *see* karma (actions: Brāhmanism)
Adam, "first man," 62n, 241
adhikārin, *see* pupil
Ādi-Buddha, 530n
Aditi, Vedic goddess, 10n
Advaita Vedānta, *see* Śaṅkara; Vedānta
Advayavajra, Buddhist teacher, 556n
affirmation: of Vedic Brāhmanism, 345-47, 349-51, 379-80, 413-14, 575; of Mahāyāna Buddhism, 558; of Tantra, 575, 595, 596, 598
Afghanistan, 134, 498, 505; art of, 132n; *see also* Gandhāra
afterworld, *see* heaven/hell
Āgamas, 570, 588, 597; divisions, 568n; sādhanā in, 591; see also *Tantras*
ages of the world, Indian theory of, 106n
Agni, Vedic god, 8, 9, 71, 204, 344, 368, 398; -Vaiśvānara, 339-40
Agnihotra sacrifice, 373
Agotra, Buddhist teacher, 533n

SANSKRIT INDEX

This index (running on the lower part of the pages following) lists, in English alphabetical order, all the Sanskrit and the occasional Pāli terms used in the text. Cited are those occurrences, one or several, which help to explain meaning and shades of meaning. Where meaning varies in different philosophical schools, variant citations are marked. The following abbreviations are used:

Br	Brāhmanism	P	Pāli
Bu	Buddhism	SY	Sāṅkhya-Yoga
J	Jainism	Skr	Sanskrit
M	Mīmāṁsā	T	Tantra
N	Nyāya	V	Vaiśeṣika

A

ābharaṇa, 583n
abhāva, 518
abhimāna, 319
abhiniveśa, 295
abhyāsa, 370, 431
acala, 385
ācamana, 583n
adharma, 271 (J)
adhidaivam, 10n
adhikārin, 51, 56
adhiṣṭhātar, 286
adhivāsa, 367
adhyāropa, 418
adhyātman-adhidaivam, 10n
adhyavasāya, 320
ādipuruṣa, 308
advaita, 375, 414, 456
advaya, 420
advitīya, 456
āgāmi-karma, 442
āgata, 133n
aghāti-karma, 273
aham ajña, 25
ahaṅkāra, 228, 319, 327, 374
ahiṁsā, 171, 250, 433
ajīva, 270 (J)
ājīva, 263
ājīvika, 263, 264n
ajñāna, 430
ākāśa, 270, 430
akhaṇḍa, 439
Akṣapāda, 610
ālayavijñāna, 526
aloka, 270
ambara, 210
aṁśa, 390
amutra, 54
anāhata śabda, 585
ānanda, 415, 425, 456, 562n

E

E
